Religious Transformation in Maya Guatemala

Religious Transformation in Maya Guatemala

Cultural Collapse and Christian Pentecostal Revitalization

Edited by **John P. Hawkins**

SCHOOL FOR ADVANCED RESEARCH PRESS | SANTA FE
UNIVERSITY OF NEW MEXICO PRESS | ALBUQUERQUE

ISBN 978-0-8263-6225-4 (cloth)
ISBN 978-0-8263-6226-1 (e-book)

Library of Congress Cataloging-in-Publication data is on file
with the Library of Congress.

Cover illustration: *La Reunión Evangélica* by Antonio
Vásquez Yojcom, San Juan La Laguna, Department of Sololá,
Guatemala.
Designed by Felicia Cedillos
Composed in Minion Pro 10.25/13.5

SAR Press acknowledges the generous support for this
publication received from the research funds of the following
Brigham Young University entities: College of Family, Home,
and Social Sciences; Department of Anthropology; and David
M. Kennedy Center for International Studies.

To Carol Lee Hawkins,
whose unfathomable support made it all possible

Contents

Part I. Ethnographies of Present-Day Religious Practices in Nahualá and Santa Catarina Ixtahuacán

Part II. Understanding the Christian Pentecostal Wail: Guatemala's Religious Transformation in Historical Perspective

Part III. Understanding the Christian Pentecostal Wail: Guatemala's Religious Transformation in Synchronic Perspective

Illustrations

Tables

Foreword

Christian Pentecostalism as Post-Protestant Weberian Religious Rationalization

THIS BOOK IS ABOUT RELIGIOUS change in two K'iche' Maya *municipios* (townships) in the western highlands of Guatemala "caught between collapse of the old and exclusion from the new." Author and editor John Hawkins gives pride of place to student ethnographies of K'iche' Maya religious traditionalists, Evangelical Protestants, and orthodox and charismatic Catholics from the field school he and Walter Adams directed in Santa Catarina Ixtahuacán and Nahualá, Department of Sololá, in 2002–2003. The centerpiece of this book, however, is the way Hawkins explains the proliferation of Catholic charismatics and Protestant Evangelicals in these ethnographies. He argues that regardless of denomination, their shared Pentecostal-style worship of high decibel, hands on, glossolalic communion with the Holy Spirit makes them sufficiently distinct liturgically and theologically from sedate, mainstream Catholicism, Protestantism, and Eastern Orthodoxy to warrant designating them a fourth branch of Christianity that he dubs "Christian Pentecostalism." He goes on to attribute the widespread appeal of this ecstatic form of Christianity in Latin America and elsewhere to the impact of global capitalism. In Hawkins's view, far from being extravagant or irrational, Christian Pentecostalism's embrace of the Holy Spirit holds a revolutionary potential for renewed civic virtue.

What most struck me on first reading the manuscript of this book was its neo-Weberian scope and significance that take it far beyond field school ethnographies of millenarian outcry against modernity. In its ethnographic rationalization of actors' changing religious orientations, its attention to inner-worldly salvation in the Holy Spirit, and its appreciation of the unintended consequences of such salvation in a neoliberal, capitalist world, Hawkins's argument speaks to the breadth of Max Weber's sociology of religion. It is important to remember that Weber (1978[1968]) wrote about religion not for its own sake, but to understand how, under different historical circumstances, value-rational social action devoted to engaging the world as a meaningful totality comes to rationalize different action orientations of religious carriers and status groups. In like fashion, Hawkins's theory of Christian Pentecostalism develops a model of religious rationalization—in Weberian terms, the interplay of religious values and social action, not progressively more "reasoned" religions—under conditions of late capitalism experienced from the bottom up in peripheral places like Guatemala. As such, this book proves a worthy, and no less provocative, sequel to Weber's *The Protestant Ethic and the Spirit of Capitalism* (1996).

In relating Christian Pentecostalism to capitalist globalization, Hawkins does more than apply Weber's Protestant work ethic to Maya production, as Sheldon Annis (1987) once did. Instead, I see Hawkins advancing Weber's Protestant ethic thesis by proposing Christian Pentecostalism as a new form of Christianity that he might have called (but modestly chose not to) "post-Protestant" in its ecstatic redemption of life worlds brought to crisis by the very capitalist order that Weber argued Protestantism helped rationalize in the first place. If, as Weber concluded, Calvinist anxiety over preordained, otherworldly salvation begat a Puritan worldly asceticism of living life as a divine calling in which success became proof of salvation but inevitably succumbed to the ceaseless striving for material gain dictated by modern capitalism, Hawkins argues that Maya Christian Pentecostals try to alleviate the disruptions of global capitalism by personally renouncing worldly vices in order to garner acceptance and respect from fellow congregants and sanctification from the Holy Spirit. Together, these aspirations allow Maya Christian Pentecostals a meaningful alternative to past religious imperatives and to inveigh morally against a present fallen world. Hawkins's Christian Pentecostals become the spiritual heirs of Weber's Puritan saints to the extent they embody what happens to the Protestant ethic as the world that that ethos unintentionally made possible further transforms under neoliberal globalization. Theoretically, they reveal what otherworldly salvation looks like in the face of the inescapable, this-worldly, materialist morality Weber attributed to the modern economic order.

This rich, provocative argument holds intriguing neo-Weberian implications that John Hawkins, ever the generous and gracious colleague, has invited me to speculate on here as a complement to his own probing Durkheimian concerns with community renewal, moral revitalization, and life-affirming reciprocity. First, and perhaps most incidentally, the reversal of terms and inversion of relationships between his theory and Weber's meet almost too perfectly Lévi-Strauss's (1955:442–443) definition of structural equivalence: Puritan preoccupation with otherworldly salvation becomes Christian Pentecostal dispossession by global capitalism; worldly asceticism as a calling from God becomes inner-worldly self-discipline against congregationally declared vices; worldly success as a testament to God's glory becomes sanctification of the dispossessed through this-worldly baptism in the Holy Spirit; eternal salvation as God's unknowable justification by grace alone becomes a self-actualized, if provisional, communion with the Holy Spirit before fellow congregants; the loneliness of the Protestant believer before God becomes mutual acceptance in self-selective congregations; and the irresistible temptation of capitalist wealth that corrupts the priesthood of all believers becomes the holy if sectarian wail of all prophets for personal redemption in a fallen world. Hawkins proposes no Lévi-Straussian structure here, but in focusing on the same concerns as Weber's—inner-worldly asceticism, otherworldly salvation in the face of this-worldly morality, the search for meaning in an unknown fate—his theory suggests that the confluence of historical circumstances and action orientations that Weber identified as central to the emergence of modernity still shapes its aftermath in these so-called postmodern times. Indeed, the rise of Christian Pentecostalism as a new form of Christianity may mark a comparable moment of historical transformation in modernity's global reach as experienced from below.

Second, as modernity runs historically to global crisis, Hawkins tempers Weber's pessimism about the inevitable triumph of capitalism's compulsory competition for wealth by affirming the enduring power of ecstatic charisma to heal the world. For Hawkins, Christian Pentecostalism represents a direct response to late capitalist globalization, especially as economic hyperintegration binds local places to a mystifying complexity of distant but interdependent elsewheres. Hawkins knows that explaining the incongruity of ecstatic possession within advanced capitalism calls for more than the reductive functionalism of millennial recursion to the past, defiant (or despairing) emotional release, or redirected postcolonial protest against marginalization in the present. Although he considers each of these, rather than settle for what Christian Pentecostalism *does*, he focuses on what it *is* to the people who practice it. As Weber might, he attends closely to how Christian Pentecostal worship—most distinctively, speaking in tongues—resonates with the occult truth-telling of traditional Maya shamans and diviners even as it forsakes their ritual revelations for a Holy Spirit open to and self-evident before all. Ecstatic possession by the Holy Spirit becomes more compelling as failing K'iche' Maya subsistence maize cultivation ceases to justify shamanic exchanges with local earth lords and ancestors, and as the necessary improvisations of survival in a globalizing Guatemala favor more personal spiritual empowerment against a world now indifferent to old Maya covenants with land, place, and ancestors.

Third, Hawkins's treatment of Christian Pentecostalism as both rationalized by received Maya religiosity and rationalizing of morally compromised Maya entanglements in modernity fits theoretically with Weber's broader conception of rationalization as a double-sided historical process derived from constellations of accepted values but driven by actors' felt need to reformulate those values as new circumstances challenge established actions and understandings (Kalberg 1980). Like the good anthropologist he is, Hawkins recognizes that if Christian Pentecostalism represents a new form of Christianity, its wide occurrence requires more than local rationalization. Similarly, in good Weberian fashion, he looks to global capitalism's top-down importunities on local ways of life and livelihood as the relevant circumstance that Christian Pentecostalism religiously rationalizes from the bottom up. To the extent that Weber was right, and capitalism already presumes Protestant-derived values, this Christian Pentecostal religious rationalization becomes all the more "post-Protestant" in reshaping Weber's "Protestant ethic" of hoped-for salvation through unceasing work into a response to the increasingly macrocosmic capitalist commodification of people's microcosmic efforts to save themselves materially and spiritually with what they have at hand. (For the interplay of microcosmic "mystics" against macrocosmic markets in North American religious revivalism, see Rodseth and Olsen 2000.) As unseen markets and the demand for alienated labor make self-sanctifying worldly success more problematic for people on the margins regardless of identity, abode, or religious orientation, Christian Pentecostalism reorients the Protestant-cum-capitalist ethic of ceaselessly striving in the world to a post-Protestant but still very much this-worldly spiritual sanctification by promising microcosmically oriented converts the personal moral surety of the Holy Spirit's macrocosmic—but appropriately unintelligible—gift of tongues.

More speculatively, this possible association between the Holy Spirit and macrocosmic capitalism's enigmatic dictates and inchoate promise may help further clarify how Christian Pentecostal trancing and speaking in tongues rationalizes the instrumental opportunism of striving in a capitalist world. Far from senseless, possession by the Holy Spirit powerfully answers the felt need for individual self-affirmation before the mystifying fluctuations of work and wages, production and profit in global marketplaces, and the indifference (if not corruption) of state regulators and enforcers. Such personal affirmation, however, involves more than the Holy Spirit alone. It depends equally on what could be called the "collective individuation" in Christian Pentecostal worship itself. Long distinctive of Pentecostalism, congregations gather to deafening music, song, and preaching—what Hawkins knowingly calls the "pentecostal wail"—but members pray individually in a cacophony of voices to the Holy Spirit that answers only the chosen with trancing, healing, and speaking in tongues. Unlike distant markets or official regulations that appear arbitrarily to advantage or disadvantage, the Holy Spirit presumably sanctifies only the truly worthy. This not only empowers the individuals so blessed before their own congregations to transcend old moral covenants and the moral failings of a wider world beyond local control or suasion. It also inspires them to find their way in that world—itself glossolalic in too often obscuring understanding or anticipation but now made meaningful in each devotee's internalized cacophony of speaking the speech of all nations as proof of their own living salvation.

Such empowerment in turn raises the prospect that

this post-Protestant Christian Pentecostal religious rationalization of sanctifying collective individuation ultimately, if unintentionally, promotes capitalist values of possessive individualism. That is, the gift of the Holy Spirit comes from on high, but spiritual possession from above becomes a personal possession of those below already "gifted" with their own charisma of moral virtuosity to resist the worldly vices prohibited by their congregation. This moral rectitude, along with the fervency of their faith in cult song and prayer, defines the unceasing work they must do to save themselves in the Holy Spirit—and in the eyes of their congregation. Should their gift fail, revocation by the Holy Spirit—or rebuke from other congregants—makes their failings public to the congregation that then calls them to redouble their moral, if not practical, striving for personal repentance, redemption, and repossession of (not just by) the Holy Spirit. To the extent they comply, Christian Pentecostals become ever more responsible—and liable—for saving themselves, and congregational collective individuation prepares the way for further capitalist alienation and possessive individualism. Whether in this world or the next, salvation demands the self-sacrifice not just of hard work, but of rendering up that part of oneself drawn to worldly affairs and indulgences in favor of the self-sanctifying gift that inclines the religiously minded to the Holy Spirit in the first place. In both form and substance, the literal incomprehension in the Holy Spirit's gift of tongues helps rationalize the unseen, incomprehensible workings of global capitalism, just as sanctifying collective individuation in Christian Pentecostal worship literally embodies unfathomable marketplaces as potentially, if inconstantly, accessible to the appropriately, if imperfectly, gifted.

Last, Weber's (1946a) observations on the congregational organization of Protestant sects further clarify the post-Protestant direction of Christian Pentecostalism. For Weber, Protestant sects differ from churches (to which anyone can belong) in their self-selective election and the equality of members. Admitted only after adequate preparation and examination, congregants must hold their own by constantly proving their worth to each other through appropriate knowledge and behavior. The resulting social self-esteem of mutual acceptance enhances exclusivity in the congregation, even as it licenses members to speak out equally on matters of doctrine, practice, and propriety. This privileged egalitarianism extends to priests and prophets, whose authority no longer flows solely from their charisma (or routinized status) as intermediaries with the sacred. Instead, like oracles or diviners before them, they are expected not only to provide services for the congregation as a whole, but also to pastor congregants individually on their path to salvation. While this helps attract and retain members in competition with other sects, parsing prophetic revelations into prescriptions for everyday life risks "casuistically" depreciating their sacred source and cosmic truths (Weber 1978:464–465).

At each turn, Christian Pentecostalism's emphasis on individual responsibility and evangelization ordained in the Holy Spirit intensifies, if not transforms, these Weberian congregational dynamics. While still predicated on individual election through conformity to God's word and the rule of law (expressed most immediately in congregational injunctions against immoral behavior), Christian Pentecostal sanctification in the Holy Spirit pushes congregations in contradictory directions. As assemblies of all prophets, congregations become ever more exclusive, but personal righteousness can also make them more exclusionary—and inspire self-sanctified dissenters to leave and found their own congregations. Sectarian schisms result, but the collective fervor essential to Christian Pentecostal sanctification necessitates tempering doctrinal disputation enough to attract new converts to keep congregations viable. The Holy Spirit obliges by minimizing, if not dispensing with, pastoral authority over adepts, who become their own intermediaries with the sacred. Collective individuation also obviates the relativization of charismatic revelations through each congregant's own direct religious experience, and doctrine comes to focus increasingly on procedures and on the vices singled out for intolerance by the congregation. This, however, increases the risk of "idolatry" in Roy Rappaport's (1999:444) sense of "oversanctification of the specific" by too closely equating congregational acceptance (or disapproval) with divine will, creating further grounds for both sectarian intolerance and righteous disputation.

The egalitarian, exclusionary, experiential tensions in Christian Pentecostal congregations result more in what sociologist Émile Durkheim (1949[1893]:130–131) called the mechanical solidarity of likeness, as opposed to his organic solidarity of complementary interdependence. Despite the worldwide appeal of Christian Pentecostalism, the fact that congregations tend toward tight-knit insularity may limit the extent to which their moral imperatives can generalize on larger, more diverse social scales. This may occur most readily when state power

appeals to Christian Pentecostals' respect for the rule of law, God's or otherwise, or to their moral rectitude as subjects in the sense of a political constituency instead of as self-actualizing, moral selves (Foucault 1982). Cynicism aside, however, Weber (1946a:307–310) noted that congregational organization in turn-of-the-twentieth-century North America had diffused into secular society through the growth of self-selective, voluntary associations—from mutual aid and burial societies among the aspiring middle classes to "the Boys' Club in school . . . the Athletic Club or Greek Letter Society . . . the notable clubs of businessmen and the bourgeoisie . . . [and] the clubs of the metropolitan plutocracy." All of these presumed election by merit and ongoing, appropriate conduct that helped to foster not only sober bourgeois respectability, but also the wider bonds of "civil society" that made the United States more than a "sand heap" of grasping opportunists. Whatever the ultimate import of Christian Pentecostalism under late capitalism, Weber reminds us that it will be mediated by its congregational organization as well as by the resulting action orientations of its individual converts.

All this said, these Weberesque ruminations remain incidental to John Hawkins's deeply humanistic concern for the fate of Mayas in Guatemala and how Christian Pentecostalism as community building, cultural revitalization, and moral reciprocity links their mountain fastness of Sololá to the heartland of the United States and beyond. This ambitious book reflects the courage of Hawkins's convictions as an anthropologist, ever committed to both careful ethnography and comparative generalization. In tracing the wider causes and consequences of his and his students' ethnographic findings, Hawkins argues here for the revolutionary potential of Christian Pentecostalism as "the only response so far devised that enables a growing sector of the poor to conceptualize and construct a meaningful and workable response to state failure, societal chaos, economic exploitation, and exclusion." While many (most?) secular humanist readers may well decry—and thus perhaps not see coming—a Christian Pentecostal revolution under God's rule of law, Hawkins again demonstrates the courage of his convictions to follow his evidence where it leads and at least consider the possibility. Given how convincingly he roots Christian Pentecostalism in the same cultural and economic crises of dispossession, dislocation, and disregard that drive current populist politics across the globe and the demagoguery at the heart of capitalist modernity, his proposition is one we need to take seriously.

As Weber (1946b) counseled, however, the path forward remains historical, as much evolutionary as revolutionary. It seldom leads where actors themselves envision, and our task as social scientists is to seek clarity—about actors' values and orientations, the means available to them, the consistency (or not) between their means and ends, and the capacitating or countervailing circumstances working for or against either or both. This book draws clarity out of complexity in identifying and rationalizing Christian Pentecostalism. While some may contest the answers it presents, the agenda it sets in the questions it poses and where it looks for answers will prove its own enduring, redemptive gift.

JOHN M. WATANABE
Dartmouth College

Preface

A Field School Approach to the Ethnography of Religion

JOHN P. HAWKINS

GIVEN THAT THE REST OF this book describes and analyzes religion in Guatemala and around the world, let me briefly describe the methods we used to bring the data together. This is the fourth volume of ethnography derived from the Brigham Young University (BYU) Department of Anthropology's Nahualá/Santa Catarina Ixtahuacán Ethnographic Field School. (The first three are Hawkins and Adams 2005a; Adams and Hawkins 2007; and Hawkins, McDonald, and Adams 2013.) In other publications, we (Hawkins and Adams 2005b; Hawkins 2014; and Hawkins and Adams 2014) describe the field school rationale and procedures in some detail, so I do not say much about our field school or field methods here. Suffice it to say that the time period for most of the descriptive fieldwork of this volume is mid-May through mid-August 2003, the exception being Larson and colleagues' chapter, which is based on fieldwork from mid-August through late December 2002. Subsequently, several of the lead authors of ethnographic chapters returned to these townships for further fieldwork, which enriched their analyses. Hawkins and Adams directed the field school in 1995–2006 and have been doing fieldwork in Guatemala at various times, thinking about it frequently, and writing about it for more than fifty and nearly forty years, respectively.

In the ethnographic chapters of part 1, each lead author uses a variety of well-known qualitative and quantitative methods. All were functionally fluent Spanish speakers from the outset. Each had a K'iche'–Spanish translator who also functioned as a field guide and companion. All of the BYU students had attended a one-semester K'iche' language course that effectively drilled language basics: phrases, vocabulary, and grammar. (Some completed two semesters.) This language exposure helped students maintain the quality of translations since most could follow enough K'iche' to determine whether the translator was doing a reasonably good job of translating into Spanish, rather than summarizing or skipping. All conducted interviews and kept field notes and transcriptions of tape-recorded interviews in Spanish or in K'iche'. The translators produced interlinear translations from K'iche' to Spanish and added commentary on interviews conducted in K'iche'. Prior to discovering anthropology, Winston Scott already spoke fluent Q'eqchi', one of the Maya family of languages along with K'iche'. Consequently, he quickly became functionally fluent in K'iche'.

In each of the town centers or their associated *aldeas* (rural hamlets) in Nahualá and Santa Catarina Ixtahuacán, field school members and faculty lived, one to each household, with families of traditionalist shamans, healers, Ortho-Catholic leaders, Catholic *carismático* group leaders, Pentecostal *evangélico* congregational ministers, or quite ordinary people participating in one or more of these ways of worship as experienced in that location. Throughout this volume, first-person singular pronouns refer to the experience and perspective of a chapter's lead author. "We" refers to collectively massaged insights that involved the lead author, the field school directors, and fellow students. All lead authors chose the pseudonyms used in their chapter; any reuse between chapters is purely coincidental and does not denote the same person.

The substantial number of willing team members who coordinated their work on interrelated segments of Guatemalan religion made possible this distinctive, comparative, multisited approach. The term "multisited" references goals elaborated by Marcus and Fischer (1986), Marcus

(1995), and Falzon (2009), among others. They advocate the study of an issue, process, concept, material substance, social network, or symbolic "flow" by paying attention to it at multiple locations and by trying to portray its various interconnections and implications throughout a large or even global cultural, symbolic, and social system. This we have tried to do with regard to religion by distributing the field school students throughout the diverse religious system as experienced in Nahualá and Santa Catarina Ixtahuacán. I could not have achieved this ethnographic result alone, nor could I have arrived at the theoretical interpretations I did based just on my own experiences. I benefited from the wealth of their data and social connections over the years.

Thus, I restate the claims I made in Hawkins (2014) and in Hawkins and Adams (2014). A well-run ethnographic field school can be a life-changing and effective pedagogy for students of any major. In addition, the undergraduate field school mobilized for publication can be a powerful research method that ought to be among the techniques available to any anthropologist. Our field school's multisited format made possible our simultaneous documentation of multiple faith practices. Had I been doing fieldwork solo, I would not have had the time to study all these strands of faith myself. Nor would I have been allowed such diverse access to so many "pathways to God" (Morgan 2005:90–91) by the sometimes jealous faith groups promulgating their truths. Simultaneous documentation by students in multiple locations and habitats, as well as their social connections and my own, enabled me to attend to all styles of religious practice in an atmosphere of trust and provided me a much richer and broader range of experiences. The range of religions we delved into allowed me to see similarities among Pentecostals and charismatics that I would not otherwise have seen. It enabled me to recognize them as "Christian Pentecostals." Thus, the conclusions of this book emerge as a direct product of collaboration in undergraduate research using the field school format. I recommend this approach to others as a legitimate research method and a rich source of theoretical stimulation.

Acknowledgments

In 1974 I chanced to meet an older researcher—an economist fomenting development projects—in the street at the border between San Marcos and San Pedro Sacatepéquez in Guatemala's western Department of San Marcos. We chatted. He asked what I was doing. I told him that I was a doctoral student studying ethnicity, family, and economy in the two towns for my dissertation, a study that eventually became *Inverse Images* (Hawkins 1984). My description of this research topic bored him. Across the street in front of us, the largest non-Catholic church in San Pedro had just finished its noisy services, broadcast by rooftop speaker. Its Pentecostal worshippers came pouring out. Pointing to the church and its members, he blurted enthusiastically: "*That* is what you anthropologists *should* be studying; that is where the *real* social action is!" I have forgotten his name and university; I have not forgotten his injunction. It took me thirty years to act on his suggestion for this fieldwork and another sixteen years to think it through and write it up, I hope coherently. This book shows how prescient he was.

I have many to thank. Indeed, *we* have many to thank, for this is a collective research effort. But the impossibility of the task daunts us. How can we possibly thank adequately the many people who have helped so much to make this project possible?

We—the editor and chapter authors—profoundly appreciate the innumerable Guatemalans who guided our steps, explained to us their actions and dilemmas, and tolerated our presence. Think about it! Maya families opened their lives to us. They allowed us to live with them in their homes, no matter how small. In some homes they shoved belongings out of the way to clear a room for one of us. In others, they hammered together frames and tacked up opaque plastic sheets to create privacy-granting screens that divided a single room. They cooked nutritious and healthy food for us. They nursed us, prayed for us, and cheered us on. They guided our footsteps to help us avoid cultural pitfalls and physical risks. In a word, they mothered and fathered us as they would their own. Whole flocks of Pentecostals received us as *hermanos* and *hermanas* (congregational brothers and sisters). The charismatic communities warmed to us, too, and called us, like they called each other, *qachalal*, the K'iche' term for "we kin" or "our sibling." Over the years, traditionalist shamans repeatedly blessed us, anointing our bodies from crown to calf with the soft sweep of the sacred ears of silk-tasseled corn so dear to Maya lives. Catholic priests in three town centers and bishops in department and national centers answered our every question and brokered us into their communities. Each of our students had a translator or shared a translator who not only made access to K'iche' possible, but also guided the students into the culture, advised, fixed problems, translated tapes, typed interviews, and coached in whatever the topic was.

All these families, communities, and individuals forgave our cultural sins and taught us how to be better local citizens, how to be proper men and women, and how to be more understanding practitioners of their cherished beliefs and religious activities. Religious leaders, congregational members, community citizens, and translators did this knowing full well that we were not real adherents to their faiths nor permanent members of their religious communities. The host families of this volume's fourteen coauthors deserve much recognition and thanks. And so do the many families who received previous and subsequent cohorts of about 200 field school students throughout the years 1995–2006 and 2009. These students from before and after the 2003 religion-focused cohort also deserve thanks for their professional behavior: they made it possible for the 2003 group to be trusted from the first day.

In particular, I thank Pascualino Tahay Ixtos; his

wife, Catalina Perechú y Perechú; and their children, with whom I lived for five summers. Pascualino has helped me learn culture and language, translated innumerable recordings, and been a true friend. At Brigham Young University, David Shuler's visionary direction of the field studies section of the David M. Kennedy Center for International Studies made our administrative and recruitment work for each field school cohort much easier. First as a field school student, then as a field school student facilitator, later as a Kennedy Center employee, and finally as David Shuler's replacement, Malcolm Botto Wilson guided generations of students through K'iche' classes, helped them fill out forms, and prepared them for the field. From an idea in 1993 to the present publication, we received support from Joel Janetski, David Crandall, Charles Nuckolls, and James Allison, as successive chairs of the Department of Anthropology. Two patient and savvy department administrative secretaries, Evie Forsyth and Tami Pugmire, facilitated the work. Deans Clayne Pope and David Magleby opened purses and doors throughout the university, as did Dean Ben Ogles during the write-up phase.

From 2002 through 2006, funding from the National Science Foundation's program Research Experience for Undergraduates made it possible for students from six universities to participate in the field school at a much lower cost than otherwise would have been the case. The SES grant 0139198 covered 2003, the year most focused on religion, but the SES grant 0354014 for 2004–2006 had lingering effects that also deserve recognition.

John Monaghan from the University of Illinois at Chicago, Jon McGee from Texas State University–San Marcos, and Servando Hinojosa from the University of Texas–Pan American (now renamed University of Texas Rio Grande Valley) recruited and advised students from their respective universities and helped them craft papers from the experience. Walter Randolph Adams, who coedited previous volumes from the field school and who coauthored with and advised students as codirector of the field school from 1995 to 2006, has been a constant support. James McDonald, likewise, has helped me think through many an issue during our collaborations from 2006 to the present.

John Clark rendered a particularly incisive critique of my introductory and concluding chapters when they were in a dismal state of organization. Anonymous reviewers were also most helpful and quite patient; they saw the vision of what we were up to and gave profoundly good advice. Stephen Houston and James McDonald read and critiqued the more or less penultimate draft and penned evaluations that helped bring it to our publisher's attention. Norman Schwartz read, discussed the issues, and encouraged me to finish this manuscript up until the day before he died. Henri Gooren and John Watanabe both unmasked their reviewer status and gave more than one round of enormously insightful suggestions. Sarah Soliz, director of the School for Advanced Research Press, provided a detailed edit, with nearly every recommendation used. Merryl A. Sloane rendered an extraordinary copyedit that helped me smooth the manuscript, clarify its meaning, and eliminate many infelicities. I thank you all; to raise up a manuscript, as with a child, it takes a village.

Richard N. Adams (now deceased) and Betty Hannstein Adams hosted our annual assessment conference in their home in Panajachel (Department of Sololá, Guatemala). We thank both of you for your hospitality and gracious intellectual and physical support over the years. Several of our students recovered their health in the sunny warmth of your patio guest bedroom. As a result, they could return to Nahualá or Santa Catarina Ixtahuacán to enrich their studies.

All the coauthors owe debts to the spouses, fiancées, friends, parents, siblings, nieces and nephews, children, grandparents, and grandchildren who in one way or another made a three-month stint of undergraduate fieldwork possible. Again, collectively, we thank you all!

It would appear that Santa Catarina (the patron saint of the Catholic people in both communities that we studied), Mary as mother of Jesus, Maximón as Judas Iscariot, and a legion of living local ministers, *pastoras*, healers, priests, *ajq'ijab'*, *sobrenas*, and prophets have interceded for us with God, Jesús, Espíritu Santo, qatat/qanan, Santo Mundo, ancestors, and the members of these communities of Mayas. We appreciate the willingness of both the intercessors and the importuned to let us intrude on their domains. We hope that in this book we have represented these K'iche' people, their communities, their divinities, and their diverse yet related religious practices and beliefs fairly, meaningfully, analytically, and with dignity.

Religion in cultural and historical context is a complex topic that cannot be dealt with briefly and cannot ever be done completely. On both counts I have suffered. Every time I went through the manuscript to shorten and remove duplications, I also discovered new interconnections that needed to be analyzed. In the end, the length is needed to show the complex ways that Nahualá and Santa

Catarina Ixtahuacán are excellent windows on worldwide religious processes.

I thank chair Jim Allison and the faculty of the BYU Anthropology Department, Renata Forste as head of the David M. Kennedy Center for International Studies, and Dean Benjamin Ogles of the College of Family, Home, and Social Sciences for their help in many ways and for matching grants that have made the publication of this complex analysis and its underlying ethnographic and historical data a purely intellectual decision based on the merits of the argument. This book could have been seen as an economic impossibility and rejected out of hand (and it was, many times). I thank Sarah Soliz for having perceived the merits rather than rejecting on the economics.

The mistakes and shortcomings that surely exist in this book are our own—and mostly my own, not anyone else's. Any strengths you may find in this book had their genesis in the wisdom of the people of Nahualá and Santa Catarina Ixtahuacán or were inspired by the many teachers and authors who shared their perspectives with us in person, in class, or in print over the years.

JOHN P. HAWKINS
Provo, Utah
July 10, 2020

An Introduction to the Ethnography of Religion and Religious Change among the K'iche'

JOHN P. HAWKINS

IN THIS BOOK WE INVESTIGATE religious variety and religious transformation among the K'iche' Mayas living in Nahualá and Santa Catarina Ixtahuacán, two townships (*municipios*) in the Department of Sololá, an administrative province located largely in the highland region of western Guatemala. These Guatemalan Mayas are undergoing a rapid and massive religious transformation via individual conversion. From varieties of stately and relatively sedate Catholicism and a Maya Catholic traditionalism wherein spirit visitation to the shaman and considerable alcohol use can give the impression of excess but in which both the shaman's and client's behavior is quite sedate, many have converted to one or another of several varieties of ecstatic, motile, noisy Christian Pentecostal faiths.

I attach a special meaning to the phrase "Christian Pentecostalism": I coined the term to include both Protestant-derived ecstatic religious practices and denominations called *evangélico* as well as the Catholic-derived ecstaticism called Charismatic Renewal. In these Christian Pentecostal faiths, ordinary adherents and their leaders become bodily agitated during worship meetings. Some adherents may fall into trance during these religious services, many may speak in tongues, and any can be healed. In most congregational meetings, the sound output from electronic amplification can be literally deafening. Why? What is the meaning embedded in the increasing acceptance of this style of worship, and why has that style expanded rapidly from the 1950s to the present?

Some academics find the Christian Pentecostal style of worship rather off-putting if not downright illusory, although the judgment is seldom seen in print. I rather prefer the approach implied by Émile Durkheim (1858–1917). Durkheim (2001[1912]:62) asserts, "It makes no sense that systems of ideas like religion, which have held such a major place in history and from which people have always drawn the energy needed to live, are merely tissues of illusion." Rather than be put off by a style, Durkheim and a long line of successor anthropologists of religion would say we should find its meaning or its social value to the group.

My thesis is simple and not at all illusory. Throughout the twentieth century and especially since the 1950s, Mayas have been experiencing culture collapse and systemic exclusion. Those who change from traditional *costumbre* (a term for traditionalist religious performance) and Roman Catholic practice to Christian Pentecostal make this person-by-person conversion because Mayas, and indeed all Guatemalans, are currently undergoing the collapse of their colonially organized way of life. This collapse disrupts ideologies, symbols, life practices, and social structures that have undergirded the society of colonized Mayas and colonizing Catholic Ladinos for almost 500 years.

For the Mayas, the collapse swirls around the high cultural value placed on corn. Indeed, both physically and mentally, corn is their staff of life, the key substance on which they exist. Yet in the present day, they encounter grave difficulties in producing sufficient corn for their needs. This is so for two reasons. First, Mayas have experienced a century-long population increase that has quadrupled and quintupled, on average, the number of mouths each highland Maya village must feed (with an elevenfold increase in the country as a whole). Second, the Mayas have experienced colonial expropriation and the outright theft of indigenous lands, and they must contend with the simple fact that one cannot grow new land except by destroying forest on ever-steeper mountainsides, which are subject to erosion and depletion when put to corn production. Thus, the fast-rising Maya population and a relatively static base of arable land have combined to produce from the 1950s to the present a condition in which the average Maya family has been increasingly unable to support itself with a sufficient quantity of the primary substance of Maya well-being, which is also a major component of Maya religious and cultural symbolism: corn.

This shortage of a cultural essential has produced a crisis of cultural faith in a society that ideologically, relationally, and symbolically centers on corn as the key life-giving substance. With the increasing cultural crisis brought on by land and corn insufficiency has come a crisis regarding family and municipal autonomy as well as the increasing irrelevance of those religious ideas, symbols, and practices that connect to corn and autonomy and have represented and guided Maya residents in this colonized society. In a word, corn and land crises led to cultural crisis; cultural crisis led to religious crisis; and religious crisis has, ultimately, precipitated religious change on a massive scale.

At the same time that the Mayas' corn culture has been collapsing, substantial numbers of Guatemalans—especially poor urbanites and indigenous Mayas—have been effectively excluded from secure participation in the emerging neoliberal global order that increasingly penetrates their villages and hinterlands and seems to be the only visible alternative to the old colonial corn-raising and tax-extraction regime. This exclusion has added to the crisis. Exclusion from any apparent viable alternative has exacerbated the people's consternation regarding corn culture collapse and has increased their sense of desperation. Thus, exclusion also fuels their interest in and style of religious change.

These two factors—cultural collapse and systematic social and economic exclusion—explain the recent religious transformation of Maya Guatemala and the way, style, and emotional intensity in which that religious transformation gets expressed in current Christian Pentecostal ritual. Convert by convert and sometimes community by community, Mayas move from relatively sedate Maya traditionalism and thoroughly sedate Ortho-Catholicism to various forms of trance-inducing, tongues-speaking, bodily animated, electronically hyper-amplified ecstatic Christian Pentecostalisms.

To explore and understand this phenomenon of religious change, we need three components: description, history, and theory.

Part 1 of this book provides the description. It includes twelve ethnographies of current religious practice as the various religions were experienced in Guatemala in 2002–2003, ranging from a disappearing *cofradía* collective Catholic traditionalism and a vigorous individualist shamanic traditionalism, to Ortho-Roman Catholicism, Protestant *evangélico* Pentecostalism, and Catholic renewal charismaticism. As I describe in the preface, these studies derive from a coordinated undergraduate field school effort. Suffice it to say that none of what follows in this book—neither the ethnography nor the theory—could have been developed without the extraordinary and diverse observations and writings of a remarkable group of young students who were willing to live with and practice the dominant religion to which each of their adoptive families adhered. In part 2, I develop the historical sequence that has resulted in Guatemala's current religious diversity. In part 3, I lay out the theory that interlinks and makes overall sense of the data presented in part 1 from the student ethnographers and my own living with shamans, Ortho-Catholics, and Pentecostals over the thirteen years we held the field school. The same theory taps into the history developed in part 2 and illuminates our understanding of how the past became the present.

What theories and theorists should we use to think about religious belief and practice changing from relatively sedate forms of traditionalism and Roman Catholicism to the ecstatic forms of Christian Pentecostalism? First, this inquiry confirms the fundamental value of taking a Durkheimian perspective on the relation of religion to society. Durkheim suggests in *The Elementary Forms of Religious Life* that religion reflects the underlying sense a people have of their society's structure and of that society's fit to their surrounding ecological universe. In Durkheim's (2001[1912]:314) words, "If religion generated everything that is essential in society, this is because the idea of society is the soul of religion." On close inspection, this phrasing is quite circular. Durkheim has the ideas and practices of religion generating or regenerating and continuously reconstituting society; at the same time, he has a people's overall perception of the society and its key social relationships being apprehended and incorporated as symbols into religion even though no one individual may apprehend it all. Moreover, according to Durkheim, participation in religious rituals anchors individuals to society by renewing their sentiments of attachment to the collectivity. Participation in ritual makes those individuals into whatever kind of person they are by imbuing them with the ideology and guiding symbols needed to lead a successful life in that society. In a word, rituals make people into what they are, as van Gennep (1960[1909]) and Victor Turner (1967, 1968, 1969) have so adroitly shown. For Durkheim (2001[1912]:11), "rituals are ways of acting . . . within assembled groups . . . meant to stimulate and sustain or recreate certain mental states in these groups." Durkheim, however, neglected to address how fast a society's relation to the sustaining universe can change when the idea of compound interest applies to population increase accelerated by twentieth-century health conditions. Population growth, it turns out, changes a society's relation to its sustaining environment, as Malthus early observed. Rappaport (1968) details the cyclical linkages between population and religion among the Tsembaga Maring of New Guinea; Cancian (1965, 1972, 1992) lays out the long-term transformations of Maya traditionalist *cofradía*-embedded religious practice induced by population expansion.

Change in the environment-to-population balance, however, can eventually alter modes of production and in the process inject stress and conflict into society. So, Durkheim's emphasis on a current social structure and its linkage to an environment being maintained by ritual, symbol, and cosmological ideas constitutes the solid base for this study of religion, but Durkheim's thought is not enough because its circularity leads to too static an analysis. Yet Durkheim, too, acknowledges the impact of material conditions, although it is not the central focus of his argument. Thus, he says, "Of course, we take it as obvious that social life depends on and bears the mark of its material substrate" (Durkheim 2001[1912]:318–319). Since materialist explanation was not Durkheim's forte, I seek help from the very sources he argued against: Karl Marx (1818–1883) and Friedrich Engels (1820–1895).

Conflict introduced by population-forced changes in modes of production and material distribution require us to add the insights of Marx and his intellectual companion, Engels. I tease out the rather Marxian relations of religion to changes in political economy in part 2. There I document the material and political bases of the theses I offer: a corn crisis precipitated a culture crisis, and that culture crisis has been met with a religious crisis followed by a religious change toward ecstaticism, which expresses the untenability of the human experience of culture collapse and exclusion. Now the corn shortage crisis is a material condition. But Marx and Engels would not have wanted us to fall into the trap of a purely materialist explanation of changing religion. In a more reflective

mood than when in his politically argumentative persona, Engels (2008a[1890]:274, 276–277, emphases in original) concedes:

> According to the materialist conception of history, the *ultimately* determining element in history is the production and reproduction of real life. More than this neither Marx nor I have ever asserted. Hence if somebody twists this into saying that the economic element is the *only* determining one, he transforms that proposition into a meaningless, abstract, senseless phrase. . . . Marx and I are ourselves partly to blame for the fact that the younger people sometimes lay more stress on the economic side than is due to it. We had to emphasize the main principle vis-à-vis our adversaries, who denied it, and we had not always the time, the place or the opportunity to give their due to the other elements involved in the interaction.

So even though leaning on the strength of the materialist influences, Marx and Engels were eclectic, as I hope to be here. Material change can result in ideational change, and vice versa.

We must remember, however, that people do not go down the rabbit hole of change, particularly religious change, blindly and with easy acceptance. Quite the contrary. Some are early adopters, to be sure. But most people struggle with change—they resist it—for they must make new decisions and thereby take chances rather than simply follow the rutted paths of their forebears. Indeed, I suspect that most people resist change because they intuitively recognize that all changes have unintended and unforeseeable consequences. They find the old comforting—even if it increasingly pinches. Thus, some resist change while others accept it, and the divergence introduces additional stress through adverse judgment of each other. Thus, conflict emerges in their society.

Moreover, change affects people's emotions. Among the Mayas, some men (and I mean explicitly and mostly people of male gender) try to douse their emotional reactions to change with alcohol; some men strike family members violently out of frustration; some join revolutionary movements. A tiny fraction of women have tried each of those paths too. But most women who change have tried a softer approach, one culturally accorded to them as appropriate for women: family-oriented spirituality that portends religious change rather than political revolution or anesthetizing inebriation. Some choose the path of intensified religious performance according to their village tradition of Catholicism. Many women and some men respond to change by using religion to try to correct and resymbolize the difficult situation in which they find themselves. They use a new religion to recognize their social situation—their existing and emerging society—and thereby adopt a new approach to making sense of the social swirl that is happening around and to them.

To handle theoretically these changes in people's thoughts and the impact of changes in their thoughts and practices regarding religion on the society around them, I turn to Max Weber (1864–1920). He helps us think about the consequences of new religious ideas and the effects of charismatic leadership and ascetic practice in religion on society, with the third-order consequences of societal changes arising from changes in religious ideology and symbolism.

Understanding a people's changing responses to difficult and existentially threatening conditions requires the additional conceptual services of Anthony F. C. Wallace (1923–2015), who extends Weber's ideas of charismatic leadership regarding religion and change. Wallace shows how a societal crisis can be met with purposeful, transformative, deliberate, and rather rapid restructuring of society via religious revelation. In Weber's terms, the shift from traditionalism and Ortho-Catholicism to Christian Pentecostalism in Guatemala exemplifies a charismatic movement. In Wallace's terms, the surge in Christian Pentecostalism constitutes a revitalization movement and an adjustment cult. Christian Pentecostalism in Guatemala is indeed both charismatic and revitalizing; moreover, Christian Pentecostalism partakes of Weber's attributes of an ascetic sect in that congregations of people themselves put rather strict limits on what constitutes acceptable practice and membership. Having noted that both Durkheim and Marx-Engels are eclectic, if leaning in opposite directions, it is worth noting that Weber, too, recognizes the mutual interactivities between society, materiality, and ideas. He may push the importance of "religious consciousness," but he recognizes that consciousness does not go unaffected by circumstance, whether social or material. Thus, Weber (2002[1905]:122) makes his main pitch: "Modern man, on the whole, is rarely able, with the best will in the world, to imagine just how significant has been the influence of religious consciousness on conduct of life, 'culture,' and 'national character.'" But in the immediately succeeding sentence, he

mellows the thrust: "However, it cannot, of course, be our purpose to replace a one-sided 'materialist' causal interpretation of culture and history with an equally one-sided spiritual one. *Both are equally possible*, but neither will serve historical truth if they claim to be the conclusion of the investigation rather than merely the *preliminary work for it*" (emphases in original). In short, Durkheim, Marx and Engels, and Weber largely concur on the interactivity of these components of social life, but they then proceed to focus on dissecting the anatomy of different parts of the beast.

Wallace fleshes out Weber by describing cases of charismatic innovation in the face of social, cultural, and material stress. According to Wallace, characterization as an adjustment cult or a religious revitalization movement applies to the worship (and other) activities of any religious group that advocates transformative change toward a new cultural practice that they deem better for society—and the individuals or groups in it—than the practices of the old social order. Leaders of adjustment cults and religious revitalization movements advocate deliberate change of the basic culture and social institutions of a society because the cult's adherents see that society as "unsatisfactory," sick, or defective (Wallace 1956:265). Guatemalan Pentecostals do indeed see their society as defective and corrupt, as do Catholic charismatics and others in the society. The objective facts of social breakdown are there for all to experience, among them lack of land, hunger, alcohol abuse, domestic violence, governmental corruption, and civil war.

Indeed, from around 1980 to perhaps 2010, we witnessed—and Guatemalans experienced—what was perhaps the high-crisis phase in the century-long collapse of the Maya people's way of life. We observed the meltdown of their once secure cultural, symbolic, social, and economic systems, the disruption of their long-practiced social relationships, and a fast-rising crisis in their culturally preferred means of production. We saw the unraveling of Spanish-derived internal colonial exploitations and patronage. We watched as Mayas culturally dependent on corn reached and passed the point where their micro plots of land and their meager corn harvests could fill their bellies adequately, let alone produce enough for some to be sold for cash to buy other things they now are enticed to need. For the better part of a century, Mayas have had to choose and to invent what to do as their cultural order has eroded and broken down. They have experienced what Marx and Engels (2008[1850]:94) call a "great . . . upheaval of social conditions" and Durkheim (2001[1912]:158) calls a "great collective upheaval." Indeed, as I detail in part 2, Mayas have experienced several upheavals. Moreover, caught between the collapse of their decaying colonial system, which depended on ethnically identified and municipally segmented Maya peasants, and the failure of any new system to give Mayas adequate alternative access to a sustainable and secure means of production, Mayas presently experience "a spiritless situation" and stand at the "heart of a heartless world" in the dispirited, nonreligious sense that Marx (2008[1844]:42) intended. Under such conditions, we would expect, as Marx predicts, a restlessness of ideas in general. We would expect a considerable transformation of the "religious ideas" that have anchored their society. We would expect men and women to express the "ideas and outlook" of "religious distress" and legitimately "protest" the "real distress" they experience in their daily lives (Marx 2008[1844]:42). And they do all of this in Maya Guatemala. But contrary to Marx's expectations, Maya Guatemalans and many others around the world have voiced their protest and real distress not so much with political revolution (although Guatemalans and others have tried that too) as through religious change.

Both Protestant Pentecostal and Catholic charismatic versions of Christian Pentecostalism envision and emotionally represent the pain of experiencing the end of a way of life and the anxiety of having no accessible alternative in view. They do so in trance, in glossolalia, and in hyperamplification tending toward cacophony. As decision-making agents, Christian Pentecostal participants respond to their predicament with religious symbols appropriate to and representing it, as Durkheim would expect. Their experience of collapse and exclusion in society has come to constitute the soul of, the core idea of, their new religion. At the same time, their decisions based on that new perception change the cultural and religious patterns they follow and, they hope, will suitably alter what they consider to be a corrupt and failing society.

I find two additional theorists essential to unraveling the complexity and meaning of religion. Ferdinand de Saussure (1857–1913), a linguist, argues that meaning resides within contrapuntal oppositions in a set of terms. I apply that perspective to help extract the meanings of religion in the two *municipios* of Guatemala we studied. Finally, I use Marcel Mauss (1872–1950) and his ideas of the obligations (or reciprocities) inherent in the gift to tidy up our understanding of the processes of religious

conversion in Guatemala and clarify a society- and universe-embracing redefinition of religion.

In many respects, Durkheim's, Marx's, Weber's, and Wallace's approaches are quite compatible. We need the root ideas of all four theorists, plus the ideas of Saussure and Mauss, to think through and come to understand religion and religious change in Guatemala because movement toward ecstatic religions also constitutes the most important social change affecting Christianity today. I. M. Lewis (1971) popularized the term "ecstatic religion" with his book by that title. Lewis devotes detailed attention to ecstatic aspects of religious practice among the more traditional, seemingly autochthonous, shamanistic sectors of religious practice in societies around the world. He sees ecstaticism primarily as trance behavior that helps protect and give voice to sectors of society whose structural position is either greatly repressed (as is often the case among women) or under cultural transformation (as among the Macha Galla or the Tungus). Ecstaticism in Christianity is not his focus.

Ecstaticism in Christianity is, however, a focus of this book. And we can do no better in stating the theoretical intention of this work than to follow Lewis's lead as to what is needed in the discipline to deal adequately with ecstatic manifestations in Christianity and at the interface of Christianity with traditional, autochthonous, popular religious practices present at various locations where colonialism spread Christianity. Lewis (1971:26) rebukes social science and anthropology for paying too much attention to and for being too "enthralled" by the "theatrical aspects" of ecstatic religious performance. He holds that anthropologists and sociologists thereby fail to deal with an important sociological grounding intertwined with the presence of trance and other forms of ecstatic performance. What, he asks, are the sociological correlates of ecstaticism? Thus, Lewis writes, "few of the more substantial works . . . of comparative religion pause to consider how the production of religious ecstasy might relate to the social circumstances of those who produce it; how enthusiasm might wax and wane in different social conditions; or what functions might flow from it in contrasting types of society" (21).

A pursuit of the sociological grounding of Christian ecstaticism in Guatemalan society is precisely the goal of the present book, in which we analyze Christian ecstaticism and its interface with (supposedly) autochthonous traditionalism in postcolonial societies impacted by the Christian West. Thus, I depart from Lewis's focus on the more traditionalist shamanism of what has usually been thought of as the largely non-Christian traditional sector of religious practice in postcolonial societies. Instead, I examine the rapid pentecostalization of Christianity—a manifestation of ecstatic religion—both in Guatemala and throughout what were once the Christianized European colonies of the Global South. Christianity's center of gravity is being driven southward by expansion in the Global South of the ecstatic religions on what was formerly Christianity's periphery and by diminution of the sedate Christianities traditionally rooted in what might be called the Global North or the Digital North (Johnson and Chung 2009:50–53). Guatemala thus serves as a window revealing the nature of worldwide religious processes. These processes have led to the religious diversity manifest in the increasing pentecostalization of Christianity and its parallels in the expanding fundamentalism in other world faiths.

Indeed, much religious diversity exists in Guatemala. Various formal denominations of Catholic and Protestant/Pentecostal affiliation coexist with independent congregations and with "unchurched" expressions of indigenized and Mayanized faith traditions. Moreover, many people attend the religious practices of more than one faith style. As already noted, the main styles of religious practice in Nahualá and Santa Catarina consist of a Maya Catholicism called traditionalism, the local variant of Ortho-Roman Catholicism, Protestant-derived Pentecostalisms, Pentecostal-derived Catholic charismaticism, and neotraditionalism.

So far, I have been a bit unorthodox in using the word "Pentecostalism" in both a lowercase and a capitalized form. I have referred also to "Christian Pentecostalism." In addition, I have discussed religion without defining it, relying on ordinary notions of the term. Now, however, I must define these terms at least to a first level of accuracy and usage so that we can arrive at a second level of understanding in subsequent chapters.

INITIAL DEFINITIONS OF SOME KEY TERMS

I have neither the talent nor the will to engage in a fight about the definition of religion, but I do need to be more clear. Stringer (2008:16–17) argues that a precise and inclusive definition is impossible. Rather than define, he holds that we should look at a people's—any people's—ordinary daily practices and ideas associated with belief in the immaterial, in Stringer's case, among the English. We do so to arrive at a working notion of religion, rather than a tightly specific definition. I agree, at least for now.

In this book, we examine the ordinary beliefs and activities of Guatemala's Maya indigenous peasant people. This leads me to challenge ordinary understandings of what might be considered religion. I come back to that late in part 3. For now, suffice it to say that in this book I consider religion to be the set of interconnected beliefs, symbols, practices, and social relations that cognitively and socially link living humans—via gift giving and mutually understood expectations of reciprocity—to usually unseen entities considered to be empowered, interventionist, sacred, special, and set apart. These unseen entities or their visible instantiations in images or lived experience affect living humans through the rewards, punishments, interventions, or interactions believers say they may confer upon or have with living humans. The members of all current religious traditions in Guatemala understand these ideas of reciprocity and believe in the existence of generally unseen powers or beings. They know that humans and sacred beings exist in covenant relations with each other. They believe they owe each other generalized reciprocity. Guatemalans—both Maya and non-Maya—know that both humans and divine entities manifest their covenant relatedness with each other through mutual, bidirectional gift giving: rewarding gifts for proper behavior or punishing reciprocities for dereliction or neglect. Living humans and the unseen beings of the spiritual realm—whether good or evil, indifferent or attentive, predictable or capricious—should exchange gifts and uphold reciprocities. All humans and divinities should keep their contracts or pay a price. Humans and the unseen thereby take care of, placate, or remember one another and their expected covenants.

Nevertheless, the possibility of either human or divine indifference, inattentiveness, or capriciousness adds an element of unpredictability to human-divine relationships and lays a foundation for possible excess in behavioral responses when humans, experiencing a run of bad luck, try ever more insistently to placate or even bribe the unseen powers.

Because this definition of religion includes unseen beings, it resonates with historical and current Maya and non-Maya Guatemalan cultural heritages. It is a sufficient definition of religion for the purposes of this book, and it allows for differences of religion or different religions to coexist and operate within a region, an ethnic sector, or a nation. Except for the part about gifting and covenant, it is a definition well within the tradition of Edward B. Tylor (1871:1:383–385), in which religion orients around "belief in Spiritual Beings."

Are there religions that do not subscribe to the existence of some unseen but interventionist being, religions that do not have a concept of a deity or deities? Likely yes. Herbrechtsmeier (1993) and others have argued that certain strands of Buddhist practice, for example, deem deities irrelevant, although many Buddhists give gifts to the unseen. But we have to explore the Maya ethnographic data and theory before I take on this wrinkle in chapter 25, largely through the idea of the gift.

What religions, styles of worship, or ideas about the conduct of the honorable life, in the Guatemalan senses of the term, does this volume treat? We studied five styles of religious practice in a variety of semi-urban and hinterland rural settings in Nahualá and Santa Catarina Ixtahuacán. At this point I only want to lay out the synonyms used for each of these five styles and offer perhaps a distinctive feature or two about each.

I use "traditionalist," "Maya traditionalist," "Maya Catholic," and "traditionalist Catholic" interchangeably to refer to a strand of Mayanized Catholicism or Catholicized Mayanism that appears to its participants to be simultaneously the "correct" form of Catholicism, "the old ways," "older" than the practice of today's Ortho-Catholicism, "traditional," and "Maya." Today, traditionalist practice centers around the ritual leadership of a shamanic or divinatory *ajq'ij*, often with the participation of his wife.

I contrast the term "neotraditionalist" and its variants with "traditionalist," "Maya Catholic," and the other synonyms just noted. In this study, "neotraditionalist" refers exclusively to the recently politicized form of traditionalist religious practice largely used for Maya identity politics. Neotraditionalist leaders seek to establish a pure Maya religion by removing what they perceive as Catholic and Christian content and by enhancing what they perceive as Maya-derived and "ancient." Neotraditionalist practice is also led by an *ajq'ij*, but generally one who is younger and more political than the local and older *ajq'ijab'* (*-ab'* and *-ob'* pluralize nouns referring to people) performing the Maya Catholic rites.

I use "Roman Catholic," "Ortho-Catholic," and "international Catholic" interchangeably to refer to those Catholics who recognize the local parish priest and, through him, the region's bishop, the nation's archbishop, and ultimately the pope of the Holy Roman Catholic Church as their guides to correct religious practice, belief, tradition, and change.

I use "charismatic" and its variants to refer to that strand of Catholicism that has adopted many attributes of Protestant Pentecostal worship and that seeks to "renew" traditionalist Catholics and Ortho-Catholics by infusing in them the bodily reception of the Holy Spirit as evidenced by exuberant, ecstatic worship practice, including electronic amplification, bodily movement, trance falling, glossolalia, and healing. Each local, small charismatic community in a hamlet or urban canton worships under the guidance of a married couple approved by the Ortho-Catholic parish priest.

I use "Protestant" in reference to the historical or mainline sedate denominations and derivatives of the Reformation's opposition to the theology and practice maintained by the Roman Catholic Church. I use *evangélico* and the English translation "Evangelical" as this term is understood today in the Guatemalan villages: it applies to people or congregations that identify with energized, Spirit-engaged Pentecostal Protestant worship emphasizing anti-Catholic contrasts and ecstatic worship in pursuit of repeated bodily experience of the Spirit via electronic amplification, bodily movement, trance falling, glossolalia, and healing. Occasionally, even in the Maya villages, *evangélico* is used with a wider meaning to refer to any non-Catholic religious congregation or person. This might include Mormons, Mennonites, Jehovah's Witnesses, or mainline Protestants trying to contrast themselves with Pentecostals who, nevertheless, might be performatively Christian Pentecostal.

And, as indicated above, I have coined the term "Christian Pentecostal" to enable the analytical discussion of both Pentecostals and Pentecostal-mimicking Catholic charismatics, classed together. I seek to understand this Christian Pentecostalism, this newest style of Christian worship.

Anderson (2000) provides a solid approach to a definition of Christian Pentecostal that certainly works in the two *municipios* we studied. What I call Christian Pentecostal, he calls Pentecostal (in 2013) and pentecostal (in 2000), which includes classic Pentecostal denominations, charismatics from the historic denominations, and neo-Pentecostal independents. The Pentecostal movement, he suggests, should not be defined by some specificity of doctrine as to how, when, or in what sequence or name the stages of salvation come. Rather, Anderson (2000:24–25, emphases in original) argues, a religious congregation is pentecostal—my Christian Pentecostal—if its leaders and members engage in an effort "concerned primarily with the *experience* of the working of the Holy Spirit and the *practice* of spiritual gifts." Some years later, Anderson (2013:8, emphases in original) again asserts that Pentecostalism "includes all those movements and churches where the emphasis is on an ecstatic *experience of the Spirit* and a tangible *practice of spiritual gifts*." In my studies in Guatemala, such "working" or ecstaticism entails embodiment, sensoriality, and participation. It is almost always associated in major meetings with the electronic hyperamplification of coordinated music and sermon. The liturgical practice exudes energy in waves of ecstaticism that include bodily motion, some speaking in tongues, occasional immobility from having fallen to the floor in apparent trance, and, notably, healing. Indeed, speaking in tongues, intense movement sometimes followed by trance, and healing are central to a Maya's perception of having experienced a bodily engagement with the Holy Spirit, even if that experience is not achieved in every meeting nor by all participants in a given meeting. Thus, a pentecostal liturgy that fosters the acquisition of the Spirit can be extraordinarily—at least, in my perception—noisy and active.[1] Moreover, the speaking-in-tongues component of pentecostal verbal behavior is not syntactically, morphologically, or phonologically complex enough to be classed as a human language. The unlanguaged aspect of glossolalia highlights the shift from a Protestant emphasis on mental apprehension of the theo-*logical* "word" to a pentecostal emphasis on bodily *experience* of the Spirit. It is this experientiality—this exuberant bodily behavior, this speaking in tongues, and this path to healing—that documents that one's body has been imbued and infused with, or penetrated and taken over by, the Holy Spirit. That is what distinguishes pentecostal worship and pentecostal faiths from other varieties of Christianity, not the denominational name or any Protestant versus Catholic derivation. I use the term "pentecostal wail" to describe this form of worship. I do so not to denigrate it; rather, I hope it appropriately expresses the angst and insecurity of contemporary Maya life in rural Guatemala.

The analytical term "Christian Pentecostal" (and, occasionally, deliberately lowercase pentecostal) helps us explore more effectively the observed data. It enables us to perceive and analyze a set of relationships otherwise hidden in the data of daily life because their patterns are categorized under separate terms—Protestant Pentecostal and Catholic charismatic—for these religious groups tend to be studied separately by anthropologists and sociologists of religion, and members of the two groups see themselves as distinct. They are distinct. But they also share close resemblances that should be recognized more and studied together. With the notable exceptions of Chesnut (2003a), Althoff (2014), and Gooren (2010, 2012), however, scholars generally have researched either Protestant Pentecostals (many studies) or Catholic charismatics (rather fewer studies) separately, as one-off examinations of a distinct religious community. By contrast, our method of simultaneously produced comparative fieldwork highlights the considerable similarities between Pentecostal Protestant and charismatic Catholic practices and beliefs.

To underline those similarities and make their collective analysis transparent and unambiguous, I initially followed the lead of Brown (2011:4) and Yong (2005:18–19). Both signal important similarities between Protestant and Catholic ecstatic practices as a collective type by using lowercase "pentecostal" to discuss the commonalities of ecstatic worship in twentieth-century Christianity. Both Brown and Yong reserve uppercase "Pentecostal" to refer to ecstatic denominations, congregations, practices, beliefs, and church traditions derived from mainstream Protestant denominations, the Evangelical Protestant holiness tradition, and Pentecostal backgrounds that have remained denominational or become indigenized and independent. Likewise, Anderson (2000) chose the lowercase "pentecostal" to emphasize the diversity in the movement. I chose to do the same, for a while.

Eventually it dawned on me that analytical pentecostalism, combining both Protestant and Catholic versions of pentecostalism, was in fact a distinct fourth type or branch of Christianity, as different from the other main branches of Christianity—Eastern Orthodoxy, Roman Catholicism, and Protestantism—as each of these is different from the others. I detail and defend this proposition in chapter 22. Here let me say that it simply looked disrespectful and unequal to capitalize the names of the three recognized branches of Christianity and treat the fourth branch—the one I propose—in lowercase. Using the new term "Christian Pentecostalism" remedies this problem; it allocates equal respect in the capitalization. As a practical matter, I use the variants "pentecostal" and

"Christian Pentecostal" interchangeably throughout this book.

One might ask, is the distinction between Pentecostal Protestant and generic Christian Pentecostal (Catholic and Protestant combined) worth the fuss? That is, do we need a conjoined Christian Pentecostal category to analyze Christian religious behavior insightfully? Steigenga (2007) provides an answer. He surveyed both Catholics and evangelicos to explore statistically the impact of religious differences on political "apathy" and levels of political participation. To his credit, Steigenga asked all those he surveyed, independent of denomination, if they had spoken in tongues, an indication of ecstatic religious activity. This enabled him to segment his data not just in terms of *evangélico* and Catholic, but also in terms of pentecostalized versus non-pentecostalized, regardless of formal Catholic or Protestant denomination. Steigenga (2007:266–268) shows that Catholics and Protestants who exhibit the pentecostal/charismatic attribute of speaking in tongues are—at a statistically significant level—more like each other on a number of attributes (wealth, education, political participation) than they are like the non-charismatics of their own religious denomination, whether *evangélico* or Catholic. He notes this "high degree of pentecostalization across religious groups in Guatemala" and concludes that "*religious charismaticism and not religious affiliation* is the crucial factor" in determining the social and political impact of religious change in Guatemala (268, 266, emphasis added). On the basis of our qualitative and quantitative data for Nahualá and Santa Catarina Ixtahuacán, I concur with Steigenga. The distinction is very much worth the fuss. With these terms in hand, I can now outline the issues that we address throughout the book.

RELIGIOUS CHANGE

All these strands of religion coexist in Guatemala. Each is practiced in Nahualá and Santa Catarina Ixtahuacán in the "present day" of 2003–2019. I explore the meanings that these faiths have had for their adherents, describe the worship practices in these religions, and examine the broad social conditions in which religious life has been lived and how the practices have evolved. I seek in this book to account for the fact that the distribution of Guatemalans among these faith traditions has undergone rapid change over the last eighty years. Guatemalans and Mayas have moved increasingly from sedate to ecstatic and from Catholic to Pentecostal and pentecostalized Catholic.

The massive distributional change of religious practice compels scholarly attention. These religious changes have proceeded even more quickly in Nahualá and Santa Catarina Ixtahuacán than in the rest of Guatemala in spite of having gotten a later start. Thus, in a mere fifty or so years, these two towns and their hinterlands changed from being nearly 100 percent sedate, wary Maya Catholic traditionalists and a few Ortho-Catholics in the late 1950s to about 70 percent exuberant Christian Pentecostal religious practitioners in the present. Today, roughly 40 percent of the people throughout the communities we studied are Pentecostal Protestants (*evangélicos*). Of the remaining 60 percent, roughly half are pentecostal Catholics (*carismáticos*). Most of the rest are Ortho-Catholic, cultural Catholic, traditionalist/Catholic, and neotraditionalist. Finally, there are a few people who assert they are completely unaffiliated with religion, and there are some Mormons (a faith tradition that one student studied but did not write up) and Jehovah's Witnesses (a faith tradition that we did not study).

Given how implacably conservative and inward-oriented the Mayas were reported to be in the 1930s–1950s ethnographies—taciturn and evasive, focused inwardly on cultural maintenance in their communities of refuge, unexpressive of emotion in public, and even surly toward outsiders at times—this transformation in which many Mayas have turned toward outwardly emotional, expressive, and exuberant religions is remarkable and needs to be understood. Why did this transformation from non-electronic to hyperamplified electronic religion happen? And why did the move from largely sedate (except in fiesta inebriation and the shamanic trance of the most respected traditionalist senior leaders) to largely ecstatic happen? What do the different faith practices mean to their adherents? How can one account for the accelerations in Christian Pentecostal growth, first in the 1950s, then in the early 1970s, and again in the 1980s–1990s? What does the religious landscape of Guatemala now look like, and how does it now operate?

ORGANIZATION OF THE BOOK

In chapter 1, I describe briefly the social and economic conditions and geographical setting of the two *municipios* we studied. These *municipios* are in the process of moving from relatively autonomous corn-based economies rooted in Maya culture to globally peripheral economies of corn agriculturalists forced to sustain their families with added artisan and wage labor. This is the setting for the ethnographies of religion produced by our collaborative field school. The chapters of part 1 deliver intimate ethnographies of religious practice and belief as they existed in 2002–2003 in these two *municipio* centers and their rural hamlets. As Kovic (2007:201), Hall (1997:vii), Orsi (2005), and de Certeau and Rendall (1984) advocate, these ethnographies lay out "lived religions" and their everyday practices in various ecological niches in these *municipios*.

The first five chapters in part 1 focus on traditionalist and Roman Catholic practices, and chapters 7–10 turn to *evangélico*/Pentecostal worship. Chapters 11–13 explore the Catholic charismatic style of worship, which explicitly mimics the major attributes and perceived strengths of Pentecostal worship.

None of the chapters in part 1 should be taken as theoretical statements. Rather, they are intended to be descriptive, depicting varieties of religious life as they are lived. Nor are they the whole story of religious change in Guatemala. Guatemala is a diverse country, and each of its 331 *municipios* in 2002 and 340 municipios in 2020 have their particular story of religion, religious change, and historical and social processes to tell. Yet the experience of religious change in Nahualá and Santa Catarina Ixtahuacán that we document here offers a window that helps us see and think about much of what is going on regarding religion elsewhere in Guatemala and, indeed, throughout the world.

In part 2, I account for the meaningfulness of the Christian Pentecostal wail by exploring the history of religious change and religious conflict in Guatemala. In chapters 14–21, I move through successive periods of Guatemalan history, focusing in each on a stage of Guatemala's political economy and how it connects to religion: pre-Spanish on corn, colonial on submission, independence on coffee and modernization of infrastructure, and conservative military governments on control and terror during war. Each chapter details how a major change in Guatemala's society and political economy links to a substantial shift in its religious behaviors and beliefs. In particular, I elaborate the importance of corn in Maya culture, and I show that the decline in per capita land and corn production accounts for the phenomenal rise of Christian Pentecostal conversions, the decline in the importance of land-symbolizing traditionalism, and the fall in hierarchically

oriented Ortho-Catholic affiliation. In addition, I use statistical methods to show that the standard (and previously unexamined) academic presumption that the disruptions of earthquake and civil war generated the surge toward Protestant and Pentecostal membership is incorrect. Statistical tests of the available data confirm only the explanation of culture collapse occasioned by a fall in land and therefore corn per capita. Given that culture collapse and exclusion produce liminality, I argue that the Christian Pentecostal wail is a rational and appropriate emotional expression of the angst of collapse and exclusion, an expression that needs to be understood rather than disparaged by academics and believers of other faiths.

Part 3 develops the theoretical interpretation of the previous ethnographies and history using a synchronic approach. My explicitly Saussurean approach to meaning complements the one derived from historical sources in part 2. These data lead to two conclusions. First, the most interesting process of change in Christianity today is not from Catholic to Protestant, but from sedate religions (Catholic or Protestant) to ecstatic religions (Pentecostal or charismatic). Here the term "Christian Pentecostal" comes to center place, for Christian Pentecostalism represents the most important social movement of the twentieth and twenty-first centuries in the postcolonial, Christianized Global South. Second, Christian Pentecostalism is so different in its base premises and practices regarding the proper pursuit of a relation with God that it deserves to be considered—nay, it demands that we consider it—a distinctively fourth branch of Christianity, equal to and alongside Eastern Orthodoxies, Roman Catholicism, and the world's Protestantisms. Of equal importance, I argue that gifting provides a better understanding of the individual conversion process than religious marketplace metaphors and that gifting, reciprocity, and their effect of incorporating the universe into human society constitutes a better approach to a definition of religion.

In the book's conclusion, I explore the following question: if Christian Pentecostal success is a response to collapsing culture and subsistence systems and exclusion from alternatives, how does one account for Christian Pentecostalism's increasing presence in middle-class and even elite sectors of Euro-American society where, presumptively, one sees neither collapse nor exclusion? I suggest that elites increasingly understand that the growing complexity of developed nations make them ever more subject to threat of collapse. Secularization may be a trend in northern globalized, digitized societies, but that mounting risk of collapse produces increased angst and nutures the spread of Christian Pentecostalism into the most digitized economies and societies. I conclude with the notion that the idea of the gift is both the soul of religion and the basis of society, reaffirming and specifying more carefully Durkheim's social and symbolic take on the nature of religion as a representation of the nature of society.

THE GOAL OF RESPECTFUL UNDERSTANDING

In sum, I argue that the cacophony, glossolalia, and trance states of Christian Pentecostal practice accurately reflect—indeed, they literally decry—current Maya social conditions, and they resonate culturally with deeply held Maya premises. In those senses, this practice is fully rational and accurately connected to reality. Academics and everyone else must take Christian Pentecostalism seriously. They must understand Christian Pentecostalism for what it is: a cry of angst in a culturally collapsing world.

Like many who are reading this, neither I nor my field school codirector, Walter Adams, nor any of the chapters' lead ethnographers are or have been Pentecostal or charismatic. Personally, I have found the cries of the Christian Pentecostal wail emotionally wrenching, just as wrenching as I have found the tears of Ortho-Catholics on their knees as they plead with saints for some blessing to be gifted or reciprocally exchanged. So much pain from their lives gets poured out in prayer. In Christian Pentecostal meetings, however, the cacophony of the electronically boosted liturgy can be physically distressing; my ears have buzzed for as much as an hour after some meetings, a sign of physical damage being done. Yet the loudness and the energy and the glossolalia are there for a reason. They symbolize and communicate the urgency of the unspeakably harsh and chaotic realities many Mayas experience today—living as they do in a liminal state, caught between ongoing cultural collapse and systematic exclusion.

We must therefore respect the multiple religious traditions of Maya Guatemala: traditionalists, neotraditionalists, Ortho-Catholics, historic Protestants, Pentecostals, charismatic Catholics, and others we were not able to study. We have tried to find out what each style of Guatemalan religious practice means to its adherents, how and why each religious style is lived the way it is in contemporary Guatemala, and what the various religions do for the individuals, families, and communities in the Guatemalan context.

This goal of respectful understanding is implicit in Durkheim when he suggests that Australian Aboriginal religion, and indeed all religion, cannot be a "mere tissue of an illusion." For Durkheim, Aboriginal religion is a social and cultural fact, a symbol system that speaks to and works toward social cohesion within a society and that links and relates that society to its known environmental universe. I argue for the same conclusion regarding present day Christian Pentecostalism in Guatemala and elsewhere. It is not a tissue of illusion; it is a tightly woven canvas of socially transformative power. In being emotional, in being cacophonic, in being end-of-the-world oriented, and in calling the world corrupt, Christian Pentecostalism is a thought-filled, emotionally cathartic, and quite accurate statement about the nature of society and the universe as experienced by these Mayas. In addition, it is a reasoned prescription for what to do about collapse, exclusion, liminality, and powerlessness in a chaotic society operating within a failing state.

In this journey toward respectful understanding, we begin by examining how religion is lived in the daily lives of ordinary Maya Guatemalans in Nahualá and Santa Catarina Ixtahuacán, and to do that I must introduce the communities.

NOTE

1. In June 2017 I used a decibel meter app I had installed on my cell phone to establish that in one Pentecostal meeting in Nahualá, participants worshipped for two hours within a sustained sound level of 103–108 decibels, with crescendo music bursts that reached 114 decibels.

Chapter One

The Communities of Nahualá and Santa Catarina Ixtahuacán

JOHN P. HAWKINS

ÉMILE DURKHEIM IS JUSTLY FAMOUS for directing attention primarily to the importance of understanding the power inherent in the social nature of society; largely he analyzes the social structures and social institutions whose participants make social facts of the shared cultural ideas he calls the *conscience collective*, the collective consciousness. Nevertheless, he also recognizes the impact of physical conditions, what he calls the "material substrate," on how people handle their lives (Durkheim (2001[1912].318–319). In this chapter I lay out some notes on the material setting that constrains the lives of the Mayas inhabiting Nahualá and Santa Catarina Ixtahuacán, two contiguous *municipios* located in western highland Guatemala.

The *municipios* of Nahualá and Santa Catarina Ixtahuacán lie on the south-facing slope of the Pacific coast volcanic chain that is the backbone of Guatemala. They drape from the cold passes at 10,000 feet and higher (more than 3,070 meters) to the much hotter and lower *bocacosta* coffee piedmont at some 600 feet (approximately 200 meters) above sea level. As one can see in maps 1 and 2, the two *municipios* lie northwest and west of Lake Atitlán, separated from direct access to the lake by other *municipios*. Both claim to share borders with the Departments of Totonicapán and Quetzaltenango, although common maps tend to show just Nahualá touching these departments. A forty-five-minute bus ride to the southeast takes a Nahualense to the *municipio* of Sololá, which hosts the department capital's offices. Sololá provides markets, hospital access, and, above all, the necessary legal and administrative services that connect *municipios* and residents to the nation.

For most of their out-of-community economic needs, Nahualenses and Ixtahuaquenses travel west an hour by bus to Quetzaltenango—commonly called Xela—Guatemala's second-largest city. People from the northern half of these two *municipios* go to Xela when they need something from the globalized world that they cannot find (or wait for) in Nahualá's large, sprawling Sunday market, which supplies much of their foodstuffs, purchased clothing, hardware, housewares, music tapes, CDs, and small radio, telephone, and audio equipment.

POPULATION, LAND, LANGUAGE, AND ETHNICITY

Table 1.1 reveals some salient comparisons of Nahualá and Santa Catarina Ixtahuacán with other *municipios* in the nation regarding land area, population, and density. One notes that the *municipios* of Nahualá and Santa Catarina Ixtahuacán are large in population and densely inhabited compared to other rural *municipios*, even in the high-density western indigenous departments. Figure 1.1 shows how the populations of Nahualá and Santa Catarina Ixtahuacán have increased dramatically over time. Figure 1.2 shows how that population increase plays out as a density increase.[1] Because Santa Catarina Ixtahuacán has had a higher rate of annual population increase, its population gradually has become denser than that of Nahualá.

Ethnically and linguistically, the *municipios* of Nahualá and Santa Catarina Ixtahuacán each give residence—overwhelmingly—to indigenous, K'iche'-speaking people. K'iche' speakers in Guatemala number about 1.27 million, according to the 2002 Guatemala census. K'iche' is one of the larger of some twenty-one to twenty-six Maya family languages spoken in Guatemala, and one of some thirty to thirty-four languages in the Maya family in Mesoamerica (England 2003:733; https://en.wikipedia.org/wiki/Mayan_languages). How many languages there

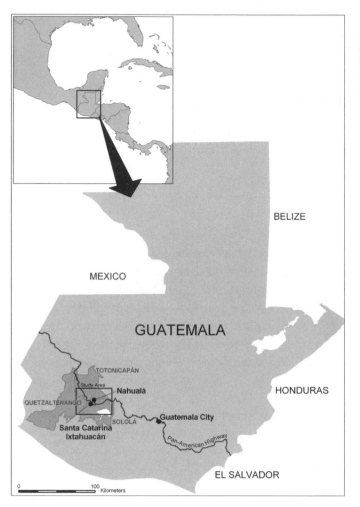

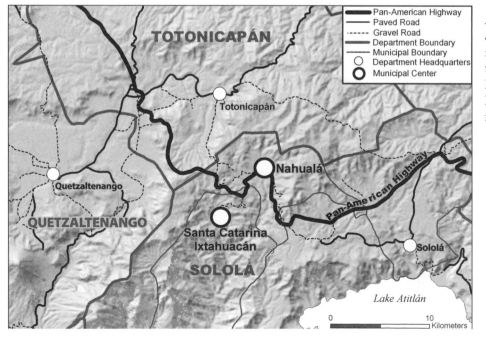

TABLE 1.1. POPULATION AND LAND AREA COMPARISONS (2002 CENSUS)

	GUATEMALA[a]	GUATEMALA EXCLUDING DEPARTMENTS OF PETÉN AND GUATEMALA[b]	WESTERN HIGHLAND DEPARTMENTS[c]	DEPARTMENT OF SOLOLÁ	MUNICIPIO OF NAHUALÁ	MUNICIPIO OF SANTA CATARINA IXTAHUACÁN
# of departments	22	20	7	1	n/a	n/a
Total area (km²)	108,892	70,921	25,630	1,061	218	127
Mean area per dept. (km²)	4,950	3,546	3,661	1,061	n/a	n/a
2002 census of inhabitants	11,237,196	8,328,880	4,014,769	307,661	51,939	41,208
Mean inhabitants/department	510,782	416,444	573,538	307,661	n/a	n/a
Inhabitants/km²	103	117	157	290	238	324
% increase 1973–2002	117.7	108.9	116	141.7	137.4	155.8
# of municipios, 2002	331	302	148	19	1	1
Mean # of municipios/department	15	15	21	19	n/a	n/a
Mean inhabitants/municipio	33,949	27,579	27,127	16,193	51,939	41,208
Mean area/municipio (km²)	329	235	235	56	218	127

Notes: [a] Excludes Guatemala's nominal claim on Belize.

[b] Department of Petén is excluded because of its unusually expansive forests and low population for much of its history; Department of Guatemala is excluded because of unusual urban density.

[c] Includes Departments of San Marcos, Huehuetenango, Quetzaltenango, Quiché, Sololá, Chimaltenango, and Totonicapán.

Sources: Morales Urrutia 1961; Prado Ponce 1984 (areas); INE 2002a, 2003a (population figures).

Figure 1.1. Populations of Nahualá and Santa Catarina Ixtahuacán. *Sources*: Secretario de Estado del Despacho de Fomento, Sección de Estadística 1880; Dirección General de Estadística 1897, 1921, 1924, 1942, 1957, 1971–1972, 1974, 1982b; INE 1994, 2002a, 2002b, 2002c.

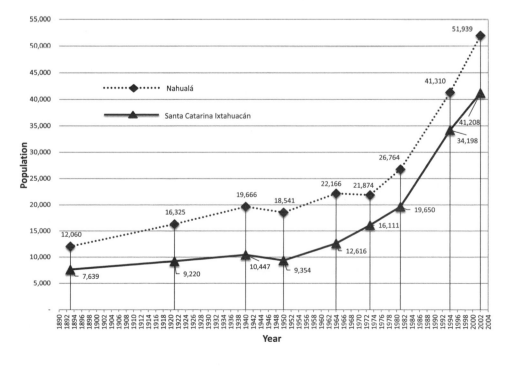

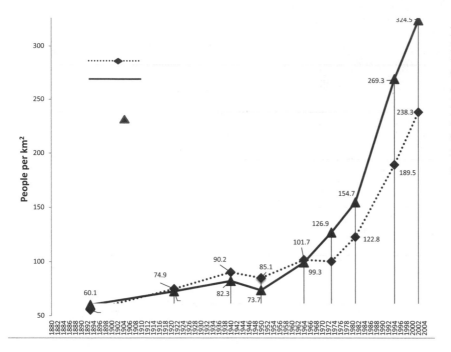

Figure 1.2. Population densities of Nahualá and Santa Catarina Ixtahuacán. See the note in the text for concerns about the *municipios'* areas. *Sources*: Secretario de Estado del Despacho de Fomento, Sección de Estadística 1880; Dirección General de Estadística 1897, 1921, 1924, 1942, 1957, 1971–1972, 1974, 1982b; INE 1994, 2002a, 2002b, 2002c.

are depends on how finely linguists parse the dialect differences that characterize each municipality. As one can see in figure 1.3, from 1880 to 1999, Nahualá and Santa Catarina did not drop below 99 percent indigenous Maya first-language speakers, except in the 1994 population census. The variations are probably due more to foibles in census procedures than to real trends in the percentage of Maya speakers in the two *municipios* over the 136 years for which we have census data. Table 1.2 compares the two towns with the nation, the western region's departments, and the Department of Sololá regarding ethnicity and language use in 2002. At 99.5 percent or more Maya, Nahualá and Santa Catarina Ixtahuacán remain among the highest percentages of Maya ethnicity and Maya language retention in the nation.

Mostly endogamous marriages have led to genealogies that have largely remained within their communities for generations. Until recently, little use has been made of hospitals in the department capitals or significant cities. As a result, place of birth identifies one ethnically, ties one to kin, and places one on the land or in a trade from one's community of origin. Origin by birth, based on one's parentage in a particular *municipio*, has long been recognized as a defining feature of indigeneity. Thus, Guatemalan census figures spanning 136 years confirm the overwhelmingly dominant indigenous linguistic and ethnic character of these communities.

Most Nahualenses and Ixtahuaquenses grow up in

K'iche'-speaking families and encounter a need to learn Spanish for the first time in elementary school. However, a few resident adult K'iche' Mayas, mostly schoolteachers, try to speak Spanish in the home because they recognize that Spanish serves as the lubricating language of trade and administrative control throughout the country. By speaking Spanish at home, they feel they give their children an advantage in school.

In the urban centers of Nahualá and Santa Catarina Ixtahuacán, many men under age forty to fifty speak Spanish as a second language rather well, especially those whose work includes some government employment or outside trade. Likewise in the town centers, a few women under thirty speak some Spanish willingly, but those over thirty usually prefer to be monolingual K'iche' speakers, though they often can muster a few words in Spanish. Except for children of people returned from recent international labor migrations and a few children whose parents want them to learn Spanish rapidly by not speaking K'iche' in the home, all indigenous residents of Nahualá and Santa Catarina Ixtahuacán prefer K'iche' to Spanish as the natural language of home and neighborhood. In the rural hamlets, K'iche' use strongly predominates. There, a few men manifest some facility with the trade language, while most women say they speak very little to no Spanish. Within this general statement on language use, I should note that Pentecostals and Mormons tend to have better Spanish than do Catholics because significant

TABLE 1.2. POPULATION, ETHNICITY, AND LANGUAGE COMPARISONS (2002 CENSUS)

		GUATEMALA[a]	GUATEMALA EXCLUDING DEPARTMENTS OF PETÉN AND GUATEMALA[b]	WESTERN HIGHLAND DEPARTMENTS[c]	DEPARTMENT OF SOLOLÁ	MUNICIPIO OF NAHUALÁ	MUNICIPIO OF SANTA CATARINA IXTAHUACÁN
TOTAL INHABITANTS		11,237,196	8,328,880	4,014,769	307,661	51,939	41,208
INDIGENOUS INHABITANTS	Total	4,610,440	4,153,824	2,703,079	296,710	51,924	41,190
	% of total	41.03	49.87	67.33	96.44	99.97	99.96
	Mean/department	209,565	207,691	386,154	296,710	n/a	n/a
	Mean/municipio	13,929	13,754	18,264	15,616	51,924	41,190
% OF TOTAL INHABITANTS LEARNING THIS AS FIRST LANGUAGE[d]	Maya	30.9	38.6	54.8	89.5	99.7	99.5
	Spanish	67.8	61.2	44.8	10.4	0.3	0.5
	Other[e]	0.2	0.2	0.4	0.08	0.002	0.005

Notes: [a] Excludes Guatemala's nominal claim on Belize.

[b] Department of Petén excluded because of its unusually expansive forests and low population for much of its history; Department of Guatemala is excluded because of unusual urban density.

[c] Includes Departments of San Marcos, Huehuetenango, Quetzaltenango, Quiché, Sololá, Chimaltenango, and Totonicapán.

[d] Calculated from figures based on population three years of age and over.

[e] "Other" includes non-Spanish and non-indigenous languages as first languages learned, including English, German, French, and Arabic. The residual percentage includes the Xinka and Garifuna speakers in the country.

Source: INE 2003a.

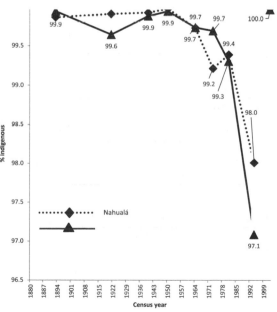

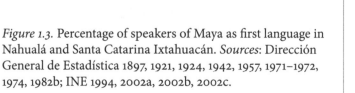

Figure 1.3. Percentage of speakers of Maya as first language in Nahualá and Santa Catarina Ixtahuacán. *Sources*: Dirección General de Estadística 1897, 1921, 1924, 1942, 1957, 1971–1972, 1974, 1982b; INE 1994, 2002a, 2002b, 2002c.

parts of non-Catholic ritual involve reading the Bible and singing hymns in Spanish, and both Pentecostals and Mormons use Spanish to interact regularly with visiting regional leaders of their faith.

When speaking, the Mayas of Nahualá and Santa Catarina Ixtahuacán sharply contrast their indigenous status with the outsider Ladinos, called *mu's* (pl. *mu'sayib'*) in K'iche', literally "strangers, foreigners, aliens." A few non-Mayas do live in the communities. In the former municipal head town, now known as Antigua Ixtahuacán, the resident priest was an American during our study period.[2] Some years, he was helped by an American volunteer who fomented development aid projects with Catholic funding. In Nahualá during the years we held the field school, one or both of the resident priests were Spaniards, while the other was from another country or was Guatemalan. Some of the nuns have been non-Guatemalan. In the early years of the field school, a Peace Corps volunteer worked and resided in Nahualá. Before the field school, there had been one also in Santa Catarina Ixtahuacán. No one seems able to remember when either terminated, and there has been none that I know of since 2000 in either *municipio*. Perhaps a half dozen anthropologists of foreign extraction have resided in one or the other of the two towns, and occasionally a student or church group has visited. The state system assigns medical personnel and other government officers in Nahualá to work, but they do not usually live there, preferring to commute.

Thus, in both *municipios*, the few Ladinos who work in the governing towns arrive each Monday morning. They come on buses and motorbikes to the municipal centers to work in schools, NGO offices, and government agencies. In Nueva Ixtahuacán and Nahualá, many commute daily because of the ease of transportation access. In Antigua Santa Catarina, there have been none since 2000. Prior to the fission in 2000, on weeknights, some Ladinos overnighted in a dingy municipal services rooming house and left the *municipio* each Friday afternoon. Nahualá and Nueva Ixtahuacán supply many of their own teachers, but a substantial number still commute from nearby cities. During the week, the resident foreigners, the handful of commuting Ladinos, and the traveling salesmen resupplying stores in Nahualá are hardly noticeable but for their *cargo* vans and trucks. On weekends, any Ladinos overnighting during the work week have gone home. Except for the priests, the town centers and surrounding hinterland of rural hamlets of both Nahualá and Santa Catarina Ixtahuacán seem virtually 100 percent indigenous.

When speaking of themselves, Nahualenses and Ixtahuaquenses often use the Spanish term *indígena*, frequently the term "K'iche'," and occasionally the term "Maya" to identify their ethnicity.[3] Most readily of all, however, they give their Nahualense or Ixtahuaquense township of birth and residence as an ethnic identifying marker: They are, respectively, *ajNiwala* or *ajCatalin*. Indeed, Guatemala remains divided not only by language and ethnicity but fiercely by a municipalization of identity. These people are "Nahualense" or "Ixtahuaquense" (or "Catalineco") first and "*indígena*," "K'iche'," or "Maya" a distant second, third, and fourth. Despite the inculcation of daily salutes to the flag and renditions of the national anthem in schoolyard ceremonies, Guatemalan identity rates as a distinct fifth, although with migration and increasing penetration of state services into the indigenous *municipios*, people's Guatemalan identity is now expanding rapidly in importance. The municipalization of indigenous identity that Tax (1937) found so compelling in the 1930s nevertheless remains strong.

ECONOMIC AND SOCIAL OUTLINES OF THE TWO TOWNS AND THE REGION

Corn dominates the agricultural economy of highland Nahualá and Santa Catarina; indeed, at some times of the year corn literally hangs over their lives (plate 1). McBryde (1945), Early (1982), and Annis (1987), among others, have described the Maya peasant agricultural system in rich detail. Except for the use now of chemical fertilizers, little has changed. Thus, I offer only a brief review.

The people of Nahualá and Santa Catarina Ixtahuacán cultivate their corn by human labor. With a large handheld hoe (Sp. *azadón*; K'i. *asaron*), they turn the ground for planting, weed, rick up a supportive dirt mound around the growing plants, and do other chores. With a machete, men, boys, and occasionally women clean brush, weed, and trim and harvest wood. With a planting stick, machete point, or even an *azadón*, they easily plant in the cleared and overturned fields. With an ax or machete, they can take down a tree or some of its limbs and prepare and split wood and kindling. While chain saws are common among those who make a living from harvesting wood, none of us saw an engine-powered tiller or a tractor in these *municipios* during the years of field school operations (1995–2006, 2009).

In the fields—*milpas* in Spanish, *ab'ix, awex,* or *tiko'n* in K'iche'—people plant corn primarily, and they inter-plant beans frequently. Corn supplies people with energy. Beans provide protein. The two plants live symbiotically: beans climb the corn stalks while they provide rhizome fertilization to the corn. At the ground level, most fields are kept weed-free and dirt-visible. Planted squashes sometimes cover patches of a *milpa* at ground level. Useful wild herbs and medicinal plants as well as volunteer cultigens from a previous season are allowed to grow and are harvested as needed. Such plants reduce soil erosion and supply nutritious spices, vegetables, vitamins, and medicines.

Occasionally one sees a patch of vegetables raised as a cash mono-crop. Neither Nahualenses nor Ixtahuaquenses, however, have entered significantly into exportable vegetable production of such cash crops as broccoli, cauliflower, lettuce, cabbage, carrots, or onions, which one sees predominantly in Panajachel, Zunil, Almolonga, and across the flat fertile plains between Chimaltenango and Tecpán (Fischer 2006; Goldin 2011). The 2003 agro-census reports only 112 *cuerdas* of vegetable truck crops planted in Nahualá and 320 *cuerdas* in Ixtahuacán compared to 36,304 *cuerdas* of corn in Nahualá and 19,984 *cuerdas* of corn in Santa Catarina Ixtahuacán.[4] Just to be complete, Nahualenses also harvested 48 *cuerdas* of potatoes and 208 *cuerdas* of wheat while Ixtahuaquenses harvested 208 *cuerdas* of potatoes and 288 *cuerdas* of wheat. (The census rounded to the nearest *manzana*, equal to 16 *cuerdas*.)

In addition to the common corn and its associated bean and (less frequently) squash complex, one sees domestic animals. Some families raise a few sheep for meat and wool but mainly to sell for ready bursts of cash. Some raise goats. A few households have a cow; some feed a pig their household garbage. Ownership of a horse helps a few families transport firewood from mountain to home or market and carry agricultural products to market, but a considerable amount of local firewood and crops is carried on Maya backs. That is changing, however, and pickups increasingly do more of the local heavy transportation. Local access roads branch and rebranch, spidering out to all of the hamlets and sometimes beyond the last hamlet into forest or field. But the pickups and other manufactured objects owned by these Mayas come from outside the *municipio*, from the global world. They must be purchased. The expanding presence of purchased manufactures in these villages represents either the sale of corn from the fields or family labor sold locally or internationally. Of course, many families sell their excess labor

because most have insufficient land to absorb their available labor or to feed the demanding mouths. Purchases are made because of obvious convenience; pickups haul much more wood or corn than pack animals and do the work much more comfortably than by human portage.

Indigenes find themselves subject to incessant marketing. The global system creates new needs through billboards, radio and television ads and programs, and the visibility of high-status Ladino ethnic styles, which are much displayed in windows and worn in Guatemalan cities. Marx and Engels (1948[1848]:12–13) comment on this process as they saw it among the peasant farmers of Europe: "In place of the old wants, satisfied by the production of the country, we find new wants, requiring for their satisfaction the products of distant lands and climes. In place of the old local and national seclusion and self-sufficiency, we have intercourse in every direction, universal inter-dependence of nations." This "economic intercourse," these purchases from the global world, put added strain on the family farm, which from time immemorial has run under the cultural premise (and goal) of self-sufficiency. Today (our experience from 1995 to 2019), the farms and families of Nahualá and Ixtahuacán must not only provide for more Maya mouths than a generation or two ago, but the farm or the family's labor must also feed the far-away makers of products that supply the expanding wants of indigenous people.

How much land have the inhabitants of these *municipios* had through time? Figure 1.4 gives landholdings in agricultural service, including farmed land in annuals and perennials, pastures, and forest, held in possessed *fincas* (estates). Of these kinds of land, annual crop land is most important as it produces the corn and beans that undergird the Maya diet.

Corn not only dominates Mayas' fields, it also dominates their minds. Corn forms the axial symbolic system around which these K'iche' people organize gender relations, family interactions, and notions of personal worth. Annis (1987) argues that the corn production system is driven by interwoven cultural premises he dubs "*milpa* logic," a conceptual system that prioritizes focusing a family's available labor in its corn-cropping land and investing the excess beyond subsistence needs in ways that enhance the family's local municipal social status.

So how much land is needed to sustain an indigenous family? While the figures are somewhat variable, there is reasonably close agreement between both official estimates and the ethnographies that discuss the matter.

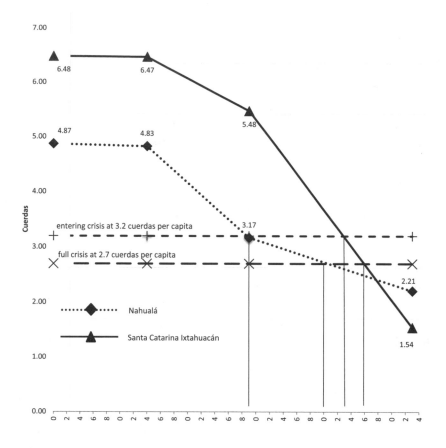

Figure 1.4. Per capita landholdings, Nahualá and Santa Catarina Ixtahuacán. *Sources*: Dirección General de Estadística 1957, 1968, 1971a, 1971b, 1971–1972, 1974, 1982a, 1982b; INE 1994, 2002a, 2002b, 2002c, 2003, 2004a, 2004b.

Officially, in national census data, possession of 16 *cuerdas* or less is considered "subfamilial"—inadequate for family subsistence. Annis (1987) computes the minimum land needed to produce 1.1 pounds of corn per person per day for an average family of 5.1 people. His figures in *God and Production* are based on the fact that the residents of San Antonio use the 40 × 40 *vara* measure for a *cuerda*.[5] Converted to the standard 25 × 25 *vara* measure used in most of Guatemala, Annis's (1987:38) calculations work out to 15.1 *cuerdas* of the 25 × 25 variety needed for corn production. If the average family size of 5.9 in the Department of Sololá is used instead of 5.1 to calculate land needs for corn production, then 17.5 *cuerdas* are needed. So Annis's corn production method both underbrackets and overbrackets the national figure of 16 *cuerdas* depending on whose family size is used. In any event, under Annis's calculations, no land is added for the extra needs of minimal purchases in an indigenous cultural economy. Thus, 16 *cuerdas* severely underestimates the amount of land a family actually needs to survive in present-day Guatemala. We ask again, how much land is needed?

Nash (1958a) provides a Maya answer from the 1950s time period when Maya indigenes had much less need for externally produced products than they do today. The Mayas of Cantel identify "a definite notion of a style of life . . . which they call 'adequate' or 'customary' or comfortable. . . . Over and over it is said that 20 *cuerdas* of good, flat, well-watered land is what a family needs . . . [which] turns out to mean that a man, a woman, and three children can grow all the staples of corn, beans, and squash they consume, and still have enough surplus to sell in the market so that they may purchase the other things they will need" (Nash 1958a:21). We know that Nash and Cantelenses are using the 25 × 25 *vara cuerda* because Nash tells us a *cuerda* is equal to 0.108 acres (21).

Is twenty *cuerdas* of "good land" still enough? To be sure, current use of fertilizer tends to double production on a given piece of land. But with the passage of time, the number of "the other things they . . . need" has more than doubled. Nevertheless, with chemical fertilization, twenty *cuerdas* is still a good minimum figure for a "comfortable" existence. Recognizing that the government figure of sixteen *cuerdas* for minimum family subsistence is about 20 percent below what Mayas say is actually needed, in this book I will use the government figure. By doing so, I can easily make comparative calculations among all *municipios* in Guatemala because Guatemalan census operations have used one *manzana* as a breakpoint in agricultural figure tabulations since the first agro-census in 1950. Two provisos are needed. Proviso one: because I am using the government figure of sixteen *cuerdas* instead of the Nash figure of twenty, in the calculations and discussions in the rest of this book, remember that if we were to take Nash's figure as the cutoff point for minimum subsistence, things are either about 20 percent worse or crisis points arrive somewhat earlier than those given in this book. Proviso two: Nash speaks of "good, flat, well-watered" land as the basis of the requisite twenty, and Annis apparently uses flat agricultural land to calculate his average family's minimum nutritional needs but says nothing of land for forest access or pasturage. The government census figures for total agricultural land, however, include any *cuerda* put to agricultural service, and the census specifies neither "good" nor "flat" nor "well-watered." The same is true for the category of arable land, which does not include pasturage or forest and says nothing of goodness or flatness or water conditions. So also for land planted to "annuals": such lands are cropped (rather than pasture or forest), but the census indicates nothing regarding the quality of land. Thus, in the figures that follow, the crisis point of minimum land needed is in fact much higher than sixteen *cuerdas* of any land, which for government purposes includes land planted to annuals or perennials, pasture, or forest. Because of proviso two, the crises discussed in the rest of this book are even worse and even more immediate than the 20 percent worse specified under proviso one. But sixteen *cuerdas* as the crisis point gives us a very safe place to presume the existence of acute crisis.

Given the rapid rise in population that began around 1950, the relatively static land base, and the necessity of dividing inheritance among sons and daughters per Guatemalan law, by 1995 one saw steep hillsides and valuable flats covered with a patchwork of small corn plots (see plate 2).[6] The multiplicity of small plots does not in itself indicate inadequate land, for a family typically has several fields assembled through inheritance, marriage, purchase, and rental. But the facts are grim. From our 2010 survey, in the Antigua Ixtahuacán town center, 3 percent of the population had no land whatsoever, compared to 5 percent in Nueva Santa Catarina Ixtahuacán. In Antigua Santa Catarina Ixtahuacán, 12 percent controlled a quarter or less of the minimum sixteen *cuerdas* of land requisite for supposedly comfortable indigenous farming; in

Nueva Santa Catarina Ixtahuacán 60 percent had a quarter or less of the land area deemed minimally adequate. In Antigua Santa Catarina Ixtahuacán, 56 percent of families had half or less of the requisite land; in Nueva Santa Catarina Ixtahuacán, 97 percent had half or less of the requisite sixteen *cuerdas* needed for family maintenance. Only two people (6 percent of Antigua Santa Catarina Ixtahuacán families surveyed) had the requisite sixteen or more *cuerdas*; no families from Nueva Santa Catarina Ixtahuacán had sixteen or more.

National agro-census figures let us calculate the per capita holdings of arable land in annuals, which in these *municipios* means corn and beans, and see that resources deteriorate over time (figure 1.5). I inserted two horizontal lines in figure 1.5 to mark the per capita minimum viable subsistence of an average household consisting of between five people (the upper line, at 3.2 *cuerdas* per capita, representing a small family in crisis and an approximate entry into crisis for all) and six people (the lower line, at 2.7 *cuerdas* per person, representing slightly above the actual average family size throughout the Department of Sololá and a condition of clear crisis for most families). The landownership line segments above the upper (3.2 *cuerdas*) horizontal indicate the time span in which the local average family's corn production has stood above the minimum needed for household nutritional subsistence. Figure 1.5 comes closer to representing the existential needs of good agricultural crop land described by Nash than does figure 1.4, but there is still no provision in the agro-census that the croppable land in annuals be flat, good, or well-watered. In each *municipio*'s trend line, the segment between the two horizontals reflects the time span in which the individuals and, cumulatively, the families in each community are on average moving from incipient crisis toward acute crisis. The trend-line segments below the lower horizontal represent the time span in which individuals and households in these *municipios* on average have existed in acute subsistence crisis.

One can see that in the 1950s, the two *municipios* clearly entered this zone of cultural crisis wherein the available arable land of the municipality as a whole is insufficient to feed and sustain the total number of its inhabitants and households. Nahualá entered crisis in approximately 1953, while Santa Catarina Ixtahuacán entered crisis in 1954. By 1956, Nahualá was clearly in full crisis while Santa Catarina Ixtahuacán entered full corn crisis from about 1959. Both have remained in clear and worsening crisis since the 1960s.

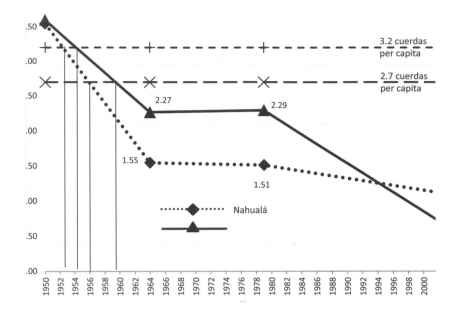

Figure 1.5. Cuerdas per capita in annual crops, Nahualá and Santa Catarina Ixtahuacán. In 1950, Nahualá's residents averaged 3.55 and Santa Catarina's 3.60 *cuerdas* per capita of land in annual crops. *Sources*: Dirección General de Estadística 1954, 1957, 1968, 1971a, 1971b, 1971–1972, 1974, 1982a, 1982b; INE 1994, 2002a, 2002b, 2002c, 2003, 2004a, 2004b.

Yet these per capita "average" figures do not adequately represent the extent of the crisis. In part, the representation fails because a few large landholders are averaged in, masking the precariousness experienced by the bulk of the people. Nevertheless, the available figures are instructive: in 1964, 3.4 percent of Nahualá's households and 9.5 percent of Santa Catarina Ixtahuacán's households were landless (having less than one *cuerda*). At the same time, 42 percent of Nahualá's households and 28 percent of Santa Catarina Ixtahuacán's households had at least one *cuerda* but less than the requisite sixteen *cuerdas*. This gives a total in 1964 of 45.4 percent of Nahualá's households and 37.5 percent of Santa Catarina Ixtahuacán's households living in corn-insufficient crisis. By 1979, these figures had risen: 17.3 percent of Nahualense households and 39 percent of Santa Catarina's households were effectively landless (possessing one *cuerda* or less) while 49 percent of Nahualense families and 23.4 percent of Ixtahuaquense families had at least one *cuerda* but less than the minimal sixteen. Thus, by 1979, 66.3 percent of Nahualense households and 62.4 percent of Ixtahuaquense families were in clear subsistence and cultural crisis, having less than the minimum sixteen *cuerdas* considered requisite for bare indigenous family survival in a corn-based economy. In a word, by 1964, crisis was palpable for nearly half the families in both communities. By 1979, the subsistence and cultural

crisis regarding land and corn gripped nearly two-thirds of the families in both communities. Unfortunately, I have not been able to extract comparable figures from either the 1950 or the 2003 agricultural censuses. Nevertheless, the presence and direction of increasing crisis in corn was clear well before the added disruptions of the 1976 earthquake and the 1980s escalation of brutal civil war.

With so many families having inadequate land (plate 2, figure 1.5) and given few good job options for earning from their excess labor capacity, one sees signs of nutritional stress in everyday life: streaks of red-brown in otherwise jet-black hair suggest widespread malnutrition, as do the subnormal heights marked as "severe malnutrition" on many children's growth charts at the local health clinics. The frequent complaint of "gastritis," the word used to describe the burn of stomach acidity, also suggests insufficient food and skipped meals, leading to hunger. Finally, the commonplace stunting and bodily thinness in the population suggest both malnutrition and hunger. John Early's (2012) lament about the food and culture crisis throughout Maya Guatemala certainly applies with full force in Nahualá and Santa Catarina Ixtahuacán.

The extreme shortage of croppable land challenges physical survival, the gendered order, family structure, and even one's sense of personal worth. Given the value of land in affirming indigenous identity, small plots of croppable land have become extremely expensive. High prices have put agricultural land out of reach of many indigenous residents. The population-induced shortage of land, the culturally induced values invested in corn growing, the debts of migration, and the inflation of prices induced by remittances have raised the price of croppable land throughout the region (Stoll 2013:85–96). Good, relatively level agricultural land in the rural areas around Nahualá that in 1990 cost at most Q5,000 a *cuerda* in 2019 cost Q65,000 to even Q90,000 a *cuerda*, a thirteen- to eighteenfold increase. Yet the price of corn produced on the land has only risen fourfold. At these prices, growing corn is simply not an economically rational choice, but it is a culturally valued choice. The problem is that at such prices the land is beyond the reach of families who have not produced international migrants. Moreover, land price inflation caused by migration remittances forces more migration. Migration, population increase, and the cultural value of corn and land thus have placed the prime substance that maintains Maya culture—corn *milpas*—out of the reach of those who remain to maintain the culture. Indeed, the ability to meet one core Maya value (having adequate land on which to raise corn) requires that one violate other Maya values (being present to personally work the cornfields and the goal of maintaining relative isolation within a *municipio*). This is so because one must migrate out of the community for years in order to secure the funds needed to add to the sliver of land one acquires by inheritance; this diminishes one's participation in the activity of raising corn, diminishes one's community connection, and undermines community isolation and self-sufficiency. The teenagers and young adults who migrate even lose K'iche' language skills and become Spanish speakers primarily. Thus, land shortage and consequent corn shortage severely challenge the underlying indigenous cultural logic and valued premises that circle around family-centered and inwardly oriented safety, family subsistence on corn, and self-protection through municipal autonomy and self-reliance.

The shortage of access to land and corn also affects gender roles. Corn not only must be raised, the job principally and preferably (but not exclusively) of men. Corn also must be dried, stored, and processed into food, and food preparation is quite exclusively the cultural job of women. If adult men are not nearby, having migrated to find wage work, who does the agricultural work? If men are gone in pursuit of wealth or if they are incapacitated, women must do more to earn cash and tend the fields for the family economy, thereby adjusting gender practice and expectation.

As part of the gendered economy of corn, almost all households have one or more sets of a mano and metate, with which corn can be ground into edible flour. Traditionally, women spent hours grinding the lime-soaked corn (nixtamal) into a mash from which they could make tortillas (*lej*) and tamales (*sub'*).

Today, most households lean their big metates against the kitchen wall or relegate all but one to an out-of-the-way corner where they gather dust—seldom used, but never thrown away. Women and children take heaping bowls of wet nixtamal to the loud motor-driven mills where, for a quarter quetzal, they can have the grinding work that once took hours kneeling over a metate done in two or three minutes. Today, women grind chilies in small stone bowls or on small metates. Some women occasionally use the big metates to regrind corn brought back from the nearby mill. Such regrinding takes more time but adds to the taste, the fineness, and the appropriate femininity of the resulting foods and is done when there is time or a festive reason to display one's devotion to culture and to others.

Wa, the K'iche' domain cover term for all corn foods, remains the primal food category. Only *wa*—corn-based edibles—are classed as "real" food, indicative of the importance of corn in Maya culture. All of the rest of things eaten are *riki'l*—they are considered condiments, flavorings, spices, garnishes. Thus, condiments (anything but corn) contrast explicitly with *wa* (corn foodstuffs)—the only real food. Only *wa* satisfies food cravings. The only edible really desired, and absolutely required, is *wa*. Only corn satisfies the belly, the body, and the mind, as Rode (2007:71–79) shows in detail. Against this cultural expectation that only corn is real food, the Maya man's inability to produce enough corn to feed a family, due to land shortage, constitutes a significant personal and cultural crisis; by the cultural expectations that define their gender, men ought to produce the corn that feeds their family. (For more on the impact of corn and land shortage on male gender roles, see Wells, Hawkins, and Adams 2020.)

Beyond the corn plots, Nahualá's huge twice-weekly market drives the local economy. The Sunday market—biggest by far—spills out of the large market buildings. Provisional stalls, vendors, and hordes of purchasers choke the main and side streets for a half kilometer along the axis of the main roads on both sides of the town and along two parallel roads in town. On Thursdays, the central plaza provides sufficient space, and all but the main street remains mostly clear. During the rest of the week, a few vendors open shops in the market buildings, and others tend stands or sit on tarps and woven pads in a cobble-covered rectangular area perhaps fifteen by thirty meters between the showy garden plaza and the stone-buttressed cross standing in front of the large old Catholic church (plate 3). Throughout the week, in small shops and larger stores lining the main street of Nahualá, local resident merchants sell a profusion of cell phones, tools, building materials, school supplies, CD players, pocket cameras, medicines, wood furniture, coffins, plastic chairs, kitchen utensils, fresh meat, packaged foods, and even ritual supplies for both mainline and traditionalist Catholics. In a word, Nahualá supplies much of the basic material stuff that garnishes today's indigenous life. Meanwhile, old men often sit on the benches of the decorative and restful central plaza (plate 4).

In the year 2000, the *cabecera municipal* (administrative center) of Santa Catarina Ixtahuacán fissioned, with the leaders moving some five-sixths of the families to a new location that they call Nueva Ixtahuacán. The Nueva Ixtahuacán center has a new market building. But its market days—the same Sundays and Thursdays as Nahualá's—do not generate the agglomeration of street stands and crowds seen in Nahualá. Nor does Nueva Santa Catarina Ixtahuacán have a thriving business district during the week: just one shop sells agricultural tools and supplies; a few one-room stores sell "first necessities"; and a half dozen or so people lay out fresh produce in the market building. Antigua Ixtahuacán, now no longer a *cabecera* but still trying to remain significant, has even less to offer: a tin shed covers a few of those who come on Sundays for the market. But its market plaza and the number of people providing goods on Sundays are smaller than either Nueva Ixtahuacán's or Nahualá's markets.

In both *municipios*, craft productions supplement some people's agricultural incomes. Nahualenses in particular, but also a few Catarinecos, carve and paint wooden objects, including diverse forms of animal life, saints for tourist or local markets, low tables, small and simple chairs, chairs with armrests and carving on the back slats for use beside the shaman's altar, and the boxes in which to store clothing and other objects to protect them from the damp. Nahualense carvers suffer from a shortage of raw timber. By contrast, in Santa Catarina before the split and in and around Antigua Santa Catarina

today, one can hear sawyers fell timber with chain saws or watch them saw logs into planks using two-man saws. One stands above on the log, while another stands below, availing themselves of the advantage conferred by a steep mountain slope.

In both towns and throughout their hamlets, women weave on backstrap looms to provide their own clothing needs, for almost all women dress in the home-woven navy blue *corte* (K'i. *uq*) and the red or purple brocade on white huipiles distinctive of the town. Only since the time of the move in 2000 have residents of either town frequently substituted sweaters and machine-made blouses for the labor-intensive brocaded cotton huipil. Likewise since about 2000, a few women have taken to purchasing the generic *jaspe*-woven *cortes*—the tube skirts woven mostly by men operating foot-treadle looms of eighteenth-century design—rather than weave their town's distinctive deep-blue, seam-embroidered, backstrap-woven *uq*. Today, however, the economic situation is desperate. Consequently, many women also weave to try to sell something to tourists, neighbors, or pan-Maya-oriented women in other communities, who now display their indigenous universalism and pan-Maya sympathies by wearing a variety of huipiles, which until the 1980s had sharply distinguished and separated the residents of different municipalities.

Beyond this, the craft patterns of the two municipalities diverge. Some Nahualenses specialize in the hand production of stone manos and metates. They use the local volcanic rock quarried from land high on the western slope of the *municipio*. The volcanoes near Nahualá supply a particularly suitable rock for making the hand-held quern (K'i. *uq'ab ka'*; Sp. *mano*; grinding stone) and the slightly concave, three-legged grinding platform (K'i. *ka'*; Sp. *metate*). Nahualenses mine suitable boulders from their ash and sand encasement, split the larger ones, and then shape rough blanks that they then carry home on their backs. In the convenience of their house patio, they chisel the blanks into grinding platforms (plate 5). On any sunny morning on the western slopes of the *aldeas* close to the quarries, one can hear the steady ratta-tap-tap of a man somewhere nearby hammering a metal chisel against the stone, working without safety glasses, chips flying, slowly shaping the stone blanks into the gracefully curved manos and metates that characterize the town. (For technical details on this industry, see Searcy 2011; Hayden and Nelson 1981.) One sees Nahualense mano and metate products in Nahualá's local market, and they are carried from town to town by men, some of the oldest of whom still wear Nahualá's (and Santa Catarina's) distinctive indigenous clothing style: a red and orange striped home-woven shirt and white embroidered shorts covered by a wool *koxtar*, the checked (dark and light brown), knee-length, wrap-around men's skirt distinctive of Nahualá and Santa Catarina Ixtahuacán. It is usually left open at the back like an apron and is tied down with a leather belt known as a *pas*.

Development projects run by nongovernmental organizations (NGOs) have tried to introduce a number of crafts and occupations into both *municipios*. They have succeeded in educating a few new crafters, to be sure, but not in numbers sufficient to become distinctive to either community or to solve their root economic problems. In spite of numerous economically oriented NGO development projects, little economic development has resulted from NGO teaching. NGOs do contribute significantly to the economy, but not by training many new artisans. Rather, they contribute first by finding and then funneling significant outside donations to families with children defined as "in need." Second, NGOs contribute by employing local bilingual people at favorable wages as go-betweens to organize, manage, and distribute humanitarian donations from Euro-American sources to K'iche' families (Checketts 2005; Nuttall 2005; Sinclair 2007).

Few other reliable sources of wages exist. One of them is teaching in government-run schools or, less favorably, in private schools. Another wage source is employment in the mayoral office or one of the state-run agencies. The forest management office, the post and telegraph office, and the government health center, for example, provide services in the *cabecera* of most *municipios* and sometimes even in hamlets. Each agency needs at least one employee. Working for the municipal or state offices provides secure, regular, and relatively high salaries compared to the wages of local agricultural or craft production daywork. Nevertheless, while wages from an NGO are comparatively ample, they are not secure long term, as many of these organizations come and go based on NGO priorities and funding; further, government jobs can come and go based on the party in power. But both government and NGO wage earners have an advantage compared to the bulk of agro-dependent families. NGO and government employees can save their wage money and buy corn and land from the traditional agriculturalists whose fortunes are not so stable.

I cannot end the story of the economy without noting the substantial contribution from international wage labor remittances from migrants. Remittances push needed cash into present-day Maya life. The combination of micro parcelization of the land, new and more reliable access to roads, phone connections to relatives who have made the migration, and economic desperation has driven many to mortgage their lands to relatively rich locals or to outsiders bankrolling the cross-border human trafficking. With the mortgage money, Mayas hire "coyotes" to guide them through Mexico to gain illegal entry into the United States, the Mayas' dreamland of fabulously well-paying work in food services, landscaping, and construction. Once in the United States, they must quickly find a job and work feverishly to pay back the mortgage loan, which accumulates interest at an exorbitant rate (Stoll 2013:103–104). If a migrant does not connect with a job or if he (or sometimes she) gets caught in Mexico or in the United States and deported, the sending family loses the land it had mortgaged as collateral and the family descends further into impoverishment (Stoll 2013). With luck, however, the migrant secures adequate work, pays off the loan, and begins sending home money that can help the originating family. The resulting remittances maintain kin and family connections across thousands of miles during years of separation. Families frequently use those funds to finance construction of a multistory concrete and cinderblock home, which replaces the family's much smaller one-floor adobe house roofed with tile or tin. Without exception, the owner of every two-, three-, or four-story house or commercial building situated in a rural hamlet or in Nueva Ixtahuacán had one or more sons or the male household head in the United States sending remittances, which made these constructions possible.

Massive migration to the United States has impacted the character of local families. Adult men and older teenage boys often migrate. Among the K'iche', authority has long been vested in the senior adult male of a household compound. When these men migrate to the United States, remaining family members find their authority and order-maintenance systems substantially disrupted. Women do not easily acquire the respect needed to keep young men in line. If a grandfather is not alive and active in child supervision, young men may drift to the authority and security of peer gatherings, which adults fear and call "gangs—*maras*" (Edvalson et al. 2013; Call et al. 2013; Burrell 2013).

We see the impacts of migration and the absent male

family members not only in gangs but also in religion. Migration and male absence show up in the inability of charismatics to retain male youths in affiliation (Bradshaw et al., this volume). They also appear in the urge women feel to join small congregations where they can acquire surrogate male authority through close attachment—frequently a relationship by kinship or marriage—to respected male pastors (see part 1 and chapter 25).

Young men and women talk frequently about their desire to *superarse* (advance), "get ahead," and "progress" (*progresar*). Migration is one way to get ahead. The primary alternative to migration is education. Clearly, high school or post–high school educations and bilingual talents have enabled a few from Nahualá and Ixtahuacán to secure favorable salaried employment as teachers and municipal employees. Moreover, the necessity of education to garner these jobs has transformed the local view of education. Corn farming is no longer seen as the path to security. Education is.

But the education path is fraught with unseen traps. Among them is the fact that the first achievers have filled the locally available teaching positions. Moreover, Hatch (2005) has shown that discrimination against indigenous people, a lack of networks, and simple patronage graft militate against a teacher from an indigenous community getting work anywhere in an education bureaucracy run by Ladino government appointees. Thus, while education is believed to be the way out of agricultural impoverishment, escape through education is not a sure thing. Institutionalized exclusions persist. As a result, poverty, hunger, insecurity, and marginality haunt the K'iche's of both the Nahualá and Santa Catarina town centers and, even more so, the tens of thousands inhabiting Santa Catarina's and Nahualá's peripheral rural hamlets.

Many additional aspects of K'iche' society and culture could be treated in an introductory chapter such as this. I and my colleagues have, however, already published a good deal on family, education, gender, and international development (Hawkins and Adams 2005a); ethnomedical beliefs and practices and the K'iche' access to national medical systems (Adams and Hawkins 2007); and political, land, and K'iche'–state integration and penetration issues (Hawkins, McDonald, and Adams 2013). Because there is much that needs to be said here about religion, I refer the reader to these other sources for more on general K'iche' culture as it is expressed in Nahualá and Santa Catarina Ixtahuacán.

THE POLITICS OF VILLAGE FISSION

While the municipality in Guatemala provides a primary first identity (Tax 1937:425, 433–444), in fact that identity can be fractured. First, there is a tendency toward smaller, more local self-identification that increasingly emphasizes one's rural hamlet or town barrio. Second, there can be significant political disputes between people representing sectorial interests within a *municipio*. So it was between Santa Catarina Ixtahuacán, the original colonial municipality, and Nahualá, the more recently founded municipality (plate 6). These two fissioned following an 1860s dispute between two *principales*, Manuel Tzoc, who people claim founded Nahualá, and Miguel Salquil, who, the myths claim, led the Santa Catarina Ixtahuacán population that remained in place (Asociación CODEIN 2008; see also Jardine, Hawkins, and Adams 2020).

More recently, some of Santa Catarina's urban center residents, among them many of the more educated, have envied the educational access and economic success Nahualá has had as a result of its fortuitous location next to the Pan-American Highway (see Morgan 2005; Hawkins and Adams 2020). Until the year 2000, the governmental apparatus of the municipal center of Santa Catarina Ixtahuacán, now called Antigua Ixtahuacán, lay nine kilometers away from the international highway at the end of a rough, sinuous, unpaved mountain road frequently closed in the rainy season by mudslides and washouts (plate 7). Ixtahuaquenses had been debating the possibility of moving at least since the 1960s and had used geological reports of their *cabecera*'s alluvial instability as one justification. But the matter merely simmered, with no action taken for decades. In the last days of October and the first days of November 1998, the town suffered major flooding, mudslide damage, and alluvial slippage as a result of the drenching it received from Hurricane Mitch. The damages renewed the call to move the head town center to a place of greater safety. Of course, the location they chose for safety also provided easy access to the east-west bus transportation that frequented the Pan-American Highway, giving them entrée to schools in Quetzaltenango and Totonicapán and to jobs in department centers throughout Guatemala. Five-sixths of the population—about 500 families—decided to move to what is now called Nueva Ixtahuacán (plate 8). About 100 families stayed. Among other things, those who stayed had significantly larger agricultural landholdings (Hawkins and Adams 2020).

The story of the motivations behind the split, the politics of the relocation, the following development of the two centers, and the increasingly bitter interactions of each town with the other and with the government is complicated. We tell it in the fifth volume of reports from this field school (Hawkins and Adams 2020). I mention this town-center division and relocation here because we followed cultural and religious life in both Antigua and Nueva Santa Catarina's head town centers from the split in 2000 through 2010 via the field school, and from 2010 until 2019 via occasional visits of Hawkins, Adams, and several student lead authors. Some of the reasons that Santa Catarina's residents have given for moving physically from their old town site to a new location—including a desire for progress and access to modernity—parallel several of the reasons they and other Guatemalans give for moving spiritually from traditional and Ortho-Catholicism to Evangelical Pentecostalism and Catholic charismaticism.

Durkheim (1949[1893], 1965[1895]) vigorously preaches the importance of examining social structure and ideologically "collective," shared mental constructs—what we call today "culture"—as a basis for understanding human behavior. But he also recognizes that there is a physical reality that interacts with the social and the cultural, which he calls the "material substrate" of population, land, climate, and other factors that leave their constraining "mark" on social life (Durkheim 2001[1912]:318–319). I have sketched some of these materially related factors in this chapter, although it is not possible to keep them strictly separate from the social and cultural. We now turn to religion in these two *municipios,* their town centers, and their many rural hamlets.

NOTES

1. Density per square kilometer is entirely dependent on the accuracy of the area attributed to each *municipio.* Here is the problem. I used 218 km² for Nahualá and 127 km² for Santa Catarina Ixtahuacán. I no longer can document where I got the 127 figure for Santa Catarina. Gall 1981, 1983, suggests the two *municipios* had 218 km² shared between them (*mancomunado*) and does not attribute to each its portion. Prado Ponce 1984 gives Nahualá at 218 km² and Santa Catarina at 137 km². If this is correct, the line in figure 1.2 for Santa Catarina is about 7 percent too high above the x axis at each point, drawing it closer to Nahualá between 1974 and 2002. FUNCEDE 1994 and 1995 show

each *municipio* at 218 km². That would considerably (and proportionally) drop Santa Catarina Ixtahuacán's line and density. However, FUNCEDE 1997a:4 and 1997b:4 give Nahualá 97 km² and Santa Catarina Ixtahuacán 121 km². This would more than double all of Nahualá's density figures and raise Santa Catarina's density only modestly. Scott Ure (pers. comm., 2020) says that "the most recent GIS survey data show Nahuala = 187.11 km² and Santa Catarina Ixtahuacán = 190.67 km²," making them almost equal. This would make Nahualá about 20 percent more dense than Santa Catarina because of its higher population. Of course, this is dependent on the accuracy of the lines drawn on the GIS maps and photos. Leaders of Nahualá and Santa Catarina Ixtahuacán hold that their border is in active dispute and has been for a century or more. What is certain is that both *municipios* are big in area and densely populated compared to other indigenous *municipios* of the region.

2. In July 2017 Santa Catarina Ixtahuacán's resident priest ended forty-two years of continuous residential service in the Ixtahuacán parish.

3. As John Edvalson (pers. comm., 2013) points out, when ordinary Nahualenses use the term "Maya," they do not refer to an ethnic sector of society as a whole. Rather, they identify the cultural and religious practitioners of a specific religious tradition, that of traditionalist, syncretic Catholic Mayas and the now reconceived and reworked neotraditionalists, both of whom see their religious practices as "pure Maya religion." For the 95 percent of ordinary Nahualenses and Ixtahuaquenses who publicly (but not always privately) reject the old-style religious rituals and the powers of the beings of the old ways, the traditionalist Maya Catholic and neotraditionalist practice of *costumbre* feels folkloric and embarrassing.

4. The national census and the citizens of Nahualá and Santa Catarina Ixtahuacán measure land by the *cuerda* (from Spanish for "rope" or "cord"), which is a square 25 *varas* to a side. The *vara* is a colonial measure of a "rod" or "staff" about 83 centimeters long, although sources vary on the official length. In my experience, Mayas generally guesstimate their land areas based on the time it takes to work their plots rather than on exact measurements. For census purposes, 16 *cuerdas* constitute a *manzana.* One *cuerda* equals 0.108 acres or 0.04 hectares; one acre equals 9.27 *cuerdas* or 0.41 hectares; and one hectare equals 22.90 *cuerdas* or 2.47 acres. See Hawkins 1984:421n9 for more details on larger local measurements.

5. Using the same *vara* of 83 centimeters, the *cuerda* used in San Antonio Aguas Calientes is 2.56 times larger than the *cuerda* used in this study's region and in most of the nation. It is approximately a quarter of an acre and slightly more than a tenth of a hectare.

6.   As a young undergraduate in Guatemala doing linguistic fieldwork in San Ildefonso Ixtahuacán, Department of San Marcos, during the sumer of 1968, I marveled at the fields perched on steep slopes. At the time, I naïvely wondered how they farmed such precarious fields; now, I better understand the forces that drove them to that solution.

PART I

Ethnographies of Present-Day Religious Practices in Nahualá and Santa Catarina Ixtahuacán

In this part, we describe the parameters and processes of lived religion and its diversity in town centers and hinterlands in the *municipios* of Nahualá and Santa Catarina Ixtahuacán. As Durkheim (2001[1912]:3) says in *The Elementary Forms of Religious Life*, "We shall not study . . . religion, then, just for the pleasure of recounting its oddities and singularities. We have made it the subject of our study because it seems most likely to yield an understanding of . . . an essential and permanent aspect of humanity," that of our "religious nature."[1] Durkheim affirms that it is "axiomatic that religious beliefs, as odd as they sometimes seem, have a truth that must be discovered" (333). He asserts that "there are no false religions. All are true in their fashion: all respond, if in different ways, to the given conditions of human existence" (4). It is our task to describe the religions of present-day Guatemala and find their social truth by analyzing the conditions of their existence and the words and behaviors of their adherents.

While each chapter may contain a modicum of references to issues in the literature, none claim to be theoretical contributions. Description is what is needed, description is what endures, and thus description certainly trumps analysis (Hawkins 2014:554). Diachronic and synchronic analyses follow in parts 2 and 3, respectively.

NOTE

1. Early translations of this work used the title *The Elementary Forms of the Religious Life*. Later translations dropped the second "the."

Chapter Two

The Religious *Cargos* and Fiestas of Santa Catarina Ixtahuacán and Their Decline

CLAYTON G. LARSON, JOHN P. HAWKINS, AND WALTER RANDOLPH ADAMS

UNTIL THE EARLY TWENTY-FIRST CENTURY, a system of *cargos* (public offices) organized public life in Santa Catarina Ixtahuacán, as it has done in many other indigenous villages in Latin America. *Cargo* derives from the Spanish verb *cargar*, which means "to carry a burden." Likewise, *eeqele'n*, the K'iche' word for public office, is related to the verb *eeqaxik*, which means "to carry a burden" or "to cast blame." Indeed, *cargos* could be onrous in terms of the time, money, and toil necessary to fulfill them. *Cargo* holders were also subject to public scrutiny and condemnation if they failed to meet expectations. In Mayas' conception, however, Mayas did not "hold" such offices in the US cultural sense of grasping it in one's hand as a personal possession; rather, they each bore the burden temporarily for all, as if it were suspended from a tumpline on their backs. If the *cargo* bearers completed their obligations properly, however, *cargo* service could secure them the respect of their community throughout their lives. Thus, the incentives for escalating one's investment in the institution appear quite obvious. All religious participation, including *cargo* involvement and fiesta participation in older styles under the supervision of *ajq'ijab'* and experienced *k'isib'alib'* (*pasados*), is seen as performance of *costumbre* (custom or old-style traditionalist religious practice). In this chapter I describe Ixtahuacán's religious *cargos* during the final years of their full operation, outline their decline, and discuss the political, economic, and historical contexts that led to their discontinuance. My fieldwork took place from late August through late December 2002.

BACKGROUND

The *cargos* of Ixtahuacán can be divided into two categories: civil and religious. The elaborate civil-religious hierarchy model outlined by Nash (1958a:66–67), where individuals alternated between civil and religious *cargos* as they completed their public career, did not exist in Ixtahuacán during the time frame captured in my informants' memories. The only blending of civil and religious authority my informants noted is that on completion of a senior *cargo*, be it civil or religious, a person was recognized as one of the *k'isib'alib'* (the finished ones) or chief citizens (Sp. *principales*), a group with significant de facto political authority.

While senior serving civil *cargo* holders had a monopoly on *formal* political power and constituted the primary interface with the national government, for many significant internal affairs, the consensus of the *k'isib'alib'* reigned supreme. Civil leaders, such as the *alcalde municipal* (town mayor), would gather the *k'isib'alib'* and ask them to discuss important political matters. Their consensus was always respected. Collectively, however, the *k'isib'alib'* were not a formal political body governed by the sort of administrative rules typical of political bodies in national governments. While membership in the *k'isib'alib'* was generally clear, some of the secondary *cargos* generated claimants that could have been disputed.

The *k'isib'alib'* determined the community's position on such important matters as land disputes with other villages or how to punish social deviants. For example, the *k'isib'alib'* were instrumental in organizing lynchings as punishment for extreme crimes, such as murder. For such extralegal actions, it was critical that all decisions be formed by common consent so that no one could be distinguished as a mob leader subject to punishment by the national judicial system (see Bybee et al. 2013). In these circumstances, the diffuse but powerful authority of the *k'isib'alib'* was ideal. In such delicate matters, the community did not ask the *k'isib'alib'* to formally approve their actions; rather, community members watched the *k'isib'alib'* for passive signs of consent. Only people who had held senior religious *cargos*—which were entirely ceremonial offices—belonged to this powerful group.

In contrast with the civil *cargo* holders, who still interact with the national government and organize the mundane activities of everyday life in the village, the religious *cargo* holders interacted with the ethereal world of saints, angels, and deities, and organized the ritual activities of sacred holidays. The principle of *mayordomía* (sponsorship) governed these *cargos*: "Certain families are appointed stewards (called *cofrades, mayordomos,* or *fiesteros*) of the village saints, and are responsible for the celebrations. After serving for a year they relinquish their posts and responsibilities to new delegates" (Smith 1977:1–2).

Ixtahuacán once had an elaborate fiesta system with dozens of *cargos*, including offices distributed among five *cofradías* that sponsored fiestas for their corresponding saints, *nikodeems* who organized ceremonies for Lent and Holy Week, *sacristanes* who adorned the church for fiestas, and *pixcariyib'* (*fiscales*) who directed the activities of the *cofrades* and *sacristanes*. All of these services were rendered without financial compensation and often at great personal expense. While the civil *cargos* increased in power and importance in the 1980s and 1990s, the religious *cargos* have declined to the point that most have been abandoned.

THE RELIGIOUS *CARGOS* AND CATEGORIES OF PARTICIPANTS

Compared to other pueblos, the *cargo* system in Santa Catarina Ixtahuacán had an unusual focus on the communal images kept in the Catholic church (see table 2.1).[1] In other pueblos, the *sacristanes* were responsible for caring for and protecting the communal images in the church, and *alcaldes* and mayordomos were responsible for caring for and protecting the images of their individual *cofradías*. In Ixtahuacán, each *pixcar, chajal, sacristán, alcalde,* and mayordomo was expected to give rotating service at the church. When they were on duty, they cleaned the church during the day and slept in the church at night to protect the images from thieves. When all the *cargos* were filled, the images at the church had a twenty-four-hour security force of eighteen men (see table 2.2). In contrast, the images of the *cofradías*, which were kept in

the first *alcalde's* home, were cared for only after duties to the communal images had been fulfilled. On those weeks when the first *alcaldes* slept in the church, the images of their *cofradías* were entrusted into their wives' care. That so many *cargo* holders were willing to commit so much of their time (up to half the total year) to the service of communal images suggests that a strong sense of unity prevailed in Ixtahuacán. In turn, the experience of serving the communal images reinforced this unity and strengthened the cult of the patron Santa Catalina throughout the municipality.[2]

Cofradías

The most important ritual-sponsoring organizations in Ixtahuacán were the *cofradías*. *Cofradías* are groups of men and women who give one year of service to a saint. Ixtahuacán had five *cofradías*, which were sponsored by specific barrios (neighborhoods) in Ixtahuacán's municipal center and outlying *aldeas* (villages) and *caseríos* (hamlets) throughout the municipality (Baronti 2002:16). This system encouraged people from rural hamlets to identify with the municipal center.

Members of *cofradías* were called *cofrades*. Traditionally each *cofradía* in Ixtahuacán had twelve *cofrades*: two *alcaldes*, six *martomuyib'* (plural of *morto'm* [mayordomos]), and four *chuchuxelib'* (plural of *chuchuxel*, female *cofradía* assistants; the root *chuch* means "mother"). As these *cargos* became more difficult to fill, however, *cofradías* sometimes only had one *alcalde*, a few *martomuyib'*, and one or two *chuchuxelib'*. Men served as *alcaldes* and *martomuyib'*; women served as *chuchuxelib'*. Each *cofrade's* title indicated his or her rank and position. For example, the two mayors were called *nab'e* (first) and *ukab'* (second) *alcalde*. Thus, the saints' images, the *cofrade* mayors, and the civil office mayors paralleled each other in structures of substitution. Higher positions and ranks carried greater prestige and responsibility. For example, *uwaq* (sixth), also called *ch'i'p* (last, little), *morto'm* was an entry-level position that could be filled by a youth, while the *nab'e morto'm* was a position of honor occupied by an adult.

Alcaldes were the ranking authorities in the *cofradía*. They hosted the most important images of the *cofradía* in their home and fed the *martomuyib'* who came from distant hamlets to give service in the church. *Alcaldes* and *martomuyib'* were responsible for caring for the communal images at the church and the *cofradía* images in the

TABLE 2.1. HIERARCHY OF THE IMAGES OF SANTA CATARINA IXTAHUACÁN

TOWN PATRON			
Large Catalina			
Medium or Second Catalina			
Little Catalina			

SECOND MUNICIPAL PATRON			
Saint Michael the Archangel			

OTHER IMAGES ON THE ALTAR			
Saint Paul	Sacred Heart of Jesus	Saint Peter	Virgin of Suffering

IMAGES FROM THE OLD ALTAR (NOW IN STORAGE)						
Saint John	Saint Joseph	Saint Raphael	Christ Child	Saint James	Resurrected Christ (stolen)	Qajawaxel (God with the World in His Hand)

OTHER IMAGES IN THE CHURCH	
Christ Crucified	Two Angels

IMAGE FORMERLY KEPT BY THE FIRST NIKODEEMS
Christ in the Tomb

COFRADÍA IMAGES				
Santa Cruz	Korpus	Qajawal/Jesus/San Francisco	María del Rosario	María de la Concepción
two images of Christ Crucified	Christ Riding a Donkey	Christ	Mary of the Rosary	Virgin of the Conception

SECONDARY COFRADÍA IMAGES				
Santa Cruz	Korpus	Qajawal/Jesus/San Francisco	María del Rosario	María de la Concepción
Saint Helen, Saint Michael the Archangel	a silver-plated box for the host	Saint Francis of Assisi, Saint Raphael	Saint George	many smaller virgins of conception

TABLE 2.2. FULLY STAFFED ROTATION OF *CARGO* SERVICE

FIRST WEEK	SECOND WEEK	THIRD WEEK	FOURTH WEEK	FIFTH WEEK	SIXTH WEEK
first *pixcar*	second *pixcar*	first *pixcar*	second *pixcar*	first *pixcar*	second *pixcar*
first *chajal*	second *chajal*	first *chajal*	second *chajal*	first *chajal*	second *chajal*
first sacristan	second sacristan	first sacristan	second sacristan	first sacristan	second sacristan
first *alcalde**	second *alcalde**	first *alcalde**	second *alcalde**	first *alcalde**	second *alcalde**
first mayordomo*	second mayordomo*	third mayordomo*	first mayordomo*	second mayordomo*	third mayordomo*
sixth mayordomo*	fifth mayordomo*	fourth mayordomo*	sixth mayordomo*	fifth mayordomo*	fourth mayordomo*

*One from each of the five *cofradías*, for a total of five serving people in each of these positions.

home of the highest-ranking *alcalde*. The *chuchuxelib'* were required to wash the clothes of the images every twenty days and to prepare traditional foods and beverages for the fiestas. All *cofrades* shared the costs of their fiestas equally. Each *cofradía* was expected to host seven fiestas each year. On the saint's day of a particular *cofradía*, that *cofradía* would have a large celebration to transition its leadership; in addition, the other four *cofradías* would sponsor their own smaller but nonetheless elaborate parties. Also, for the saints' days of Santa Catalina and San Miguel, the town's first and second patron saints, each of the five *cofradías* would host a separate fiesta.

During their year of service, *cofrades* had the most onerous burden of all religious *cargo* holders. During any given week, when fully staffed, one *alcalde* and two *martomuyib'* from each *cofradía* stood guard and cared for the saints at the church. Much of their sacrifice was in the form of lost labor time. During the weeks that they were on duty, *alcaldes* and *martomuyib'* were unable to work in their fields or do other gainful employment. This meant that each *alcalde* would give about twenty-six weeks or 182 days of service throughout the year, while *martomuyib'* would each give seventeen or eighteen weeks (119–126 days) of service. However, as people lost interest in the *cofradías* in the 1980s, fewer and fewer *cofrades* served in the rotation, creating more work for those who did. One man said that when he was *nab'e alcalde* in 1987 and 1990, he had no second *alcalde* and only four *martomuyib'*. As a result, he was only able to keep two *cofrades* on duty each week on a three-week rotation. As first *alcalde*, his time contribution increased to about thirty-five weeks or 245 days, two-thirds of the total year.

Apparently, no record was ever kept of the contributions made by *cofrades*. I therefore asked several former *cofrades* to list all of their *cofradía*-related expenses during their year of service. According to one estimate, the total annual cost of the *cofradía* was Q18,794. Each *morto'm* and *chuchuxel* contributed approximately Q832, and each *alcalde* contributed approximately Q5,237. These numbers seem inflated and should be considered only an estimate of expenditures. The technique, nevertheless, revealed a wealth of information, summarized in table 2.3, about the kinds of purchases *cofrades* made, probable costs, and the allocation of their responsibilities.

To get a better handle on the costs, I decided to re-create a *cofradía* fiesta. I received permission from the *k'isib'alib'* of the *cofradía* Concepción to re-create their traditional saint's day fiesta, provided I paid for all expenses.

Several former *cofrades* were invited to play the part of *ajb'e* (guide to the proper road; literally *aj-*, "belonging to, master of," and *b'e*, "the road"), *alcalde*, *chuchuxel*, or *morto'm*. I tried to be as frugal as possible in my purchases and still do everything that was appropriate for a *cofradía* fiesta. My purchases for the one-night fiesta totaled Q876.25 or US$111.20 (using the conversion rate of Q7.88 = US$1), a significant sum considering that a typical day's wage in Ixtahuacán at this time was Q40.00 or $5.08.[3] In the past, there were about fifteen nights of celebration a year, and the cost was split among all *cofrades*, ranging from six to twelve, in each *cofradía*. Each *cofrade* was also responsible for procuring the appropriate costume. I spent Q945 or $119.92 to have such an outfit made for me, which friends assured me was a reasonable price. It seems conservative to say that if the *cofradías* were to celebrate their fiestas today in a culturally appropriate way, each *cofradía* member would have to spend more than $100, and perhaps much more if they wanted to do it well, while the expenses of the first *alcalde* would be in the hundreds of dollars.

In return for their service, *cofrades* were granted ceremonial privileges. For example, Baronti (2002:17) reports that positions of honor were reserved for *cofrades* during mass. Likewise, *cofrades* held prominent positions during all the processions of Ixtahuacán and were allowed to wear ceremonial dress that resembled the clothing of nobility from earlier generations. *Martomuyib'* were permitted to wear the *kapa'n* (a black tunic with decorative sleeves), the *sutib'al su't* (brocaded headscarf), and the *saaka'w* (brocaded shorts) (Baronti 2002:17; see plate 9). Beneath their *kapa'n*, they wore hand-woven shirts with an embroidered collar and brocaded cuffs, the daily garb of all the men in Ixtahuacán twenty years ago that is still worn by some older men. *Alcaldes* also wore the *sutib'al su't* and *saaka'w*. They were further permitted to wear a woolen fedora hat and a *raxa k'ul* (a *kapa'n* adorned with red ribbons) and to carry a silver staff adorned with the insignia of their *cofradía* (Baronti 2002:17; plate 9). The *chuchuxelib'* wore sleeveless *po't* (*güipil* ~ huipil, the traditional women's blouse) brocaded with a *kab'ajwil* (two-headed eagle) and adorned with red ribbons (plates 1, 10).

The clothing worn by a headman from Ixtahuacán in a drawing by Von Tempsky (figure 2.1), a Prussian adventurer who stayed in Ixtahuacán briefly during the early 1850s, resembles the recent traditional dress of *alcaldes* and mayordomos (compare figure 2.1 with plate 9). The dark tunic with decorative sleeves worn by the headman in the

TABLE 2.3. ESTIMATED COSTS OF THE *COFRADÍA* CONCEPCIÓN IN 1982

EVENT	ITEM	PRICE/UNIT	# OF UNITS	TOTAL (QUETZALES)	PAID BY
	incense	25¢/ounce	2 pounds	8.00	all *cofrades**
	candles	Q3.00/pound	5 pounds	15.00	all *cofrades*
	flowers			100.00	all *cofrades*
	fireworks	Q1.50/rocket	3 rockets	4.50	all *cofrades*
	marimba	Q30.00/night	2 nights	60.00	all *cofrades*
	food for the band	Q5.00/meal	10 people, 3 meals/day for 2 days	300.00	all *cofrades*
EACH OF FIVE *COFRADÍA* FIESTAS	homebrew liquor	Q5.00/gallon	4 gallons	20.00	all *cofrades*
	traditional cross buns	2.5¢/bun	2,000 buns	50.00	all *cofrades*
	ceremonial grain coffee	Q3.00/bottle	2 bottles	6.00	all *cofrades*
	coffee cups	20¢/cup	50 cups	10.00	all *cofrades*
	coffee	25¢/pound	3 pounds	0.75	all *cofrades*
	sugar	30¢/pound	50 pounds	15.00	all *cofrades*
	Subtotal for 12 *cofrades*	Q589.25	Cost/*cofrade*	Q49.10	
	Total for 5 fiestas	Q2,946.25	Cost/*cofrade*	Q245.52	
	incense	25¢/ounce	5 pounds	20.00	all *cofrades*
	candles	Q3.00/pound	5 pounds	15.00	all *cofrades*
	flowers			100.00	all *cofrades*
	fireworks	Q1.50/rocket	3 rockets	4.50	all *cofrades*
	marimba	Q30.00/night	3 nights	90.00	all *cofrades*
FIESTA OF SANTA CATARINA	food for the band	Q5.00/meal/person	10 people, 3 meals/day for 3 nights of playing	450.00	all *cofrades*
	homebrew liquor	Q5.00/gallon	4 gallons	20.00	all *cofrades*
	traditional cross buns	2.5¢/bun	1,000 buns	25.00	all *cofrades*
	ceremonial grain coffee	Q3.00/bottle	2 bottles	6.00	all *cofrades*
	coffee	25¢/pound	3 pounds	0.75	all *cofrades*
	sugar	30¢/pound	50 pounds	15.00	all *cofrades*
	Subtotal for 12 *cofrades*	Q746.25	Cost/*cofrade*	Q62.19	
	incense	25¢/ounce	2 pounds	8.00	all *cofrades**
	candles	Q3.00/pound	5 pounds	15.00	all *cofrades*
	flowers			100.00	all *cofrades*
	fireworks	Q1.50/rocket	3 rockets	4.50	all *cofrades*
FIESTA OF SAN MIGUEL	marimba	Q30.00/night	2 nights	60.00	all *cofrades*
	food for the band	Q5.00/meal/person	10 people, 3 meals/day for 2 days	300.00	all *cofrades*
	homebrew liquor	Q5.00/gallon	4 gallons	20.00	all *cofrades*
	traditional cross buns	2.5¢/bun	1,000 buns	25.00	all *cofrades*

TABLE 2.3 (CONTINUED)

EVENT	ITEM	PRICE/UNIT	# OF UNITS	TOTAL (QUETZALES)	PAID BY
FIESTA OF SAN MIGUEL	ceremonial grain coffee	Q3.00/bottle	2 bottles	6.00	all *cofrades*
	coffee	25¢/pound	3 pounds	0.75	all *cofrades*
	sugar	30¢/pound	50 pounds	15.00	all *cofrades*
	Subtotal for 12 *cofrades*	Q554.25	Cost/*cofrade*	Q46.19	
EASTER WEEK	incense	25¢/ounce	3 pounds	12.00	all *cofrades*
	candles	Q3.00/pound	5 pounds	15.00	all *cofrades*
	flowers			100.00	all *cofrades*
	traditional cross buns	2.5¢/bun	1,000 buns	25.00	first and second *alcaldes*
	fish	Q4.00/pound	6 pounds	24.00	first and second *alcaldes*
	Subtotal for all *cofrades*	Q127.00	Cost/*cofrade* for 2 *alcaldes*	Q10.58	
	Additional subtotal for 2 *alcaldes*	Q49.00		Additional cost/ *alcalde*	Q24.50
CHRISTMAS	incense	25¢/ounce	3 pounds	12.00	all *cofrades*
	candles	Q3.00/pound	5 pounds	15.00	all *cofrades*
	flowers			100.00	all *cofrades*
	Subtotal for 12 *cofrades*	Q127.00	Cost/*cofrade*	10.58	
FOOD FOR 2 *MARTOMUYIB'*	tortillas, tamales, coffee, beans, eggs, vegetables, beef broth (during fiestas)	Q4.00/meal	2 people, 3 meals/ day for year	8,760.00	first and second *alcaldes*
	Subtotal for 2 *alcaldes*		Q8,760.00	Cost/*alcalde*	4,380.00
DAILY OFFERING TO THE SAINTS	incense	25¢/ounce	2 pounds/week for 52 weeks	416.00	all *cofrades*
	candles	Q3.00/pound	3 pounds/week for 52 weeks	468.00	all *cofrades*
	Subtotal for 12 *cofrades*	Q884.00	Cost/*cofrade*	Q73.67	
MISCELLANEOUS	clothing	Q300.00/uniform	12 uniforms	3,600.00	all *cofrades*
	reed mat for Semana Santa	Q50.00	1	50.00	all *cofrades*
	reed mat for the images	Q50.00	1	50.00	all *cofrades*
	presents of traditional dress for the images	Q800.00	1	800.00	all *cofrades*
	tablecloth	Q50.00	1	50.00	all *cofrades*
	curtain	Q50.00	1	50.00	all *cofrades*
	Subtotal for 12 *cofrades*	Q4,600.00	Cost/*cofrade*	Q383.33	
ANNUAL COST OF ALL FIESTA EVENTS	Q18,793.75	Annual cost/ *morto'm/chuchuxel*	Q832.06	Annual cost/ *alcalde*	Q5,236.56

Note: *By 1982, the number of *cofrades* had declined from the ideal of twelve to an average of ten per *cofradía*. Nevertheless, the per person cost for the *mortomuyib'* and *chuchuxeles* and the two *alcaldes* is calculated as though there were no loss of personnel.

1850s drawing resembles the 1985 male *cofrades' kapa'n*. The scarf on the head in the 1850s resembles the 1985 *sutib'al su't*. However, the Von Tempsky headman's adornments lack brocaded designs. The headman seems to be wearing a short skirt or tunic, while the 1985 *saaka'w* is essentially baggy shorts gathered tightly at the waist; however, the headman's skirt/tunic in the 1850s extends to about the same length as the 1985 *saaka'w*. Also, the staff carried by the *alcaldes* in 1985 is reminiscent of the cane the 1850s headman bears. This suggests that the ritual garb worn by the *cofrades* in the recent past was originally an imitation of the outfits worn by nobility. These similarities suggest that *cofradía* costumes were meant to be a conspicuous form of adornment. In an inward-focused community like Ixtahuacán, such ceremonial privileges would have been instrumental in signaling and according status.

Figure 2.1. Drawing of an indigenous headman, ca. early 1850s. *Source*: Von Tempsky 1858:facing page 363.

Ajb'e, Soline'l, and *Secretarios*

Other *cargos* were associated with *cofradías* but did not make the holder of the office a *cofrade*. These included *ajb'e, soline'l* (brother), and *secretario* (secretary). Unlike *cofrades*, who served one-year terms, people who filled these *cargos* served for life. Two *ajb'ejab'* gave the *agradecimiento* or prayer of thanksgiving at *cofradia* fiestas, one for the incoming and one for the outgoing *cofrades*. They would also join the *cofrades* in procession wearing the ceremonial *saq usu't* (white brocaded headscarf). *Ajb'e* were older men who could pray in archaic, formal, and rhythmical phrases. An *ajb'e* often served as *k'amal b'e* (matchmaker and marriage officiator) as well (see Araneda 2005; Ajpacajá Túm 2001). An *ajb'e* may also have been an *ajq'ij* (Maya priest) who burned offerings of incense, sugar, fragrant botanicals, and other objects to heal his clients or make other petitions (see Scott et al., and Hanselmann et al., both this volume). A *soline'l* was responsible for finding people to serve as *cofrades* each year. His status was lower than a *cofradía alcalde* or *ajb'e* because he only served a few months out of the year, but, like the holders of senior *cargos*, a *soline'l* was allowed to wear the *saq usu't* during important ritual functions. *Cofradías* also had one or two secretaries who were responsible for recording the names of the *cofrades* and writing notes for the *alcaldes*.

Pixcariyib' and *Sacristanes*

Cargos specifically associated with the Catholic church included two *pixcariyib'*, two *sacristanes*, and two *chajalayib'* (plural of *chajal*). Like *cofrades*, these were year-long, ranked *cargos* that required rotating service at the church. Each *pixcar, sacristán*, and *chajal* cared for the church and its images every other week, sleeping in the church with the *cofrades* at night. The *pixcariyib'* supervised and directed the *cofradías* and disciplined wayward *cofrades* if necessary. Baronti (2002:18) says they also managed the *cofradía* funds. *Pixcar* may be a K'iche' adaptation of the Spanish word *fiscal* (treasurer). Each *pixcar* had a *chajal* as his personal assistant.[4] The *chajal* performed such tasks as cleaning the *pixcar*'s bedroom and bedding at the church, carrying his hat and

Figure 2.2. Drawing of an indigenous high priest, ca. early 1850s. *Source*: Von Tempsky 1858:facing page 368.

staff during mass, and adorning the altar in the *pixcar*'s home with flowers and pine needles.

Sacristanes functioned as assistants to the Catholic priest. They helped the priest perform mass in the church on Sunday and traveled with the priest to perform mass in other communities during the week. During fiestas, they were also responsible for adorning the church with curtains, fruit, flowers, pine needles, and balloons.

Nikodeems

The *nikodeems* constituted another *cofradía*-like sodality. The term comes from the biblical figure Nicodemus, a member of the ruling political body in the ancient Jewish state who was an advocate of Jesus Christ and brought spices to anoint his deceased body (compare the King James Version of John 3:1, 19:39–40). The *nikodeems* memorialized this mortuary service by caring for the image of Christ during Lent and Holy Week. There were four *nikodeems*, ranked *nab'e* (first) to *ukaj* (fourth). The *ajwi pasyoon* (also known as *ajwi cruz*) was closely associated with the *nikodeems*, making a functional group of five.[5] The *nikodeems* and *ajwi pasyoon* were older men of spiritual maturity who were required to fast extensively during Easter season. The *ajwi pasyoon*'s wife was called the *ajwi censaria* (master of censer/incense). She acted as a sort of *chuchuxel* for the *nikodeems*. She washed the clothing of the Christ images during Lent and carried a large censer in front of the cross during the Lent and Holy Week processions. The *nikodeems*' wives also joined in processions, but they did not have a named *cargo*.

Baronti (2002:20) notes that *nikodeems* wore the *saaka'w* along with "a white cape that resembles a sheet, and a lightly embroidered ceremonial hat, somewhat in the form of a miter, and made of the same material." This resembles Von Tempsky's (1858:368) description of the costume of the high priest of Ixtahuacán's native religion. The high priest wore "a long spotless white robe, with red embroidery round the neck, chest, and sleeves . . . also a white cap, in the shape of an antique helmet, embroidered also in red with a small cross in front. . . . There were besides these parts of his costume a white sash of cotton for his waist, and a sort of half towel, half cloak, that he wore over his left shoulder." Von Tempsky's illustration

shows that the high priest's cap was also shaped like a miter (figure 2.2).[6] This suggests that the *nikodeem*'s costume was originally a form of conspicuous adornment like the *cofrade*'s costume. The *ajwi pasyoon* wears the same traditional ceremonial dress as the *cofrades*.

K'isib'alib' and Pasado Sacristanes

Ixtahuacán also had two sodalities made up of past *cargo* holders that served as advisory or supervisory bodies. I have described some of the activities of the first sodality, the *k'isib'alib'*, which functioned as both a political and religious organization. Just as the *alcalde municipal* consulted with the *k'isib'alib'* on important political matters, the *soline'l* would consult with the *k'isib'alib'* to determine who should be named as *cofrade* each year. Formerly, the *k'isib'alib'* also named people to be *alguaciles* (constables), the lowest-ranking civil *cargo*, given as a punishment to people who did not have the right comportment to be a *cofrade*. The *k'isib'alib'* were older men who had held one of the chief religious *cargos*, such as *pixcar* or *alcalde* of a *cofradía*, or one of the chief civil *cargos*, such as *alcalde municipal*, *bisalcalde* (vice mayor), or *rixtool* (councilman).

The second sodality of former *cargo* holders still functions: the *pasado sacristanes*. As the title suggests, these are men who have previously served as *sacristanes*. *Pasado sacristanes* still are responsible for naming new *sacristanes* each year and for assisting the serving *sacristán* in procuring adornments for the church for important fiestas.

Dance Groups

In addition to *cofrade* participation, some Ixtahuaquenses joined dance groups to mount the elaborate pageant dances that represented the conquest, the Moros, the deer, and other facets of indigenous life, as widely reported in the literature (Municipio de Cantel 1991; Montoya 1970; Jiménez de Báez 2002). They spent considerable sums to rent or purchase the requisite costumes for their parts in what amounted to outdoor historical plays enacted in the town plaza or some suitable field.

Comités

Ixtahuacán's *comités* (committees) currently provide other *cargos* that are nonceremonial but are still useful in building prestige. The *comité de la iglesia* (church committee) is responsible for raising funds for the construction and maintenance of the church. The *comité de la feria* raises money to hire expensive marimba *orquesta* (orchestra) bands to play in Ixtahuacán during the saints' day celebrations. Another *comité* guards important municipal documents, such as the *título municipal* (town title), an early colonial document with (we were told, but not allowed to see) a jaguar skin binding, which has proved instrumental in settling numerous land disputes in Ixtahuacán's favor. Each barrio in the municipal center also has its own *comité* that carries out public service functions as need arises. Typical *cargos* in a *comité* include *presidente*, *secretario*, and *tesorero* (treasurer).

THE FIESTA SYSTEM AND CYCLE

In 1858, Von Tempsky (373) wrote of the Ixtahuaquenses' "custom of dancing round the images of saints and stimulating themselves by strong drink, until, overcome by fatigue and drink, they would sink at the feet of the altar, a sacrifice of themselves believed to be exceedingly agreeable to the saint, and thus beneficial to their interests in Heaven." Dancing for hours to marimba music in front of the images and drinking *kuxa* (home-brewed alcohol) are still, with the modifications noted below, a vital part of the celebration at the town fair. Von Tempsky (1858:374) claims that about every two weeks, Ixtahuaquenses celebrated saints' days with drinking. Though perhaps exaggerating, he asserts that they "prepared for each *fiesta* so much before the day of its celebration, and extended the celebration so much after that day, that the only intermissions came to be those produced by mere exhaustion of body and means." In the 1970s, Ixtahuaquenses still celebrated twelve major fiestas (see table 2.4), most of which were marked by drinking and dancing before the images.

Saints' Days of the *Cofradías*

The five *cofradías* in Ixtahuacán were each associated with a specific saint's day: Santa Cruz (Holy Cross), Korpus (Corpus ~ Body [of Christ]), Transfiguración/Qajawal (Our Lord Master [or Our King]), María del Rosario (Mary of the Rosary), and María de la Concepción (Mary of the [Immaculate] Conception). On the saint's day corresponding with each *cofradía*, the images of that *cofradía* were carried in procession from the home of the old *nab'e alcalde* to the home of the new *nab'e alcalde*. All of the *cofradías* joined in these processions. Each *cofradía* held its own fiesta in the home of their *nab'e alcalde*, making five simultaneous celebrations each holiday. Fiestas for the saints' days of the *cofradías* lasted two or three days, while the fiesta for Santa Catarina lasted a week, though that of San Miguel was shorter.

In preparation for these fiestas, the *martomuyib'* collected wild plants to adorn the home of the *nab'e alcalde* where the images were kept. From the mountains near the municipal center, they gathered green pine needles to spread across the floor, the leaves of the *ch'yu't* (an agave) to bind flowers to the vertical poles supporting a protective canopy over the saint, cypress branches to hang on the walls, and a white flower called *kartuch*

TABLE 2.4. CALENDAR OF THE FIESTAS OF SANTA CATARINA IXTAHUACÁN

Lent Ash Wednesday to Palm Sunday	Day of Mary of the Rosary/María del Rosario October 7
Holy Week/Semana Santa Palm Sunday to Easter Sunday	All Saints' Day, Day of the Dead November 1, 2
Day of the Holy Cross/Santa Cruz May 1	Town Fair/Day of Saint Catherine November 25
Corpus Christi/Korpus Thursday after Trinity Sunday	Day of Mary of the Conception/María de la Concepción December 8
Day of Transfiguration/Qajawal August 6	Posadas December 16–24
Day of Saint Michael the Archangel September 29	Christmas December 25

(calla lily, from Sp. *cartucho*, "cartridge"). The *martomuyib'* from hamlets in the *boca costa* (Pacific piedmont, literally "mouth of the coast") also brought tropical fruits (e.g., pineapples, bananas, plantains) and flowers as decorations.

Cofrades made substantial purchases for these fiestas. *Cofrades* hired musicians to play the marimba, the *tambor* (drum), and the *chirimía* (double-reed flute; see plate 11). If money permitted, they hired a large marimba orchestra with a marimba, brass instruments, keyboards, drums, and singers (see plate 12). The *cofrades* purchased *bombas* (loud, colorless, mortar-fired or rocket-type fireworks) manufactured in San Andrés Xecul and procured abundant *cohetes* (firecrackers). *Cofrades* and honored guests received *kuxa*, the musicians received meals from a restaurant, and the crowd at large received *panes de avión* (cross buns) and *atol ceremonial* (a cornmeal drink), coffee, or hot chocolate.

Officials set off *bombas* to let the community know that the fiesta was beginning. People gathered, listened to the musicians, and danced if sufficiently inebriated. The ceremonial part of the fiesta began when the *ajb'e* offered the *agradecimiento*. People remember the *ajb'e* talking about the history of the town and its *cofradías*, praising the saints, expressing thanks to the outgoing *cofrades*, and explaining the duties to incoming *cofrades*. The outgoing and incoming *cofrades* formed separate lines, facing each other, and performed a dance. In the dance, the line of incoming and the line of outgoing *cofrades* approached

each other and receded repeatedly, coming together in the middle of the dance field to give each other a double hug (switching cheeks), at which point they also switched sides. This sequence was performed as many times as there were pairs of incoming and outgoing *cofrades* replacing each other. The dance thus represented them exchanging positions in the ritual life of the community. Throughout this dance, the *cofrades* distributed and drank shots of *kuxa*.

Lent

The traditions of Lent involved the *cofradías* and the *nikodeems*. During the six Fridays of Lent, the *nikodeems* carried a large wooden cross from the Catholic church to a small chapel at the cemetery in Barrio Calvario, where they held a prayer service. They then returned the cross to the church (Baronti 2002:20). The *nikodeems* were accompanied by the *ajwi pasyoon*, the *ajwi censaria*, the *nikodeems'* wives, all *cofrades*, the *ajtunab'* (trumpeters), and the Hermandad de María (Ajrusatayib'). On the fourth Friday, the *chuchuxelib'* washed the saint's clothes. The *martomuyib'* assisted them by carrying the clothes and placing them on a large *petate* (reed mat) to dry. On the fifth Sunday, the *nikodeems* removed the clothing from the icon of the Entombed Christ (Cristo Sepultado), and the *martomuyib'* created a pool by arranging twelve stones (representing the twelve apostles) around a spring. Then the *ajwi censaria* washed the clothes, assisted by the Hermandad de María. They also washed the *k'erk'er* (crotalus; Sp. *matraca* ~ rattle), a large, cogged, rotating wooden clacker/noisemaker played in lieu of bell ringing when the icon of Christ was ritually crucified (and in Roman Catholic rites, until his resurrection). On Palm Sunday, the final Sunday of Lent, processioners carried *cofradía* Korpus's icon of Christ riding a donkey from Barrio Calvario to the church.

Holy Week

In the evening of Holy Wednesday, the *nikodeems* and all *cofrades* processed through town along a course marked by twelve stone crosses (Baronti 2002:18). On Holy Thursday, the *chuchuxelib'* prepared eggs that the *nikodeems* and *cofrades* served to the purple-robed *kab'lajuuj apoxtaliib'* (twelve apostles) (Baronti 2002:18). The *apoxtaliib'* were children from six to twelve years old who were selected because they had an infirmity that people believed could be healed by their participation. The *apoxtaliib'* joined the *nikodeems* and *cofrades* for the Holy Week processions. On the evening of Holy Thursday, the *ajtunab'* played their trumpets for two hours, signaling that tomorrow would be Good Friday.[7] On Holy Thursday and Good Friday, approximately sixteen young men staged a mock battle in front of the church. Half were costumed as Jews and the other half as soldiers. Purportedly, this represented the Jews' attack on Christ and the Roman soldiers who tried to defend him.

Also on Holy Thursday, the *martomuyib'* hung the icon of San Simón from a tree (see plate 13) and left it there until Good Friday.[8] David Radtke (pers. comm., 2006), a Peace Corps volunteer who lived in Ixtahuacán in 1982, reports that women tried to walk under San Simón to increase their fertility, and the *martomuyib'* would chase them away with sticks.[9] Informants (all nontraditionalists) claimed that veneration of San Simón was witchcraft, but people involved with traditional Maya shamanism in other communities often claimed that San Simón was a benevolent deity associated with the pre-Columbian religion of their ancestors. The fertility powers the women of Ixtahuacán ascribed to San Simón hint at this traditional aspect. (See also the descriptions of San Simón in the communities of our study area in Morgan 2005:78, 80; McDonald and Hawkins 2013c:3–5, 11n2; and Scott et al., this volume.)

On Good Friday, the *ajwi pasyoon* read Ixtahuacán's apocryphal passion narrative from an old manuscript (Baronti 2002:20). Then the *nab'e nikodeems* and *ajwi pasyoon* climbed up the cross and nailed the icon of the reclining Christ to it, creating what Baronti (2002:20) calls "the 'still point' or center of the Holy Week services." At this moment, the *nikodeems* played the *k'erk'er* (see plate 14), the wood clapper's staccato snap contrasting sharply with the clang of bells throughout the rest of the year (see plate 15). The *ajwi pasyoon* read the death narrative of Christ. After he finished, the icon was removed from the cross and placed in a glass coffin.

On the Saturday of Glory, the icon of Christ in the glass coffin was carried in procession throughout the municipal center. Families had erected huge soccer-goal-shaped arches that spanned the streets (plate 16). These arches were adorned with leaves and messages such as "Dios Es Amor" (God Is Love), "Jesús Salva" (Jesus Saves), and "Jesús Resucita" (Jesus Resurrects). The families filled water jugs (*tinajas*) with offerings—candles, money, plantains, flowers—and suspended them from the arches by ropes. After the image of Christ passed under each arch, family members loosened the ropes and lowered the jugs to the *nikodeems*, who accepted the contents as an offering to the image of Christ. The *nab'e nikodeems* managed these donations.

The *nikodeems* then carried the icon of Christ in the glass coffin to the cemetery. People formed a line there, and as they passed before the icon, the *ajwi pasyoon* whipped them as a reminder of the beating Christ received before he was crucified.[10] The notion of whipping transgressors has cultural resonance in Ixtahuacán, the practice having endured for at least a century.[11] Von Tempsky (1858:384) describes how the people "administer[ed] justice among themselves": "Trespasses of any kind, of man or woman, against the laws of their community are punished, without any distinction of sex or age, by whipping. They have in an open square a tall whipping-post, to which the unfortunate individual is drawn up with a rope round his hands, until his toes just touch the ground, and then a hard and stiff cowhide is laid vigorously on his or her bare back."

On Easter Sunday, humorous dancers called *saqwi'n* (Sp. *grasejos*) danced through town. They wore monstrous-looking masks and torn clothing and carried rope whips. The *saqwi'n* danced to a specific type of marimba music. They also mocked each other, screamed, and tried to make the crowd laugh. When they reached the church, the *saqwi'n* knocked on the door to "wake up" the newly resurrected Christ. When the church doors opened, the resurrection was complete, and the Holy Week fiesta was over.

ADDITIONAL RITUAL AND FIESTA CYCLE *COSTUMBRES*

Several additional fiesta cycle *costumbres*, which were celebrated in the past and continue in the present, deserve some description. They remain the active portion of the fiesta cycle, perhaps because the *cofradía* organizations were less involved in their execution; they are carried out as an individual or family obligation or as a secularized municipal event. I base my description of these rituals on observations of them made between August and December 2002.

Todos Santos and Día de los Muertos

Like Catholics around the world, the people of Ixtahuacán celebrate Todos Santos (All Saints' Day) on November 1. During Todos Santos, the *sacristanes* decorate the church with strings of *k'exwäch* flowers (marigolds, also seen on the bells in plate 15).[12] In the past, the mayordomos would go from home to home requesting money for the saints. That night was called Noche de los Difuntos (Night of the Deceased), a holiday that developed from the same tradition as Halloween. People believe that the spirits of the dead wander during Noche de los Difuntos, and current Ixtahuaquense folklore is full of ghost stories associated with this night. November 2, Día de los Muertos (Day of the Dead), is a holiday that resembles Memorial Day in the United States. People visit the graves of their relatives and decorate them with *k'exwäch* and other flowers, incense, candles, wreaths, and pine needles and branches. The living—who literally replace the dead in both name and generational succession, who stand in the place of the ancestors in life and "before the face [*chuwäch*]" of the ancestors at their graves—honor their deceased relatives with these offerings.

The chapel in the cemetery is decorated with pine needles, and several *ajq'ij* say prayers there and pour sugar and alcohol into ceremonial fires as offerings. People in the market sell snacks, such as peanuts, tamales, oranges dipped in chili powder, and baked *güisquil* (chayote, a fruit boiled and eaten as a vegetable). On the hilltops, children fly kites.

Feria Municipal

From November 22 to 26, Ixtahuacán holds its *feria municipal* (town fair) honoring its patron saint, Santa Catalina. A few weeks before the *feria*, traveling vendors begin to set up stalls in the town. By the time the *feria* begins, the town is inundated with vendors selling treats, toys, clothes, beer, and trinkets of all types. Others set up foosball and air hockey tables, and there are video games. In provisional sheet-metal sheds, pirated movies are played on a television. Other nonceremonial activities during the *feria* include soccer matches, marimba concerts, or a *campo de toros* (bullfight field) where men dressed in drag put on a humorous mock bullfight. The *comité de la feria* raises money from private sponsors to hire the marimba bands. In 2001 and 2002, the *alcalde municipal* sponsored the *campo de toros*.

On November 22, the sacristanes adorn the Catholic church with balloons, squashes, pineapples, oranges, flowers, bananas, and bunches of leaves that resemble palm fronds, called *ramas de kip*. Colorful lights are placed around the *nab'e* Catalina image in the church. That day, the *ukab'* (second) Catalina image is carried to the home of a sponsoring family who will keep it throughout the *feria*. The family has strewn the floors of their home with festive, aromatic, honorific pine needles. Flowers and other decorations are placed before the image. The family hires musicians to play and gives *panes de avión*, coffee, and *kuxa* to their guests. Many masses are held that week, and people form long lines to give gifts of flowers, candles, and money to the *nab'e* Catalina image at the church.

On November 24 and 25, the *ukab'* and *ch'i'p* (youngest sibling) Catalina images are carried in procession throughout the principal streets of the town (plate 17). As processioners exit the church carrying the saints, they walk on elaborate "carpets" of colored sawdust that decorate the streets with pictures and geometric patterns to honor the saint. They were traditionally joined by the five *cofradías* and all of their images. The procession stops periodically at houses, where people give offerings to the image, light fireworks, and give coffee and *panes de avión* to the processioners. They also stop at the *municipalidad* (city building), where the *alcalde municipal* praises the *patrón*, and they stop before marimba bands, which play for the *patrón*. As the images of Catalina return to the church's main entrance, designees light thousands of firecrackers.

Traditionally (but no longer in Santa Catarina

Ixtahuacán), several dance dramas were performed during the *feria*, including the Baile de la Conquista (Dance of the Conquest) or the Muerte de Tecum Umán (Death of Tecum Umán). As described by Ixtahuaquense informants and following the well-documented script of the conquest play (Montoya 1970; Municipio de Cantel 1991), indigenes dressed as Spanish soldiers and K'iche' warriors danced opposite each other and provoked their cultural opponents; Tecum Umán and Pedro de Alvarado engaged in face-to-face single combat while the soldiers watched; Alvarado slew Tecum Umán and a general battle broke out; and the dance concluded when Tecum Umán was lifted into a coffin and carried away. Other traditional dances reported for Ixtahuacán include *bailes de los moros* (Moors), *mexicanos* (plate 18), *toritos* (bulls), and *venados* (deer).

Posadas

Like many pueblos in Mexico and Central America, families in Ixtahuacán host small fiestas called *posadas* from December 16 to 24. Each night, a different family hosts the communal images of Joseph and Mary in its home, in commemoration of the struggle Jesus's parents had in finding shelter before his birth. These families adorn their homes much as the *cofrades* or the hosts of the *ukab'* Catalina did for the fiestas they hosted. The families spread pine needles on the floor and place pine or cypress branches on the walls. At a *posada* I attended in 2002, the host family played recorded marimba music rather than hire musicians. In contrast to public fiestas of the *cofradías* and *ukab'* Catalina, the fiestas of *posadas* are generally invitation-only events, and full meals are served to the guests.

Having described the *cofradía* practices and their practitioners both past and present, I turn now to discuss the issues surrounding their decline.

DECLINE OF *COSTUMBRE* IN IXTAHUACÁN

The *costumbres* (traditions) of Ixtahuacán have always drawn criticism from outsiders. Here, I explore early twentieth-century Catholic efforts to modify the *cofradía* and associated *costumbres*, the rise of Evangelical and charismatic religions and their direct assault on *costumbre*, and world economic change, especially from 1970 to the present, which has contributed to the decline of *cofradía costumbres*.

Cofradía and the Early Catholic Struggle for Orthodoxy

In Von Tempsky's day, Ixtahuacán's Catholic priest, Vincente Hernandez Spina, made it his special agenda to undermine the tradition of drinking and dancing before the saints. For this, the people of Ixtahuacán twice tried to lynch him (Von Tempsky 1858:374–384). During the 1960s, on three separate occasions, the priests in Ixtahuacán confronted the people who were dancing and drinking on church grounds. In one instance, the priest took the marimba players' mallets, and in the other two instances, the priests forcibly removed people from the church who were drinking and dancing. On these occasions, the people of Ixtahuacán vigorously defended their right to drink and dance before the images. In one case, they sent a letter to the departmental government requesting that the priest be relocated, and in another, they considered lynching the priest (Larson 2006:33–34).

Beginning about 1935, efforts to modify Ixtahuacán's *costumbres* to conform to the practices of the international Roman Catholic Church began to take a more ideological approach. As part of the Catholic Action movement, two men from Ixtahuacán were trained to be *catequistas* (catechists, adult catechism instructors), and they began promoting standard Catholicism. Soon there were two groups of Catholics in Ixtahuacán: the *catequistas* (here referring to those who accepted the teachings of the catechists) and the *costumbristas* (traditionalists). According to a son of one of the original *catequistas*, early *catequistas* were the object of scorn and ridicule from the *costumbristas*. He believes that his father's enemies had him arrested on what he claims to be false charges of embezzlement during the mid-1940s because they did not like his religious beliefs.[13]

Even though they were selected by the priest and trained to be his ministers of orthodox outreach, *catequistas* did not directly oppose the fiesta system. Rather, they advocated reforms, though these reforms made the *costumbres* less appealing to many people. For example, one *catequista*, who was simultaneously the first *alcalde* of the *cofradía* Transfiguración (also called Qajawal)[14] in 1987 and 1990, refused to pay for the alcohol consumed during the fiestas. He allowed the other *cofrades* to bring their own alcohol and to drink, but he refused to consume any or to pay for the consumption of others. As noted above, drinking and dancing before the saints was the focus of traditional fiestas. It is doubtful that the "dry" *cofradía* system that the *catequistas* advocated would have been sustainable.

Charismatic and Pentecostal Alternatives as Assaults on *Cofradía*

Evangélicos (Pentecostal Protestants) and *carismáticos* (pentecostal Catholics) overtly opposed the practice of *costumbres*. Both of these religious groups eschewed alcohol consumption, rejected dancing of any sort, and banned marimba fiesta music. Ixtahuaquenses who converted to these religions were directed not to participate in the *cofradías*. Thus, increasing conversion to Christian Pentecostal religion greatly accelerated the decline of the *cofradía* system in Ixtahuacán.

The rise of these new religions requires a brief historical description from the perspective of Ixtahuacán. In the 1940s, one family in Ixtahuacán's municipal center practiced Protestantism at home. They were unsuccessful, however, at proselyting their neighbors, and after the daughters married, the parents returned to Catholicism. About 1973, Protestantism was reintroduced after a young student from Ixtahuacán was converted by the family he boarded with while attending school in nearby Santa María Visitación. The family from Santa María used the connection to begin preaching in Ixtahuacán and formed the first Evangelical church there, Iglesia Evangélica Asamblea de Dios Bet-el. By the late 1980s and early 1990s, several *evangélico* congregations worshipped in Ixtahuacán, seriously eroding the will of the remaining Catholics to sustain the total fiesta system.

The Charismatic Renovation began when a handful of Ixtahuaquenses, men who had apparently encountered the charismatic movement independently, began to hold charismatic prayer meetings in the community. In October 1976, Ixtahuacán's Catholic priest (of US nationality) legitimized these services. He believed that the emotional nature of charismatic services would reach and retain people who otherwise would be drawn into the Pentecostal denominations. The priest hoped these charismatic services would eventually lead his parishioners to the more standard, meditative form of Catholicism practiced by the *catequistas*. To this end, the priest helped to establish charismatic congregations in hamlets throughout the municipality. As the fledgling Evangelical and charismatic

Catholic congregations began to swell in numbers during the 1980s, they experienced repeated schisms. These rifts typically developed from disputes between the principal families of a particular congregation and led to the formation of new congregational groups.

In 2002, during my fieldwork, seven Evangelical congregations, three charismatic congregations, and one Seventh-day Adventist congregation held regular services in Nueva Ixtahuacán. I counted attendance at all of the Sunday (or Saturday for the Adventists) religious meetings during November 2002. Average attendance at Catholic mass (359) was slightly higher than the average total of all Evangelical services (344), but on three of the five Sundays, Evangelical services drew a larger total crowd than did the Catholic mass (see table 2.5).[15] In a survey of 115 households in Nueva Ixtahuacán,[16] 60.9 percent of the households identified themselves as some type of Catholic (sum of 43.5 percent Catholic, 14.8 percent Catholic and charismatic, 1.7 percent Catholic and Maya spirituality, and 0.9 percent as Evangelical and Catholic), while 37.4 percent identified themselves as some type of Evangelical (36.5 percent Evangelical plus 0.9 percent Evangelical and Catholic). In addition, approximately 3.5 percent identified as practicing some kind of Maya spirituality (1.7 percent Maya spirituality and 1.7 percent Catholic and Maya spirituality) while 0.9 percent identified as Jehovah's Witnesses (while none of the above, these people might be classed analytically as Evangelical on account of not being Catholic nor practicing Maya spirituality) (table 2.6). Thus, Catholics are still in the majority in Ixtahuacán, but self-identified Evangelicals are more likely to attend worship service than self-identified Catholics are. While 24.3 percent of Catholics in the survey identified themselves as charismatic, attendance at the afternoon charismatic services averaged 155, which was 43.2 percent of that of Catholic mass, suggesting that charismatics are among the most active of Catholics, at least at their own services. Unfortunately, I could not ascertain how many of those attending mass considered themselves charismatics. We know, however, that charismatics feel an obligation to attend mass weekly, and our sense is that most do.

Cofradía and Recent History

In the 1970s, Ixtahuacán's *cofradías* experienced a brief period of elaboration before their decline became evident. Such an end of the dominance of *cofradía* has been reported for other Mayas (Cancian 1965), and they seem

TABLE 2.5. ATTENDANCE AT THE PRINCIPAL WORSHIP SERVICES IN NUEVA SANTA CATARINA IXTAHUACÁN, NOVEMBER 2002

STYLE OF WORSHIP	CHURCH NAME	ATTENDANCE					
		11/3/02	11/9/02– 11/10/02	11/16/02– 11/17/02	11/23/02– 11/24/02	11/30/02– 12/01/02	Average
ORTHO-CATHOLIC	El Templo Católico	280	348	303	503	362	359
CHARISMATIC CATHOLIC	Católica Carismática de la Primera Comunidad (Paxocol)	68	0*	57	38	98	65
	Iglesia Católica Carismática de la Segunda Comunidad (Calvario)	48	0*	0	0	35	21
	Iglesia Católica Carismática de la Quinta Comunidad (Chuijuyub)	67	0*	66	70	73	69
EVANGELICAL/ PENTECOSTAL	Iglesia Evangélica Metodista Primitiva Belén	6	8	2	1	0	3
	Iglesia Evangélica Alfa y Omega	30	46	54	0	29	32
	Iglesia de Dios Evangélico Completo	39	48	45	38	38	42
	Misión Evangélica del Príncipe de Paz Pentecostés	134	98	65	109	86	98
	Príncipe de Paz Visión	6	9	4	0	0	4
	Iglesia Evangélica Asamblea de Dios	32	43	35	19	37	33
BET-EL	Iglesia Misión Evangélica Casa de Oración Pentecostés Central	124	116	71	76	150	107
ADVENTIST	Iglesia Adventista del Séptimo Día	nd	25	47	9	14	24
SABBATH TOTALS	Ortho mass	280	348	303	503	362	359
	Charismatic churches	183	0*	123	108	206	155
	Evangelical churches	371	368	276	243	340	320
	Adventist church	nd	25	47	9	14	24

Notes: nd = no data.

*There was no service in the charismatic churches on November 10, 2002, because the leaders attended a regional meeting.

TABLE 2.6. RELIGIOUS AFFILIATION IN NUEVA SANTA CATARINA IXTAHUACÁN, 2003

SURVEY DATA, 2003 FIELD SCHOOL			ANALYSIS		
Religious Affiliation Claimed	# of Adherents	% (N = 115)	Major Orientation	Adherents	% (N = 115)
Catholic	50	43.5		70	60.9
Charismatic	0	0.0			
Catholic and charismatic	17	14.8	Some Catholic affiliation		
Catholic and traditionalist	2	1.7			
Catholic and Evangelical	1[a]	0.9			
Evangelical	42	36.5	Some Evangelical affiliation	43	37.4
Catholic and Evangelical	1[a]	0.9			
Jehovah's Witness	1	0.9		3	2.6
Adventist	0	0.0	Non-Catholic/ non-Evangelical		
Maya spirituality	2	1.7			
Total	115	100		115 + 1[a]	100.9[b]

Notes: [a] Claimed in both the Catholic and Evangelical analytical columns.

[b] Total exceeds 100 percent because of the double claiming.

worthy examples of Marx's (2008[1855]:127) observation that "obsolete social forces" often "summon all their strength before their agony of death, pass from the defensive to the offensive, challenge instead of giving way," and thereby seek to reassert the validity of "premises which have not only been put in question but already condemned."

At that time, a wealthy man from the Aldea Guineales on Ixtahuacán's tropical piedmont sponsored one of the cofradías for several years and staged Ixtahuacán's most expensive fiestas to date. Other cofradías began to compete, seeking wealthy sponsors and hiring expensive marimba orchestras. These increased expenditures may have burdened cofrades so much that the costumbres became difficult to sustain.[17]

During the 1980s, many people declined invitations to be part of the cofradías. Whether this was a result of the increased violence of the insurgency or the increased population and diminished per capita yields, we cannot be sure. But cofradías often had fewer than the ideal twelve cofrades. As it became evident that the cofradías were on the downslide, there were some attempts to buttress them with public subsidies. One informant reported that during the 1980s, President Marco Vinicio Cerezo

Arévalo gave Q6,000 to each of the cofradías so they could purchase new clothing. In the 1990s, Ixtahuacán's Catholic priest began offering scholarships to those who agreed to participate in the cofradías.[18]

By 1992, however, the cofradías of Santa Cruz, María del Rosario, and Transfiguración/Qajawal stopped holding regular fiestas. These cofradías still had martomuyib' who served in the church until about 1996, but they no longer sponsored celebrations. In 1999, after a few years of intermittent sponsorship, the last two cofradías, Korpus and María de la Concepción, held their fiestas for seemingly the last time. In 2000, some men from the cofradía Korpus functioned as martomuyib' in the Catholic church in Nueva Ixtahuacán, but they did not sponsor fiestas. No other cofrades have been named since the relocation in 2000. All of the cofradía images except those belonging to the cofradía Concepción are now locked in the church. From the relocation in 2000 until 2002, the icons of Concepción had remained in the same home rather than rotating each year, and the host family had not sponsored any fiestas in their honor.

The decline of Ixtahuacán's cofradías can also be illustrated in terms of the shifting forms of sponsorship that maintained them. The forms of sponsorship employed in Ixtahuacán corresponded with the four strategies described by Smith (1977:1–2, 5–6): *mayordomía* or rotating service, which prevails when the fiesta system is sound; the "administered" strategy, which relies on permanent sponsorship by certain individuals; the "appended" strategy, which relies on increasing the number of sponsors; and the "truncated" strategy, which relies on limiting festivities.

In the earliest memories of Ixtahuaquenses, *cofradías* were supported by *mayordomía*. *Cofrades*, who changed every year, donated funds to the *cofradía* and made investments, such as purchasing livestock, which the *martomuyib'* were expected to raise and then sell to help finance the celebrations.

As *cofradía* expenses escalated in the 1970s, the administered strategy was employed: wealthy Ixtahuaquense families began to financially sponsor the *cofradías* year after year. In the 1980s and 1990s, the *soline'l* in each *cofradía* chose increasingly younger, even adolescent, *cofrades*, and the appended strategy was used. Youths were probably selected to avoid adult labor loss, but the parents and extended family members of the young *cofrades* were expected to contribute to *cofradía* expenses. Thus, a regularly employed schoolteacher might assist a younger nephew. The scholarships offered by the Catholic priest in the 1990s as recruitment incentives are another type of appended strategy. Ultimately, the *cofradías* resorted to truncating *costumbres*, until there was little left.

Many other *costumbres* in Ixtahuacán have declined or transformed. The *cargo* of *pixcar* has been completely abandoned. Baronti (2002:18) claims this *cargo* disappeared in the late 1970s after the *nab'e pixcar* was accused of embezzlement. Several informants deny this incident occurred. One claims that the *pixcariyib'* never controlled funds, and this office continued until 1980 when two men, neither of which are the man Baronti claims embezzled funds, were the last *pixcariyib'*.[19]

Baronti (2002:21) also discusses the decline of *costumbres* among the *nikodeems*. He notes that in 1994, one of the three remaining *nikodeems* withdrew from his *cargo* because his son, a charismatic Catholic, claimed that venerating images contradicted the Bible. Then in 2000, the remaining two *nikodeems* were separated from each other by the *traslado* (relocation) of Ixtahuacán's government center to Chwipatan. Although the remaining *nikodeems* seek to preserve their Lent traditions, their desire seems unlikely to be fulfilled as these two *nikodeems* grow older and the younger generations lose interest.

As the *cofradía* system went into collapse, the community began to deploy a *comité de la feria*, which now sponsors the week-long festivities for the town's patron, Santa Catalina. Dance groups, which until 2000 performed complex traditional dances during the town fair and other holidays, now sponsor a simplified generic masked dance that no longer tells a story. Individual families still host the *ukab'* Catalina image in their home during the town fair or the images of Mary and Joseph during *posadas*.

The national holiday, Día de la Independencia (Independence Day), celebrated on September 15, has waxed stronger while many of Ixtahuacán's religious holidays have waned. This holiday incorporates many aspects that refer to and reflect traditional activities, but now often in modified and simplified forms that contrast with current religious practices and adopt iconic pieces of traditionalism. During the children's parade in 2002, many classes of students dressed in traditional costumes: some wore white cloaks and carried a cross, like the *nikodeems*. Others wore jaguar and monkey suits like dancers, and still others dressed like the *saqwi'n* and danced to marimba music. Most of the others wore the traditional homewoven and brocaded clothes that their ancestors wore. Sometimes speaking Spanish, sometimes K'iche', children also recited poetry that they considered traditional, performed traditional dances, and put on plays depicting traditional activities at the *salón municipal* (municipal auditorium). These activities express the desire to teach children about *costumbres* so the traditions are not forgotten. Still, it is significant that some of the activities, which were once considered sacred acts of devotion to be carried out by adults, are now preserved only as amusing diversions for children in a nonsacred national celebration. Also, the increasing elaboration of a national holiday at the same time that most communal religious holidays have been neglected suggests that the people of Ixtahuacán are trying to integrate with the national society.

CAUSES AND EXPLANATIONS: THE DECLINE OF GUATEMALAN *COFRADÍA* IN POLITICAL, ECONOMIC, AND HISTORICAL CONTEXT

A variety of scholars have advanced explanations regarding the decline of *cofradía* sponsorship. Before laying out a few of these, however, I describe my personal experience as a sponsor of a *cofradía* event, because it sheds light on why people in 2002 resisted *cofradía* service and have not reinstated certain of its customs.

A Personal Account of *Cofradía* Decline

Unsatisfied with fallible memories of expenses and activities in prior decades, I decided to re-create a *cofradía* fiesta to supplement my interviews with observational data. When I first suggested that I could host this fiesta, many people in the community expressed enthusiasm for the idea and encouraged me to do it. However, when I approached the man who had housed the images of Concepción, he seemed reluctant. Most likely, he did not trust me as an outsider, and he knew that if anything went wrong, he would be blamed. His son, however, advised him that holding this fiesta would be a great idea, but suggested it should end early and that not much alcohol should be served so the party would not get out of hand. I agreed to pay for all expenses except for the alcohol.

I invited several people in their thirties and forties who had formerly been *cofrades* to play the role of *cofrades* in this fiesta, but none of them accepted. One of them said that these days, it is too embarrassing for young people to wear *cofradía* costumes. Today, only the oldest men in Ixtahuacán wear traditional dress. One elderly woman whom I invited to be a *chuchuxel* initially responded with great enthusiasm. However, shortly before the fiesta, she decided it was not a good idea. She felt that because I was a foreigner, I could not be trusted. I might steal the images. A foreigner had stolen the image of Christ Resurrected from the church altar in 1996. That night she visited several of my invitees, trying to persuade them not to attend. When another invitee found out what this woman was doing, he also circulated through the village endorsing the project and encouraging everyone to participate. When I learned of this dispute, I considered canceling the fiesta, but I was told not to worry about the woman, because no one took her seriously. My idea of sponsoring this fiesta had taken on a life of its own, and I felt I had become an unwilling participant in a conflict I had generated.

As the festival approached, the man who hosted the images sent word that I could not expect him to pay for any of the expenses associated with the fiesta, including the alcohol and the firewood to cook the food. I capitulated and agreed to pay for the alcohol. The morning before the fiesta, people told me that the amount of alcohol I had purchased was insufficient—though I had been told previously it would be enough—and they needed money to purchase more.

That day, I accompanied the man who had circulated through the village telling people that they should support the fiesta as he visited the homes of other invitees to encourage them to participate. In one home, a man seemed hesitant; he kept turning to his wife for a response. I could not follow the conversation in K'iche', but I later found out that his wife was reluctant for her husband to go because he had a sickness of worms "in his stomach," which Mayas associate with alcoholism. In the end, both husband and wife participated in the fiesta, and the other *cofrades* prevailed on the husband to have some *kuxa*. He died a little over a month later of unknown causes presumably complicated by an alcohol binge.

In the end, six men and two women accepted the role of *cofrade*, and a large crowd came to watch. These "*cofrades*," ranging in age from fifty to eighty-six, were much older than most *cofrades* in the past. Indeed, in the later phases of *cofradía* collapse, *alcaldes* were sometimes as young as eighteen, and juveniles were often selected to be *martomuyib'*. The celebration started at about 12:30 p.m. and ended abruptly at 8:30 p.m., after a notoriously impaired alcoholic came into the party very drunk and fell onto the marimba, breaking one of the mallets.

These experiences suggest a number of reasons that *cofradía* fiestas are no longer celebrated or restarted. First, people fear exposing their precious images in public because that could give robbers a chance to steal them. Second, there is disagreement and anxiety about the proper role of alcohol in *cofradía* fiestas. For the biggest supporters of *cofradías*, who are generally older people who served as *cofrades* during their young adulthood, alcohol consumption is an irreplaceable part of *cofradía* fiestas. Still, there is a growing feeling in Ixtahuacán among Catholics as well as Evangelicals that the drinking associated with *cofradías* is excessive. There are obvious pragmatic health reasons for limiting alcohol consumption, as the death of one participant may illustrate, but it seems that for young people there is an additional element of shame associated with drinking. I suspect that they are trying to avoid hated stereotypes about "drunken Indians." Third, there is an unwillingness to support *cofradía* fiestas financially. I found that many people were willing to participate in the fiesta when I bore the costs, but no one was willing to share the costs with me. Fourth, the ceremonial aspects of *cofradía* fiestas, such as dressing in traditional costumes and performing traditional dances, are embarrassing for young people today, even those who formerly participated in *cofradías*. They seem to feel that these *costumbres* are old-fashioned and parochial. They want to represent themselves as modern and cosmopolitan.

Cofradía Decline in the Literature

Scholars have suggested various reasons that Mayas and their communities have abandoned the religious *cargos* and fiestas. Nash (1958b:72–73) associates the breakdown of the traditional hierarchy in Cantel, Guatemala, with the period of sweeping political reforms between 1944 and 1954 during the presidencies of Juan José Arévalo and Jacobo Árbenz Guzmán. As a result of these reforms, access to political offices depended more on party affiliation than on completion of communal *cargos*. Young adults who had not completed junior *cargos* began to hold high political offices. This undermined the authority of the *principales*. Service in the *cofradías* was no longer mandatory for prestige or high civil office, and the long-term viability of the *cofradías* became unclear.

Cancian (1965:192–194) predicted that the fiesta system in Zinacantán, Mexico, which was still healthy at the time, would soon decline. He suggests that with the rapid population growth that was then taking place, there would not be enough *cargos* to allow everyone in the community to participate in the traditional hierarchy. Those excluded from the *cofradía* system would therefore be attracted to economic activities in the Ladino world as an alternative mode of developing status. This would create economic inequality in Zinacantán that would result in the abandonment of the *cargo* system.

Hinshaw (1975:63–71) associates the decline of the *cofradías* in Panajachel with "shifting attitudes and values." He notes that some people seem to have used military service or Protestant conversion to avoid *cofradía* service. At the same time, young people in Panajachel increasingly engaged in new, more remunerative occupations. Hinshaw suggests they felt that status could more effectively be obtained by amassing and displaying wealth than by fulfilling ceremonial *cargos*.

Brintnall (1979:170–181) connects the decline of the fiesta system in Aguacatán, Guatemala, with economic changes occasioned by the introduction of garlic and onions as cash crops. These endeavors created surplus wealth among young people, making them economically independent of their parents, whom they traditionally needed for land inheritance, and of Ladinos, who traditionally provided contract work in the *fincas* (plantations). Because of this independence, the cash croppers seemed immune to social pressures and rewards that otherwise would have drawn them into traditional service.

Warren (1978:168–169, 170–177) documents a native perspective about why the *cofradía* system declined in San Andrés Semetabaj. There, the people associated the Catholic Action movement with the decline of the *cofradías*. *Costumbristas* sought to limit Ladino oppression by maintaining a communal system that was independent of the national government. *Cofradías* were central to this system. Indigenous Catholic Action members, in contrast, tried to challenge Ladino dominance by engaging in traditionally Ladino political and economic activities. Those linked to Catholic Action felt that the burden of religious *cargos* precluded them from displacing the Ladinos, and they therefore undermined the *costumbristas* as they sought to displace Ladinos.

W. R. Smith (1977:6–7) associates the vitality of the fiesta system in three Guatemalan towns with their relative economic conditions. He claims that the fiesta system declined in San Miguel Ixtahuacán because the people there became too poor to bear the costs of sponsorship due to their dependence on plantation agriculture (Smith 1977:73–102, 133–144). On the other hand, San Pedro Sacatepéquez, a prosperous regional economic center, had become so affluent that other forms of status building had supplanted the fiesta system (103–132, 145–160). The fiesta system remained most intact in San Pedro Petz, an *aldea* of San Pedro Sacatepéquez. With economic strength between the other two, Petz had remained agricultural yet not desperately impoverished because of its close proximity to a variety of coastal and escarpment resources (161–168).

Baronti (2002:20) gives two reasons that Santa Catarina Ixtahuacán's *costumbres* have declined. First, he claims that as young people increasingly began to study, they were precluded from participating in the *cofradía* system, and they began to associate these traditions with "illiteracy and backwardness." Second, he writes, "iconoclastic Evangelical Protestants and charismatic Catholics . . . waged an unremitting propaganda war on the *cofradía* system" (20) because use of religious icons was interpreted as idolatrous paganism. Baronti also implies that the relocation of Santa Catarina Ixtahuacán further undermined its *costumbres*.

Larson (2006) links the maintenance of *costumbres*

in Santa Catarina Ixtahuacán with two successive economic processes. First, the experience of proletarianization and subordination when working on Ladino plantations—necessitated by rapid population growth and an increased need for cash from wages—reinforced the value of *costumbres* as an expression of ethnic identity and even resistance to change when they returned to the village. This resistance was both symbolic and psychological. Via *cofradías*, the people of Santa Catarina resisted the loss of economic self-sufficiency as they experienced the transition from family-based, landowning agriculture to serving as hired labor at *fincas*, and the religious and ideological subjugation of indigenous customs to non-indigenous priests and the non-indigenous society at large. Honoring the customs in these circumstances gave them the psychological space to feel dignity and independence from the emerging world around them, in which they felt they had a diminished role. The second facet of this process showed itself in conflict with successive priests. Priestly resistance to *costumbre* in fact endowed *costumbre* with native value as a symbol of resistance to Maya subordination in the economic system.

Countervailing this tendency, Ixtahuaquenses recently have become more comfortable with the market economy, and that involvement has increased their dependence on cash income. Through treadle-loom weaving and government jobs based on outside education, Ixtahuaquenses' cash economy involvement has undermined *costumbres* because it entices people to realize their personal desires through commodity consumption.

Global Explanation and Ultimate Cause

All of this helps us understand the decline of the fiesta and *cofradía* system in Santa Catarina Ixtahuacán. In evaluating these hypotheses, however, it is useful to distinguish proximal causes from ultimate causes. Proximal causes are local conditions or events that catalyze or speed up larger ongoing processes in the local area. Proximal causes are useful for explaining why certain events took place sooner or had a relatively larger impact in one area than in other similar areas. Significant proximal causes for the decline of the fiesta system in Santa Catarina Ixtahuacán include the religious movements of Catholic Action, Evangelical Protestantism, and charismatic Catholicism; historical events such as the reforms of 1944–1954 and the *traslado* of Ixtahuacán's municipal headquarters; and economic trends such as the introduction of treadle-loom weaving

and the acquisition of government jobs through increased education.

However, because fiesta and religious *cargo* systems have declined universally among Maya communities in Guatemala and Mexico, as they have elsewhere in Latin America, and because many parallel institutions (such as the potlatch systems in the Pacific Northwest or ancestor worship in East Asia) have declined around the world, none of these local or regional phenomena can justly be called an ultimate cause or adequate explanation. Nor is it sufficient to merely gloss these changes as "modernization" without explaining the specific processes that caused them.

Clearly there is an ongoing global trend that undermines certain institutions that have been relatively stable for hundreds of years. The institutions most affected are those that demand huge outlays of personal wealth while yielding only local status, those that maintain the political dominance of the elderly, and those that promote communal ideals over individual desires. To understand the ultimate cause for the worldwide decline of diverse institutions, including the *cofradía* system, that embody these attributes, we need to do more than examine the local history of a community in the decades preceding the decline. Rather, we need to study the global expansion of capitalism over the centuries and document local human responses to global processes in both the past and the present.

The psychic and social costs of *cofradía* participation spiked when a rising population made resources increasingly inadequate and when the simultaneous penetrations of global capitalism and Guatemalan nationalism—which made health-based population growth possible—unseated local status investment from its dominance as literally the only game in town in the insular indigenous community. Under this competitive pressure, the relatively unquestioned but never monolithic indigenous ways became the questionable "old ways." As the old ways declined, the pressing question soon became, how do I get connected to the "new ways"? But indigenous Maya culture is not I-centered. And it certainly is not irreligious. As we show in succeeding chapters, the Maya response to the decline and collapse of the old ways was we-centered—but with a more local, congregational focus rather than a municipal, group focus embodied in the parish—and enthusiastically religious to an astonishing degree.

Even though the collectivist, municipally oriented *cofradía* system declined, there remains today a relatively vibrant but quasi-covert individual- and family-oriented shamanic form of the old ways, tied to the good earth, which gives blessings, helps in healings, and supports good mental health.

NOTES

1. In former times *cofradía* images were kept by the *cofradía* in the home of the first *alcalde* (in one of the *cofradías*, a secondary image was kept by the *nab'e morto'm* as well), and the Entombed Christ image was kept by the *nikodeems*. Today, most of the *cofradía* images are kept in storage, locked in the back of the Catholic temple (the temporary Catholic church building in use while the new church facing the mayoral offices across the plaza is being constructed).

2. Residents call the patron saint of Nahualá and Santa Catarina Ixtahuacán either Santa Catarina or Santa Catalina. Although the latter is more common, both are acceptable. Her formal designation is Santa Catalina de Alejandria.

3. One night of a three-man *marimba pura* band, Q300.00; marimba transport, Q100.00; two pounds of candles, Q9.00; two candles in glass, Q15.00; half pound of incense, Q12.00; twelve six-inch rockets, Q95.00; two yards of string fireworks, Q7.00; cypress branches and pine needles, Q30.00; one bouquet of yellow flowers, Q15.00; one bouquet of white flowers, Q10.00; two meals for the musicians, Q60.00; a large basket of cross buns, Q100.00; five pounds of chocolate, Q22.50; fifteen pounds of sugar, Q26.25; eighteen pints of home-brewed liquor, Q48.00; and three packages of cigarettes, Q26.50.

4. *Chaj-* is the root for caretaker or guard.

5. The *ajwi* constructions combine the following: *aj-* (master of, from the place of, devoted to, or with the desire of); *-wi* (when prefixed or possessed implies extruded from or an extension of the noun construction).

6. Either Von Tempsky made an error and confused the left and right shoulder, or the image was reversed at some point in production. We do not know.

7. In classical Maya, the *tun* was a stone slab monument that heralded in its engravings the reigning lord's accomplishments and genealogy. In modern K'iche', the root word *-tun-* refers to a drum or a trumpet, and its verbal forms suggest gathering as well as announcing.

8. San Simón is a heterodox saint who is popular throughout western Guatemala. He has a dark, curling mustache and wears a business suit (or, in some communities, a military uniform) and glasses and smokes a cigar. San Simón is associated with hedonistic desires. People offer him gifts of money, alcohol, cigarettes, and candles and petition him for riches or lovers.

9. The hanging of San Simón seems to be a representation of the suicide of Judas Iscariot, but it also creates a striking parallel with the crucifixion of the image of Christ on Good Friday. Though not confirmed by interviews, we suspect that the hanging—what in modern terms might be called a *lynchiamento*—represents the castigation due to one who upsets or betrays the Mayan value of solidarity with community, represented by the solidarity of Christ with his apostles in the Last Supper, prior to his betrayal to the Roman governing elite and their military.

10. Children were whipped softly to help them remember to be good, while adults who were considered to be serious sinners were whipped repeatedly and forcefully. Thieves were whipped on the hands, and people who danced too much were whipped on the feet.

11. John Watanabe (pers. comm.) notes, "Whipping was the primary form of public punishment for offenders throughout the colonial period; every cabildo had its whipping post in front of it."

12. *K'ex* means "change, exchange, or replacement," and *wäch* means "face, surface, or image." In K'iche' cosmology, grandchildren replace grandparents and are often given the name of a grandparent whom they replace. Those so named frequently call each other *nuk'ex*, "my replacement." Casual namesakes also hale each other as *nuk'ex*.

13. Both Brintnall 1979 and Falla 1978 describe the process of priests using youths to help them and, in the process, setting up significant factionalism in the municipalities: Ortho-Catholics and youths versus traditionalist Catholics and elders. For the perspective of Ixtahuacán's parish priest regarding Ixtahuacán's transition to partial orthopraxis, charismaticism, and Protestantism, see Baronti 2002:20–25.

14. Qajawal: *q-* = first-person plural possessive, *ajaw* = lord, *-al* = intensifier, exemplar of category, supreme.

15. Note that November hosts the week-long fiesta *patronal* of Santa Catarina. This, along with Easter and Christmas, is one of the few times that casually cultural Catholics feel an obligation to attend mass, and the central provisional church building fills to capacity. This holiday seasonal factor may account for the two Sundays in which attendance at mass exceeded attendance at Evangelical meetings.

16. In 2002, I procured a map of Nueva Santa Catarina Ixtahuacán and walked all of its streets, identifying and numbering individual households. Defining an individual household was problematic because in Ixtahuacán, a household complex is usually composed of a few separate, freestanding structures. However, each household complex had one standardized, original identical structure, a two-room cinderblock home constructed by the Guatemalan federal government and nongovernmental organizations as part of the recovery effort after landslides associ-

ated with Hurricane Mitch in 1998 (Hawkins and Adams 2020). I defined a household complex as a group of structures associated with one of these standardized homes. I identified 546 complexes, 15 of which were not occupied in 2002, which created a target population of 531 household complexes. I selected 133 household complexes, one-quarter of the population, by using a random number list to create a surveyable sample for my questionnaire. Because of time constraints and some nonparticipation, the questionnaire was completed in 115 of these 133 homes, 86.5 percent of the sample and 21.7 percent of the population.

17.   In 1979, Guatemala floated the quetzal, its currency, and thereby devalued it. Prior to that time, the quetzal had been tied to a par value (one-for-one exchange) with the US dollar. Concurrently, massive imports of goods and other economic forces, including population growth, made it impossible for the traditional Mayas to live in relative economic self-sufficiency. In effect, the *cofrade* families' living costs and external needs shot up at the same time that *cofradía* expenses escalated. They escalated both competitively as officeholders tried to out-fiesta one another, and they escalated in absolute terms because the devaluation forced up prices immediately while wages lagged, and few had excess corn to sell because of the underlying land crisis.

18.   This American priest's behavior may have been unusual. Others in the Ortho-Catholic clergy were sometimes hostile toward traditionalists. John Watanabe (pers. comm.) notes that Maryknolls in Huehuetenango were by turns strict orthodoxists, cutting down crosses where *costumbre* was done, or communitarian developmentalists less concerned with traditionalists (but perhaps only after they had the traditionalists in decline).

19.   I mentioned this to Baronti, and he responded that the office may have lasted longer than he indicated.

Chapter Three

"Come Now!"

Current K'iche' Maya Traditionalist Shamanic Ceremony and
Cosmology in a Rural Hamlet of Santa Catarina Ixtahuacán

WINSTON K. SCOTT, JOHN P. HAWKINS, AND WALTER RANDOLPH ADAMS

IN THIS ANALYSIS OF TRADITIONAL cosmology and shamanic practices in a contemporary indigenous community in Guatemala, I lay out the K'iche' Maya view of the sacred from a physical and spiritual perspective, establish the relationship between deities and living beings, and show how the interaction between the deities and humans works in shamanic ceremonies.[1] In doing so, I follow Durkheim (2001[1912]:4): "We must reach beneath the symbol to the reality it embodies and which gives it its true meaning." By traditional cosmology and ritual, I do not mean beliefs and ritual practices that existed at some time and place in the past, now dredged out of the memories of older informants. Rather, I refer to the ideas and practices of a ritual system currently believed and practiced but referred to as "traditional" by indigenous people to contrast it with a panoply of new doctrines and religious practices. These new religious practices include Ortho-Roman Catholicism and its activist and outreach branches, such as Acción Católica, *cursillistas*, and charismatic Catholicism; Evangelical Protestantism's many fractious Pentecostal congregations and denominations; and a smattering of other recently introduced religions that may not consider themselves either Catholic or Evangelical, such as Seventh-day Adventists, Mennonites, Jehovah's Witnesses, and Mormons. In contrast to all these, traditionalist religion—called *costumbre*—is believed to be ancient. I emphasize, however, that it is currently practiced.

Traditionalist rituals are often led or performed by older, respected members of the community, called *ajq'ijab',*[2] who have learned them. Those who commission the rituals on their own behalf, however, include the old,

the middle-aged, and some younger couples. Traditional K'iche' cosmology and ceremonies center on spiritual entities and fuse theological figures and the geographical environment through a Trinity composed of a Creator, earth lords, and ancestors.

I was fortunate to gain quite intimate access to the community of Xekakixkan, an *aldea* of Santa Catarina Ixtahuacán about a half-hour drive from the municipal center. Upon arrival in Santa Catarina municipality, I was the only student in the field school who did not have a host family already set to greet me. Rather, John Hawkins led me to a small hamlet high above the municipal center where a certain daykeeper, Baltazar, well known throughout the region and addressed locally by his Mayanized name, Tix, received us into his home.[3] We discussed the possibility of Tix hosting me as a student who wanted to document his work as a daykeeper, thereby preserving his knowledge of the Maya cosmos for the young people who were not learning it. This daykeeper's most pressing concern was whether or not I would eat the way they did. We assured him that I had spent a great deal of time previously in Alta Verapaz with Q'eqchi' Maya–speaking communities and that I felt right at home consuming chilies, tortillas, and *süb'* (a steamed corn tamale). More important, I assured him that I had worked with Q'eqchi' communities in their fields and knew how to plant, clean, and harvest maize; that I was experienced at chopping and carrying firewood; and that I was willing to help him in all these tasks. He agreed to consult his wife, Mikaela. I returned to Ixtahuacán.

A few days had passed when I received word that the couple had agreed to host me. The next day, I went to work in the fields with Tix, helping with the chores as we slowly began to discuss his thoughts about his work with revered Maya spirits and the natural world that surrounded us in our mountain setting. I have no doubt that my language facility and familiarity with a rural Maya lifestyle convinced my hosts to accept me into their home. They did not speak Spanish, so I had to speak K'iche'. As a fluent speaker of Q'eqchi' Maya, I readily picked up on the many linguistic similarities and soon could proficiently communicate with my hosts and the community. All of the interviews, questionnaire surveys, and conversations that I present in this chapter were conducted in K'iche' Maya, and I am the translator thereof.

Three *ajq'ijab'* supplied the bulk of the information on which I base this study, collaborating to answer specific inquiries concerning Maya cosmology and ritual. The practical application of Maya cosmology and ritual comes from my host, who is the eldest of the three. Tix used spiritual invocation, ancestral communion, place-based ritual, and divination in his work as a daykeeper. Much of the information in this chapter derives from my observation of Tix's ceremonial practice and my involvement as his novice assistant in the ceremonial realm. Tix taught me not only about what he, as an *ajq'ij*, believes concerning spirituality, but also how spirituality is practiced. From Tix's examples, and later by participating in some of the smaller spiritual duties of ceremonies, I gained information regarding traditional cosmology through action, as opposed to explanation. Tix never explicitly told me what was going on. Rather, I discovered that when I made statements summing up my understanding of an issue or procedure, either he would confirm my observations with a smile of pleasure or he would correct my misunderstandings.

Although previous literature, such as Tedlock (1982), details Maya calendrics and divination in traditional K'iche' culture and the forces that have led to the displacement of traditional spirituality with new religions, we lack in-depth documentation of ceremonial practice and its philosophical underpinnings as well as a full description of the divination and related trance states. Falla (2001) and Brintnall (1979) document aspects of traditional Maya beliefs and temporal shamanic hierarchies. However, these authors focus on cultural transformation and religious conversion from traditional post-conquest Maya Catholic religious practices to orthodox Catholicism and Evangelism, not on the symbolism of current "traditionalist" or "customary" ceremonial practice and interaction

between spiritual and temporal beings. Although Tedlock (1982) provides an in-depth and personal documentation of K'iche' shamanic works, her account focuses on recruitment of shamans and on the symbolic meanings of the contemporary twenty-day Maya calendar. In this chapter, by contrast, I document the shamanic ceremony and trance-state divination that sustains a working cosmological system by maintaining balance and order between spirit entities and humans who actively petition them for guidance and knowledge.

I show that the traditional cosmology of the community of Ixtahuacán reflects characteristics of both sacred and temporal philosophies that find grounding in the environmental surroundings and that empower the souls of the dead in a supernatural existence connected to the living. Suffused with Christianity but distinct from its standard variants, the traditional cosmology creates a spiritual hierarchy and base for believers by which they live, both culturally and religiously. The Trinity of spirit entities—Creator, earth lords, and ancestors—make up a spiritual hierarchy that a shaman calls through prayers and offerings to "Come now!" to a ceremonial space where the living await instruction. Traditionalist rituals thus establish a forum in which the realms of living clients and supernatural beings interact to ensure a harmonious balance among the living, the deceased, and the spiritual guides of the K'iche' Maya cosmology.

K'iche' shamanic ritual embodies aspects of van Gennep's (1960[1909]) and Turner's (1969) analyses of rites of passage and their three corresponding states of separation, liminality, and reaggregation. This process, as experienced through shamanic K'iche' ceremonies and divination, is solely concerned with creating a sense of certainty and understanding in life through maintaining a harmonious relationship between the spiritual and temporal realms of spirit entities and the living. Harmonious balance looms central to those who employ a shaman to perform ceremonies because they attribute all negative occurrences that might befall them to imbalance in life and to neglect of the earth lords and ancestors. Ritual allows people to establish, or reestablish, the desired balance through communication via a shaman and the spiritual gifts that he possesses. While other scholars (Tedlock 1982; Fischer 2001) have documented the importance of balance in Maya thought, how shamans establish this balance through traditionalist ritual has not been adequately described.

In the community of Ixtahuacán, so experienced with

the uncertainties of life, a shaman acts as a holy figure. Following Douglas's (1966:51) terminology, a shaman is "set apart" from other people by spiritual gifts and a divine calling to direct individuals, interpret spiritual messages, and counsel members of a community.

In western thought, key words, phrases, practices, and symbols characterize and divide religious belief systems from the secular. However, in the tradition (costumbre, "custom") and spirituality of Ixtahuacán, a fusion of Catholic and Maya theology, practice, folklore, and mythology combine with contemporary cultural idiosyncrasies to create a distinct cosmology of sacredness that in the minds of its adherents, suffuses all places and all times. The fusion creates a sphere that is both sacred and secular, mixing cultural identity with religious ideology, all of which is expressed through ritual. In the traditionalist's life sphere, there is no distinction between sacred and secular.

In this chapter I also show that Ixtahuacán's traditional religious community does not separate and classify magic, mysticism, and religion as distinctly different. Rather, traditionalist religion eclectically mixes these facets that drive the cosmology and ideology justifying traditional ritual behavior. Simply put, without aspects of both magic and ritual functioning in the same context, religion would simply be thought without action. However, Maya culture is praxis-oriented. Action takes precedence over logocentric approaches that dissect and contemplate the coherence of the thought embedded in performance. I show these distinctly Maya cultural syntheses of sacred with secular, of magic with religion, and of thought with action in an analysis of the traditional K'iche' ceremony, the characters involved, and the purpose behind it.

DAYKEEPERS AND THE SHAMAN

Daykeepers—the *ajq'ijab'* who deal in matters concerning Maya spirituality and Maya calendrics—perform the traditional rituals. Tix explained his work as a spiritual mediator and a mouthpiece to deities: "My work, what I do, is to find what your life wants. Perhaps there is sickness; perhaps something of yours was lost. The Santo Mundo [Sacred Earth ~ Holy Earth = earth lords] tells me what is necessary to find what you need to do so that your life is good."

In K'iche' Maya, *ajq'ij*, a single title, refers to three orders of daykeeper distinguished by differences in the

type of work that they perform with spiritual entities, differences in their symbols of power, and differences in the spiritual gifts they have received. "There are three [types] of daykeepers," said Diego, a Maya student who had participated in various Maya ceremonies. "One uses the *tz'ite* [divining beans]; the second can communicate with the Santo Mundo; and the third can talk with both of these and the *antmas* [ancestral spirits]."

The lowest order of daykeeper is a man or woman (though usually a man) who deals only with the *tz'ite*. The diviner draws from a supply of beans and counts the extraction to determine the proper approach to accomplish desired events and whether those events should be linked to or initiated on a proposed day in the twenty-day Maya calendar or, more wisely, tied to some other day. An individual who has come with some type of worry or question approaches the *tz'ite* daykeeper (my term). Having heard the question, this daykeeper inquires further about actions to be taken by ritual means to appease the Creator, earth lords, and ancestors. By separating and counting the beans, the daykeeper allows the earth lords to determine the day and the necessary offering to be performed. For the performance of the restorative ritual, however, the *tz'ite* daykeeper must refer the client to a daykeeper of a higher order since this first level of *ajq'ij* cannot perform the necessary ceremony; rather, his work only determines a time on the Maya calendar when a ceremony will be accepted.

Daykeepers of the second order—those with a higher ability and higher authority of a spiritual nature—perform ceremonies that correlate to things of this world, but their authority and practice exclude contact with ancestral spirits. Using the *tz'ite*, this order of daykeepers can determine the days on which a ceremony will be accepted by the Santo Mundo and perform the needed ceremony on behalf of a client. The second level of daykeeper, however, has limited communications with the Santo Mundo, only being able to call earth lords to a ceremony and interpret their messages through burning candles and incense. The third and highest order of daykeeper, exemplified by Tix, possesses gifts to communicate directly with spiritual entities—specifically the Santo Mundo and ancestors—and to be their mouthpiece through divination. When in communication with spirit entities—when in a trance—the shaman becomes the medium connecting the living to beings in the spiritual realm; the third-order shaman conveys verbal messages between them. Tix explained that the ability to enter into the trance state happened *through* him, but not *because* of him. He described the trance state in these terms: "They [ancestral spirits] are the ones who come before my face and talk in my mouth. I call them, but if the offering is not good, they will not talk with me."

Tix emphasized that this third order of daykeeper had the greatest gift: the ability to talk with ancestral spirits—the *animas*—through entrance into a trance state: "Miguel is a daykeeper [*ajq'ij*], but he only works with the *tz'ite*. Alonso is a daykeeper [*ajq'ij*] who can perform a ceremony and call the Santo Mundo, but he cannot talk to the *animas*. What I work in—I am able to do all of these things, plus the *animas* and Santo Mundo talk to me when I call them. I never chose to have them talk with me, but they do, and I tell people what the Santo Mundo wants."

In this chapter, I concentrate on this third or highest level of daykeeper. Because of the disparities in their duties and abilities, it is necessary to analytically separate the shaman—the third-level *ajq'ij*—from the other two levels of daykeeper. The gift of verbal communication and physical visitation between temporal and spirit worlds is a gift held only by the shamanic—the highest—order of daykeepers.[4] Through the gifts of the third-order daykeepers, clients seek answers to their most troubling concerns. I summarize the capacities, responsibilities, and gifts of the three orders of daykeepers or shamans in table 3.1.

Although Tix, Alonso, and Miguel were all addressed as *ajq'ij* in K'iche', Tix was clearly treated with greater deference. According to Alonso, Miguel, and other daykeepers, Tix held the highest status because of his work as a medium to spirits and a mouthpiece of the earth lords and ancestors.

To illustrate this point, I examine an interaction among Tix, Alonso, Miguel, and two daykeepers from a neighboring hamlet. On this occasion, all five *ajq'ijab'* had gathered to discuss what to do with a large rock, deemed by them Le Portuna (derived from the Spanish word *fortuna*, "fortune, luck"). The heavy stone was said to contain gold and acted as a voice and guide to a shaman who used it to communicate with spirits. This rock had been dormant; it was in the hands of a family whose patriarch had been a Maya shaman and had recently died. The gathered *ajq'ijab'* decided unanimously that Tix would inherit the Portuna, as he was the only man among the five who possessed the gifts to use it correctly. Among the five daykeepers, Tix was neither the eldest nor the youngest (figure 3.1). Yet he was deemed the beneficiary of the large stone because, as one of his counterparts stated, "The rest of us—we can't speak to the Portuna, and the Portuna will not speak to us." Among these ritual specialists, the difference between a daykeeper and a more capable shaman was not marked with titles or words but recognized in abilities and gifts.

TIX'S CALLING

Tix felt strongly that his role as a medium derived not from his own choice to become a daykeeper, but by having received the calling and by the will of the Santo Mundo and the *animas*.[5] As a young man, Tix had not

TABLE 3.1. THE THREE ORDERS OF MAYA DAYKEEPERS AND THEIR DUTIES

ORDER OR LEVEL	DUTIES				
Third or highest	Calendar and seed divination	Performs ceremonial prayers and chants	Medium to Sacred Earth (Santo Mundo)	Medium to ancestors	Performs divinations and enters trance states
Second or middle	Calendar and seed divination	Performs ceremonial prayers and chants to Santo Mundo			
First or lowest	Calendar and seed divination, occasional chanting at the request of one in a higher order				

Figure 3.1. Tix with flower offering. The high altar is behind Tix's left; the middle or world surface altar is in front of it; and the divination chair is half-obscured by his body. Tix sits in this chair when he goes into trance and becomes the voice of Santo Mundo, the earth lord. Courtesy of Winston K. Scott, 2003.

I never learned Spanish. I tried to speak Spanish, but could not. But I was able to learn the prayers. They stayed in my head. I learned them well, and after some time I began to be able to hear the Santo Mundo and the *animas* speak to me. They surrounded me."

Mikaela (figure 3.2) elaborated the events that led her husband to start his work as a shaman. Her description reviewed sad memories of losing their children, yet she was reassured by the events that followed. "We have work," Mikaela noted as she spoke of divining and performing ceremonies. Directing her eyes toward Tix, she continued: "If we have problems, if we have sickness, or if someone sends malice, we can ask the *animas* and the Santo Mundo to help us and to take it away. They talk to him, and we know what we can do to help ourselves. Life was hard before, but now they watch us and help us."[6]

Mikaela derived a sense of recompense from Tix's calling as a spiritual leader and medium to and for spirit entities. She viewed the calling as a reward because of the protection a shaman's gifts provide and his ability to obtain answers to the difficult questions in life. Moreover, the process of training and the initiation of her husband brought Mikaela a feeling of closeness to her deceased children, a by-product of a shaman's link to the spirits of the deceased and to the earth lords. Earth lords and the spirits of ancestors watch over and protect living beings; a client's participation in ceremonies and his or her offerings to the spirit entities enable the earth lords to protect these living beings. Mikaela further explained Tix's role in the relationship between living beings and earth lords, emphasizing that Tix was a necessary participant and officiator in ceremonies on behalf of others:

> He entered to be a daykeeper [*ajq'ij*] by luck [*portuna*]. It was his luck.[7] They [earth lords] told him to go and to perform the ceremonies before them. He saw them in his dreams. They told him, "Enter now. Enter now to perform the ceremonies." He dreamed about it. He dreamed that he was saying the prayers and performing the ceremonies so that offerings

sought his ritual gifts or shamanic status. Rather, a series of events—his luck/fortune—brought him to the work.

Tix had lived in the same community—Xekakixkan—his entire life. He married at the age of fourteen, living patrilocally with his wife, Mikaela, in his parents' home, as most do in Maya communities. He never attended school and had always worked as a shepherd and agriculturalist.

Six of Tix and Mikaela's seven children had died at an early age. Tix noted that their deaths were the primary catalyst for his close connection with spirits. In his middle age, he became sick. Bedridden, Tix began to have dreams that he did not understand. He dreamed of three women in a gully, motioning to him to follow them. Tix only described the identity of one of these women—Santa Catarina, the patron saint of Ixtahuacán.

Having always participated in traditional Maya ceremonies, Tix sought interpretive answers from an *ajq'ij* in a neighboring community. The shaman determined that Tix's date of birth was that of a shaman, although to this day Tix does not know what that date actually was. He began training with the shaman that he had engaged, later describing this two-year process as a "hard time." Tix explained: "In those days, I wanted to learn the prayers and to perform the ceremony. It took a long time to learn.

Figure 3.2. Mikaela kneels to grind corn with mano and metate in the kitchen/fire area of their one-room house. The bed is to the left, and an agricultural backpack sprayer and water containers are in the left foreground. Courtesy of Winston K. Scott, 2003.

Mikaela begins each ceremony by singing and reciting the Lord's Prayer, opening the way for Tix to welcome the earth lords and ancestors into the divination. As the voice, she interprets what the spirits say through Tix and repeats their answers to clients in her familiar, normal voice and in the K'iche' language to ensure that they understand what an earth lord is telling them when Tix's speech—in trance—transforms to a deep, staccato, rudimentary Spanish. She also relays any client responses to Tix, and thus to the spirits within him, during the divination.

When in trance, Tix relays the utterances of an earth lord to Mikaela. When the client asks a question, Mikaela reformulates it and relays it to Tix, acting as the earth lord. The earth lord answers immediately through Tix, and Mikaela relays the answer to the client. If further instruction is needed, Tix switches back to his regular voice and repeats the answer in K'iche' Maya before switching back to the fused Spanish-K'iche' mode of communication that the earth lords employ.

Mikaela's work as *sobrena*, as voice to the Sacred Earth, and her duties as an officiator at the divinations have conferred on her great respect in the male-dominated community and culture. Although Tix was not part of any organized temporal hierarchy of daykeepers, he said that he was never alone in his religious duties because he was always accompanied and aided by Mikaela, earth lords, and ancestors.

could be made to the Santo Mundo. He was doing the work of the daykeeper.

Tix did not, however, work alone.

THE VOICE (*SOBRENA*)

Tix considered Mikaela an important actor in his work. Mikaela worked with Tix as a spiritualist, guide, and shaman in her own right. Indeed, she played a critical role in divination by communicating messages to clients from the spiritual entities that had been welcomed to the ceremony. Mikaela was *sobrena* to the Santo Mundo.[8] In these ways, her role in ceremonies and in divination supports new analysis describing the distribution of spiritual duties between husband and wife.[9] Acting as an officiator during the divination, she becomes a voice and a medium when Tix remains suspended in a trance state. The shaman and his wife both take part in the initiation and some of the training; they share the duties of the shaman. Hence the plural pronoun in Mikaela's earlier statement: "*We* have work."

BARA

Another ritual tool that aided Tix in his work was the *bara*.[10] The *bara* is a small bag or tied cloth wrap—a prayer bundle—the contents of which are for the most part hidden from observers. When questioned about the contents of the bag, Tix would usually smile and say that it was full of *mu's*, a word that is ripe with meaning and expresses the idea of a foreign or otherworldly element.[11] Later, Tix did reveal the contents of the bag to me. The *mu's* were Maya figurines that he had found in his cornfields, once again "by luck." These were termed *mu's* because they had a foreign appearance compared to the living. Tix also referred to the prayer bundle itself, on two occasions, as the Santo Mundo.

The connection between earth and shaman in Ixtahuacán is strong. Indeed, the shaman provides a link to the sacred nature of the earth, represented in this case by Tix having dug the figurines out of the earth. Though ascribed to fortune or luck, several underlying factors determine who comes into possession of a *bara*. Tix occasionally told clients that he owned the prayer bundle because he was a man faithful to the ways of the ancestors. Tix claimed that he remained faithful because he was an agriculturalist, someone who had not attempted to assimilate into modern society by seeking a profession away from his *milpa*. "I work in the field and clean the field because it is sacred work," he explained. "Our fathers and mothers showed us how to work in the field, and their spirits are there, in the earth." Tix continued to wear traditional clothing as opposed to the western-style garb employed by many contemporary indigenous males, a characteristic that further separated him from a "modernized" K'iche' man and tied him to his Maya ancestors.[12] Tix felt these conditions explained his luck—his fortune, his destiny—in finding the contents of the *bara*. He implied that by maintaining a close relationship to the land in all of his activities, he was more alert and aware of the treasures that had been left in the fields and caves by ancestors compared to someone preoccupied with modern ways of making a living.

The contents of the *bara* are central to the work of the shaman, his authority, and his power. Along with the figurines, the *bara* includes translucent stones with the texture of obsidian core, distinct from the usual stones and rocks that one might find in the *milpa*.[13] Tix's explanation of the *baras'* origin of power ("they are made by our fathers") evoked ancestral participation. The earth-found contents manifest the relationship of the past to the present and of earth to humanity, constituting a physical connection that generates a psychological and symbolic link to the lives of the revered ancestors who lie buried in the earth. In K'iche', the word for translucence and the word for these stones derive from the same root as the word used to describe the sun's iridescent radiations.

The *bara* was stored in a sanctuary on an altar in Tix's home. Since it is an important tool, Tix never left the *bara* behind when he had to perform a ceremony away from home. Prior to removing it from the sanctuary, Tix blessed the *bara* with prayers and chanting. Tix then presented the *bara* to the earth lords, stating the purpose of his journey, and then took the *bara* to the ceremony.

OFFERINGS

To receive help from spiritual entities, a client commissions a ceremony in which he or she, through the daykeeper, presents goods and offerings to the divinities, hoping for a positive reciprocation and response from the earth lords and ancestors. Tix fulfills the role of guide and mediator by presenting clients to the spiritual entities. Moreover, Tix communicates with the entities regarding the perceived problem. Each ceremony thus provides spiritual guidance. The client delivers the offerings to the shaman as a sign of sincerity, a token of respect for the shaman and the spiritual entities. Feeling inadequate before spirit entities and believing that the shaman-priest has the necessary skills through his calling, the client hires a medium.

One client who employed Tix three times while I assisted explained why he believed that Tix could mediate with his ancestors to help him in his desire to acquire new land to cultivate: "I ask Tix for help because I don't know how to call the Santo Mundo nor the *animas*. Tix talks to them, he knows how to do the work of a daykeeper, and he helps me understand what our fathers and mothers need so that they can help me.[14] The *animas* tell Tix if they will help me, or if they need more nourishment."

All of the residents of Tix's hamlet who participated in a survey acknowledged a belief in ancestral spirits and their ability to help or hinder the living. We see in the ritual, its symbols, its exegesis, and the corresponding aspects of Tix's life an intense connectedness to agriculture, the earth, the ancestors buried therein who granted inheritances of cornfields to the living, and the earth lords as well as a concern for the adequacy of "nourishment" in life and in ritual.

The living, however, do not worship the deceased; rather, they participate in a reciprocal relationship in which each cares for the other to maintain a harmonious balance in life through ancestral communion. Clients who took the survey said the offerings provided their ancestors with spiritual nourishment and were a sign of care and respect to both ancestors and earth lords. Clients expected the ancestors would reciprocate by watching over them and ensuring harmony in their lives. As Tix explained, ancestral communion supplies a spiritual connection to the earth lords and allows clients to draw from the knowledge of the ancestors.

Clients supply offerings that Tix presents "before the face of" (*chuwäch*) the ceremonial altar. The offerings include four large candles, representing the four cardinal points of the Maya world. These are set and burned on the corners of the high altar. The fifth element of the Maya world, the *uk'ux mundo* (heart of earth),[15] sits in the center of the four cardinal candles, usually as a fifth large candle. These five candles burn throughout the ceremony. Tix confirmed to me that the *uk'ux mundo* was the place, any place, where a ritual was being enacted.

In addition, Tix places sixteen smaller candles on a second altar, which he also burns as an offering. These smaller candles represent the earth lords and Catholic saints. Twenty yet smaller candles represent the *animas*, or ancestral spirits. Tix places these candles on a third altar, a stone slab that sits on the floor between the legs of (and therefore under the surface of) the second altar table or immediately in front of the second altar (but below its surface level) toward where the officiant and clients sit. Incense, chocolate, sugar, copal (an aromatic resin that fuels the burning and produces smoke), bread, and one pint of liquor are also placed at the altar. Any client who has seen Tix work before brings at least two pints of liquor. One pint is used as an offering to the deities; the other is given to Tix to consume during the ceremony.[16] Tix considered the failure to provide the correct amount of offerings (see table 3.2), particularly the liquor, as a sign of disrespect because the failure to provide sufficient offerings creates disharmony for the client and increases the probability that the deities will not care for the client.

Clients give offerings to nurture the souls of the deities and *animas*, to secure help from them in times of uncertainty and trouble, and to give thanks in times of prosperity. Tix explained: "They [*animas*] do not actually eat or drink the food. It makes them happy to see it, but they do not have bodies. But the candles, the incense, and the copal are food for their souls. It calls them to the ceremony because it smells good, and then they consume it into their souls. Their souls get hungry, and they need nourishment, [they need] to eat, or they will not help us in our lives." Tix averred that bad things happened to people because they did not take care of the deities. The deities did not cause bad things to happen; rather, through a lack of care and, literally, a lack of providing substance to their souls, the deities could not protect people from harm.

COME NOW!

Come now, respected kingdom of God,
Come now, respected kingdom of Sacred Earth.
Here there is mercy, offering, permission, forgiveness, charity.
Here [client's name] is being presented for a work of ceremonial service.
Here he asks for mercy, permission, forgiveness, charity, miracles, and blessings
From God of Cold, God of Wind, God of Possibility, [God] of Spirit, and Blessed Holy Ancestors.[17]

Before a ceremony began, Tix interviewed the client to discuss the purpose of the visit and the desired outcome. The most common desire that clients expressed was to "help ourselves" with the aid of earth lords and ancestors. In each of the ceremonies that Tix performed, clients were present because of a perceived problem, concern, or anxiety, often regarding a monetary venture. Some men had come to ask where to find a wife, some to seek advice on what to do with a disobedient wife. A mother came, struggling to handle the problems associated with alcohol that had "taken control" of her son.

Facing the ceremonial altar, Tix began each ritual by kneeling at the side of the high altar; later, standing directly in front of the altar, he presented clients to the Trinity of deities. He chanted, full of energy, in his powerful, resonant baritone, renowned throughout the region. Clients who employed Tix regarded his charismatic voice as a sign of his divine calling as a shaman (figure 3.3).

The chanting invoked the entities from the spiritual hierarchy of Creator, earth lords, and ancestors, all tied to the sacred space of Ixtahuacán. Tix called them to present themselves at the time and place of the ceremony. The space was tied to the spiritual hierarchy through the representation at the altars of deities who dwell in the heavens (the high altar), on the earth (the second altar), and below the ground (under the second altar). Tix highlighted the notion of sacred space at the onset of the ceremonial chants with the words, "This is a place of mercy, of permission, of forgiveness, charity, miracles, and blessings." The sanctuary at Tix's home was a sacred space because of the shaman's presence, his *bara*, the proximity to his place of initiation, the images on the high altar, and the second altar, which houses the Santo Mundo. Tix's home

TABLE 3.2. RITUAL OFFERINGS, 2003

OFFERING	AMOUNT OFFERED	OFFERED TO	COST (QUETZALES)*
Large candles	.5 pound, 4–5 count	Creator (*mesa* 1)	3.00
Medium candles	1 pound, 20–24 count	earth lords/saints	4.00
Small candles	.5 lb., 16–20 count	ancestral spirit deities	6.00
Copal incense	24 pieces	all deities	12.00
Pine incense	4 ounces	all deities	4.00
Sugar	1 pound	all deities	3.50
Liquor (*tz'am*)	minimum of 1 pint	all deities and shaman	7.00
Chocolate	4 ounces	all deities	2.00
Bread	usually 8 pieces	all deities	2.00
Tobacco (*puro*)	optional	shaman for smoking	1.00
Total Cost			Q44.50

Note: US$1.00 = Q7.75.

Figure 3.3. Tix in prayer. Note the roof tile (*foreground*) used to contain the fire that Tix (and every shaman) tends during the ceremony. Courtesy of Winston K. Scott, 2003.

thus was the *axis mundi*, the place where the majority of ceremonies were performed.

When holding a ceremony outside his home sanctuary, Tix re-created the altar and brought with him elements of his sanctuary to create a sacred space. Tix could always make a space sacred because "in the valleys and in the mountains there are the spirits of the Santo Mundo. They are outside in the wind and in the cold. They are near." Tix thus transformed an otherwise normal and ordinary space, which in K'iche' thought has sacred attributes and sacred beings near but not in obvious touch, into a set-apart center suited to interaction with the supernatural.[18]

Tix often warned his clients that he was not certain if the deities would bring good news—a statement that caused them anxiety. Such anxiety and uncertainty placed the client in a state of liminality, unsure whether spirit entities would confirm a positive outcome or render helpful guidance during the ceremony (see Turner 1969).

Tix's sanctuary (and the sacred space he created if away) housed an altar complex whose three distinct altars replicated the believed physical nature of the dwelling places of the three levels of spiritual entities in the universe. Moreover, the altars symbolized their spiritual relationship and place in the hierarchy. Tix explicitly made these connections between the altar components, their spatial and physical characteristics, and the three levels of beings in the sacred hierarchy. I have not imposed or surmised their symbolic meanings. The three altars (*mesas*) each held spots for their particular associated spiritual entities and were separated into three distinct physical levels. Tix attended to the *mesas* in successive stages of the ritual as he invoked the class of deities associated with each altar through offerings, calling the respective entities to make their entry into the ceremonial realm.

When Tix began to call deities to come to the ceremonial space, he first invoked God the Creator, the Christian God who is part of the Catholic-infused ceremony, directing attention to the images on the high or first altar. Tix then invoked the earth lords, calling them while attending to the second altar, the place of spiritual favors (*tab'al toq'ob'*). The earth lords were told the name of the client being presented before them and that they were being called on to help that person by according him or her mercy, forgiveness, and charity. The earth lords were then specified by the places in which they dwelt: in the air, in the cold, in spirit, and in other named geographic locations familiar to people. Finally, Tix called the ancestral spirits to present themselves and help the client. I outline the spiritual hierarchy in table 3.3. To make the process more clear, I now describe the three altars—each referred to as a *mesa* or table—and the behaviors, images, objects, and spiritual entities associated with each.

Mesa 1: Ri Ajaw (Designer, Creator, Owner of the Universe)

The first and tallest of the three altars is a long, narrow table (about two feet in depth and six or eight feet in length) that sits against the back wall of the sanctuary, creating a working shelf. Situated on top of the altar is a collection of Maya figurines, Tix's *bara*, and antique coins: *q'ana' pwaq, saqa' pwaq* (literally, "yellow money" [gold], "white money" [silver]). Among the symbols sitting on this high or sky-vault altar representing heavenly beings, Tix includes a crucifix wrapped in maize leaves and a picture of Jesus Christ (plate 19). Flowers and pine needles envelop the sides of the altar and are changed on a weekly basis in order to maintain the *mesa* as an "altar of life": *jun tab'al k'aslik*, a "living altar."

Although the three altars separate the deities into categories of Creator (Ri Ajaw),[19] earth lords (Santo Mundo), and ancestors (*animas*), Tix referred to the first altar, the altar proper, as the collective Santo Mundo. As a group, the altars make up the place of initiation, "the spirit seat/spirit altar" (*nawal silla/nawal mesa*). This first altar, pertaining to the Creator, provides the central spot from which Tix invokes the deities associated with the traditional Christian concept of the Trinity. At this altar, Tix presents the clients and blesses them before the deities. The high altar is also where offerings are placed before the ceremony begins. Once Tix begins his petition, he gathers and presents the offerings to the spirit entities on the high altar, showing what offerings the client brought and stating for what purpose.

For positive reciprocation to occur, Tix must accept the offerings on behalf of the deities. A typical ceremony requires a standard list of gifts. The offerings are denoted by the Spanish loan word *multo* ("fine" or "penance"), indicating that they are offered so that the client will

---

TABLE 3.3. TRADITIONAL SPIRITUAL HIERARCHY IN SANTA CATARINA IXTAHUACÁN

Creator/Christian Trinity/Santa Catarina

Sacred Earth/Earth Lords of Cold, Wind, Possibility

Ancestors (Mothers, Fathers)

Shaman-Priest

Living Beings

receive exculpation for weakness or sin. The notion is that paying the fine will bring help, luck, or relief; it provides a reprieve from misfortune or the punishing hardship of life.

Apart from the offerings that a client brings to the ceremony, Tix places his own paraphernalia on this high altar, including his *bara* and two crucifixes. One crucifix represents the spirits of the altar; the other is designated as the spirit of the shaman who occupies the *silla*.[20] The client provides candles and incense for Tix to burn throughout the stages of the ceremony and liquor for Tix to drink and pour on the ground in libation. Before Tix makes the offerings, he places them on the altar until the time comes to consume the goods before the designated deity.

Tix also places on the first or main altar a statuette of Jesus Christ on the cross, which he said represents the overarching Creator God of the Trinity.[21] At this altar, Tix addresses the three entities of the Trinity by separate names: Dios Qajawaxel, Dios K'ojolaxel, and Dios Uxlab'axel (God Our Lord Master, God the Supreme Son, and God the Main Spirit).[22]

The high altar (plate 19 and figure 3.4) is also the place of origin of the power and authority of the shaman. Tix begins the ceremony and assumes control by telling the client to kneel before the altar, and Tix presents and blesses him or her before the deities. Tix blesses the client by rubbing the latter's body with the unlit new candles that the client has offered as *multo*. This act cleanses and sanctifies the client as he or she approaches the sacred altar. Tix chants prayers to present the client before the deities and cleanses, blesses, and advocates on behalf of him or her—asking for forgiveness, miracles, blessings, and mercy.[23]

When Tix blesses and presents the client before the first altar, he removes the client from his or her initial condition in the ordinary world and moves the person into the more sacred but also more temporary liminal space established by the altar.[24] Once this is done, the client is excused from the altar and takes a seat on a bench along the side wall of the sanctuary. Tix begins the work of invocation, seating himself on a chair at the center of the room, facing the three altars. The client remains silent and seated throughout the ceremony, rising only to offer Tix a shot of liquor and speaking only in response to any questions that Tix may ask.

As Tix invokes spirit entities, he places sugar, copal, and incense (the offerings that the client has supplied) in a vessel directly in front of his chair, between it and the altars. Tix uses the sugar to draw the four cardinal points of the Maya world, including the "heart of earth and heart of sky" at the center, the Mayas' fifth cardinal point. Tix ignites the contents of the vessel and continues his petition as the flames and aromatic smoke gather strength.

Because the offerings that Tix burns in the vessel nourish the spirits, Tix keeps a vigilant eye on the flames and any fluctuation in their strength, stirring the fire with a stick to discern if spirit entities accept or reject his petitions along with the client's offerings. As the ceremony progresses, Tix replenishes the offerings in the vessel until all of the material brought by the client is consumed. Tix is able to read the flames: "The flames speak to me; the fire has life. If the fire is strong during the ceremony, it is because the offering is good, and the beloved work [*loq'alaj chak*] nourishes the Sacred Earth."

Mesa 2: Santo Mundo (Sacred Earth)

The second part of the ceremony focuses on the earth lords and invoking manifestations of the multiple deities that make up the Santo Mundo. Spatially, the top surface of the second altar is slightly lower than the top surface of the high altar that represents the heavens. The second altar is separated from the high (and back) altar by a passage space that Tix can access (figures 3.4 and 3.5). The second altar physically represents the surface of the earth existing in a realm lower than the heavens. The altar represents the geographic space of the souls of the earth lords, who reside not in the heavens but in the geographical framework of the community, on and about the surface of the earth. Mikaela emphasized the immediacy of the earth lords' presence in everyday life: "They see us. They help us when we are on the road or in the town. Wherever we go, they can see us and help us so that we don't find trouble on the way. If I am walking on the path to the market and find trouble, and if I am living a good life, then they will help me so I don't fall in the gully or in the water."

The candles that burn on this second altar represent three realms: deities close to the earth, living people, and prophets/saints. Tix explained that each candle corresponds to an individual: "I have a candle, and so does Mikaela because of the service we do. The person looking for help has one because he is presented. There are candles for the Sacred Earth because they speak to me in the divination. God and Jesus have candles because they are able

Figure 3.4. Tix kneels and censes the high altar (*right*). The world surface altar is to the left. Courtesy of Winston K. Scott, 2003.

entities that dominate the worldview: the Creator, earth lords, and ancestors.

In ceremonial terms, *qatat, qanan* (our fathers, our mothers) and *animas* are terms used synonymously to refer to ancestral spirits. Four candles burn on the third altar, representing God of Spirit (two candles), God of Wind, and God of Possibility ("possibility" refers to economic prosperity and wealth). Tix confirmed that like the earth lords, the souls of the ancestors exist in the elements and the environment.

This stone slab altar lies on the ground, either between the table's four legs (as seen in figure 3.4, lower left foreground) and therefore directly under the symbolic surface of the earth, or on the ground immediately to the front of the second altar but lower than the level of the earth's surface represented by the top surface of the second altar. The third altar, designated for ancestors, symbolizes death and the burial place of the deceased, below the surface of the earth as represented by the flat top of the second altar.

The client now provides names that he or she has chosen from family lineages so that Tix can call them to come to the ceremonial place and aid in the client's life. Clients interact with the shaman as he calls the ancestors' names and supplicates their involvement in the ceremony. A powerful connection exists during this part of the ceremony among client, ancestors, and shaman because of lineage affiliation. As Tix invites the ancestors to present themselves, he literally bridges the gap separating spheres and connects the client with his or her patrilineal ancestors who have died and become gods (figure 3.5).

to help. It is the same with the prophets." Thus, at one end of the middle or second altar, two conjoined candles burn, representing Tix and Mikaela as masters of the sanctuary. Next to them flickers the candle that represents the client, followed by one for the Creator, and another for Jesus. One candle each represents San Rafael and San Gabriel. Behind these, Tix places and lights three candles, one each for God of Wind, God of Cold, and the Sacred Earth.

Mesa 3: Animas (Ancestors)

During the ceremony, Tix analyzes the candles burning on the first two altars, noting the rate at which they burn and whether they burn out. The answers that he receives from the candles allow Tix to move on to the third aspect of the ceremony, ancestral communion.

In this part, the client participates by giving the names of specific ancestors that he or she wishes to take part in the ceremony. Concerning the ancestors, "they are now gods," says Tix. Ancestors become deified through living a good life when alive, by not offending others through grudges and jealousies, and by respecting the three

DIVINATION AND TRANCE STATE: "WELCOME, SACRED EARTH"

Welcome, respected fathers, respected mothers.
Welcome, respected God of Earth, respected God of Cold, respected God of Wind,
Welcome, respected Gods of Spirit, Possibility, and Blessings.[25]

Figure 3.5. Tix conducts a ritual in the windowless chapel outbuilding in the dark (photographed without flash). He arranges candles while standing between the high altar (*behind him*) and the world surface altar (*in front of him*). On the floor, a stone slab altar to the *animas* supports twelve candles. In the immediate foreground is the tile with the fire that Tix tends while in prayer. Courtesy of Winston K. Scott, 2003.

Tix uses the three altars to invoke spirit entities and call them to the ceremony. When he feels satisfied that the spirit entities have accepted the offerings and are present in the ceremony, he begins to enter into the divination. Entrance into the divination changes the atmosphere, as deities are no longer implored to "come now"; rather, they are welcomed into the ceremony. The divination serves as the stage for Tix to enter into the trance state.

Throughout the ceremony, Tix consumes a considerable quantity of distilled alcohol. This heightens his ability to enter the trance state. Tix described what the trance state entails and the process by which he becomes a direct medium for divine entities: "They come before my face after I call them. They enter into my head as they walk before me. It is simple, really. They envelop me, and they talk in my mouth."

In contrast to the candles that brighten the sanctuary while the entities are called and welcomed, the divination takes place in total darkness. Tix closes the door to the sanctuary and extinguishes all the candles. Seated in a comparatively throne-like chair to the right of the high

altar,[26] across the room from the client, Tix sits in the dark as the divination commences.

Once again, the shaman presents the client to the deities, stating the purpose of the ensuing divination. Tix mentions the name of the client and then announces that he or she "asks a question, asks for counsel, asks for comfort before our fathers, our mothers, and before the Sacred Earth." Symbolically, the shaman disappears into the darkness and allows earth lords to emerge in his place. The arrival of supernatural beings is marked by sounds of wind (made by Tix), a distinct change in his voice (more guttural, raspy, staccato), and a change in the language he uses to communicate (an increased use of rather simplified, choppy Spanish mixed into his fluid K'iche').

Through Tix, the Sacred Earth acknowledges the ancestry of the client as a reason for granting responses to the questions that the client poses. Acting on his client's questions and responses, the shaman supplies a physical manifestation of the earth lords' presence during the divination.

The four entities that speak through Tix represent the Sacred Earth. These are categorized as gods and recognized through their distinct voices as independent beings. One client explained the origins of these gods who are speaking, as well as his experience of hearing a female voice named Kamel Mundo. "There are two women's voices because the earth is female and male. There is one named Kamel Mundo who talks like a woman. I have heard her talk through Tix."[27]

Through Mikaela, acting now as the voice, the Sacred Earth communicates directly with the client. This is the moment when clients ask questions and receive answers. Mikaela makes sure that the client understands the communication by prefacing each instruction with *Käkib'ij le Santo Mundo chawe* . . . (The earth lords say to you [singular] . . .).[28]

Mikaela ensures that the client understands all that the spirit entities are saying to him or her and acknowledges that understanding to Tix. When full understanding is confirmed, the spirit entity closes the ceremony, and Tix returns from the trance in the same manner that he entered into it: to the sound of the wind. The wind thus marks the end of the divination. Tix, now out of trance, relights the candles, bringing the client back from the uncertainty of the darkness and into the light. If any alcohol remains, Tix offers a cup to the client.

SYMBOLISM OF *MESAS* AND DEITIES

The altar for the Creator represents a heavenly realm where the Creator (as the Christian Trinity of the Father, the Son, and the Holy Spirit), the town's patron saint (Santa Catarina), and other Catholic saints are invoked. This altar's surface is situated on a higher plane than the two other altars, correlating with the idea that the Creator exists high above the earth. Tix says that although the altars are physically separate and the ceremony exists in three separate parts pertaining to each altar and category of deities, the ceremony has the same purpose, to help the client. "It is one *mesa*. The ceremony is three parts, but there is only one service." Symbolically the three altars sit above, at, and below the surface of the earth, incorporating in the ceremony the entire cosmos of heaven, earth, and netherworld.

Tix used a hot-cold model to identify positive and negative spirit entities pertaining to the client's state of being during the ceremony. Concerning cold-associated entities, he stated, "God of Cold is in the air. God of Wind is in the air. They are outside. That is where they live." He expressed that the entities associated with cold characteristics are positive entities and exist to combat the entities associated with hot qualities.

But Tix's notions of hot and cold diverge from the hot-cold category complex documented in other Maya communities. Wilson (1995) reports that the hot-cold categorizations of a Q'eqchi' Maya community are associated with illness, personality, and taboos, and concludes that each of the hot and cold categories have both negative and positive connotations. For Tix, by contrast, air and cold are positives, defined in opposition to the negative, heat-associated entities who reside in the *q'aq'* (fire), the term commonly meaning a place of suffering (not *xib'alb'a* ~ *xib'ilb'a*, the Maya underworld, whose root also

connotes suffering and fear). Tix never invoked a spirit entity associated with heat. Tix and Mikaela emphasized that ceremonial practices maintain cold as a positive element and that hot is the element associated with entities that hinder.[29]

The existence of beings who reside "in the fire" should not be confused with the underworld, a realm discussed through analysis of ancestors. When a person dies, their soul goes to the fire if they caused something bad to happen to another being through envy and jealousy. There is no need to call on these spirits; they neither help nor hinder and are insignificant as far as the desires of the clients and the shaman are concerned. One consults the ancestor spirits that did good for others, especially by providing descendants with land.

The shaman uses a codified language during the divination; clients know they are being greeted by an earth lord when they are welcomed with a low-pitched, guttural, staccato Spanish greeting of *buenas noches* (good evening). Tix fuses broken Spanish with K'iche' Maya (the ratio is roughly 10 percent Spanish to 90 percent K'iche') when, as the medium, he acts as the voice for the deities. He infuses basic Spanish terms that both he and the client understand, using just enough of the language of the "other" to show that a different element is communicating through him.

By employing Spanish in the divination, Tix denotes the hegemonic authority of the Ladino "other" that has long held power over indigenous life throughout Guatemala. The client becomes aware that a foreign element is present by hearing the codified commands and terms conveyed through Tix. The use of the foreign language announces the presence of an unfamiliar *mu's*, a being of power and heightened authority; the term is applied to a Ladino or other foreigner visiting the community. The familiarity of Tix's voice disappears as the multiple new voices of earth lords and ancestors emerge in the darkness.

The divination manifests the reality of spirit presence as Tix, spirit entities, and client realize direct, audible communication that acts to bring balance to the life of the client. The client comes to Tix asking for *consulto* and *consuelo* (consultation and consolement) and to have questions answered by the earth lords and ancestors. The spirits speak through Tix and give assurance that offerings have been accepted, allowing the entities to reciprocate by ensuring help and harmony to the client regarding his or her question or project.

CEREMONY AND SACRED SPACE

For K'iche' traditionalists, ritual brings about order when people feel wronged and helps them understand and accept their afflictions. The ritual centers them in a system of meaning through which they gain understanding and helps them cope with tragedy and loss. More important, through ritual, people maintain or restore balance with the cosmos.

In a psychological sense, clients who commission Tix to perform a ceremony in their behalf set in motion a rite of passage (van Gennep 1960[1909]). Thus, the ceremony begins with separation (cleansing and presentation before deities), a period of liminality (while observing the ceremony), and reaggregation into a new state of being through direct communication with deities during the divination. Moreover, the client has been transformed by the receipt of new knowledge and assurance. In K'iche' shamanic practice, one may repeat the ceremonial steps as necessary, on multiple occasions in a person's life, when the client encounters new problems that require a solution through ritual.

One sees van Gennep's principle of reaggregation in play after the completion of the ceremony. Once more, Tix converses briefly with the client about the client's state of being prior to the ceremony, during the ceremony, and in relation to the answers that the client received during the divination. Through the ceremony, Tix helps the client gain perspective on the initial problem and move toward the desired goal of helping themselves through a period of instability and misfortune into a new, harmonious state of being.

In many of Tix's divinations, the client seeks to determine the source of a serious or persisting illness. Although the ceremony will usually identify the cause of a physical sickness, be it witchcraft or neglect of the spirits, Tix is not a *curandero*, one who cures physical sickness by rubbing out the disease and physically attending to a client. Once the Sacred Earth informs Tix's client of the real cause of the sickness in his or her family, the person must seek advice from an appropriate medical practitioner as to what medicine to take or procedure to follow, either pharmaceutical or natural. Tix only divines the cause of illness; he does not attempt to physically cure the client. The curing principle relies completely on the invocation of deities so that the client may determine a solution, whether by using medicinal plants, via more traditional ceremonies, or through pharmaceutical means.[30]

CONCLUSION

Tix's work as a shaman shares many characteristics with Nadel's (1946:25) classic analysis of shamans among the Nuba:

> The shaman . . . is more than merely a temporary and passive medium through which others place themselves *en rapport* with the spirit world. He is an incarnation of the spirit, and so a person lifted above all others. He is a passive medium when possessed; but through his ability to induce possession he is also a master of these supernatural powers. He is an instrument which others may use only in the sense in which priests are instruments for the communication with deities. The shaman, then, is both a mouthpiece of the spirits and an officiant of the cult addressed to them.

In the rural hamlet of Ixtahuacán, each part of the divination ceremony centers on determining what the client's future actions should be to restore a harmonious balance to his or her life so that it proceeds well and is blessed with help from the unseen spiritual world. Clients who employ a daykeeper supplement their orthodox Catholic beliefs. They share Tix's belief that the ceremony and divination ritual are part of a greater structure of spiritual entities that they associate with "true" Mayas. Their identities become bound to the ceremony and the earth, to the deities that dwell in the environment, and to the ancestors who show them that the correct manner to live is through the means that the earth provides.

The notion that the earth is tied to Maya identity, as Tix defined it, is a concept shared by his clients. Like Tix, they are agriculturalists who depend on the land and the environment to sustain themselves and their families. Each of Tix's clients expressed a belief in a physically tangible set of earth lords living in the nearby geographic region who have the ability to help or hinder an individual and those he or she is responsible for, depending on the actions that the individual or the dependents take to care for the deities. Ancestral communion depends on the belief that the spirits of the deceased are available to aid their descendants if they receive nourishment and veneration from the living. As Tix stated, "They are gods now."

Many in Ixtahuacán's organized religious communities believe that Tix's traditional Maya spirituality constitutes a kind of polytheism. Tix, however, explained that Maya spirituality and cosmology include separate manifestations of spirit entities that function much like the three separate *mesas*. Although the ceremony is divided into three separate parts in relation to Creator, earth lords, and ancestors, they work with a unified purpose: to invoke spirit entities to come to the sacred place designated by the shaman. The tripartite ceremony that is one and the tripartite altar that is one have the same structure and unity as the Christian Trinity that is one. Likewise, whether the entities dwell above, upon, or below the earth, they have the same purpose and duty: to watch over the clients who are supplicating their help and to maintain a harmonious balance. Tix provided a similar view with regard to the relationships of the manifestations of spirit entities and how they function: "God [the Creator] created the world. He created men and the corn when he sowed the seeds. The world gives rain and sun to the earth. This gives men food, we have wood for fire, and we have mud for homes. And the ancestors learned how to take care of the earth and how to plant corn. We learn from the ancestors and they help us take care of the earth."

The ceremonial inclusion of earth lords, ancestors, and Christian deities reflects the survival strategies that people employ as a way to learn from the past through caring for different spiritual entities. The deities reciprocate the offerings that they receive by granting spiritual guidance to clients, watching over them, and protecting their paths among the uncertainties of a dangerous world.

K'iche' shamanic ritual practice connects clients to the supernatural. The ritual calls earth lords, ancestors, and Christian deities from other realms through offerings and prayers. If satisfied, these entities come and provide clients with information that helps them achieve a desired state of being in which they may function comfortably. By visiting Tix, clients access and enter into a divine realm of thought and being. Through the power of the ritual, they leave as new beings, in a psychological sense, restored and renewed to the desired harmonious state and more prepared—indeed, divinely coached—to deal with the vagaries of timing and decision in an uncertain world.

Given this description of higher-order shamanic practice in Santa Catarina Ixtahuacán, we can now compare and evaluate the scholarly expositions available. In *Time and the Highland Maya* (1982, with subsequent revised editions), Barbara Tedlock gives a marvelously detailed examination of current Maya calendrics and Maya shaman-priest sortilege divination associated with the calendar. Throughout the book, Tedlock focuses on elucidating the current cultural status and day values of the 260-day Maya calendar and the divination procedures of the shaman-priests who deal with the Maya calendar and its day values. She thus focuses on the calendar logic, sortilege procedures, divination performance, and cultural logic of the first-level shaman's interaction with clients as practiced among the K'iche' of Momostenango. Because of her focus, however, she either misses or chooses to not describe the higher-order shamanic practices in which the shaman-priest becomes the in-the-room presence and mouth of the Santo Mundo or the ancestors. Rather than the yes-no-maybe answer of sortilege with its perhaps ambiguous cultural interpretation of calendrical values, the third-order shaman-priest provides a direct language exchange between the clients present in the room and the earth lords (Santo Mundo) or the ancestors that the shaman has embodied. This permits direct, two-way communication between clients and Santo Mundo or ancestors of questions and answers and the solicitation of real-time verbal clarifications—an interrogation—of the meaning and implication of the messages coming from Santo Mundo or ancestors via the communicative mediation of the *sobrena*.

The shaman provides an invaluable service to a client seeking help and advice from higher beings as he brings deities to the people both spiritually and physically, creating a sacred space in which clients show devotion through offerings, are cleansed through ritual, and receive personal instruction. To the client, the invitation to "Come now!" is not just a part of the ceremonial prayer; the arrival of Santo Mundo or the ancestors is experienced in reality and is the manner through which a K'iche' Maya with a traditionalist, land- and corn-oriented perspective can maintain a cosmological balance among people, place, and divinities.

In Xekakixkan, the people, the place, the divinities, and their shaman-mediator are distinctly agricultural, rural, Maya, and of the land. Tix is structurally equivalent to the saints lining the walls and alcoves of the high altar in the central Catholic church. Like the saints, Tix mediates the transmission of messages, favors, and protections between the living and the high deities. But the Maya shaman of the third order mediates most directly with the earth lords (the gods that work most closely and frequently on the surface of the earth) and with the ancestors who provided the living with their land and resources (as ancestors now partaking of divinity, they concern themselves with the human activity of their living descendants on that earth). Both earth lords and ancestors are intimately land-linked, and the earth lords are closely associated with the weather—represented in the gods of cold, rain, and wind and in the attention to the sun implicit in the title *ajq'ij*—which nourishes the corn that feeds the people on that land. The earth lords are the master of human *portuna* on the surface of the earth. The ancestors, if they were responsible in life, secured for the living an agricultural inheritance on which the living now depend. That makes the ancestors good and suitable to be called on for advice. In the Maya agro-tradition, traditionalist religion as led by privately contracted shamans like Tix is the most sensible—in both the tactile and the cognitive/intellectual meanings of the word—religion for Mayas still able (or still trying) to be independent of others and dependent on the land.

Traditionalist religion ties these agriculturalist Mayas to the ancestors who gave them land and life and to the earth-surface divinities most closely concerned with nature, agriculture, weather, and the fortunes and misfortunes of luck, destiny, or *portuna* of those living on and from that surface. Tix's traditionalist shamanism embodies in its Maya-understandable symbols a preeminently Maya-suitable religion. It will no doubt continue to appeal to many of those most engaged in and still able to be sustained by the independent hand-labor subsistence agriculture that has characterized Maya life for centuries. In arriving at this interpretation, we had to "reach beneath the symbol" to plumb the agricultural and tellurian backgrounds of a Maya society still under colonial social strictures. In doing so, we have found, as Durkheim suggests, its "true meaning"—which is to say, its social meaning. We see in the next chapter that Maya traditionalist Catholicism—because of its Maya indigenous ethnic and native associations—can become a powerful symbol of cultural resistance to Ladino hegemony when its younger practitioners shear off the most obvious symbols of traditionalist Catholic syncretism.

Traditionalist shamanic ceremony and divination thus provide a powerful survival strategy and psychological strength by which the client utilizes a Maya cosmological structure to cope with life and death, prosperity and poverty, and to receive counsel from deities. The shaman is the mechanism by which balance is achieved between and for the client and deities. Shamans like Tix and the rituals they perform preserve that balance. The Tixes of the Maya world thus sustain the lives of those who subscribe to traditionalist practice and belief.

NOTES

1. Scott did fieldwork from mid-May through mid-August 2003 with repeated brief visits since. Hawkins used his eight years of contacts and prior experiences in Santa Catarina Ixtahuacán to place Scott in the home of this region's most famous shaman, Baltazar (Tix). Scott did the fieldwork and wrote the first drafts. The use of "I" in this chapter refers to Scott. Hawkins worked extensively with Scott on rewriting/revision and on the theoretical position. Today (2020), Scott notes that this piece might be entirely rewritten and retheorized.

2. Plural of *ajq'ij*, where *aj-* suggests "from," "of," "agent of," or "master of," and connotes the desire or orientation of a person. *Q'ij* means "day," "sun," or "time."

3. Baltazar asked Hawkins that he not be given a pseudonym; his wife, Mikaela, the *sobrena*, in precarious health since 2003 with a debilitating cough probably caused by spending much of her life tending the smoky cooking fire in the center of their one-room house, has died. Respecting their wishes, and seeing no danger to their lives from this revelation, we have not used pseudonyms for them. All the other names in this chapter are pseudonyms.

4. The shamanic order accounted for all but two instances of ritual that I observed and participated in.

5. Tedlock's description of K'iche' shamanic calling in Momostenango, Guatemala, is similar to the path that brought Tix into his work with spirits. The calling is one that is received, not sought out by the shaman. "In Momostenango, a daykeeper, or shaman-priest is recruited in classical shamanic fashion, with 'divine election' through birth, illness, and dreams" (Tedlock 1982:53). See also Morgan 2005; Wilson 2007; and other chapters in this volume for the linkage between divine election, illness, and dreams, even in Evangelical and charismatic practices that reject traditional specialists.

6. It is important to note the use of K'iche' in Mikaela's statement "We have work." There are two verbs: *chaqunik* (work as in labor, from *chaq* ~ work, labor, task; and *-unik*, a verbalizer, thus to "perform the work"), and *q'ijinik* (to perform the Maya shaman's duties, from *q'ij* ~ day; and *-inik*, a verbalizer, thus to "perform the days"). Mikaela spoke in terms of the latter, the working of the shaman as daykeeper, as opposed to work as manual labor.

7. In K'iche' culture, *portuna* suggests luck, but the connotations are complex. K'iche' luck is not random chance, though chance and unexpected surprise are there, but destiny and good (also sometimes bad) fortune, as hinted at in the cognate *portuna*.

8. The term *sobrena* deserves attention in order to get to its meaning in K'iche'. *Sobrena* is likely a corruption of a Spanish loan word, the adjective *soberano/a*, meaning "sovereign." In the context in which it is used as a title for Mikaela, with a spiritual and

ritual sense, I have seen fit to translate the term as the "voice." The term "voice" better describes Mikaela's work as a shaman's wife. The Spanish word *soberano*, or in the case of a woman, *soberana*, is also used as a title or honorific adjective. It is given to the queen of the beauty pageants in Nahualá and Santa Catarina. From this point of view, Mikaela may be titled as the shaman's queen or honored partner. However, I feel that the term "voice" better describes her role as an important instrument in the ceremony.

9. Tedlock 2005 demonstrates that women are often neglected in the literature analyzing shamanism and spirituality. Tix, however, consistently acknowledged Mikaela as his essential partner.

10. Tedlock (1982:69) describes what seems to be a similar object used by the shaman-priest as the *baraj punto*. According to Tix, the *baraj punto* is a stick he uses as he points to certain candles during a ceremony to explain the will of spirit entities to a client. Tix denied that Tedlock was talking of the same type of instrument and insisted that the item of most importance is the *bara* prayer bundle that he uses.

11. *Mu's* is used in Santa Catarina Ixtahuacán to refer to things that are other, ghostly, foreign, or non-Maya, and thus it is universally and frequently applied to address or refer to Guatemala's Ladinos and to visiting students. When used in personal address, *mu's* is prefixed with *a-* or *al-*, connoting male or female, respectively, and youth. John Hawkins, for example, was regularly called *a xwan* (Sp. Juan) when known to the speaker and hailed as *a mu's* (young male foreigner) when not known to the speaker.

12. See Warren's (1998:169) discussion titled "Maya *Costumbre* as Memory." Tix's use of the traditional municipal clothing for K'iche' Maya men reflects his thoughts about cultural continuity. Although Warren questions the accuracy of collective memory and traditions in Maya communities, Tix chooses to affiliate his spiritual and religious tradition with a lineage of Maya ritual.

13. Deemed "magic stones" by Friedel, Schele, and Parker 1993:55.

14. *Qatat, qanan*: "our fathers, our mothers," refers to an individual's ancestors collectively as well as to the community's ancestors. In essence, they are the same, and this is another way to refer to the *animas* of particular importance to the client.

15. The morpheme *k'ux*, signifying the physical heart and (by extension) intention or will and a variety of emotions (when modified), can also be pronounced *k'u'x*, with a glottal closure on the vowel.

16. By 2006, Tix claimed he had stopped drinking alcohol during the ceremonies for health reasons. In 2010 and 2012, in ceremonies performed with and for Hawkins, Tix had returned to the consumption of considerable alcohol in his performance of ceremonies.

17. Translation of this prayer:

Sa b'a la reino Dios
Sa b'a la reino Santo Mundo
Are wa' k'o tab'al toq'ob', licens, perdon, karidad
Are wa' le kub'an presentar we jun le chaq jun le patan [client's name]
Are wa' kuta toq'ob', licens, perdon, karidad, milagro, bendicion
Re Dios tew, re Dios kaqiq', re Dios posib, tewal, y benditos santos animas.

18. Eliade (1959:20) expresses the idea of sacred space as a place set apart and designated for supernatural activity: "There is, then, a sacred space, and hence a strong, significant space; there are other spaces that are not sacred and so are without structure or consistency, amorphous." Tix's ceremonies and spiritual spatialization show similarities to what Eliade is describing and its practical use in K'iche' ceremonies.

19. The article *ri* connotes "unseen" or "distant."

20. *Silla*, a Spanish loan word for "chair" or "seat," is used in traditional K'iche' terms to mean the place of the shaman-priest's initiation, the place where he was seated in his office. One sense here resonates with classical Maya royal seatings, which have been made apparent through decipherment of Maya hieroglyphic texts (Houston 2008). Likewise, one finds affinities with the colonial *audiencia*, the seated hearings that indigenous people experienced before Spanish lords.

21. In conversations concerning the creation of the world, Tix insisted that Jesus was the creator of both the earth and humans. He asserted that Jesus's image represented the Christian Trinity.

22. In this rendering, "master," "supreme," or "main" are mutually substitutable for *-axel*, with "supreme" possibly the best translation.

23. Eliade (1959:11) presents this as designating spaces for sacred ritual in contrast with the everyday activities of the "natural 'profane' world."

24. The act of employing a shaman demonstrates a desire to separate from a previous state of being. By presenting the client to the deities, the shaman moves the client into the state of liminality constructed by van Gennep and elaborated on by Turner.

25. Translation:
Saj la etat enan.
Saj la le Dios mundo, Saj la Dios tew, Saj la Dios kaqiq'
Saj la Dios nawal, posib, tewal.

26. "To the right" is from the perspective of Jesus or any of the saints on the altar, who all face into the room, backs to the wall, the same orientation as the shaman seated in his chair.

27. Kamel Mundo was the only earth lord that was given a

name throughout the time of my fieldwork. It is difficult to decipher if this is a given name or a K'iche' adaptation of a Spanish name. With this trouble in decipherment, I decided not to treat Kamel Mundo as a modified loan word, but to use the name in its K'iche' context through the meaning and identity that the people provided. Although during ceremonies one could hear another woman's voice occasionally and still other distinct voices of men, they were never called by a specific name, only by the general term Santo Mundo.

28. The linguistic structure of this sentence presents the Sacred Earth as a plural manifestation of one entity. "Käkib'ij" denotes a plurality, more than one deity speaking to the client even as the title implies a singular entity. Literally, *kä* (incomplete) // *ki* (third-person plural subject pronoun) // *b'i* (to speak) // *j* (transitive marker) // *le* (demonstrative, that which is nearby) // *Santo Mundo* (specified in subject position grammatically) // *ch* (to) // *aw* (second-person singular) // *e* (goes).

29. Hawkins 1984 finds that such temperature associations are linked to ethnic identity. He shows that hot is Ladino, the coast is hot, and thus the hot coast is associated with negative Ladinos (and negatively experienced plantation labor). The inverse is that the mountains are cold, indigenous communities reside in the high, colder mountains, ergo indigenous is both cold and positive.

30. For more on the curing phase, see Adams and Hawkins 2007. Nadel points out that the healing practices of a shaman traditionally deal with the psychological ailments that hinder people, not the physical. The "therapeutic effects that the shaman's practices may have are entirely psychological and rest on the suggestibility of the subject" (Nadel 1946:26).

Chapter Four

Balance of the Fire

The Neotraditionalist Maya Spirituality Movement in Nueva Santa Catarina Ixtahuacán

FREDERICK H. HANSELMANN, JOHN P. HAWKINS, AND WALTER RANDOLPH ADAMS

WISPY WHITE CLOUDS ENVELOPED US as we hiked up a hill north of the new town, Nueva Santa Catarina Ixtahuacán, its houses rendered invisible by the fog. I paused to catch my breath, unaccustomed to the thin air at this altitude. The town sits at 9,800 feet elevation, and we were climbing even higher to see an altar where Mayas held ceremonies. We passed the last terraced fields and arrived at the summit. My guide, a young college student from town, pointed out the altar. Three children accompanying us raced to get there first and clambered onto the altar itself. I asked for permission to photograph the area, which my friend granted. I got close to better discern the figures that seemed to be carved on rocks, and then attempted to take a picture. The camera malfunctioned: no picture. Puzzled, I turned around 180 degrees and took a picture of the panoramic view. The camera worked. I turned again and tried to take another picture of the altar. Once more the camera failed. I wondered if the problem was the auto-focus on the camera. My friend suggested that the gods did not want me to take the picture. In the same breath he threatened the children and ordered them off the rocks. He then turned to me and said, "Try it now." It worked. Scowling at the children, he informed me that we had not been respecting the sacred space, and for this reason I had been unable to take the photograph.

This lack of respect is not unusual because many of the people in town do not follow "traditional" belief. The younger and more educated, who are the larger constituency of the followers of traditionalism in Nueva Santa Catarina Ixtahuacán, use the term "Maya spirituality" to refer to their traditionalism. Teachers working at the Paraíso Maya, the local high school, which teaches a curriculum that advocates Maya approaches to subjects and

Maya ethnic pride, comprise the majority of those in this educated segment of what they consider traditionalist religion. For clarity in this chapter, we call this group "neotraditionalists" and their religious practices neotraditionalism. The second constituency of traditionalists in in Nueva Ixtahuacán consists of the few elder shamans (*ajq'ij*) living there. These elders have practiced their Maya rituals for many years and mainly serve individual clients. Tix, described in detail by Scott and colleagues (this volume), is one of these, as would be Lázaro, whom Morgan (2005) describes. All of these traditionalists practiced before the politics and symbols of Maya unification and resistance touched Santa Catarina and Nahualá. Traditionalists do not contest the neotraditionalists; these elders simply perform their religious practices and allow the neotraditionalists the same right.

Among the elderly traditionalist *ajq'ij* priests, a universal term that encompasses their beliefs does not exist, but many labeled their ceremonies as "Maya religion." They called themselves *ajq'ijab'* in K'iche' and, when trying to speak Spanish, *sacerdotes mayas*, a term also used self-referentially by the neotraditionalist leaders. The two groups differ in beliefs and practices. However, those that do not follow either—mainly Protestant Pentecostals, orthodox Catholics, and charismatic Catholics, which together constitute the overwhelming majority of the community—see only a single belief and practice.

Maya spirituality or neotraditionalism, the focus of this chapter, has begun to decrease in prominence and number of adherents in Nueva Ixtahuacán. A number of factors contribute to this. Doctrinal ambiguity, greater religious choice, and economic contractions related to the decline of the once flourishing pan-Maya movement have left the educated elite of Nueva Santa Catarina Ixtahuacán as Maya spirituality's main advocates and practitioners. Most are schoolteachers born in the town, although some are ethnic Maya schoolteachers from outside the community. Others are administrators in the Santa Catarina Ixtahuacán *municipio*, all locally born and raised. Whether young professionals born in Ixtahuacán or Mayas from other *municipios* working in Nueva Ixtahuacán, their embrace of Maya spirituality likely represents an effort to reaffirm their own Maya identity precisely because of their contradictory, Ladino-like professionalization and mobility.

A wide variety of research has been conducted on traditional belief and customs of the Mayas in various locations in Guatemala. One strand of research has focused on the Maya culture as a reaction to the imposed Spanish culture (Foster 1960; Hawkins 1984). Some scholars have centered on the correlation between ancient Maya and modern Maya belief (Friedel, Schele, and Parker 1993). Other works have focused on traditional belief and ritual in the *cofradía* festivals and through the Maya saint Maximón (Cook 2000; Tarn 1997). Some compare Christianity and traditional Maya ideology (Scotchmer 1986). Others have researched shamanism among the Tz'utujils, and traditional myth and ritual as seen through art (Carlsen and Prechtel 1994; Christenson 2001). Dennis Tedlock in 1996 published a new translation of the *Popol Wuj*.[1] Scholarly research also connects the pan-Maya movement and its embrace of traditionalism and neotraditionalism to such issues as the Maya exodus to Mexico due to cultural persecution, changes in traditional belief and economy, and indigenous culture and its development (Burns 1993; Fischer 1996, 2001; Gálvez Borrell and Esquit Choy 1997; Warren 1998).

My research explores the state of traditional belief in a small K'iche' municipal center after the pan-Maya movement era, especially as it exists among advocates of or sympathizers with the pan-Maya movement. I document the local rise and decline of Maya spirituality over the years, explore the reasons behind the decline, and examine the effects of the pan-Maya movement and international aid on Maya spirituality within the confines of Ixtahuacán's relocated municipal head town. The linkage of nativist religious movements to political activism in a society is not new. In the Latin American context, for example, Steigenga and Cleary (2007b:10) note, "Recently there has also been a significant movement toward native (or neonative) spirituality among a number of indigenous

groups and individuals in Latin America. From Andean spiritual leaders who seek to revive elements, practices and symbols of their Inca heritage to Mayan religious practitioners who emphasize their pan-Mayan identity in Guatemala and Southern Mexico, there is a self-reflective process of cultural rescue and synthesis underway in the region."

Living in Nueva Santa Catarina Ixtahuacán, Guatemala, from mid-May to mid-August 2003, I used participant observation and interviews to collect the majority of my data. I also used freelisting. While conducting this research, I struggled with a number of difficulties. First, not many ceremonies took place during my stay. Although I was disheartened at first, my interviews led me to recognize that the relative absence of ceremony was evidence of the decline of Maya spirituality. Second, few people knew much about or wanted to talk about the traditional beliefs. Thus, my study depended on a relatively small number of people, six of whom provided most of the information. For the most part in this chapter, I present my findings in the emic form to preserve informants' cosmologies and assumptions about the world they live in. I also include some of my own etic perspectives; hopefully my personal ethnocentricities do not distort the content too much.

After struggling for some weeks, I worried that my research had stagnated; it seemed to be going nowhere. I was having trouble finding people with whom to talk. One informant suggested that I commission a ceremony to ask for permission to conduct my research. After contacting a shaman, making the arrangements, and giving him the money to purchase all of the necessary goods—though I failed to find a dove to sacrifice—I knelt at the same altar I had tried to photograph three weeks earlier and, through the ritual, received permission to conduct my research (figure 4.1).

In Maya divination, the answers sought to questions come from within a fire tended by the responsible shaman (see figures 3.3, 3.5, and 4.1 and plate 20). If the flames spiral up together in a whirlwind column of sorts, the fire is considered to be "balanced" and the answer is positive, but if the flames spread out decentralized, the answer is negative. In my case, the fire spiraled. The balance of the fire indicated a positive answer to my request. This ceremony opened the proverbial door and solved my problem of finding informants. I had sought a Maya solution to the question of why my endeavor was not going well and whether and when I should engage in it. To the Mayas,

Figure 4.1. A neotraditionalist shaman consults deities regarding the author's concerns and acquires permission for the study. Fire and colored candles are in the left foreground. Courtesy of Frederick H. Hanselmann, 2003.

this showed that I respected their beliefs and that my interest was legitimate. Word of the positive answer in the fire traveled the community's lines of gossip. From that point on, I was granted access to any ceremony or activity among those engaged in Maya spirituality, and I could discuss any topic with them. Weeks later, it dawned on me that the results of my study might have been much different had the fire not been balanced.

CORE BELIEFS OF MAYA SPIRITUALITY

According to its practitioners, "Maya spirituality is not a religion. It is a way of life." The word *religión* is a western term, they say, which outsiders imposed long after the beginning of the Maya civilization. The followers of Maya spirituality see the Ajaw—the primary divinity—in everything: "All of nature is a manifestation of the Ajaw, so he is constantly with us and around us." Nature indeed plays a large role in Maya spirituality. One of the fundamental principles of Maya spirituality is respect for nature and all that pertains to it. As products of nature, we should

revere nature. As one informant put it, "The forefathers say that we are children of nature. We are the youngest children and for that we need to respect our elders—the other plants and animals in nature. They are our older siblings. The trees, the rocks, the water, and all other aspects of nature are alive. Material objects all have spirits like us." According to Maya intellectuals in the village, the Spanish thought this Maya anthropomorphism was idolatrous, when the Mayas were simply paying respect to the older members of their family.

How does one use the materials of the universe if it is both enchanted with spirits and related to us? A local neotraditionalist advocated: "Man needs to use nature in order to survive. He needs to kill animals for meat, use rocks for his houses, and cut down trees to grow corn, for example. Man is not superior to nature, and this is something that has been forgotten by many. This is one reason why there are ceremonies: to ask permission to use what is in nature." As a consequence, another principle of Maya spirituality is unity and its use in everyday life. No individual is better than the next. Members of the community need to respect each other and work together.

In Maya spirituality, there is no sin, but there is right and wrong. When one commits an error, it is considered a learning experience that contributes to bettering one's life. Neotraditionalist informants emphasized that the *siete vergüenzas*, or seven shames, of the *Popol Wuj* express the main principles regarding right and wrong. By seeing what is wrong, right can be effected. By avoiding these shames—*odio* (hate), *avaricia* (avarice), *codicia* (greed), *mentira* (lying), *robo* (stealing), *soberbia* (pride, arrogance), and *adulterio* (adultery)—one can better function as a part of society and not solely as an individual. Avoiding the seven shames promotes unity, communality, balance, and complementarity. The shames all result in causing harm to another person, be it bodily harm, mental anguish, or material loss. The Maya spiritualist's concept that no one is perfect relates to the idea of wrongdoing as learning.

Maya spirituality cultivates a notion that one must tell the truth, which has implications for the local legal system. The ideal of telling the truth also exists on a community level, outside of Maya spirituality. Members of the community understand when they are guilty and will generally admit to their error and correct it. (See Thompson et al., this volume; and Thompson and Hanamaikai 2005:128–129 on the fear of God and the telling of truth in legal contexts.) For example, if a man steals from another person, the two families and the elders will arrange to have the man pay off the debt implicit in the theft. Most of the town will also know what the man did; this causes shame and embarrassment that often limits repeat offenses. The man will apologize and begin to repay that which he has taken. Sometimes other punishments are passed out, such as working for the offended family for a time. The victim's family tends to be supportive of the offender and helps him atone for his wrongdoing. Everyone works together to help support both sides during the situation, and the thief learns a lesson. The people in the community use this system instead of the national judicial system, although the latter is also found in town (see Hawkins, McDonald, and Adams 2013). Going to the judge or the police is the last resort, however. Residents avoid the court system and seldom take legal action. Ixtahuaquenses agree they must tell the truth with the elders to avoid the national legal process.

Communal orientation is another principle of neotraditionalist Maya spirituality. Humans, they say, are here on this earth in order to live communally with others. We do not achieve something after this life. Rather, we gain by being here. Life is not a race to see who can do the best. People need to live in peace and harmony, respecting all others. Afterward, our souls will continue to live on. If we did well with our lives, we will function as ancestors after death and aid our offspring and later generations. The ancestors live among us, but we cannot see them. They help and guide us. On the other hand, if we did poorly with our lives, we will live in *xib'alb'a* with the other souls that have been cast into the earth.

The descriptions I was offered of the ceremonies I observed at first seemed quite problematic. One possibility is they were simplified and locally Mayanized versions of popular Maya concepts readily available on the internet. To be sure, the four colors tied to cardinal directions with meanings are in the *Popol Wuj*, as are jaguars, although they are differently stylized. I was told, for example, that the Maya cross had thirteen squares that

coordinated with thirteen orifices of the human body and with the days of the Maya week, and that twenty perimeter angles in the representation of the Maya cross reflect the twenty days in the Maya month (figure 4.2). It was so neat and modernized. My informants admitted that the use of colored candles, each color to be burned at its own cardinal point, was new (plate 21).

I was told that there were four jaguars, each also connected to a cardinal point. Thus, when a neotraditionalist *ajq'ij* prays to begin a ceremony, he invokes the forms of God and the first ancestors, which are the four jaguars. Each jaguar also has a wife. In the East is the *balam k'i tze'*, the jaguar of the thousand laughs (*balam* = jaguar, *k'i* = many, *tze'* = root for laugh, smile). To these Mayas, "he does not worry about things." Every occurrence is meant to happen, and for this reason one should not worry or stress. The understanding exists that "we need to work to survive." In the West is the *balam aq'ab'*, the jaguar of the night (*aq'ab'* = night, power). "This means that we are not afraid of the night, and we can go around at night without fear. The women are still working late at night with the corn, the weaving, the food, the clothes, and everything else." In the North is the *balam maj kuta'*, the jaguar that does not ask for anything (*maj kuta'* = he asks nothing). Such a jaguar, it is said, "can provide for himself," a core indigenous premise of autonomy and self-support, asking nothing from others or the government. In the South is the jaguar of mutual assistance.[2] When a birth occurs, for example, "everyone collaborates to help wash clothes, cook, clean, and perform other duties to help the new mother. People adhere to these communal values because they know that when they have a child, the others will

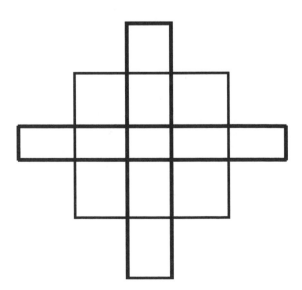

Figure 4.2. The Maya cross.

help them. If one fails to help, then one does not receive any help in return.

These are the main premises of modern indigenous Maya culture—fatalism in the face of powerful non-indigenous forces, self-sustenance at the family and community level, and mutualism with both positive and negative reciprocities—all tied to and justified by non-Christian jaguar symbols that can be shown to be rooted in a deep Maya past. Long ago, Mayas honored jaguars, even if not this particular configuration of them. Did this approach come to today's neotraditionalist Mayas by word of mouth from the uneducated Maya Catholic traditionalists like Tix? Did they get it from the internet, from academic or speculative texts of pop literature, or from university classes? Did they elaborate new meanings for old symbols on the spot? In the end, the source of a revitalization idea does not matter; one modifies tradition creatively to clarify and justify the culture that is needed in the present (Hobsbawm and Ranger 1983). What matters is the earnestness of today's presentation and the mix of the new authenticated by the presence of the old. Such is the stuff of revitalization movements and revitalization religions, of which neotraditionalist Maya spirituality is one.

BELIEF AND AMBIGUITY

Maya neotraditionalists hold that their Maya spirituality is monotheistic, albeit a complex monotheism. There is only one god, the Ajaw, they say, who manifests in a wide variety of ways. The Corazón del Cielo (*uk'ux kaj* = Heart of the Heavens) and Corazón de la Tierra (*uk'ux uleu* = Heart of the Earth) are two manifestations of the same god, who is also Tzaq'ol and B'itol, the Creador and Formador (Creator and Shaper/Constitutor). Tepew Ukumätz is yet another aspect, said to be the spirit of god on earth. Neotraditionalist Maya spiritualists believe that four beings, or jaguars, combined to create the world and that these are also manifestations of the Ajaw. Other entities, such as the gods of corn, war, family, death, and mountains, also exist. However, these are not gods in the generally understood sense of the word. They are spirits that protect the domain identified by their name. They are *dueños* or landlords, indeed, earth lords. Maya spiritualists liken these to the saints in Catholicism, since the saints are not considered gods either. None of these manifestations is seen as separate from the "One Whole," or

God, in the beliefs of Maya spirituality. Hence, neotraditionalist adherents affirm the tradition of Maya spirituality as monotheistic.

In contrast, according to neotraditionalists, the elders that follow the older form of traditionalism (such as described by Scott et al., this volume; and Morgan 2005) hold that these manifestations and entities are all separate beings. Thus, neotraditionalists suggest that traditionalists accept polytheism. Generic traditionalism therefore entails doctrinal ambiguity because of the difference between the old traditionalism and the new Maya spirituality (neo)traditionalism, since both belief systems are considered traditional at a higher conceptual level.

A tolerance for mixing religious beliefs furthers ambiguity in the doctrine. Many Maya spiritualists attend services of one or another of the Christian religions, seeing no apparent contradiction (see Morgan 2005). Because Maya spirituality is not considered a religion, attending a denominational service—be it Catholic or Protestant— is not inconsistent. Some adherents of Maya spirituality believe in both the Christian deity and the traditional monotheistic deity. Others strictly adhere to the traditional deity. One younger shaman described a vision he experienced while in a trance state, in which he saw Jesus Christ but could not speak to him. Some believe there is no need for organized religion or any regular practice of ritual if one is a follower of Maya spirituality.

Beliefs regarding the creation exemplify doctrinal ambiguity and diversity because some of the traditionalists that attend Catholic church mix traditional beliefs regarding the creation with Catholic creation beliefs. Other Maya spiritualists believe in the strictly Catholic version of the creation. One informant believes in Darwin's notions of evolution and the scientific theories of creation. A few believe that the *Popol Wuj* correctly describes the creation. The latter believe that the Ajaw, Tepeo Ukumätz, Tzaq'ol, and B'itol (which are all manifestations of the same god) came together and decided to create the world. These four, some say, represent the four elements of nature: water, fire, earth, and air. The four elements combined, and the world was created: "Then the Ajaw wanted to create someone who would take care of the earth and show him respect." The plants and animals were created, but they did not talk: "Then the men of mud were created, but they were watered down and wishy-washy." They did not do what the Ajaw wanted. They fell apart.[3] In a second attempt, men of wood were created, introducing the use of wood for fire, arrows, and other purposes. Yet, "the men of wood were awkward and unintelligent and also failed to comply with what the Ajaw wanted." On the third attempt, the Ajaw was successful, creating humans out of corn. He had Ixmucane, the moon, make nine drinks of corn, which symbolizes the nine months in the womb. This is when humans became humans. The skin and bones were created with white and yellow corn. With this successful third attempt, agriculture and civilization began. (For more on the three stages of human creation and the significance of mud, wood, and corn in the modern community, see Jardine, Hawkins, and Adams 2020; and Rode 2007.)

Thus came the world and humans into being, according to adherents of Maya spirituality. Their creation myth represents humans as the youngest creation and confirms the importance of corn, giving a neotraditional explanation for the consumption of corn at every meal. "Man is made of corn, so he must make sure to maintain himself," one man said. A creation story is vital to a working spiritual cosmology. Yet, allowing for the acceptance of differing beliefs regarding creation has led to a schism between the camps in the traditionalist community.

Despite the principle of community, a lack of *communitas* exists (Turner 1969) because adherents of Maya spirituality and the rest of the villagers do not worship collectively. Maya spiritualists believe and practice as individuals, hiring shamans as guides. Little binds them together, and I witnessed disagreements among them as to the nature of Maya spirituality, its doctrine, and its ritual. Indeed, the relative absence of collectively celebrated ritual inhibits the development of a coordinated collective conscience (Durkheim 1949[1893]).[4]

In effect, each neotraditionalist informant has a different, personal notion of Maya spirituality and creates his or her own personal doctrine, as evidenced by the multiple views regarding the creation, monotheism, and polytheism. Several adherents have a favored shaman, whom they may travel an hour or more to visit.

Maya spirituality lacks communal or collective orientation and organization (Turner 1969; Durkheim 1949[1893]), further contributing to confusion and a decline in participation. The only organization that exists is the relationship of the client to the shaman. The followers do not see an *ajq'ij* as a priest or an official with a congregation. The *ajq'ij* knows the sun or counts the days (*aj* = occupation, *q'ij* = sun or day), a mix of astronomer and astrologer: "He knows how to navigate the heavens and the Maya calendar. He communicates with the Ajaw

on our behalf. He is able to see the ancestors and communicate with them and the other spirits that exist." The *ajq'ij* functions as the spiritual leader or shaman.

The *ajq'ijab'* (plural for *ajq'ij*) are very diverse. They conduct ceremonies in different fashions and teach a variety of concepts and ideas, each relating to the *ajq'ij*'s personal beliefs. For example, the elder *ajq'ijab'*, who typically represent the most conservative traditionalism, drink *kuxa*, a homemade illegal liquor made from fermented corn.[5] They deem it sacred because man was created from the same corn and because the liquor allows them to communicate with the Ajaw. Thus, traditionalists both drink the alcohol and pour it as libation offerings (plate 22). The younger *ajq'ijab'*, who typically align with Maya spirituality, tend not to drink *kuxa*. They value it as a product of nature made from corn, but only use the liquor as a libation offering by pouring it on the ground or in the fire. The younger *ajq'ijab'* believe that one should be fully conscious—and not inebriated—before the Ajaw.

In sum, traditional beliefs and practices—splintered between the young, simplified, urbane Maya spirituality and the old, complex, rural practices—have difficulty providing consistent answers to followers in Nueva Santa Catarina Ixtahuacán. The discordant ideas in the two strands of "traditional" belief have created confusion and ambiguity in Maya spirituality, leading to its decline. Speaking metaphorically, its fire is not balanced.

DECLINE

They cut off our fruit, they cut off our branches,
they cut off our flowers, but the trunk remains.
They cannot remove our roots.
—JOSUÉ, HIGH SCHOOL HISTORY TEACHER AND
ADHERENT OF MAYA SPIRITUALITY

With the advent of the Peace Accords of 1996, neotraditional expressions of traditional Maya belief flourished and became a widespread practice, resulting in what is now termed Maya spirituality. This outward expression and practice of traditionalism also came with a sociopolitical linkage. That very political linkage, however, now contributes to the current state of decline in Maya spirituality as a neotraditionalist movement. Ixtahuaquense adherents of Maya spirituality perceive their neotraditional practice to be much less popular now than in the years immediately following the Peace Accords. During the Guatemalan civil war, the government and army persecuted and oppressed many traditional Mayas, especially the shamans, which led many ordinary Mayas either to think that traditionalism was bad or to fear for their lives and cease to participate (Burns 1993; Green 1993, 1999). Many people, among them *ajq'ijab'*, were targeted and "disappeared," most by government military forces and conservative private death squads, never to be seen again (Salazar 1996; Burns 1993). This resulted in a severe decline in the use of native languages and traditional clothing in an attempt to avoid the ethnic persecution. The process attacked the roots of Maya identity and added to the forces encouraging many to modify, hide, or give up the outward appearance of indigeneity.

The pan-Maya movement, through pro-Maya activism, demanded recognition and compensation from the state in terms of social, territorial, political, economic, religious, and linguistic rights (Fischer 1996, 2001; Warren 1998). The movement made a public and political impact (Salazar 1996). Activist groups surfaced to argue for the civil and human rights of the people before and especially after the Peace Accords established basic protections (Gálvez Borrell and Esquit Choy 1997). The Peace Accords established not only that the Guatemalan government should protect indigenous rights and culture, but that it should actually *foster* indigenous culture and tradition. With financial backing from a number of aid sources and nongovernmental organizations, indigenous leaders sought to revive the traditional beliefs and customs of the Mayas, including the reinstatement of shamans, elders, and midwives (Warren 1998). With the onset of the Peace Accords, many K'iche' took part in ceremonies and adhered to the more popular traditional beliefs. At this point in time, the division between what is now termed Maya spirituality and traditional beliefs had yet to occur in the belief system. People realized that the Peace Accords protected their culture and their history; many began to believe again and use that belief and ceremonial practice for political purposes. Many new shamans went through training during this time and began to practice. Traditional beliefs and Maya spirituality were viewed as one, and both old and young flourished. Thus, the pan-Maya political and cultural movement created a cultural revitalization of traditionalist religion. Indeed, the renovation of traditional belief and ceremony figured importantly in the pan-Maya movement's culture and political agenda. Government

organizations and NGOs funneled money into the support of religious ceremonies.

This traditional religious renewal, however, has been declining. According to Ixtahuaquense adherents of Maya spirituality in 2003, few people practice Maya spirituality in Nueva Santa Catarina Ixtahuacán compared to the number who practiced in the late 1990s. The remaining adherents in the neotraditional Maya spirituality movement are also the last remaining advocates of the pan-Maya indigenous, activist, political identity movement. Indeed, the last remaining advocates of Maya spirituality (as distinct from the tellurian shamanic traditionalism described in chapter 3) all teach or serve as administrators in the Paraíso Maya, an internationally funded bilingual high school chartered to foster education that emphasizes Maya roots and concepts. Some of the town's educated elite and a handful of young shamans who have adjusted the rituals to represent the interests of this school elite constitute the few remaining practitioners of Maya spirituality.

In addition, in Nueva Ixtahuacán, only a smattering of elders assert the efficacy of older Maya Catholic traditional practitioners, among them Tix, who from time to time resides with his daughter and son-in-law in Nueva Ixtahuacán. While the two strands of traditionalism maintain a mutual respect, practitioners rarely communicate with those of the other constituency. For example, an adherent of Maya spirituality did not know that an older man in the village was a traditional *ajq'ij*.

Greater religious choice has opened another route to decline, although few that remain within Maya spirituality understand the factors that brought about either the resurgent version of traditionalism or its decline. Some Maya spiritualists attribute the decline of both forms of Maya traditionalism to the "religious invasion" of the *evangélicos* (the Pentecostal Protestants) and the *carismáticos* (the pentecostal Catholics). Indeed, a good number of churches have found a home in the small town of Nueva Santa Catarina Ixtahuacán. As one person exclaimed, "There are more churches than people!" Nueva Santa Catarina Ixtahuacán has about five hundred families divided among seven Pentecostal Protestant congregations, four pentecostal charismatic Catholic congregations, the Roman Catholic parish (to which charismatic Catholics also belong), a congregation of Seventh-day Adventists, and the two segments that practice Maya traditionalism. Approximately eight families follow the Maya spirituality movement, and two follow the older traditional belief system. The new variety plays a large part in the decrease of traditionalism, both old and new. The majority of those once involved in Maya spirituality in the culturally resurgent years after the Peace Accords have moved on to other churches or religions; indeed, a large number converted to the charismatic and Protestant Pentecostal faiths.

Conversion from the old traditionalism also occurred, even among those considered the most stalwart and conservative. A highly regarded shaman in the nearby town of Sololá threw away all his possessions pertaining to his profession as an *ajq'ij* and joined a Protestant congregation. My informant, who knew this man personally, asked why he did it. The former shaman replied that as an *ajq'ij* he had practiced and believed in the wickedness of the devil, the standard Protestant/Pentecostal label for traditional ritual activities.

The practitioners of Maya spirituality thus see the Protestants as their main religious antagonists due to the utter intolerance of the Pentecostal churches toward Maya spirituality and older traditionalism. Indeed, Protestants are the most outspoken in condemning the traditionalists; the orthodox Catholic leaders still try to retain and transform the old traditionalists, who yet see themselves as the true Catholics. The Evangelical leaders, however, disdain Maya spirituality and its rituals, speaking of it as evil from the pulpit. Their fulminations against traditional practices in sermons are broadcast live from speakers mounted atop churches. Some even say that it is a "sin to talk about the Maya priests." They convince people to think that the traditions are "bad" or "evil." As a result, many adherents and officiants of both traditionalist and neotraditionalist orientations have ceased to practice.

To the Maya spiritualists in Nueva Santa Catarina Ixtahuacán, Protestantism functions in an inverted version of the Protestant ethic (Weber 1996). Weber holds that the beliefs of the Protestant religion lead adherents to excel. The ethic of Protestantism, he says, has played a crucial role in the political and financial success of the free market system (Weber 1996). In Nueva Santa Catarina Ixtahuacán, Maya spiritualists think the situation is the opposite, though they do not reference Weber. They assert that the Evangelical churches oppress the people. They suggest that the Evangelical attitude is that "God's will decides all": "If one is poor, it is the will of God. If a person who is poor attempts to make money and be successful, this person would be going against God." According to neotraditionalists, Evangelical Protestants lack a sense of progress and only manifest a sense of existence: "People exist to obey God's will. To go against this principle would be disobedience." Hence, capitalistic success is nothing to them: "If you are born poor, you stay poor." In the Maya spiritualists' view of the present, Evangelical Pentecostalism is the religious opiate of the masses, as Marx suggested, constituting a mode of oppression. Maya spiritualists would reject the Weberian notion that Protestantism and capitalism mutually foster each other.

In contrast, those who practice neotraditionalist Maya spirituality seem to be the most innovative in town. They have steady salaried jobs, they continue their educations, a few have college degrees, and two have computers in their homes. Some have their own side businesses to supplement their income. They feel that the Mayas can be strong and independent, not relying on others for what they need. The proponents of Maya spirituality argue that the Mayas can and should prosper and advance in society, contrary to what others might preach or say about them. The Maya spirituality version of traditionalism seems to effectively adapt its adherents to their increasing interconnection with national and global institutions and forces, rather than inhibiting that interconnection, as one might suspect of such a near cousin of agricultural traditionalism.

Adherents of Maya spirituality also sense another inverse relation to Protestantism concerning the notion of God's will. Maya spiritualists attribute to Protestants the belief that a person cannot change or resist God's will, and to do so is a sin. Thus, a neotraditionalist described the misfortune of a young Evangelical girl who had taken ill. Her illness started out as a tiny problem that would have been curable with medicine, but the girl progressively became worse. She and her family were members of a Protestant congregation in town. Due to the belief in God's will, the family believed that the girl was meant to be sick. When neighbors of another faith offered to send for doctors, the parents haughtily refused, saying that God would make her better. The treatment given consisted of the congregation's prayers, the pastor's visits, and personal prayers over the girl. When the illness became grave, they took greater measures. The pastor brought in a woman who had the gift of healing. She, too, prayed over the girl. The people had faith and believed that she would recover. When the girl died, Evangelicals said that it was the will of God. The Maya spiritualists still feel bitter about the hold of this religion over the participating Maya villagers, in part because, at a fundamental level, all are kin.

In another case, a teacher at the bilingual school, an adherent of Maya spirituality, seethed when she told of an Evangelical woman whose husband was a drunk and would beat her and the children. When the abused woman sought help from their congregation's pastor, he advised her to stay with her husband and to pray for him. She did, but nothing changed. After yet another drunken beating, the husband requested that the family fast for him. The wife "just needed to pack her bags, grab the children, and leave the husband," the teacher concluded, "but she was afraid to do so because her church frowns on divorce and separation."

Yet, while Maya spiritualists verbally condemn the Christian denominations, they also condone attending their services, particularly those of the Ortho-Catholic church. This furthers the aforementioned confusion and ambiguity. As noted, many adherents to Maya spirituality mix religious beliefs. Some of those who practice Maya spirituality also attend the Catholic church and see nothing contradictory in doing so. Some of the more influential practitioners of Maya spirituality feel that the Catholic church helps the poor and allows for some tolerance of traditional belief. However, they continue to explain that many cannot forget the well-documented history of the conquest and the role Catholicism played in the suppression of traditional religion during that time. These practitioners harbor a general distrust of organized religion and label it an instrument of colonial exploitation.

Some who remain practitioners of Maya spirituality think the exodus of their former followers to other religions or congregations occurs because of money. The root of Guatemala's financial problem, they say, is poverty: "Many people are poor." According to some informants, the Protestant churches receive a good deal of funding from wealthy foreign sponsors. These churches, in turn, give money and supplies to the townspeople, and such donations bring about many conversions. Typically, congregations support their pastor and church through tithes and donations. Instead of members supporting the pastor, Maya spiritualists think that the pastors are supporting the congregation, an inversion of the flow of congregational funds. They think such funding comes from outside sources, mostly international, of the same faith. Thus, the somewhat disgruntled remaining spiritualists identify an explanation and a culprit for their decline. Protestantism is the competitive boogeyman close at hand.

The reality is rather more complicated. In the aftermath of the 1980s war and during the pan-Maya movement, foreign governments and international aid groups donated huge quantities of money to support cultural revitalization. The surge of available funds politicized the expression of traditional beliefs and practices, as younger practitioners adapted the rituals to suit the occasions deemed appropriate by the funders and to prove their legitimate indigeneity. The reader should bear in mind that I obtained this perspective from informants that took part in the now declining pan-Maya movement in town. They did not wish to name specific groups or organizations that received the money, nor did they know exactly where the money originated. This monetary infusion from international aid nourished the florescence of Maya spirituality and traditional belief. Then, the decline in such funding two decades after the height of the war and eight years after the signing of the Peace Accords similarly undercut the outward expression of neotraditional Maya spirituality. Thus, international aid, including the role it played in the pan-Maya movement and the effect on Maya spirituality when the aid to indigenous cultural revitalization diminished sharply, further accounts for the rise and then decline in Maya spirituality. People, mainly those with education, had created "traditional" cultural organizations and received financial aid from donors. With this money, these organizations formally taught those who came to participate in their programs explaining the "Maya culture," though what they taught was a modern interpretation of traditionalism. These cultural institutions financed many ceremonies and fostered the resurgence in "traditionalism," albeit a neotraditionalism.[6]

In short, many people participated in Maya spirituality after the Peace Accords because of the financial assistance and the political expedience. Even the mayor commissioned ceremonies, which helped authenticate and show the visiting funders the indigenous roots of the town's relocation and aid-funded reconstruction. But with the town built, the funding essentially ended, and the fervor of guilt about the war over,[7] those that still follow Maya spirituality wonder what has happened. As one informant pointed out, "Who remembered that our town moved [just] three years ago? Who has said, 'Let's have a ceremony to give thanks for our town and our land?' We had a ceremony to help us move, but we don't have one to give thanks. Really, many people do not live Maya spirituality."

Now that the donations have dried up, the "people look for another source; they go to whoever gives money, food, or materials for houses." One informant noted that he does not hear much about the resurgence now. Indeed, many of the institutions that were financed by international donations have closed or are closing: "There was a time when one institution would conduct a ceremony on one side of town and a different institution would promote a ceremony on the other side. Now, many institutions have closed because they do not have funds." Four of my informants taught in the Paraíso Maya school, which explicitly encourages Maya studies and awareness and still regularly promotes Maya ceremonies and cultural activities on commemorative days. Notably the Paraíso Maya is the only institution in Nueva Ixtahuacán that still promotes modern Maya traditionalism. Thus, the school's continued international funding depends in part on the lasting attractiveness of its mission to foment Maya-aware education.

Transformations in the shaman-client relationship offer further evidence of the connection between the decline of Maya spirituality and the reduction in international cultural assistance funding. A traditional Maya shaman typically accepts a donation for his services to further the interests of the client. The client purchases the offerings necessary for the conduct of the ceremony. When the aid was available, however, institutions paid the shamans and the expenses of ritual materials. The individuals who practiced Maya spirituality during this time became unaccustomed to paying out of their own pockets for the shaman's services. Eventually, the influx of aid money designated for this type of cultural revitalization came to an end. The lack of money left the practitioners in the role of financing their own ceremonies and paying the shamans. Moreover, the neotraditionalist ceremonies conducted in Nueva Ixtahuacán were commemorative rather than determinative. That is, they commemorated or blessed institutional events; they did not help individuals resolve by divination conundrums regarding why their luck was bad, or what they should do, or when. The Ixtahuaquense version of neotraditionalism did little to help the individual adapt to life. Faced with this new situation, many opted to look elsewhere for religion. Thus, outside money played a significant but temporary role by increasing the overall participation in neotraditional belief and custom in the town, while the subsequent lack of funding led to its decline.

In neotraditionalist belief, other churches offer handouts in the form of food and supplies, which also come from outside donors. Neotraditionalists cynically say that "this is where the people go," without realizing the irony that their complaint applies to their own condition. While many townspeople are strong in their beliefs, my neotraditionalist informants say that many also "sway in the breeze." The community has experienced a shift from national and international government-sponsored funding given to traditionalist practitioners to foster a culture to a system of nongovernmental aid given to and through Evangelical church groups and orthodox Catholic institutions because the government, constitutionally, cannot foster a religion.

Neotraditionalism's insistence that it is not a religion also has contributed to its cycle of rise and decline.

Some in Ixtahuacán hold modernization at fault for the decline in tradition and for the hardships that Mayas confront. They see globalization as a threat that will "exterminate individual culture and convert us all into one global culture worldwide," echoing Lévi-Strauss's (1974:41) sentiment that modern society "pretends . . . it is investing them with nobility at the very time when it is completing their destruction" in the mass production of society. Politics and foreign aid, some assert, led people to practice traditional rites for the wrong reasons, but they harbor no grudge. Many Mayas feel that we should learn from the good things from every culture and respect each other, manifesting a principle of cultural inclusiveness and syncretism that Morgan (2005) and Fischer (1999) document (see also Erickson, Hawkins, and Adams 2020). Today, the few who practice Maya spirituality are of the opinion that the people have to experiment with and verify what they have, even if they have lost certain aspects of their culture by embracing the present while returning to the past.

One informant lamented, "I think that if the people had been left to themselves, the growth would have been more out of desire instead of need or want. It would have come from the heart. There probably would still be many practicing the traditional [ways]." Now, few in Nueva Ixtahuacán follow Maya spirituality, and some of them deliberately hide their practice from the rest of the townspeople. In the past, by contrast, shamans would announce publicly that there would be a ceremony.

One informant noted that while many do not believe, they still unknowingly comply with traditional customs and beliefs. They eat tortillas with every meal, not just because corn is what they grow, but because they believe corn products have the consistency and the moisture needed to regenerate a healthy human body. They practice many other customs having traditionalist and Maya connotations, including the ways they use the *tuj* (sweat-bath) for medicinal, religious, and birthing customs thought to be Maya rather than Ladino. For the moment, the Maya spirituality resurgence in Nueva Ixtahuacán appears largely over. Yet the adherents of Maya spirituality believe that its roots—the traditions and customs—still exist in the Maya culture in a dormant state, mostly unused.

Much evidence points to a disappearance of traditionalism and customs in Nueva Santa Catarina Ixtahuacán. Young leaders lament that many wise elders who knew much have died. New fathers do not teach their children the traditions because they did not receive traditional teachings as children either. The oral history of tradition thus fades. Nor has anyone written or documented these traditions to preserve them for future generations. Many feel ashamed to take part in the rituals. According to some informants, many have lost their Maya heritage, identity, and culture. Those who practice Maya spirituality feel that they need to put their traditions and customs into practice and develop them, but most of those who remain adherents are salaried employees of a school sustained by outside international funding based on its cultivation of Maya-content education for Mayas and thus have a self-interested reason for cultivating their perspective.

The Ixtahuaquense practitioners of Maya spirituality attempt to make a return to the past, but they do so with combinations of old and new symbols and practices that appeal to and link an educated elite and younger shamans. The difference between neotraditionalism and the traditionalists such as Tix (described by Scott et al., this volume) remains, but engenders no animosity. Leaders of both orientations attempt to further the traditions in their own manner. The elder shamans practice a form of traditionalism oriented to agriculture and one's link to ancestors through inheritance in a particular local community. The educated elite and younger shamans follow a neotraditional Maya spirituality that enhances an indigenous identity called into question by new forms of employment and consumption and an increased orientation away from the community.

CONCLUSION

Despite the apparent decline of the movement, at least as it manifests in Nueva Santa Catarina Ixtahuacán, the practitioners of neotraditionalism in general still hold on to their beliefs and push to share them with those that have left tradition to the side. Advocates do so, however, not with obvious proselyting, as the *evangélicos* do, but through teaching and admonition made possible by their official positions in schools and government. While their cosmology appears to be in disarray, the followers of Maya spirituality hold that they will change the current situation by themselves: "We have control over our culture and beliefs. We determine the future." The remaining Maya spiritualists see themselves as beginning anew, without help from outsiders, using the knowledge they gained from pan-Mayanism to further this restart.

The respected and educated elite of the town are mainly responsible for this new approach, much akin to the notion of Marx's intelligentsia who lead the people to change the system (Marx and Engels 1968[1848]). The Maya spiritualists who work as teachers in the Instituto Paraíso Maya teach principles found in the *Popol Wuj*, including the Maya method of counting, the Maya creation story, and the book's place in Maya history. They teach their native language, K'iche'. They proudly instruct their students regarding their heritage and the great civilization that their ancestors created. The students learn the symbol of the Maya cross and all that corresponds with it. They learn the Maya calendar, the meanings of the days, and their *nawals*. From time to time, they witness ceremonies staged in the school courtyard performed by a neotraditionalist shaman from Totonicapán. In all this, nationally educated schoolteachers possessing a modernized idea of indigeneity cultivate and reinvent the notion of tradition. During these school-sponsored ceremonies, the students manifest tolerance mixed with disinterest, standing around the ceremony being performed, but socializing with each other rather than paying attention. For them, the neotraditionalist ritual is not a religious event eliciting their devotion but a cultural parade soliciting their indigenous advocacy and providing a welcomed opportunity to cancel classes.

These Guatemalans are not alone in following these paths to identity and spirituality. In the Andes, Corr (2007:175) sees that "the social context in which I analyze conversion to native spirituality is one of increasing social movements and political organizations based on identity; one in which indigenous people proclaim pride in their unique cultural heritage." Corr notes that neotraditionalism "is not an organized religion to which people are converting, but rather a change in attitudes, discourse, and practice." Likewise, leaders of the pan-Maya move-ment and Maya spirituality synthesize local practices and local ideologies with new ideologies of ecological preser-vation, human rights, indigenous political mobilization, and even western and Guatemalan romanticizing of east-ern (Asian) spiritualities.

The strand of pan-Maya religious activism here described appears to have wilted in this town with the cessation of direct NGO funding of religiously linked eth-nic identity. We doubt, however, that this is the end of the movement toward traditionalist revitalization. It will no doubt find other symbolic reexpressions because identity unification as a movement toward ethnic and class power will continue unabated. How soon it becomes more prominent and permanent in Nahualá and Santa Catarina remains to be seen. Local agro-mercantile traditionalism unimpacted by the swirls of identity politics and inter-national rights, however, also appears to be contracting. The one local shaman still teaching had a collection of six Ladino university students from outside the commu-nity taking lessons. No one in town was choosing to learn from him, from Tix (Scott et al., this volume), or from the older traditionalist Hawkins had lived with in Nahualá. In the latter case, even the traditionalist's son was refusing to learn the art, in spite of the manifest economic value to be gained from assisting the old guard in dealing with the stresses and resentments of modernization.

There is an active economy devoted to protecting one-self against sorcery based on envy. And envy, built into the culture as a premised expectation that kept things equal in the old days, is generated to excess by modernization and its derivative inequalities. Thus, modernization pro-duces social space for both traditionalist practice devoted to overcoming inequalities and for growth in indige-nous identity politics expressed through neotradition-alist religion. As Corr (2007:175, 192) puts it, "any study of what people are converting to must include the 'passage' toward native spirituality" because that incorporates both the move toward indigenous pride and symbolic affirma-tion of the values of indigeneity emergent in the rapidly decolonizing world.

Although Maya spirituality in Nueva Ixtahuacán has experienced a drastic decline, it appears that its remain-ing followers have found an institutionalized locus for maintaining a presence that could generate a renewal. The tree's trunk and its roots remain. Neotraditionalism, as Engels (2008[1890b]:284–285) puts it, "presupposes certain definite thought material handed down to it by

its predecessors," in this case, Maya Catholic traditional-ism, from which neotraditionalism "takes its start." Neo-traditionalists thus follow Durkheim's (2001[1912]:277) observation that they "remain faithful" to their imagina-tion of their "past" and seek "to preserve" an indigenous "collectivity's moral profile" in the present and future, a moral profile that states they are deserving of local and national human rights as a people vis-à-vis Ladinos and the national government. Perhaps in time, this local neo-traditionalism will again have branches and flowers, and the fire will regain its balance.[8]

NOTES

1. A number of spellings of the K'iche' word for "book" or "paper(s)" have been used in transcriptions and translations of this sacred Maya text: *vuj*, *vuh*, and *wuj* are the most common variants. The form used depends on the editor's fidelity to early Spanish transcriptions or choices regarding the politics and tim-ing of modern K'iche' (or Quiché) alphabets. Throughout this text, I refer to this ancient Maya book as the *Popol Wuj*, as attested in Christenson's (n.d.) K'iche' dictionary, unless I cite someone's complete modern title. In the references, each author or editor is of course accorded their own spelling preference.

2. Hanselmann did not record the informant's K'iche' term for the fourth *balam* in his notes, but instead provided a Span-ish gloss of the term "mutual assistance." The *Popol Wuj* attests to the first three *balam*s as given here, although the translation of their names may be somewhat modern. See http://www.mesoweb.com/publications/Christenson/PV-Literal.pdf, lines 4942–4945, and repeatedly thereafter. The fourth *balam* is given in the *Popol Wuj* as *ik'i balam*. Here, the translation is dicey: *ik'* = month, but the second *i* is of unknown meaning to Haw-kins unless it is a corruption of *e*, the animate pluralizer, render-ing "month of many *balam*s" or "twenty *balam*s," perhaps. Or the initial *i*- could be the second-person plural possessive and the thing possessed is *k'i*, translatable as "many," and together literally "you-all's plurality." It is a stretch, but that could be the source of the term "mutuality" in a modern rendition. To Hawkins, this translation of the fourth *balam* seems uncertain, inscrutable, and unlikely. We regret the uncertainty we leave for some future researcher to clarify.

3. Why was the first creation of men of mud rejected? After all, mud has important uses in village life; with it, one builds houses and makes useful pots. But to the K'iche', mud also rep-resents laziness. A wet and formless lump of mud or clay is *q'ol*. It cannot do its work; it has no purpose when slick and shapeless.

Indeed, it is dangerous; on the trail, *q'ol* causes one to fall. Today, to call a person *q'ol*—lazy, muddy, formless—in a culture centered on a good work ethic, "good formation," and propriety is a severe rebuke.

4.   Hawkins has seen the young neotraditionalist shamans employed by the Paraíso Maya school offer inaugural and other celebratory rituals before a crowd of students and faculty. The students, however, seemed to be simply observing a performance, as if at a play and still being rather distracted, rather than participating in a ritual in which they were engaged in body and belief.

5.   Liquor itself is not illegal, but making home brew to avoid taxes is.

6.   We recognize that any interpretation of tellurian traditionalism has always been a current and therefore modern interpretation of itself.

7.   A good deal of funding came to Nueva Ixtahuaquenses (and Mayas generally) because postwar, the United Nations, a number of international NGOs, and some Guatemalan technocrats and intellectuals wanted to fund Maya cultural development and maintenance in recompense for the atrocities committed against Mayas during the war. See Hawkins and Adams 2020.

8.   This chapter was finished in content and argument, though not polished, by 2008. Late in the process we discovered the work of Cook and Offit (2013), which analyzes and contrasts the threads of Maya Catholic traditionalism and Maya spirituality in Momostenango. We find the same identity processes at work in Nueva Santa Catarina Ixtahuacán as in Cook and Offit's elegant book regarding Momostenango and are glad to confirm that Cook and Offit's insights apply over a wider ethnographic area. Our work seconds the conclusions advanced by Cook and Offit that Maya spirituality is essentially a newly constructed revitalization religion. It is attuned to a new era of indigenous identity politics and synthesizes elements of Maya traditionalism, "new age" beliefs, and popular modern concerns, including western stereotypes of eastern religious elements, university students' perspectives, and the needs of indigenous peoples for recognition, identity, protection, and appreciation by the people and institutions of the more Ladino nation.

Chapter Five

"The Church Protects Us"

Ortho-Catholic Symbolism in Antigua Santa Catarina Ixtahuacán

JOHN J. EDVALSON, JOHN P. HAWKINS, AND WALTER RANDOLPH ADAMS

ON A TYPICAL LATE AFTERNOON in Antigua Ixtahuacán, the K'iche' Maya family I lived with would sit in their kitchen eating a dinner of tortillas and beans.[1] The small adobe kitchen had a cooking fire on the ground surrounded by three stones, on which the family placed a *xot*, a flat piece of iron on which they cooked. The men sat on short wooden benches, warming themselves, while the women knelt on mats woven from dried reeds from nearby Lake Atitlán as they prepared the food. The fire highlighted faces in the room with a soft ocher glow.

Finishing his meal, the family patriarch would perform the Catholic ritual of making the sign of the cross by touching first the forehead, then the sternum, followed by the left and right sides of the chest, and sometimes followed by a kiss of the fingers. After this, he would hand his plate to his wife and, turning to me, say, "Maltiox, a Xwan" (Thanks, young John). *Maltiox* is most likely a contraction of *rumal* Tiox, meaning literally "because of God" or "due to God." Colloquially, it means "thanks to God" and in ordinary conversation something close to a simple "thank you." It indicates also the honored place of God in the causal cosmology of everything that happens. Typically, an honored guest is thanked first, followed by the male and then female members of the family, in hierarchical order, at every meal.

When I asked my host father when one should make the sign of the cross, he looked thoughtful for a moment and then responded confidently that it should be done "before eating, before leaving on a trip, before work, and when you have to sign some type of document."[2] This and many similar statements led to the examination in this chapter of how Ixtahuaquense orthodox Catholics employ and interpret the symbols of their religion.

Maya Catholics in Antigua Santa Catarina Ixtahuacán use religious symbols to ameliorate a myriad of fears and anxieties. They engage in Catholic rituals to help control the chaotic elements of their life. In this chapter I identify how ritual behavior surrounding the local patron saint Santa Catarina, the Catholic holiday of Corpus Christi, and the Catholic cross sheds light on the fears people in Ixtahuacán face every day and how they deal with those fears.

To better understand the nature of the fears experienced by members of this community, we must understand the context. At the time of my fieldwork in 2003, Antigua Ixtahuacán was undergoing a process of transition. In 1998, Hurricane Mitch had caused extensive damage to the town, resulting in the January 2000 migration and relocation of approximately five-sixths of the community to a location sixteen kilometers away by road and more than 3,000 feet higher in elevation, a swatch of land adjacent to the Pan-American Highway. Relocation split families, physically and emotionally divided the community, repositioned the municipal government, and resulted in the loss of infrastructure and government funding to the originating town center where I studied. The move was motivated primarily by educated members of the community who sought the economic advantages of being close to the highway. Hurricane damage to the original *cabecera* (town center) provided the pretext they needed to relocate the municipal seat, which, according to Antigua Ixtahuaquenses, was something that had been debated long before the coming of the hurricane. Those who saw an economic advantage to the move and those they convinced relocated; those who had less to gain by moving stubbornly stayed. (For more on the hurricane, the politics of relocation, and the developmental aftermath, see Hawkins and Adams 2020.)

The bold act of the one-sixth of the community that remained has been the source of a number of conflicts, including debates over land, water, and government resources. The government and international funding of the move was contingent on the uninhabitability and total abandonment of the original community. Those who remained undermined the argument that danger was imminent, and that threatened the allocation of funds to build a new town center for the migrants. Those who moved had to find financial and official backing. They therefore hid the fact of the remaining population as long as possible in order to secure government funding. As a result, the government funded Nueva Ixtahuacán and cut off funds for Antigua Ixtahuaquenses indefinitely; the latter was declared a zone of imminent danger by virtue of the better political connections of the municipal officers that had moved.

This upheaval added a myriad of anxieties and fears to those normally experienced among members of the originating community. Their local school system closed: how would they educate their children? Their weekly Sunday market shrank: how would they secure a diversity of foods and sell their corn and beans? They found themselves unable to repair the municipal sewer lines: how would they sustain this infrastructure and other services, such as electricity and potable water? How would they manage their governance and health? They could secure no public funding for home or public building repairs. For months, electricity was cut off to the whole town. Despite these losses, the people retained control over their land and continued to subsist more or less as they had. Lack of government support was nothing new to this indigenous community.

Amid these losses, the most significant remaining institution was the local Catholic church and its K'iche'-speaking American priest, who opted to stay rather than move with the majority of his flock. Over the years prior, the church had provided medical treatment, organized various food cooperative projects including a fish farm, and built a granary where people could store corn after harvest until prices turned more favorable. The parish also received periodic support from the priest's diocese in the United States. Hence, in the absence of reliable safety nets, Catholics in this community saw the church as the one remaining bastion of security. As one young man stated succinctly, "The church protects us." This statement led to two significant research questions: What are the fears that the Catholic Church protects its adherents from? And how do Catholics receive protection from these fears?

METHODS

In order to understand how the Catholic Church and its symbols function to provide the people of Ixtahuacán with relief from life's challenges, I employed the following methods in the investigation: participant observation, structured and unstructured interviews, free lists, pile sorts, and a survey.

Most of the participant observation took place during religious meetings at the Catholic church located in the town center, perhaps eighty meters from my home. I gave special consideration to ritual behavior at mass and on Catholic holy days. I also actively participated in many events, ritual and otherwise, with my host family. Living with them allowed me to observe the day-to-day ritual performances of a typical devout Catholic family in Antigua Ixtahuacán.

Ixtahuaquense Catholics expressed a number of concerns in unstructured interviews. To gain an understanding of what the local fears were, I had consultants make free lists of the fears they felt most prominently in their lives. From these lists, I designed Likert-scale questions and then asked thirty Catholic Antigua Ixtahuacán villagers to rate their fears and anxieties on a five-point scale from "most fearful" to "least fearful." I decided to include both fears and anxieties about their future and well-being because I found that fears and anxieties had a strong relationship and were quite impossible to disentangle. Moreover, both fears and anxieties are subject to intercession from divine forces. In addition, I explored how Ixtahuaquenses felt their religion protected them from what they feared. From this information I devised structured interviews and recorded the responses.

RESULTS

While people in the village feared supernatural phenomena, such as witchcraft caused by envious rivals, they also worried about their future and about educational opportunities. Table 5.1 ranks the fears and anxieties accumulated from the free lists in the thirty-person Likert-scale survey. Note that in almost every category, women express rather more fear than men; the exceptions are an equal fear regarding alcoholism and witchcraft and men's greater fear of death.

When asked how they received help in dealing with these chaotic forces, the overwhelming majority of people asserted that strict adherence to the ritual practices of the Catholic faith was necessary to receive protection from what they feared. The most common answer to the question of how religion helped them cope with fears was prayer and other rituals that Catholics associate with prayer. Catholics in Ixtahuacán pray just as often publicly as privately. One can easily observe the form of public prayers in the almost daily meetings of Catholic religious devotion held in Charismatic Renewal meetings in members' homes,[3] in the church, at weddings, and at funerals. On a daily basis, I observed the private prayers offered by the family I lived with.

Santa Catarina

To access divine power, Catholic orthopraxy in Ixtahuacán depends on the mediation and intercession of saints with ordinary citizens and of priests with saints. The local patron saint, Santa Catarina, plays many roles in the community. Her name is featured prominently on the sign that announces one's arrival at the community's edge. Catholic Ixtahuaquenses believe she watches over the community. Like many Catholic saints, she forms a part of the spiritual hierarchy and intercedes for local Catholics before God. As one local man put it, "She is the *patrón* here."[4] Many residents made similar comments. Catarina's bright, neon-lit image reigns over the back altar, the most prominent statue in the local Catholic church.

During my fieldwork, Santa Catarina was the only large

TABLE 5.1. AVERAGE FEARS AND ANXIETIES OF CATHOLIC VILLAGERS IN ANTIGUA IXTAHUACÁN

FEAR/ANXIETY	AVERAGE LIKERT SCALE (5-POINT) SCORE		
	All Respondents	Women	Men
1. Alcoholism	4.12	4.12	4.12
2. Education	3.81	4.00	3.61
3. Death	3.70	3.39	4.00
4. Illness	3.60	3.92	3.39
5. Thieves	3.60	4.00	3.33
6. Hunger	3.50	4.00	3.17
7. Earthquakes	3.40	4.08	2.94
8. Travel	3.33	3.42	3.28
9. Harvest	3.23	3.75	2.89
10. The future	3.23	3.58	3.00
11. Envy	3.10	3.73	2.94
12. Evil spirits	3.03	3.83	3.00
13. Work	3.03	3.58	2.67
14. Storms	3.00	3.50	2.67
15. Temptations	2.97	3.50	2.61
16. Ghosts	2.93	3.22	2.50
17. Witchcraft	2.93	2.92	2.94
18. Cutting firewood	2.83	3.42	2.40
19. Old age	2.83	3.00	2.72
20. Money	2.77	3.33	2.39
21. Travel in city	2.63	2.83	2.50

Note: The frame used to elicit responses was "I feel that _____ causes a great deal of fear/anxiety." Responses were coded as follows: 5 = muy de acuerdo (strongly agree), 4 = de acuerdo (agree), 3 = algo de acuerdo (somewhat agree), 2 = en desacuerdo (disagree), 1 = muy en desacuerdo (strongly disagree).

image for Antigua Ixtahuaquenses to pray to because all the other images, including the original old images of Santa Catarina, had been taken to Nueva Ixtahuacán at the relocation of the community in January 2000. The replacement statue was donated by Spanish benefactors. Most mornings, a few local parishioners came to the church and offered money and candles to Santa Catarina. In my brief exchanges with people leaving the church, worshippers remarked that they had come to ask for help with the corn harvest, health problems, or financial difficulties. However, more and more Catholics were turning to charismatic congregations for these needs.

For some, praying to Santa Catarina for help was not as powerful as praying directly to God in charismatic prayer meetings. This was especially the case in seeking healing from sicknesses. The pragmatic nature of the Catholic parishioners allowed them the liberty to try all kinds of methods to ward off sicknesses or receive blessings of better fortune. The same people who prayed to Santa Catarina could be found going to a charismatic leader to ask for healing or to a Maya *ajq'ij* (shaman/healer, a traditionalist religious practitioner, diviner, and guide). These actions were not necessarily considered *awas* (taboo, prohibited), although the leaders of each of these Catholic sectors competitively sought the patronage of attendees at others and condemned the practices of their competitors. Charismatics considered patronage of the traditionalist shamans definitively *awas*, but they allowed prayers to Santa Catarina in the local church. Presumably Santa Catarina was not a significant economic or membership threat to charismatics, whereas the *ajq'ijab'* were, since both charismatics and *ajq'ijab'* provide avenues to healing. The only religious healing that required full-scale conversion, however, was the healing conducted in an Evangelical context (see Jones et al., this volume). In general, the influence of Santa Catarina was fairly neutral to the Catholic factions, and the saint was available to bless and interact with all Catholics in the community.

In addition to sustaining the villagers in the face of immediate needs and concerns, Santa Catarina held particular significance for the students in the community. An older woman remarked that "Santa Catarina is the caretaker of the students and helps them with their studies." Indeed, the church and Santa Catarina afforded Ixtahuaquenses a source of protection and sustenance, a wellspring of power that they could access when needed.

During the move in January 2000, those who chose to relocate to Nueva Ixtahuacán contested the permanent resting place for the saints of the church. In one of their more audacious symbolic acts, the Catholic separatists from Nueva Ixtahuacán removed the massive church bells from the tower piers and took all the precious statues of the saints from the old church, including the colonial statues of Santa Catarina. A legend, widely told in the town, asserts that during another division and migration of the community, 140 years previously, the separatists going to what is now Nahualá had tried to move Santa Catarina's statue from her pedestal and could not, a reflection of her intent to remain in the correct town site. The attempt in 2000 to move her statue, by contrast, succeeded—a sign to the people in Nueva Ixtahuacán that she approved the community's move. Antigua Catholics, however, claimed that she was moved against her will. Indeed, many of those who remained at the original town site had dreams in which Santa Catarina stated variations of "they may have moved me, but I remain here to protect you."

While the significance of Santa Catarina has waned in charismatic congregations, one cannot deny the symbolic importance of Santa Catarina to the Catholic parishioners in general. The donated statue physically and constantly reminds Ixtahuaquenses that they are being protected from the unpredictable forces that prey on humankind.

Corpus Christi

The annual Catholic holiday of Corpus Christi brings Ixtahuaquenses physically together and allows them to symbolize community solidarity. In patently circular feedback, this solidarity helps the people feel the strength of being together as a religious group. How religious symbols empower individuals and groups is, of course, one of the main foci of symbolic analysis in anthropology. In Antigua Ixtahuacán in 2003, Corpus Christi as a celebration lent itself to this empowerment interpretation. During Corpus Christi, Catholics commemorate the Eucharist. By doing so, they remember the importance of attending mass and partaking of communion. During the celebration, the priest and processioners circle the town center (symbolically—and physically as much as topography and the rough cobbled streets allow) with the priest holding high the glass-cased and gold-rayed monstrance (*ostensorium*) that displays the wafer representing the body of Christ: Corpus Christi or simply Corpus. For Catholics around the world, this holiday emphasizes the doctrine of transubstantiation, wherein the bread and the wine become, literally, the flesh and blood of Jesus Christ.

Such was the case in Antigua Ixtahuacán during the celebration I witnessed, with some added cultural elements that one might not find in a Catholic church in the United States.

On Sunday, June 22, 2003, the congregation celebrated Corpus Christi. As on other Sundays, men and women coming to mass in the renovated church filed in as individuals, families, or groups of friends. Older couples tended to sit separately on opposite sides of the chapel, divided by gender; younger families stayed together. The chapel was decorated more than the norm, and pine needles adorned the front of the altar. The people had dressed as usual: the women wore the traditional Maya skirt and blouse, while some men sported traditional clothing and others rather Ladino (western) apparel. The sermon dealt with the doctrine of transubstantiation and how Corpus Christi was designed by the Vatican to eliminate any idea that the bread and wine offered in the communion was symbolic and not literally the blood and flesh of Christ. The priest remarked that while remembering Christ, the people needed to improve their lives. He asked, "What will people think that are not of our religion?" He then described how the church renovation was not yet finished, a hint on how they could serve better. However, the real emphasis was on how the change they needed to make was an inward and not an outward one.

After the sermon, the priest celebrated the Eucharist. Two women took up the bread and wine and followed the priest as he circumambulated the church, swinging the censer as he prayed. As this was done, the congregation gave offerings, which were collected by two older men who used wooden poles to place colorful, indigenously woven offering bags within everyone's reach. Then the priest offered a prayer while the congregation knelt. The priest then knelt as well, held the bread up and blessed it, and then did the same with the wine. He said, "This is the sacrament of our faith." He then invoked the power of the divine by asking not only that the holy bread and water be imbued with power but that the bishop and the pope be blessed as well. Two lines of parishioners formed to receive communion. After all had partaken that were willing and worthy, the padre made the sign of the cross over the congregation and blessed them "in the name of the Father, the Son, and the Holy Ghost."

After the mass, the priest put on more formal garb for the procession: a red and white robe over the thinner white robe he wore during mass. The formal robe, appropriately embroidered with gold for the special occasion, reflected the sacredness of the ritual he was about to perform. Over his shoulders he placed a white scarf with a red cross embroidered on the back. From the altar, the priest picked up a golden cross with the crystal display of the *hostia* (host) prominently in the center. He raised it toward God and displayed it before the audience. As the priest and the *sacristanes* left the church followed by the congregation, the explosions of hundreds of *cohetes*—chains of loud firecrackers—marked the end of mass and the beginning of the procession.

During the procession, four men held up a golden canopy that was attached to wooden poles. The priest, under the canopy, held the golden cross as he walked. Some men rang a bell in front, while the congregation followed behind, singing hymns. One man held up a portable stereo that blared disharmonious trumpets. The procession went around the block that surrounded the main church. At every corner they stopped at a tabernacle placed on green pine needles. There the padre knelt and prayed, blessing the area projecting from that corner, protecting the town and hamlets in that direction from hardships. Through the circumambulation, the prayers thereby blessed the entire municipality. Corpus Christi allows Catholics of Antigua Ixtahuacán to celebrate and remember what it means to be Catholic. The doctrine of the Eucharist unifies them with other Catholics around the world. The ceremonial act of taking the gold cruciform monstrance outside, moving from the protected area of the church into and symbolically around the community, shows the power of symbols to "make sacred" their profane surroundings and protect the congregants from harm (Eliade 1959:21, 30).

Given the difficulties of life for the Catholics of Antigua Ixtahuacán, community ritual was an essential part of their day-to-day survival. The family I stayed with spent about ten hours per week in religious devotions. They perceived benefits from this action. The ritual act of Corpus Christi invoked the power of God, making them feel safe amid the forces of an unpredictable world.

The Cross

Ixtahuaquense Catholics consider the cross one of the most powerful and pervasive of Catholic symbols. Nevertheless, informants seldom mentioned signing the cross as a help in dealing with life's economic anxieties—such as education, money, and work. Catholics felt, however, that signing the cross did have protective powers for dealing with fears regarding supernatural, dangerous, or unpredictable phenomena, such as evil spirits and bus accidents. Crosses could be seen frequently—worn around Catholic necks; emblazoned on, in, or above Catholic churches; and placed above the lintel on the interior side and, less often, on the exterior side of doors that opened Catholic households to the public street or their main courtyard.

Doña María, an elderly woman known for her "traditional" adherence to Catholic practices but not a frequenter of charismatic meetings, discussed some of the ways the cross could be used as a protective symbol: "The cross is very important for me. Not only is it present in the church but also in the roadways. The cross is formed into four paths, and if you are being followed by a ghost or an evil spirit, because of the path of the cross, these spirits will become lost and will not follow, because God is also in the cross. In every cross that has been formed, God is there."

Over the years, indigenous Guatemalans have blended Catholic and Maya beliefs. As a result of this syncretism, the cross has come both to symbolize Christ and the Catholic Church and to represent the four cardinal directions, a sacred symbol in many traditions, including Catholic and classic Maya. In this case, the "four paths" misdirect evil spirits that might be following. "Why do people often place the cross above their door?" I asked doña María.

Many people do this because sometimes they get very scared [se asustan] of ghosts and evil spirits and also curses sent to the family by witches [fantasmas, malos espíritus, y también brujerías enviadas a la familia]. The cross [that is placed on the door] is the same as the ones placed on the pathways around the town. It protects me from everything that's evil.

[I asked,] "Why do you place one around your neck as well?"

You should put a cross around your neck because that is where your heart is. It is a protection for all of the body and the mind.

The cross played other roles also. It marked one as a Catholic; indeed, local Evangelicals do not wear the cross because it so strongly connotes Catholicism. "This might be," one man suggested, "because they [the Evangelicals] do not believe that Christ . . . washed away their sins." He continued: "When a person puts the cross around their neck, it is so that others can see. The other churches do not believe that the Lord Jesus Christ died for our sins.

Maybe they don't believe in that, but when you are Catholic you put it on. And when some Protestant asks you why you put that on, you can tell them, 'I have this because I am Catholic, and my belief said that Jesus Christ cleansed us [nos lavó] of our sins, by the cross.' That is the signification." This remark may seem to have no bearing on the symbol as a means of protection. However, if we read between the lines we can see how the informant believes that the cross marks or sets him apart from outsiders, in this case Protestants, who do not share his beliefs.

We find in these passages another indication of the fear or anxiety inherent in dealing with disorder (Douglas 1966). Things or people that do not fit the categories of an accepted symbol system are dangerous. According to Douglas (1966:97), "if a person has no place in the social system, and is therefore a marginal being, all precaution against danger must come from others." The action of "putting on the cross" makes its wearers holy or set apart compared to someone who does not have the protective advantage of that religious symbol. As Douglas suggests, the act of being holy means separating or protecting oneself from harm or unpredictability. Holiness, then, is a symbolic creation of order out of chaos; it is a way to systematically separate the disharmonious from the harmonious in the world. In Antigua Ixtahuacán, this means protection from the fears and dangers they face.

A young Catholic woman illustrated how the physical presence of the cross protected: "If one places a cross [above one's door], those evils will no longer continue to come here [ya no siguen llegando esos malos]." One creates a holy space by wearing or marking something with a cross, thereby establishing a boundary or barrier against unpredictable spirits. When asked why he placed a cross above his door, a Catholic man reflected: "God is like a shield [como escudo] for the family and the house. Perhaps he will detain evil—evil spirits—from entering in the house. In other words, it is to protect us from the enemy [el enemigo]."

Travel engendered considerable fear, and for good reason. In Guatemalan newspapers, daily pictures of bus wrecks attest to the dangers of travel. More locally, the standard greeting among Mayas who meet on a mountain trail is "Ma tzaqik!" (Don't fall down!), a testament to the slipperiness of ordinary footing and of all of life. A woman averred that making the cross could protect you from harm were there an accident on the road: "When you get on a bus, make the sign of the cross so you do not encounter anything bad on the way. And if there is an accident, the person that makes the sign of the cross will be safe; nothing will happen to them. [The cross] protects against bad things [el mal]."

While the cross serves as a symbol of protection, it also unifies an entire belief system and represents how Catholics view their relationship with God. Salomón, a Catholic man in his thirties, remarked thoughtfully: "The cross represents the love of God. The love of God comes from above [pointing upward] for all of humanity. I know that the cross is directed vertically, right? [using his hands to show the shape of a cross] This is the love of God for the world."

THE FUNCTION OF RELIGIOUS SYMBOLS

The Catholic church in Antigua Ixtahuacán has a multitude of symbols present both in the material culture—religious buildings, necklaces, holy sites—and as ritualized behavior by the members of the congregation in their daily activities, such as signing the cross on their chests, lips, or foreheads at crucial moments of transition (including baptism and passage in front of a church or altar place) or danger (such as movement out of home or town, getting on a bus). Geertz (1973:89) states: "Sacred symbols function to synthesize a people's ethos—the tone, character, and quality of their life, its moral and aesthetic style and mood—and their world view—the picture they have of the way things in sheer actuality are, their most comprehensive ideas of order." Here Geertz emphasizes the role that religion plays in expressing and therefore maintaining a shared order and avoiding chaos. First, by understanding local fears, one gains insight into the pressures that affect the conceptual and physical world in which Antigua Ixtahuacán's Maya Catholics live. Such insight leads the researcher naturally to investigate the methods people employ to deal with their world, including the measures they take to avoid its dangers. Second, by understanding the local survival mechanisms for dealing with dangerous situations, we can begin to construct the local worldview, what Geertz (1973:88) calls people's "conceptions of a general order of existence."

Malinowski (1954:52–53) writes that "religion counteracts the centrifugal forces of fear, dismay, demoralization, and provides the most powerful means of reintegration of the group's shaken solidarity and of the re-establishment of its morale." In Antigua Ixtahuacán, religion indeed promoted solidarity and helped ameliorate fears

in the minds of its practitioners, although new politico-economic forces and associated new religions had made that solidarity much less communitarian than in the past. However, orthopraxy among Catholics in Antigua Ixtahuacán remained paramount as the political economy of the community was dependent on the local Catholic church as a source of international funding and a basis for community solidarity. By utilizing and interpreting the various symbols the Catholic church provided, residents of Antigua Santa Catarina Ixtahuacán created a support system to which they turned during times of uncertainty, especially during the rough period of community split and upheaval.

Mary Douglas's work helps us put the Ixtahuaquense experience in perspective. She examines how religious symbols, especially the rituals inspired by those symbols, counteract unpredictability and enforce order. By understanding the elements of disorder, she asserts, we can comprehend what people view order to be. She says of disorder that it provides material for new patterns: "We recognize that it [disorder] is destructive to existing patterns; and also that it has potentiality. It symbolizes both danger and power" (Douglas 1966:94). Ixtahuaquenses in 2003 frequently manifested key Catholic symbols in their everyday activities because of the multiple dangers they faced and the ever-present disorder that threatened to disrupt their lives. The persistent presence of danger and disorder inspired fear and worry among my consultants and was the motivation behind the Catholic Ixtahuaquenses' dogmatic adherence to the Catholic faith. As Douglas puts it, "ritual recognizes the potency of disorder" (94). In Antigua Ixtahuacán, Catholics affirmed the existence of hurtful disorder each time they invoked the protective symbols of their faith. The disorder prominent in their lives fostered the repetition of rituals and symbols that acknowledged and repelled the chaotic elements.

Part of that creation of order entails simplification. Crapo (2003:49, summarizing Horton 1967:50–52) suggests that "religious thought . . . is an effort to reduce the complexity of the world around us to a simpler system of comprehensible ideas, much as scientists attempt to reduce the world's complexity to a few simple laws." One such simplification involves compacting the multiple sources of chaos and danger into a single symbol, what Ixtahuaquenses call "the enemy" or "the devil." Ixtahuaquenses believe that religious ritual wards off evil; it is there "to protect us from the enemy." This enemy is the devil; indeed, Ixtahuaquenses believe that the evil or chaos they experience comes from the devil. A resident reflected on the impact of Hurricane Mitch on the area: "I don't think that these things can come from God. They must come from the devil."

CONCLUSION

In Antigua Santa Catarina Ixtahuacán in 2003, the powers inherent in Santa Catarina, Corpus Christi, and the Catholic cross—and the symbolic performances that connected people to those powers, protected people from dangers they believed to be real. They provided a space where predictable order could be established. Catholic residents in Antigua Ixtahuacán relied heavily on these symbols not only to provide them with a sense of unity, but also to ensure their survival. As Geertz (1973:99) attests: "Man depends so much upon symbols and symbol systems with a dependence so great as to be decisive for his creatural viability and, as a result, his sensitivity to even the remotest indication that he may not be able to cope with one or another aspect of experience raises within him the greatest source of anxiety."

For the Catholic residents of Antigua Ixtahuacán, the aforementioned religious symbols gave them sacred spaces wherein they could find refuge from the profane, the dangerous, and the unpredictable. The symbols marked a place where divine influence could be made manifest. Eliade (1959:21, 30) asserts that divine presence sets apart the inconsistent spaces of sacred, meaningful order and profane, confusing disorder:

> For religious man, space is not homogenous; he experiences interruptions, breaks in it, some parts of space are qualitatively different from others. . . . There is then, a sacred space, and hence a strong, significant space; there are other spaces that are not sacred and so are without structure or consistency, amorphous. . . . The sacred reveals absolute reality and at the same time makes orientation possible; hence it founds the world in the sense that it fixes the limits and establishes the order of the world.

In a world that seems to be in a constant state of political and economic disruption, the Catholic church and its symbols serve for the residents of Antigua Ixtahuacán as a consistent reminder of the people's belief that God is aware of them and concerned with protecting them from harm. These symbols also represent the very real political and economic stability that the Catholic church provides for a community experiencing a chaotic transition. I would argue further that religious symbolism and its rituals act as a bridge, connecting people to people, and people to their world, through the embodiment of their worldview in instantiated ritual acts. Thus, as Durkheim (2001[1912]:11) suggests, humans "owe to religion not only a good part of their knowledge but also the form in which this knowledge is elaborated."

NOTES

1. My fieldwork was conducted in 2003.

2. W. R. Smith (1977:115) recorded a similar concern about documents when his informant offered as an affirmation of his bravery that he was not even afraid to go to a government office. When you are functionally illiterate in a klepto-state, the fear and uncertainty of signing a document remain palpable and merit the protections of the sign of the cross.

3. Members were reluctant to distinguish themselves as being either charismatic or non-charismatic. Consequently, I do not make the distinction in this chapter.

4. The word *patrón* has connotations not readily available in English. A *patrón* is one's boss, employer, protector, political caudillo, benefactor, defender, and, often, landlord. Above all, a *patrón* is one's status superior. One can access the *patrón* to one's advantage through these relations provided one tenders homage, respect, labor, and political partisanship in the *patrón*'s favor. Often this is done by lower-status people asking the *patrón* to be the godparent of their child.

Chapter Six

The Unfinished Church

Accommodation and Resistance as Catholic Responses to the Declining Social Significance of Ortho-Catholicism as the Axial Religion of Nueva Santa Catarina Ixtahuacán

BENJAMIN PRATT, JOHN P. HAWKINS, AND WALTER RANDOLPH ADAMS

AS I ENTERED NUEVA SANTA Catarina Ixtahuacán (more commonly called Nueva Ixtahuacán) for the first time in May 2003, the beauty of both the town and its surroundings astonished me. Set in an elevated valley, the town seemed idyllic. Well-paved streets created a precise grid system. White cement houses perched on neatly platted properties. In the town's center stood the staples of all Guatemalan towns: the municipal building, a park, and a magnificent Catholic church. It was not until I got closer to the town center that I noticed something remarkable about this church building. While the sculpted and plastered façade of the church towered majestically over the buildings below, the other three walls were no more than ten feet high, unfinished and not yet connected to each other or the façade. They supported no roof and surrounded an unused, floorless space that had grown to weeds (figure 6.1).

Every few days during that summer, five to ten workers labored on various parts of the church building. I asked one of the local members of the Catholic church why construction on the edifice moved so slowly. He told me that the church did not have enough money or volunteer support to engage in full-time construction. As I would later find out, the unfinished church was a stark symbol of the status of Catholicism in Nueva Ixtahuacán. While Catholicism remains the most influential religion in the region, it has lost much of the social influence it once possessed.

Two weeks after arriving in Nueva Ixtahuacán, I spoke with Juan, one of the teachers at the local school. During our conversation, Juan suggested that I study the changes that had occurred in Catholicism over the previous twenty years. When I asked him what he meant, Juan explained, "Twenty years ago, people used to identify themselves by their religion. Not only was everybody in the town Catholic, but the town was Catholic." He continued, "People would come from all over the municipality to celebrate Catholic festivals. Everybody went to mass and rosary, and one or the other of those meetings took place almost every day of the week." Now, the Catholic priest who traveled to Nueva Ixtahuacán once a week to hold mass did so in a small cinderblock building with a tin roof that stood on the corner of the Catholic church's property in Nueva Ixtahuacán. Rosaries occurred less frequently than mass. Juan exemplified this shift in practice. While he attended mass and Catholic festivals as a child, and still claimed to be Catholic, he no longer participated in any Catholic rituals or ceremonies. His parents and siblings had joined a nearby Evangelical church, and Juan focused almost exclusively on his family and on teaching in the local school.

Juan had perceptively observed a shift in the religious practices of his town, a shift much remarked in academic theory and research. Sociologist Peter Berger describes this change in terms of economic theory. Using the metaphor of society as a religious marketplace, Berger (1990[1967]) explains that in monopolistic religious marketplaces, that is, in societies in which only one religion is available, people share a common weltanschauung, their concept of the world and the place of humanity in it (see also Chesnut 2003b). In contrast, in societies with multiple religions competing for parishioners, often referred to in the literature as pluralistic religious marketplaces, people do not share a single weltanschauung. Therefore, successful religions in competitive religious marketplaces,

Figure 6.1. The unfinished Catholic church in Nueva Ixtahuacán. Courtesy of John P. Hawkins, 2006.

as Chesnut (2003a:12) puts it, "tailor their production and marketing of religious goods to the exigencies of private life" (see also Berger 1990[1967]:147 for public-private distinction). In essence, societies that shift from a monopolistic to a pluralistic religious marketplace, also described as a shift from public religion to private religion by Calder (2001) and Chesnut (2003a:12), tend to lose that commonly held worldview. Moreover, secularizing forces, such as mass literacy, communication, and mobility, work in tandem with religious pluralism to intensify the social implausibility of the dominant or monopolizing religion of a region, consequently chipping away at the weltanschauung of the community (Berger 1990[1967]). Berger (1990[1967]:133–134) summarizes the cultural result: "Private religiosity, however 'real' it may be to the individuals who adopt it, cannot any longer fulfill the classical task of religion, that of constructing a common world within which all of social life receives ultimate meaning binding on everybody." Such a profound loss affects all participants of the originally monopolistic religious society.

In this chapter, I argue that mainstream Roman Catholicism no longer possesses the social significance and influence of an axial religion—a religion that organizes and underlies the social life and cultural ideology of a people—that it once held in this Maya village in the Guatemalan highlands. Thanks to religious pluralism and secularizing factors that more fully connect Nueva Ixtahuacán with the outside world, the decline in the social and cultural centrality of Ortho-Catholicism in Nueva Ixtahuacán mirrors the decline occurring throughout Guatemala.

Catholicism's social decline in Nueva Ixtahuacán elicits divergent responses from Catholic parishioners. While most Catholics have made ideological and social adjustments to accommodate the changing identity of their town, many charismatic Catholics resist social changes through rigorous adherence to tenets that facilitate their interaction with people in their own congregational community while distancing them from Catholic parishioners not involved in the charismatic movement.

Parishioners' differing reactions to Catholicism's declining influence in Nueva Ixtahuacán demonstrate potential dangers in attempting to understand significant social change through any one theoretical perspective. While many Catholics endorsed Juan's views on the social decline of Catholicism in the town, Catholics involved in the charismatic movement unknowingly diverged from Berger's (1990[1967]) theory that religion loses power and plausibility in a pluralistic religious marketplace. The responses of those participating in Nueva Ixtahuacán's charismatic movement more accurately reflect Stark's (1998) theory, which notes that competing religious worldviews typically drive innovation and increase the influence of religion on the public and private lives of believers. Despite their obvious differences, both Berger and Stark help us interpret the different Catholic responses to the decline of the social significance of their religion. That said, we should be cautious regarding any attempt to understand human religious response through singular theories constructed within and as a result of "western" experience. What should we then highlight regarding the Ortho-Catholic and charismatic Catholic practices and relationships to each other and to the Protestant Pentecostalism in this region?

THE CHARISMATIC MOVEMENT: A PREFERENTIAL OPTION FOR THE CATHOLIC GUATEMALAN

While Evangelical Protestant growth in Guatemala has been pronounced, the rise of charismatic Catholicism has been meteoric, leading Chesnut (2003b) to imply that the charismatic movement is the reason that the Catholic Church still maintains any prominence in Latin America. The Catholic Charismatic Renewal (CCR), which started in the United States in 1967, was exported to Guatemala during the early 1970s (Chesnut 2003b). The CCR mirrors the Evangelical worship experience because both consciously and unconsciously CCR members and leaders try to emulate their Pentecostal practices. Charismatic *cultos* occur more regularly than mass, and charismatic Catholics hold these meetings in smaller, more intimate settings, like the house of a member of the congregation or a small, plain cinderblock room built for worship. In Nueva Ixtahuacán, charismatic *cultos*, like those of Evangelicals, are held in the K'iche' language, as opposed to Ortho-Catholic mass, which is offered in Spanish. Charismatic worship seeks to connect with spiritual gifts, such as healing and glossolalia (Chesnut 2003b). Also,

charismatic meetings are dynamic and exciting; often involving energetic music, many even employ a live band like the Evangelical churches. In many ways, charismatic Catholicism gives parishioners the Evangelical experience without requiring them to leave the comforts, community, and identity long provided by Catholicism.

Aside from offering Catholic parishioners exciting and ecstatic worship opportunities, charismatic participation also gives Catholics the opportunity to tighten their ties to a religious community that for years had been becoming loose-knit and neglectful. Specific charismatic proscriptions serve to reinforce solidarity among the congregation, often at the expense of their connection to the greater community. Close communities also reinforce prohibitions on alcohol and infidelity, which is a major selling point among Guatemalans looking to change their lives (Chesnut 1997).

Thus, the charismatic movement represents Catholicism's move to become a "more aggressive and effective competitor" in Guatemala's religious marketplace (Garrard-Burnett 2008:84). Unsurprisingly, the Catholic Charismatic Renewal has been credited with slowing the exodus of Catholics to other faiths (Melendez 1992; Chesnut 2003b). According to surveys, 60 percent of Guatemalan Catholics classify themselves as part of the charismatic movement (Garrard-Burnett 2008). As of 2003, Nueva Ixtahuacán had five charismatic *comunidades* (religious communities), each in a different canton of the town. While each *comunidad* had only about 25–50 practicing members, charismatic Catholics comprised more than 90 percent of the 150 parishioners that regularly attended mass. The charismatic movement's widespread success shows the volatility of the religious marketplace in Guatemala. It also confirms the idea that Guatemalan Catholicism is actively competing to become a "preferential option for the spirit" (Chesnut 2003b:55), as well as a preferential option of the poor.

SECULARIZATION, THE RELIGIOUS MARKETPLACE, AND SOCIAL IDENTITY IN NUEVA IXTAHUACÁN

Small Maya *municipios* like Nueva Ixtahuacán thrived in relative isolation for generations, insulated in the western highlands of Guatemala by high mountains and late to receive minimal infrastructural amenities, such as electricity and paved roads. However, since the 1960s, advancements in state-supplied literacy, communication, and mobility have increasingly linked the western highlands to the rest of Guatemala and to the world. These connections, intensified by the relocation of Nueva Ixtahuacán in 2000 to the side of the Pan-American Highway, have dramatically enhanced religious plurality in the town and have fostered a decidedly public and competitive religious marketplace. Consequently, literacy, communication, and mobility bear the brunt of Ixtahuaquenses' blame for Catholicism's dwindling influence in Nueva Ixtahuacán.

Many Nueva Ixtahuaquenses also embrace education as a top explanation for the religious change. When Nueva Ixtahuacán was created, its location at a mountaintop saddle was ill suited for farming. It was both too cold and too high in elevation for ordinary corn, and it was highly constricted—hedged to the north and west by Totonicapán and to the south and east by prior squatter claims of Nahualenses. The new municipal headquarters town stood as a small island cut off from its former agricultural land base. Consequently, many in town pursued nonagrarian work. They sent their children to high school to get ready for such work, which helped the local Instituto Paraíso Maya to flourish. Started in 1993, the Paraíso Maya abandoned its original building, now derelict near Antigua Ixtahuacán, and relocated to Nueva Ixtahuacán in 2000. It has thrived in the new setting (figure 6.2). While the Instituto Paraíso Maya is considered a public school, it receives funding from international entities, which provide resources that help it rival schools in larger Maya towns, such as nearby Nahualá. In a survey administered to sixty Ixtahuaquenses, about 50 percent indicated that their children's education was more important to them than participation in church. Each religious group in Nueva Ixtahuacán was represented in the survey, and Catholicism had the highest percentage of those placing a higher priority on school, with about 75 percent of surveyed Catholics giving primacy to education over religion.

Though highly supportive of education, some Catholics expressed concerns over what their children learn in school. Three teachers from Nueva Ixtahuacán independently identified a trend they had noticed in their classes. As one teacher put it, "Many people in Nueva Ixtahuacán have the idea that technology can solve problems that could previously only be solved by God. . . . Since technology is moving at a faster rate than ever, belief in God is dropping at an equal rate." This Ixtahuaquense teacher validated Leslie White's (1959) theory that increasing technological control invariably leads to a contraction in things understood primarily in religious terms.[1]

The townspeople with whom I spoke indicated that science has had a particularly deleterious effect on Catholicism in Nueva Ixtahuacán. Catholic schoolteachers in particular indicated that evolution is the most spiritually dangerous subject taught in school. "Evolution," according to Juan, "teaches us that we came from monkeys and that we were not created by God, like the Bible says." Similarly, human cloning touched a nerve among some Ixtahuaquenses. Miguel, a schoolteacher and farmer in Nueva Ixtahuacán, stated that "human cloning takes part of the miracle out of the procreating process and fosters belief in science instead of God." Despite these concerns, none of the teachers felt it necessary to discontinue scientific study in order to preserve religious beliefs.

During my stay in Ixtahuacán, Nueva Ixtahuaquenses celebrated the Instituto Paraíso Maya's tenth anniversary. During the three days of celebration, influential townspeople gave inspiring speeches about the progress and advancement that the school had brought. Huge numbers of Ixtahuaquenses participated in the celebrations, clearly the most well-attended event during my fieldwork. For the event, the school hired a neotraditionalist shaman who, though young, dressed in the older male indigenous style (except for lace-up hiking boots) that was now worn only by one or two geriatric men. Seeing events such as these, some Ixtahuaquenses surmise that Catholicism's influence in Nueva Ixtahuacán is shrinking as technological and literacy advancements become increasingly important.

Technological advancements, made possible by education and infrastructure, have hastened Ixtahuaquenses' ability to communicate with one another and participate in national and international networks. When the government began to build Nueva Ixtahuacán's infrastructure starting in late 2000, it created roads, buildings, sewers, and water and electrical distribution systems. These have enriched the lives of Ixtahuaquenses. But these "advancements" have also proved detrimental to the collective religious experience of those in Nueva Ixtahuacán, as Ixtahuaquenses have used electronically amplified sound systems to skirt the culturally expected face-to-face etiquette of politeness and respect. Just as is still done via the culturally understood and feared sorcery systems they call k'oqob'al, they can attack, impersonally, other faiths and their neighbors who belong to those faiths via broadcasts

Figure 6.2. The Paraíso Maya high school in Nueva Ixtahuacán. Courtesy of John P. Hawkins, 2006.

from speakers and radio towers. They can do so with no apparent human contact and thus no shame or restraint, which would exist at the moment of a face-to-face insult.

Radio broadcast is the most common form of media-based communication in Nueva Ixtahuacán. Though only about 3,000 people live in Nueva Ixtahuacán, it has its own radio station. From dawn to dusk, one can hear radio receivers playing in all parts of town. Women listen to programs while cooking, men listen while they work outside, and children memorize the catchy radio commercials, often repeating or singing them even after the radio has been turned off. Religious radio programs ply the airwaves more regularly than any other form of radio show.

While religious radio programs undoubtedly enhance the influence of religion on daily life for some, they are a point of disturbance and contention for others. While I

understood little of the religious programs I heard on the radio, since they were mostly in K'iche', various townspeople indicated that Evangelical programs largely outnumbered Catholic radio programs. Catholic Ixtahuaquenses decried the Evangelical radio shows, explaining that they spread anti-Catholic opinions and even speaking directly of the "evils of Catholicism."

The tone of the negative messages I heard over the airwaves contradicts the otherwise polite and mannered mode of communication employed between people when they interact directly in Nueva Ixtahuacán. As with other Maya cultures, an Ixtahuaquense shows respect to others by speaking softly and by avoiding eye contact with the recipient of the message, lest the listener think that the speaker is trying to assert dominance over him or her. While interpersonal disagreements invariably occur, they are typically handled in private, sometimes by secretive witchcraft, and it is rare to hear an Ixtahuaquense shout. The anti-Catholic sentiment proclaimed across the airwaves contrasts sharply with this expected decorum and alarms Catholic parishioners in Nueva Ixtahuacán. According to them, these acerbic radio messages have already caused many Catholics in Nueva Ixtahuacán to leave Catholicism. While a few of the Ixtahuaquenses that leave Catholicism later join the Evangelical movement, many become disenchanted with organized religion in any form and refuse to patronize any faith, though they typically still claim association with the Catholic Church.

While not as prevalent as radio, television has played a major role in the secularization of Nueva Ixtahuacán. When I asked a few of the schoolteachers who reside in Nueva Ixtahuacán why they felt television had altered the role of Catholicism in their town, they invariably pointed to science and science fiction programs as the main culprits. One man explained, "Science programs teach us to believe in science instead of believing in God. Science fiction makes us think that things are real which are not. It affects our belief in God." The threat of science to religion and the displacement of religion by science perceived by these Ixtahuaquense Mayas evokes Durkheim (2001[1912]:326): religion finds itself "countered by a rival power," science, "that, born from" religion "submits" religion "henceforth to its criticism and control."

Among men, television combines with *fútbol* (soccer) to undermine Catholic ritual. Ixtahuaquense men, like other male Guatemalans, border on full-fledged fanaticism in their passion for *fútbol*. In the *municipio* (the town's administrative center and the surrounding lands that belong to it) of Ixtahuacán alone, at least fifteen soccer teams play every Sunday. Each local team bears the name of some professional team from Europe or South America. Though televisions are quite sparse in town, televised national and international soccer games draw huge audiences in Nueva Ixtahuacán. Extended families congregate by the few televisions and watch the games to the bitter end. With a few rare exceptions, televised games and town games occur on Sunday. Therefore, Catholics who are also soccer fans face a trilemma: do they participate in Catholic religious ceremony, or watch the big game, or play in the village match? Many young Ixtahuaquenses find both watching and playing soccer much more appealing than being at mass.

Though not mentioned as frequently, some Catholics think that the explicit sexual content of television undermines Catholicism in Nueva Ixtahuacán. A few of my close Ixtahuaquense acquaintances told me that television is sexually desensitizing the children of the town. Native Ixtahuaquenses never really gave a reason for why this is such a detriment to religion. However, I soon realized that sexual forwardness and disrespect go against the Ixtahuaquenses' long-standing civic and religious values, including respect. Though none of the local church officials expressed to me their church's stance on human sexuality, and common-law unions prevailed, one of the core religious values of the town is sexual fidelity and chastity for youth.[2] Indeed, until the 1980s, most young men had little opportunity to mix with young women, and in K'iche', to have "talked" with someone of the opposite sex is a euphemism for having had sex with them. Though not a huge threat as of yet, many Ixtahuaquenses foresee future problems in children learning too much about sex at what they deem to be too young an age. The scantily clad women on television and in Nueva Ixtahuacán's festival dance hall during town celebrations in no way mirror the well-covered women of Nueva Ixtahuacán, who still wear the home-woven brocades that thickly drape their body from the base of the neck to elbows to ankles.

According to some Ixtahuaquenses, movie theaters pose a larger threat to the hegemony of Roman Catholicism in Nueva Ixtahuacán than any other modern invention. I found this interesting, since the nearest formal movie theater is in Quetzaltenango, an hour by bus southwest of Nueva Ixtahuacán. These Ixtahuaquenses claim that access to on-screen pornography in distant movie houses and violence on local DVD-fed screens in homes and video parlors corrupts their youths.

A few Ixtahuaquenses identified the "I don't have to fear anybody" attitude portrayed insistently on the silver screen (and on television) as problematic. This attitude, they say, is not conducive to a good Catholic life, for a "good Catholic" fears and respects God. The movies, they hold, teach one to fear nothing. As Catholic youths lose their fear of God, the Catholic Church loses the power it could have had—had it held onto the younger generation of Nueva Ixtahuacán.

The robust infrastructure provided by the government when Nueva Ixtahuacán was created gave Ixtahuaquenses unprecedented access to electricity. Each government-funded house has electric light sockets that can be tapped for other uses. Electricity fuels the religious battle for the airwaves in Nueva Ixtahuacán. During *cultos*, local pastoral leaders of both Evangelical and charismatic congregations use microphones to preach their spiritual messages not only to the twenty to forty or even a hundred members present in their congregation but across the valley to all those within earshot of the powerful amplifiers and huge speakers in the chapels and mounted on rooftops. During non-meeting hours, the same systems play CDs of bands belting out upbeat religious music, known in Nueva Ixtahuacán as *cantos*. One Sunday evening at dusk, as I walked across the soccer field 300 meters south of the center of town, I could hear six churches simultaneously competing for auditory supremacy from different points across the valley. The reasons for amplifying the religious meetings became clearer. In a competitive religious marketplace, powerful outdoor electronic speakers attract more attention and reach a larger market share than an unamplified voice, no matter how powerful its message. From the homes of leaders or from the church buildings the local congregations built, both charismatic and Pentecostal congregations sought continuously to dominate the aural attention of all. Many played tapes or CDs of songs or sermons congenial to their perspective from early morning to late evening throughout the week.

Here is one example of a Pentecostal congregation's leaders using public address equipment to circumvent communicative etiquette. One evening during dinner with my host Catholic family, we all ate and conversed while the sermon of a nearby Evangelical *culto* invaded the walls of the kitchen and assaulted our ears. The leader, a friend of my host, preached a fiery sermon in K'iche', comparable in tone to any American televangelist. As we chatted, a sudden awkwardness filled the room. All members of my family sat in silence. Reading my puzzled expression, the father explained that the preacher had just publicly condemned and demeaned my host family over the rooftop speakers for their decision to remain Catholic. While this preacher would never condemn my hosts in a personal conversation, his amplified sermons freed him to criticize others beyond the community's cultural constraints, without serious concern for social norms. Though my host family seemed largely unaffected by this public rebuke, most individuals I interviewed told me of at least one or two families that had stopped practicing Catholicism after enduring public insults like this one.

The internet plays an increasingly vital role in the transmission of thoughts and ideas in Nueva Ixtahuacán. In June 2003, the town officially gained internet access via two computers in the Instituto Paraíso Maya computer lab. These computers were open for rental after school hours. Two of the local schoolteachers explained their concerns about the ways in which internet use might undermine religion in general, and Catholicism in particular. One teacher stated, "Since anybody can put anything on the internet, a lot of false information is being passed off as truth." He further explained, "In the future, as townspeople and especially youth increasingly interact with the internet, they will start believing anything that they find on it, including material that is against religion and God." Though the argument may seem superficial, a closer look at K'iche' etymology demonstrates its merits. In one paper, Kristine Whipple (2006) perceptively notes that in the K'iche' language, the word for "truth" is *tzij*, which literally means "word[s]." The internet, as words written, thus constitutes a form of accessible secularization because as *tzij*, it is a source of truth, whereas formerly truth in the form of written words came solely from the Catholic Church, a government office, or a court.

Increased mobility in the western highlands, which has played a vital role in opening Ixtahuacán to the rest of Guatemala, parallels electronic media in its effects. Getting on a bus that transports one to a formerly inaccessible experience seems rather like a robust media experience. The Pan-American Highway, completed between Guatemala City and Quetzaltenango during the 1960s, connects the western highlands to Guatemala City and to other major urban areas throughout western Guatemala. Commercial buses quickly populated the new highway, allowing those living in Maya Guatemala to make purchases and work outside of the western highlands. However, despite the new highway, pre-split Santa Catarina Ixtahuacán maintained some insulation from the rest of the country due to the amount of time it takes to get from the Antigua Ixtahuacán center to the highway. Though only nine kilometers in length, the dirt road that links Ixtahuacán to the Pan-American Highway winds along a relatively steep grade and requires about a thirty-minute drive. The relocation thus had an especially profound effect on Ixtahuaquenses' access to travel. Nueva Ixtahuacán sits about 600 meters by flat, paved road from the Pan-American Highway, making travel far easier for those in Nueva Ixtahuacán than those who remain in Antigua Ixtahuacán. Reliable and efficient transportation allows men looking for work to broaden their search to several relatively large urban or tourist areas offering employment. They can thus work for wages without moving their families away from extended family and friends in Nueva Ixtahuacán.

Many Ixtahuaquense men now spend one to four weeks at a time working in large urban areas, such as

Quetzaltenango, Sololá, or Guatemala City. Due to the relatively high cost of bus fare (Q20, which is equal to US$2.50 and is about half a peasant's average daily pay), men working near or beyond the capital only return home once or twice per month. Their families feel their absence, and Ixtahuaquenses acknowledge that many of the young men in town have stopped going to church and started participating in dangerous activities. Their mothers disapprove but feel unable to stop them. The Catholic church also feels the absence of these men. The parish advisory group, composed only of men, has been undermined by the lack of capable participating men. Noticeably more women than men attend Catholic religious gatherings, and one cannot help but attribute some of the gender inequity to the number of men working far from home.

In the spirit of modernization, Nueva Ixtahuaquenses have invested heavily in the "mass literacy, mass communication, and mass mobility" of which Berger (1990[1967]:169) speaks. These have accelerated the pace and spread of secularization in Ixtahuaquense society and affected the axial status Roman Catholicism enjoyed in the 1950s–1970s. At the same time, these modalities of communication and connection have given other religious movements a chance to develop in the region. As predicted by Berger (1990[1967]:135), this aspect of secularization has facilitated the spread of new religious thoughts and ideas in Nueva Ixtahuacán, creating a dynamic and pluralistic religious marketplace where Ortho-Catholicism previously dominated. This shift has hastened the end of the primarily Catholic-based weltanschauung among Ixtahuaquenses.

Every Catholic I met in Ixtahuacán expressed some degree of concern about the social decline of Catholicism in their town. When religion loses its centrality and becomes a mere compartment in society rather than society's axis, believers in the once-central axis often experience a great deal of cognitive and emotional dissonance (Crapo 2003:263).

Parishioners who have stayed Catholic have responded in many ways to the decline in the centrality of Catholicism in their town. Most Catholic responses can be generally classified under two basic but polarized categories: accommodation and resistance. The majority of Catholic Ixtahuaquenses have used accommodation in their lives and religion to form an evolving relationship with the secularization of society. Many Catholics, however, have resisted the new religious and social identity through religious proscriptions and practices embodied in the Charismatic Renewal.

Accommodation

I spent one particularly cold morning during the summer of 2003 talking with the custodian-guards of the Catholic church's interim building in Nueva Ixtahuacán. When our conversation turned to soccer, I reflected on the fact that the local soccer team played the majority of its games on Sundays during the same time period that the priest celebrated the only session of mass held each week. Knowing that many of those soccer players were Catholic, I asked the men what happens when a practicing Catholic also happens to play soccer on the local team. Both men seemed perplexed. Finally, one answered, "Well, he plays soccer." I persisted. "But what if that Catholic soccer player wants to attend mass?" "Well," one custodian-guard answered, "then he goes to church." From the reaction I received, I could tell that both men seemed surprised that I was not grasping the logic in their responses. When I asked about the possible time conflicts between soccer games and Sunday mass, the men's faces beamed with clarity. "There are no conflicts," responded one with a triumphant grin, "because the people that go to the soccer games go to the soccer games, and the people that go to mass go to mass."

Other than reminding me of the importance of asking culturally competent questions, my conversation with the custodian-guards put words to a general feeling that permeated the town at that time: religious and secular activities increasingly constituted separate, incommensurate, unmixed compartments. Moreover, a number of this chapter's quotes from Ixtahuaquenses, all ordinary Catholics, suggest an ambivalence regarding the process of secularization in Ixtahuacán. On one hand, they appreciate and extol the advancements that have improved their quality of life, literacy, and the ease with which they can perform their daily duties and recreate. On the other, they lament the effects of secularization, particularly on the religious identity and shared worldview that have now been lost.

During mass one week, the priest, a Kaqchikel-speaking Maya from Sololá, chided church members for not arriving on time. He reminded them that he had changed the starting time for mass from 9 a.m. to 8 a.m. to accommodate shopping in the market after mass, thus appeasing the indigenous women who needed to make morning purchases at the market to supply their household for a week. However, the priest indicated that he would change mass back to 9 a.m. if people did not start coming on time. After mass, I walked across town to interview a local schoolteacher named José with the priest's announcement about mass and its implications still occupying my mind.

José, a young and dynamic teacher at Paraíso Maya, typified the ambivalence felt by many Catholics dealing with the social decline of Catholicism in Nueva Ixtahuacán. I mentioned the priest's announcement and asked José about the changes he had noticed in the *municipio* during his lifetime. While excitedly describing the way in which Nueva Ixtahuacán had embraced education and modernity, José also conceded that modernity seemed to be making Catholicism less relevant in day-to-day life, as exemplified by the priest's necessity to change the mass schedule to accommodate Nueva Ixtahuacán's otherwise unremarkable marketplace. When I asked about the future of Catholics in Nueva Ixtahuacán, José responded with surprising optimism: "When the Spanish came, our ancestors did what they could to adapt to the changes that were present and survive. As this [modernization] continues, we will adapt to it and survive as well."

José's reference to colonial Mayas struck me as especially ironic and telling. During the early conquest of Guatemala, the Mayas were coerced into the Catholic religion. While many Mayas formally worshipped as Catholics, they worshipped on their own terms. They often made Catholic saints symbolic of Maya deities, which allowed Mayas to worship in their traditional style while appearing to be Catholic. Though this practice ignited an inquisition in Guatemala (Chuchiak 2005), traditionalized worship was never fully eradicated from Catholicism among the Mayas. On more than one occasion, I learned of healing rituals being performed by Catholic traditionalist leaders in Nueva Ixtahuacán. Their procedures more closely approximated traditional Maya religion than anything in mainstream Christianity.

Initially, I thought José was basing the future success of Catholicism on the attempts made by the Spanish to convert the Mayas to Catholicism, and the manner in which the colonial Mayas remade Catholicism to suit their own needs and the "larger conceptual world" (Fischer and Hendrickson 2003:95). However, as our conversation continued, it became clear that José's optimism was actually based on the continued ability of Maya culture in Nueva Ixtahuacán to both adapt and withstand identity change. His comments indicated that for José and many other progressive Catholic Ixtahuaquenses, the preservation of Maya identity means more than simply preserving Mayas' Catholic identity. It means creating a Maya Catholic identity compatible with the globalized world rapidly emerging around them, difficult and conflicted though that task may be. Thus, for a long time, survival for Ixtahuaquenses has consisted in taking what they are given and making it their own. That, by definition, is accommodation (Morgan 2005:61–62).

Resistance

While the majority of Ixtahuaquense Catholics ambivalently accommodate the social decline of Catholicism in their community by changing their practices and expectations and by compartmentalizing, charismatic Catholics insulate themselves against secularizing forces through specific religious practices, such as prohibitions, frequent worship services, and services held in K'iche'. Some charismatic Catholics further insulate themselves from secularization through a conscious rejection of modern amenities. Through these specific practices, charismatic Catholics succeed in ideologically separating from the larger society, creating spiritual mini-communities in the process. Charismatic resistance against secularization exemplifies Stark's (1998) theory that pluralistic religious marketplaces can revitalize religiosity among religious congregations. As Stark (1998:197) almost peevishly remarked, "By now it probably is no surprise that competition stimulates Catholic commitment."

Adherence to specific prohibitions separates the charismatic Catholic from the traditional Catholic in the western highlands of Maya Guatemala. The most obvious prohibitions are on alcohol, dancing, parties, and even marimba music. Though alcoholism in Nueva Ixtahuacán seems less common than in most areas of Guatemala, it is considered one of the most dangerous plagues. Conversion stories of *catequistas* (those who lead charismatic *comunidades*) and parishioners praise their participation in the charismatic movement as essential in their own sobriety or the sobriety of a loved one. The prohibition on alcohol consumption is universal across the five charismatic congregations in Nueva Ixtahuacán.

Since alcohol had long been associated with both religious and nonreligious celebrations in town, in 2003 most charismatic *comunidades* in Nueva Ixtahuacán also prohibited attending town celebrations. Charismatic Catholic responses to these celebrations varied by *comunidad* and ranged from full support to boycott. Some of the more "modernized" *comunidades* had little to no prohibitions on celebrations, while more "traditional" *comunidades* prohibited their members attending even the most venerable of Catholic processions and celebrations.

Given that dances were organized only during celebrations, charismatic prohibitions on dancing, both masked and not masked, seem logical enough. Charismatic adherents' compliance with these prohibitions, however, varied by generation: youths were frequently noncompliant regarding the nonmasked dances, which played pop music and offered the opportunity to gyrate near a member of the opposite sex. At one point, a famous merengue band came to Ixtahuacán and played at a community celebration. Ixtahuaquenses filled the community hall, though most stood or sat around the perimeter of the dance floor. Some stared quietly. Others wore disdain on their faces. For the first two hours of the concert, only a handful of Ixtahuaquenses, all quite drunk, danced. However, as the evening continued, sober individuals casually joined the dancing until by the end of the evening about forty to sixty people were dancing, most of whom were fully sober. When I commented to the son of my host family that his mother, a charismatic Catholic, had taught me that *are awas ri xajoj* (dancing is prohibited), he forcefully stated that dancing is *not* prohibited. The fervor in his disagreement indicated that this had probably been a sore issue between them. Though popular dances seem to be mostly prohibited, I found that many charismatic youths in the village disagree with this proscription.

One of the more interesting prohibitions among more traditional charismatic *comunidades* is against marimba music. Marimba music is common and popular throughout Guatemala; the marimba is the iconic national instrument. While the mental connection between marimba and nation is superficial at best for Nueva Ixtahuaquenses, I found it emblematic that the charismatic communities, which seem to be working so hard to insulate and isolate themselves from the greater society, would reject the national instrument. Three charismatic teens taught me a more utilitarian purpose for this prohibition. While scanning through the various radio frequencies one afternoon, we stopped briefly on marimba music. One of the boys commented in K'iche' to the others, and all three laughed. When I asked what the boy had said, one of the other young men responded in Spanish, "Dice que es música de los bolos" (He says that this is music for drunks). Marimba music is synonymous with annual saints' and municipal

celebrations and, consequently, alcohol. As I learned from other charismatic Catholics, the charismatic prohibition against marimba music has more to do with prohibitions on alcohol and celebrations than anything else.

While *catequistas* informed me that prohibitions on alcohol, celebrations, dancing, and marimba music keep charismatic Catholics safe from vices, such as drunkenness and promiscuity, these prohibitions also seem to bring secondary gains. Such stringent taboos separate charismatics from non-charismatic Catholics. Separation from those of the mainstream Catholic faith seems to weaken previous friendships and familial relationships with those outside of the CCR, which enhances charismatics' ability to fight worldly influences.

Charismatic Catholics also differentiate themselves from traditional Catholics by adhering to a rigorous worship schedule. Primera Comunidad, the oldest charismatic community in town, holds meetings three times a week, sometimes more if specific prayer meetings are needed on behalf of sick or afflicted members of that congregation. While charismatic meetings lack specific regulations for duration, meetings of the Primera Comunidad usually last about three hours. They occur in K'iche' and are led by the *catequista* of the congregation. These meetings are often dynamic, interlacing cycles of sermons, singing, group prayers, and instrumental music. Ixtahuaquense charismatic worship services often appear more Evangelical than Catholic, a fact also noted by Chesnut (2003b) in his description of Brazilian charismatic Catholicism. Indeed, charismatics consciously model their meetings on Evangelical Pentecostal practice. By worshipping together on a regular basis, charismatic Catholics are able to form strong relationships with other members of their congregation, relationships based on shared experiences. These bonds promote adherence to charismatic policies since relationships motivate members of the *comunidad* to remain in good standing with their congregation and compliant with prohibitions.

Catequistas also differentiate themselves from mainstream Catholic priests by holding religious meetings in K'iche' as opposed to Spanish, the language of the mass once Nueva Ixtahuacán left the parish of Antigua Ixtahuacán, where the American priest had learned K'iche' and used it in all church activities. The circuit priest normally assigned to Nueva Ixtahuacán allows teachings and Bible readings in K'iche', but he does not speak the language, thus precluding him from building the type of rapport *catequistas* can create with their parishioners. As indicated by Hoenes del

Pinal (2008), the use of native language in worship gives credibility to religion in Maya Guatemala and helps parishioners internalize spiritual messages more deeply. At the same time, the rise of charismatic Catholic communities and worship led by local leaders in the *comunidades* make the Ortho-Catholic priest increasingly peripheral; the priest, too, is now less solid as an *axis mundi*, even though his services are required to perform mass.

Pablo, the *catequista* and pastoral leader of the charismatic Primera Comunidad in Nueva Ixtahuacán, preaches and lives a traditional Maya life. He wears the *kamix* (thick shirt with embroidered cuffs and neck, from Sp. *camisa*) and *koxtar* (kilt-like men's skirt) traditionally worn by K'iche' men and still works in his fields in Antigua Ixtahuacán, even though he and his family live in Nueva Ixtahuacán. When Pablo arrived with his family in Nueva Ixtahuacán, he did not like the new cement house built by the government for him on his property, so he built his own traditional K'iche' adobe house and kitchen alongside the government-issue house, using the cement block house for storage. In 2003, he and his family did not have a TV, not because they could not afford it, as he assured me that they could, but because they chose not to have one. I remember Pablo as the only Guatemalan man I met with whom I did not converse about soccer; most Guatemalan men will discuss soccer at the slightest provocation. Pablo routinely preached the importance of staying separate from the world; his inattention to soccer certainly supported that.

Pablo regularly taught from the Bible during even the most mundane of conversations. One afternoon as we sat in his kitchen, he proclaimed, "We have humble living conditions because that's the way God likes it. I'd rather my children live here than in some mansion without having Christ in their hearts." For Pablo, life without outside influences and the technologies that can bring those influences is the true and proper way to live. Admittedly, Pablo does not represent the whole of the charismatic movement in Nueva Ixtahuacán. Rather, he represents a more traditional side of the CCR. I found it interesting that despite the fervent nature of his views, Catholic Ixtahuaquenses respected and admired Pablo. Though they did not share all of his strong views on prohibitions and the dangers of "the world," no one considered Pablo crazy or overzealous. But inevitably, respect and a place for Pablo depleted the respect and place of the Ortho-Catholic priest.

Through prohibitions, frequent religious meetings, services held in K'iche', and even the rejection of modern amenities in some cases, charismatic Catholics in Nueva Ixtahuacán isolate themselves from the external world and even the greater municipal community they live in. At the same time, they reinforce the tight-knit *comunidades* to which they dedicate themselves. Charismatic approaches to building community support Stark's (1998) claim that increased competition in the religious marketplace increases participation in religious organizations and activities.

CONCLUSION

As with many significant social and cultural shifts, a complex web of events, ideas, and factors have led to significant changes in Guatemalan religious practices. Evangelical Pentecostalism has spread rapidly across Guatemala, becoming a significant religious force. In response to Pentecostalism's rapid growth, Ortho-Catholicism fosters (sometimes quite begrudgingly) its own pentecostal charismatic movement, which has gained an enormous following in Guatemala. Vibrant worship services and tight-knit congregations make both Evangelical Protestantism and charismatic Catholicism attractive options in the Guatemalan religious marketplace.

By studying Nueva Ixtahuacán as a microcosm of Guatemala's religious shift, I have more clearly identified specific factors that, woven together, have created a dynamic religious marketplace where a previously monopolistic market existed. Evangelical and charismatic ideologies arrived in Antigua Ixtahuacán during the 1970s. Evangelical and charismatic success was then accelerated by technological advancements, such as radio, which has allowed both Pentecostals and charismatics to compete for a larger number of adherents.

While facilitating the growth of both Evangelical and charismatic congregations, advancements in literacy, communications, and mobility also played a role in secularizing Antigua Ixtahuacán. Secularization hastened during the 1990s and especially in the 2000s, when many Ixtahuaquenses relocated to Nueva Ixtahuacán, benefiting from easy access to the Pan-American Highway as well as a more reliable electrical infrastructure, paved roads, buried sewers, and new municipal buildings built by the government. Technology and mobility, as well as the inability to successfully farm in Nueva Ixtahuacán, have made education a high priority for Nueva Ixtahuaquenses. This focus on education, coupled with the fierce technological competition between charismatic and Evangelical groups to convert increasing numbers of people in Nueva Ixtahuacán to their ideologies, has diminished the public role of the Catholic church in Nueva Ixtahuacán.

Since Catholicism had long provided a shared world-view (weltanschauung) for Ixtahuaquenses, Catholic parishioners in the Nueva Ixtahuacán of diminished Catholic centrality now face uncertainty. Many Catholics in Nueva Ixtahuacán have accommodated to the changes in their town, making concessions that allow them to compartmentalize their religion when needed and sometimes adhering more proudly to their Maya identity than their Catholic identity. However, those involved in the Charismatic Renewal have redoubled their efforts to resist secularization and religious pluralism in their congregations. Through prohibitions on alcohol, dancing, celebrations, and, for some, even modern amenities, charismatic Catholics in Nueva Ixtahuacán separate themselves from non-charismatic townspeople. Frequent worship services held in the K'iche' language help charismatics build strong bonds and rapport with other members of their charismatic *comunidades*. These relationships reinforce adherence to the charismatic way of life, making religion once more for them the "sacred canopy" (Berger 1990[1967]) under which all other facets of life reside.

In Berger's (1990[1967]) seminal work on secularization, he indicates that literacy, communication, and mobility, aided by a pluralistic religious marketplace, lead to the secularization of major religions. Indeed, his theory proves quite accurate in describing not only the social decline of Catholicism in Nueva Ixtahuacán, but also those Catholics who accommodate their culture in relation to their religion, reducing religion to a more restricted realm. However, Berger's theory falls short, unable to account for the widespread popularity of Pentecostal and charismatic congregations, the zealous nature of both movements' adherents, and the overall increased religiosity in Nueva Ixtahuacán that both movements have brought. Stark (1998) explains those phenomena by theorizing that religious competition revitalizes religious participation. However, Stark's theory does not account for nonreligious factors that also affect the rate at which religion is practiced, making his theory a bit too narrow to describe the changes that have occurred in Antigua and Nueva Ixtahuacán since 2000. The factors involved in the social decline of Catholicism in Nueva Ixtahuacán and the variables involved in parishioners' responses to that decline are reminders that complexities of human behavior render societal shifts unpredictable and often inexplicable through singular sociocultural theories.

Nueva Ixtahuaquenses often think of "modern" and "secular" as synonyms. As they move boldly into a rapidly changing twenty-first century, many orthodox Roman Catholic Ixtahuaquenses brace themselves for the alterations they feel will come, hoping to bend and accommodate as their Maya ancestors did when the Spanish arrived. They adhere to the idea that accommodation to and acceptance of outside beliefs and practices can be beneficial, especially in promoting survival.

The charismatic Catholics, on the other hand, try to resist the changes at hand. They currently resist through an ideology that promotes a distrust of things from "the world." Their prohibitions promote isolation from the rest of the community, while their worship structure maintains unity among the members of their small *comunidad* through regular, powerful, boisterously Spirit-infused meetings held in K'iche'. As the Catholic scholar Louis Bouyer (1990:85) suggests, these charismatics liberate themselves from "all the ties that imprison [them] in the jail of [their] modern and so comfortable but so flatly materialistic way of life." Shades of Weber's "iron cage" of materialism. Only time will tell how these two reactions to secularization will change the face and centrality of Roman Catholicism in Nueva Ixtahuacán.

NOTES

1. This idea of course has deeper roots. It figures prominently in Marx, in this case via Engels (2008[1873–1886]:192): "One fortress after another capitulates before the march of science, until at last the whole infinite realm of nature is conquered by science, and there is no place left in it for the Creator." In Weber (2002[1905]:317, 356–357, 364–365), passages implicitly credit science with western and capitalist success versus religion restraining technology and science. Likewise, one finds in Durkheim (2001[1912]:326) reference to the primacy of science over religion: "Once the authority of science is established, it must be reckoned with. . . . One can affirm nothing that science denies, deny nothing that it affirms, establish nothing that does not rest, directly or indirectly, on the principles borrowed from it. From then on, faith no longer exerts the same hegemony as before over the system of ideas that we can continue to call religious."

2. However, a good deal of the research on public health issues from this field school shows that sexual behavior does not follow the restraint that the values would indicate.

Chapter Seven

Conversion to Evangelical Protestantism

The Ritual Reconstruction of a Disrupted Worldview
in Antigua Santa Catarina Ixtahuacán

MICHAEL H. JONES, JOHN P. HAWKINS, AND WALTER RANDOLPH ADAMS

ANTHROPOLOGISTS, PSYCHOLOGISTS, AND OTHER SOCIAL scientists have long tried to understand religious conversion. They have explored the definition of conversion, the social roles attendant to conversion, and the psychological importance of conversion. In this chapter we explore the conversion experiences of *evangélicos* (Protestant-derived Pentecostals) and argue that conversion stories (*testimonios*) attain consistency and meaning in a small congregation in Antigua Santa Catarina Ixtahuacán through socialization.

Some converts have understood and described their conversion as a physical change. Similarly, certain researchers see physical change as a metaphor for the change that occurs in an individual upon conversion (Kilbourne and Richardson 1989:15–16). In one such physical change, a convert might speak of having an illness, being healed, and then converting. The healing of an illness—whether it be physical, mental, or spiritual—is equated with change and becomes a metaphor for conversion.

Some anthropologists, such as López Cortés (1990), view conversion and incorporation into a congregation as a psychological phenomenon. A rupture in the normal symbolic order, also referred to as a "crisis of meaning," leads to a search for an understandable "construction of the world" (López Cortés 1990:31). Similarly, George Saunders (1995:324) uses ideas of Ernesto de Martino to posit a "crisis of presence," a concept of alienation as a result of difficulties that arise in the individual's life prior to conversion, which sets the stage for change.

Conversion is also seen as a form of socialization, as in Long and Hadden (1983). In this framework, scholars view conversion as a process of incorporation in which the individual learns to emulate the members of a group (Balch 1980; Beckford 1978; Taylor 1976) and thereby incorporate themselves into the new group. The socialization approach sees conversion as a ritualized process that brings an individual from a disrupted social situation into a new and more coherent system (López Cortés 1990; Saunders 1995).

In trying to understand conversion conceptually, socially, and psychologically, scholars have explored the role of the personal conversion story. Lawless (1988:3) explains, "The narrative accounts of that conversion serve to guide the religious experience of subsequent conversions." Others (Booth 1995; Saunders 1995) also discuss the function of the conversion narrative in defining the acceptable socialization process among new converts. In a conversion narrative, the individual reveals his or her concept of conversion and sheds light on the psychological function of the conversion process. Although researchers have looked at various aspects of conversion, they have not looked at the specific conversion and socialization process revealed in conversion narratives.[1] In our experience, the conversion narrative comes to reflect the social—that is, shared—understanding held by the receiving group, toward which the convert eventually modifies her or his testimony. In this sense, conversion is social, a matter of separation from one set of relationships and eventual inclusion in another set of relationships. This is all based on understandings of differences in ideology or orientation toward the world as held by each group, and the convert trying to construct a workable ideology for dealing with the world and the social groups that compose that world and work in it.

During fieldwork,[2] I found that in the process of telling

their conversion stories and listening to those of others, individuals participated in a socialization process leading to greater incorporation in the receiving group. The individual, through repeated recitation of the narrative, formed an understanding of his or her conversion and benefited from the psychological reformation of a disrupted symbolic system. The convert's symbolic system was disrupted in the sense that the premises that had previously guided her or his life under a given religion and social network simply had not worked. The person's life stood in some degree of chaos or collapse. The narrative, however, seems most important in that it formed, revealed, and reiterated the practices that constituted the status quo of proper behavior (socialization) in a particular congregation: the new (religious) social group at the core of the convert's changing social network. That is, the testimony of conversion came to increasingly reflect the expectations and ideology of failure and renewal anticipated by members of the new group of converts: the convert's life had been one of chaos or failure and was now improved and renewed.

I suggest that conversion among Pentecostals is a process of socialization through a ritualized reconstruction of an individual's disrupted symbolic system as described above. In the historic and social contexts of Santa Catarina Ixtahuacán, I explore three aspects of the conversion process among Pentecostals: motive, mode, and choice of congregational affiliation after an individual's acceptance of *el evangélio* (the gospel).[3] The ritualized telling of one's conversion narrative reveals how these three aspects of conversion socialize people into an existing church group essentially new to the convert.

THE PENTECOSTAL CHURCHES OF ANTIGUA SANTA CATARINA IXTAHUACÁN

In 2000, a *traslado* (mass relocation) of some 500 families from the municipal center of Santa Catarina Ixtahuacán to a new municipal center left only 100 or so families in the original village, which no longer served as the official *cabecera* (municipal seat). All of the Pentecostal ministers and most of their congregants migrated. The Pentecostals who remained in Antigua Ixtahuacán were left without an organized church. One month after the *traslado*, they organized the Cordero de Dios (Lamb of God). About a year later, a family that had abandoned the effort to live in the new town center returned to the originating town

center and formed another church, the Iglesia de Cristo (Church of Christ).[4]

In 2003, the two Evangelical churches in Antigua Ixtahuacán each had fewer than fifteen adult members who attended the Sunday *culto* (meeting). In each church, between three and ten of those adults also attended the other two weekly meetings that each church held on Tuesdays and Thursdays. One or two teenagers could usually be found in either of the *cultos*, and between six and sixteen younger children accompanied their parents. In a well-attended *culto*, approximately twenty-six people were present. Compared with the Evangelical churches in the surrounding *caseríos* (hamlets), these congregations in the old municipal center were relatively small.[5]

I inquired concerning members who had become inactive. According to the *obrero* ("worker" or "laborer," a title similar to assistant pastor) of one of the *evangélico* churches, four people living in the town who had been going to *culto* no longer attended. The *obrero* of the other Evangelical church estimated that two individuals plus one family that had formerly attended did not come now. Recognizing the possibility that the *obreros* may have mentioned some of the same people, I estimate that no more than ten *evangélicos* lived in the community who did not now go to *culto*. With an estimated thirty or so adults who attended *culto* weekly and the ten or so who no longer attended *culto*, around forty adults living in the community considered themselves *evangélicos*.

Cordero de Dios

After the *traslado*, in which the pastors and congregations of all the *evangélico* churches moved to Nueva Ixtahuacán in early January 2000, four men—Samuel, Carlos, Miguel, and Venicio—decided that those remaining in Antigua Ixtahuacán needed an *evangélico* church. They sent Carlos to nearby Totonicapán to speak with the *hermanos* (brothers ~ leaders) of the central church of the Cordero de Dios mission. The Totonicapán Cordero de Dios group was connected to—but independent of—a group from North Carolina, which sent visitors on occasion. On February 2, 2000, the central Cordero de Dios church established a "mission" in Antigua Ixtahuacán with Samuel, Carlos, Miguel, and Venicio as its leaders.

That year, the Cordero de Dios group (figure 7.1) met in a fifteen-by-thirty-foot building that was part of the Suey (Samuel's patronymic) family's residential complex. The core membership of the church consisted of eleven adults.

Figure 7.1. Cordero de Dios Pentecostals in worship. Courtesy of Michael H. Jones, 2003.

Six were related to each other by birth or marriage and resident in the Suey complex; three were related to members of the other *evangélico* congregation; and two had no close familial connection in the congregation.

Iglesia de Cristo

In January 2000, the Tzep family moved with some 500 other families to Chwipatan, the location of Nueva Ixtahuacán. However, they felt that it was wrong to accept international aid, which was available in Chwipatan, because they did not know the source of the money (see Checketts 2005 for a detailed discussion). Soon after, unhappy with conditions in the new setting of Chwipatan but convinced that it was not safe to return to the unstable ground of Ixtahuacán (the reason they had left in the first place), the Tzep family moved from Nueva Ixtahuacán to a *caserío* about twenty minutes by pickup from the original village. After a year, the wife of the oldest son of the Tzep family received a prophecy that they should return to their homes in the Antigua Ixtahuacán center and found a church.

On July 9, 2001, they started the Iglesia de Cristo in Antigua Ixtahuacán. Of the fourteen adult members attending the church, twelve were related by birth or marriage, while two had no close familial ties. They held *culto* in a room of an abandoned house near the Tzep family compound (figures 7.2 and 7.3).

CONVERSION NARRATIVES

As I interviewed the members of these two congregations, I became aware of a ritualized conversion process. This process entailed the recitation of personal narratives that recounted the events of each person's conversion to Pentecostalism. Members drew on and incorporated aspects of *los testimonios* of the other members to form their own story. A conversion story was thus shaped through time, collectively, as it was told and retold, until an appropriate narrative form was created. That form, in turn, prescribed and described the proper conversion rituals (Lawless 1988). Lawless (1988:3) claims that recounting the narratives "constitute[s] an important function in the complete conversion process." As Wightman (2007:244) puts it, "Narrating one's conversion experience through specific Pentecostal genres (such as testimonies) and tropes (such as being 'born again' and healing) is not merely a reflection of one's changing identity as a *cristiano*, but an integral part of forming a new Pentecostal identity." Lindhardt (2012:93–121), following Susumu (1986:158), sees conversion as a long-term process related to shifts in social networks and experience that is cultivated and transformed by the processes of talk in congregations. Likewise, McGuire (1982:49–50) notes that conversion involves a transformation of perceptual processing and premises.

In the remainder of this chapter, I analyze Ángela's conversion text and the conversion stories of others in the light of theorists who have addressed the nature of conversion and conversion testimonials. First, I present Ángela's narration; the mix of verb tenses suggests the ongoing immediacy of her experience:

Well, [I converted] on account of an illness. When the illness began, I had a high temperature. And at that time I had no strength, and I did not eat or drink— nothing. For about fifteen days, around that, I am sick and I cannot walk, and I cannot get out of bed. That's where I was, just in my bed. And I thought about that there is a God, that God exists. And I began to pray and I said to God, "Dear God [*Dios mío*, literally, "my God"], help me in this illness! Lord, pardon my sins! I promise you, Father, [that] if you let me live, I am going to work for you. I will preach your holy word. I am going to preach your word for you if you will let me [live] still," I said to God. It was about the fourteenth day when I thought this, but I was really sick,

Figure 7.2. Iglesia de Cristo members in worship. Courtesy of Michael H. Jones, 2003.

Figure 7.3. Iglesia de Cristo worship with a woman leading the congregation in prayer. Courtesy of Michael H. Jones, 2003.

seriously ill. I think that God hears my prayer. At that moment, I felt a presence [*un ambiento*]. I felt something very different in this moment when I am praying to God. I continued this, saying these words. I am begging [*clamando*, "importuning," literally, "crying to"] God, "Lord, if you permit [me] my life, do [your] works on me," I am saying to God. And God did works on me. And the next day, I drank some cups of coffee, and I ate a tortilla, and I was well, almost well. And when things calmed down, I feel very happy because I made a promise to God. Then, in subsequent weeks, I went to the Evangelical [church] and there I accepted.

I have always heard them, when they are preaching. The Evangelical pastors, they were [always] preaching, but I never paid any attention. But because of my sickness, I thought [about it].

ANALYSIS

Conversion narratives, which "constitute a reiterative authentication of the original experience" (Lawless 1988:13), reveal a personal and communal understanding of the conversion process. Because this process is revealed in the recitation of narratives, the process cannot be analyzed as an observed event. It can only be seen as an oral account of the event, told at a removed time by an individual who is categorically different from when the conversion occurred. Whether an event reported by a convert did or did not occur is not important.[6] What matters is what the conversion narrative reveals about the

present socialization and integration of an individual into the community. Booth (1995:371) claims, "The true story is . . . the one that makes narrative sense." A narrative is held as true if it makes sense in the cultural and social context in which it is told. In Ángela's case, the story that "makes narrative sense," and therefore is true, centers on an episode of severe illness followed by healing delivered in an Evangelical context. Ángela does not specify a direct Evangelical intervention in the cure, such as by receiving a blessing or laying on of hands in a particular Evangelical meeting. She only states that she had heard the Evangelical message continuously, as background, without paying attention to it. But when gravely ill, she pondered her condition against that background presence and accepted the Evangelical message and fellowship.

The formation of a proper conversion narrative and its socialization affect an individual as he or she enters into a new system. Individuals' understanding of their appropriate role changes as they learn to be a member of the group. As this understanding evolves, so does the person's narrative that explains the process. When a member becomes sufficiently socialized, the narrative both matches and reveals the proper form for conversion. The conversion narrative is thus a socializing and didactic tool created by individuals in a group and used to convince one another of proper conversion behavior (Booth 1995; Lawless 1988). Booth (1995:385) explains that the stories offer a hope of being "lifted temporarily . . . out of the fallen world into a 'world' that one would prefer to live in." Thus the narrative reveals how one becomes a "better [person] living in a superior world" (386). In effect, the narrative becomes an important part of the reconstruction of the symbolic order by providing the symbols (Geertz 1973; Turner 1957, 1968, 1980) that form that reconstruction. The story, as it describes the appropriate motive and mode of conversion and subsequent choice of congregational affiliation, also works to illustrate the proper way in which one should interact with one's new associates via the newly formed symbols. Clearly Ángela has been "lifted" by God "out of the fallen world" of illness-caused-by-sin. Moreover, Ángela has become a better person by virtue of no longer being thoughtless or failing to pay attention. Her conversion narrative implies she is now more cognizant of the things of God.

Motive

In every conversion narrative I recorded, individuals described a crisis as the motive for conversion. What people narrate as a crisis seems like a factual experience to them. But that account is not a statement of fact or condition. Rather, it is an exposition of the narrator's desired and reworked perception of the fact or condition. This fact, now rendered as a crisis, causes a disruption in the person's existing symbolic organization by showing the disparity between what the prior symbols and premises say should be the condition of his or her life and what that condition seems to be. Put differently, one's prior cultural guide seems not to be working well to set up or maintain one's life experience (López Cortés 1990). This leads the individual to seek a means of reordering that system by changing social networks, thereby seeking to be included in a network that seems to manifest a religious symbolic order that might, or clearly does, guide or contribute to a more desirable life. According to López Cortés, in the specific Mexican Pentecostal movement that he studied, the church's rituals and ideology function to control the loss of symbolic meaning through the construction of a new symbolic system. This same phenomenon seems to occur among the Pentecostals of Antigua Ixtahuacán. For Ángela, the crisis was a disease that went beyond a normal length and severely debilitated her. The reconstructed order entailed a direct connection to God rather than the former order of a mediated connection through a saint.

I refer to a motivating crisis—like that experienced by the members of the Pentecostal congregations of Ixtahuacán—as the "motive for conversion." The motive, then, is the event or state of being that inspired the desire to change the action or behavior that caused the crisis or disruption. All the motives mentioned in the Antigua

Santa Catarina Ixtahuacán conversion narratives fall into one or both of two categories: alcohol abuse and illness. Ángela's clearly concerns illness.

Alcohol Abuse

Sixteen of the twenty-five adult *evangélicos* in the community mentioned alcohol as part of the reason they accepted *el evangélio*. Of the sixteen, six stated "alcohol use" was the primary motive for conversion. The story of Carlos and Carla illustrates the role of alcohol in triggering the conversion process and its prominent place in conversion narratives.

Carlos and Carla had been married six years, and at that time had three of their eventual nine children. He was drinking "a lot," and this caused "problems" with his wife. He later defined the problems, in part, as *pegando mi mujer* (hitting my woman). Before this time, his brother-in-law had been telling him about *el evangélio*, but Carlos felt that he "was good" with the Catholic Church, and so paid no attention to his brother-in-law. Then, in what he termed a *llamado de Dios* (a [wake-up] call from God), he decided to quit drinking, and he and Carla accepted *el evangélio*.

Those who were brought up in the religion by *evangélico* parents mentioned that when they converted, they were trying to leave behind *cosas mundanas* (worldly things). When I asked Ixtahuaquenses to explain *cosas mundanas* or *prácticas mundanas* (worldly practices), I received descriptions of certain activities. This list always included alcohol, usually included cigarettes and fiestas, and often included the playing of the marimba. After not participating in these *prácticas mundanas* for a time, these individuals would accept the gospel. In the case of Ángela, while she does not mention worldly things, she clearly admits having been insensitive to the spiritual messages she had been hearing and, if asked, probably would have called that being "of the world."

The results of a survey given to the twelve Pentecostal households in the community demonstrate the emphasis on and preoccupation with alcohol in the group. Fifty-eight percent of the households said drinking alcohol was *awas* (taboo). Though the results show that only a slight majority of the houses mentioned alcohol as *awas*, they do suggest that the concept of alcohol avoidance, which is found in almost all of the narratives, is a socializing factor. This finding is even more interesting if one considers that at least 90 percent of the adult members, when interviewed, mentioned alcohol avoidance as being associated with Pentecostalism.

Illness

Of the eighteen people interviewed about their conversion story, eleven (including Ángela) reported *la enfermedad* (sickness illness) as the reason for conversion. In the narratives, converts described *la enfermedad* sometimes as a spiritual illness and sometimes as a physical illness—perhaps a fever or an ulcer on the arm. Irma related the story of her husband, Pedro's, sickness, which led to his desire to join the congregation of Cordero de Dios: "They took him to the hospital, and he was not cured. And when we go to another hospital, the doctors say that he has no sickness, that there is nothing that is in his body. There is nothing."[7] (Again, the present tense suggests that the crisis is experienced as something still ongoing.) After the hospitals and doctors failed to alleviate Pedro's illness, he and his family sought a Pentecostal healing, which led to his conversion. Irma explained that an *hermana* (female member, literally, "sister") from another town prayed for Pedro, and he was healed.

Though Pedro experienced physical sickness, some converts felt their illnesses were spiritual. Marta, for example, explained that she felt no desire to attend services with the *carismáticos* (a movement in the Catholic Church) with whom she normally worshipped. She described a desire to go to the Pentecostal church out of "a necessity" she felt. Soon after, she felt "healed in her relation toward God" and converted to *el evangélio*. Her husband claimed that she was healed of a spiritual sickness in that, upon going to the Pentecostal *evangélico* church, she was healed from her lack of desire to worship God.

The presence of spiritual illness, not just physical illness, in conversion narratives suggests an importance placed on the existence of some kind of illness that has to be healed at conversion. While I am not doubting the validity of Marta's experience, she related her conversion in terms similar to those used by people who had converted following a physical illness.

As with alcohol avoidance, the importance of healing showed up in many parts of the Evangelical Pentecostal culture other than conversion. If a relative or neighbor was ill, members prayed for them to be healed. These prayers occurred in *culto*, in the home of a member, or in the home of the sick person. One congregation prayed for sick members in organized *velorios* (night prayer vigils)

in the person's home or in the building in which they regularly met.[8] I asked one *obrero* the reason that they pray. He explained that prayer is for "sins, to give thanks, for necessities, and for the sick." Ángela's narrative, however, does not mention the intervention of or interaction with living *evangélicos*.

The emphasis on physical and spiritual sickness not only in the conversion narratives but in many aspects of the religious life of the *evangélicos* of the town might suggest that individuals are socialized in their congregations to have a newfound concern with illness. However, sickness and healing are also major themes in the greater K'iche' Maya culture. Thus, Morgan (2005) relates the illness and calling of Lázaro, a Maya traditionalist shaman. Scott and colleagues (this volume) document Tix's illness and calling in even greater detail. Finally, several chapters of Adams and Hawkins (2007) describe the place of illness and healing in the calling of medical/religious traditionalist practitioners in the K'iche' health care system. Thus, although alcohol avoidance is a newly constructed signifier in the new system, for *evangélicos*, sickness and healing reconstruct and reapply central K'iche' symbols deeply embedded in the greater cultural context.

Mode

The motive of conversion relates what the convert saw as the fundamental crisis or discomfort impelling his or her change. The mode of conversion is the means, the trigger of that change, the event the individual describes when asked how he or she overcame the crisis.[9] In every case of conversion, a spiritual experience followed the individual's recognition that his or her life was out of order or *estaba mal* (was bad). Most converts, like Ángela, mentioned healing (spiritual, physical, or psychological) in their conversion narratives as being the trigger that converted them. Many of those who did not experience a healing mentioned dreams as part of their conversion and saw dreams as a legitimate mode in which the call to change takes place.

Healing

Many converts chose to be *evangélicos* following their own healing or the healing of a family member. They spoke of these healings in very matter-of-fact ways. Consultants repeatedly said that if one has faith, one will be healed. When I asked for biblical verses that explained conversion as a result of sickness, *obreros* cited verses connecting conversion to healings. Among them, they cited Luke 17:15 (English Standard Version), "Then one of them, when he saw that he was healed, turned back, praising God with a loud voice"; Luke 17:19, "And he [Jesus] said to him, 'Rise and go your way; your faith has made you well'"; and Jeremiah 33:6, "Behold, I will bring to it health and healing, and I will heal them and reveal to them abundance of prosperity and security."

Healing in the context of a religious setting has a socializing effect in two senses. First, a religious healing is conceived of as a gift from God mediated or brought to the healed by the congregation attended. That gifting has reciprocity implications, a social fact. Second, the congregation has a socializing effect; the healed come to see the worldview of the healers as of increased value. The healed come to be socialized by and inculcated with the symbols and ideologies of the healing Evangelical community.

For example, Irma, who accepted the gospel fifteen years ago with her husband, gave this account of her conversion: "With a sickness God touched me, and I was sick for one month. I didn't eat anything, not even tortillas, nothing. I drank only hot water. And then after a month . . . [*pausing and starting again*] Before, I was Catholic. And when I was sick, I went to the other church, and God healed me. God gave to me, and I am free." For Irma, the illness was the motive for her conversion, but it was through the healing that the conversion was effected. While I cannot document the changes in a testimony due to socialization, given that I was in the community only three months, there is a hint of the existence of a socialized form in the similarities between Irma's and Ángela's accounts. Irma was sick for "one month," Ángela for something like "fifteen days"; Irma "didn't eat anything, not even tortillas, nothing," while Ángela "did not eat or drink—nothing," but the day after her prayers she "drank some cups of coffee, and . . . ate a tortilla."

Healing was also a common theme among those who had been members for many years. Members commonly prayed over each other. In one case, a preacher brought in from Totonicapán prayed over a member, who was thereby healed. Often, inactive members reconciled with or came back to the church after being healed. Those who included healing in their conversion story placed it in relation to Evangelical church activities, such as attending *culto*, being prayed over by an *evangélico*, or heeding direction that came in the form of a dream.

Dreams

Miguel was very sick. A large sore festered on his arm; he drank alcohol three times a week. His mother told him he was suffering for his vices. The pain became so bad that he often cried. After "fifteen days and fifteen nights," he had a dream. In his dream he was told, "When you accept the gospel, your healing is assured, but if you don't, you will lose your arm." He accepted the gospel and was healed.

Miguel mentioned sickness and alcohol problems as the means by which God called him. But the mode by which he was converted was the dream. His sickness and alcoholism were his motive to change, and it was through the dream that he was told how to be healed.

Antonio and Carina were the oldest *evangélicos* and had been members longer than any other *evangélicos* still in the community. They recounted the story of how the gospel arrived in the village thirty-three years ago. The man who would become the first convert in the town was a student in a Catholic seminary in the nearby city of Sololá. Through his studies, he developed a question about the baptism of babies. He saw a conflict between what the Bible teaches and what was taught by the Catholic Church. He left the seminary and returned to the village. He had a dream that someone would come to the town and bring the truth. Within a month, an Evangelical preacher arrived and began to preach the gospel in the town. The man soon converted.

This story describes an early dream conversion that occurred in the village. In many of the narratives, the theme of dreaming as part of conversion constituted a retelling and imitation of the now-mythological first conversion. Ten members reported experiencing dreams in connection with their conversion.

The Cultural Rootedness of Healing and Dreams

Here, we draw attention to the deeply embedded place of dreams in greater K'iche' culture. Tix, a male diviner (Scott et al., this volume), and a female traditionalist midwife (Yukes 2007:67n7) both had dreams that, as revelations, they associated with their healing.

In the narratives, the manner by which Evangelical converts switched religions is interesting, especially in light of historically documented modes of conversion to religious and healing activity in the greater K'iche' cultural context. Ixtahuaquenses are not alone in being affected religiously by healing and dreams. Falla (2001) describes religious intensification, in which a person converts from being an ordinary Maya Catholic citizen to being a traditionalist shaman after he has been healed. Falla (2001) also documents the common occurrence of individuals and families changing to a different kind of religion, usually Catholic to Pentecostal *evangélico*, after a healing event has taken place. Barbara Tedlock (1981, 1987, 1991) discusses the importance of dreams in the K'iche' Maya culture in many of her writings. She claims that in the culture, emphasis is placed on dreams and dream interpretation in the activation of sacred callings among traditionalists as well as in initiating secular behaviors.

Thus, dreams and healing have played a role historically in the greater K'iche' traditional culture and in the local traditional root culture of Ixtahuacán. Among the Pentecostals of Ixtahuacán, the dream or healing event comes in conjunction with the answer as to how the individual will or should reorganize his or her life, just as it did for traditionalist Tix in Scott and colleagues (this volume).

Choice of Congregational Affiliation

With only two Evangelical churches in Santa Catarina Ixtahuacán, one would think that discovering why a person would choose to go to one *culto* instead of the other would be easy. Indeed, the two congregations were divided along family lines with only a few exceptions. From an outsider's point of view, it seemed that converts went to a congregation where their family went. This assessment may very well be true, but in light of the reasons people gave as to why they went where they went, the answer may be more complicated.

In explaining congregational and denominational switching, some researchers have tried to determine if the convert's personality changes with conversion or if personality determines conversion (Paloutzian, Richardson, and Rambo 1999; Poling and Kenny 1986; Weiss 1987; Weiss and Comrey 1987). In reviewing conversion narratives in Santa Catarina Ixtahuacán, I did not find evidence to support conclusively either of these theories, but I did find that personality plays an important role in deciding with which *culto* a convert affiliates.

I found three attributes—familial ties, *testimonios*, and personality preference—that seem to explain at least in part one's congregational choice.

Familial Ties

Both congregations had a patriarch and matriarch from whom almost all members of each congregation descended. The congregations did not simply consist of extended relatives, that is, distant cousins. Rather, they included four generations of a stem family. Mothers and their married daughters, who now lived outside of the paternal home, commonly used the time before and after the *culto* to talk and be together. Even the location of each *culto* building in the paternal family complex demonstrated the central nature of the family group in each congregation.

In the K'iche' Maya community, it makes sense for people to remain within and strengthen the patrifocal family group. Indeed, the patrifocal family has been a central part of much of Guatemalan indigenous societal structure. Many members mentioned in their conversion narratives that they were informed about the *evangélio* by a family member or that they themselves gave *testimonios* that helped convince members of their own families. The congregations of both churches seemed to have entered the *evangélio* in a snowball effect. Wives typically followed their husbands, and siblings often converted one after the other.[10] Some converted at ages when they were under strong parental pressure and so followed their parents. Only the first conversion in the family complex deviated from this pattern.

The importance of parental pressure—in conversion and in other aspects of local society—does not completely disappear with age. Family pressure continues into adulthood and can be a factor in conversion and religious activity among the K'iche's (Falla 2001). Parental pressure certainly impacted the Suey family in Ixtahuacán. When the Suey father converted, he brought with him his spouse, their youngest single son, and all of their daughters but the eldest. The eldest son remained with a charismatic group; the youngest son, who was married, and the eldest daughter remained Catholic. This variation in reaction by children to their father's conversion suggests that there are varying degrees of parental influence on the individual, depending on age, sex, position in the family, marital status, and the more intangible issue of personality.

Testimonios

The theme of *testimonios* emerged when I questioned individuals regarding how someone should choose which *culto* to attend. *Evangélicos* in Ixtahuacán defined *testimonio* as how a person or a congregation as a whole behaves and acts. It was also understood as the act of testifying verbally about *el evangélio* and its action in one's life. An individual decided which congregation had members whose *testimonios* seemed good by noting which individuals behaved consistently with their view of the gospel or biblical dictates.

Irma and her husband, Pedro, decided to attend *culto* again after three years of not participating. They had stopped going to *culto* after the *traslado*. Irma explained that they stopped participating in the Pentecostal church they had joined after their conversion because the congregations and pastors left for Chwipatan. After three years, Pedro became ill and was healed while in the hospital by *evangélicos* from another town. After the healing, Irma and Pedro decided to go to Cordero de Dios and reaccept the gospel with *obrero* Samuel's group. When asked why they chose to attend that *culto*, Irma responded, "Because Samuel is there. They [the members] stayed here and were faithful, just as the word of the Lord says."[11] Irma thus indirectly criticized the Iglesia de Cristo congregation members, who were implicitly "unfaithful" because they had moved to Nueva Ixtahuacán. Irma and Pedro chose the *culto* they would attend based on how they felt about the *obrero* of the church and because the congregation acted in a way that conformed to their understanding of the Bible.

Personality Preference

One member's explanation of *culto* preference suggested that congregational affiliation was based on who one gets along with best. Juan and his family did not go to *culto* until the Iglesia de Cristo was founded locally by those returning from the *caserío*. They already had the option of attending *culto* with Cordero de Dios, but they chose not to. He explained, "They have other *hermanos*, and their conduct doesn't seem right to me, so I don't go to that place."[12]

When asked if it is permissible for a person to start another church if he fights with another member, Juan responded, "That is how the church is."[13] In a word, congregational fission is expected practice. Although these congregations had not split in the one to two years since their founding, such fission is widespread among *evangélico* congregations.

Juan's account adds another aspect to *culto* affiliation besides those of family and *testimonios*. In fact, Juan was related more closely to the members of Cordero de Dios than to his congregation of choice. According to Juan, one should affiliate with those whose personalities seem most congenial or compatible. Even so, the concern that "their conduct doesn't seem right" affirms the importance of *testimonios* in justifying congregational choice.

CONCLUSION

When individuals realize that they do not fit into their cultural setting because of a crisis brought on by illness or a failure to act in a manner consistent with a shared culture, they often find a means of incorporating themselves into a new system. This phenomenon accounts, in many cases, for the decision of individuals to reject Catholicism, accept the contrastive *evangélio*, and choose a new congregation to which they will belong.

In the story of Carlos and Carla, alcohol use created a setting where the couple's social relationship was under stress; Carlos drank and beat his wife. A breakdown or crisis occurred. The symbolic structure of Catholicism—well grounded in local tradition and custom—that had anchored their lives had become disrupted. Through the *llamado de Dios*, Carlos was told how to be healed of his alcoholism. As the couple was socialized into the receiving group, Carlos and Carla began to organize what was for them a new symbolic system in a new congregation. But that congregation already had a working symbolic system to which Carlos and Carla needed to conform. Over time, they developed their newly formed construct and refined it by making the repeated tellings consistent with what they heard among their peers in the receiving congregation. By repeated declaration and refinement through *testimonio*, they could then function in their new group as the new system dictated.

Stromberg (1993:ix) argues that "it is through the use of language in the conversion narrative that the processes of increased commitment and self-transformation take place." Booth (1995) claims that the narrative not only functions as a teaching and socializing tool, it also allows an individual to lift him- or herself into another, ideal world. I suggest that this "ideal" world is the reconstructed symbolic system that emerges upon social acceptance and integration into a specific congregation.

I have argued that Pentecostal conversion in Ixtahuacán, as revealed through conversion narratives, reorders one's life after some circumstance caused a serious disruption. Older members socialize converts; converts learn the fundamentals of the *evangélio* through the ritualized expression of common themes in the telling and hearing of conversion testimonies. Moreover, the converts increasingly validate their own authenticity as their conversion story approaches the congregation's norm. The oral recitation of the motive and the mode of conversion offers new symbols around which one forms a new worldview.

Individuals completed the reordering of their disrupted symbolic system when they joined a particular congregation. The choice of the particular group with which they affiliated seemed to be a function of family connection, though this was sometimes overridden by personality clash. I infer that factors such as familial ties, acceptance of certain *testimonios*, and preference for a personality type helped determine the *culto* an *evangélico* of Ixtahuacán would attend.

Flinn (1999:56) discusses a model that breaks conversion into "(1) a turning away or separation; (2) a state of suspension; and (3) a turning toward," presumably following van Gennep (1960[1909]) and Turner (1969). Flinn (1999:57) refers to the "separation" as experiencing "spiritual dissonance." This dissonance places the individual in an "in between state" (58) or a liminal phase (Turner 1967, 1969) comparable to Flinn's "crisis of presence." The "turning toward" phase is defined as a change in lifestyle and behavior that cements the individual in the group.

The Ixtahuaquense Pentecostal conversions, as revealed through the recitation of conversion narratives, demonstrate the phases of Flinn's (1999) conversion model. A separation occurs due to the individual's state of being, which I call the motive for conversion. The in-between state is the crisis or disrupted symbolic system that precedes the mode of conversion. The conversion narrative itself, as it informs the socialized individual about proper behavior, is part of the final stage of turning toward, comparable to van Gennep's and Turner's reintegration or reaggregation.

The conversion narratives of the K'iche' Maya Pentecostals of Ixtahuacán reveal the proper way in which one is supposed to convert and subsequently behave as a newly socialized member of the organization. The narrative, in demonstrating the proper way for new converts to act, builds solidarity and bonds the individual in the group, thus reconstructing the convert's formerly disrupted world and reforming their previously inadequate worldview. Pentecostal ritual is, as Weber (2002[1905]:96, emphasis in original) intimates, above all else an experience of "*feelings* [that] flow from the direct witness of the spirit." And like the Australian Aborigines whom Durkheim (2001[1912]:175, 177) analyzed from the ethnographies that he had access to in his day, the Pentecostals in each congregation of Antigua

Santa Catarina Ixtahuacán do indeed "shout the same cry, pronounce the same words, make the same gestures to the same object." In socializing the new converts to this conformity, congregants and converts alike "bear witness" to each other that they have arrived at, that they have achieved, a community in which, as Durkheim suggests, they "share the same moral life."

NOTES

1. Chesnut (1997:51) notes similarities in the conversion stories of Brazilian Pentecostal Protestants, but he does not explore the *process* of convergence.

2. I gathered the data using four methods: participant observation, extensive interviews, a basic survey, and an attempt at freelisting. While these methods garnered different types of data, they often supported one another, lending confidence to these conclusions.

3. All translations are my own.

4. There is no relation to the worldwide Church of Christ.

5. By comparison, one meeting I attended in a *caserío* about a kilometer away from Ixtahuacán had, in a conservative estimation and not counting those who hung around the back door, seventy to eighty people in attendance.

6. Like others (e.g., Lawless 1988), I do not wish to judge the individual accounts as being "true" or "untrue." The issue of truth is not important. I only want to show that the particular ritualized language used in the recitation of conversion narratives reveals the social (and sacred) process wherein the converts reconstruct a disrupted symbolic system.

7. "Se llevaron en hospital y no se alivió, y a pasar en otro hospital y los doctores dice[n] que no tiene enfermo, no hay nada que está en el cuerpo, no hay nada."

8. This *evangélico velorio* represents an interesting continuity with the *velorio* in Catholic practice and local tradition, in which a deceased person receives nine nights of prayer vigil to cure his or her soul of the burden of sin and facilitate its union with God.

9. If not offered freely in the conversation, I probed with the question, "Cómo se convirtió?"

10. These two congregations differed from the women-first conversion experiences reported in other chapters in this volume and in the larger literature, such as Brusco 1993, 1995.

11. "Porque está Samuel. Ellos se quedaron y fueron fieles, como dice la palabra del Señor."

12. "Tienen otros hermanos y su conducto no me conviene, entonces no me voy a este lugar."

13. "Así es la iglesia."

Chapter Eight

"Clap Your Hands and Sing"

Three Functions of Music in Nahualá's Evangelical Protestant Churches

JENNIFER PLEASY PHILBRICK WAYAS, JOHN P. HAWKINS, AND
WALTER RANDOLPH ADAMS

IN THIS CHAPTER, WE PROVIDE a description of
the uses and consequences of music in two Pentecostal Protestant congregations of Nahualá. As Durkheim
(2001[1912]:258) puts it, "If religious ceremonies," including music and song, "have any importance, it is because
they set the collectivity in motion. . . . Their first effect
then, is to bring individuals together, to increase contacts
between them, and to make those contacts more intimate.
This in itself causes a change of consciousness." We highlight not just the ways music organizes by setting the collectivity in motion, but how it indeed changes the consciousness of the Pentecostal participant.

While the majority of Nahualá's citizens are Catholic,
since the 1990s there has been a sharp increase in the number of members attending other Christian denominations.
We use the terms "Christian(s)" and "Christian music" as
these words are used by Evangelical Protestants in the area
to contrast themselves with Catholics and, not inconse-
quentially, to claim a certain moral high ground, for the
implication of this phrasing is that Catholics are not Christian. Protestant Pentecostals use variants of "Christian" to
designate Evangelical people, activities, and other things,
such as music, as distinct from Catholic people, activities,
or music. Many of these denominations use high-powered
electronic amplification and speakers the size of large filing
cabinets to project music and sermons within and beyond
the small churches that house the congregations. Thus,
while the large old Catholic church that faces the town
plaza may be the most obvious *visual* sight in Nahualá,
the loudest *sounds* come from the Evangelical Protestant
church music being played in their chapels and from chapel
rooftops all over town throughout the week.

In Nahualá's urban center during my fieldwork in 2003,
nine church buildings (*templos*) provided space where the
largest Evangelical Protestant church organizations and
their members met. Many smaller groups assembled in
private homes. One pastor estimated that in the entire
municipio of Nahualá more than forty distinct *evangélico*
church groups congregated. Some of these churches had
been in the area for more than thirty-five years. Others
were relatively new. In this chapter I focus on two of the
congregations, to which I give pseudonyms.

The first I call the "International Church," and it had
been established in Nahualá for more than thirty years,
one of the first three Evangelical Protestant churches in
the town. Introduced to Guatemala by foreign missionaries, the church has grown to be one of the country's
largest Protestant churches. Originally the International
Church met near the town center, but early on, as the
church membership grew, it purchased a large piece of
land within ten minutes' walking distance of the market.
The local members raised the money to build a large *templo*, living quarters for the pastor, and a *colegio* (primary
school). The large multistory *templo* seats up to 3,000.
In 2003, the pastor claimed around 500 members, with
approximately 200 regularly attending *cultos* (meetings).
Seating was gender-divided, with women on the left and
men on the right. That pastor hailed from Mazatenango.
He had formal training by the local headquarters in Guatemala City and served in Nahualá by assignment.

In contrast to the large International Church, the "Oasis
Church" had only been in Nahualá for a couple of years.
Its membership was small and largely consisted of one
extended family. The pastor had been a member of the

International Church but felt like he wanted something more. His brother introduced him to the Oasis Church, which was founded in Guatemala. They attended services in a neighboring town before establishing a *templo* in Nahualá. Thirty to fifty people regularly attended *culto* at the Oasis. Men and women sat intermixed in the congregation. The church was growing, and seating had become limited. A special *culto* was held to solicit funds for new chairs. Members were encouraged to bring new white plastic chairs or donate money so that more could be purchased. Inside the church, several banners hung from the rafters, each displaying an epithet for God: Jehovah, Jesucristo, Jireh, Shalom, El Shadday, Rey de Reyes (King of Kings), Consejero (Counselor), and Admirable.

Each church held weekly *cultos* either in the *templo* or in believers' homes. Sunday *cultos* usually garnered the largest attendance. Weekday meetings sometimes had special purposes, such as a birthday celebration or an *acción de gracias* (thanksgiving).

All *cultos* (plate 23) followed a basic pattern that involved worship through music, prayer, and hearing the word of God. Other activities included collection of offerings, the Lord's Supper, baby blessings, and fasting. *Cultos* generally lasted two to three hours. I also experienced brief meetings, full-day events, and all-night worship services. Members spent at least half of the time in any *culto* worshipping through music and song. The amount of time dedicated to music was either planned or dictated by the spirit, depending on the church and the occasion.

Two languages are widely used in Nahualá, Spanish and K'iche'. Both were used in *culto*. The majority of the sermons and liturgical portions of the services were conducted in K'iche'. Although the Bible was available in both Spanish and K'iche', pastors read from the Bible in Spanish. Most hymns were sung in Spanish.

In addition to the Sunday and weekday *cultos* and other religious activities common to the process of Evangelical religion in Nahualá, I attended two special Evangelical musical events. In the first, a Nahualense church celebrated its twenty-fifth anniversary in Nahualá's central plaza. With an electronic band and speakers positioned on the open-air balcony of the town market building, the meeting dominated the public plaza throughout the day. Everyone was invited to attend, though they had to attend if they walked through town or conducted any business in the center. The celebration mixed the attributes of a concert and a *culto*, with speakers and special musical guests. In the second event, held in Quetzaltenango, an hour away by bus, a popular Christian singer from Mexico and his band performed in a large church. It was similar to a rock concert: attendees waited in long lines, and the singer offered for sale logo-branded T-shirts with added religious motifs and CDs of his Evangelical music. At least 2,000 people attended.

METHODS

During three months of participant observation in Nahualá, I attended various *cultos* and spoke with members associated with different congregations. I held formal interviews with pastors and church members. I spent the last month of my fieldwork interviewing specifically on the subject of music, and I attended the two special musical events noted above and interviewed people about them.[1]

During my time in Nahualá I collected compact discs and hymnals of the music used in the *cultos*. I also took pictures, made sound recordings, and recorded video footage when appropriate.

I interviewed in Spanish for two reasons: first, to reduce the need for a K'iche' translator; and second, because the majority of the interviewees preferred Spanish when speaking on religious subjects.

Because of time conflicts (such as meetings being held at the same time) I was limited in the number of churches that I could visit regularly and include in my study. Although I attended one or more *cultos* with ten Evangelical congregations in Nahualá, I focused on two contrasting organizations: the large International Church and the small Oasis Church.

Although I started fieldwork with a broad interest in all aspects of Evangelical Protestantism, I continually felt drawn to the music and its role in worship. Indeed, music dominated the ambience of the Evangelical *culto*. In picking such a focus, however, I worried that I was unqualified. How could I study Evangelical Protestant music given my limited musical knowledge or ability?

My concern was not unique in ethnomusicology. Some scholars consider competency in both anthropology and music—a double specialization—to be necessary. Other ethnomusicologists, however, argue that the dual requirement has thwarted the study of music-as-culture in anthropology (Merriam 1955:1173). Instead of trying to understand music at the technical, descriptive, note level, I focused on music as part of the community's social and religious experience. Thus, my fieldwork approximated the position of Feld and Fox (1994:25), who observe, "In recent years, work in ethnomusicology has moved decisively toward a fully anthropological perspective. . . . Ethnomusicological perspectives are increasingly social, linking the structure and practice of musical performances and styles with music's deep embeddedness in local and translocal forms of social imagination, activity, and experience." In this chapter I share my observations on Evangelical Protestant music as experienced in the lives of Nahualense Evangelicals by looking specifically at how the church members interacted with and participated in musical activities.

FINDINGS

Pentecostals in Nahualá use hymns to exalt and worship God. According to these Evangelical Protestants, heavenly music heralded the birth of Jesus Christ and has always been a part of the religious experience. "And when Christ comes again the angels will sing out" (King James Version: 1 Thessalonians 4:13). Indeed, these Evangelical Protestants felt they based everything they did on some passage in the Bible, and they used scriptural references to justify the importance of music in their worship. Indeed, music was inseparable from these Evangelicals' lives and represented their devotion to God.

Analytically, one can see music playing a broad role in the Pentecostal Evangelical community. As Owen, Walstrom, and Michelsen (1969:99) put it, "[Alan] Merriam . . . discerns ten general functions . . . of music in human culture: emotional expression, esthetic enjoyment, entertainment, communication, symbolic representation, physical stimulation, social control, the 'chartering' of ceremonies and institutions, assisting continuity and stability, and aiding general cultural integration."

I saw all ten of Merriam's functions of music at play in Nahualá, and there are glimpses of each function throughout this chapter. My emphasis, however, is on what Merriam calls "aiding general cultural integration." I focus on three aspects. First, the music organized people's religious participation on both the individual and group levels. This participation reinforced belief and group membership. Second, music acted as a bridge to unite believers not only with God but also with surrounding communities and the world in which they lived. Third, even though music united people and groups, it simultaneously served

to distinguish one group from another. I describe each of these functions in turn.

Music as Organizer of Participation, Belief, and Membership

Participation is an active and contributive sharing process in an activity or organization (Keil 1987:276). Music sung by a group instigates collective participation and foments group identity. The Evangelical Protestant churches relied heavily on the participation of their members, who were involved in many ways. They contributed to the church by means of monetary donations or physical labor. Members were assigned or volunteered to help clean up or hold a *culto* in their home.

Evangelicals participated in a number of socially recognized roles, among them pastor, *pastora* (wife of the pastor), *diácono* (deacon), *diaconisa* (deaconess), and *ujier* (usher). The pastor was the principal leader of the church; he coordinated the efforts of all other members, including the musicians. Deacons and ushers helped with ceremonies, such at the Lord's Supper, and the collection of offerings.

During a *culto*, not only were all activities accompanied by music, but literally and figuratively they were orchestrated by appropriate types and levels of music. The band would punctuate the pastor's main points with a percussive explosion or a trill of keyboard or guitar. The band would use specific types of music to transition the pastor or others into or out of a particular activity, whether it be prayer, collection, sermon, glossolalic communion, or trance state. Music brought the congregation together in united song and emphasized the intensity of their prayers, giving audible signals of when to cool down, stop one activity, and begin another. Thus, music instigated participation in worship, organized it, and made it collective and meaningful. Indeed, Merriam (1964:227) observes, "Music . . . provides a rallying point around which the members of society gather to engage in activities which require the cooperation and coordination of the group." And so it was in these Evangelical congregations (plate 24).

Worship through music allowed for various levels of participation by church members. Band members, singers, music directors, and pastors led, incited, performed, or soloed; members sang as directed.

Each church had a small band. Leaders and congregants interpreted biblical references to King David's musicians as authorization for the type of instruments used in *culto*: "And David and all the house of Israel played before the Lord on all manner of instruments made of fir wood, even on harps, and on psalteries, and on timbrels, and on cornets, and on cymbals" (King James Version: 2 Samuel 6:5). Thus, the ancient use of acoustic stringed instruments validated today's use of electric stringed guitar and bass and electric keyboard. Bibilical cymbals justified today's drum kits and percussion synthesizers. Bands occasionally played trumpets, but the flute, mentioned in some scriptural passages, was not used in the groups I studied. The electrically amplified keyboard was the central instrument of the band.

The players taught one another and learned their instruments by trial and error, without formal training. Some exercised their musical talent as an aside to their regular occupation. Others dedicated themselves to musical vocations. Musicians were members of the specific church community in which they regularly played. In some cases, musicians were called to the position. Due to their limited number, musicians learned as many instruments as possible. Even though women outnumbered men at the Sunday *culto* meetings, I observed only male band members.[2] Women were allowed to play instruments in the Oasis Church, but only in *cultos* directed by and organized for other women.

While singing hymns was essential for a *culto*, surprisingly the band itself was not. At the International Church, the band only played on Sundays and at special *cultos*. During my fieldwork in 2003, this band only had one keyboard player; the second had recently moved to the United States. When the lone keyboarder was available, the church had music at *culto*; when he was not, it did without. In the Oasis Church, the band rarely failed to play. After one *culto* in which the band did not play, the pastor explained that the band had not practiced or held the required special prayer service. He thus withheld the "honor of playing" because "they lacked preparation and worthiness."

However, instrumental music almost always accompanied singing and sermon if a band was available. If no band was available, people sang without accompaniment. In addition to congregational singing, some churches used small choirs; other churches relied on individual singers. Both men and women sang in the congregation as well as individually from the podium or at the microphone. Like playing in the band, an opportunity to sing was sometimes given as a calling and carried with it certain obligations. This provided individual members with very specific roles that helped to facilitate the church meeting. In a neighboring town, Thompson and colleagues (this volume) observed that a rebellious girl was given the assignment to sing in her Evangelical Protestant church as an opportunity to show humility and reintegration following her punishment period of forced abstention from performance at the podium. In both the International and Oasis Churches in Nahualá, singing or playing in the band was a privilege and honor, never a punishment.

A music director led the band and singers. Sometimes the music director read a psalm and announced the songs to be sung, or he simply sang as the lead vocalist. The music director sometimes changed, either during a specific *culto* or from one *culto* to the next. The pastor could also serve as a music director and might incorporate additional singing into his sermon and prayers (for parallels, see Horwatt 1988:130). The music director had the responsibility of picking the songs and establishing the order in which they were sung.[3] Importantly, the progression of songs influenced the pace and feel of the meetings. While leaders created the music and organized its flow, the congregation provided the numeric bulk of the participants.

It was difficult to measure the level of attention given throughout the meeting. Often, individuals seemed distracted by their children, fellow worshippers, or what was going on outside. During the sermon, older members sometimes fell asleep while the young girls gossiped and talked among themselves. By far, the music of the *culto* elicited the most physical and audible responses from the congregation. Worshippers were encouraged to sing along. The words sometimes were posted on a placard or could be found in a printed hymnal. Most often, however, members sang the simple and oft-repeated refrains from memory.

The large, one-room, open-design, cinderblock construction of most *templos* produced very poor acoustics. Little concern was given to using a mixer to balance the sounds. Rather, the emphasis was on making the music as loud as possible, while the poor acoustics often made the words of the songs distorted and unintelligible. Regardless, people knew the words—whether by practicing them, singing along with the radio, or just from hearing them over and over again in church—and continued to sing along.

Most hymns consisted of a single short and simple text. Repetition established the length of a particular rendition. Most songs were much repeated until the desired emotional effect or function (such as monetary collection) had been achieved. The lyrics derived from Bible stories and ideals. Singing helped members learn Evangelical principles in general as well as a congregation's particular take on those principles. Key concepts were repeatedly reinforced through song. The songs taught whom to worship and how to worship.

Learning through song was not limited to time spent in *culto*. *Evangélicos* listened to Evangelical music on the radio and sang hymns throughout the week, either accompanying the radio or singing solo. Even the elderly who did not otherwise speak Spanish could be heard singing the hymns throughout the week, out of church. One pastor explained that some older K'iche' monolingual people have their grandchildren explain the meanings to them at home. They become familiar with the Spanish religious words, which are used over and over in these songs.

Singing, of course, is not the only way that the congregation participated in the *cultos*. Because the music was seen as a conductor for the Holy Spirit, many "manifestations of the Spirit," according to the attendees, emerged as the musicians played and moved the songs or instrumental renditions toward intense crescendos, followed by diminution and transition. The people wailed, cried, prayed aloud, or even spoke in tongues. They also clapped, raised their hands, or laid their hands on one another to give each other blessings (figure 8.1)—all, most often, to the orchestration of music.

The pastor of the International Church recognized that these were emotional reactions but pointed out that they were also dictated by the teachings of the Bible. In the Oasis Church, the congregation on some occasions waved flags and veils and danced in the meeting room using spinning and jumping motions. Such extended freedom of motion, however, was unusual for Evangelical Protestant churches in Nahualá. At the outdoor anniversary event attended by the community, the visiting musician encouraged the crowd to jump. No one did, even though the lyrics they sang along with said *salta al Señor* (jump to[ward] the Lord).

Each church taught its congregants the appropriate ways to participate. Even though in the climactic moments, body activities and noise levels became almost chaotic, they were still within certain bounds set by individual pastors and established as congregational custom.

Spiritual manifestations—such as body movement, prophecy, and speaking in tongues—sometimes occurred without the immediate presence of music, but they were most likely to occur against a foreground of loud, climactic, fast-paced music (figure 8.2) (Pitts [1991] documents a similar association of music style to receptivity to manifestations of the spirit among African American Baptists). In Nahualá, the songs of each *culto* were arranged to illicit emotion at crucial moments. The band controlled the speed of each song. Certain songs began slowly and built to a feverish pace. At the fastest tempos, the wailing intensified and the singing became less recognizable. Individuals became consumed in the moment. Mothers who may have had children tugging at their huipiles did not give them heed. In the Oasis Church, worshippers became so transformed and oblivious of their surroundings that certain people were designated to make sure that no one ran into the walls, chairs, or other participants, or hurt themselves if they fell to the floor as an expression of

Figure 8.1. Pastor healing a congregant in a Pentecostal church. Courtesy of Jennifer Pleasy Philbrick Wayas, 2003.

Figure 8.2. Women in the pre-trance mobility phase of worship at a Pentecostal church. Courtesy of Jennifer Pleasy Philbrick Wayas, 2003.

the spirit. The impact of music on these congregants confirms Durkheim's observation that, in Keane's (1997:53) words, "ritual form can create a unified congregation by regimenting vocal and bodily movements and, by its emotional effects, may transform individuals' subjective states."

Music was used to introduce and give background ambience to participatory rituals, such as the giving of offerings. Bands played slower music at these times; leaders suggested that the slower pace allowed congregants time to "reflect on the goodness of God." Music, both instrumental and sung, provided background while members and leaders prepared for and consumed the sacramental Santa Cena (Lord's Supper). The song's repeated chorus intoned, "Su amor no termina, / Su gracia no acaba, / Un limite no hay al poder de Jesús" (His love has no end, / His grace does not run out, / There is no limit to the power of Jesus).

Specific hymns may have special purposes. One pastor identified three basic types of hymns: one for God, one for the individual, and one for the nonbeliever. A hymn for God exalts and adores God and is directed to him, such as in the lyric "No hay Dios tan grande como Tú" (There is no God as great as Thou). One hymn for the individual or perhaps for the nonbeliever talks about the change that takes place as one is converted to the gospel. Other hymns express what the individual is or should be feeling and allow the congregants to give thanks to God. One such hymn states, "Hay momentos que las palabras no me alcanzan para decirte lo que siento" (There are moments when words do not suffice to tell thee what I feel). An example of a lyric that might "call a friend" to belief would be "Yo tengo un amigo que me ama, / Tú tienes un amigo que te ama: / Cristo Jesus" (I have a friend that loves me, / You have a friend that loves you: / Jesus Christ). Evangelical Protestants actively encouraged others to find and accept Christ. Music was one proselyting tool used to invite others to share or participate in the religious experience.

In accordance with their interpretation of the Bible, Evangelicals placed additional loudspeakers on the rooftops of church buildings or the houses used for services.[4] They felt that many people had accepted Christ by listening to a hymn or sermon that was amplified and delivered well beyond the physical bounds of the church compound. Indeed, given the amplification and reverberation within the cinderblock walls, I often found I could hear the words and messages better when I was fifty or a hundred meters away in the street than in the meeting room

itself. And if I could not remember exactly where a specific church was, or when its meeting started, I could wait for the service to begin and easily follow the sounds of the music right to the place.

In addition to the technology of electronic amplification in meetings and from rooftops, Evangelicals used other modern technology to put out the word. While television and the internet were not readily available to town members—in 2003 cable was just coming in, and internet was expensive—the local radio waves were used extensively to reach out to others. The town had two small Christian (which is to say, Evangelical-oriented) stations. Different churches purchased time and showcased their church through music and preaching. Some congregations mounted speakers and amplifiers on trucks, which drove around playing Christian music. They used such systems throughout the town and its hamlets to petition for funds, announce events, and invite people to church. The churches also held cultos or sponsored highly amplified special music events in community spaces. The anniversary event—held in the community space above the market, visible throughout the town plaza, and audible well beyond—drew in many more people than actually belonged to the particular church or its Evangelical cousins. Although the pastors spoke, the emphasis was on the music and the special musical guests. Because of the highly visual and accessible location, many people just passing by were attracted to attend, to listen, or to be entertained.[5]

Music as Social Uniter

Because religious music played such a large role in the Evangelical Protestant experience and involved the participation of not only the church members but also the community at large, such music acted as a bridge or common ground between member and God, between fellow members, and between one Evangelical church and another. "Musical performance," Basso (1985:253) asserts, "is associated with powerful beings and is a means of communicating with them." For worshippers, the main purpose of the hymns of adoration and alabanza (praise) was to worship God and to direct praise to his name.[6] Music thereby united people with God. Such a union can be reached in other ways, but, as expressed by one pastor, "you get there faster by car than on foot." Music was the vehicle of that more direct, speedier channel to connection with God and bodily reception of the spirit.

The music also served to prepare listeners to receive the words of the preacher and thus God's message for his people. The pastor of the Oasis Church explained that in biblical times, before God sent manna to the earth, he sent dew to cover the earth. Music serves as the precursor dew that prepares for the word of God.

Music also bridged differences that existed in the congregation. Much of the religious music used a tempo, loudness, and style or genre that mimicked the pop music enjoyed by the younger generation, but it was not limited to them. Old and young alike found themselves moved by religious music. Moreover, in *culto*, individuals shared spiritual experiences in a congregation. Physical interaction and pan-congregational rhythmic motion, such as unified swaying, sometimes became part of the musical experience, creating additional bonds between members.

While the majority of preaching during a *culto* was in K'iche', most of the songs were in Spanish. The vast majority of the songs a congregation sang were composed by Evangelicals from outside the town. Lyrics, and sometimes the musical scores, appeared in published pamphlets that circulated throughout the country. Tapes, CDs, radio broadcasts, and visiting ministers and traveling congregants further ensured that music was widely distributed. Shared music thus bound local congregations to their sister or parent churches and bridged the ethnic boundary.

Shared music also linked Nahualense *evangélicos* to other denominations of Evangelicals throughout Guatemala and to Pentecostal coreligionists throughout the world. A song from a popular Christian group called Apocalipsis illustrates how the musical lyrics themselves reinforced these links. The first refrain notes, "Men don't want to recognize thee, / that thou art God. / But we recognize that thou art God of all nations." The song goes on to say, "Thou art God of ——" and repeats this phrase inserting in the slot, one by one, the nations (or territories) of Costa Rica, Honduras, Mexico, Puerto Rico, Argentina, Brazil, and North America. In the second verse, the song repeats the initial refrain of worldly rejection and affirms that "we recognize that thou art God All-Powerful." The song then uses that same frame "Thou art God of ——" and inserts departments and well-known city centers throughout Guatemala itself: Guatemala, Quetzaltenango, San Marcos, Mazatenango, Zacapa, Cobán, Escuintla, Totonicapán, Quiché, and Chichicastenango. Thus, the song links the congregant to God, and through God to the nations of the Western Hemisphere and the people

and places of Guatemala. The concept of the song is that God, as defined by Evangelical Protestants, is the God of every nation and community, and thus unites everyone, worldwide, who sings the song.

Wightman (2007:245) finds a similar orientation toward global connection and national orientation embedded in the Pentecostalism she studied in Bolivia: "Pentecostal affiliation provides an identity in the community or the nation, and Pentecostals see themselves as part of a global social movement. Through these connections with a global movement, Pentecostals in Cochabamba"—like those of Nahualá and Ixtahuacán—"can tap into a discourse that offers an alternative vision of globalization to the secular, capitalist one that has restructured their lives and increased their marginalization and alienation from the state."

Owen, Walstrom, and Michelsen (1969:100) note that "music and musicians often serve more than merely local social 'functions.'" They suggest that musical events and musical personnel tend to be intersocietal and thus help integrate diverse societies and cultures over larger regions. Because many of the songs were used across churches, Christian music linked the relatively isolated congregations of Nahualá to multiple denominations within the larger Evangelical Christian world. In the International Church, the marimba could have been used as a base and style for songs, but the congregation preferred songs, music styles, and rhythms from outside Nahualá and Guatemala.[7]

When a popular singer from Mexico came to Quetzaltenango, a small delegation from Nahualá attended. At the concert, people from all over Guatemala—Ladinos and indigenous people alike—enjoyed the same religious music. The singer encouraged everyone to jump and dance. The people from the town I studied did not dance and jump around like others did at the concert,[8] but they participated in their own way by singing along. They enjoyed sharing their love for God in such a large gathering of Christians.

Thus, a large selection of Christian music exists that is not specific to one church or another. One could easily purchase this music at Nahualá's weekly market from the various stands selling religious music cassettes and CDs. These stands displayed dozens of groups and hundreds of titles. To a large degree, the same music was used across different Evangelical Protestant churches. The unity brought on by the shared music manifested itself at the anniversary party. Not only did pastors and members from other churches attend, they also gave support that was verbally recognized in the meeting. To be sure, church members were encouraged to listen only to Christian music, but that did not limit them to specific songs sung only in their congregation. Moreover, at another level of unification, Evangelical songs are increasingly being adopted into the liturgy of the Catholic church in Nahualá, especially among the rapidly growing charismatic Catholic congregations.[9]

In general, the styles of music played in church mimicked popular music. Frequently, Christian bands pirated recent "worldly" musical scores and gave them religious lyrics. For this reason, one might recognize a Beatles tune or a particular *ranchera* song in a religious setting. Evangelical leaders and parents pushed their children to "not be of the world"; they set rules to distinguish Christian behavior from worldly behavior. I believe that the religious adaptation of secular music allowed Evangelical youths to enjoy modern music, like their Catholic peers, while still remaining connected with the Evangelical church.[10]

Music as Social Divider

Just as religious music bridges gaps between groups, it can also divide groups, distinguishing one from another. Christian music serves to separate Evangelical Protestant churches from Catholic, charismatic Catholic, and other churches. Evangelical music differs greatly from the music used during Ortho-Catholic mass. Although charismatic groups have adopted many Evangelical Protestant songs, they follow in the Catholic tradition of directing praise to Mary, and they have adapted Evangelical songs to include occasional reference to her. An Evangelical Protestant song, on the other hand, would never accord honor to the mother of Christ.

This type of music also distinguishes Pentecostal Evangelicals from other Protestant groups. The music used in the Church of Jesus Christ of Latter-day Saints (Mormons) and that used by Jehovah's Witnesses are very different from the type of music used in these Evangelical Protestant groups. Mormons, for example, use a piano (or recorded piano music if no piano or player is available); emphatically, and therefore contrastively, they do not have bands or use electronic amplification beyond what is needed to hear a speaker's words at the back of a room. Other than singing, Mormon music does not invoke extra participation, such as clapping, shouting, or dancing.

Music selection also distinguishes the Evangelical Protestant groups from each other. The Oasis Church is widely recognized as being different from the rest, especially in the type of music that is played and the dancing that accompanies it. Other churches, as mentioned, have adapted popular forms of music; Oasis has not. Oasis leaders and members have written all of their own songs and believe it a holier music. Not surprisingly, a pastor of another church believed the exact opposite. He saw Oasis's music as anything but God's music. Rather, he considered it "the devil's music" because it was not like his. Music indeed divides as well as unites.

Although melodies and lyrics from outside the community of Nahualá are often utilized, local churches also create their own religious music to retain their regional heritage and preferences. Even though an international Spanish hymnal was available, the International Church chose to make its own informal version. The leaders picked songs they liked, the majority of which were not in the international version. They also sang a few songs in K'iche'.

As mentioned earlier, it is important for "good Christians," that is, Evangelicals, to separate themselves from the world. They are not allowed to listen to music that is not Christian. Even though the only difference between Christian music and worldly music is the text, the Evangelical Protestant churchgoer sees them as totally distinct; one is sacred, the other profane.[11] Some pastors regarded music that they denominated "rock" to be not just worldly, but of the devil. This music, they explained, talked about things such as the pleasure of sinning. Susceptible listeners, they feared, would be easily caught in Satan's trap. Thus, music not only divided and distinguished some styles of religion from each other, it also separated the religious from what they saw as the irreligious.

CONCLUSION

Music facilitates spiritual experiences. Music can influence which church a person joins and how they interact with others. Through shared music, churches are tied together; through distinct music, the separateness of congregations can be emphasized. Regardless of their denomination, Evangelical worshippers are invited, even commanded, to sing out and participate. As one of their songs reminds them, they must "raise their voices and ring out" songs "to Jehovah because he showed them enormous goodness."

Music such as this highlights important traits of Evangelical Protestant groups, including their reliance on the Bible, the role of the Holy Spirit, and the nature of personal religious experience. As Durkheim (2001[1912]:258) says, Pentecostal ritual, especially the music, "set[s] the collectivity in motion, . . . bring[s] individuals together, [and] increase[s] contacts between them," making "those contacts more intimate." I have shown that in association with music, Pentecostal ritual does indeed cause a change of consciousness in religious and national orientation. Music, in sum, serves as an embodied organizer of Pentecostal belief and practice. Through it, the Pentecostal worldview can be observed, compared, and understood.

NOTES

1. My fieldwork and focus on music shares some productive resonances with Barbara Lange's (1996:67) study of musical performance among the Isten Gyülekezet.

2. In corroboration of the much higher female-to-male ratio of attendees in Evangelical meetings, see Jones et al., and Smith et al., both this volume. On the predominance of male band members in Evangelical congregations, see an interesting parallel in Lawless 1983:434. We have, however, observed women as solo vocalists closely associated with church bands.

3. In mixed-gender cultos, I only saw male song leaders.

4. "Preach ye upon the housetops" (King James Version: Matthew 10:27).

5. By all these means, Catholics absorbed the insistent message that they needed to change. See Morgan 2005; and Pratt et al., this volume.

6. Hymns of adoration are slower songs. Hymns of *alabanza* are fast-paced. They serve to rejoice in the goodness of God and give him thanks.

7. In addition, marimba music, though theoretically available, had strong Catholic fiesta connotations and might have been discouraged on those grounds also.

8. Neither in Nahualá nor in this special concert did the *evangélicos* dance in their church meetings in the sense of couples dancing with each other or individuals orienting to the opposite sex in courtship. "Dancing" here means standing and moving one's body and feet to the rhythm of the music, oriented to the pulpit and as an expression to God.

9. The availability of informally printed booklets of Pentecostal songs, modified in places to accommodate Catholic interests, suggests this musical adoption is at least a nationwide phenomenon.

10. Youths, male and female, still found ways to listen to popular worldly music, in spite of the prohibitions.

11. I (Hawkins) well remember my first encounter with this cultural parsing. I was chatting with the Evangelical daughters of traditionalist Maya Catholic parents. The daughters explained the things that were *awas* (prohibited), among them *música*. I laughed and said they listened to *música* all the time.

"No we don't," they claimed.

But I had caught them! "Yes you do! Right now, right there!" as I pointed to the radio blaring *ranchera* music.

"That is not *música*, that's *alabanza*!"

"What is the difference?"

"In *música*, the words talk of worldly things; in *alabanza*, the words talk of God."

I paid close attention to the words for a few minutes. Indeed, these were Evangelical gospel lyrics, in K'iche', set to Mexican *ranchera*.

I learned respect, and I learned to listen.

Chapter Nine

Taboos and Togetherness

*Religious Prohibitions and Evangelical Community Boundary
Maintenance in Nueva Santa Catarina Ixtahuacán*

AMELIA SISCO THOMPSON, JOHN P. HAWKINS, AND WALTER RANDOLPH ADAMS

WHEN I WALKED INTO THE room, I smiled at Teresa and Enzor, the parents in the home where I lived while in Nueva Santa Catarina Ixtahuacán.[1] They sat in the parlor area with their daughter Antonia and a young man I did not know. Their subdued and unintelligible (to me) K'iche' words generated a background hum. Slowly, I became aware of an uncomfortable feeling and had the thought that perhaps I ought not to be in the room. I slipped out through the cloth-draped doorway. Seeing María, the daughter-in-law, in the kitchen, I asked what was going on. María replied, "He's Antonia's boyfriend." I raised my eyebrows, looking for more information. She explained that the boyfriend was angry with Antonia's parents, because Antonia had gone to the dance. Not sure if I didn't understand because of the language difficulties or the cultural differences, I asked for clarification. Going to dances is *awas*—forbidden or taboo. Antonia's boyfriend was angry with her parents for not keeping her under control. This was not an easy task, I would learn.

Later, Antonia was summoned to the room again. She emerged shortly thereafter, head down, a fresh bruise high on her left cheekbone. As we walked up the hill to church together, I lagged behind, unaccustomed to the stiff Maya women's skirt the family requested I wear. Antonia stated matter-of-factly, "My mother hit me." "Oh," I said simply, unsure yet what the proper response should be.

AGENDA

In this chapter, I discuss the prohibitions particular to the Evangelical congregation Antonia and her family attended, explaining why they existed as they did and what function they served in the larger society. Durkheim (2001[1912]:40) suggests that prohibitions define and identify the sacred realm by "protecting" and "isolating" "sacred things." Strong correlations exist between the system of prohibitions and social actions. To explore this connection, I first examine the literature on religious prohibitions. Then I discuss the cultural context of prohibitions in this specific congregation. Finally, I analyze the data from my observations of natural practice, natural discourse, and elicited discourse in Nueva Santa Catarina Ixtahuacán regarding the function of prohibitions in this cultural community. I discuss my methods during the analysis.

A THEORETICAL CONTEXT FOR UNDERSTANDING PROHIBITIONS

Clear membership in a group seems a prerequisite for sharing a sense of unity, equality, comfort, and acceptance in that group. Victor Turner (1969) calls that feeling or experience *communitas*. From Durkheim's initial work to such summaries as Crapo (2003), anthropologists have long known that participation in group rituals fosters interpersonal loyalties among members.

In describing the religious practices of an Appalachian Evangelical group in the United States, Scott (1994:227) notes that a revival "served as a discursive arena through which participants identified and interpreted broader social issues relating to class, gender, and the foundations of community solidarity." She notes the "anti-worldly"

spirituality of the congregation (228) as well as its association with poverty, social marginality, and rapid social
change. Believers were prohibited from engaging in
worldly pursuits, such as drinking, dancing, and gambling. Such prohibitions provided a means to solidify
group identity (229). Scott observes that seating patterns
during worship services reflected a member's gender
identity as well as their spiritual state. For example, sinners sat toward the back of the hall, while those in good
standing sat in the front. Women took the left half of the
room, men the right. Thus, behavioral prohibitions and
restrictions identified one's status and state of grace in the
congregation. Similar processes operated in the Nahualense congregation I studied.

Gill (1990:709) describes an Evangelical group in La
Paz, Bolivia, among whom religion created a feeling of
opposition to the prevailing norms and practices of the
dominant society. The religion served to establish a sense
of order and to instill feelings of hope in people living in
an uncertain or alienated social environment. Like Scott,
Gill (1990:712) found that prohibitions, such as those
against drinking and dancing, solidified social bonds,
creating in turn a shared sense of community not unlike
Turner's notion of *communitas* and constituted popular
reasons for conversion.

After studying Evangelical groups in the Ecuadorian
sierra, Maynard (1993:247) observes, "Identity implies a
social process of contrast with, or opposition to, other
possible identities." In answering the question "What is
a Christian?" the Evangelicals Maynard studied strongly
emphasized orthopraxy over orthodoxy: "All the
responses emphasized action by saying, 'One who does
the commandments of God,' 'One who does the will of
God,' and 'One who has a good testimony'" (252). Thus,
Maynard underscores the role of behavior in constructing one's identity. As Crapo (2003:182) notes, participation in ritual publicly communicates acceptance of the
community morality symbolized by that ritual. Even if a
participant is privately not truly committed to the rules
and values expressed in the ritual, the act of public acceptance obligates him or her to abide by them, and such
compliance connotes membership in the group. Thus,
anti-rituals—which is to say, the avoidances encoded in
certain taboos—function to create a social identity for
those who abide by the taboos.

My research sought to extend the observations of the
above-mentioned scholars regarding opposition, prohibitions, identity, and group cohesion within a larger society.

To do so, I searched for answers to these questions: What
societal stresses helped shape the Evangelicals' use of
prohibitions in Nueva Ixtahuacán? What role did prohibitions play in strengthening their sense of community?
And what rituals and anti-rituals solidified membership?

SETTING

During my fieldwork in 2003, Nueva Santa Catarina
Ixtahuacán was a fledgling village, newly founded in the
highlands of Guatemala. Villagers remembered fondly
the homes, lower down the mountain and much warmer,
that they had left a mere three years previously in January 2000. María reminisced, "In Antigua Ixtahuacán, my
house had a garden, and I would grow things there." Her
home in Nueva Santa Catarina Ixtahuacán, by contrast,
had a yard of hard-packed earth surrounded by a corru-
gated tin fence; patches of cold-tolerant bunch grass stubbornly survived around the fringes of her cinderblock
home.

Nueva Ixtahuaquenses expressed sadness when they
discussed their old village and home, lost to them in a
mudslide. But they mixed with this nostalgia a sense of
looking forward, of banding together and striding into the
future. Their new high school was stocked with USAID-
and government-provided computers wired to the internet. Many families in Nueva Ixtahuacán emphasized education and moving up. Naturally, there was tension as new
changes pushed tradition into the shadows of the past.

The concept of "the world," an oft-overheard phrase,
was linked in many people's minds to forward progress,
westernization, and sin. More often than not, these concepts existed in people's minds as a tangled mass, inex-
tricable from one another. While some embraced change
and welcomed it into their families, homes, and churches,
others shunned it as the harbinger of sin and corruption.
The community was divided thereby into three distinct
groups. Each group was roughly homogenous within
itself, based on education, economic status, and view of
"the world." Loosely, the three groups can be described
as follows: Catholics were the most well-off, the most
well-educated, the most involved in the world, and the
least involved and/or committed to their religion in the
sense that religion constrained their lifestyle. Evangelicals were less well-off, less well-educated. They built
their social connections through their religion and were
generally more committed to their faith than Catholics

were. Charismatics were similar to Evangelicals in that they were less well-off and less well-educated than non-charismatic Catholics, although I am not familiar enough with them to say whether they were slightly more or less so than the Evangelicals. It was quite apparent, however, that charismatics typically came from the lowest economic strata.[2]

The Evangelical religious group I studied, Voz Que Clama en el Desierto (Voice That Cries Out in the Desert), had notably dense social ties within the congregation. Their social lives revolved around the church. While the religion forbade parties of the world, parties with a religious spin were another story. I attended numerous revival gatherings that could easily be described as praise and worship parties, complete with food and live music.

The local Catholic church claimed to welcome all and counted all who believed in Jesus Christ as members of its faith, including those that did not attend or that belonged to other congregations. Charismatics and Evangelicals, on the other hand, had stricter sets of rules for who could and could not be counted as a member. They formed tight-knit groups and clearly identified those within and those without.

The Catholic church anchored the nucleus of the town, its large building facing the central square. Its white stuccoed façade loomed large, its twin bell towers rising high above the community. It was indeed impressive—until one walked around the corner to realize that its incomplete side and back walls supported no roof. The incomplete shell stood unused—quiet and empty—evidence, as Pratt and colleagues (this volume) argue, of the Catholic church's fading influence in this town.

In Lévi-Straussian (1967[1949]:xxix, 136; 1974) contrast, around the perimeter of the village, Evangelical and charismatic meetinghouses dotted the hills like wildflowers gone to seed, brightly painted spots of color and vibrant sources of sound. One such church housed Voz Que Clama en el Desierto, the congregation to which my host family belonged and that I attended while in Nueva Ixtahuacán (plate 25).

At nearly any hour of the day (including late at night and well before dawn), one could hear the word of God being pounded out of one or more of these buildings. The building housing my congregation sat to the southeast, on the outer fringe of Ixtahuacán's homes, perched on a hill overlooking the town. The pastor of Voz Que Clama en el Desierto proudly told me that their church was built entirely from locally donated money, supplies, and labor.

Congregation

In Guatemala, family ties are strong. My congregation behaved like one big extended family. Between eighty and a hundred members (including children) attended regularly, and nearly all were related to Pastor Manuel through blood or marriage. Indeed, throughout the community, family ties were a common reason for belonging to a particular congregation. Many members lived in households that bordered the church plot or that touched the property of other congregants in the immediate neighborhood of the building. Across the street from the church, Pastor Manuel's compound was surrounded by a web of cinder-block complexes, yards spilling into one another, property boundaries blurred by children scurrying from house to house. The majority of the households near the church were related. They saw each other at church several times a week and in passing on the street on a daily basis. Children were raised by many "parents" in the church family. People seemed to feel a responsibility to each other and a heightened sense of accountability.

The pastor, the grand patriarch of the whole group, had had a life-altering experience through which he found God after a long love affair with the bottle. His experience changed the lives of his family members; like dominoes, one after the other, the majority of his kin eventually came into his church.

One friend who was my age, still fresh with the glow of conversion, attempted to explain the appeal of the gospel to me and bring me into the group as well. I noticed several such attempts, both literal and symbolic, to identify me as a member of the group. In this congregation, sharing religious ties is an important way of cementing social relationships.[3]

In the first initiation I went through with my host family, my sisters dressed me in their traditional indigenous clothes. Speaking little Spanish, they simply held out a huipil, their traditional hand-woven pullover blouse, and indicated that I should hold up my arms so they could slide it over my head. Next they held out the traditional skirt, a large cylinder of cotton cloth that wraps around the body and is secured high and tight on the waist with an embroidered belt. They waited for me to remove my pants. "My pants?" I asked. They giggled and nodded. I stood awkwardly in my long johns while they swaddled me with this distinctive tube, which, surprisingly, was even warmer than my multiple layers of pants.

The girls ushered me outside and into the kitchen

building to present the new me. I was greeted with laughter, clapping, and approval. "So, would you like me to wear these clothes?" I asked. When they answered in the affirmative, I questioned, "All the time?" Yes again. I was then informed that these clothes were better than my own. I later understood that for a woman to appear in pants was relatively scandalous. We came to a compromise: when I went out with the family or around town, I would dress traditionally (figure 9.1), but when I went into the city or traveled alone, I would wear my own clothes (figure 9.2). Clothes certainly functioned to maintain boundaries of inclusion and exclusion in groups, a matter of great cultural concern to the family, the congregation, and the community.

The second initiation happened when they informed me that it was time for church, leaving it unsaid but understood that I would attend church with the family. This was the first time I sat with them in the congregation. Before moving in with my host family, I had attended church and sat in the back, taking notes, unwittingly taking a seat in the section reserved for sinners. Now I walked in with Antonia, María, and Teresa and joined the other women on the central benches. The unspoken statement: I was part of the family and therefore part of the church.

Worship Practices

A typical meeting began with singing. Often we came in late while everyone was already standing and singing praise and worship songs, often to vaguely familiar tunes. (The Beatles' "Ob-La-Di, Ob-La-Da" was a common one.) The women's side of the meeting hall was generally twice as full as the men's and took about twice as long to fill. Women straggled in, having just finished dinner preparations, or rescuing the hanging laundry from the threat of afternoon rain, or gathering up the children. Children wove in and out of parishioners' legs on both the men's and the women's sides, often dancing and running around in the center aisles. The deacons, whose responsibility it was to maintain order in the meeting, occasionally attempted to corral the children and deposit them with an adult, though not necessarily their parent; any available lap would do. Generally, though, the children simply wandered. Because of the typically high levels of noise and energy in the meetings, scurrying children did not distract.

Along with singing, which privileged members took turns leading, members read aloud from the Bible. In

Figure 9.1. The author as dressed by her host family. Courtesy of Amelia Sisco Thompson, 2003.

Figure 9.2. The author in traveling attire. Courtesy of Amelia Sisco Thompson, 2003.

the last third of the meeting, the pastor always said a few words. Typically, he mentioned not being "of the world." From the pulpit, the idea was ambiguous and expressed more as an overarching theme to guide one's life. Specific applications of the idea were elaborated and rules were taught in the home as well as in the social sphere outside the meetinghouse.

While singing, Bible reading, and praying were the three major activities of the meetings, eating together after a service was a close fourth, or perhaps rated a higher ranking, depending on whom you asked. Francisca, one of my favorite informants, always knew when food would be served and had no qualms about sneaking an extra serving or two when the baskets were passed around. Often, when I felt myself fading toward the end of a two-and-a-half-hour-long meeting, Francisca would lean over with a grin and whisper, "There's food coming!" She would pocket several small loaves of the sweet bread and wrap a few tamales in the cloth all women carried, which served a multiplicity of purposes from hat, to baby carrier, to umbrella, to shopping bag. "I'll get extra, and we can share," she would whisper conspiratorially as the baskets neared. And she always made good on her word, pressing torn pieces of bread into my hand on the sly or pouring more hot chocolate from her cup to mine. Regularly breaking tortillas together bonded these people, especially the women, to each other, and they used food to bond me to them.

Despite the aura of should-nots that hung over the group, they made their own kind of fun. Since being of the world was denounced, they created exciting alternatives. Every week or two, we traveled to neighboring towns for what were essentially religious parties. Sometimes the event celebrated a baptism or an anniversary of membership. Sometimes visiting pastors or famous religious singers would visit. All such gatherings meant even more singing and mountains of more food. The whole congregation piled into two or three pickup trucks and flew down the mountain to attend these events. Each pickup held about thirty bodies, intertwined like puzzle pieces, utilizing every inch of available space. It was at these times—as we clung to each other in one colorful mass of humanity, fighting the centrifugal force of curves that threatened to pull us from the speeding truck, whizzing past waves of intensely green hillsides—that I really felt a part of that group.

These religious gatherings evoked the feeling of being at a festival. Vendors gathered outside the doors like flies—knowing they had a captive, hungry audience—and sold such treats as halved oranges sprinkled with salt and chili powder, frozen bananas, ice cream, sodas, and grilled chicken. The speakers tended to have a bit more showmanship than our quiet, subdued local pastor. They strode the length of the stage, waving their arms and shouting praises to the Lord, expounding on his virtues or his suffering.

Typically the speakers focused more on ideas than on actions. Faith, mercy, and salvation were common themes. Peppered among these, the common refrain to not be of the world echoed, though typically in an abstracted sense. Once people arrived at home, however, parents made this abstract idea more concrete.

PROHIBITIONS AS SOCIAL MARKERS

While I never heard specific rules listed from the pulpit, all the members of the congregation were familiar with each one. When I interviewed the pastor and asked him directly what things were prohibited, he said rather ambiguously, "It is prohibited to be part of the world." I had better luck questioning the parishioners, who were all eager to talk about the nitty-gritty details. Outside church, prohibited things—those which were *awas* and, especially, who in particular was doing them—were favorite topics of conversation. María, Antonia's sister-in-law, often informed me of the host of prohibited acts that Antonia committed. Always there was a note of disapproval in her voice as well as a glint of excitement in her eye. There seems to be something universal about the attraction of the forbidden.

They knew that I did not follow all their rules and were curious to know of the things I did, like dancing. Dancing, in particular, was forbidden to them, though not unknown, especially to girls like Antonia. Indeed, going to parties and dancing were on the tip of everyone's tongue when I asked about prohibitions. They would often ask me, giggling, to dance for them.

While it was common knowledge that I was not a member of their faith and did not live an Evangelical lifestyle, they still wanted me to be part of the family and part of their social circle. One evening, not long after my first trip to church with the other women, a cousin, Marco, stopped by. He came into the bedroom with Antonia in tow. "Do you want to sing tomorrow?" he asked me. There was a special event, and he wanted me to sing some songs and play my guitar. I explained that I didn't know any religious songs or Spanish songs. "That's okay," he replied. "I have a book right here." He handed me a book of lyrics in which he had marked three songs for me to sing. The lyrics had no music with them since the tunes were simply learned by hearing them at church over and over. He assured me that I could just figure out what chords sounded good with the songs. After some convincing on his side, and some bargaining on my side, we decided I would learn one song, and he would teach me the melody.

One of the first things I learned after attending a few Evangelical meetings in Guatemala is that by US standards, most of them can't sing in tune. Their meetings are full of cacophonous, disorganized, yet heartfelt praises and rejoicing. So when Marco and José (his cousin and the pastor's son) sang for me, picking out the melody was like untangling a mangled spider's web. I recorded the song and listened to it over and over. My version of "Divine Companion" was likely different than any they had ever heard.

The typical style of singing in their meetings is a combination of shouting, crying, and singing, which I didn't attempt to imitate. Instead, I opted for a melodic interpretation, which was not greeted by the typical shouts of "Hallelujah!" and "Glory to God!" Rather, I received an awkward silence and several polite "Amens." As I took my seat, the pastor's son, who was about my age, grinned and shook his head with an "Oh, my, oh, no" implication, mirroring my feelings exactly.

While the experience left me feeling rather sheepish, I realized I had gone through another ritual. Only members in good standing were allowed to sing in front of the congregation. Menstruating women were also forbidden to stand and sing in front of the congregation. It was common knowledge that I did not meet the first criterion, and they had no way of knowing the second. I realized that the greater purpose of the prohibitions was to mark who was part of the group and who was not. Because they wanted to identify me as a member of their social group, the fact that I did not abstain from all things prohibited was less important than using that same system to identify me as at least an honorary member.

PROHIBITIONS DETAILED

For bona fide members, the expectations were higher. Through a system of social policing that included rampant gossip, a strict code of conduct was enforced. The prohibitions included going to parties, drinking alcohol, being part of the world, attending fairs or festivals of the world, adultery or having more than one boyfriend or girlfriend, singing in front of the congregation while pregnant or menstruating, attending church or praying while menstruating, wearing makeup or jewelry, being angry, not attending church meetings, smoking, divorce, living together before marriage, chewing gum in church, cutting your hair if you were a woman, lying, participating in traditional Maya customs, harming others, and giving the evil eye.

The common phrase "of the world" encompassed all these prohibitions. Most frequently, however, it was used synonymously with "going to dances and parties." The subject came up often in my home since Antonia had a penchant for dances. After the trip to the dance that earned a bruise on her cheek, she told me proudly, "I've been to three other dances!"—all on the sly, of course. A dance that Antonia and I both attended was put on by the town. A rock band was hired. Ten quetzals (about US$1.25) bought entry. I was surprised to see normally docile people pushing and shoving to force their way into the gymnasium through the one small door. Two young men guarded the doorway, calling over the throng, "Tickets? People with tickets?" "Yes, we have tickets!" we shouted back. Ten quetzals—almost a third of a peasant laborer's daily wages—was too much for most people to pay. For women, Q40.00 a week was an average salary. So, most resorted to sneaking or forcing their way into the dance. As we made our way to the front, people clung to our sides, hoping to squeeze in with us. Strong arms reached out through the doorway and pulled me through, lifting me off the ground and depositing me on the other side.

I looked around, expecting to be in a tightly packed room, bodies pulsating to a pounding beat like one might see at a dance club in the States. What I encountered was more akin to an awkward middle school dance. This type of music and dance throbbed well outside the culture of the Nueva Ixtahuaquenses. The band played mightily to scattered clusters of men and women clinging to the periphery of the gym, their traditional clothes bright color spots along the wall. As the evening wore on and people had more to drink, some ventured onto the dance floor. I was again reminded of a middle school dance, as men awkwardly attempted moves that they had likely seen on television. I was asked to dance by a man my age, who was no less than six inches shorter than me. We teetered around in circles, his hands on my waist, arms sticking straight out. This type of atmosphere epitomized "the world" and for members of Evangelical groups was to be avoided at all costs.

When I asked María what was so bad about going to dances, she said that people who go to dances of the world also drink. Drinking was a serious problem in the highlands, as was the familial abuse that tended to accompany it. There was drinking in abundance at this dance. It seems that for *evangélicos*, it was the association with alcohol, more than the act of dancing, that was the problem.

Manuel related how he came to be the pastor of his congregation: "Before, I used to get drunk all the time. My family was very sad. Sometimes I wouldn't come home. One day, I had an experience. I saw God and began to read the Bible. I studied it all the time." Eventually he came to know the book so well that he began to teach others, developed a following, and has built his own church to preach in.

Such stories of a life changing event were common. Religion was often the antidote to alcoholism and the problems that surrounded it. However, while the ideal was to trade the bottle for the Bible, many people had trouble making a clean switch. Thus, there was still fear and caution around anything to do with alcohol, or the world, the two often being synonymous, especially for men. While the phrase "being of the world" was decidedly a religious notion, I heard it discussed most often around the stove in the kitchen or while the women were washing clothes or weaving.

CONSEQUENCES OF SIN

The sins I learned of varied categorically and in severity, though the consequences in every case were forms of isolation of varying length. María explained the repercussions of drinking: "First the pastor talks to him [the sinner] and says, 'If you drink again, you can't come back to church.' Drinking is not of God. It is of the devil. It is better for someone who has decided to drink not to come to church at all, because now they are part of the world." María's imagined pastor drew a distinct line between those within and those outside the congregational fold. Certain behavior excluded one from belonging. Such behavioral markers were used to identify the insiders and outsiders. As Lambeck (1998) asserts for the Malagasy, taboos functioned in Nueva Ixtahuacán to create a social identity for the *evangélicos* who followed them.

More than professions of belief, one's actions, such as attending meetings, identified one as an insider. If a person did not abide by the rules, only two possibilities existed: either that person was already part of the world and not part of the congregation, or they were part of the congregation but their sinning placed them in a liminal state. In the latter case, they were neither fully of the world, nor fully or deserving of the congregation. The pastor would assign such an individual a period of punishment in the form of separation from participation in the full round of congregational worship activities. After that, the repentant sinner could be reintroduced to the congregation.

Thus, when a person sinned, and gossip or chance encounter brought it sufficiently to the pastor's attention, the sinner received a visit from the pastor. He told the offender, for example, that he or she should attend all meetings, but may not stand up and sing in front of the congregation, bear testimony, visit the sick with other members, or bring flowers to decorate the church. The secretary of the church recorded the specific strictures, as well as the duration of the punishment. According to José, "A person can't participate in the world and then come and worship and bear testimony because their testimony isn't valid. When people see them at the fiesta and then at church, it isn't good. If someone goes to a party and another person sees them there, the pastor will talk to them and give them discipline."

Always there was the concern that "someone would see you sinning." When I asked what happened if no one saw you at a party, José, after some contemplation, replied, "Well, then you only have to pray to God and ask for pardon." "You don't have to talk to the pastor and receive punishment?" I probed. "No, only if someone sees you," he answered matter-of-factly. This focus on being seen (or not) shows how heavily the emphasis was placed on social relationships and roles. In this Evangelical congregation, as in the much larger K'iche' community that had moved and even in the municipal unit as a whole, identifying those that belonged to the group and keeping them within the bounds of that group mattered greatly. The system of prohibitions and disciplinary actions unified the congregation, visibly showing who was part of the inner circle of inward-facing members, who was on the fringe, and who was on the outside.

The awarding of privileges in my case was not based on my behavior. Rather, it told the congregation and the community at large that this particular gringa belonged to this specific group. During my time there, I was cared for, looked after, gossiped about, and confided in like any other member of the group.

Other forms of discipline included having to sit on the back benches while the rest of the congregation normally filled up the front two-thirds. If you committed *awas*, you were not allowed to participate with the women who brought fresh flowers and decorated the dais You also could not visit the sick. I asked one woman for clarification on this: "So, if your mother is sick, you aren't allowed to go visit her?" She replied, "Oh no, I can go visit her alone. I just can't go with other members of the congregation." Here again was a technique of separation and isolation wherein the importance was placed not so much on the act but on where one fit in the group. The physical separation symbolically showed one as standing outside the group, as defined by its norms. An important part of the punishment process, the separation established the liminal and therefore dangerous state of the guilty party.

ANALYSIS OF PROHIBITIONS AND CONSEQUENCES

I became aware early on that going to parties and dances was taboo in this Evangelical community. Disobedience to this particular prohibition was the first major "social drama" (Turner 1957) I encountered, the slapping incident described at the beginning of the chapter. Throughout the remainder of my fieldwork, dancing, its prohibition, and the infractions thereof recurred frequently in discourse within families, between friends, and, implicitly or explicitly, in church meetings. Moreover, it provided the basis for a value dispute that underlay several dramatic flare-ups. It was, in short, a recurrent theme.

From where did these value disputes emerge? Partly they came from generalized processes of modernization and increased inclusion in the global world. Partly they also came from the stresses Ixtahuaquenses experienced as a result of their recent relocation. Thus, the community of Nueva Santa Catarina Ixtahuacán roiled with change and flux. Because of the move, the town had to secure a workable new infrastructure. At the same time, old ways of life were passing away in the face of increasing contact with the nation of Guatemala, with the United States, and with the products of globalized trade. In Nueva Ixtahuacán, a division or demarcation separated those who wanted and encouraged the change and those who pushed it away and

attempted to maintain a more traditional lifestyle. While the two camps coexisted peacefully, people wanted to identify one another as being from one school of thought or the other. Evangelicals talked about and therefore identified those who did not belong to an Evangelical church and who, therefore, embraced what they called "the world." In this congregation and this community, the great emphasis placed on avoidance of certain sins and abiding by certain prohibitions directly resulted from the social tensions having to do with secularization and globalization, and the challenges of reconciling changes with tradition—all exacerbated by the recent relocation. The Evangelical community tried to maintain its boundaries with an us-versus-them attitude that kept outsiders and their philosophies at bay. The observance of prohibitions by oneself and others helped maintain those boundaries.

The upset about Antonia and the dance happened within a few days of my arrival at their home. It was obviously a topic of serious social volatility and piqued my interest. I began asking questions: "What is prohibited?" and, more important, "Why?" This led to more formal research methods. Through freelisting, pile sorting, a survey,[4] and paired comparisons, I found that the proscribed doctrine of the religion and the casual discourse of its followers as to what is cardinal sin differ. Officially, killing is the worst sin one can commit, followed by getting drunk, going to Maya ceremonies, fornication, being angry, cutting your hair, and going to parties. However, in natural discourse, interviews, and freelisting, the sin of going to dances and parties, or being of the world, nearly always came up before the subject of killing. I interpret this difference by considering the natural discourse prohibitions and sins as the most socially volatile and at the forefront of members' minds. After all, in daily life one is more likely to be tempted to go to a dance or party or to be presented in the marketplace with a choice regarding something defined as a sin of the world than to face the option of murder. Thus, figure 9.3 shows the percentage of cases in which each sin was mentioned in a free list offering open slots for up to five responses. The percentages provide a ranking as to which sins were the most socially significant in the daily lives of Nueva Ixtahuaquense Pentecostals.

THEORETICAL IMPLICATIONS

In the Evangelical church I studied, members found a sense of community and solidarity. Indeed, in church

Figure 9.3. Socially significant sins.

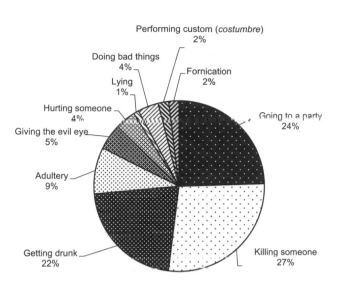

they participated in something that is closer to a family than an organization. With so much change going on in the village of Nueva Santa Catarina Ixtahuacán due to the relocation of the village and the increasing influence of the western world, they derived from their church community a haven of continuity and togetherness. In this sense, the small religious group picked up where the greater society and the narrower nuclear family fell short in meeting people's needs.

The members' sense of community was strengthened through the ritual avoidance of defined prohibitions. In abiding by those prohibitions, they used their bodies as markers to communicate that they were not part of the "other" or of the world. When the rest of the town celebrated a fiesta, the Evangelicals stayed at home, met in church, or attended a celebratory religious event, though it would not be called a fiesta, for that was *awas*. This clear demarcation both set them apart and bound them together. By identifying the "other"—those that participated in things of the world—they made their own identity clearer.

Yet within the church, I found gradations of belonging. Those who had recently broken a taboo were pushed to the outer fringes of the circle of belonging through exclusionary techniques, such as being required to sit at the back of the meeting hall and being forbidden to participate in religious activities in front of other members. To remedy this ostracized state and reintegrate with the group, the sinners had to redouble their efforts to avoid the world and to attend all meetings. Meeting attendance was required in order to be a member in good standing.

The mutuality of required attendance in turn helped solidify social relationships and strengthened the sentiment of "us" in contrast to "them."

One even sees in figure 9.4 a slight breakdown in separation from the world in the attire of my own family in Nueva Santa Catarina Ixtahuacán: one daughter is not dressed as *indígena*, and a son is dressed in the long-established and nearly universal male attire approximating Ladino style.

Durkheim (1961[1912]) has said that religion is the worship of the social order. Guatemalan Evangelical Protestantism—which is to say, Pentecostal Protestantism—replicated and worshipped the ideal social order. Prohibitions, and the decision to abide by them or not, marked where people stood in the community. By talking about what acts and/or prohibitions various individuals did or did not commit, church members defined themselves and those around them.

Even if one were not fully committed or converted to the religion, rituals and prohibitions marked one's place in the group. This was the case for Antonia. She attended church immediately after being punished for sneaking off to the dance. Her disobedience was public knowledge; likewise, her penitence was public. She went through the traditional stages of ritual, a reintegrative rite of passage, and, certainly, in Victor Turner's terms, a social drama. First, the pastor separated her from the group for having sinned. Next, in the liminal state of neither belonging nor not belonging, she publicly wept and praised God in church. I knew from talking with her that her heart was not breaking for having committed this prohibited act. In fact, I suspected she would not hesitate to do it again, since it was the fourth dance she had attended. What was at stake, however, was her standing in the church community, broader than her residential family but narrower and more effective than the *cabecera* village of Nueva Santa Catarina. For this reason, she strove to rebuild her place in it. After faithfully attending all her meetings and refraining from breaking any more prohibitions, she would eventually be reaccepted as a full member with full privileges. Knowing Antonia, I think she preferred to live comfortably on the fringe, maintaining her painted lips and arranging an occasional late-night rendezvous. Previous research has identified the role of the Evangelical

Figure 9.4. Part of the author's host family in Nueva Santa Catarina Ixtahuacán. Courtesy of Amelia Sisco Thompson, 2003.

faith in creating identity for people, especially those in the midst of flux and change. I observed similar processes of identity formation.

CONCLUSION

The people in Nueva Santa Catarina Ixtahuacán faced changes from every angle. Some embraced the changes; some tried to push them away while rebuilding the crumbling foundation of the past. In an effort to build group solidarity and create a personal and group identity, Evangelicals of the congregation I studied employed a strict set of prohibitions that served to identify outsiders and insiders—those of the world and those who were not—and that bound together a supra-family interaction and support system. Consequences for disobedience served as markers for where people stood in the circle of membership. Clearly identifying those who were of the world, or "not one of us," the prohibitions strengthened both their Evangelical identity and the unity of their tight-knit, gospel-linked, complexly extended family. Durkheim was right that prohibitions—taboos—marked the sacred and

separated it from the profane. Observance of those prohibitions also marked people, gave them identity, and clarified their group affiliation.

Weber turned out also to be right. The prohibitions of this Pentecostal group set up an extreme regimentation of daily and weekly schedules and of domestic and public life that was much different than the relatively "relaxed, practically imperceptible, and scarcely more than formal authority" (Weber 2002[1905]:2) that guided life among the cultural Catholics and even the thoroughly engaged Ortho-Catholics. Moreover, the locus of judgment had partially moved from the ethnic identity of the *municipio*, which had been coterminous with traditionalist Catholicism and parish-defined Ortho-Catholicism, to the small congregation of those meeting with and judging one another quite intensely. Just as happened in the original Reformation, this Christian Pentecostalization in Nueva Ixtahuacán "meant less the entire *removal* of ecclesiastical authority over life than the replacement of the previous form of authority by a *different* one" (Weber 2002[1905]:2, emphases in original). As can be seen in Larson and colleagues, Scott and colleagues, and Edvalson and colleagues (all this volume), the forms of Catholicism and of Pentecostalism "penetrated every sphere of domestic and public life to the greatest degree imaginable" (Weber 2002[1905]:2).

NOTES

1. All personal and family names in this chapter are pseudonyms.

2. If the pattern holds, charismatics in Nueva Ixtahuacán would be the most religious, would be the least educated, and have the strongest social ties in their congregations. For the charismatic family I knew well, this was indeed the case. But charismatics were not the focus of my study.

3. These kinship and family-centric congregations reproduced aspects of support and sustainment long embodied in Catholic *compadrazco* (fictive kinship) ties, which often and likewise confirmed important political, economic, and social relationships.

4. I administered a survey to the entire congregation of Voz Que Clama en el Desierto living in Nueva Santa Catarina Ixtahuacán. The other student researchers in the field school, most of whom are authors of chapters in this book, administered the same survey to the congregation or religious disposition that they studied intensively. Each researcher supplied questions pertinent to the particular emphasis that had emerged in her or his study, and the cross-administration in all the qualitatively studied congregations enabled comparison. Trained bilingual speakers, college students, and teachers from the community elicited responses from each family using a survey form written in both Spanish and K'iche' and administered in K'iche'.

The question I devised for the survey, which I analyze in this chapter, was "In your religious group, which are the activities most prohibited?" I hoped to gain insight into the sins that were at the forefront of people's minds. My theory was that those freelisted in the top three to five would be the most socially significant. Indeed, the same prohibitions listed were the hot topics of everyday conversation, gossip, and concern.

Chapter Ten

"We Dance Together and Sing and Pray, We Unite as Women"

Maya K'iche' Women's Evangelical Conversion and Participation in Nahualá

ADRIANA SMITH, JOHN P. HAWKINS, AND WALTER RANDOLPH ADAMS

A WALK AROUND THE RAPIDLY growing indigenous town center of Nahualá in 2003 revealed several brightly colored Pentecostal Protestant churches, most often on the urban perimeter (plate 26). Frequently, they blasted messages about God and "coming to Christ" through large sound systems. Peering through the front doors of many of these churches, one could see a large, open room with several benches facing a podium set on a raised platform. Often, a mural painted on the entire back wall displayed majestic nature scenes of paradisiacal mountains, waterfalls, and grazing animals. One of the Pentecostal churches I frequented depicted God's hands reaching down from a clear blue sky as if to beckon people into the room (plate 27). Evangelical music—often repetitive religious chants set to synthesized electric guitar and keyboard beats—could be heard any hour of the day from these churches through rooftop speakers or out the doors and windows via large indoor speaker banks. In addition to amplifying live, energetic music in meetings—from midmorning to late at night—mobile public address systems on the backs of trucks played Evangelical music and religious messages as they passed through town. In addition, some Evangelical churches used their outdoor speakers to continuously play prerecorded religious sermons or music during non-meeting hours, from predawn to late night. Thus, Evangelical messages pulsed across the valley every day of the week.[1]

These modes of communication called people into the church, offered them blessings from God and promises of prosperity, and admonished them to repentance. La palabra de Dios, the Evangelical word of God, reached into every corner and hamlet of Nahualá. Likewise, Evangelical influence has been spreading to all parts of Guatemala.

Although Guatemala is predominantly Catholic, the number of Pentecostal Protestants is growing rapidly. The term most commonly used to describe Pentecostal Protestants in Guatemala is evangélico; therefore, I refer to this style of religious practice as "Evangelical" throughout this chapter. Because a much higher percentage of Evangelicals than Catholics regularly attend church meetings, Stoll (1993b:2) refers to Evangelicals as "the movers and shakers on the religious scene." Here, Stoll suggests a Pentecostal dominance not only in numbers, but in the boisterous manner in which they worship and the enthusiasm with which they demonstrate their faith.

The changing political and economic forces imping-ing on indigenous communities and families in high-land Guatemala have played an important role in the high rates of conversion to Evangelical religions from the more traditional Catholicism. Women stand at the forefront of this change. Indeed, a large percentage of the Protestant boom in Guatemala is based on wom-en's conversion to the Evangelical churches. In Nahualá, 60–70 percent of those who participate in Evangelical meetings are women, indicating that women are the real "movers and shakers" on the Evangelical scene. Despite these facts, much ethnographic and survey work that addresses Latin American Evangelicalism fails to recog-nize women's considerable conversion and participation in the Evangelical church. In this chapter I attempt to fill in some of this gender gap. I suggest, as others have, that women in Nahualá convert to Evangelical churches to seek relief from strains in the family, particularly abuse and alcoholism (Eber 1995), empowerment through church participation and leadership roles, and a shared community through women's prayer meetings (Brusco 1993).

BACKGROUND

Much of what has been written on Latin American conversion to Evangelical faiths falls under two categories of thought. The first is a Weberian approach. Annis's (1987) work, for example, suggests people are drawn to Evangelical faiths because economic gain is built into and results from the ideology to which they convert. The second approach claims that conversion is a response to political strife, particularly the 1980s civil turmoil, which has driven Guatemalans to seek other sources of comfort and protection (Garrard-Burnett 1998; Fischer 2003). Although both of these may be factors in Guatemala's wave of Evangelical conversion, much of this research fails to distinguish the gendered differences between men's and women's experiences of conversion into Evangelical churches (Wilson 1995:164; Brusco 1993:144).

The deficit of research informed by a gender perspective proves to be particularly important when one considers the number of women, compared to men, participating in Evangelical faiths. Women constitute a two-thirds or better majority of lay members, yet researchers seldom analyze, let alone describe, their participation in Guatemalan Evangelicalism, with Brusco a principal exception. Those studies that do discuss women's participation "tend to focus purposefully on female leaders—preachers, evangelists, educators, missionaries, and founders of religious organizations—and leave less influential women and their devotional lives unexamined" (Griffith 2002:187). In this chapter, I try to remedy these voids by focusing on understanding ordinary women's religious experience in a few of Nahualá's Evangelical congregations.

CONVERSION AS RESPONSE
TO FAMILIAL STRESS

Indigenous Guatemalans find themselves stretched between the social and ecological limits of traditional life, where a static land base and rising population threaten age-old subsistence patterns, and the difficulties of accessing all that is implied by "modernization." (For a deeply empathic analysis of these forces in Nahualá, see Morgan 2005.) The K'iche's suffer from ethnic discrimination; geographic and linguistic forms of isolation; geological and economic hardships; and biased governmental, educational, and political practices. These impediments simultaneously imply increased contact with and opportunities

from the economic and political forces of the national and global society. Through confronting this mix of constraints and opportunities, Maya people change the way they live their lives. Today, no single outside coercive force makes them give up their indigenous ideologies. Rather, indigenous people hybridize foreign cultural characteristics with their own traditions as they seek to adapt to a complex and changing world. In Nahualá, shifts in language usage, dress, and subsistence strategies clearly exemplify this hybridization.

The changes in production from traditional *milpa* agriculture to a cash economy affect cultural values and assumptions, including women's labor. Speaking of women in San Pedro Chelnahó, Chiapas, Mexico, Eber (1995:237) suggests, "Changes in men's productive roles, including their decreasing capacity to support their families off the land and their increasing dependence on wage labor, seem to offset benefits for women." The changing role of men in the cash economy likewise affects women in Nahualá. Nahualense women confront more discrimination in the cash economy and more violence by men who have devalued women's noncash contributions to family and society.

Women in abusive relationships, who sometimes leave their male partners and seek help from their natal families, often also look for support in Evangelical churches: "Old cooperative units of domestic production have mostly broken up. Men are frequently unemployed and frequently leave women husbandless. . . . The woman finds her refuge in the church and tries to bring her husband along too. . . . Conversion follows and the atmosphere of the home changes" (Martin 1990:181–182). Martin's description of religious conversion in Latin America, in which women in husbandless homes seek "refuge in the church," closely parallels the patterns I saw in Nahualá. Julia, for example, reflected on her life prior to converting to an Evangelical church: "Before, my life was horrible, because before—[*she paused*] that was when we would drink. My husband and I would get drunk during celebrations, and he would sometimes hit me. There were problems, like him hitting me a lot. This is why we are in the church now. Now he doesn't drink. Neither do I. Now, thank God, he doesn't drink."

Isabela revealed her personal conversion story as we spoke in her small textile store. Before she found her church, she and her husband drank frequently, and he would abuse her. Her friends told her that the Catholic church could not help and brought her to the Evangelical church. She said, "I noticed a great change in my life and left behind all the bad things. And when I went to [the Evangelical] church, I felt the presence of God, and I was very happy." However, when she got home, her husband would continue to abuse her. So she prayed and asked God for help until her husband converted too. He eventually did, and she claims, "Everything is fine now."

More often than not, it is the woman—a wife and mother—who converts first in the family, looking for domestic support. Often, she is seeking help for problems of sickness, alcohol abuse, physical abuse, or other domestic strife. (See Jones et al., this volume, on alcohol abuse as a reason for Evangelical conversion.) Frequently, her partner and the rest of the family convert after her, one by one over a period of time. Eber (1995:222) describes similar trends in her research among Mayas of Chiapas, where women were the first to convert because of their role as monitors of household resources and family health. Evangelical churches appeal to Nahualense Maya women in these crisis situations because the ideology of Evangelicalism is similar to the Maya ideology of control over one's life through community support (see Green 1993:175).

Evangelical churches condemn drinking alcohol, violence, self-absorption, and having multiple sexual partners, and they monitor behavior through tight-knit social groups. By emphasizing a responsibility toward family well-being, Evangelicalism disparages many behaviors associated with machismo and realigns women's and men's priorities toward strengthening family units (Brusco 1993:144; Flora 1976:187–203). When a woman brings her husband into an Evangelical church, he is expected to fulfill his obligations to the family. Ideally, he stops drinking and abusing his wife and children. Of course, the husband does not always follow his wife into conversion, or he may not be willing to stop drinking or change his abusive behavior. In these cases, Evangelical women often find in their community and ideology the strength to leave such men. In her study of Bolivian Evangelical churches, Lesley Gill (1993:193) argues, "The rigid, puritanical rules of most congregations allow women to develop greater self-esteem because abusive male behavior[s], such as drunkenness and sexual harassment, are controlled." The rules give women a basis for rejecting abusive behavior.

Nahualenses, too, appreciate this religious justification for leaving an abusive partner in the Evangelical community. Juana, for example, indicated that her husband did not stay very long in the Evangelical church after he converted. While he was in the church, things were fine. But after he left, he started drinking again and hitting her. She took her two children and left him. She said, "Now, he doesn't go to church, but I always do because I know that there is a God in heaven, and I know that there is a God that helps me with my things, my business, and taking care of my boys." Juana's faith in her church gave her the strength to leave her husband. Thus, reasons for conversion to Evangelical churches are far more extensive than just orientations toward economic advancement (Garrard-Burnett 1998:124).

Beyond problems related to alcohol and abuse, Nahualense women often reported that they converted because of sickness. The pastor and other members of the Evangelical church extended blessings to anyone who requested them. Women often converted after Evangelical members visited them in their homes and offered healing prayers. Elena, a Catholic at the time of her sickness, recounted how she had been very ill and was not getting better: "Members of the [Evangelical] church came here to help and pray for me. They were always with me so that my sickness would go away. . . . After I was baptized, I didn't have the sickness."

Roberta, an older woman, suffered from bad eyesight. She converted when the pastor of the Evangelical church would come to her home and pray for her eyes. She recalled he was very friendly and made frequent visits. Although her eyesight did not completely recover, his healing prayers and constant visits helped her to feel better. She, too, was the first in her family to convert and eventually led her husband and children into the Evangelical faith. Many Nahualense women followed this pattern; they converted following sickness-related problems and subsequent healing (see Jones et al., this volume, for modes of conversion).

Powerful healing prayers characterize Evangelical churches. "To enter into the church membership meant joining a quasi-familial network of brothers and sisters who would gather round and (literally) touch you in time of sickness or trouble" (Martin 1990:166). In Nahualá, these healing prayers took place in the general Sunday meetings, during home visits at any time, or during smaller prayer meetings held throughout the week. In a rather dramatic and intimate experience, several people would pray for an individual, usually with some of them touching the ill or bereaved person, with hands on their head, with a Bible touching the body of the person being blessed, or sometimes with the Bible held high in the praying person's other hand.

CULTO MEETING DESCRIPTION

In Nahualá, Evangelical religious meetings (*cultos*) produced loud live music, passionate song, and soulful prayer. People attended the meetings for spiritual enlightenment and worship, but also for the opportunity to participate in the healing prayers. The size of the congregation varied according to the church. In the largest Evangelical groups, seventy-five to a hundred people attended Sunday *cultos*.

One Sunday afternoon, I accompanied Mariana, my translator and good friend, to her church, one of the largest Evangelical congregations in Nahualá. The bright pink and brown building crowned the top of a low hill at the edge of town. Both its colors and location made it stand out quite dramatically. As we walked toward the church, I could already hear the band playing the welcome music. Nahualense Evangelical music is repetitious and upbeat; it often inspired people to stand, clap, sway, or even dance.

Walking through the main doors of the building, I saw the huge mural painted across the entire wall behind the raised platform and podium. The mural depicted a romanticized natural landscape of a glistening brook flowing by a wood of flowers and evergreens. Bouquets of pink flowers lined the small podium. The building consisted of one large meeting room, with high rafters supporting a zinc sheet-metal roof (plate 27). Huddled on the left side of the platform, the band consisted of two electric guitars, drums, and a keyboard. The congregation sat on rows of wooden benches; Mariana and I took our seats in the back with a few of Mariana's friends.

The *culto* meeting began with vibrant singing. During the first hour, the singing transitioned into a prayer directed by the pastor. From gleeful songs and light-hearted clapping, the mood shifted to more intense, fervent worship; people cried out, their faces buried in their hands, tears streaming. Some people moaned their prayers under their breath, while others praised loudly and clearly. The intensity of prayer and music diminished gradually. One by one, people ended their prayers; these sat and waited for the others to finish. To conclude, the pastor announced loudly and boldly, "En el nombre de Jesucristo, amén" (In the name of Jesus Christ, amen). This ended the first hour of the *culto*, and the pastor began his sermon. He spoke in K'iche', skillfully projecting his words with varying intonation and inflection, and he often read directly from the Bible in Spanish. He preached for about an hour (figure 10.1).

The third hour of the meeting was devoted to more prayer (figure 10.2). Fifteen to twenty women walked forward and knelt on the floor in front of the podium.

Figure 10.1. Pastor preaching in a general *culto* meeting. Courtesy of Adriana Smith, 2003.

Figure 10.2. Pentecostal congregation in worship. Courtesy of Adriana Smith, 2003.

I leaned over and asked Mariana what they were doing. "They have a special need," she said. Throughout the prayer, the pastor touched their heads. Calling them each by name, he blessed them regarding their specific needs. At the same time, the rest of the congregation included them in their simultaneous prayers. The band played throughout the long prayer. People cried; women, especially, cried in their *pañuelos* (meter-square, multipurpose, home-woven wraps). Mariana, next to me, quietly wept her own sorrows. When the prayer ended, the women who had gone to the front filed back to their seats, the marks of tears still on some of their faces. The meeting concluded with another round of boisterous song.

EMPOWERMENT THROUGH CHURCH PARTICIPATION

Nahualense women were highly involved in church meetings, and they held *cargos*—appointments or positions—in which they helped carry out various duties in the church. The number of women often was double or triple the number of men in the congregation in any *culto* meeting. There also were *cultos* throughout the week designed specifically for different categories of people in the congregation, including a *culto feminil* just for women, a *culto para jóvenes* for youth, a *culto*

familiar for smaller groups of families to get together in households, and, the largest of all, a *culto general* on Sundays for everyone to come together. A pastor told me that they had tried to have a *culto* for men, but not many attended, so they canceled it.

Evangelicals in Nahualá noted the greater numbers of women in the congregations and offered several explanations for it. A woman highly involved in her church congregation said: "The men, because of their jobs, they can't come. They can't get done until four in the afternoon, and by that time it's too late to go. So they come to the house and pray here." An *anciano*, a church elder, said:

Sundays, sometimes the men have business to do, so they don't go. They prefer their businesses. So now, women are much more punctual. . . . I think since Christianity began,[2] the women have given more importance in the service of God because of the examples when Jesus Christ lived, giving the message of repentance. The women were with him, with Jesus Christ. It didn't matter to them to leave their work to listen to the word of God. In contrast, the men busied themselves with work. The women were with Christ, listening to him. . . . I think that they [women] are more sensitive. Wait, I *know* that they are more sensitive. They have hearts with more true feelings. Men busy themselves with daily tasks. I think that is the difference.

An Evangelical pastor explained, "[The men] are doing other things, like working outside the community, in jobs, and also there are a lot of them in the States. There are 25 men from the [my] church in the [United] States, out of 200 members."

Two hundred members would constitute about thirty-five or, at most, forty residential families. Thus, in all likelihood, more than half of the families had an adult or teenage male working in the United States, usually for several years. A large number of men also left Nahualá to work in other areas of Guatemala. In part, this could explain the disproportionate absence of men in *culto* meetings. It also demonstrates the idea that women seek out the Evangelical community because of the lack of social support from their absent husbands and sons.

Because the majority of the congregation was female, Evangelicals experienced a trend that promoted gender equality. According to Steigenga (2001:129–130), the change manifested in two ways: "Evangelicalism provides a kind of moral autonomy that supports women's increasing independence in the domestic sphere. . . . A second argument relating to Pentecostalism and gender suggests that the evangelical belief in spiritual equality may also lead to increased opportunity for associational participation for women outside of the home." In Nahualá, Evangelical leaders and members fostered female leadership; they spoke of powerful women in the Bible during sermons; and they invited women to hold positions and testify in the church. Such women leaders provided support to other women in dealing with their domestic needs,

Women held several *cargos* in the Nahualense Evangelical churches. They helped plan and carry out the activities throughout the week for the church. North American Protestant churches have often been criticized for not allowing women equal power and privilege in church positions. To the contrary, my research and that of others demonstrates that Latin American Pentecostal Protestantism accords women more place and participation (Brusco 1993:144; Flora 1976:196–199). Martin (1990:166) argues similarly, "Women have long been accepted into the church in Pentecostal churches as evangelists . . . and Pentecostals have offered women roles of unprecedented leadership." The most common positions women held in the Evangelical churches in Nahualá were the *diaconisa*, members of the *directiva*, and the *pastora*.

I was first introduced to the *diaconisas* (female deacons) while sitting in a *culto* meeting. Several women went to the front to pray for a baby girl. As the father held his baby, the *diaconisas* kneeled in front and prayed aloud along with the pastor. I asked someone next to me who those women were, and she answered, "They are the *diaconisas*. . . . they take care of the building and bring the flowers for the meetings." Antonia, a *diaconisa*, explained further: "There are twelve *diaconisas*, and we go visit the sick, [go] to women who are planning to accept Christ, or [go] to women who just need their spirits lifted [*animación*]. . . . For example, we have the custom here that as soon as you have a baby, we bathe the woman, make something for her to eat, and ask her for her clothes to wash."[3] The *diaconisas* got together to delegate duties, such as cleaning the church building or providing the flowers for Sunday *culto*, and they planned *visitas* (visits) to other women. In general, the *diaconisas* took care of the church and the members of the church that needed their help. *Diaconisas* were often the older and more respected women of the church.

Women also held positions in *directivas* (councils); each type of meeting had its own council. For example, each congregation had a *directiva* for youth, a *directiva* for women, and a *directiva* for family *cultos*. The *directiva* for the women's *cultos* planned and organized the weekly women's meeting and any other activities that involved women specifically. Sara, the treasurer for the women's *directiva* in one congregation, said: "There are nine women in the *directiva*. . . . Every Sunday we get together, and we plan the activities that go on in the church. . . . When we go on *visitas*, we go when there are sick people, or when there are those that don't participate in the church. So we go to these women to lift their spirit so that they will come back." The *directiva* members visit about four or five women a week and pray for them.

In one particular *directiva* meeting after *culto*, seven or eight women casually grouped together to talk while everyone else filed out of the building. They sat on the benches, huddled close together, and talked while keeping an eye on their young children. As no women needed support that week, they did not plan *visitas*. They discussed an upcoming event for which they were in charge of preparing food: several pastors from other hamlets of Nahualá were coming for a *culto* meeting and dinner afterward. The women of the *directiva* planned what food to prepare and who would help (figure 10.3). They also discussed the next day's women's *culto* meeting. *Directivas* took care of many of the logistical tasks inherent in carrying out meetings.

Sometimes the wife of the pastor referred to herself as *pastora*, an officially recognized position in these Evangelical churches. A *pastora* is head of the *diaconisas*, and she is

Figure 10.3. Sharing food after a women's *culto* meeting. Courtesy of Adriana Smith, 2003.

in charge of the religious duties they carry out. Paula was a *pastora*. Her husband was a prominent pastor in the community, and she was a strong-willed, influential woman. In women's *culto* meetings, she was recognized as the leader.

On one occasion, Paula and I went to a women's *culto* where I witnessed the role of the *pastora*. The woman who had been directing the meeting (who often served as a member of the *directiva*) introduced Paula as the *pastora* and invited her to conduct much of the rest of the meeting. Paula stood in the front of the small adobe room facing fifteen or twenty women sitting on *petates* (woven mats) on the floor. A table covered with locally woven cloth and decorated with a bundle of flowers stood between Paula and the other women. "It is so nice to worship God if we do it from the heart," she said, after which she invited the women to stand and led them in a chain of songs for about thirty minutes. Her voice cried out much louder than most, and women followed her lead as she chose song after song. She initiated each new song with nothing more than a small pause to take a breath. The other women joined her by the second phrase, all having memorized the repetitive songs.

After singing, the women found their seats again on the floor, and Paula welcomed all of them, calling each by name. "Does everyone feel the presence of God?" she asked. "We are serving the Lord and no other. We have to worship with all our heart." Then she noted, "Not all of the *diaconisas* are here, and neither are all [members of] the

directiva participating. We should pray for these women. We shouldn't hold any envy or anger for others because God does not appreciate that." After this brief message, she appointed another woman to pass a plate for the offering and then introduced her son, who gave the message.

In Paula's *culto* meetings, either her husband (the pastor) or her son gave the message. In some congregations, women delivered the main message. A different *pastora* in Nahualá gave the message in all her women's *culto* meetings. Although Nahualense women participated energetically in women's *cultos*, only men preached during the general Sunday *culto* meetings, and only men were recognized as pastors—in the sense of trained theologians.

I asked a pastor of a prominent international Pentecostal church in Nahualá if women were allowed to preach in the general meetings. He responded, "Some churches don't allow women to preach." "Why?" I asked. "A woman shouldn't be allowed to speak in church if she doesn't know the Bible, if she hasn't learned the doctrine. It's not allowed. Otherwise, she would give bad interpretations of the Bible." "What about the women who do know the Bible?" "Yes, they can preach. We have pastors who are women—lots of them." He pastored in an international Pentecostal church with branches in almost all countries of the world. "But I am the only pastor here [in Nahualá of that denomination]," he concluded, perhaps reflecting the lesser educational access of women in this indigenous community.[4]

Even though a certificate from a seminary is not required to be a pastor in smaller independent churches, at least some training is helpful. Women, however, have found it difficult to leave Nahualá to acquire training in theology and public speaking because of the expectation for domestic responsibilities.

In their various positions in the church, women helped carry out necessary church functions, and their designation as holding *cargos* also gave them a sense of empowerment, paralleling the findings of Steigenga (2001:27). In Nahualá, Catalina, a young woman just married, said being part of the *directiva* helped her: "I have never before had the experience of working with a group, with these women. I am learning more now." Rosa, who had served for two years as a *diaconisa* and was in her second term, observed, "When they called me for the first time, it scared me. Yes, I thought that I could never carry out this duty. . . . Now I can. Now I am not timid."

WOMEN'S *CULTOS*: THE ATTRACTIONS OF GENDER INTIMACY AND MESSAGE RELEVANCE

Nahualense women found the women's *culto* meetings held on weeknights to be attractive because of the social atmosphere they created, because the messages and discussions directly related to their lives, and because the *cultos* offered an intimate environment wherein women felt comfortable sharing their struggles and praying for each other. In summary, women's *culto* meetings gave women the opportunity to unite as a support group.

I attended the *cultos de mujeres* for three Evangelical churches each week. Carried out and conducted by women in their own homes, these meetings were often smaller versions of the larger *cultos* on Sundays. Women also referred to the women's *culto* as the *sociedad de mujeres* (women's society), the *grupo feminil* (female group), or the *grupo para damas* (group for ladies). In one of the three congregations I attended regularly, the women's *culto* was exclusively for and attended by women; the other two were mostly women with a few men who gave the sermons or played instruments. A fourth Evangelical church did not have a weekly women's *culto*; rather, its women went on retreats with sister chapters in other communities (figure 10.4). These much larger combined women's *cultos* occurred once a month.

On a rainy afternoon, my translator and I made our way to a women's *culto* in town. We climbed a steep hill toward the house of Marisa, a member of the *directiva*. From her courtyard decorated with potted plants, we took a flight of stairs, following the sound of women's voices singing cheerfully and loudly; the meeting had already begun. We found a place on the tiled floor with the other

Figure 10.4. Regional women's *culto* meeting. Courtesy of Adriana Smith, 2003.

women in the small room. We all sat on *petates*, facing the woman in front leading the song. Of the eleven women present, many had brought small children or infants.

Marisa conducted. After the song, she announced that the pastor would now give his sermon. He stood up and gave a vivid twenty-minute speech. He used his whole body as he swung his arms and paced back and forth in front of the moved audience. At times, he spoke loudly and profoundly and at other times almost in a whisper. Once in a while, the women would call out in K'iche' *eau*, a word often used to agree with or acknowledge someone. His sermon led into a prayer. The pastor initiated the prayer, and the women got on their knees and began to pray as well. Their voices filled the room; all around me were the sounds of repetitive, rhythmic, and fervent prayers from the women. The praying slowed to a stop, and women returned to their seated positions on the *petates*, wiping tears from their faces.

Marisa then stepped to the front of the room. She spoke about the specific needs of a sick woman who was not able to attend the *culto* meeting. Then Marisa asked if there were any women present who also needed a prayer. A woman's hand went up, and she explained to the group that her son was sick. The women knelt on the floor again, and Marisa directed another vocal group prayer for the woman who was sick and the woman with the sick son. As the group members prayed, they used the women's names, asking God to bless them and bring them the things they needed. The chorus of women's voices lifted and reverberated through the space of that small tiled room for several minutes more. The pastor, who had found a seat in back, prayed in Spanish, his loud, low voice almost completely drowned out by the cries of the women.

The prayers trailed off to a stop, and a different woman stepped to the front, picked up a dish from the table, and carried the dish around the room to collect offerings. Marisa then made some announcements as the pastor slipped out the back. Marisa's announcements quickly turned into friendly conversations between many of the women, and the *culto* soon took on the form of an informal, social gathering. As the women talked, they smiled and laughed with each other.

A few women left and returned with food and drinks. They walked around the room, giving each member a large piece of sweet bread and a small plastic cup of hot chocolate. For the next half hour, the women chatted in small groups, laughing and sharing stories. A few of the women expressed interest in what I was doing there. I joined them on the *petates*, and we communicated in a mix of Spanish and K'iche'. They made jokes about how I should marry their sons and smiled at me as we sipped our hot chocolates.

I asked Marisa why they had women's *culto*. She responded, "It's for the women. When we have needs, we pray for each other. When there is sickness, we go to the sick to pray for them and make them feel better." Women were attracted to these meetings because of the intimate social environment that they provided and because the *culto* messages directly related to women's experiences and struggles. They did not get this personalized attention in general *culto* meetings. I have recorded, transcribed, and translated seven complete women's *cultos*. In each meeting, the speakers gave messages directed to the women and relevant to their personal lives.

During one, the pastor delivered the story of Hannah. He emphasized these points: Hannah was an older woman who was infertile. She wanted a child so she asked God for help. She prayed fervently "with great faith." The pastor asked the women to turn to 1 Samuel 26–28 and read with him in Spanish. "The theme," the pastor said, "is God listens to your requests. This woman in the Bible has a need, [so] she asks God for a child." The pastor then asked the women, "Are there things you ask from God that you need for your children?" He continued the story of Hannah, explaining that she went to the temple and prayed hard for a son. In exchange for her request, she promised to devote the son's life to serving the Lord. The prophet Eli saw her and told her to go home and wait until God granted her petition.

The pastor interrupted this account and told the story of two people he knew. The couple could not have any children, and the husband beat his wife because she was infertile. The pastor explained that this was the wrong way to treat a woman who can't have children because it is not her fault. He then referred back to the story of Hannah and applied it to the women's lives: "The women that have kids, they don't need to ask God for kids, their needs are different. You have to ask God—for example, if you have adolescent boys—you have to ask God to bless them so that they don't drink or use drugs. . . . Whatever problem presents itself, you can put it in the hands of God. He is the one that can solve them." He explained that just as Hannah was granted her petition with a son, God would bless them, too, with the things they needed.

In the prayer after the message, the pastor's voice cried out in K'iche': "Oh God, you know these women, help them and their children. . . . [Grant them] health, intelligence, welfare. . . . Our purpose is that we all prosper in you, in your salvation. . . . Bless the mothers."

On another occasion when I was visiting a women's *culto*, Marta, a woman from another K'iche' community, was invited to give a personal testimony as the main message for the meeting. Marta stood in front of the room on a platform and told her story in K'iche'. She spoke for about a half hour, and the other women were visibly moved by her words. Throughout her speech, women called out *amén* and *aleluya*. The pastor, standing in the back of the room, listened intently and often called *aleluya* as well. After Marta related her story, she led the congregation in prayer; they prayed for her, for themselves, and for everyone else. At one point, Marta asked the women to put their hands on their own heads and bless themselves as they prayed.

After the meeting, the women sipped hot pineapple juice and passed around sweet bread. A woman seated next to me provided an account of the story in Spanish. She told me that Marta had been having horrible stomach pain and other problems. She fasted for three days and prepared herself to go to *culto*, and she was healed through God's grace. The *pastora* overheard our discussion and piped in, "We come to *culto* to look for God, to lift ourselves to betterment, and to become stronger and more valiant." Marta's faith-promoting example gave the women a more personalized connection to their religion as they heard the experience from another woman.

Women relished these *culto* meetings because they provided an intimate environment in which women could comfortably share their struggles. At one women's *culto*, the entire meeting was devoted to praying for all the women who expressed concerns.

Congregations held special prayer *cultos* about once a month. One meeting began when the woman whose turn it was to conduct the *culto* stood behind a podium set below the dais and spoke in a soft voice: "*Culto* is necessary, and we are going to have a prayer *culto* to ask for blessings from God and sing the songs of worship so that we may feel the presence of God in our lives." The timid woman conducting then asked the seated women for *peticiones* (requests for help from God). Women expressed their requests in detailed accounts of the problems they were facing, and the members of the church then prayed for them, often by name. One of the women asked for help because her husband had stopped coming to *culto*, and she wanted the group to pray for him. Two or three

other women shared their problems, but not all the attendees did. Then all the women and the pastor, who had been silently sitting in the back, knelt at the front next to each other, resting on the edge of the raised platform. The pastor began to pray aloud, using each woman's name and touching her head as he prayed for her individual needs. This prayer lasted twenty minutes. The pastor led the prayer loudly, and the women cried out to themselves. One woman put her hand on the head of another woman to pray for her, holding, comforting, and helping her through her problems. They all stood up when the pastor eventually ended the prayer.

The intimate and personal environment made the women feel more comfortable expressing their concerns and praying for each other individually. The tasks provided a chance to develop their skills and confidence in a society where the female gender has little other opportunity to lead or interact. Moreover, it was clear that the pastor and the pastor's wife play key roles in the lives of women in this community. Pentecostal ministers in Nahualá (and throughout Ixtahuacán) fulfill a decisive role in organizing life by guiding ritual and providing "pastoral care, church discipline, and preaching" (Weber 2002[1905]:105) in ways that are quite encompassing and, as Weber suggests, in ways that challenge our comprehension and our expectations.

When prompted about the purpose of women's *culto* meetings, many women expressed ideas of unity. I was traveling in the back of a truck with several women after a women's *culto* that had been held about an hour away from Nahualá. One woman reflected, "We are happy [during women's *culto* meetings]. We want to join together and worship God and help in the needs of the women, together. On your own, you can't help much. Now with the help of other women, it is possible." Another woman in the truck agreed, "When it is just women, we dance together and sing and pray, we unite as women. . . . It makes us happy to be together."

CONCLUSION

The Evangelical church serves as an empowering institution for women because of the high percentage of women who attend meetings, the assistance women receive in their familial struggles from their peers in those meetings, the personal satisfaction and decision-making power women gain in church positions, and the comfort they receive in women's *cultos*. Because women make up the majority of Evangelical church attendees, these churches extend more opportunities for women to get involved in religious leadership, and they teach less male-centric doctrine. The Evangelical church in Nahualá also offers women relief from strains arising from gender inequalities, alcohol use, domestic violence, and illness in their families.

Evangelical doctrine preaches against the macho behaviors that are reinforced when men transition from traditional Maya gender-complementary productive roles to the wage labor economy, which devalues women's labor and worth and undervalues gender complementarity. The Evangelical church attracts women who seek relief from problems associated with alcohol and domestic violence. They convert, hoping that their partners will convert after them and give up their drinking habits and abusive behavior. The Evangelical church also offers its members emotionally intense healing prayers when they or members of their family suffer illness. Male and female leaders welcome women and coach them in leadership positions in the church. The leadership positions women experience give them a sense of belonging and importance.

Last, *culto* meetings organized and conducted by women offer women an opportunity to worship in an atmosphere that is their own. They talk about issues relevant to their lives and unite together as women in a social environment. Contrary to much academic assertion, Evangelical religions in Nahualá do indeed empower women.

NOTES

1. This practice ended in about 2010 with the institution of noise abatement laws.

2. In Evangelical discourse, the words *cristiano* and *evangélico* were used synonymously, implicitly excluding Catholics and traditionalists from the category "Christian."

3. For more detail on the birth-care customs hinted at in this statement, see Wilson 2007. For details on the *tuj* used to bathe women after birth, see Rode 2007. The need to lift the woman's spirits suggests the possibility of symptoms of depression or postpartum issues. In this regard, see Sullivan's 2007 work on mental health issues in nearby Nueva Santa Catarina Ixtahuacán.

4. See Hanamaikai and Thompson 2005 for a depiction of women in Nahualá in 1995. Their paper, by inference, gives comparative background on how much Evangelicalism in Nahualá has advanced the participation and equality of women.

Chapter Eleven

A Fervor of Hope

The Charismatic Renovation in Antigua Santa Catarina Ixtahuacán

AILEEN S. CHARLESTON, JOHN P. HAWKINS, AND WALTER RANDOLPH ADAMS

THE CATHOLIC CHURCH DOMINATES DAILY life in Antigua Santa Catarina Ixtahuacán, much like its church building towers over the center of the town. Brass church bells had marked time, audible to the edges of the village and valley fields, before being taken—Antigua Ixtahuacán's residents would say "stolen"—by those who left to colonize the site of Nueva Ixtahuacán. Now, an electronic recording of a bell rings the hour throughout the remaining small village. Most adults living here were born Catholic, as were all their parents and grandparents. Although many devout Catholics do not attend Sunday mass regularly, until recently most people found it difficult to think of themselves as anything else but Catholic.

Catholicism, nevertheless, is changing. One of its variants is charismatic—which is to say, pentecostal ecstatic—Catholicism. In this chapter I describe two charismatic Catholic communities—groups or congregations meeting separately from the services offered by the parish priest in the parish church—one in Antigua Ixtahuacán center and one in a nearby rural hamlet. In particular, I show that healing is woven into the warp of daily religious life and stands at the center of the movement's growth in the region.

HOW THE CHARISMATIC MOVEMENT BEGAN IN IXTAHUACÁN

According to Santa Catarina's priest, the Charismatic Renewal began in Ixtahuacán mostly because of the influence and interest of Salvador.[1] As Salvador told his story, he was eighteen years old and married when a sickness left him bedridden for two years. One night,

Salvador had a dream, a dream, he said, that changed his life forever:

> I was sitting under a tree when from far away I could see a figure approaching me. I could hear him calling my name really well, but I could not see his face. I remember feeling really happy at that time, and I could see myself in bed, but this time I still heard the same voice, and now it told me, "Salvador, jala la cuerda" [pull the cord]. "No tengas miedo, Jesús sana, Jesús salva" [Don't be afraid, Jesus heals, Jesus saves]. I remember in my dream I was really afraid to pull the cord that hung but there was no ceiling. I finally pulled it, and after that I woke up. Two weeks later I was cured and ready to testify the word of God and serve him.

Salvador said this dream "saved his life."

Salvador did not further interpret the key symbol in his dream, "the cord that hung but there was no ceiling," which he was ordered to pull. We offer this possibility: in Maya life, the only cord that hangs down but is not attached to or from a visible ceiling (being threaded through holes in the lower ceiling until it reaches down from the highest point in town, an open belfry) is the pull cord for the bells in the church's two towers. But only the church's designated *catequistas* are allowed to pull the dangling cord, sounding the bells that call the parishioners to mass or meetings.

After his dream, Salvador did continue his devotion with the church, and in fact he became a catechist who would pull the cord on the bells. He learned to cook for the resident priest of Ixtahuacán. In 1974 or 1975, when the Renovación Carismática movement began in earnest in Guatemala, Salvador was sent to El Novillero, a hamlet of another *municipio* and the center of a Catholic outreach program, where he was temporarily assigned to cook for a new priest. That priest, brought from the United States, had been tasked to foster the spread of the Charismatic Renovation in Guatemala. Salvador converted during his time of service there.

In 1979, when Salvador came back to Ixtahuacán, he received the consent of Ixtahuacán's priest and began to spread the word of this new movement. Thus, the local priest, Salvador, and some other members of the community invited people not only to renew their lives as active Catholics but also to rejuvenate their spirituality through pentecostal ecstatic worship. The first official meeting, a novelty, drew 400 people eager to learn about the movement. The movement's local leaders hoped to bring people more fully into, and even back to, the Catholic Church by encouraging more joyful encounters with the Holy Spirit.

THE CHARISMATICS OF IXTAHUACÁN AND THEIR RELATION TO THE PARENT CHURCH

In 2003, three *comunidades* ("groups" or "congregations") of charismatics operated in Antigua Ixtahuacán. Two more met in a neighboring *caserío* accessible to and attended by many Antigua Ixtahuacán residents. All were within the parish of the resident priest.

To remain Catholic charismatics in good standing, a group's leaders and followers must follow the hierarchy of the church, attend Sunday mass and other activities of the core Roman Church, respect the seven sacraments, be humble, and pray daily. Every charismatic congregation submits to the command of the Catholic Church by responding to the administrative advice of the town's appointed local priest. Charismatics certainly do not think of themselves as a different church; they simply implement a different style of being Catholic. When asked if they were Catholic, typically Ixtahuaquenses would answer yes. When asked if they were charismatic, those who were would say *también* ("also" or "that too"). Most people did not see a difference between the two. Only the more religiously educated, such as the *catequistas*, members of praying groups, and some students could identify the differences between a charismatic Catholic and an ordinary Catholic.

Nevertheless, tensions exist between charismatics and the core Catholic Church for at least two reasons. In the first place, charismatics distinguish themselves from Catholics with regard to certain doctrines and associated practices. For example, in order to eliminate alcohol abuse and sexual excess, charismatics proscribe alcohol use and dancing, even when part of a religious fiesta. Yet alcohol consumption and dancing have been central to Catholic-oriented municipal fiestas at least since the Spanish conquest. Most charismatics also eschew any special orientation to the saints that decorate the Catholic church building and circulate in the traditional *cofradía* fiestas or, nowadays, on the fiesta days of the town's patron saint (see Larson et al., this volume). These proscriptions on drinking, dancing, and saint adoration as well as other restrictions are points of friction with the originating Catholic Church.

In the second place, the perspective of charismaticism as a "renewal" casts a negative light on the source church. Today, many people consider the *renovación* a renewal of one's physical life in addition to a renewal of one's spiritual life. "That is how the Renovation should be understood: as a privileged moment of the Spirit" (CELAM 1977:x). Thus, for many charismatics, the word "Catholic," semantically, has come to represent inadequate behavior or even misbehavior. As Juana, a charismatic in Antigua Ixtahuacán, stated, "The difference between a Catholic and a charismatic is that a Catholic still frequents bad things. They still do whatever they want, and it's not good what they are doing. Charismatics are better because they separate from the bad things and do God's will, and what God wants for the people is that they do good in order to follow him. [But] Catholics still drink and go to parties; perhaps that is not what God wants." The tension, of course, will not go away. How closely can a movement mimic its mother institution and still have its members perceive it as a *renewal* movement? Conversely, how closely can a renewal movement mimic the mother church's archrival, the Pentecostals, and not be a rival itself?

The latter is more ominous for mainstream Catholic leaders. In essence, how far can a renewal movement move away from the mother institution and not become breakaway Protestant? Charismatics avoid alcohol, dancing, and the excesses induced by venerating the saints, explicitly modeling themselves on Protestant Pentecostal doctrine and practice. Likewise, charismatics use highly amplified electronic music to set the conditions for "feeling the spirit." Charismatic congregations in fact use some of the same music and lyrics as the *evangélicos*, as the Pentecostal Protestants are known. (See Wayas et al., Jones et al., and Smith et al., all this volume, for other parallels.) Thus, the charismatic unit that I call "Manuel's group" frequently sings "El Evangélio es Poder de Dios" (The Gospel Is the Power of God) and "Esto es el Espíritu Santo" (This Is the Holy Spirit). These are both hymns that prior to the charismatic movement, only Evangelical Protestants sang.

Moreover, the charismatics' rejection of the saints leads them naturally to the Protestant positions that Christ provides the only source of strength and protection in this life and that one should not venerate the Virgin Mary or appeal to her for religious favors at all. Some, like Manuel's group, have taken this anti-Marian position. Other charismatic groups, however, believe that "Mary represents the way that human beings should be affected [i.e., transformed] by [the Holy] Spirit" (Centro Carismático el Minuto de Dios 1976:6). Hence the second tension: the Catholic movement into pentecostal renewal constitutes a movement toward Pentecostal Evangelicalism, yet this latter movement presents itself as the radical expression of truth and is vigorously anti-Catholic. This line of tension can become a basis for fission in a charismatic congregation and separation from the core church and its local priest.

A third line of tension emerges from the individualism inherent in charismaticism. This individualism takes three forms. The first revolves around submission, in this case to the parish priest. How can one submit to church law and custom *and* be charismatic, an advocate for needed renewal? A second form develops around the character of the group leader: how does a group leader manage the charisma needed to attract a congregation and animate them with the spirit without becoming the egoistic center of attention, thus displacing the priest and the core church? Ixtahuacán's priest described how a charismatic group leader in his parish did in fact gain the trust of its followers and carry them out of the church.

Finally, a distinctive group whose members make contributions can provide a group's leader with a source of income. The background poverty of all indigenous areas opens the temptation for a charismatic leader who has become the center of attention and affiliation in a charismatic *comunidad* to become independent of the priest, keep the collection offerings, and make a living off pentecostal enthusiasm, thereby becoming *evangélico*.

Thus, in some charismatic congregations, the leaders and members started to use the movement as an instrument for accomplishing their personal interests rather than as a communal effort that, according to fundamental charismatic beliefs, should be rooted in the hierarchy of the Catholic Church. On various occasions, personal interest fomented schisms, ultimately resulting in the creation of many *comunidades*. The propensity to split congregations may have ebbed somewhat with the division of Antigua and Nueva Ixtahuacán; nonetheless, much friction has persisted between the charismatic groups and the central church in Antigua Ixtahuacán.[2]

Manuel, the leader of a charismatic *comunidad* in a nearby hamlet, claimed to have the gift of prophecy, which he received through prayer a few years ago. Ana, Manuel's wife and a very devout believer in her husband, reflected, "He has cured many people[, bringing them] to God. Maybe that is why a lot of people criticize us, because others went with him [as his congregants] after his sickness [and cure]." Manuel's call to healing had split a charismatic congregation, and gossip and criticism along with defense by his parishioners were widespread throughout the town center: he charged for his services versus he only took gifts as offered; he performed witchcraft to extract illness versus he did not; and so on.

Thus, Manuel epitomized the processes of sectarian subdivision even in the administration of healing. Moreover, ideas about witchcraft and the removal of candles and objects from a person's body already existed in the traditional healing systems of both Nahualá and Ixtahuacán. To Evangelicals and even to some charismatics, Manuel's practices bordered on witchcraft. In the orthodox worldwide Catholic charismatic movement, object extraction as a form of healing practice is rejected. The more charismatic Manuel became, the more he suffered censure from the orthodox Catholics and the further he distanced himself from the Catholic center.

Despite internal conflicts between groups, the church, and the members, the words "charismatic" and, especially, *renovación* (renewal) unite followers as a whole, regardless of membership in a specific *comunidad*. There are still questions: How has the charismatic movement impacted the lives of Ixtahuaquenses? And how has the tendency toward fission and doctrinal and behavioral difference worked out in practice? In the remainder of this chapter I examine two congregations of charismatics, one more closely affiliated with the priest and the church, led by Salvador, and one representing the tendency to evolve into breakaway status, led by Manuel.

JESUS HEALS AND SAVES

Salvador named his congregation Jesús Sana y Salva (Jesus Heals and Saves), the words he heard in the dream that changed his life years before when ill.[3] A fifty-four-year-old man at the time of my fieldwork, Salvador wore his *rodillera* (K'i. *koxtar* ~ an apron-like kilt open at the back) and other traditional clothing with pride. He had attended many seminars beyond the seven weeks of charismatic training given to all those who want to receive "el bautismo en el Espíritu" (the baptism in the Spirit), which is, according to charismatic beliefs, the basis of the *renovación*. A respected man in the community, Salvador was twice elected mayor of the *municipio*. Some refer to him as "la mano derecha del padre" (the priest's right-hand [man]). Indeed, during Sunday mass, Salvador sat at the front of the Catholic church facing the body of congregants, helping the priest. The priest considered Salvador's congregation the only charismatic *comunidad* that did not pose problems for him.

Worship Style

Worship in Jesús Sana y Salva did not involve any musical instruments. This lack of a band and amplification distinguished his congregation. But some probably dismissed his group, finding its meetings boring, because spirited electronic music anchors most charismatic and Evangelical meetings in Ixtahuacán (see Wayas et al., this volume). His widely known *grupo de oración* (prayer group responsible for conducting healing rites), on the other hand, had considerable success.

Before a meeting began, one typically saw colorful *pañuelos* covering the backs and heads of women, children running around the room, and men sitting seriously, some of them up front, waiting for the service to begin. According to Salvador, "The church taught women long ago and they got used to it because in Corinth the apostle Paul said that if the head was not covered while in church, one's hair would be cut off."

To worship, Salvador's small flock entered a large room (about five meters wide by eight meters long) called the *casa de oración* (house of prayer), which he constructed on his household compound's property. First, parishioners usually knelt in front of the altar, which consisted of a table situated at the far end of the room with religious posters on the wall behind it, a candle, and a basket for offerings. They made the sign of the cross. Women usually sat on the right side of the room, while men usually sat on the left. Generally, no more than ten women and five men attended the services.

The altar had two posters of the Virgin Mary, three of Jesus Christ, and one of the Holy Ghost. Salvador's members behaved sedately, rather like in the Catholic church. The congregation seemed more reserved than other charismatic *cultos*, in that they did not speak in tongues as frequently, perhaps because Salvador lived and thought traditionally, or because he had more Catholic religious instruction than other charismatic leaders, or because he was an employee of the priest.

Salvador strongly advocated the seven sacraments, supporting the mainline Catholic Church, during his *cultos*. He never failed to explain a scripture to the congregation after reading a passage from the gospel. He also used examples from daily life, so that his parishioners could understand the gospel better. At the end of the sermon, the congregants participated in an oral review with call-and-response quizzing regarding the content of Salvador's sermon. Then, the congregation sang several hymns and recited prayers. Toward the end of the ceremony, while kneeling, the congregation began to pray in louder tones of voice. Given the small size of the group, one could easily perceive each individual's emotions. Only four people (including Salvador's wife) seemed to go into a trance and manifest the "charisma" (gift) of speaking in tongues. According to charismatic doctrine, to obtain the gift, one must "pray with fervor" (Pastor 1998:42–43). Leaders and laity feel that speaking in tongues moves prayer to a more profound, efficient, or meritorious level of communication, though no one is precisely sure how (Gutiérrez González 1977:99–103).[4]

Seldom did Salvador reserve time for parishioners to give offerings. A small basket for offerings rested on the altar but remained empty most of the time because Salvador did not solicit funds from his congregation. At the end of the meeting, the ill went to the altar, where the healing group, consisting of six members of the community (four women and two men), placed their hands on the heads of the ill and prayed for their recovery. This phase lasted about twenty minutes. The healing group in Salvador's congregation then knelt in front of the altar and prayed.

Membership Composition

Salvador's *comunidad* was small compared to others, having not more than fifteen regular members. It consisted primarily of elderly widowed women and men, one or two young children, and older couples. Given the infirmities of age, these members expended considerable effort to go to the meetings, held four times a week. Salvador's parishioners had been cured by him or had been part of his group for a very long time. Twice as many people attended Salvador's meetings before the town split, when about 80 percent of the residents of Ixtahuacán emigrated in 2000 to Nueva Ixtahuacán. Those who stayed in what became known as Antigua Ixtahuacán remained faithful to Salvador; his wife, Catalina; and their small charismatic community.

None of Salvador's family, other than his wife, belonged to the congregation or attended his services. His youngest sons participated from time to time, but they did so mainly to play with the other children who accompanied their parents. Of his six sons and three daughters, none considered themselves charismatic. They had a basic idea of what their father did as a minister and healer and regarded his work as "good deeds," but they expressed no interest in joining his congregation. However, his children regularly attended Catholic Sunday mass. Most of Salvador's sons were married and lived in Nueva Ixtahuacán. His daughters said that even if they wanted to join, they did not have the time to participate due to the amount of work they had to perform both in and out of the house. (On youths' nonparticipation in charismatic services, see Bradshaw et al., this volume.)

CHRIST, THE ONLY HOPE

Manuel and the regular members of his congregation chose the name Cristo, la Única Esperanza (Christ, the Only Hope) for their *comunidad*. Manuel, a forty-four-year-old catechist, lived in a nearby *caserío*. He drew his congregation from other surrounding *caseríos* and from the village center of Antigua Santa Catarina Ixtahuacán. He had founded his group in 2000, three years previous to my fieldwork, after being cured of "stomach cancer." Manuel attributed the cure to the power of prayer. Others said that he founded his group as a result of disagreements he had with the leader of the only other *comunidad* in his *caserío*. In 2003 he had more than eighty members in his congregation, more than half of them men. Since the founding of his *comunidad*, Manuel claims to have had conflicts with the local priest. Therefore, although some of his members attended mass in Antigua Ixtahuacán,

Manuel rarely did so. Finally, in contrast to Salvador, Manuel seemed much less traditional. He owned a car, used a cell phone, and dressed in black jeans and brand-name shirts, silver chains adorning his neck.

Worship Style

Manuel's prayer house was much smaller than Salvador's, but he had many more members. His prayer groups consisted of at least thirty people; Sunday services generally had eighty or more in attendance. The men usually sat in the front and on the left side of the room, while women sat on the right and behind. Latecomers abandoned this gender decorum and sat wherever they could find a place.

Manuel's *culto* felt more modern than Salvador's. Manuel had at least two elements for a successful charismatic group: musical instruments and people who knew how to play them well.[5] His group held meetings on Thursdays and Sundays. More attended, however, on Sundays. Two young informants said that they liked this congregation because of the music group that played there; they noted the band frequently received invitations to play to charismatic meetings in other towns. Indeed, many charismatics affirmed the importance of instruments in their worship.[6]

A member of Manuel's congregation described a typical meeting as "una fiesta con Jesús" (a party with Jesus).[7] From the pulpit, during *culto* meetings, Manuel frequently asked the parishioners, "¿Están contentos?" (Are you content? happy?). Those present enthusiastically yelled back, "Si, gloria a Dios, aleluya" (Yes, glory to God, hallelujah), to which Manuel instructed, "¡Entonces un aplauso para nuestro Rey!" (Then a [round of] applause for our King!), to which a loud clash of cymbals would ring out.

When a new member joined the congregation, the leader yelled, "Todos: uno, dos, tres" (Everyone: one, two, three). Pointing to the new member, the congregants shouted in unison: "Hermano/a [name], bienvenido a esta comunidad que sigue adelante en la obra del Señor" (Brother/sister [name], welcome to this community that moves forward in the work of the Lord). These events seemed much like a late-night television show, with the host constantly animating the audience through clapping, jokes, special guests, and loud music—all emphasizing the points made by the person preaching or leading.

The first time I went to Manuel's congregation, I had to go to the front of the hall where they formally welcomed and introduced me as *hermanita* (little [familiar, endeared] sister) Aileen. Hymns followed. Then they began the ordinary conduct of the meeting, including several hymns and prayers. The people seemed to go into a trance. They cried, closed their eyes, and rocked back and forth, singing out loud. Others just raised their hands in the air while facing the altar.[8] From time to time, congregants or leaders spoke in tongues, uttering a series of repetitive syllables. The hymns combined religious lyrics with a kumbaya style of music typical of many religious congregations, both charismatic and Evangelical, throughout Guatemala.

Manuel's congregation always reserved time to solicit offerings. As at mass, people deposited their offerings in a basket placed on the altar. According to Manuel, most of the collection paid for the instruments and funded *acción de gracias* events to buy food and drinks. Members of Manuel's congregation felt obliged to contribute to these activities.

Membership Composition

Manuel's group consisted primarily of middle-aged men and women. Ironically, most of Manuel's members came from Antigua Ixtahuacán and neighboring *caseríos*, but very few people other than his family attended from the *caserío* in which Manuel lived and the church building stood. Manuel's congregation included many of his kin and was quite family-oriented. Both Manuel's and Ana's parents were active members of the congregation, as was his oldest daughter. Indeed, Ana played an important role in the congregation. Other members included couples who attended Sunday service with their children. The parishioners consisted of men and women in about even numbers.

The congregation continued to grow rapidly because of Manuel's success as a healer. When someone joined Manuel's congregation, many of their family members also joined. Manuel and members of his congregation also actively invited people to attend their *comunidad*. Some felt so impressed—by the hymns, the musical instruments, the spontaneous prayers, the healings, and the testimonies—that they chose to return.

HEALING AS CORE BENEFIT

Healings constituted one of the most important benefits of attending a charismatic congregation, a fact recognized

both officially (Pastor 1998:20) and locally. Both Salvador and Manuel, often with the help of selected members, engaged extensively in healing. Healing not only helped the parishioners, it attracted new members to the group. As a high school student in Nueva Ixtahuacán said, "The more people a person can cure, the more members he is going to have."

Sickness constantly threatens people in places like Ixtahuacán due to the lack of hygiene, inadequate nutrition, poverty, and isolation. Moreover, as Adams and Hawkins (2007) show, the modes of secular healing are quite limited, and the ones judged best—the hospitals—are largely inaccessible. Thus, the topic of healing came up during all interviews and conversations, and both charismatics and ordinary Catholics agreed that health and healing were major reasons people joined charismatic congregations. In part, the charismatic movement spread rapidly because many people—including priests—claimed to have been healed miraculously of diverse ailments, and this has been so in other areas of the world (see Freixedo 1983:56). As one Ixtahuaquense charismatic said, "Prayer and faith are more important than anything else. Faith is bigger than any doctor and even bigger than any medicine."

Ixtahuaquenses believe in two causes of illness: one is a mere strike of unfortunate luck or natural causation (*yab'ilal*); the other is a result of *mal hecho* or *brujería* (*k'oqob'al* ~ curse, witchcraft) (see Harris 2007 for medical approaches to these two categories of disease). In charismatic belief, prayer can cure either. Every charismatic congregation had a *grupo de oración* (prayer group) that performed prayers for those in need. One did not have to be a charismatic to ask for a healing intercession. When a non-charismatic Catholic got sick, he or she tended to try home remedies (prayers, herbs) first. If this did not work and if the family had enough money, it would take the sick person to a doctor.[9] If the person lacked sufficient money to visit a doctor or if the doctor's remedies yielded no result, the family called on a prayer group or charismatic healer. In Catholic Ixtahuacán, the choices for healing were Salvador's or Manuel's congregations and their respective prayer groups.

The two congregations had very different methods of working. Salvador's prayer group went to the houses of various patients, where they performed the healing rituals after *culto*. Salvador entered the house, followed by his six-member prayer group. The six would kneel on the floor while Salvador talked to the patient. Salvador explained that this made the ill person feel "closer to God" and "hopeful." After a short talk, Salvador knelt down next to the patient's bed, and with the other members of the prayer group began the healing ritual by singing the hymn "Divino Espíritu Baja" (Divine Spirit Descend).[10] From my field notes, I offer this slightly edited extract of one session in a series of three:

> The man closed his eyes while Salvador and his wife, Catalina, got close to him and touched his face with their hands. During this time, Salvador rubbed the patient's body with a pomade of balsam. In the background, all the other members really concentrated on praying. Two of them especially, a man and woman, lifted their arms while kneeling down and began to speak in what appeared to be another language. The patient's family knelt and prayed behind the visiting prayer group. Although there were kids running around the house, the concentration from both the praying group and the family members was so intense that it could not be interrupted.
>
> Toward the end of the intercession, Catalina, who has the gift of prophecy, approached the patient and put her hand on his head for the second time. During this time, she felt God interceded, revealing Psalms 29, 34, and 40 to her. Everybody knelt down again and together prayed the Padre Nuestro (Our Father or Lord's Prayer) and the Ave Maria. After this, the sign of the cross was made by everyone, and the session ended.

The patient claimed to have had visions toward the end of these sessions, when Salvador's wife prayed over him. Catalina, however, manifested her gift of prophecy only once in this treatment sequence.[11] The patient stated that he felt better after each of the three sessions. The family offered the prayer group bread and coffee in gratitude.

Before I left the field, my translator and I returned to the patient's house to see if he had gotten any better. I found him in a lot of pain, lying in his bed. He said that he was very thankful to Salvador and his group and that he had had visions and felt better after every session. The relief did not last more than two hours, however, and pain forced him to lie on his back again. When asked if he had tried other healing groups, he responded that he would like to, but the other groups charged for their services, and he did not have any money.

Some of Salvador's parishioners claimed that Salvador

had cured them, and consequently they had joined his congregation. For example, Leticia said:

> I joined Salvador's group three years ago because I had a pain in my back that would not go away, so I went to him, and they healed me. They did not take a lot of time to cure me because God told me many things through Catalina's prophecy. He told me that I had to repent from all the things that I had said and that I had to repent of all of my sins. I believed this was true because I had said a lot of things to my parents, who are now dead, that I now regret. God told me, "I will heal you" but that I had to repent from all those things I said and did to [my parents]. After doing what he said, my sickness ended.

This case interests us because doctrinally "for the Charismatics, healing and salvation (*sanación y salvación*) are almost synonyms. He who gets healed is saved and he who wants to be saved ought to be healed. First in his heart so, after, if it's God's will, he will be [healed] in his body as well" (Pastor 1998:19).

Manuel is more renowned as a healer than Salvador is. When people related cases of themselves or others having been cured of a "mal hecho por una persona" (harm done by a person), they had turned to Manuel.[12] One woman testified:

> One always knows when a sickness is a *mal hecho* ["bad deed," referring to a witchcraft curse; in K'i. *k'oqob'al*] because if you don't get cured with a doctor, at a hospital, clinic, or any place where they give you pills, the only solution is to go with God or a servant of God so, there, he will heal you, and one will know if it's a *mal hecho*. When my son was sick [in] his stomach, we went to Manuel. By means of prophecy, he told us that his sickness was a *mal hecho*. He rubbed olive oil into my son's body and took out a little red candle, and my son did not hurt any more.

Some would argue that these healings work because "the mind controls the body" (Pastor 1998:22), that such cures depend on psychological suggestion, and that the sickness still remains in the body. Psychological suggestion or not, even if the residents of Antigua Ixtahuacán wanted to go to a doctor, getting out of town and having the money to pay for both the doctor and medicines were virtually impossible. Even those who might have had the money preferred healing intercessions, having heard the testimonies of other people who claimed to have been healed.

OTHER BENEFITS OF CHARISMATIC GROUP MEMBERSHIP

What does the charismatic community and worship service offer adherents in addition to healing? Charismatic meetings offered one of the few opportunities where people not only could, but should, express freely the stressors to which they found themselves exposed. Only in *cultos* could one speak openly of one's troubles or joys and cry and laugh in rapid succession. They felt comforted. People's faces changed by the time a meeting ended. Ixtahuaquenses said this was because they felt better after they prayed and sang. I believe that through charismatic ceremony—whether or not it includes amplified instruments—adherents attain an emotional state that both expresses and relieves stress. Ixtahuaquenses refer to this state as experiencing *la presencia de Dios* (the presence of God).

People experienced solutions to the grievous problems they faced and in turn devoted themselves more fully to the institutions and people that provided them with relief. Manuel's wife, for example, remembered how her husband "drank a lot. After he gave himself to God, there has been a lot of peace in our family."

People also join charismatic congregations because life in Ixtahuacán can become very depressing. Against this background, charismatic worship entertains. To Ixtahuaquenses, every day that passes produces more people to feed and less money to support them. A never-ending cycle of extreme poverty leads to deficient nutrition and poor hygiene, which in turn engenders more poverty. The charismatic movement offers an escape, for a while, from their daily routine and oppressive lives. Charismatic music, adapted from the music "of the world," delivers joyful, repetitive, noisy, vigorous entertainment. Ixtahuaquenses treat themselves to a rock concert every time they attend an instrumented charismatic meeting. The town has few other modes of entertainment.

Clearly, frequent assembly and participatory contribution in small groups with the same congregants create bonds of sociality missing in the more anonymous core Catholic practice, where one attends mass at any of several times in the week, if at all, and with no one in particular guaranteed to be there except the priest. Thus, "it is not surprising that relaxation [*distensión*] and joy reign in charismatic meetings,[13] where everybody there feels at ease because they are recognized, appreciated, valued, and loved" (Centro Carismático el Minuto de Dios 1976:6–7).

CONCLUSION

People join groups of their own free will. But what pushes them to a specific group are their personal experiences of healing, the testimonies of friends, or connections to family members who have been cured by a prayer group or healer. People also join to receive support for avoiding vices, especially alcohol abuse, and such support also is a form of healing. The success of a charismatic group in Ixtahuacán, in many cases, depends not on its relationship with the Catholic Church and the local priest, but on the charisma of the local congregational leader(s), the entertainment it offers its members, and the testimonies of people healed.

Although the Catholic Church has local priests and nuns that encourage Catholics to become leaders and laity in the charismatic movement, upper-level clerics do not really know what to think about the charismatics (Freixedo 1983:57). The priest in Antigua Ixtahuacán nurtured the beginnings of charismaticism in his parish. Yet now he says that the movement has become so threatening because of its success that he is "demoralized" by it. Regardless of the position of the church or the priest in this matter, charismatic groups in Antigua Ixtahuacán will most likely keep growing. The old, sedate Catholic Church stands at risk.

NOTES

1. All names in this chapter are pseudonyms.

2. During the relocation to Nueva Ixtahuacán, most Evangelicals moved, leaving few Evangelicals in Antigua Ixtahuacán today. A larger percentage of charismatics than Evangelicals stayed put, refusing to relocate.

3. The lead author, Charleston, had excellent access to and participatory involvement in this group because she lived in Salvador's household. See Tedlock 1981, 1982, 1991; Scott et al., this volume; Morgan 2005; Harris 2007; and Wilson 2007 on the

importance of the dream in one's calling to traditional religious/medical community service among the K'iche's.

4. Antigua Ixtahuacán's priest, however, considers trances dangerous to the church. In his view, they can lead one to have a false sense of prophecy. Anyone, he says, can claim to have visions and use them to portray a negative view of the church and to encourage other parishioners to leave the church. The church, therefore, does not believe that charismatic reception of the Spirit constitutes the sole manner in which one can experience the Holy Spirit. For charismatics, however, the Spirit "can blow anywhere" (Centro Carismático el Minuto de Dios 1976:14), meaning it is not constrained by Ortho-Catholic expectations. This, of course, constitutes another point of tension between the core Roman Catholic Church and its charismatic segments.

5. If instruments were unavailable, or when the electricity needed to play them failed, I noticed that people became shyer and less willing to participate in the songs and prayers.

6. When asked about the role of bands in charismatic congregations, the priest replied, "Most priests will want a congregation without instruments because they have an effect [on] you, and if it is *la presencia de Dios* [presence of God] that you want, then you shouldn't need instruments."

7. "Party" does not do justice to the connotations of "fiesta." One must add the connotations of celebration (both religious and secular), event, publicly available grandeur—contrasting against a background daily grind of monotony—plus a dash of craziness.

8. Trances seemed to occur more often during the smaller prayer meetings than during the Sunday services. They also seemed to occur more often in congregations that used electronic musical instruments. However, given that Salvador's group is the only one I know of that did *not* use musical instruments, this latter observation may be tenuous.

9. Although most of the informants considered doctors to be important, many of them stated, "God is before any doctor."

10. Note the similarities to the traditionalist *ajq'ij*, who invites the divinities to "come now" (Scott et al., this volume).

11. Catalina, as a Catholic charismatic prophet who assists Salvador, reproduces the structural position of Mikaela, who served as the *sobrena* (interpreter) and assistant to Tix, the traditionalist *ajq'ij* whom Scott et al. describe in this volume.

12. The issue that caused the priest the most concern about Manuel was that he cured patients by himself without the help of a praying group, claiming to heal people by removing candles, toads, and bees, among other things, from their bodies. See Harris 2007.

13. *Distensión* hides an ambiguity: it also means heightened tension or an excitement that gives way in catharsis.

Chapter Twelve

The Catholic Charismatic Renewal in Nueva Santa Catarina Ixtahuacán

A Movement of Women

NICOLE MATHENY HUDDLESTON, JOHN P. HAWKINS,
AND WALTER RANDOLPH ADAMS

THE TOWN CENTER OF NUEVA Santa Catarina Ixtahuacán is home to a group of about 3,000 K'iche' Mayas who live in an environment of uncertainty and social problems. Being indigenous people, they occupy the lowest social status in Guatemala, and concordantly, they have the lowest access to adequate health care, nutrition, education, and land (Adams and Bastos 2003). In the late 1970s and 1980s the country went through a civil war that resulted in the genocide of thousands of Mayas and instilled terror in those left alive. In response to these social strains, scholars suggest, many of the population turned to new religions (Garrard-Burnett 1998:120–137).

In this community, the main religious organizations are the Roman Catholic Church, various independent Evangelical churches, and those who are associated with the Catholic Charismatic Renewal (or charismatic movement). I focus on charismatics in this study. I found that the overwhelming majority of people involved with charismaticism are women. In this chapter, I explain why.

The charismatic Catholic movement in Guatemala offers its followers advantages that are normally found in Pentecostal churches, whose participants are called *evangélicos*. At the same time, being a charismatic allows them to remain under the banner of their traditional Catholic religion, for *carismáticos* are Catholics just as Jesuits or *cursillistas* are, and all understand this. A number of studies have attempted to explain why women constitute a substantial majority of participants in Evangelical or Pentecostal religions. Most ascribe the disproportion of women to the advantages they gain from being involved with the Pentecostal ritual and lifestyle. These advantages include an encouragement for both spiritual

and economic self-improvement (Gooren 2002; Slootweg 1998), a more personal connection to God (Siebers 1991), and a sense of power and control over one's life (Kamsteeg 1991). While these explanations provide valid possible reasons as to why women are drawn to these religions, they fail to explain why these advantages would attract women more than men.

In this chapter, I demonstrate how these so-called Pentecostal Protestant advantages play a role in appealing to Catholic charismatic followers and in particular to Catholic charismatic women. I assert that the characteristic of the movement that particularly appeals to women is its nature as a social support group. It is culturally acceptable for men in Nueva Santa Catarina Ixtahuacán to gather in social settings where they play sports or drink alcohol, but women do not have such opportunities. Therefore, in addition to other benefits gained, the Charismatic Renewal serves as a locus of acceptable sociability and support for women, which they may not generally find elsewhere.

HISTORY OF THE MOVEMENT

The Charismatic Renewal in the Catholic Church began in the United States in 1967 at Duquesne University when a small number of dissatisfied Roman Catholic faculty members engaged in discussions with Protestant Pentecostals. These Catholics felt a lack in their faith and asked the Protestant Pentecostals to help them find a way to return to a type of Christian community similar to that of the early Christians in the Bible. Four of the faculty members were baptized in the Holy Spirit under the guidance of Pentecostal Protestants and went on to influence a small number of students attending a religious retreat at Duquesne University. At the retreat, student participants also experienced baptism in the Holy Spirit. These faculty members and students subsequently shared the experience with other Catholic universities and groups of people, and the movement quickly spread to Catholics of all continents (Bord and Faulkner 1983:10–11).

Thus, laypeople, not ordained priests, fostered the rapid spread of the charismatic movement, and it was intended for laypeople. By 1975, charismaticism had spread to Latin American Catholics. Since the 1980s, according to Siebers (1991), the charismatic Catholic movement has been increasingly popular in Guatemala among indigenous people, paralleling the rise of Pentecostal Protestant religions. Siebers (1991:84) argues that the rise of Pentecostal churches coincided with the civil war in Guatemala and the fear evoked in the people by the violent actions of the state.

CHARACTERISTICS OF THE MOVEMENT

Because so many have turned to Protestant Pentecostalism and charismatic Catholicism, both of which reject the notion of intercession by saints, the people of Nueva Santa Catarina Ixtahuacán do not call upon Santa Catarina, their town's patron saint, or any other saints of the Catholic Church for intercession, blessings, or healings as readily as they once did. In this, they follow the many *evangélico* churches in the town and surrounding area that have long rejected veneration or even respect for the saints. That rejection is a central point of difference between *evangélicos* and mainstream Ortho-Catholics. Yet many Catholics now practice this different kind of Catholicism, this hybrid Catholicism, which the participants call La Renovación Carismática (Charismatic Renewal). It is a movement that some call Pentecostal Catholicism or Evangelical Catholicism because it embraces many aspects and beliefs of Evangelical Protestant Pentecostal churches—which have vociferously rejected Catholicism—while still maintaining some distinctively Catholic beliefs and Catholic affiliation.

Social Organization

I focus in this chapter on the charismatic group that calls itself La Quinta Comunidad, the Fifth Community.

Elder leaders in this *comunidad* say the first charismatic community was established in Santa Catarina's municipal center in the mid-1970s. Since then, members of the Charismatic Renewal in Nueva Ixtahuacán separated themselves into four additional *comunidades*, one of which collapsed. These communities fissioned from one another after conflicts developed between members concerning proper worship methods and theologies, or when a group became too large for its worship facility. In Nueva Ixtahuacán, charismatic groups hold some general beliefs and practices in common but differ on particular issues.

The essential religious practice of each community is the *culto* (prayer meeting worship service), held in addition to mass. In *culto*, those affiliated with that particular *comunidad* meet together and worship. In La Quinta Comunidad, participants meet in a building they constructed for themselves. They hold *culto* every Tuesday, Friday, and Sunday. In addition, members are expected to attend Catholic mass every Sunday with other congregants, some of whom do not participate in the Charismatic Renewal.

Male *catequistas* (catechists) or *predicadores* (preachers) lead each community as pastors. The group's leaders are required to meet once a month with their parish's priest, church officials, and other catechists to receive instruction on proper worship and conduct. Although they meet with church officials, the *catequistas* preach whatever they feel is appropriate at the *cultos*. No other parish official or parish priest attends *cultos*.

In La Quinta Comunidad, four *predicadores* preach and lead the community. These men are expected to teach the "true word of God" to all who will listen, testify of Christ and of the power of God, and heal the afflicted. The *predicadores* alternate with one another in preaching in the *cultos*, though often two of them preach during the same service. Toward the end of the service, the *predicadores* offer healing prayers for those who wish them. They also form prayer groups (*grupos de oración*) that heal people in *culto* meetings or during house visits by collectively laying their hands and Bibles on afflicted individuals and praying to God for their restoration to health.

Even though men hold the official leadership positions, women make up most of the congregation in all of the communities I visited in Nueva Ixtahuacán. More specifically, in La Quinta Comunidad, the average number of women present was triple the number of men, and most of the men present were the *predicadores* and the members of the band that provides the music for the meetings (see Boudewijnse 1991:182). Women of all ages attend La Quinta Comunidad meetings, with married and childbearing women age eighteen to forty-six the dominant presence.

Worship Meetings

The congregants hold *culto* meetings in a separate church building located at a distance from the village's more imposing and central Roman Catholic edifice, which is still under construction, and the temporary building that houses the saints and hosts the mass. At charismatic *culto* meetings, members play a keyboard, trumpets, drums, and a bass guitar—all hooked up to four very large speakers. The band accompanies singers, who offer their *testimonios* of Jesus Christ and the Holy Spirit through song. This music is played at a loud volume on the speakers; I could feel its sound waves vibrating in my chest, and the music and preaching are audible to all in the surrounding neighborhood. At almost the same time on *culto* days, several nearby Evangelical churches play their music loudly over speakers as well.

At the beginning of each meeting, the congregants sing songs inviting the Espíritu Santo (Holy Spirit) to come and visit their congregation.[1] A *catequista* with a microphone frequently initiates a prayer, after which congregants quickly begin calling out prayers of their own, their wailing and moaning sometimes obscuring the lead of the *catequista*. Indeed, members may kneel and pray at any time throughout the services, and often do so regardless of the activities of the congregation's leaders. Congregants

desperately plead with God. Some people call out loudly, while others mumble. Some congregants pray for their families, asking God to bless them. Others pray for a sick member of the community, while some ask for help to feed their families. Some pray in such a moaning and whimpering tone that their words are indiscernible, and some speak in tongues, using a few repetitious syllables in tonalities varying from soft to shouted and sometimes highly amplified from the podium microphone.

At the end of each *culto*, officiants invite the ill in the congregation to come to the front of the room to be healed by *catequistas*. The afflicted advance to the dais and kneel in front of the podium, which is decorated with a picture of a dove descending into two hands. The band plays. Closing their eyes and praying aloud, some *catequistas* place a Bible on the head of the sick, using both hands, while others hold a Bible up in the air with their right hand while placing their left hand on the head of someone sick.

The *culto* building looks like other churches in the town in that it is painted a bright color and is shaped differently than the uniform-looking government-built houses. But unlike the surrounding *evangélico* churches, the building of La Quinta Comunidad does not have a sign or name on the front that marks it as a separate entity. The charismatics symbolize their adherence to Catholicism by not separating themselves by name (figure 12.1). They are simply a "fifth community" or another such number in that parish. Indeed, I found it difficult to separate charismatics from traditional Roman Catholics when asking people what their religious inclinations or

Figure 12.1. A charismatic Catholic meeting place. Note the absence of any name identification. Courtesy of Nicole Matheny Huddleston, 2003.

affiliations were, because the charismatics of Nueva Santa Catarina Ixtahuacán do not readily make that distinction when labeling themselves. Charismatics see themselves as a part of the Roman Catholic Church and not a separate religious group.

Nevertheless, charismatics consciously reject some aspects of the core church, creating interesting paradoxes. Charismatics still consider themselves to be good Roman Catholics, yet they participate in religious practices and rituals that are not always consistent with traditional Catholic ideology (by having a religious experience unmediated by a priest, for example), and they reject practices (such as attention to saints, consumption of alcohol, participation in fiestas honoring the saints, use of marimba) that have been traditional in Guatemalan and Latin American Catholicism for centuries. While Catholic Church leaders and the charismatics themselves expect charismatic parishioners to attend mass in addition to culto, the behaviors played out in culto starkly differ from those enacted in the mass. Mass, for example, may include guitar music amplified only enough to make it heard at the far end of the large church, but there are no drums or highly amplified guitar or other instruments. Moreover, in the mass, people have no opportunity to call aloud their own prayers or to outwardly express intense emotion. In a mass, one cannot come to the front of the church and be healed if ill.

Indeed, charismatic Catholic culto differs little from the practice of the surrounding Evangelical worship meetings. Moreover, charismatics openly acknowledge that similarity. As one catequista of La Quinta Comunidad said, "We are almost the same. It is just that we have the holy mass, and they [the Evangelicals] do not have that." Likewise, non-charismatic Catholics frequently asserted that charismatics "act like Evangelicals."

Charismatic music and style of worship in the prayer meetings differ from those in the Catholic mass. In culto, the congregants stand, clap, and sing along with the music and take turns leading songs with the microphone. Others spontaneously walk to the podium and read from the Bible or give testimonio of their conversion experience and their faith in the Holy Spirit and in Jesus Christ. Laymen chosen by other members of the community to be preachers give weekly sermons. Thus, the charismatic congregants have a much more active role in their small satellite charismatic worship services than they do as parishioners in mass. Moreover, in all these details, they are active in the same ways one sees among congregants in a Protestant Pentecostal culto evangélico.

Charismatics not only worship like Evangelicals, they also reject key aspects of the local practice of Latin American Catholicism. In the first days of my fieldwork in 2003, one of the main preachers of La Quinta Comunidad made certain I understood some of the elements that differentiated them from traditional Roman Catholics. "We do not attend the fiestas for the saints, and we do not dance to marimba music . . . and we do not drink alcohol, because Jesus does not want that." Dancing in any form (such as school dances) is prohibido (prohibited), as is going to the traditional Catholic celebrations for any of the saints, including the annual fiesta for the town's patron, Santa Catarina.

WHY THE MOVEMENT?

According to van den Hoogen (1991:128), anthropological studies demonstrate that women have traditionally played the chief role in the daily practices of Catholic beliefs, and women have the most contact with priests and the church. To van den Hoogen, it therefore seems logical that women would play a large role in the Charismatic Renewal. Her answer, however, does not explain why I found the numbers of men and women attending Sunday mass to be closely balanced (44 percent men, 56 percent women), while the numbers were so disproportionate at charismatic culto: under 18 percent were men, and 82 percent were women. Clearly, something about charismatic Catholicism especially attracts women. What might this be?

Action versus Passivity

Until the 1970s, when a new attitude emerged in some segments of the Catholic Church about increasing the role of the laity, indigenous people in Guatemala played a passive role in the church, as had been the practice throughout Latin America (Siebers 1991:90). Members of the Catholic laity were passive subjects of a religious hierarchy set in a political and social system that demanded similar passivity and subjection. In the 1970s and especially in the 1990s and 2000s, such attitudes did not mesh well with making good choices in a complex emerging global economy where choices had to be made (Stoll 1990:13). These attitudes were especially hurtful to women because land loss, corn shortage, unemployment, increased alcohol abuse, and male absence for international labor made dependence on men precarious. This paved the way for a more active role for the laity, especially for women, in the charismatic movement.

The charismatic worship services demonstrate how active a role the women play. During *culto*, women clap and sing aloud. They may go individually to the podium and use the microphone to sing songs, accompanied by the band. Other women have opportunities to go up to the podium and tell the rest of the congregation about their trials and how Jesus saved them. Unlike men in the Catholic Church, who have traditionally been able to at least belong to brotherhoods (*cofradías*), women have had little opportunity to be independently active members of a group. Reina (1966:100–104) and others argue that women did have an active coordinate role in the *cofradías*, at least in the 1950s–1960s. Then, the wives of *cofradistas* served as *chuchuxelib'*. *Chuchuxelib'*, however, were dependent on their spousal attachment for their call to service, whereas their charismatic sisters a generation or two later (except the *catequista*'s spouse acting as *pastora*, the pastor's wife) were not dependent on spousal attachment. Moreover, *chuchuxelib'* served men and the community the food and drink of the fiestas; charismatic women, by contrast, lead men in prayer and admonish them in sermons and testimonies. In a word, charismatic women have considerably expanded independence and voice.

A Personal Connection

In conjunction with this active style of worship, charismatics believe in a more personal connection to God. This aspect of the charismatic movement sharply differentiates their ideology from traditional Catholicism. Like adherents of other Pentecostal (Protestant) religions (Siebers 1991), charismatics believe that common people can communicate and connect with God as individuals without the help of a religious official, such as a priest or sainted intercessor. Charismatics do not consider it necessary to have a priest present at the prayer meetings, and I never observed one in attendance.[2] Charismatic independence, however, contradicts a core belief of Catholicism that truth resides in tradition as interpreted by the ecclesiastical hierarchy, flowing through the priest to the parishioner (Smith 2019:sec. 6). To be sure, charismatics agree that they should attend the Catholic mass, which requires a priest. To a *carismático*, however, the other half of what

is essential—receipt of the Spirit—requires no priest and does not occur in mass. Although the priest must officiate for charismatics at mass each week and at baptismal, marital, and mortuary sacraments, he is not needed nor present for the three and sometimes more long meetings each week conducted by the charismatic groups.

These practices have put members of the Charismatic Renewal at odds with Catholic officials at times. On two occasions while I was attending mass in Nueva Santa Catarina Ixtahuacán, the officiating priest reprimanded charismatics in the congregation for not attending mass on a regular enough basis and for believing that attending *culto* was sufficient.

Encouragement for Self-Improvement

Gooren (2002), taking a neo-Weberian approach, contends that in Latin America, and in Guatemala in particular, Evangelical Protestant churches have been such strong competitors with the traditional Roman Catholic Church because they tend to foster elements of asceticism and self-improvement, while Catholicism tends to support the status quo. I apply this approach to the Charismatic Renewal movement. Charismatic *predicadores* indeed preach Protestant-like asceticism and self-improvement, both of which help explain the popularity of the movement. The approach works, apparently, across cultures. Thus, Slootweg (1998:65) states that the material conditions of the majority of Pentecostal women in Chile with a husband who had converted to Pentecostalism were significantly improved because the husband stopped spending money on alcohol or other personal matters.

The prohibitions that charismatics have placed on themselves in Nueva Ixtahuacán demonstrate their desire for improving their situation. Catholic charismatics impose strict sanctions against drinking alcohol. Congregants should not attend celebrations for the Catholic saints or go to dances. Charismatics hold that traditional Catholic religious celebrations and both traditional and secular dances directly foster the consumption of alcohol, which results in excess. Indeed, the celebrations held for the saints have always been known as occasions to consume alcohol in large quantities as a community. Whether it be dancing to traditional fiesta marimba music or listening to modern rock bands at the schools or in the community salon, charismatics (and Evangelicals) hold dances and drinking in contempt. This renouncing of any activity associated with alcohol, even to the point of renouncing certain community-sponsored or Catholic Church–sponsored events, demonstrates a desire to ameliorate the desperate conditions generated by alcohol abuse in the Maya community (Eber 1995).

Charismatics strictly prohibit alcohol consumption, which is mostly directed at men, but the majority of the people attending charismatic meetings are women. In Nueva Santa Catarina Ixtahuacán, women generally do not consume alcohol, but their husbands often do. My interviews indicated that in the congregation of the charismatic movement in Nueva Santa Catarina Ixtahuacán, there did not appear to be a significant decrease in the consumption of alcohol as compared to Catholic families in the overall community. Women of La Quinta Comunidad affirmed that their husbands drank alcohol and that most of them did not attend *culto*. That fact surprised me. Upon arriving in the community, I had thought that because the charismatics prohibited drinking alcohol, I would see a substantial decrease in alcohol consumption among the families associated with the movement. I found that was far from the case.

Power and Control

In addition to the movement offering women an active role in their religious community and a way to express their religious beliefs, charismaticism enables women to exert power and control over their circumstances. Most often, women find power over illness or injury through faith healing. Kamsteeg (1991:211) describes the same phenomenon in Pentecostal churches in Peru, where he identifies two types of faith healing. In one, men and women physically touch, laying their hands on an ill person's body and praying over them. In the other, people pray for other people's health without actually making physical contact with them. In both cases, healers who are successful gain prestige and power in their religious community because their faith has been proved to be strong enough to heal others.

In a more general sense, Boudewijnse (1991) found that more than 80 percent of the charismatic women in Curaçao affiliated with the movement during a period when they were being challenged with serious problems in their lives. "The Charismatic movement met people in their need for 'more security' and their need to express themselves more openly. Next to this, the movement offered material as well as immaterial support" (Boudewijnse 1991:185).

In Nueva Ixtahuacán, men and women are not given equal privileges in faith healing. Groups of select men called *grupos de oración* heal people by laying their hands or Bibles on afflicted individuals. Women only pray, at a distance, for others to be healed. Women feel empowered to call on the men to heal them and their families, and they also possess the right to pray for healing and well-being themselves.

Women also gain a sense of protection for themselves and their families by being members of the charismatic movement. A sixty-five-year-old charismatic woman said, "It is good to participate in the Charismatic Renewal, because if one does not participate, one does not have a life, or one could die, or one could have problems in one's family." When asked why she first began attending *culto*, she related that she had been ill for three years and nothing would help her, so she asked a *grupo de oración* to come and pray for her, and she was healed.

In La Quinta Comunidad, the *catequistas* and *predicadores* form the prayer group that goes to individuals' houses when called upon to heal. Informants described two types of illness that prayer groups could heal. The first, called *enfermedades normales* (normal illnesses), includes a variety of ailments. Prayer healings, used in place of or in conjunction with western medicine, can treat such normal illnesses. The second type includes any malady believed to be caused by witchcraft (Sp. *brujería*; K'i. *k'oqob'al*). Illnesses that seem inexplicable in how they arise and progress get attributed to witchcraft (see Harris 2007).

A *catequista* told of taking ill one day while working. Suddenly, he felt so sick he could not walk and had to stay in bed. He could not work to support his family. After three months of being severely and inexplicably ill, a *grupo de oración* came to his house to try and heal him. The men informed him that he was not sick with a normal illness, but that it was due to *brujería*. After the men prayed for him and laid their hands on his body, he saw a black shadow leave his body and float out of the room. He was cured.

Conversion stories in the charismatic movement often tell of cures. Many of the women in the congregation find an attractive sense of security and well-being for themselves and their families not found elsewhere, rooted in the prospect of prayerful intervention in their problems and illnesses. As one thirty-five-year-old woman remarked about the Charismatic Renewal, "If we [women] don't participate [in the renewal], who knows what will happen? Who knows if I will die or have sickness in my life?"

While many of the women converted because of personal healing, most of the men said they converted because their wives or family members were healed or because they decided to give up alcohol. A fifty-three-year-old charismatic woman suggested that women rely on the church because they "get ill a lot, but men do not. Women get sick every twenty-eight days, and men do not. Women also have to give birth to children, and men do not." Indeed, the K'iche's refer to both menstruation and pregnancy with variants of the K'iche' term *yawab'* ("to be sick").

In short, the charismatic movement acts as a source of empowerment, control, and protection, though the power exerted by individual women is still minimal and therefore doesn't answer the question about why so many more women than men are drawn to the movement. Clearly, "all *de jure* authority in Charismatic communities is male" (Bord and Faulkner 1983:17). Thus, if power or control were the leading factor in drawing people to the movement, it would seem to have greater appeal to men, because men still hold nominal control and authority in the movement. Why, then, the greater appeal to women?

Some feminist theologians believe that because women have traditionally been denied full participation in the Roman Catholic Church, they "must either withdraw from all mainstream associations, or at least have spiritual events and movements consecrated to the needs of women" (Starkloff 1997:662). If, indeed, as Ruether (1989:5-6, cited in Starkloff 1997:662) argues, women in the church desire to build "a community of liberation from patriarchy," I can only state that in Nueva Ixtahuacán, charismatic women have yet to become liberated from patriarchy because the movement and local worship are still controlled by men.

Social Support Group

Each of the benefits discussed above is valid. I have shown where scholars have identified each of them in other Latin American contexts, and I have demonstrated that these same advantages can be seen in Nueva Santa Catarina Ixtahuacán. But they do not succeed in fully explaining why so many more women than men find charismaticism attractive, because such advantages would seem to be equally appealing to men. To account for the extra appeal to women, I suggest that the charismatic movement provides women with a culturally acceptable form of social interaction and support that men readily have found elsewhere. In the words of a *catequista*, "Women don't do the

same things that men do, because men play football [soccer], and they play ball with their friends, and they do not attend church. On the other hand, women do not play ball, and so they attend church. Men also drink alcohol, but women do not."

Other charismatic men and women proffered these same reasons for fewer men at *culto*. Women are looked down on if they drink alcohol or play soccer. They participate relatively little in the formal public politics of the town. Indeed, most women have been quite limited in their social interaction outside the family by cultural expectations that they secure permission from husband or father for each out-of-home activity. Thus, the women's social space has been quite limited. But attending to religion for the household has always been a domain accessible to women, though it is rather individuated, private, and domesticated under Ortho-Catholicism (Hawkins 1984). *Culto*, by contrast, creates for women a place and a means in which they can socially interact outside of their homes and, recently, develop group activities (Checketts 2005; Nuttall 2005; Sinclair 2007).

Anthropologists have argued that alcohol establishes bonds between people and facilitates social events and interactions (Heath 1987, 1988, 1991; Baer, Singer, and Susser 1997:81). Short of drunkenness, it is socially acceptable for Roman Catholic men in this K'iche' community to drink alcohol with other men. Drinking together generates social acceptance in a male group. The male drinking pattern in Nueva Ixtahuacán accords with Heath's observation that "inclusion with a group where drinking [alcohol] is a focal activity is often a mark of social acceptance" (Baer, Singer, and Susser 1997:82).[3]

Sports, especially in the form of soccer, provide another basis for male interaction in groups. Pratt and colleagues (this volume) show the prevalence of men's interest in and interaction around soccer. Therefore, while men in this community have long found social interaction and social acceptance through alcohol and sports, Catholic women can meet these needs through associations in the charismatic movement. Because Catholic women in Latin America have traditionally maintained religion in the home and kept up religious ties to the church, their new sociality through charismatic religion is seen as legitimate and socially acceptable.

The *culto* is very much a social as well as a personal experience for congregation members. Congregants all kneel at several points during the service and pray together aloud for health, for assistance with their problems, and to worship God. They also pray frequently for each other. Several informants said that if a woman's husband has a problem with alcohol and she is involved in the charismatic movement, then she can get help from the group. The congregation will pray for her, and the *catequistas* will come to her house and help her. While alcoholism is not actually controlled through this charismatic movement—I discussed above that although prohibited in charismatic doctrine, many women report continued excessive use by their husband—small-group charismatic sociality buttressed by a hopeful, helpful spiritual ideology mitigates alcohol's impact on women and their families.[4]

CONCLUSION

In multiple ways that Durkheim (2001[1912]) comments on, the charismatic meetings, like the Pentecostal ones, "reaffirm feelings" (157) deemed essential, especially the sense that one has been embodied by God through spiritual possession as it manifests in tongues, trance, and excitement. Congregants who share this experience are in the process bound "together into a closer and more active relationship" (157), and they do indeed feel "stronger" (256).

The charismatic movement thus fulfills a social and spiritual need among the women of its congregations and provides security against illnesses and social problems that cannot be controlled or cured in other ways. Throughout Latin America, more women than men attend the charismatic worship meetings. Researchers have discussed different advantages that possibly contribute to the movement's attraction to women, but they have failed to convincingly explain why men would not also be attracted to these benefits. This chapter demonstrates how the charismatic movement offers support to women from other women involved in the group. Charismatic practice allows women a place and means in which to socialize and receive social support, a type of support already available to men in the form of social drinking and playing sports. In addition, women whose husbands drink alcohol to excess find support from this movement because they gain access to a small group of men in the church whom they consider stable and who can pray for them so they can receive God's help.

The charismatic movement allows women to receive this needed support and security—including health security. Such support and security are not found in the ordinary Roman Catholic Church practice. In charismaticism,

women get this support without having to leave their traditional church. By contrast, to acquire similar support from Evangelicals would require the complete shedding of traditional Catholic symbolism and ideology.

In these regards, charismatics not only mimic the protective avoidances (alcohol, dancing) of Evangelical Protestantism, they also acquire the small-group sociality and support for women that have so clearly emerged as crucial in the literature on Protestantism and in the chapters on Evangelical religion in this volume, particularly that of Smith and colleagues. We have, then, a clear instance of parallel and imitative evolution in this development of Catholicism—and for similar functional reasons as those of Evangelicalism.

NOTES

1. We note the parallel here with the traditionalist's call for the spirits of Santo Mundo and the ancestors to "come now" (described by Scott et al., this volume).

2. Indeed, none of the fieldworkers in 2003 saw a priest attend a charismatic meeting.

3. These authors cite "Heath 1990:270" as their source for the quote, but I have been unable to confirm it as the correct source.

4. This observation makes us suspect that the formally and vehemently anti-Catholic (and therefore anti-old-culture-and-society in Durkheim's sense of "religion is the soul of society") characteristic of Pentecostal Evangelical Protestantism is a necessary attribute of Pentecostal success in treating alcohol abuse. Of course, we don't know whether Pentecostals are quite as successful as they might seem or claim. A good study would compare the full social and ideological contexts of Protestant Pentecostal and Catholic charismatic approaches to and success in treatment of alcohol abuse in families. Clearly, we also need a more detailed comparative examination of conversion in these two styles of religion. We note that all of the chapters on Pentecostal Evangelicalism in this book emphasize use of the word "conversion," more so than the word is used in the chapters on charismatic practice. It may be that Evangelicals have a qualitatively different conversion experience, which is phrased as rejection of the old as a total system. Charismatics cannot quite reject Catholicism; they can only reject attributes of Catholicism or deny that certain behaviors were ever properly a part of it. Here, too, we suggest the need for a detailed comparative ethnographic study of the similarities and differences between charismatic Catholic and Protestant Pentecostal "conversions" and conversion stories, treating ideological, symbolic, and social factors.

Chapter Thirteen

A "Modern Generation of Youth"

Secularization and the Alienation of Charismatic Catholic Teenage Males in Nahualá

GILBERT BRADSHAW, JOHN P. HAWKINS, AND WALTER RANDOLPH ADAMS

SIZABLE GROUPS OF CHARISMATIC CATHOLICS, a form of Catholicism introduced to Guatemala in the 1970s, reside and worship in Nahualá. They call the movement La Renovación Carismática, the Charismatic Renewal, or simply *la renovación,* and they refer to themselves as *carismáticos* (charismatics), as do people outside that practice.

I found that Nahualense Catholic male youths, especially among the charismatics, do not exhibit as intense a level of commitment to religious observance as their parents. Through interviews and participant-observation, I acquired perspectives on male youths in the charismatic faith as I sought to determine why their religious attitudes and intensity of attachment differ from their elders. In particular, alcohol consumption, drug use, and gang affiliation blocked youths' participation in charismatic religious life and weakened the charismatic youths' religious zeal. Additionally, the families of these young men sent them off to school, leaving them no time to participate in the religious meetings that dominate the family culture. The families, anxious for their youth to leave the community and get jobs, sacrificed the continuity of their religious observance to provide their children with educational opportunities. Moreover, families supplied their children with commodities previously considered unnecessary and that were, in previous decades, relatively inaccessible in their culture and way of life.

In lieu of devoting themselves to and organizing their lives around religion, whether it be the now mostly defunct pursuit of service to the gods by carrying out *cargo* obligations (see Larson et al., this volume) or engagement in Ortho-Catholic or Christian Pentecostal denominational religions more prominent today, Nahualense charismatic youths increasingly interest themselves only in devotion to and accumulation of material productions of the new capitalist markets. This new orientation seems to be a modified version of Marx's "commodity fetishism," which Taussig (1980) describes among Bolivian tin miners and Colombian plantation workers, but without the symbolic accoutrements in which the capitalist system's crimping distortion of peasant life is personified as "the devil." In Nahualá, such demonization seems to be left to the devoted Renovación Carismática parents as they rail against "the world" being "of the devil." The youths, rather, seek solace in the accumulation of modern, personal commodities—clothes, electronics, music—and an older commodity, alcohol, rather than involve themselves much in a formal religion. All these factors combine to leave a vacuum of absent male youths in the Nahualense community of charismatic Catholics.

THE NATURE OF MALE YOUTH ACTIVITY AMONG CHARISMATICS

A prominent Charismatic Renewal preacher and I hiked from his house to a charismatic meeting, walking about two miles uphill in the thin mountain air. He had invited me to accompany him. Cresting the hill, we descended into a lush green valley cradling a little cluster of houses. As we arrived, several men smiled warmly and welcomed him. A man with a black book that looked like a weekly calendar spoke; other men, surrounding him, talked of upcoming events. The only teenager present stood in a small alley formed by the houses. He kicked a nearby puppy and stormed off down the path, ignoring his mother, who chased him, pointing and beckoning to the room where the others had congregated.

Eighteen men, twenty-three women, and six small children attended the service.[1] Some of the children came and went, but none of the adults left. Unmarried male youths between childhood and adulthood—*jóvenes* in Spanish and *alab'om* in K'iche'—were noticeably absent. Afterward, I remarked on the lack of *jóvenes* at the meeting. The respondents affirmed my observation. I asked if the youths would attend the next meeting. It was possible, they said, but not likely. When I asked for more information about why young men were not attending, an uncomfortable silence lingered until someone changed the subject.

Each of the fifty-four Charismatic Renewal communities (*comunidades*, congregations) in Nahualá hold at least one meeting (*culto*) almost every weekday (plate 28).[2] They attend at least two meetings on Sunday. The morning mass (*misa*), lasting about an hour, is held in the central Catholic church building facing the municipal plaza and is attended by charismatics from all the charismatic congregations in the parish *municipio* and by the local non-charismatic Catholics. The other meeting, their own hamlet's or canton's charismatic *culto*, is held locally in a nearby *comunidad* building or a member's home. Each *culto* lasts nearly three hours and is accompanied by a band that according to members of the congregation and band alike, plays "happily, the music of God" (figure 13.1). The loud music and joyful meetings require commitment. Devoted members try to attend most if not all of the meetings of their congregation. Many of the members of the Charismatic Renewal spend more than twenty hours a week at worship or celebrating religiously energized birthdays, open houses, and other commemorations of good fortune.

The charismatic meetings I attended in Nahualá paralleled in structure and content those described by Huddleston and colleagues and Charleston and colleagues (both this volume) in Nueva and Antigua Santa Catarina, as well as the local Evangelical meetings. I do not duplicate descriptions of worship here. What drew my attention was the absence of participating male youths. Charismatic practice clearly attracts and sustains adults but not young men. The question is, why are so few male youths present?

THE CHARISMATIC RENEWAL IN NAHUALÁ

Like the charismatics described elsewhere in this volume, participants in Nahualá's renewal not only attend the weekly Sunday morning mass, they also divide into smaller communities that meet as often as six times a week, and regularly three or four times a week, in the congregations' meetinghouses, simple buildings that lie scattered throughout the town's barrios and its rural hamlets. In these meetings, they "celebrate and preach the word" to the "brothers and sisters" of the community with whom they so frequently associate. They meet together much more often than do traditional Catholics, explicitly so that they can have a "unified congregation" (plate 29). Members may also host rituals at their homes where, at their own expense, they share celebratory thanks for personal or family good fortune.

A number of charismatic Catholic practices differ from those of traditional Roman Catholics. For example, many charismatics do not chant (*rezar*) the Padre Nuestro (Our Father or Lord's Prayer) in the manner that Roman Catholic tradition dictates. They also claim they do not pray to the Virgin Mary. Additionally, charismatics prohibit drinking alcohol and dancing. "[We] don't dance, don't drink, can't pray to images, and many of us don't chant prayers." On the positive side, the faithful members recognize that they enjoy certain "gifts of God," including glossolalia, prophecy, and visions during their small-group meetings.

As in Santa Catarina Ixtahuacán, these differences with the core Ortho-Catholics substantially mimic the practice of Evangelical Pentecostal Protestant faiths. Charismatics' emphasis on Jesus Christ, rather than on the saints or on Mary, resonates strongly with Protestantism. Moreover, Nahualense charismatic Catholics, like their counterparts in Santa Catarina, are fully conscious of their similarities with Evangelicals. Indeed, one Catholic priest observed that the church regained some *evangélico* converts when the renewal became popular among Catholics.

CHARISMATIC CATHOLIC WORSHIP

Energy is the defining characteristic of charismatic meetings. During the weeknight meetings, the public audio systems can blaze loudly—penetrating the calm night air with sermons, music, and prayers. The entire town

Figure 13.1. Band in a charismatic church. Flowers and an altar table are in the foreground. Courtesy of Gilbert Bradshaw, 2003.

center can hear the charismatic meetings because of the amplification. The *voz* (voice)—the group leader giving announcements—can sound like some kind of advertisement or a natural disaster warning.

Jorge, one of several people loitering outside the house one night, said that the amplified voice offered an *oración* (prayer) to God and that they kept it loud because "the louder it is, the happier the meeting." He further explained how the Charismatic Renewal differs from Ortho-Roman Catholicism: "We go to the mass on Sundays. And on weekdays those of us in the renewal have other meetings. . . . The difference [between charismatics and other Catholics] is that the traditional [Catholics] don't go to church every Sunday." By contrast, he noted that charismatics go to several activities or meetings a week *plus* the weekly mass. He felt that the smaller communities provide for very interesting meetings because the manifestations of the Holy Spirit (speaking in tongues/glossolalia, healings) occur more often in smaller congregations.

THE DECLINE IN CHARISMATIC MALE YOUTH INVOLVEMENT

The family hosting a charismatic *reunión de cumpleaños* (celebration of a birthday) filled their house with flowers, loud music, and, most of all, people. Members crowded into the steamy rooms; hardly any standing room

remained. The crowd consisted entirely of middle-aged to elderly people and very young children; few, if any, teenagers or young adults celebrated inside.

The four or five male youths who came to the meeting stood outside, the atmosphere of their gathering decidedly different from the one inside. In low tones with long pauses, they talked about David's brother in the United States and his truck, the high-paying jobs in the United States, and DVD players. Instead of traditional Maya clothing, they wore westernized baggy pants that resembled popular gang attire of North Americans. When someone attempted to talk to them, they would avoid eye contact and ignore that person.

The mother of one of the boys came out of the meeting, found her son, and ordered him inside. Miguel reluctantly obeyed. The other boys, knowing that their mothers and grandmothers could do likewise, immediately left to go somewhere else, leaving Miguel the only male teenager in the meeting.

The male youths of the charismatic Catholic church seldom attend the afternoon prayer meetings during the week. Given the fervor and enthusiasm of adults, what prevents these youths from participating in their family religion? When I asked a member of a local youth group how the young people are doing in church involvement, he said, "Not all [the youths] are faithful. There are some that don't trust [God]."

Priests, teachers, and other leaders all consistently

noted the pervasive lack of respect among the teenage males. Jesús, a teacher at a local school, mentioned that because of the lack of education among youths, they do not take the things of God as seriously as those who have more education. Felipe, a parochial council member said, "[The youths] have problems with alcohol, drugs, and gangs. These things are what are affecting our youth the most." Indeed, people consistently gave two reasons for youths not going to church: either they were going to school during the meetings (junior high schools and high schools hold classes in the afternoon and into the evening on weekdays, overlapping with the charismatic meetings), or they were involved in gangs or substance abuse.

Mainstream Catholic leaders admit their limited ability to combat the lack of participation by male youths, claiming that the teens "lack excitement" for the Ortho church. For example, the Ortho church sponsors an annual youth community concert. Although it publicized the activity for months in advance, the concert did not bring nearly the numbers of young people that its organizers had anticipated. A member of the council said that the council had decided to give the concert to "energize the youth" and to engage them in the church. He lamented the large decline in attendance even from five or six years ago. On the day the band played, the whole village could hear them as if attending a rock concert, complete with amplified music, lights, and background singers. Rural citizens could hear it from miles away. The council had chosen to hold the concert on the church's elementary school playground because of its size and proximity to the town center. Hundreds of *jóvenes* gathered, easily the largest gathering of youths that I ever saw in Nahualá. Many of these *jóvenes* were accompanied by their parents, who then split off and stayed fairly close by in the town center, mingling with the other parents who had walked with their *jóvenes* to the event. Yet, if the church had wanted to foster excitement and enthusiasm in these teens, it seemed to fail. Everyone stood in complete silence. No one applauded when the band stopped playing. When band members tried to get the youths to clap along to the beat, no one joined in. Even though the Ortho church allows dancing, nobody entered the large open space in the middle of the crowd to dance—leaving a noticeably awkward vacuum.

The songs ended, and the priest spoke: "So, how many of you pray [*rezar*] to the Virgin every day?" He waited for a positive response. Only silence answered him. The priest repeated: "Raise your hand if you recite your prayers to the Virgin every day!" Only a few timid hands went up. *Ay*

Dios mio! the priest exclaimed, showing disappointment in his young followers.

Escúchanme! he commanded. "Listen to me! If you are not [praying] to the Virgin, you are against the Virgin. If you are against the Virgin, you are against Jesus Christ himself. The Virgin is the mother of Jesus Christ, and if you are not praying, you are showing Jesus that you do not respect him or his mother." Still more silence. "You are against Jesus!" The priest showed annoyance and distress with the lack of participation and respect that the youths showed him.

The concert ended, and everyone quietly filed out of the schoolyard without excitement or cheering for the band by anyone but the adults who organized the event. One adult started to clap and chant the name of the band and visibly attempted to engage the youths in applause, to no avail. The young people simply left, the noise of their banter and the shuffle of their feet the only acknowledgment the band received for three hours of performance.

Many of the leaders and organizers showed visible frustration with the concert. Manuel, an organizer, lamented that they had spent such a large portion of their budget on the band. He did not feel that the band or the audience enjoyed the concert. He observed that many *jóvenes* snuck out as soon as they could. The disinterest seemed symptomatic of the overall lack of youth participation in the local Catholic church—especially in the Charismatic Renewal.

ADULT PERCEPTIONS OF YOUTH IN THE CHARISMATIC RENEWAL

Many adult Catholics see teenagers as pursuing a different course than these adults took in their youth. Statements that adult informants made about the youths shared many features. Some adults expressed embarrassment about the behavior of *jóvenes*; others evinced hostility toward youths' attitudes, which they considered "rebellious." When I asked adults if they regularly attended Catholic meetings when they were young, they overwhelmingly answered yes. For them, a good Catholic attended religious meetings regularly.

Adult members of the Charismatic Renewal perceived the charismatic youths as violent. "The youth are cruel and *malcriado* [poorly raised, misbehaved]," one man explained as he watched a large number of teens beating a dog. "The youths here are bad people," said another man, trying to get to the safety of his home before dark because, he said, youths bring guns from Guatemala City and rob people.[3]

Other adults expressed a sense of despair when talking about the teens. "This is the modern generation of youth. They are *malcriado*, and they despise people," stated one man while expressing worry for his children who did not attend church. While witnessing two young boys laughing at an old woman who had fallen down in the street, the town pharmacist said, "We don't know what to do with this generation." As we walked the woman home, he indicated that the *jóvenes* do not obey their parents, do not wear traditional men's clothing, nor do they attend mass. He became very emotional about his fear for the future of the Charismatic Renewal.

Adults asserted they never acted the way that the youths act today. However, when today's adults showed signs of rebellion in their youth, they did so by joining the charismatic or Evangelical Protestant movements. Some of them are now leaders therein (see figure 13.2).[4] Maybe the adults acted just as rebelliously as their children act now—but in their own way. When asked if older generations, as youths, had acted rebelliously, adult informants responded that the teens today are much more rebellious than any previous generation.

AN ANALYSIS OF SECULARIZATION IN THE CHARISMATIC CONTEXT

Nahualense adults did not portray the "what's the matter with kids today?" attitude familiar in the United States. Rather, they intimated a much more profound and important change between two generations. They felt their youths had strayed from the traditions, specifically the religious traditions, of their parents. In particular, young men were failing to participate in the charismatic Catholic church and preferred to live a more secular lifestyle. In a word, the youths exhibited secularization as well as alienation from their parents.

Nahualense youths attend church at a much lower frequency than their parents and even older siblings. Local church leaders estimate that only 15–20 percent of youths born to the Catholic Charismatic Renewal (CCR) congregations attend services. In the dozens of meetings I observed, however, the percentage seemed even lower. This is a curious and compelling new condition given that religious participation in the *cargo*/fiesta system defined a Maya's social status a mere two generations ago, and Ortho-Catholic orientation was seen as coterminous with Guatemalan nationality. Yet this segment of the new religious movement seems unable to retain its male youth.

When asked why youths did not attend meetings, the

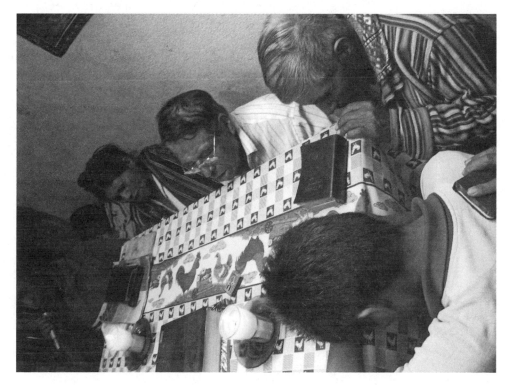

Figure 13.2. In a charismatic church, a pastoral lead couple kneels at the altar with two male congregants. Courtesy of Gilbert Bradshaw, 2003.

responses did not vary: alcohol and drugs, gangs, education, and a concern with material acquisition—all signs that secularization had occurred and was occurring. In this transformation, Maya male youths mimic Ladinos more and more as time passes.[5] I did not collect sufficient information on drugs in Nahualá to be able to elaborate on that aspect; I did, however, detect an additional issue, which I call quasi-commodity fetishism.

Alcohol

Although alcohol use and abuse has long been a feature of indigenous society, alcohol relates to both modernization and secularization in that its use is increasingly decoupled from ritual fiesta use. Once, I witnessed a group of young people watching a boy stagger around in the street. Initially, I looked for a crime scene or a fight. It soon became apparent that he was seriously intoxicated. The incident occurred on a street cutting across a steep hillside: one side of the street was tight against the face of the hill, and the other side offered a twenty-foot drop only protected by a four-inch curb. The lad fell down in the middle of the street, got up, and then fell down again in the same place. He arose from the ground and staggered uncertainly toward the side of the street with the drop-off, apparently oblivious to the danger. No one in the crowd did anything; it seemed likely the boy would fall off the ledge. Stunned that no one offered help, I grabbed him before he could seriously injure himself and took him to his home.

I inquired what had happened. The youth said he had just received his monthly wages. His friends convinced him that they should all go drinking. They encouraged his inebriation. When he was intoxicated, they stole his wallet. The thieves had all been his friends since childhood. He belonged to the Charismatic Renewal. His father, distraught because of his son's situation, expressed disappointment because his son had always attended mass with the family until he started to drink. The young man had dropped out of school, found menial work, and lived from payday to payday, waiting to buy his next drink.

This young man represented the many *jóvenes* who abused alcohol in Nahualá. A walk near the plaza at any time of day revealed a number of young people (and many others who were older) drunk, passed out, lying in the streets. Although Guatemalan law prohibits the sale of alcohol to minors, vendors around the plaza commonly sold alcohol to underage youths. Jorge, a public

health specialist who is also a prominent member of the Charismatic Renewal, said this practice "is a grave social problem in the community." He further noted, "Twelve bars in Nahualá sell alcohol to young people. . . . There are young people that come in every day with alcohol problems, like damage to the liver or kidneys." Many young members of the Charismatic Renewal, he affirmed, buy liquor illegally.

The police chief commented, "The younger generation gets together and bothers a lot of people. They are always in the street. When it comes to alcohol, they all look for it and get together at a cantina [bar] and then share the bottles." There are so many bars in Nahualá that it is difficult to keep them adequately patrolled. "In one particular bar," stated a local health official, "approximately fifty to seventy-five young people go [drinking] every Sunday afternoon, the majority of whom are minors." Some informants blamed inadequate parental supervision; others blamed the owners of bars who do not monitor to whom they sell alcohol.[6]

The bartender and the police chief both agreed that Catholic youths comprise the majority of the teens who solicit alcohol. They did not distinguish between charismatic, Ortho-Roman, or traditionalist Catholics, but collectively cited "all types of Catholics."[7] Moreover, the police chief felt the Charismatic Renewal did not have social programs sufficient to deal with these problems.[8]

The officials of the Catholic church in Nahualá, although aware of this problem, encounter limits in what they can actually do. Antonio, a church official who works with troubled youth, reflected:

We try to help, but sadly, we do not have the resources so that we can help people indefinitely. For example, to materially help them to get out of their addiction and start a normal life, we lack a lot to get there. We believe that this has to be voluntary though; the person that wants to change has to have his own will. . . . We are trying to persuade all the young people that are within our reach to . . . motivate them. With Father Juan, we are treating a juvenile. We believe that he was involved with some gangs, but we are giving him the opportunity so that he is able to work with us in physical education.

Notwithstanding these concerns, the Nahualá parish does have programs to encourage youth involvement. The priest has organized youth committees that have activities every month for teens. The youths themselves, however, report poor attendance at these activities.

Charismatic Renewal congregations are supposed to have special meetings for youths. One girl said she thought that many young men fail to attend these meetings because they regularly drink alcohol. Since the renewal prohibits consumption of alcohol, such youths may feel uncomfortable attending because of a sense of guilt. When asked how the renewal controls alcohol use, one leader stated, "We give sermons in church about it [drinking], and we watch out for one another because the Bible says, 'No drunks can enter into the kingdom of God.'"

Gangs

Gangs, primarily composed of young men, have become a significant problem in Guatemala, and Nahualá gets no exemption. On one occasion, two boys, age seventeen or eighteen, engaged in a fistfight in the street. They staggered, barely having the strength to hit one another. Their friends watched and waited in silence for one to emerge victorious. A spectator, dressed in gang attire, commented on the drunken state of both fighters, adding that they both recently had smoked marijuana. They fought because one had prematurely destroyed the marijuana cigarette. "Normally they do not fight," he said, "because they [are] members of the same gang."

"The fear of gangs is real here in Nahualá," remarked a police officer. "Every year among the youth in Nahualá, anywhere from two to four deaths are caused by a mixture of both gangs and alcohol." The police officer noted that because many teens have given up their religion, their morals have changed.

The police chief seemed concerned because the Nahualá station did not have enough officers to handle the gang situation. Other informants indicated that because of media influences, gangs are becoming more and more common among the youths of the Charismatic Renewal. Marco, a gang member, remarked, "Here in Nahualá, we don't have gangs with pistols that shoot each other, but we have people that carry slingshots and machetes, and they can do damage with those." He affiliated himself with the Charismatic Renewal until he realized that "the renewal did not mean anything" to him. The renewal, he said, "restricted [me] too much," and he did not consider renewal membership "worth the sacrifices." Marco described the process of gang initiation:

There are groups here [in Nahualá]. And if there is someone that wants to be part of the gang, they don't just accept someone easily. They have to do things before [admission], so they can become part of the gang.[9] If they cannot do it, they are rejected from the gang. Sometimes, among the gang, they will choose about ten or fifteen men, who are thieves, to hit this person [the candidate]. But the person does not have the right to defend himself. If he lives through a span of five minutes' beating, they will let him be part of the gang. Here [in Nahualá], there are gangs, and they run around hitting, but there are not that many rivalries. They will take people and, if they hate [them], they will take them and hit them. There are gangs that run in the streets and rob—but not that many—[not] like in the capital [Guatemala City].

Marco felt that because the Charismatic Renewal teaches against drugs, alcohol, and violence, many gang members do not feel welcomed by the communities of charismatic Catholics. Also, because of the gang members' lifestyle, many of them are not interested in an intensely emotional religious meeting. Indeed, Edvalson and colleagues (2013) argue that the gangs in Nahualá are explicitly antireligious.

Nevertheless, at least some gang members affiliate themselves with the Charismatic Renewal. At the thirty-first anniversary celebratory meeting of the charismatic congregation called the Alpha and the Omega, two boys dressed in gang apparel visited from Guatemala City. During the meeting, the older teen fiercely tried to make the younger one cry. He grabbed the younger boy's finger during the prayer and viciously wrenched it backward until the younger boy cried out in pain. In spite of their extreme unruliness, the members of the congregation made an effort to exhibit patience with them. The older youth hit one worshipper in the face when his arm slipped off the younger boy's head in a failed attempt to put him in a headlock. The man simply ignored it and smiled. Later, the man noted how seldom youths attended his congregation, and he wanted them to feel welcome in spite of their behavior.

Education

Acquiring an education further impinges on one's charismatic church participation. To consider oneself faithful in most organized churches, one must participate in its meetings. Because the members of the Charismatic Renewal attend meetings for more than twenty hours a week, those who study full time find it difficult to keep up. When asked which has the higher priority during the week—secular studies or church attendance—prominent church members, without hesitating, answered: "Their studies. They will get a job; this [a job] makes it impossible for them to come to meetings as well, because they will have a boss. That is okay though." According to some, even the teens that study all week still do not go to mass or prayer meetings on Sunday because that is the popular day to drink. Note, in figure 13.3, the gaggle of male youths gathered outside the *culto* meeting; one is reading a book.

The Catholic church has a seminary-linked school system that is significantly cheaper to attend than other private schools and reportedly is better. Although typically reserved for those that want to become priests and nuns, Catholic seminary is available to all local Catholics. One priest remarked, "Many around here have gone to the junior seminary. They say, 'I want to be a priest.' However, it seems to me like they go to take advantage of the studies of the junior seminary because it is very cheap. It is cheap, and in other institutions it is much more expensive. I get the feeling that this is what they are doing. I think they are only lying to themselves." Because "they are having trouble encouraging youth to go into the ministry," the priest allows any young people to study in the church school system because he hopes that some will be inspired to go into the ministry as

either priests or nuns (on education, see Hatch 2005; De Hoyos, Hawkins, and Adams 2020).

Quasi-Commodity Fetishism

Many youths display intense interest in the entertainment aspects of capitalist production, and I adapt Marx's "commodity fetishism" to call it quasi-commodity fetishism. Nahualense youths have a strong desire to acquire commodities, even when it alters their cultural or religious values. This behavior is widespread. When, however, they acquire the commodities, they often associate these material items with the blessings of God.

At least some youths of the Charismatic Renewal showed signs of such commodity enthrallment.[10] For example, a young married couple, Marianna and Davíd, both sets of their parents having played prominent roles in the Charismatic Renewal, wanted to buy a new pickup truck. Marianna worried about the purchase because it would consume the funds she needed to go to school. Together, they decided that they would use their life savings to cover her school expenses. Approximately one week after this joint decision, however, her husband came home with a shiny white Toyota Tacoma pickup truck—funded by their savings account.

Although Davíd had bought the truck without consulting her, Marianna was ecstatic. She screamed with excitement and praise about the beautiful truck and vigorously exhibited her pride in ownership. When her father asked how she planned on continuing her studies, she simply

Figure 13.3. Male youths of charismatic families gather in their church's exterior courtyard. Note one of the seated young men studying a book. Courtesy of Gilbert Bradshaw, 2003.

responded, *Dios sabe* (God knows), meaning that she did not know but trusted fate. She later commented that she would rather have the "most beautiful pickup truck in [the Department of] Sololá" than the education.

This type of desire—to own a pickup truck, build a large house, buy a DVD player, acquire a cell phone—is a new trend. "When I was a boy, we didn't worry about having houses made of stone or brick," explained Santiago. "We were too worried about the needs of our brothers and sisters to worry about a large house. The youth are becoming too worried with things that won't save them." He opined that the things that will save them are God and religious devotion—things that in his view, the youths have forgotten.[11]

Although migration, no doubt, is a factor, it is not the only thing that fuels quasi-commodity fetishism. From every angle, western consumerism affects Nahualenses. They see the cars that whiz by on the international highway a kilometer away from the town center. They see store windows full of showy goods, which are held at arm's length by their poverty and the thick glass. Above all, various media now penetrate the village to the core. When walking the streets of Nahualá, one occasionally sees a satellite dish on the side of an adobe or cinderblock house. Most houses have pirated cable connections. Televisions hooked to DVD players in dingy basement parlors offer cheap movie theater substitutes. Only recently have the wage remittances from migrated family members made pickup trucks common elements in the town.[12]

CONCLUSION

A number of problems remain that need to be addressed by long-term doctoral research or team-based field school research focused on youths and a comparison of youth responses to religion in this multireligious context. Do CCR-raised teens respond differently in the Nahualense and Ixtahuaquense context than do Ortho-Catholic youths? Preliminary but rather anecdotal evidence suggests there is not much difference. Do CCR-raised youths respond differently to religious indoctrination than do Pentecostal or Mormon youths? Again, anecdotal evidence suggests yes, but we need a focused comparative study of teenagers in different religious contexts. In this chapter we have provided only a preliminary hint of what may lie still undiscovered in the nature of youth responses to the swirl of change in religion and society in this region. Nevertheless,

evidence suggests that the secularization of youth, enthrallment with commodities, and a rebellion against organized religion have induced a precipitous decline in teens' religious involvement in Nahualá's Charismatic Renewal communities.

The adults in the community believe that religion is important. In Weber's (2002[1905]:35, emphasis in original) phrasing, religion and "*the salvation of their souls*" lie "at the heart of their life and work." They know that spiritual beings exist and intervene in the affairs of people. Many proclaim a lifelong religious zeal, even as young people. Practicing members of the Charismatic Renewal attend significantly more meetings than do practitioners of ordinary Catholicism; the latter tolerate a lot of nonparticipating, cultural Catholicism. In spite of their parents' convictions, the youth of today's charismatic Catholic families seldom attend religious functions for several reasons: the prominent use of alcohol, the rise of gang membership, the need to leave the community to obtain an education or a job, and the substantial (perhaps even captivated) interest in commodities. All are significant changes for this culture.

In an attempt to fashion a new identity, youths are rejecting age-old Maya traditions. The teens are cruel instead of passive; antireligious instead of pious; and involved with gangs instead of family members. They leave Nahualá instead of adopting the tradition of working the same plot of land that has belonged to their family for generations. All of these changes suggest that among Nahualense charismatics, youths and adults are heading toward divergent social and religious paths in a failing intergenerational transmission of K'iche' culture, religious values, and religious behavior. If the present trend of youth disengagement continues, charismatic Catholicism as a denomination will end with the death of its last elderly member. However, this assumes the group replenishes itself primarily by reproductive replacement.

Another possibility is even sadder. When these wayward youths grow up, form families, and get married, the problems these marginalized men have acquired with alcohol, violence, and an inability to farm or find work will precipitate another round of familial crisis. Their wives will then join a charismatic or Evangelical group for support, thus replenishing charismaticism with a renewed membership of desperately aggrieved women and a few men who need and offer support to each other. These souls will continue to lay their personal tragedies before God and seek healing through enthusiastic, tense, mournful worship. Their worship will continue to reflect, according to Durkheim (2001[1912]), the structural limitations and personal anxieties inherent in finding a way to live in their local context, a context thoroughly disrupted by this globalized world but to which they are neither admitted nor adapted. And perhaps yet again, *their* youths will find themselves marginalized, enthralled by commodities, and repeating the cycle.

Nahualá's adult charismatics did not expect that they would so substantially lose their male youths. Quite the opposite, they consciously engaged in a new practice of religion to help their offspring. But they did not reckon with the impacts of permissiveness in Ortho-Catholicism, which they had not sharply broken with as the *evangélicos* did. Who would have thought that in seeking the salvation of their souls through what they deemed a more purified and spirited version of Catholicism that the parental generation in fact erected roadblocks for their male youths? These are truly "unforeseen and indeed *unwished for* consequences of the work of the Reformers" of which Weber (2002[1905]:35, emphasis in original) spoke; in this case, the consequences are for the charismatic parental reformers. Just as Weber predicted, it appears that the results among today's youth in charismatic families have been "far removed from, or even in virtual opposition to, everything that" the parents and congregation leaders "themselves had in mind" (35).

NOTES

1. According to Bradshaw, not many female youths attended either. They may have been tending younger children so that their mother could attend *culto*. He speculates about this, however, as he did not try to research or document female youth involvement in the charismatic movement.

2. Another fieldworker reported fifty-seven communities, and fifty-seven is the number Hawkins was told by a member of the Nahualense parish council. The point is not that two student fieldworkers disagree about a number that is in fact changing and expanding by fission, but that a large number of subgroups meet within the geographic confines of each Catholic parish, groups that are essentially beyond the reach and control of the parish priest.

3. Once, several residents said that a gang fight was scheduled in the town square that Friday night. The fight consisted of a group of friends pelting another boy with a slingshot. No gang members flashed guns. On gangs and gang perceptions in the study region, see Edvalson et al. 2013 and Call et al. 2013.

4. Informants casually estimated that 40 percent of local Catholics abandoned Catholicism for Protestant Pentecostalism, and another 40 percent joined the new Charismatic Renewal. We have no way of ascertaining the validity of these estimations.

5. The term "Ladino" identifies people that claim a non-indigenous cultural heritage.

6. Nahualenses commonly drink *kuxa*, a clandestine alcoholic brew, or its legal, purified, and glass-bottled cousin, aguardiente. Both are inexpensive, potent, easily acquired, and very popular, especially among youths. Bar owners often have their young children serve drinks to customers. This both facilitates underage access to alcohol (a younger server cannot easily refuse an older, yet underage, buyer) and accustoms bartending children to consider alcohol as a normal drink.

7. The comment that Catholics are those who typically drink is probably a reflection of the lore that Protestants do not drink because they are not *supposed* to drink. In a study on alcohol use among youths, Adams (1999) finds that those identifying themselves as Catholic and as Protestant were equally likely to drink.

8. The police chief declared that every time one sees a religiously active youth, "they are either Mormon or Evangelical." The few religiously active youths I met in Nahualá were, indeed, either Mormon or Protestant. Only during the celebrated ordination of the first K'iche' Catholic priest did I see Catholic youths present in noticeable numbers in a church setting.

9. That is, they must commit one or more crimes, and submit to being beaten by the rest of the gang. See Edvalson et al. 2013.

10. This evidence is admittedly inconclusive because of my inability to quantify signs of commodity fetishism. However, there seems to be enough evidence to warrant further investigation.

11. We saw hints of this quasi-commodity fetishism emerging in our earliest field schools. For example, Morgan's (2005:63) interaction with his host brother, and the difference between this host brother and Morgan's host father can enrich our understanding of the quasi-commodity fetishism trend.

12. In 1995, the first year of our field school, it took Hawkins two hours to find and hire someone with a pickup to take us from Nahualá to Santa Catarina. By the year 2000, one could usually see ten or more pickups lined up in informal taxi queues at two strategic locations, awaiting business from early morning to after dark.

PART II

Understanding the Christian Pentecostal Wail

Guatemala's Religious Transformation in Historical Perspective

The previous twelve chapters laid out some of the diversity of current religious practice in Nahualá and Santa Catarina Ixtahuacán as examples of worship in Maya Guatemala. How are we to understand such diverse data? How are we to grasp the meaning and consequence of these varied religious beliefs and practices? There are at least two routes.

First, any attempt at understanding should try to clarify some approximation of causality: what happened to create this condition of religious diversity? The answer to that lies in history, in diachronic analysis. That is the task of this part of the book. In linking religious change to the history of material conditions, I am guided by the shared ideas of Marx and Durkheim and, more implicitly, Weber. Marx and Engels (2008[1850]:94) blurt out the idea most explicitly: "It is clear that with every great historical upheaval of social conditions the outlooks and ideas of men, and consequently their religious ideas, are revolutionized." Durkheim's (2001[1912]:318–319, 329) emphasis on social structure leads him to a more muted statement of material impact: society "bears the mark of its material substrate . . . [and] only events of sufficient importance can manage to affect society's mental position." Weber was less certain of directionality. Implicitly in his work, the social fact of expanding mercantile colonial capitalism influenced the ideas of the Protestant reformers while the ideas of the reformers helped consolidate and purify expansive capitalism. Regardless of the differences, in the work of all three, material context is seen to impact

the forms of religion. Indeed, it is because of this interaction of ideas with material and social circumstance that Durkheim (2001[1912]:127) advances his fundamental insight: "The reality that religious thought expresses is society." Marx and Engels (2008[1846]:74–75) develop the same concept: "It is not consciousness that determines life, but life that determines conscoiousness." Because all human life is social, for Marx, like Durkheim, "consciousness is therefore from the start a product of society."

In my analysis of Guatemalan religious change, each chapter of this part treats a phase of Guatemalan history that is also tied to some aspect of what Marx and Durkheim would have called a "great upheaval" of material and social life as well as a change of religion. Of course, I am an imperfect historian. I depend largely on secondary sources, and history is always a simplification, a summary, and a personal interpretation hopefully fenced and guided by the guardrails of reasonably well reported evidence. But simplifications, summaries, and interpretations all have their limitations. Therefore, so does this study.

To help overcome some of the limitations of a historical interpretation, I use a second approach that helps refine, verify, cross-check, and flesh out the study of current behavior and meaning. That avenue is synchronic, rather than diachronic, analysis. Synchronic analysis entails the examination of actual speech and described action to derive meaning by teasing out their implications given their current full-bodied social context. Thus,

I attend to what people say and do, examine what they say about what they say and do, and juxtapose structurally the implications of what they could have said but did not and what they could have done but did not.

In short, according to Saussure, meaning inheres not wholly in any given speech act or behavior (however deeply interpreted in context), but derives also in part from understanding the opposition of any given statement or act with other members of the set of things that could have been said or done. That is the comparative, contrastive, contextualizing task of part 3.

But first things first. We must look at the changes in society and ecology through time. I seek to show the historical origins of Guatemala's religious diversity and ground my analysis in the observation that the underlying thrust for transformational change toward ecstatic religion in Guatemala today derives from the collapse of maize subsistence agriculture entwined with exclusion from viable alternatives. Of course, this condition of corn culture collapse and exclusion did not happen all at once. At each step of religious change represented by a chapter in part 2, there was an accompanying change in the political economy that reflected a transformation or "upheaval" in people's mode or organization of subsistence. For the Mayas, the focus regarding those transformations begins with and must always remain on corn.

Chapter Fourteen

Corn

The Significance of Maize in Pre-Conquest Maya Society and Religion, circa 3000 BCE–1523 CE

JOHN P. HAWKINS

CORN MATTERS TO THE MAYAS. Indeed, my argument is that the religious diversity and the success of the Pentecostal and Catholic charismatic religions portrayed in part 1 stem from a cultural crisis rooted in the collapse of maize subsistence agriculture accompanied by a failure of Guatemalan and global society to include Mayas in any viable economic strategies that might mitigate the failure of the corn supply, which Mayas thought was guaranteed by religious covenant. Thus, to appreciate the cultural implications of the twentieth and twenty-first centuries' shortfall in corn and to fathom how troubling that shortfall must be to anyone with a Maya cultural orientation, one must understand the deep cultural origins of the value Mayas place on corn, on land, and on the importance of covenant.

To say that corn matters is to say that corn is a value in and of the society. It is an idea. Durkheim (2001[1912]:317–318, emphasis added) suggests: "A society is not simply constituted by the mass of individuals who compose it, by the land they occupy, by the things they use, by the movements they make, but *above all by the idea that it fashions of itself.*" The values placed on corn, land, and covenant are essential ideas that Mayas have of themselves and of their world. They are core symbols and physical and behavioral sustainers of their indigenous society. Indeed, corn has undergirded Maya and other indigenous societies in Mesoamerica for thousands of years. Archaeologists have shown that corn sustained precursors of the Maya way of life since at least 3000 BCE (Marcus 2003:78; Zier 1980). The importance of corn early entered Mesoamerican religious symbolism. Taube (1992, 1996, 2000), for example, finds symbols of the divinity of corn and of a corn god in the Olmec pantheon in the Formative period (1500 BCE–400 BCE). These Olmec corn god symbols reverberate throughout the cultures and societies nurtured in Mesoamerica, among them, the Mayas.

To the Mayas, corn mattered both culturally and religiously. Corn sustained their lives. Corn mattered so much that the classic Mayas tied boards to the heads of their babies to elongate their skulls, thereby replicating in their heads the tapered cylindricality of healthy ears of corn topped by shocks of silken hair (Houston, Stuart, and Taube 2006:45; Miller and O'Neil 1999:106–108). Maya glyphs, stelae, and ceramics depict a corn god in human form, tasseled and nascently emerging from a trifoliate bract of growing corn leaves.

The *Popol Wuj*, a document that emerged late in the pre-conquest period, makes both overt and covert reference to corn and a deity in the process of creating humankind (Christenson 2003; Stross 2007; Garrard-Burnett 2004:546). In this Maya sacred book, the God of Corn makes three attempts to create humans. Out of earth, God of Corn creates mud humans, but they slump in laziness. That doesn't do, for laziness is a wholly unacceptable character trait among today's Mayas (Wells, Hawkins, and Adams 2020; Hawkins 1984) and probably the early Mayas too (Christensen 2000:46, 149–151). God of Corn as Creator/Shaper tries again and creates humans out of wood, but they are too stiff, rigid, and dry. They are rejected because they cannot worship their creators, and they have no liquid sweat (Christensen 2000:47–49, 151–155). In a final attempt, the God of Corn successfully creates humans out of nine grindings of corn dough. These are indeed sentient beings that, like corn, have skins filled with the juices of life, hold their shape, grow upward, are topped with dangling hair, and display a proper corn-like, humid consistency (Christensen 2000:129, 265). In conceiving themselves as made by the gods out of corn and nothing else, and in physically shaping themselves to be more like corn, pre-conquest Mayas centered and elaborated the notions that humans depend on corn, that the gods provide corn, and that the gods—and therefore humans—see corn and society as essentially and insepa-rably linked.

The creation of humans out of corn—the stuff and staff of Maya life—makes humans physically and mentally suc-cessful. Corn satisfies the mind and the belly. Corn pro-vides the substance, fluids, and consistency requisite to a healthy Maya's body in the year 2000 (Rode 2007) as well as in the year 200. The place of corn in Maya thought and religion made sense to the classic Mayas, made sense to Mayas in the past hundred years, and made sense in 2003 (when students were doing their fieldwork). Corn continues to hold a central place in the Maya diet, and until the twenty-first century, a substantial proportion of most Mayas' labor activities was devoted to procuring corn, obtaining the firewood needed to prepare corn, and engaging in all the activities that turn dry, storable corn into moist, hot, palatable corn foods suitable for family consumption. By sacralizing corn, both the classic Maya religion and its modified derivative, the present-day tra-ditional Maya religion, reflect and communicate this fun-damental reality of corn centrality and corn dependence.

In today's Maya world, the importance or meaning of being "traditional" does not lie in the authenticity or purity of a practice's derivation from pre-Columbian activities. Rather, the importance and meaning of today's traditionalism lies in the claim of ancient derivation pre-sumed to be proved by its contrastive relationship with what Mayas experience in present-day Ortho-Catholi-cism and in Pentecostal or Catholic charismatic practice. Unfortunately, many anthropologists exploring the Maya religious experience often interpret a belief or behav-ior as traditional and seek its sources in Maya history rather than extract its current meaning from its multiple usages and positioning vis-à-vis other rituals, regardless of historical provenance. The approach that sees mean-ing inhering in connectedness to what is perceived as an ancient form remains in use today in Maya studies, exemplified by Stanzione (2003), Hart (2008), and Mole-sky-Poz (2006).

Cook and Offit (2013:xiii) offer a more nuanced critique of the idea that a presumed historical connection is sufficient to establish meaning among the Mayas by showing that the distinctive religious practices that Mole-sky-Poz, Hart, or Stanzione portray as ancient are nei-ther simply "an indigenous religious system with roots in pre-conquest Maya culture" nor even a synthesis of Maya and Catholic systems. Rather, the distinct practices that living Mayas say are traditional are a constantly evolving adaptation resulting from the interaction of village-level politics and conditions, national events and pressures, and global intrusive processes. Cook and Offit (2013:159) conclude:

The notion of a continuing tradition of Maya religious thought and practice as put forward in Hart (2008) and Molesky-Poz (2006) is more problematic . . . than their conceptual frameworks suggest. In fact, what seems to have developed over the past two decades is two coexisting syncretized traditions lacking common roots, with *costumbre* here understood as a very local syncretizing of Spanish Catholic and indigenous reli-gion with colonial period roots and Maya spirituality as a late twentieth-century regional or national (and "Maya" rather than Momostecan [Momostenango is the mostly K'iche'-speaking *municipio* they studied]) syncretizing of Protestant and indigenous forms of worship, with hybridization of indigenous traditions, readings of the *Popol Wuj*, and new age cosmology.

Pre-Columbian Maya religion symbolized, empha-sized, and sacralized the deeply held importance of corn in establishing the identity of Maya humankind. The cen-trality of corn in sustaining Maya life has persisted into the present. Its importance in part lies in its food value as the Maya basic staple and in part lies in its iconic eth-nic contrast to the Ladino group, which sees wheat-based breads, rather than corn-based tortillas, as the pres-tige food. So pre-conquest Maya corn symbols and pre-conquest ideas about corn's sacredness persist by being caught up in present-day structures of symbols that con-trast with early versions of Ortho-Catholicism and help maintain the ethnic hierarchies and ethnic boundaries essential to colonial and present-day Maya life.

The cultural centrality of corn is further symbolized in a number of cultural aspects, beliefs, and avoidances that focus attention on the continuing value of corn. The Maya root word for "food" (*wa*) refers only to corn sub-stances. One cannot step over spilled corn; one must pick it up even if it must be dug out of the dirt kernel by kernel. To avoid a miserable fate, one never takes a second tortilla until one has finished eating the tortilla in one's hand or on one's plate. A shaman blesses the body of the person being healed in ceremony with a cob of corn, touching forehead, shoulders, arms, and legs with sweeping motions that envelop the body completely in the curative value of corn. The ethnographies are replete with references to the importance of corn to the Mayas, some indicating that importance in their titles. Thus, Valladares writes *The Cult of Corn in Guatemala* (1993) and *Man and Corn: The Ethnology of Colotenango* (2002[1957]) while Rojas Lima offers *The Culture of Corn in Guatemala* (1988). Corn matters to the Mayas.

Ethnographers such as Vogt (1976), Monaghan (1995), and Early (1982) have found the logic of mutual covenant—godly protection and provision for humans in return for humans feeding and praising the gods and maintaining moral conformity—central to twentieth-century Maya thought. With population growth and land loss, however, the increasing difficulty of seeing themselves as protected by covenant has become a crucial element in the Mayas' turn to Pentecostalism and Catholic charismaticism and the related slow decay of traditionalism. The subsistence difficulties documented in the 1930s ethnographies became a manifest food crisis for many by the mid-twentieth century.

Reciprocity matters, however; people monitor their own behavior and that of the gods. Covenant can be broken through inattention by either party to the reciprocities expected. What might be the implications of a corn shortage? Here is the logic of religious crisis. If humans do not perform rituals to please the gods and show them respect, or if humans fail to conform to behavioral

expectations as to proper Maya social comportment or give inadequate offerings to the gods, the gods can rescind their protections. Conversely, if well-behaving Mayas find the expected protections lacking, they could feel betrayed and assume the covenant has been broken. As Early (2012:19) notes, "usually there is no strict accounting." Nevertheless, "if a receiver does not eventually make a return, especially when the previous giver is in need, the pact is broken" (19). The expectant but offended receiver or the offending nongiver can be either a Maya person or some divinity. Therefore, the culprit or source of a breach evidenced by hard times would not always be clear or ascertainable to a Maya. One might wonder, for example, "Did I/we offend a divinity or ancestor by inattention? Or did an earth lord neglect me/us out of caprice?" Only a "no" answer to the first question implies humans need do nothing more than they are already doing. However, given the difficulty of getting any answer to either question, the most logical human response to hard times would be to lay on more rituals or increase ritual expenditures to get the gods' attention or end their caprice; this would ensure an acceptable offering as well as demonstrate behavioral conformity to the most rigid or expansive of possible expectations (Early 2012:19 32). In effect, one doubles down on the value of the gifts offered the gods in an effort to reacquire divine pleasure and protection. Hence the pre-collapse expansion in *cofradía* offerings described by Larson and colleagues (this volume) and Cancian (1965).

In following the structural impacts of pre-conquest Maya corn and covenant beliefs into the present, however, I get ahead of myself. I must now explore the impacts of a radical intervention in the lives of early Mayas: the Spanish conquest.

Chapter Fifteen

Colonialism

Catholicism and the Spanish Control of Land and People, 1524–1821

JOHN P. HAWKINS

IN 1524, A BAND OF some 420 Spanish conquistadores and perhaps 300 Tlaxcalan allies, led by Pedro de Alvarado, crossed into the Mam political and language territory of southwestern Guatemala via western Soconusco. No doubt, the Mams had heard rumors about what had happened to the powerful Aztecs to the northwest when the subordinated Tlaxcalans rebelled against the Aztecs by allying with the Spanish. So the Mams sent their ambassadors to these Spaniards and likely thought they had found a possible salvation from the overbearing K'iche' kingdom that had subordinated them. Alvarado negotiated an alliance with the Mams and promised them long-term protection and special status under the Spanish Crown in return for the Mams' help in defeating the overlord K'iche' polity. The strategy mimicked exactly Hernán Cortés's exploitation of the Tlaxcalans' resentments in order to conquer the superordinate Aztecs (Hawkins 1984:48–53). With these Mams helping, Alvarado succeeded and subjugated the K'iche' empire.

The Spaniards quickly imposed a new order of *encomienda* and *repartimiento* work enslavement in their new territories. In a process called *reducción*, the conquistadores, administrators, and Catholic priests collectivized and resettled the dispersed indigenous people into compact villages (*congregaciones de indios*), which were laid out around a central plaza that anchored rectilinear streets and blocks—all meeting Spanish urban expectations. The invaders subjected the indigenous people to Spanish colonial state law and, later, to local Ladino whim. According to Martínez Peláez (1970), they thereby changed the various polities of Mayas, turning them into "Indians."

Ladinos, an often unruly class of people, first emerged as an interstitial category composed of biological mestizos and indigenous people who had learned Spanish, adopted Spanish attire, and moved to Spanish town centers to take up nonagricultural trades (Martínez Peláez 1970:306–307, 368; Hawkins 1984:50–80; MacLeod 1973). Independence from Spain, however, eventually led to Ladino replacing Spaniard as the prestige category in the provinces. Over time, Mayas and Ladinos became mutually defining oppositional categories, and this opposition led to the elaboration of complementary and often inverse differences of self-identifying and self-protecting behavior.

Inverse differentiation appears to be a universal process in cases of colonial contact, class boundary maintenance, and ethnic distinction. The process I brief here (detailed throughout Hawkins 1984) appears to have resonances with Bateson's (1936) schismogenesis; Leach's (1965[1954]) oppositions, interactions, and bidirectional passings between Shans and Kachins in Burma (now Myanmar); and Barth's (1969) foundational notions of ethnic maintenance in *Ethnic Groups and Boundaries*. All these approaches seem rooted in the fundamental processes of differentiation by opposition in a set, which Saussure (1966[1959]) holds central to the emergence and maintenance of meaning. The oppositional expectations between Ladinos and indigenous people defined and stabilized each other (Hawkins 1984).

The Spanish colonial economic and political order included a religious facet: aggressive missionization by sixteenth-century Spanish Catholics. The Spanish Catholic Church attempted suppression of the old order pre-conquest Maya religion. It sought both forced and unforced conversion to the new Christian religion. The process brought to the villages formal Catholicism, including Spain's *cofradía* practices, the Dance of the Moros, the Dance of the Conquest, mass, Mary, Jesus, Judas, and a pantheon of saints who became sacred protecting patrons and iconic representatives of each of the *reducción* Maya towns (Early 2006, 2012). Catholic parish organization mirrored the colonial organization; Spanish *reducciones* that eventually became municipalities were made parishes. The Catholic faith at the center of the colonial government and culture supported the government's "feudal organization," which "gave a religious consecration to the secular feudal state system" (Engels 2008[1887]:269).

Nevertheless, the many other functions of religion ensured that the local popular religion, laden with long-held Maya insights, persisted. Yet change in the quasi-hidden religion of the Mayas did occur. In the local popular indigenous synthesis, the Spanish and their cultural and social structural descendants, the Ladinos, became the new lords of the earth. Physically, they became such as colonial governors of expropriated land. Spiritually, they became such in ways Durkheim would have appreciated, for the *witz* of the Mams and the earth lords of the K'iche', as documented by the 1930s ethnographies and into the present, came to have European and Ladino features, dress, and language. During three centuries of Spanish colonialism, both local Ortho-Catholicism and local traditional religion evolved and redeveloped as ongoing religious syntheses, each taking meaning from its relation to the other. Today, if a given belief or practice is not sponsored or approved by the current local Ortho-Catholic priest, that belief or practice is labeled "traditional" and "Maya"—even if it is primarily older-style Catholicism. As Hobsbawm and Ranger (1983) have shown, tradition is readily invented.

As Scott and colleagues (this volume) detail, in the twenty-first century that traditionalist synthesis consists of a tripartite spiritual division of labor that reflects the current situation of indigenous Mayas, the tasks they must accomplish, and the perspectives they must hold to succeed in the corn-based village isolation they have developed to protect themselves. At the most removed level, Santa Catarina (the Catholic patron saint of the two *municipios*), Jesus, Michael (the weighing and slaying archangel), and, frequently, Santiago Matamoros (Saint James the Moor Killer, with "Moors" understood as indigenes) stand as icons on the back high table (Scott et al., this volume; McDonald and Hawkins 2013a, 2013b). They inhabit the vault of the heavens. These high divinities do little obvious work and intervene only occasionally if Mayas ask for favors, thus reflecting the distance between the Guatemalan governing elites and the indigenes.

The more earthy spiritual beings, the earth lords that come to Tix and Maximón the Apostolic Betrayer, are more likely to interact with a Maya. These divinities act on the surface world, the *uwäch uleu* ("face of the land"), represented by the second table, lower than the first and closer to the client, where today's Mayas eke out their living. One can access the earth lords through rituals performed at the shaman's house altar or near portals that connect the surface of the earth to the underworld (such as caves, springs, seeps) or where the earth's surface intrudes into the sky vault (such as mountain peaks or saddles on a trail between *municipios*). Indeed, in present-day traditionalist religion, divinity is present in natural phenomena that likewise transition between and connect earth and sky, such as wind, rain, lightning, and cold.[1]

At the third level, a Maya's ancestors reside under the world's surface, where Mayas are buried. This is represented by the stone slab altar placed on the floor under the second altar table that depicts the surface of the earth. Candles placed on the floor slab honor the client's buried ancestors. By hiring the services of a respected *ajq'ij*, today's traditionalist Maya can call on the ancestors and the earth lords to seek help for the living.

The ancestors gave life to the living. They did so by giving birth to successive generations of humans and by securing and then conveying to their children a sufficient amount of land on which to grow each generation's necessary substance of life: corn. The living can call the dead to their aid through shamans, as Scott and colleagues (this volume) describe. But the living know that to be appreciated as an ancestor, they need to endow their children with the ability to make a living, which, for the Maya, centers on access to inheritable land. That is part of the mutual caring covenant. Giving one's children an inheritance thus is urgent within today's traditionalist Maya culture and practice; land transmission helps one be remembered and have the proper post-death Ortho-Catholic sacraments performed by one's descendants. One sees here the centrality of land and the corn complex carried into present-day traditionalist religious practice and culture and expressed as covenant.

Today's traditionalist worship practice, derived from both pre-conquest and post-conquest forms of indigenous control, thus effectively symbolizes the centrality of the subsistence corn economy and the municipal isolation of the Mayas. The man who would become a remembered and revered ancestor has a moral obligation to provide corn to his family and to give corn plots to his children; the child reciprocates by obeying the father in life and, eventually, consulting him and other ancestors for their proven wisdom when they are dead. This urgency of land, as reflected in today's traditionalist religion, helps us understand the existential and religious crisis Mayas experience as their ability to provide corn comes under assault.

At least two religious symbols make clear the indigenous person's place in the colonial hierarchy. First, in present day traditional shamanic practice, an earth lord introduces himself to an indigenous client seeking knowledge by speaking Spanish through the mouth of the *ajq'ij*. Second, the source of the two-faced capriciousness of the treacherous but apostolically holy Judas/Maximón figure gets represented in the clothes he wears. Maximón figures are usually dressed in a Ladino military officer's uniform complete with aviator sunglasses and a "saucer" hat, or in a Ladino plantation owner's business suit and tie, complete with felt Stetson. What could better symbolize the source point of the caprice, the excesses, and the uncertainties of indigenous life under Spanish and later Ladino administrative law in an appointive and thoroughly corrupt bureaucracy than an apostle betrayer dressed in the icons of a military officer or plantation owner? That symbolism was colonially accurate and, to a considerable degree, still reflects Maya reality. So the traditionalist symbols of land, corn, and colonial control remain viable today for those who still possess and are able to work their own land. And the structural uncertainties symbolized by Maximón still powerfully affect indigenes, for they must interact to some degree with their ethnic opposite: the often prejudiced Ladinos who, from the Maya perspective, live their lives according to an inverse and therefore perverse, inscrutable, unreliable, and even dangerous cultural code.

What gave rise to this duplicity? On the one hand, the Spanish and the Ladinos have been givers of orders and laws that indigenes must obey. On the other, Spanish governing elites have been corrupt: protection and impunity could be bought for a price, and the right to exploit indigenes could be purchased for a suitable coin (Martínez Peláez 1970; Hawkins 1984:112–113). Judas/Maximón remains today the perfect symbol of such duplicity, derived straight from the colonial roots of these contradictions: state-sponsored extraction/exploitation, religious protection by the state's church that justifies the exploitation, and an ethnic hierarchy that confers de facto impunity on the elites. The beliefs and social practices of this hierarchy, which foster privileged Ladino control, subordination of indigenes to Ladinos, and extraction of wealth from indigenes while elites remain above the law,

still remain key premises of Guatemalan culture and the expectations embedded in Maya lore (Hawkins 1984:50–83, 112–113; McCreery 1994; Martínez Peláez 1970; Bauer Paiz 1965; Skinner-Klee 1954). So Maximón as both sacred apostle and betrayer still watches over the surface of the second-level altar table in many an *ajq'ij*'s divining room.

During the last hundred years of the colonial period, the emphasis of Guatemala's Catholic priesthood migrated from evangelizing and protecting the Mayas toward staying connected with elites and the cities' populace (Sullivan-González 1998:6; García Añoveros 1995:65–68). Mayanized Catholicism as practiced in the indigenous *municipios* descended from the colonial *congregaciones* thus became a power in itself, distant from and rather independent of the Ortho priests. Ortho priests, greatly reduced in number, largely abandoned the indigenous villages to serve the higher-status Spanish and Ladino elites. Nevertheless, Mayanized Catholicism absorbed and retained colonial notions of hierarchy, for example, in the positional steps on the ladder to high religious status through *cofradía* service. Again, as Marx and Durkheim predicted, the great societal upheavals embodied in Spanish governance, taxation, exploitation, ethnic separation, and village formation brought religious change in the form of imposed Ortho-Catholicism and evolving hierarchies in each village of indigenous gerontocratic and largely independent *cofradías* and traditionalist shamans.

One sees here the signs of the culture gulf between Maya and Spaniard/Ladino. Maya religion persisted in modified forms to provide for Mayas the symbols of the key premises of their land, work, and insular ethnic status. Popular Maya religion's panoply of spiritual beings acted in ways that showed Mayas how Ladinos would act toward them. On the opposite side, Spanish colonialism brought its religion of hierarchy and submission. Engels understood this essentially feudal and hierarchical Catholicism (Engels 2008[1886]:264). The question then becomes: What great social and historical upheaval could possibly exceed the disruptions of Spanish colonialism and even partially overturn it? The answer in Guatemala involves a growing worldwide craving for caffeine.

NOTE

1. Here and elsewhere in this book, my debt to John Monaghan's *The Covenants with Earth and Rain* (1995) is obvious.

Chapter Sixteen

Coffee

Independence, Global Markets, Liberalism, and Religion, 1821–1944

JOHN P. HAWKINS

BETWEEN 1800 AND 1850, GUATEMALANS slowly discovered that they could grow, harvest, and roast the pit in the fruit of an imported ornamental and medicinal plant: the coffee tree. They could therefore profit from the coffee-drinking rage that had already swept well-to-do Europe and elsewhere. The new product required much hand labor, and that labor need pulled Mayas further into an expanding worldwide cash economy. In the 1850s and 1860s, the national government encouraged landowners to plant enough trees to harvest a commercially viable crop and supply coffee to world markets (Wagner 2001:29–45). Guatemala's elites found they could grow coffee trees best on the middle and lower slopes of the country's rain-watered, steep, deeply ravined mountains. Prior to the possibilities opened by coffee, such mountain lands had seemed worthless to elites and were therefore left largely to indigenous municipalities to be used as communal forest resources for firewood gathering, house timber production, and corn plot expansion by swidden agriculture (McCreery 1994; Wagner 2001:87–89, 145).

Once the rain, slope, and drainage needs of coffee trees were understood, Spaniards, Germans, and Guatemalan Ladinos seeking wealth from coffee began a program of land acquisition. They bought, connived, tricked, and captured much of the coffee-suitable woodland slopes in two ecological bands: one along the lower third of the south-facing mountain escarpments paralleling the Pacific Ocean and the other on the slopes of the northern ranges facing the Petén and the Caribbean (McCreery 1994). Thus, coffee production brought Guatemala and Guatemalan Mayas into the world market and in that process, as Marx and Engels (1948[1848]:10) noted, "pushed into the background every class," including the

Mayas. Ladino exploitation of forests for coffee production put the wood needs and corn production of indigenous people at risk.

To get indigenous hand labor to the coffee plantations and to get coffee product to the ports, liberal governments built roads, telegraphs, railroad lines, and other features of infrastructure that further penetrated indigenous communities and affected their autonomy. Securing indigenous labor required coercion. A plethora of scholars treat the various permutations of work requirements imposed on indigenes from independence (1821) to the democratic opening (1944) (e.g., McCreery 1994; Martínez Peláez 1970; Wagner 2001:90–93; Bauer Paiz 1965; Skinner-Klee 1954:110–120). National leaders justified these changes and labor demands under patriotic liberal slogans of national "order and progress," which included improvements in education and attention to science (Wagner 2001:93–96; Garrard-Burnett 1998:1–20). These labor needs set in motion the basic conflict between liberals, who favored the process of "progress and modernization" to make worldwide coffee sales possible, and conservatives, who inclined toward maintenance of the simpler Spain-oriented, colonially extractive, and quite Catholic status quo.

As Engels (2008[1887]:270) observes, "The Catholic world outlook, fashioned on the pattern of feudalism, was no longer adequate for this new class and its conditions of production and exchange." Engels was speaking generally, but the insight applies to Guatemala. The liberals indeed leaned hard on Catholicism and pressed for Protestant alternatives. Maya traditionalist religion and popular culture changed also and came to reflect Ladino labor demands. In foundational myths recorded in the 1930s and 1940s ethnographies, Mayas represented hell as a form of labor slavery under Ladino-featured earth lords possessing capricious power. Given the premises of the image of the limited good (Foster 1965), indigenes who became wealthy in this life were thought to do so at the expense of their peers in the community. They must have gotten wealthy, it was thought, by making pacts with the devil, for there simply was no other way to get rich. The devil, of course, was the Ladino. But such individuals would eventually have their eternal comeuppance. Those who made the pact for wealth in this life would suffer forever after death; in one ethnography they were said to be chained to coffee trees to labor throughout eternity (Wagley 1949:56–57).

The technology of coffee production has not changed much since 1860 except for today's use of chemical fertilizers and plague-controlling sprays containing heavy metal compounds. In spite of the production increases due to fertilizers and sprays, coffee is still a hand-tended and hand-picked crop dependent on indigenous labor and grown on scarped mountainous hillsides. From the Maya perspective, however, two things have indeed changed. First, the amount of hillside land taken into non-Maya custody and converted from a communally held indigenous resource supporting household subsistence to private, market-oriented, export coffee production has increased drastically. Mayas have lost land and forest resources crucial to their mode of production survival (LaFarge 1947:3–4; McCreery 1994). Second, the amount of indigenous labor required to plant, care for, and, especially, hand pick the coffee cherries has increased prodigiously, directly in proportion to the increased number of sacks of coffee produced annually.

In 1870, coffee surpassed cochineal as Guatemala's main export (Wagner 2001:51). Coffee soon came to dwarf all the previously dominant export crops. From 1870 to 1899, coffee production expanded sevenfold in weight exported and four and a half times in value produced (Wagner 2001:111). Between 1900 and 1918, export production rose steadily until it peaked in 1917 at 892,596 *quintales* (hundred-pound sacks). Export production then plateaued and stayed between 900,000 *quintales* of green (commercially ready) coffee and 1.2 million sacks from 1918 to 1954. In the next few years, however, coffee production for export jumped 71 percent, from 1.17 million sacks in 1955–1956 to 2 million sacks per year by 1961–1962, nearly doubling the need for indigenous labor. Production hovered around 2 million sacks from 1961–1962 to 1971–1972. In 1972–1973 production jumped again to 2.67 million sacks

(an increase of 34 percent), and then rose to 3.29 million *quintales* by 1981–1982 (an increase of 65 percent from 1971–1972). Production then fell to 2.6 million sacks from 1982–1983 to 1984–1985, perhaps disrupted by the height of the insurrection (Wagner 2001:148, 155, 172, 182, 185, 197). What are the implications of these production increases for indigenous life?

To appreciate the impact of these jumps in coffee production on both indigenous labor and religious change, one needs to know how much labor coffee requires. In the twentieth century on one of the most efficient coffee plantations in Guatemala, each *quintal* required, on average, sixteen days of human labor, with six days of that labor required to pick enough wet cherries to produce a hundred pounds of green coffee (Adams n.d.). While not all that labor is indigenous or performed by trucked-in temporary *cuadrillas* (indigenous labor is especially concentrated in the picking process), the threefold expansion of coffee production between 1956 and 1981 required an approximately threefold expansion of indigenous people drafted into the national economy over the same period. By 1981, just the tasks of completing the coffee harvest seemed to have required the on-plantation labor of between one-third and two-thirds of all male and female Mayas age fifteen to sixty-four for a month.[1]

The 71 percent expansion in coffee production that occurred between 1955–1956 and 1961–1962—and the cultural stress that implies—corresponds quite closely both with the initial flourishing of Protestant Pentecostalism and with the emerging population-driven land-shortage crisis of corn subsistence. The second surge in coffee production, from 1972 to 1982, and its attendant stresses corresponds with a further burst of Pentecostal Protestant membership expansion (Garrard-Burnett 1998:120–124) and with the 1970s start-up and rapid expansion of pentecostal charismatic Catholicism. Thus, coffee increase, corn shortage, and religious ecstaticism seem closely linked in ways that I draw out as I proceed with this history. In Marx's terms, when the social economy of corn and coffee quaked, so did religion.

At about the same time that coffee production demanded more workers, Maya labor increasingly became available because Mayas were forced by land and corn shortages to sell their unused labor in order to buy food. At first, however, force had to be used. From the 1871 revolutionary success of Justo Rufino Barrios to the 1944 democratic opening, the government required that Mayas work by using various forms of corvée, imposing severe penalties if people did not deliver. In a presidential decree of May 1934, Jorge Ubico issued the last and perhaps the most famous of these labor laws. He used the notion of ending the vice of "vagrancy" as an excuse to force indigenous people to labor on the plantations. The law required that the Mayas be able to prove their progress to completing 100–150 days of labor on a plantation by carrying an employer-signed work registry in a *libreta* (booklet) (Skinner-Klee 1954:118–120; McCreery 1994:317; Martínez Peláez 1970:577–581; Jones 1940:162–163). Days were to be both paid for and signed off by plantation management. But given that failure to carry the booklet or to complete the assignment resulted in jail time at hard labor, plantation managers often signed the book without paying the wage or paid the wage without signing the book. Either course harmed indigenes severely and extended their exploitation beyond the considerable coercion and theft embedded in the law.

In addition to serving as a mechanism of labor theft or exploitation, possessing the labor book had other consequences. To merit the lesser labor obligation, Mayas had to prove ownership of the requisite land by registering in the national system the land they worked. But the registry process exposed Maya land to theft by Ladinos. The dilemma: if Mayas left their land unregistered, they had to labor for wages and neglect the land; if they registered, they risked losing the usage by losing the land (McCreery 1994; Dabb et al. 2013). As intended, the labor laws forced indigenous people out of their communities and into the urgently needed labor pool, which benefited the new coffee capitalists. In parallel, the required registration of land in order to have a reduced labor obligation forced the land into the open in a bureaucratic structure that Ladinos understood and controlled more than Mayas did. Registration of land thus eventually resulted in partial loss of land. By making indigenous land identifiable, it became available to the coffee capitalists if it suited them; as a result, land passed out of the indigenous communities.

Among the elites, coffee production and distribution had consequences that triggered an evolutionary cascade of changes in the nation. Coffee exploitation demanded connection with markets outside the colonial governance and mercantile trade connections with Spain. Producers or intermediaries had to make transactions quickly with outsiders and ship coffee promptly to Germany, New York, or other places. Under the liberals, new lines of communication—telegraph, telephone, roads—were built rather quickly.

With independence from Spain and within the global coffee culture, the direct governance of Mayas became less important. The coffee capitalists needed surges of labor—gangs of Mayas to help at the high points in the agricultural season of coffee—but it cost plantation owners less if indigenous people maintained themselves in their own villages between these surges of labor need. Thus, the colonialist forced labor of one-fourth of the indigenous population each week on rotation, as was done under *repartimiento* and *mandamiento*, gave way to more flexible labor markets, wherein Mayas came to the plaza voluntarily to get loans against their promises to labor during the times when plantations needed workers. Labor became a market commodity rather than a state asset assigned to favored cronies or a required state activity, such as road maintenance.

Of course, once the liberals acquired the reins of government and achieved their modernization project to get coffee to market profitably, they became "conservatives" in the sense that they used the power of government to help them and their patronage hierarchy stay in power and maintain their coffee-linked wealth. Liberal government and liberal laws focused on the arts of controlling the indigenous population and extracting from indigenous communities the cheap labor needed to profit from Ladino- and European-owned plantations. From the Maya perspective, each successive government was as indistinguishable from the previous or the subsequent as the segments of a millipede on the march. To Mayas, it seems, all outsiders exploited them. Therefore, contact with "foreigners"—meaning Ladinos (*mu'sayib'*)—should be avoided as much as possible. As Early (2012:41–43, 50) puts it, the Mayas' goal was to pay the costs exacted, minimize contact with Ladinos and outside institutions, and get on with their indigenous life.

How did this liberal, elite Ladino interest in coffee work out in terms of Ortho-Catholic and Maya Catholic religions? Liberals differed from conservatives in that liberals forged a pro-Protestant agenda. They did so in part because an anticlerical and anticonservative effort to remove Catholic institutions and personnel from power and control in the government helped liberals gain access to Catholic land and gave more direct access to indigenous villages as labor pools unprotected by resident Catholic clergy. The mainline Protestant interest in education, science, and progress also helped develop the infrastructure needed to raise and distribute coffee efficiently. Barrios, for example, invited American Protestant ministers to Guatemala to help counterbalance Spanish Catholicism and to internationalize his modernization effort (Garrard-Burnett 1998:3, 10–15). Liberals sought roads, railroads, ports, and telegraph connections to bring coffee to market. Protestantism helped. Conservatives, by contrast, sought to maintain or, following periods of liberal government, to restore Catholic institutions to power. Both liberals and conservatives, however, shared a mutual interest in controlling indigenes and extracting wealth from them via that control.

Calder (1970:11–23) tells in detail the story of the Catholic Church's decline in the face of liberal government "reforms." Following independence in 1821, conservatives and liberals alternated power every three to six years for some fifty years. Each time the liberals won the government, they imposed more restrictions on Catholic institutions. Each time conservatives won, they retrenched and protected Ortho-Catholicism. By 1871, however, with Barrios's victory, liberals clearly and finally dominated, expelling all foreign-born priests and nuns. Attrition and failure of replacement further reduced local clergy. Barrios ended the Catholic Church's hegemony as the sole permitted religious confession by embedding religious freedom in Guatemala's constitution.

Calder (1970:20–21) concludes that the various liberal government restrictions imposed on the Catholic Church between 1870 and 1944 "were the cause of the principal problems faced by the Church in the twentieth century" and contributed to the "severe problems faced by the Mayas." One such problem was recruitment for the priesthood. Not only did "Guatemala c[o]me to have one of the lowest proportions of priests to population throughout Latin America," but "the few priests available" to serve the Mayas (or anyone else in Guatemala) "were poorly financed, deficiently educated, and often mis-directed or incompetent" (20–21).

Lacking personnel, priest-mediated Ortho-Catholicism retreated from the indigenous *municipios* to the Ladino department capitals to serve Ladino interests. That left the indigenous small town centers and countryside virtually vacant of Ortho-Catholic supervision. The occasional visit of an itinerant priest did little. Sullivan-González (1998:30) asserts that only the permanently assigned resident priests made a difference in the Maya communities, and they were often run out of the indigenous parishes.

Thus, Ortho-Catholic leaders lost adequate contact with their indigenous faithful for a long period. As this loss of contact evolved, the 1930s ethnographies

recounted visits by a priest to a given municipal parish church once every decade or less, or at most once a year (LaFarge 1947:xii, 79; Early 2012:3–4, 110–111). Calder (1970:100–101) asserts that until 1944, "many zones" of rural Guatemala had not been serviced by a priest "in the last twenty or thirty years." At the time of Calder's study of Catholicism in the villages (1944–1966), "some" had not been visited "since the decade of 1870," or between seventy and ninety years, and others had not seen a priest "since colonial times," which amounts to no visits for some 130 years (100–101). Perhaps this exaggerates, but if so, not by much. Speaking of the period 1821–1871, Sullivan-González (1998) notes Catholic efforts to overcome the shortfall in priests by giving temporary rotating assignments with obligations to visit multiple parishes. But, he notes, these were ineffective at establishing control. Sullivan-González makes no attempt to specify the frequency of visits in the best and worst cases. To characterize the period, however, he gives an example from Cajabón (now Cahabón). There the priest was murdered over a minor argument with the traditionalists. No priest tried to enter the *municipio* for the next sixteen years, and when priests were finally assigned for short terms, there is no evidence any succeeded in having an Ortho impact in the parish (Sullivan-González 1998:77–80). One bishop "lamented" the "loss" of "three centuries" of Christianization effort among some Mayas (33). Through it all, however, Mayas called themselves Catholic and felt themselves to be the truest of Catholics. To the Mayas, the occasional visiting priest was little more than a deluded but conveniently useful administrative interloper—the performer of occasional masses, the provider of collective baptisms and marriages, and the maintainer of records. The *cofradistas* and the *ajq'ijab'*, by contrast, anchored the important religious festivals and guided the key mediations between people and the world's unseen powers, mediations needed for health and peaceful relations in the community. In addition to consulting the earth lords and ancestors through the *ajq'ij*, Catholic Mayas bereft of priestly input elaborated the practice of petitioning the saints by visiting and importuning their iconic representations in the church buildings.

According to Calder (1970), locally run Maya Catholicism and Maya Catholic traditionalism remained largely uncontested in many indigenous *municipios*, sometimes for as much as a hundred years. As a result, indigenous Maya Catholicism evolved, diverged, and became deeply entrenched in Maya community leadership and cultural structures. Indeed, Early (2012) thinks that traditionalist Maya Catholicism became a distinct version of Christianity.

Liberal suppressions of Catholic institutions and the absence of Ortho-Catholic priests in the Maya *municipios* allowed Maya reinterpretations of sixteenth-century Ortho-Catholicism to flourish. Indeed, *cofradía* and festival life expanded in ways that would become unacceptable to later-arriving Ortho-Catholic priests. As Annis (1987) shows, these *cofradía* activities were a manifestation of an indigenous "*milpa* logic" of local focus and intensive investment in the sphere of religion. *Cofradía* service reflected one's concern about local welfare and the development of one's local status via ritual. Just as Mayas prodigiously poured their labor into their corn plots, they sank their accumulated material wealth and labor into the community's *cofradía* activities in order to please the gods and increase their social status. But that prestige was only valued in the local indigenous community. To this summary of what Cancian (1965) found for Zinacantán in Mexico and Annis established in Guatemala, I add Early's (2012) and Monaghan's (1995) observations that the culture of covenantal expectation to secure divine blessing was also at work. *Milpa* logic applied to religion was also local logic. It constituted a doubling down by investing in local religious endeavors to achieve local security and status both on earth (regarding local food adequacy and social prestige) and in heaven (regarding spiritual security) (Cancian 1965; Vogt 1976; Larson et al., this volume).

The place connection, the experiential earth- and corn-grounded orientation, and the information derived from ancestors and divinations rendered the *ajq'ijab'* shamans as crucial to the indigenes as the *cofradía* leaders and both more so than the occasional visiting Ortho-Catholic priest. The system of symbols and the bodily performances in these strands of Maya Catholicism made good sense as long as the available land produced enough corn to feed modestly the Maya people and as long as the community could stay relatively autonomous politically and economically, thereby limiting exploitation by the ethnic "others" of the nation.

If one needed social status outside the community, however, one needed to speak a different ritual language. Two main options emerged: Ortho-Catholicism and the recently invited mainline Protestantism. But mainline Protestantism, it would turn out, was only an initial catalyst that would be absorbed in a transition to the ritual language of Pentecostalism.

Why were there so few mainline Protestant converts drawn from among traditionalists, Maya Catholics, and Ortho-Catholics during the time before the democratic opening? I suggest this: the Ladino exploitation of indigenous communities for coffee laborers had not changed the country's social structure significantly from the prior Spanish colonial exploitation and extraction of *encomienda* and *repartimiento* labor. Coffee's social structure from independence in 1821 through the democratic opening in 1944 was in fact a form of internal colonialism, as Aguirre Beltrán (1967) and Stavenhagen (1970, 1975) show. In a Durkheimian sense, little had changed socially or structurally for the indigenous people, so little needed to change religiously, given that the idea people have of their society "is the soul of religion."

Even until the mid-1940s, there was still enough land, together with wage supplements from labor on the plantations, to enable most Maya families to make ends meet and preserve the partial fiction of an indigenous culture living in corn-based, self-subsistence, and village isolation (McCreery 1994). Moreover, the historical Protestant emphasis on verbal logic, which came out of European and American elite education systems, was relatively incompatible with the Maya cultural focus on experientiality. Mainstream historical Protestantism therefore appealed to few indigenes. In addition, Protestant individualism did not fit Maya culture. Mayas were still exploited as a group, and these indigenes saw their collective, municipally linked ethnicity as more important (and more protective) than their individuality. So, on three counts, religion as the soul of society did not much change: the primary colonial structures of exploitation were still in place, subsistence had not yet been degraded much by population expansion, and the Protestant individualistic and text-oriented alternative was culturally incompatible with Maya ways of thought and action.

Early (1982:66), however, lists ethnographies from the 1930s through the 1960s that indicate indigenous communities had begun to experience considerable stress regarding corn and land shortage.[2] It is not hard to add to his list; one merely needs to read carefully the ethnographies he might not have consulted, among them, Gillin (1951:12–13, 31), referring to corn and land shortage in 1942–1948; the not quite ethnographic reportage and adventures of Oakes (1951a:81) for 1945–1947; and Reina (1966:41–42, 47), regarding 1953–1955 fieldwork in a community near

Guatemala City where the average family had but a fifth of the government required minimum for self-sufficiency. Land was getting increasingly scarce because of population increase, but perhaps was not scarce enough yet to drive many Mayas to seek other kinds of religion or permanent wage work beyond their *municipio*.

As Ortho-Catholics and traditionalist Catholics increasingly felt the pressures of corn shortage and culture collapse, which challenged their faith in covenanted protection, Pentecostalism's experiential, oral, embodied practice appealed more to peoples of Guatemalan indigenous culture than theological, verbal, rational, discursive mainline Protestantism. Although growth was still slow, Pentecostal varieties of Protestantism grew faster than mainline denominations. Moreover, many mainline Protestant congregations of Mayas, who were converted by North American missionaries, later transitioned their liturgical style toward the more Maya-compatible Pentecostalism. They did not, however, always indicate that transformation with a change of denominational name to include the word "Pentecostal." Nevertheless, many congregations became quite independent of their originating Euro-American sponsors (Garrard-Burnett 1998:36–40). Even so, after eighty years of missionary work, the combined number of mainline Protestants (which languished) and Pentecostals (which grew) constituted just 1.47 percent of the population in 1940 and did not become significant until after World War II (Wilson 2003:164).

After the 1940s, however, Early (1982) shows that population growth brought indigenous corn land into palpably short supply. Indigenous people's subsistence on their own land became increasingly precarious if not impossible. To eat, many indigenes had to leave their villages annually to find work. So coffee plantation owners no longer needed coercive labor laws to force the indigenous citizens out of their *municipios*. Hunger, familial love, and gender-based duty forced Mayas out. Thus, by 1944, the Arévalo government could drop the corvée laws. Economic necessity would now drive indigenes to do what ethnically discriminatory labor extraction laws had done formerly.

But why did mainstream, mission-delivered Protestant membership not prosper much in the 1940s indigenous communities in spite of growing food shortage and increasing culture collapse? First, traditionalist symbolism captured the importance of corn, land, and physical labor better than *evangélico* symbolism, and second, the land and corn crisis was new and emerging. Moreover,

both Maya Catholic traditionalism and Ortho-Catholicism better symbolized the collective submission of indigenes under Spanish rule. On the one hand, traditionalism's sortilege, Judas/Maximón duplicity, and divination by calling ancestors and earth lords when someone was troubled and uncertain better represented the factors of luck, caprice, and random risk that life under the Spanish and Ladinos imposed. On the other hand, Ortho-Catholicism's administrative hierarchy and required performative obedience to sacramental obligation better represented the essence of submission to imposed colonial obligations. Finally, Maya Catholic and Ortho-Catholic attention to municipal-wide fiestas and the place of the town saint better symbolized the collective focus still socially regnant in the *municipios* than did the new teachings of the mainline Protestants, who ignored collective municipal celebrations and emphasized individual salvation.

Early Protestantism did, however, foment education in order to provide an individual with direct access to the Bible, which in Protestantism is the sole source of authority and truth. But the very act of learning to read corroded both community and subordination because it gave congregants the ability to evaluate the affirmations of a minister against their own interpretation of the biblical text. Biblical access made the individual ultimately responsible to construct her or his own ethical framework, a movement away from common culture and toward fissiparousness. Nevertheless, this orientation toward reading encouraged Protestants, and thus Protestant Mayas, to acquire the education that might help them succeed in the diverse, modernizing, increasingly capitalist economy that was penetrating their world.

The process first of Protestantization and then of Christian Pentecostalization, however, was not instantaneous. For one thing, the expansion of coffee plantations occurred slowly, taking more than a century to come to full production and therefore full impingement on the Mayas; this culminated in the late 1970s to mid-1980s. For another, it took time for the Protestant thrust for education and health services to be modeled by Catholics and generalized to state services, resulting in widespread reductions in infant mortality. Thus, the expansion of Guatemala's Maya population resulting from better health conditions also took time. But the coffee and population expansions had a coordinated impact.

In the next chapter I show in detail how the population expansion progressed. That population growth, along with land loss due to coffee encroachment, resulted in Mayas increasingly coming to perceive their culture as under attack and in collapse, the covenant with the gods broken, their deserved bounty withheld. In response, either Mayas moved to cultural excess through an expansion of the *cofradía/cargo* offerings in a desperate attempt to appease the gods or, bit by bit as they saw no response from the gods, many Mayas chose cultural abandonment through conversion from traditionalism and Ortho-Catholicism to Evangelical Pentecostalism. To lay the groundwork for understanding this process, I step back a bit in time and detail the emergence of the land-corn-population imbalance that propelled Mayas into cultural crisis.

NOTES

1. The *finca* requiring 16 days of labor per *quintal* was Oro de Flama. In a parallel work, the United Nations Food and Agriculture Organization (1958:6) suggests that in Colombia on family farms of sufficient size to be dependent on hiring outside workers, the average labor input to produce a hundred pounds of green coffee was 8.35 days of eight hours each. In El Salvador, each *quintal* of green coffee required 13.24 eight-hour days of labor input in one year's agricultural cycle, and if the labor required to establish the plantation and raise the coffee trees is included, "a reasonable amortization of this input" plus the annual labor input "would raise to about 3 man/hours the human labor necessary to produce 1 kilogram of green coffee" (105). That works out to 17 eight-hour *jornales* (days of human labor) per hundred-pound sack, quite close to the 16 days suggested by Adams n.d.

Adams (n.d.) says that picking alone required six days of labor per hundredweight, and the UN conversion tables suggest five days of labor per hundredweight (United Nations Food and Agriculture Organization 1958:144). These figures provide some idea of the labor surge needed for the relatively brief harvest period and the consequent seasonal intrusion of coffee production on the isolation of indigenous villages. Here is the math of it: 3.29 million sacks produced in 1981–1982, at six days of harvest labor per sack,

equals 19.74 million days of labor, or 658,000 person-months of labor during the harvest season, assuming no Sabbath or other days off. The 1981 census shows an indigenous population of 2.537 million. Of these, 68.3 percent (1.732 million) were classed as rural residents. Since 52 percent of all Guatemalans are between the ages of fifteen and sixty-four, the approximate number of rural Guatemalan Mayas in this age span is 901,000 people. For this group to supply 658,000 person-months of labor, the math suggests that about 73 percent of all rural Mayas (male and female) age fifteen to sixty-four had to be enticed or coerced to labor one month each just to complete the 1981–1982 coffee harvest. Alternatively, about 36 percent would have had to work on the coffee plantations for two months each to bring in the harvest. If we assume one day off a week for Sabbath, personal maintenance, and market attendance needs, then 760,000 months of labor were needed. To complete that level of labor requirement, about 84 percent of Guatemala's entire indigenous rural population (male and female) age fifteen to sixty-four would have had to devote a full month of labor just to accomplish the coffee harvest in 1981–1982. If Maya labor accomplished two-thirds of *all* the coffee production tasks in 1981, then all of Guatemala's Mayas age fifteen to sixty-four would have had to work 2.25 months (of twenty-six labor days) on the coffee plantations. Even if Guatemala's census figures are inaccurate, as Early (1982) avers, the percentage of rural Mayas necessarily engaged in coffee labor is substantial and the impact on Maya life almost incalculable.

2. Early's (1982:66) list: "Chichicastenango in 1940–41 by Bunzel (1959:88–90), Santa Eulalia in 1932 by LaFarge (1947:5), Sololá in 1932 by McBryde (1933:107), Santa Catarina Palopó in 1935–36 by Tax (1946:124), San Antonio Palopó in 1941 by Redfield (1946:50), Todos Santos in 1945–46 by Oakes (1951b:40), Quezaltenango (now Quetzaltenango) basin in 1945 by Horst (1956:163), San Juan Laguna by Rojas Lima (1968:291, 310), San Lucas Tolimán by Woods (1968:207), Santiago Atitlán in 1966 by Douglas (1968:247), Sumpango and Patzún in 1967–69 by Elbow (1972:46, 183, 185). Although no data are available, a similar shortage appears to have taken place in the Ladino areas."

Chapter Seventeen

Crisis

Population and the Failure of the Maya Corn Culture Covenant, circa 1930–1960

JOHN P. HAWKINS

HERE I DOCUMENT THE LAND and corn bases of the emerging Maya crisis introduced in chapter 16. I use three approaches. The first puts time-series information about land and corn into graphed formats for various social units. I discuss the crisis in corn production per capita and per family in Nahualá and Santa Catarina Ixtahuacán, and I document the corn crisis issue in the entire Department of Sololá, where the two *municipios* are located, and in the nation as a whole. The second approach uses the statistical procedures of correlation analysis to test hypotheses about land, corn, and religious change. These statistics constitute a stronger but less intuitive and less visual form of relational argument regarding the linkage of collapsing culturally essential resources and religious transformation. The third approach examines the parallel findings of other ethnographers.

A GRAPHIC APPROACH TO A LAND AND CORN CRISIS, 1950–2003

Guatemala's population experienced a rapid increase stimulated in part by better public health and somewhat reduced infant mortality. From 1778 to 1940, the country's population rose from 396,000 to 2.4 million. Over this period, the compound annual rate of population change was 1.1 percent. From 1940 to 1950, the compound annual rate of change in population increased to 1.52 percent. From 1950 to 1964, the emergence of a land and corn population crisis became even clearer as the compound rate of population change jumped to 3.12 percent per annum. By 1964 the population living on the same land base had risen to 4.3 million, having almost doubled in the space of

twenty-four years—a generation and a half in a population that marries young (table 17.1, figure 17.1).

Guatemala's fast-rising population is significant in relation to the country's land and productive agricultural base. Guatemala implemented agricultural censuses in the years 1950, 1964, 1979, and 2003. National population censuses were taken at the same time as the first two agricultural censuses, so those data can be correlated and used together. For the other two agricultural censuses, I calculated the probable population for 1979 by taking the 1981 census and mathematically backing off the population by two iterations of the compound annual rate of change between the 1973 and 1981 population censuses. Similarly, I arrived at the population for the 2003 agro-census by calculating from the 2002 population census. Figures 17.2 and 17.3 show the populations for Guatemala and the Department of Sololá, respectively.

In chapter 1, I demonstrated how the *municipios* of Santa Catarina Ixtahuacán and Nahualá experienced similar rises in population (see figure 1.1). I now examine the land and the land-population ratio through per capita figures. For the country as a whole, as seen in figure 17.4, arable lands decreased slightly (7 percent) between 1950 and 1964, rebounded substantially (19 percent) in the 1979 agro-census, and then resumed the decline, finishing in 2003 with an overall increase of 360 *manzanas*, effectively no change at all for the country. The Department of Sololá, however, differs from the national pattern. Figure 17.5 shows that Sololá experienced a more modest 4 percent decline by 1964, but had no rebound, declining 20 percent by 1973 and another 2 percent by 2003 for an overall 1950–2003 decline of 25 percent in agriculturally useful land. I speculate here, but I presume this

TABLE 17.1. POPULATION AND COMPOUND ANNUAL RATE OF INCREASE IN GUATEMALA, 1778–2014

CENSUS YEAR	POPULATION	COMPOUND ANNUAL GROWTH RATE THIS CENSUS TO NEXT (%)
1778	396,149	1.11
1880	1,224,602	0.84
1893	1,364,678	1.38
1921	2,004,900	0.95
1940	2,400,000	1.52
1950	2,790,868	3.12
1964	4,287,997	2.08
1973	5,160,221	2.02
1981	6,054,227	2.49
1994	8,331,874	3.81
2002	11,237,196	2.78
2014	15,607,640	

Sources: Secretario de Estado del Despacho de Fomento, Sección de Estadística 1880; Dirección General de Estadística 1897, 1921, 1924, 1942, 1957, 1971–1972, 1974, 1982b; INE 1994, 2002a, 2002b, 2002c, 2003a.

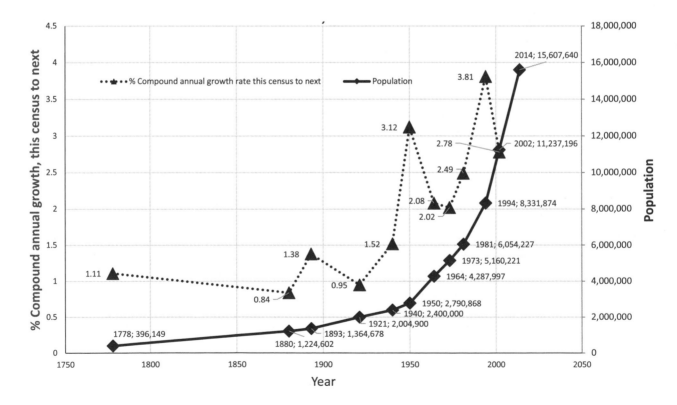

Figure 17.1. Population and compound rate of increase in Guatemala, 1778–2014. *Sources*: Secretario de Estado del Despacho de Fomento, Sección de Estadística 1880; Dirección General de Estadística 1897, 1921, 1924, 1942, 1957, 1971–1972, 1974, 1982b; INE 1994, 2002a, 2002b, 2002c, 2003a.

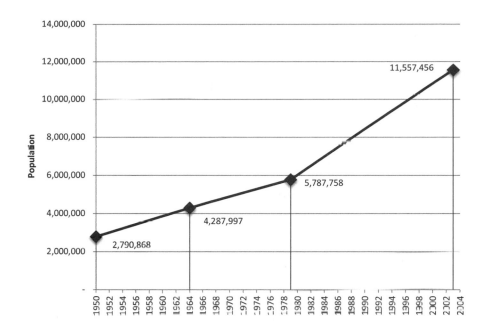

Figure 17.2. Population of Guatemala in agricultural census years. *Sources*: Dirección General de Estadística 1957, 1968, 1971a, 1971b, 1971–1972, 1974, 1982a, 1982b; INE 1994, 2002a, 2002b, 2002c, 2003a.

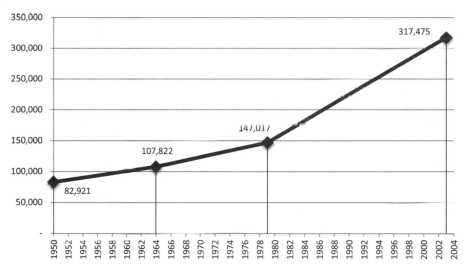

Figure 17.3. Population of Department of Sololá in agricultural census years. *Sources*: Dirección General de Estadística 1957, 1968, 1971a, 1971b, 1971–1972, 1974, 1982a, 1982b; INE 1994, 2002a, 2002b, 2002c, 2003a.

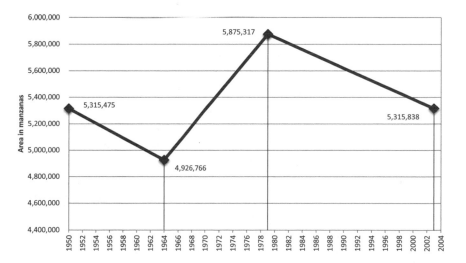

Figure 17.4. Arable land in Guatemala. *Sources*: Dirección General de Estadística 1957, 1968, 1971a, 1971b, 1971–1972, 1974, 1982a, 1982b; INE 2002a, 2002b, 2002c, 2003b, 2004a, 2004b.

decrease in the country and in Sololá is due to such things as expanded building plots to house the growing population, construction of road networks, and exhaustion of lands due to overuse, mismanagement, and erosion. In the 1970s, however, both official policy and unofficial migration expanded the nation's utilized land base by fostering migration to and pioneering of homesteads in the Departments of Petén and Izabal and in the northern reaches of Quiché and Huehuetenango along the Franja Transversal del Norte. This resulted in the countrywide arable land expansion recorded in the 1979 agricultural census. The Department of Sololá, however, experienced no such expansion and had a rather substantial drop in arable land, for it was a mature department not buffered by the ability to open new land in the relatively uninhabited Petén and northern reaches, like other departments that touched the Franja Transversal del Norte. By 2003, however, the countrywide population expansion and land needs for nonagricultural development resulted once more in a modest decline in the national land base from the 1979 high, with the Department of Sololá moving in a parallel drop, presumably for the same reasons just mentioned. The net result, seen in figure 17.5, shows an unrelenting decrease in usable agricultural land of all types in the Department of Sololá. Such a drop in absolute agricultural land area is particularly ominous given the rapid expansion over the same time period of the population needing support from that land.

Such problems show best in per capita figures. While the national arable land base did expand modestly in absolute area between the 1964 and 1979 agro-censuses, the national arable land base per capita fell throughout the 1950–2003 period due to population increase. This is most clearly seen in figure 17.6 for the nation and in figure 17.7 for Sololá. The nature of Sololá's crisis becomes more visible when one looks at the lived experience behind this fall in per capita landholdings. Although we do not know precisely how much Maya private and communal land was lost, McCreery (1994) reports a sad litany of land depredations that suggests that enough was lost to throw the indigenous system into crisis.

In graphs of key types of land and production in Sololá at the per capita level, one can see how people's lived experience could include a cognitive recognition of emerging crisis. Figure 17.7 shows the per capita arable land, that is, landholdings of all types growing useful products, including annuals, perennials, and pastures held by residents in the Department of Sololá. Figure 17.8 graphs the

per capita holdings planted to annuals in the Department of Sololá. Annuals are crops replanted each year, usually from seed, most of which produce food. For indigenous people, corn and beans are the most important annual subsistence crops, but annuals also include squash, vegetable cash crops, potatoes, wheat, and so forth. The category of annuals excludes forests and coffee or fruit trees, for example; these are, however, the food and cash crops that support Maya life and culture.

Remember that one *manzana*, equal to 16 *cuerdas*, constitutes the government's notion of the minimum landholding of all land types needed to sustain an autonomous family, that Nash (1967[1958]:29) argued the minimum was 20 *cuerdas* of "good" land (in the 1950s), and that Annis (1987) calculated that 15 *cuerdas* of land was needed just to provide minimum calories for a family of five. So, the government figure of 16 *cuerdas* per family for all lands already shortchanges 1950s Maya needs, let alone present-day Maya needs. Given a 5.9 average family size in Sololá, and a 5.1 average family size in Annis's (1987) sample, we may divide the 16 *cuerda* minimum family farm by 5 people per family to yield 3.2 *cuerdas* (0.2 *manzanas*) per capita as the boundary of incipient crisis, and by 6 people per family to yield 2.7 *cuerdas* (0.17 *manzanas*) per capita, which demarcates the boundary of having entered fully into personal and family crisis. Per figure 17.7, note that in 1950, the average individual in the Department of Sololá, which continues to be mostly indigenous and rural, had four times the minimum requisite. By 1964 that average individual had 2.9 times the minimum requisite, by 1979 1.7 times the requisite, and by 2003 but three-quarters of the requisite. Bear in mind also that this series of figures concerning arable land includes and averages in the holdings of rich Ladinos. If one calculates the same figures for land planted to annuals, which better represents the Maya condition, then (per figure 17.8) in 1950, the average individual in the Department of Sololá possessed 1.76 times the minimum. In 1964 that average individual held exactly the minimum, in 1979 71 percent of the minimum, and in 2003 29 percent of the minimum. Again, these averages are skewed by a few large landholders, among them Ladino coffee plantation landlords who devoted some land to corn. Consequently, a higher percentage of indigenous families stood in crisis in any given year than is indicated by the averages. In addition, even families with adequate landholdings could see the coming difficulty, given their experience of population expansion and inheritance subdivision with each succeeding generation.

Figure 17.5. Arable land in Department of Sololá. *Sources*: Dirección General de Estadística 1957, 1968, 1971a, 1971b, 1971–1972, 1974, 1982a, 1982b; INE 2002a, 2002b, 2002c, 2003b, 2004a, 2004b.

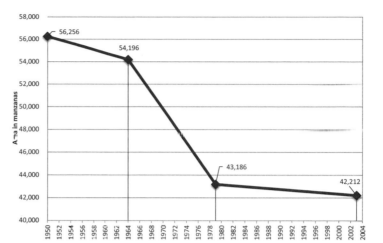

Figure 17.6. Per capita arable land in Guatemala. *Sources*: Dirección General de Estadística 1957, 1968, 1971a, 1971b, 1971–1972, 1974, 1982a, 1982b; INE 2002a, 2002b, 2002c, 2003a, 2003b, 2004a, 2004b.

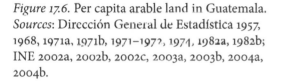

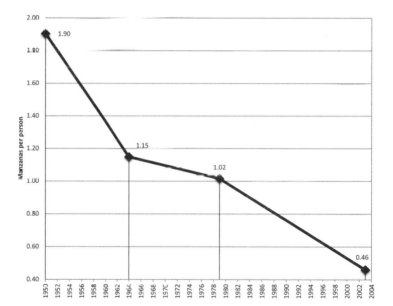

Figure 17.7. Per capita arable land in Department of Sololá. *Sources*: Dirección General de Estadística 1957, 1968, 1971a, 1971b, 1971–1972, 1974, 1982a, 1982b; INE 2002a, 2002b, 2002c, 2003a, 2003b, 2004a, 2004b.

A quick reference back to figure 1.4, figure 1.5, and plate 2 shows that the residents of the *municipios* of Nahualá and Santa Catarina Ixtahuacán have followed the same trends in land and food shortages as the rest of the people in their department and in the nation. In figure 1.5, referring to land in annuals, Nahualá entered initial crisis in about 1953 and full-blown crisis in about 1956. Santa Catarina Ixtahuacán entered initial crisis in about 1956 and manifested full crisis by about 1960. Nevertheless, as can be seen by subtracting the croppable land in annuals (figure 1.5) from the total land owned (figure 1.4), both Nahualá and Santa Catarina Ixtahuacán had large pasture and forest resources (as well as some perennials, such as coffee, in the lower elevations) compared to other *municipios*. These additional resources likely delayed the arrival of religious crisis in both *municipios* until the 1970s and 1980s. Both *municipios* adopted Catholic charismaticism in 1973–1975, expanded their acceptance of Protestant Pentecostalism, which by some accounts had entered via a few converts in the late 1940s, and experienced the collapse of the *cofradía* system in the late 1980s. In a word, the trends toward crisis are consistent at the local, regional, and national levels with subsistence crisis and related religious crisis delayed and amelioriated in both Nahualá and Santa Catarina Ixtahuacán by their relatively large nonarable land resources.

Indeed, the land-corn-population crisis had begun to enter Mayas' consciousness by the 1920s and 1930s. Early (1982:66) reports a dozen monographs from the 1930s to the 1960s that suggest Mayas already sensed land shortage as an issue. Green (1993:166–172) follows McCreery's (1994) historical analysis of land loss in indigenous communities and concludes: "It was not until the early twentieth century that population increases exerted substantial pressure on communal lands throughout the highlands" (Green 1993:178n18). Given that land and corn were essential to indigenous cultural identity, it is likely that indigenous cultural identity was likewise under "substantial pressure."

The crisis in corn can best be seen in the decline in per capita corn production, for example in the Department of Sololá (figure 17.9). Here there is not a straight decline, as in the other graphs. Corn per capita was quite low in 1964, amounting to just 31 pounds per person for the year. That calculates to 0.085 pounds per person per day, less than a tenth of a pound. Annis (1987:38) argues that a minimum calorie intake requires 1.1 pounds of corn per day, so the average corn production at that time in Sololá, where Mayas dominated and corn was the staff of cultural life, was one-thirteenth the requisite consumption. But why was there a jump in corn production in the 1979 agro-census? Some might be accounted for by an increase in land devoted to corn production; after all, land can be deforested and put to new use cropping corn, although such is never the good land nor without follow-on problems of erosion, water loss, and loss of fuel resources. Most of the increase, however, is explained by the introduction and increasingly heavy use of fertilizers among Mayas during

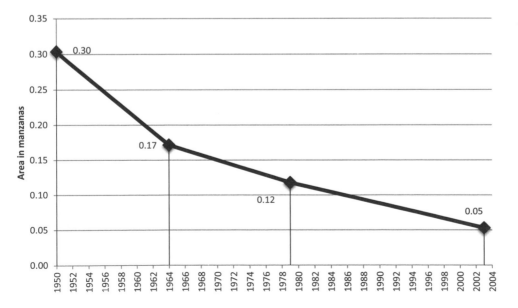

Figure 17.8. Per capita land area in annuals, Department of Sololá. *Sources:* Dirección General de Estadística 1957, 1968, 1971a, 1971b, 1971–1972, 1974, 1982a, 1982b; INE 2002a, 2002b, 2002c, 2003a, 2003b, 2004a, 2004b.

Figure 17.9. Annual per capita corn production in *quintales*, Department of Solólá. *Sources*: Dirección General de Estadística 1968, 1971a, 1971b, 1971–1972, 1974, 1982a, 1982b; INE 2002a, 2002b, 2002c, 2003a, 2003b, 2004a, 2004b.

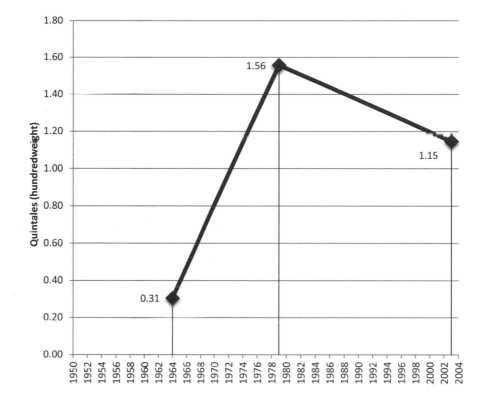

the 1970s. After 1979, however, corn production per capita dropped because oil cartel policies led to greatly increased fertilizer prices and therefore reduced fertilizer usage. And in any event, corn production in 1979, the high point, still amounted to a mere 0.43 pounds per person per day, which is 39 percent of Annis's suggested minimum daily requisite. In 2003, corn production had declined to 0.32 pounds per day per person, 29 percent of the requisite minimum. From 1950 through 2003, average corn production per person was well below indigenous maintenance for the department as a whole. For most Mayas in the Department of Solólá, this meant living in the midst of an acute food and culture crisis.

The shortfall in land and corn, combined with the increasing loss of indigenous isolation, put the mental visualization and covenant logic of the Maya lifestyle in doubt. The crisis also made Maya life precarious, difficult, and for some impossible. Early (2012:49–61) documents the nutritional crisis in detail. Both as a thought system and as an action pattern, indigenous lifeways have been in crisis throughout the Maya region. Early (2012:19–20, 72–84) asserts that corn shortage leaned hard on the Mayas, tore at their kwashiorkor-distended bellies, made them sick by wrecking immune systems,

and challenged their belief in a covenant of protective reciprocity.

Indigenous life also depends on the ability to cook corn with firewood gathered from available forest resources. Guatemala's agricultural censuses also recorded forest resources held as part of a *finca* (landholding). I do not know if the censuses recorded *all* forest resources, especially those in municipal, state, or national commons holdings that were exploitable but unowned or unclaimed by particular households. But the holdings recorded by the agricultural surveys do reflect a precipitous decline in what individuals and (at least) private corporate entities perceived they held (figure 17.10). Without access to local forest resources, Mayas had to enter further into the cash economy to pay for wood or propane gas. This steady decline in forest resources per capita added to the perception of subsistence threat, which had been made obvious by the inadequate quantity of corn produced by households for their own consumption. In these graphs of available resources through time, one can see that Mayas experienced over several generations an inexorable increase of hunger and resource deprivation, a loss of community isolation, and forced entry into the cash economy as merchants or laborers. Taken together, these graphs may be seen as indexes of culture collapse regarding the sacred reliability of corn, land, and forest access. Recall that in the *Popol Wuj*, the gods created humans first from mud, second from wood, and third from corn: the three elements that are the basis of Maya existence. Throughout the twentieth and twenty-first centuries, the project of modernity operated on these three elements to severely undermine the work of the Maya gods. Land—the mud from which humans were created—was lost to Ladinos and micro parcelized by inheritance and population expansion; wood for cooking and building was depleted by deforestation; homegrown corn became inadequate as land grew short.

Beyond the graphs, one can get a sense of the problem from photographs. Plate 30 and figure 17.11 show the profusion of housing splayed into the only suitable, flat, productive agricultural land, while plate 2 shows acute deforestation in favor of corn production.

A STATISTICAL APPROACH TO THE CORN CULTURE COLLAPSE HYPOTHESIS, 1950–2003

I shift now from exploring visually and graphically the census data regarding the indigenous corn crisis to interpreting the same data using statistical tests of hypotheses. I connect the data on corn insufficiency per capita by department with Protestant/Pentecostal membership change by department throughout Guatemala. The figures from the 1950 and 1964 agricultural censuses show negative correlations between arable land per capita with the available records of the number of Protestant/Pentecostal congregations per capita in 1981. That is, the lower the per capita available arable land or corn production across the departments of Guatemala, the higher the number of Protestant/Pentecostal congregations per capita in those departments. The relationship is statistically significant and quite strong.[1]

The agricultural censuses of Guatemala provide the *quintales* (hundred-pound sacks) of corn and beans produced per department in 1950 and 1964, as well as total arable lands, lands in annual crops, and land specifically in corn production by department and *municipio*. The population censuses give inhabitants per department. From these figures I easily calculated the change in *quintales* of corn over the ten-year period, both in absolute quantity and per capita per department or per *municipio*. When one

compares these figures with each department's percentage of Evangelical members, the correlation is significant and negative. That is, across departments, the greater the absolute reduction in *quintales* of corn or beans produced per capita between 1950 and 1964, and/or the greater the percentage loss in per capita production during that period, the greater the percentage increase in *evangélico* membership per department in 1981 (as measured by congregations per capita). The correlation is significant ($p < 0.05$) but not strong (Pearson's $r > -0.4$ for 1981).[2] (See table 17.2.)

I note that these correlations of corn reduction and shortage with 1981 Pentecostal congregations do not occur most strongly in the 1979 harvest and landholding data. Rather, corn and land shortage in a given census correlates more strongly with *evangélico* increase in the next generation, twenty and more years on. Presumably, parents hold on to their religion (and their landholding) as best they can throughout their lives. But their children are likely to change a generation later, when the children receive (or perceive the likelihood of receiving) a comparative pittance for an inheritance. Parents may sense an oncoming stress, but it is their children, as they become parents themselves, who react to the stress of lifeway collapse by engaging in religious and other change. The children, as they mature, change their religion, their gang affiliation, and/or their willingness to submit to their elders, as each generation grows into adulthood and evaluates the mix of culture, contradiction, and opportunity—or lack of it—that they face (see Call et al. 2013). At that point, they contemplate the task of raising their own families in the new, constrained, and much transformed subsistence environment. They reform their idea of the nature of society, the "soul of religion." Thus, culture collapse and a sense of exclusion result in religious change only mildly in the immediately stressed parental generation, but much more strongly when the successor generation matures some twenty years later (see tables 17.3a and 17.3b).

ETHNOGRAPHIES OF CORN AND CULTURE COLLAPSE

I am not alone in observing this relationship between production insecurity and changing choice of worship style, although no one seems to have documented the relationship through time or with statistics in the ways I have. Here, I broaden my argument by adding other anthropologists' evidence.

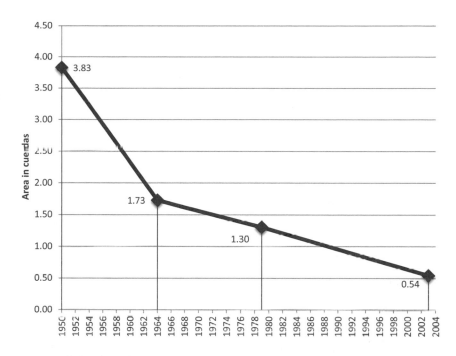

Figure 17.10. Per capita landholdings in forest, Department of Sololá. *Sources*: Dirección General de Estadística 1957, 1968, 1971a, 1971b, 1971–1972, 1974, 1982a, 1982b; INE 2002a, 2002b, 2002c, 2003a, 2003b, 2004a, 2004b.

Figure 17.11. In Nahualá, the flat agricultural land is consumed by expanding housing stock. The Nahualá *cabecera municipal* is in the midground, and one of the rural hamlets is in the foreground. Courtesy of John P. Hawkins.

TABLE 17.2. CORN AND POPULATION DATA WITH PROTESTANT CONGREGATIONS PER CAPITA

DEPARTMENT	POPULATION, 1950	POPULATION, 1964	AVERAGE ANNUAL GROWTH RATE, 1950–1964	POPULATION, 1973	CORN PRODUCTION PER CAPITA, 1950 (QUINTALES)	CORN PRODUCTION PER CAPITA, 1964 (QUINTALES)	CORN PRODUCTION PER CAPITA, 1979 (QUINTALES)	% CHANGE CORN PRODUCTION PER CAPITA, 1950–1964	% CHANGE BEANS PER CAPITA, 1950–1964 (QUINTALES)	PROTESTANT CONGREGATIONS PER CAPITA, 1981
Alta Verapaz	189,812	260,498	2.3	280,524	4.596	4.054	4.534	−11.8	−34.4	0.0006615
Baja Verapaz	66,313	96,485	2.7	106,957	3.388	4.431	2.654	+30.7	+13.4	0.0002941
Chimaltenango	121,480	163,153	2.1	194,735	3.224	2.738	4.044	−15.1	+8.1	0.0009606
Chiquimula	112,841	149,752	2.0	158,177	3.056	2.169	2.256	−29.0	−1.9	0.0004619
El Progreso	47,872	65,582	2.3	73,122	1.334	2.261	2.154	+69.5	+189.3	0.0008499
Escuintla	123,759	270,267	5.7	277,031	3.410	3.283	4.469	−3.7	−35.6	0.0009622
Guatemala	438,913	810,858	4.5	110,8186	0.781	0.397	0.129	−49.2	−33.2	0.0005217
Huehuetenango	200,101	288,088	2.6	368,567	4.125	2.961	2.736	−28.2	+19.6	0.0008021
Izabal	55,032	116,685	5.5	169,818	4.659	2.936	4.867	−37.0	−22.5	0.0015723
Jalapa	75,190	99,153	2.0	118,074	3.743	2.904	4.323	−22.4	+23.6	0.0008156
Jutiapa	138,925	194,774	2.4	233,232	3.451	2.944	4.669	−14.7	+9.0	0.0009320
Petén	15,880	26,562	3.7	64,114	5.690	3.985	15.063	−30.0	-51.3	0.0020087
Quetzaltenango	184,213	270,916	2.8	312,787	3.028	2.204	2.109	−27.2	−38.1	0.0010165
Quiché	174,911	249,939	2.6	298,686	3.658	2.960	3.368	−19.1	−5.0	0.0007161
Retalhuleu	66,861	117,562	4.1	127,235	7.135	5.193	7.340	−27.2	−62.2	0.0007752
Sacatepéquez	60,124	80,942	2.1	99,988	2.049	1.161	1.261	−43.3	−37.1	0.0005697
San Marcos	232,591	336,959	2.7	389,760	2.852	1.875	2.251	−34.3	−61.3	0.0009951
Santa Rosa	109,836	157,040	2.6	1,771,159	3.212	2.730	2.756	−15.0	+5.0	0.0006077
Sololá	82,921	107,822	1.9	127,268	0.789	1.222	1.557	+54.9	−38.0	0.0008363
Suchitepéquez	124,403	186,634	2.9	202,253	2.540	2.799	3.047	+10.2	−43.4	0.0009387
Totonicapán	99,354	141,772	2.6	166,809	1.369	1.162	1.651	−15.1	−37.8	0.0004158
Zacapa	69,536	96,554	2.4	105,739	2.751	1.936	2.519	−29.6	+3.4	0.0015469

Sources: Dirección General de Estadística 1954, 1957, 1968, 1971a, 1971–1972, 1974, 1982a, 1982b; IINDEF and SEPAL 1981.

TABLE 17.3A. LAND AND RELIGION

DEPARTMENT	ESTIMATED POPULATION, 1979[a]	POPULATION, 1981	# OF FINCAS, 1979	AREA OF FINCAS, 1979 (MANZANAS)	# OF FINCAS < 1 CUERDA, 1979	AREA OF FINCAS < 1 CUERDA, 1979 (MANZANAS)	# OF FINCAS ≥ 1 CUERDA AND < 16 CUERDAS, 1979	AREA OF FINCAS ≥ 1 CUERDA AND < 16 CUERDAS, 1979 (MANZANAS)	AREA IN ANNUALS, 1964 (MANZANAS)
Alta Verapaz	311,115	322,008	45,949	634,294	4,543	128.91	8,248	3,929	90,668
Baja Verapaz	113,402	115,602	15,201	183,829	2,351	60.08	2,325	1,049	36,945
Chimaltenango	220,726	230,059	27,784	157,107	2,527	58.04	8,052	4,273	46,827
Chiquimula	166,121	168,863	18,158	116,010	5,543	169.35	2,589	1,229	34,986
El Progreso	79,108	81,188	6,693	98,572	1,349	38.97	847	447	17,923
Escuintla	319,208	334,666	18,149	688,422	12,229	400.4	6,100	1,944	121,281
Guatemala	1,256,833	1,311,192	17,702	169,785	4,567	151.18	4,853	1,948	34,225
Huehuetenango	414,822	431,343	58,496	319,595	2,619	79.28	15,906	8,338	87,754
Izabal	188,114	194,618	14,953	360,111	3,485	71.96	1,617	755	22,078
Jalapa	131,336	136,091	15,731	147,677	1,745	45.58	1,317	726	34,452
Jutiapa	246,553	251,068	28,567	273,344	4,893	138.43	2,682	1,195	59,586
Petén	110,156	131,927	15,036	803,742	2,648	92.94	1,358	251	7,687
Quetzaltenango	352,664	366,949	30,403	192,277	3,048	97.55	16,657	7,562	38,692
Quiché	320,467	328,175	52,227	343,269	1,292	34.6	14,201	7,964	75,162
Retalhuleu	144,641	150,923	12,708	187,553	1,882	70.48	5,624	2,311	55,387
Sacatepéquez	115,481	121,127	9,871	34,847	693	22.34	3,608	1,879	14,563
San Marcos	450,153	472,326	52,781	280,918	4,207	119.38	17,668	8,696	58,858
Santa Rosa	189,740	194,168	21,364	343,668	3,611	98.54	3,852	1,682	35,948
Sololá	146,988	154,249	18,301	43,186	2,072	50.54	8,955	4,200	18,514
Suchitepéquez	228,172	237,554	15,437	282,325	4,679	102.38	7,473	2,662	32,193
Totonicapán	194,241	204,419	27,682	40,889	1,584	52.37	18,856	7,794	20,082
Zacapa	113,114	115,712	8,430	173,897	1,771	45.94	1,352	557	21,865

Note: [a] Computed from each department's compound annual rate of growth from 1973 to 1981.

Sources: Dirección General de Estadística 1968, 1971a, 1971b, 1971–1972, 1974, 1982a, 1982b.

TABLE 17.3B. LAND AND RELIGION (CONTINUED)

DEPARTMENT	AREA IN ANNUALS, 1979 (MANZANAS)	% OF 1979 POPULA-TION WITH SOME LAND BUT LESS THAN 1 MANZANA[b]	% OF 1979 POPULATION WITH NO AGRICULTURAL HOLDINGS[c]	% OF 1979 POPULATION WITH NO OR INADEQUATE AGRICULTURAL SUPPORT[d]	LAND PER CAPITA IN ANNUALS, 1964 (MANZANAS)	LAND PER CAPITA IN ANNUALS, 1979 (MANZANAS)	% CHANGE IN LAND PER CAPITA IN ANNUALS, 1964–1979	% NON-CATHOLIC CHRISTIANS, 1964	PROTESTANT CONGREGATIONS PER CAPITA, 1981
Alta Verapaz	242,336	24.3	12.9	37.1	0.348	0.779	123.9	1.70	0.0006615
Baja Verapaz	58,123	24.3	20.9	45.2	0.383	0.513	33.9	2.68	0.0002941
Chimaltenango	45,222	28.3	25.7	54.0	0.287	0.205	−28.6	10.82	0.0009606
Chiquimula	46,985	28.9	35.5	64.4	0.234	0.283	20.9	4.50	0.0004619
El Progreso	24,455	16.4	50.1	66.5	0.273	0.309	13.2	5.50	0.0008499
Escuintla	205,920	33.9	66.5	100.3	0.449	0.645	43.7	11.11	0.0009622
Guatemala	35,591	4.4	91.7	96.1	0.042	0.028	−33.3	7.36	0.0005217
Huehuetenango	136,289	26.3	16.8	43.1	0.305	0.329	7.9	25.87	0.0008021
Izabal	93,825	16.0	53.1	69.1	0.189	0.499	164.0	13.18	0.0015723
Jalapa	53,384	13.8	29.3	43.1	0.347	0.406	17.0	3.88	0.0008156
Jutiapa	87,840	18.1	31.6	49.8	0.306	0.356	16.3	9.04	0.0009320
Petén	229,798	21.5	19.5	40.9	0.300	3.086	928.7	10.79	0.0020087
Quetzaltenango	50,856	3.3	94.9	98.2	0.142	0.144	1.4	6.46	0.0010165
Quiché	13,209	28.5	3.8	32.4	0.301	0.041	−86.4	3.38	0.0007161
Retalhuleu	71,207	30.6	48.2	78.8	0.471	0.492	4.5	7.40	0.0007752
Sacatepéquez	13,892	22.0	49.6	71.5	0.180	0.120	−33.3	6.76	0.0005697
San Marcos	83,892	28.7	30.8	59.5	0.175	0.186	6.3	5.93	0.0009951
Santa Rosa	54,518	23.2	33.6	56.8	0.229	0.287	25.3	4.01	0.0006077
Sololá	17,339	44.3	26.5	70.8	0.172	0.118	−31.4	7.10	0.0008363
Suchitepéquez	63,569	31.4	60.1	91.5	0.172	0.279	62.2	6.29	0.0009387
Totonicapán	19,145	62.1	15.9	78.0	0.142	0.099	−30.3	8.97	0.0004158
Zacapa	40,262	16.3	56.0	72.3	0.226	0.356	57.5	13.47	0.0015469

Notes: [b] Calculated by summing the number of fincas smaller than one manzana and multiplying the result by 5.9 people per finca. This assumes one finca per household and may modestly overestimate on two grounds: the national average household size is likely smaller, and one family may have more than one finca.

[c] Calculated by multiplying the number of fincas in 1979 by 5.9 people per household and subtracting that from the 1979 estimated population.

[d] Sum of the department values from prior two columns.[a]

Sources: Dirección General de Estadística 1968, 1971a, 1971b, 1971–1972, 1974, 1982a, 1982b; IINDEF and SEPAL 1981.

Sheldon Annis, for example, clearly recognizes the important relationship between economic change and religious change in Guatemala. Regarding the Mayas of San Antonio Aguas Calientes, Annis (1987:142, emphasis in original) says, "Certainly *something* has gotten their attention. But was it God? . . . Was it the earthquake? Was it a zealot evangelical president, army repression, a guerrilla war? Perhaps all of these, and also something more subtle: each individual translating the growing chaos of a disordered world into his or her consciousness." I quote Annis extensively as I develop my corn and culture collapse argument. But let me be clear: my argument follows—and, I hope, extends and clarifies—the initial path set out by Annis (Annis 1987:10) when he gave his thesis that changing "religious behavior" in Guatemala "is rooted [in] economic production" and that "Protestantism makes its entry at the frayed edges, where stable systems of economic production, culture, and social relations are beginning to come apart."[3] However, I go beyond Annis's astute linkage of God and production by focusing on the generalized culture collapse entailed by corn insufficiency in a culture symbolically dependent on corn and land dedicated to corn production, rather than on the literal shortfall in calories arising from insufficient corn production as the cause.

I find further confirmation of my collapse and exclusion hypothesis in Cook and Offit's (2013:13–14) analysis of indigenous religious change in Momostenango, a K'iche' community about an hour by bus from Nahualá or Nueva Santa Catarina Ixtahuacán:

> Primarily as a result of land shortage, the true peasantry was declining in numbers and influence, and proletarianization and the emergence of a mercantile indigenous petite bourgeoisie were occurring simultaneously. Thus it could be argued that the festival of Santiago observed in 1975 or 1976 was in many ways an anachronism that retained the outward forms of a spectacle that had been constructed over several decades as part of liberal social engineering and had crystalized a good half century before. . . . [Thus,] the community appeared to its anthropological observers . . . to be a conservative repository of indigenous religiosity. But in hindsight it is increasingly clear that the cofradías, the dance teams, and the religious complexes of rural patrilineages (alaxiks) whose chuchkajaws performed ceremonies for the ancestors at inherited family altars were all undergoing the early

stages of what became massive damage because of their lack of fit with the practical, emotional, and spiritual needs of the land-scarce and financially pressed proto- and post-peasants who made up an increasing proportion of the population. During the crisis of the counterinsurgency war and violence many of these culturally, if not geographically, displaced Momostecans would convert to Pentecostalism and to radical evangelical sects.

While the last sentence of this quote gives the impression that Pentecostalism surged as a result of disruptions and pain caused by the counterinsurgency war, the rest of the quote and much of Cook and Offit's book show that there had been much prewar movement toward Pentecostal and Mormon religious communities as well as to Catholic Action. Thus, the war may have sped things along, as I discuss below, but not by much. The culture collapse drivers of religious resymbolization were already in place, and the annual rates of gain by Pentecostal faiths were already at 6–10 or 11 percent per annum between 1950 and 1964, which is two or three times Guatemala's natural rate of population expansion, well before either earthquake or war (see figure 19.5). As I discuss in the next chapter, one neither needs nor finds a reliable postquake and postwar increment in the compound annual rates of Protestant conversion. The prequake and prewar rates of (Pentecostal) Protestant increase were higher than the postquake and postwar rates and thus document rather different stresses generating twentieth- and twenty-first-century levels of Pentecostal membership in the country.

CONCLUSION

To see the implications that Marx and Engels (2008[1850]:94) would draw from this crisis is easy: "every great historical upheaval of social conditions" changes "the outlooks and ideas of men, and consequently their religious ideas." Durkheim (2001[1912]:318–319, 329) also saw the implications of material change on society; the structure of society "bears the mark of its material substrate," and "events of sufficient importance can manage to affect society's mental position." In a society that valued corn above all, lack of corn would instigate that change in mental position. In short, traditionalism was in distress and decline because increasing land and corn shortage put the legitimacy of the mental covenant between traditionalist divinities and traditionalist Maya Catholic practitioners in question.

Through escalating *cofradía* practice, Mayas tried to rebalance the covenant in which humans and gods agreed to attend to each other's needs. But with land and corn in ever shorter supply and the expectation of indigenous cultural isolation increasingly violated, Mayas felt that the hardships they increasingly experienced implied that someone was failing to maintain their end of the covenant. There were but two options. If humans had neglected the gods, were the gods punishing humans as a result? Such human neglect could be remedied by increased *cofradía* and shamanic offerings. Conversely, what if the gods had neglected or forgotten the humans? The gods could be reminded of human need by increasing ritual offerings to draw their attention. Either option resulted in the same behavior: an increased quantity of *cofradía* gift giving, as Mayas tried to secure spiritual attention, reestablish covenantal balance, and reduce the apparent punishments or inattentions implied by the experience of an increasingly constricted Maya life. Throughout Guatemala the tactic of increased *cofradía* offering was tried. But the tactic didn't work, and the effort in various towns collapsed of exhaustion in the 1960s–1980s. Third and fourth logical options actually lay in the background. What if the gods didn't care about the Maya cultural covenant? If that were the case, Mayas could abandon worship and religious denominations altogether. For most Mayas, that was a step too far. But what if the Mayas were addressing the wrong gods? If that option were the case, Mayas could abandon the *cofradía* path and worship with the Ortho-Catholics or the Pentecostals.

Given the facts of corn, land, and forest resource crises, Pentecostalism's end-of-the-world preaching, the clangor of its electronically amplified liturgy, and the unspeakability of its glossolalia started to make symbolic sense. That is, Pentecostal worship style reflects the tensions, ambiguities, and anxieties of social life in a cultural system based on corn when corn production no longer is sufficient. Pentecostal glossolalia, by definition, is prayer or other speech in repetitious and rhyming syllable sequences. The sequences abide by a few of the phonological options available in a given local language or colonial trade language. Glossolalic "morphemes" do not carry meaning nor are they embedded in a decipherable syntax. As such, glossolalia does not make sense. Nevertheless, glossolalia *does* make sense. It is meaningful in that it states that social and cultural circumstances are unutterable, indescribable, untenable, and thus unspeakable—that conditions are so bad they are unable to be put into words. Indeed, contemporary Pentecostal theologians, such as Macchia (2006:282), assert that through glossolalia, Pentecostals "groan in the Spirit with sighs too deep for words."

Thus, Maya population rise and Ladino predation of indigenous lands were the "great social upheaval" that drove the Maya land and corn shortage and the massive subsequent religious change. Corn shortage in a corn-centered culture pushed the Maya lifeway to collapse. Collapse among both Ladinos and Mayas drove the people into contention for control and access, and that eventually led to the 1980s political insurrection and suppressive ethnocidal war, which paralleled but did not precipitate the rapid religious transformation. Thus, corn, land, and other resource shortage, not earthquake or war, was the great collective upheaval that affected both political society and religion. It is true that both insurrection and religious change were extended consequences of corn shortage, while war responded to the added political factors of exploitation, graft, and mismanagement. But in working out this economic and culture crisis appraisal, I have gotten ahead of the incremental logic and process of Guatemalan political and religious history. Thus, in the next chapter, I step back to what Guatemalans call the "democratic opening" (1944–1954) and examine the contributions of that period's political and religious history.

NOTES

1. By contrast with 1950 and 1964, the correlation of per capita arable land in annuals (corn, beans, etc., but not coffee, bananas, or sugarcane) in 1979 with Pentecostal congregations per capita in 1981 is not statistically significant.

2. Correlation of per capita Protestant congregations in 1981 with change in per capita corn *quintales* between 1950 and 1964: Pearson's $r = -0.404$, meaning as corn per capita went down, Protestant congregations per capita went up ($p = 0.031$, one-tailed). Correlation of change in per capita beans *quintales* between 1950 and 1964 with Protestant congregations per capita is similarly inverse: Pearson's $r = -0.421$, $p = 0.026$, one-tailed.

3. Annis (1987) speaks of "Protestantism (or Protestant-like brands of Catholicism)." Given that the only "Protestant-like brand of Catholicism" is the highly pentecostalized Renovación Carismática, Annis is clearly talking about Pentecostalized *evangélicos* whenever he speaks of "Protestants." Annis's "Protestants" are in fact Pentecostals.

Chapter Eighteen

Clemency

The Democratic Opening, 1944–1954

JOHN P. HAWKINS

ONE CAN DIVIDE THE HISTORY of Guatemalan politics and religion on the fulcrum of 1944. In 1944, a new government led by Juan José Arévalo ended the coercive labor laws and colonial-style indigenous registration. Shortly thereafter it established a new constitution that enshrined freedom of religion. Thus, for a brief period, 1944–1954, Guatemalan leaders tried to work out the mechanics of a generalized democracy and somewhat improve indigenous access to arable land for the many who needed it.

But why did the Guatemalan congress end the labor requirements specifically in 1944? The cynic would note that by that year, due to indigenous population expansion, Maya labor was "willingly" sold (and the labor laws therefore could be lifted) because Maya land and Maya-produced corn per capita had dwindled below the maintenance level for nearly half the population. Elites no longer needed compulsory labor laws to get Mayas to do their work; hunger alone sufficiently drove the indigenous villagers to labor outside their *municipios*.

With authentic religious freedom promulgated by the new democracy, the Catholic clergy could reenter and expand services in Guatemala. From 1944 to 1954 the contingent grew from 114 to 192 clerics, an expansion of 68 percent, with most of the growth from foreign nationals (Pattridge 1994:529). While that expansion was woefully inadequate to the need for pastoral services, the Catholic institution started to rebuild its place as a major player in the Guatemalan societal and political scene. Calder (1970:48) notes, however, that although the democratic opening was authentic and available to Catholicism, the Catholic Church had been too weakened to make much progress in self-restoration during that time. Moreover, in the second half of the ten-year democratic opening, during

the increasingly left-leaning Árbenz years, the Catholic Church faced the government's increasingly negative attitude toward religion in general. The archbishop of Guatemala at the time became increasingly anticommunist and therefore, given perceptions and propaganda that Jacobo Árbenz Guzmán's land reforms represented communism, the archbishop became increasingly anti-Árbenz. Catholic recovery thus proceeded slowly.

Given the low prestige and low rates of graduation from Guatemalan seminaries during the liberal and democratic opening periods, the Catholic Church had to import clergy from overseas to help with recovery and to extend its pastoral coverage into the indigenous *municipios*. The presence of foreign priests had major consequences in Catholicism's relations in indigenous communities. Moreover, because the church had fallen into too low a status to recruit from the wealthy or the educated (Calder 1970:20), Guatemalan-born priests were drawn from poor Ladino populations. When sent to indigenous *municipios*, the Guatemalan Ladino priests also felt alien, effectively separated from their indigenous parishioners by national ethnic prejudice. Ladino prejudices concerning Mayas often left these priests incapable of empathy toward Maya Catholic practice. The foreign-born and foreign-educated priests perhaps bore less prejudice toward the indigenous people than Guatemalan priests did, but they, too, had their problems with cultural difference. To their credit, the foreign priests often promoted innovative development and education projects in indigenous communities. On the other hand, the American and northern European priests had no cultural experience with Spain's medieval *cofradía* heritage as worked out in Guatemala, and they didn't know how to deal with entrenched independent shamans and *cofradía* personnel who saw themselves as the purest of Catholics and as custodians of indigenous politics and religious propriety.

Thus, when the foreign-born and the Guatemalan priests went to the indigenous *municipios* during the Ortho-Catholic Church's effort to reestablish contact with its indigenous parishes, many priests reacted rather negatively to the traditionalist Maya Catholicism they found operating there after a century or more of largely unsupervised change. Many Ortho-Catholic priests given responsibility for Catholic affairs in the indigenous villages tried to suppress indigenous Maya Catholic ritual. The Ortho priests saw *cofradía* practices and divination by *ajq'ijab'* (shamans) as rank heresy or as folk deviation from appropriate Ortho-Catholicism (Brintnall 1979; Falla 1978, 2001; Early 2012; Calder 1970; Pattridge 1994). Of course, the Ortho priests thought of themselves as the rightful custodians of correct Catholic tradition (Adams and Bastos 2003:205–212). But so did the *cofradistas* and the *ajq'ijab'*! Ortho-Catholic priests sought to regain control of Catholic properties and to assert religious leadership in the indigenous municipalities. They worked to reclaim and manage the use of the lands and physical buildings in the hands of the indigenous civil-religious hierarchy. Ortho priests sought to purify, internationalize, and reestablish what they deemed to be properly Catholic religious practices, symbols, and doctrines. Thus, beginning in the democratic opening and certainly continuing into the next decades of conservative governments, many Ortho-Catholic priests came into sharp conflict with the indigenous *cofradía* leaders and the *ajq'ij* diviners that had evolved for a century and that constituted the center of religion in their Maya communities.

Following the pattern of their European experience, foreign-born priests sought to make themselves welcomed and trusted by creating medical clinics, schools, and development projects. They sought to evangelize the rural indigenous populace and move them toward the orthopraxis of the Catholicism that they, as priests, knew. To achieve all this, they formed units of Catholic Action and they trained helpers, called *catequistas*, from among indigenous people whom the priests had weaned away from a core orientation toward the *cofradías*. Among others, they enlisted young bilinguals still in or just out of school. These youngsters brokered the priests' efforts to penetrate the communities. Such work provided an economic and social alternative to waiting years for the inheritance of land that would make them functioning

Maya adults (Brintnall 1979; Watanabe 1992). The use of youths, however, undermined the control and authority of the indigenous gerontocracy, which was based on ownership (in some communities), communally approved use rights (in communities like Nahualá and Santa Catarina Ixtahuacán), or rental from the wealthy of corn plots needed to sustain a family in the indigenous mode of production. Thus, Catholic Action—part of the Ortho-Catholic play for presence and control in their "own" church—tore at the cultural fabric of gerontocratic Maya village leadership and undermined the *cofradía* mechanism that fostered covenantal gifting to the gods in return for sustenance and protection (Molesky-Poz 2004:524). Indeed, the split in Catholicism between priest-oriented Ortho-Catholicism and traditionalist-oriented *cofradía* and Maya Catholic shamanic divination and healing shattered the perception of a unified cultural Catholicism in Maya communities.

Members of mainline Protestant, historic Pentecostal, and independent indigenized Pentecostal denominations, groups, and churches, who constituted but 1.5 percent of the Guatemalan population by 1940, exploited the gap opened by a divided Catholicism at war with itself. Moreover, by the mid-1950s, the corn supply in the corn-centered Maya culture was clearly inadequate. That inadequacy further pushed Maya youths to seek both economic and religious alternatives.

Given the corn shortage and the cultural collapse indicated by fission and conflict in Catholicism, some Mayas took culturally desperate alternative measures. Some opted for Ortho-Catholic affiliation exclusively and refused to take their turn celebrating in the expensive traditionalist *cofradía* system. Some physically and permanently left their indigenous communities, ladinoizing themselves externally by migrating to urban settings, changing their clothing style to mimic poor urban Ladinos, and adopting the Spanish language.

For other Mayas, the age-old covenant and its logic seemed broken, and they concluded that the breakdown was not due to human neglect. Catholicism stood divided and was making war on itself. The gods seemed not to provide. The religious path of the old ways did not work (Morgan 2005). Something different had to be done. Why not try a new religious path? Perhaps it would work. Protestantism's extreme anti-Catholicism and its critique of the culture of alcohol and celebratory expenditure thus began to make sense and provide an alternative view and path, especially given the Ortho versus traditionalist conflict in Guatemalan Catholicism. Between the 1950 and 1964 censuses—in the midst of corn crisis but before quake or war—the Protestant/Pentecostal indigenous rate of expansion was 8 percent, while the national compound annual population growth rate was 3.12 percent. In the decade 1940–1950, the Protestant/Pentecostal compound annual growth rate was 11 percent per annum, more than seven times the population's rate of growth. The difference between the rates of Protestant growth and population growth accounts for the expansion of Protestants/Pentecostals as a percentage of Guatemala's population. These Mayas had rejected all factions of the Catholic system. They had challenged the old Catholic community and left it mentally by becoming Protestant, but they had not left the *municipio* physically.

Stanzione (2003:7–8) phrases the implications of the traditionalist versus Ortho Catholic conflict in the Maya *municipio* of Santiago Atitlán thus:

> One of the end results of these mid-century village changes was massive bloodshed in Atitlán throughout the 1980s because of the intense hatred the religious of Atitlán developed for one another. Another result was the ruin of the *cofradía* system with its many remnant Mayan ways of celebrating religion in Santiago Atitlán. Meanwhile, as the Catholics and Traditionalists dreamed up ways to ruin one another, the Protestants became rich off coffee cultivation, production, and merchandising, alerting the rest of the Atitecos that it was time for a much-needed change. The "Old Ways" no longer seemed to speak the language of the new way of being Tz'utujil in a rapidly transforming world soon to become a global plantation.

Through this fracturing of Guatemala's Catholicism, the modernist priests and the traditionalist *cofradía* leaders created space for the flowering of Protestant Pentecostalism in the indigenous villages. In essence, the liberal-conservative split among Catholics that had invited Protestants into the country in the 1870s was reproduced in the indigenous *municipios* during the democratic opening and the two decades thereafter (Pattridge 1994). Ortho-Catholic priests acted like Justo Rufino Barrios's modernizing liberals; *cofradistas* and *ajq'ijab'* traditionalists played the part of conservative irredentists. Moreover, this second liberal-conservative split among Catholics effectively invited Protestants to expand in the villages. Protestants benefited both times, but by the mid-1940s

to mid-1950s, the corn crisis had turned Mayas favorably toward the crisis-style ritual embodied in Pentecostalized Protestant practice. As a result, the annual rate of *evangélico* expansion in the nation more than doubled: from 4.95 percent growth per annum in 1940 under Ubico to 11.1 percent per annum starting in 1950, the midpoint of the democratic opening. In the Department of Sololá, where the annual growth rates likely reflect more closely those of the Maya population of western Guatemala, the annual growth rate of Protestants/Pentecostals rose from 8.3 percent to 10.1 percent, a 23 percent increase in per annum growth (see figure 19.5).

In addition to crisis, issues of culture compatibility pushed those who were changing their religion in the direction of Pentecostal practice. The theological and theoretical vein of mainline Protestantism still appealed little to experientially oriented Mayas. Maya Protestantism thus turned largely Pentecostal, for Pentecostal practice is largely experiential. Moreover, through its inherent spirit- and revelatory-based fissiparousness, Pentecostalism rapidly "went native" in the form of adaptive independent churches.

In 1954 at the national level, mostly conservative Ladinos again reacted to the rather liberal changes of the democratic opening and, with US help, toppled the Guatemalan government. Containment and control under repressive military leaders became the new order of the day. But the damage to the supposed unity of the Catholic Church had already been done. the traditionalist-Ortho division and tension expanded as Ortho-Catholicism continued its return to the indigenous villages under conservative auspices and military governments post-1954. Protestant-derived Pentecostalism flourished in the space opened by the rupture between local traditionalists and the external Ortho hierarchy. Governmental repression of indigenes also expanded.

Engels (2008[1882]:202) suggests that not all of a society's distressed citizens respond to crisis with political and violent revolution. Some, indeed, seek "spiritual salvation." I have shown two threads of Maya spiritual salvation: (1) the continuing expansion of Pentecostalism, and (2), the 1944–1954 effort to establish the spirit of democracy throughout Guatemala. They ran in parallel as nonrevolutionary ideologies aiming to deal with growing cultural collapse and unsustainable inequality. Revolution would come later.

Chapter Nineteen

Containment

Military Control, Outbreaks of Insurrection, and Religious Responses, 1954–1978

JOHN P. HAWKINS

THE LEADERS OF THE DEMOCRATIC opening responded to the emerging land and corn crisis. President Árbenz began to expropriate unused lands of the large plantation estates, delivering land parcels to peasants, including land taken from the United Fruit Company. This redistribution threatened the interests of the United Fruit Company's American owners, who were tied by kinship and marriage to high-level officers in the US State Department and the US Congress (Schlesinger and Kinzer 2005:76, 106–107). These men of compromised interest pushed for restitution to United Fruit by claiming that the expropriation of their lands in Guatemala smelled of communism on the loose in Latin America (Schlesinger and Kinzer 2005:107). In the fearful, McCarthyite, Cold War environment of 1950–1954, the mere mention of the word "communist" generated a swift US reaction and catalyzed an American-backed coup d'etat.

In 1954, with US planning and armaments—and Central Intelligence Agency personnel piloting aircraft that bombed military targets—Colonel Carlos Castillo Armas led an insurrection that ended the democratic experiment in Guatemala. During the insurrection and following its success, Castillo Armas exterminated his opponents or drove them from the country. Some 8,000 died—disappeared and executed extrajudicially—mostly in the capital city and in eastern Guatemala (Weiner 2007).

Thus began a series of conservative military governments lasting almost without interruption from 1954 to 1986.[1] They protected and projected the conservative agenda of containment, control, extraction, and impunity that had operated since the beginnings of the Spanish colony (Hawkins 1984:91–134). The disempowered Mayas continued to suffer.

In spite of this conservative retrenchment, the changes set in motion by the democratic opening of 1944–1954 continued to evolve for many years. Religious freedom remained and expanded, in part because it had been built into the constitution. Ortho-Catholic administrative expansion accelerated because conservative military governments saw Catholicism as a bulwark of anticommunist strength and an instrument with which to undo the power of traditionalist Mayas in the rural hinterlands. Yet other changes evolved in spite of Guatemala's renewed efforts at internal control because by 1954, Euro-American colonialisms were in decay around the world.

But Guatemala's internal colonialism, in which a superordinate Ladino class lorded privilege over a subordinate Maya class, was more subtle than transoceanic colonialism. World politics reoriented from empires toward nations as principal actors, and the United States desired stable anticommunist nations. If the Guatemalan state would be overtly anticommunist, the United States would reward its anticommunism and tolerate or ignore its internal colonialism and human rights issues. So challenging internal colonialism in Guatemala's now "stable" anticommunist state would take longer. But the challenge came.

Part of the challenge began with an outbreak of insurgency in Guatemala beginning in 1960. This insurgency and the government's military pushback percolated at a relatively low level for some years. Nevertheless, there were government escalations, among them during the presidencies of Montenegro (1966–1970) and Carlos Manuel Arana Osorio (1970–1974), with many state-sponsored disappearances that culminated in torture and death. In 1981–1983, the government response intensified sharply in a spasm of ethnocidal brutality.[2] Several additional reactions to the succession of conservative military regimes emerged. Various popular social-union movements of laborers, peasants, and women began and drew strength, some of them hiving off from groups and goals originally instituted by Catholic Action. Whether strictly secular or openly Catholic Action, these movements of labor and women protested government and private violence and disappearances, corruption, and elite impunity. As the decades went by, military units or privately hired thugs increasingly intimidated, attacked, killed, kidnapped, tortured, and disappeared the leaders and members identified with any such protest organization. Detailed studies of the politics and the appalling machinations of this period abound (e.g., Perera 1993; Manz 2004; Montejo 1999; Arzobispado de Guatemala 1998; CEH 1999; Carmack 1988; Stoll 1993a; Schirmer 1998; Weld 2014; Sanford 2003; Glebbeek 2003), so I do not detail the violence here.

The politics of control enforced by violence added to the destabilization of the Maya way of life and had consequences that fostered a variety of religious responses. Among these responses, I note the Ortho-Catholic challenge to elite control via structural interventionism, the rise of Catholic Action, a flourishing of liberation theology, the pentecostalization of Protestantism, and the rise of charismatic Catholicism.

THE ORTHO-CATHOLIC CHALLENGE TO ELITE CONTROL

In Guatemala, the Catholic clergy directly confronted state abuses and also fomented a greater participation of Catholic laity in political activity through Catholic Action groups. But how did this direct challenge emerge in an organization as essentially conservative and allied to conservative governments as Guatemalan Catholicism? It did so along three lines. First, the Catholic Church's opposition to state abuses began when the Catholic hierarchy sought restoration, as much as possible, of clerical control of formerly expropriated Catholic assets. This brought the clergy into contrastive tension with the government even though senior Guatemalan clerics were conservative and allied with the control and anticommunist agenda of the military government.

The second line of direct clerical tension with the government evolved from the necessity of bringing foreign priests into Guatemala because the former reductions of the Catholic seminary system (discussed above) had resulted in insufficient priests for Guatemala's needs. A history of the Catholic Church issued by the archbishopric of Guatemala calls the entire period from 1821 to 1989 a time of "crisis" and states that because of expulsion, the church at one point had only eighty secular priests in Guatemala to serve about 1.5 million inhabitants (Diez de Arriba and Luis 1989:2:461). Repairing that deficit required importation of foreign-born and foreign-educated priests. These imported priests had three characteristics that are of interest here. First, they tended not to be prejudiced against working closely with indigenous peoples. Consequently, they often moved into the indigenous periphery to advance pastoral Catholicism. Second, they had internationally formed Ortho-Catholic ideas of what the church should look like. Accordingly, many sought to suppress the indigenous elaborations of sixteenth-century Spanish *cofradía* and the Maya Catholic shamanic practices that indigenous populations and the gerontocracies managing the political affairs in Maya villages held to be true Catholicism. That process, begun during the democratic opening, substantially accelerated as Ortho-Catholicism gained strength and expanded its Catholic Action programs and missionization among traditionalists (Falla 1978, 2001). This exacerbated the split with traditionalist Catholics that I elaborated above and that is detailed in Falla (1978, 2001), Brintnall (1979), and Watanabe (1992). Third, the foreign Catholic leaders disapproved of state oppression and abuse on ethical grounds and also because much of the violence touched their Catholic parishioners.

The third line of direct clerical response to authoritarian control resulted from the foreign priests expanding the adjunct institution of Catholic Action and promoting the ideas and goals of liberation theology into Maya and many non-Maya parishes. While much of the Guatemalan clergy and Guatemala's early Catholic Action remained conservative, the version of Catholic Action espoused by Belgian and other European priests in Guatemala was not. In Belgium, the Jeunesse Ouvrier Catholique (Young Catholic Workers), the initial version of Catholic Action, started in 1912, urged small cells of young workers to meet, criticize the government and society, and actively seek to change the structures of society that fostered poverty and injustice (Bidegain 1985:7). In Guatemala, many of the priests educated in the European milieu had synthesized the idea that their pastoral responsibility consisted in service and care for the poor via the core ideas of Marxism, which suggested that they should directly confront material and institutional structures that fostered poverty. The clergy sought to increase the involvement of the laity in the Catholic Church's outreach to the larger populace. The priests who had made this synthesis urged the necessity of struggle against the institutions generating urban and indigenous immiserization. In adopting stances supporting institutional transformation and material development, these priests challenged Guatemala's conservative governing elites. The irony is that these elites had originally sought the reinstantiation of Catholic institutions as a support against communism. When Catholic resistance to communism and support of conservative control seemed less than obvious, relations between government and church soured, and conflict and distrust escalated.

In a parallel effort in the 1960s, the Second Vatican Council (1962–1965) and the Conference of Latin American Bishops (meeting in Medellín, Colombia, in 1968) sought further involvement of the laity and additional direct action against the institutions maintaining structural impoverishment. These efforts culminated with the 1971 publication of Father Gustavo Gutiérrez's *Teología de la Liberación*, a book that formalized and consolidated the logic of a "preferential option for the poor" as a central point of Catholic pastoral theology. Gutiérrez advocated that Catholic laity should organize to directly confront and change the governing social structures that maintained poverty and enriched elites. Catholic Action (the involved laity) and liberation theology (an orientation toward direct opposition to the structures fostering poverty) became increasingly central to Catholic pastoral practice in Guatemala. Among other things, the peasant labor union Comité de Unidad Campesina (Committee for Peasant Unity), so much at the center of Guatemalan 1970s–1980s challenge politics, had its origins in this Catholic nursery for organizational change. It is in this context that one can better understand Ricardo Falla's (1994) penetrating study of violence and Protestant conversion in the Maya Catholic parish where he served as an activist priest.

Catholic Action and liberation theology elicited brutal reactions at the nation-state level. Catholic Action explicitly pursued structural changes that its members thought would ameliorate the plight of the poor by granting them increased access to education, government services, and a modicum of wealth. It thus threatened elite control of Guatemala's people and wealth. This put Catholicism on a collision course with Guatemala's governing elites and

their army representatives, police, and thuggish private security bands tasked to maintain control of the structures that had made elites politically powerful, wealthy, and socially prestigious. Collide they did.

The conflict had heartrending reverberations in indigenous communities. By the 1970s, Guatemala's Acción Católica had become the action arm of liberation theology, wielded as an instrument to confront and undermine the country's control-oriented regime by challenging institutions that Acción Católica leaders and church theologians thought upheld, fostered, or structurally sustained the country's continued poverty. Given this, so far as the Guatemalan army was concerned, the Roman Catholic priesthood, Ortho-Catholic lay leaders and members in Acción Católica, and the leaders of other Catholic lay and labor organizations became organizers of opposition to the state and were persecuted. Mayas were both thought to be Catholic and known to be peripheral. On both counts they seemed to be in opposition to the state. Mayas were, therefore, to be exterminated. Elites enacted their self-preservation effort through executions, kidnappings, torture, murder, disappearances, and rape—in short, through terror. Terror tore through the cities and extended into the Maya villages where ethnic hatreds escalated the state brutalities to an ethnocidal level. Thus, Guatemala's dirty war, simmering since the 1960s, became ever dirtier and more brutal as the 1970s rolled into the 1980s.

PENTECOSTAL CONVERSION RATES, 1950S–LATE 1970S

In contrast to Catholic teachings of a preferential option for the poor, urging direct structural change and the confronting of institutions maintaining poverty and powerlessness, Pentecostals teach that the solution to social problems consists in individual self-reform via prayer and mutual support in meetings, resulting in self-control. They preach a withdrawal from contact with the degeneracies of "worldly" politics to avoid self-corruption and compromise. They advocate individual honesty and submission to law—especially a higher law. Pentecostals' self-reform and withdrawal from overt confrontation with social and political institutions suited non-Pentecostal elites and government officers.

There is some indication that as a result, Pentecostals suffered less direct assault than Catholics did during the government's efforts to stamp out subversion. Unpredicted by the elites, however, the Pentecostal approach turned out to be at least equally subversive to the conservative military agenda, and perhaps more so, than Catholic Action's confrontational approach. Pentecostal self-reform was not so obvious an attack. The conservative military agenda entailed control of the masses and of the Mayas, extraction of wealth by all means possible, evasion of the application of law to the elites themselves, and impunity through institutional control (Hawkins 1984). By contrast with Catholic Action's confrontation, the Pentecostal project entailed an individualized freedom from worldly hierarchy (via direct access to power from the Holy Spirit) and a relaxation of controls at the emotional/expressive level. Pentecostal preaching often included a message of acquisition of wealth through faith in God, giving to the church, and self-discipline. Importantly, the Pentecostal notion of self-discipline also embodied a resolute determination to obey the laws both of God and of the nation. At the same time, in the Pentecostal view, given the all-seeing eye of God, no such thing as impunity existed. Nevertheless, Pentecostals' disinclination to challenge directly the existing institutions of power made them seem less threatening than Catholics' activism. Pentecostals simply participated in ritual and prayer to change themselves, prayed for others and for good governance, and sought converts.

In spite of vigorous Catholic efforts to ameliorate poverty, the increasing perception of crisis in the reliance of Maya culture on failing corn production set the stage for a transformation of religious needs and expression. The old ways were not working (Stanzione 2003:8; Morgan 2005:74–93). The existential crisis made Pentecostalism's focus on end-of-the-world apocalypse, experiential reception of the Holy Spirit as a bodily transformer, and personal angst regarding sin all the more appealing. Pentecostalism made sense to Mayas because it made body and emotion connect with and express the crisis of their social condition and because it made liturgical participation and active reception of the Spirit more important than the study or hearing of words and theology. As a result, Pentecostalism successfully indigenized and began to grow prodigiously.

Between 1950 and 1980, many sedate Protestant congregations morphed into increasingly Pentecostal practice (Althoff 2014:10–14, n42). In Nahualá and Santa Catarina Ixtahuacán, all of them did so. Pentecostals still called themselves *evangélicos*, as did the few still-sedate mainline Protestants remaining in other municipalities.

Mainline Protestants and Pentecostals shared at least one thing: both engaged in a strong missionary/conversion assault on Ortho-Catholic and traditionalist beliefs and practices. The rise in Pentecostal affiliation and the waning memberships of Protestant congregations was not unique to Nahualá and Santa Catarina Ixtahuacán or even Guatemala. Steigenga and Cleary (2007b:8) note that this decline in historical or mainline Protestant membership numbers occurred throughout Latin America. Gifford (2004:23, 27, 33, 199) affirms the same for Ghana. Barrett, Kurian, and Johnson (2001:1:10) in their massive *World Christian Encyclopedia* argue the same decline of mainline Protestant denominations vis-à-vis the rise of Pentecostal affirmations throughout the world, with mainline denominations reduced from 41 percent of Christians in 1970 to 35 percent in 2000.

Before I proceed, I need to clarify the main points of the history of anthropological interest in the rise of Protestantism in Guatemala. The early ethnographic studies of the Mayas for the most part hardly mentioned Protestants in the community. If they noted them at all, Protestants were treated as another intrusion of modernity that, like cars, roads, and airplanes, could be conveniently ignored as the analyst pursued a description and interpretation of traditional Maya religion. By the 1960s, however, the Protestant presence had become substantial enough that at least two ethnographers, Brian Roberts (1968, 1973) and Ruben Reina collaborating with Norman Schwartz (1974, based on 1960s research) devoted direct attention to Protestantism in their areas of study. By the 1980s, Protestants, most of whom were Pentecostals, had become so numerous that they could not be ignored, although Annis (1987) tried to. He went to the field intending to conduct a study of tourism but found the Protestant presence so strong that he had to deal with the issue. Out of that self-redirection came his book *God and Production in a Guatemalan Town*, a study of the relation of economic and cultural change with Guatemala's increasing Protestantization.

Subsequent to *God and Production*'s publication in 1987, scholars such as Stoll (1990:10–13), Green (1993:161–162), and Garrard-Burnett (1998:120–137) attributed the now quite apparent Protestantization to social disorganization and stress caused by a major earthquake in 1976 and a spike in counterinsurgency violence occurring in 1981–1984. That became the received wisdom, and most analysts lump the earthquake and war together in a single theoretical breath, although Annis (1987:7) challenged such analysis as too "easy." I agree, and at the end of this chapter I deal firmly with the relation of the quake in 1976 to the Protestantization timing and theory.

A visual approach to data interpretation for Guatemala's religious changes seems to show a turning point in rising rates of Pentecostal membership sometime between 1940 and 1950. One can see this apparent upturn in the changing curvature of Garrard-Burnett's (1998:273) graph of Protestant membership over time. In Garrard-Burnett's graph, Protestant membership begins to curve upward for one of the churches in the 1930s–1940s. For three others, the data show a sharp lift-off in the 1950s–1960s. One can see the same phenomenon and reach the same conclusion through charting Protestant membership in the Guatemalan population from the national census records, as I have done in figure 19.1. The same steeply upward trend is visible in my graph of the Protestant population as a percentage of the national population (figure 19.2).

Nevertheless, no conclusion should be drawn from any chart manifesting a change in curvature that graphs compound growth over time. The same occurs in the graphs of Sololá's parallel data (figures 19.3 and 19.4), and it is one of the most indigenous of Guatemala's departments. All such charts display a similar bend upward in the last third of the time span covered and become asymptotic in the last fifth or so of the time scale. This is so even if the annual growth rate stays constant, for that is the nature of compound annual growth when graphed over a long time span. To diminish the temptation to assume a rate or system change at the point where the curve begins to arc upward asymptotically, in figure 19.5 I graph the compound annual rate of change for Protestant (both mainline and Pentecostal because the national census does not distinguish between them) membership for the periods between the censuses for which there are data on religion. There is no evidence of an overall increase in compound annual growth beginning in 1976 or during the 1980s escalation of violence, even though Gooren (2015) provides figures from selected denominations that self-report considerable increases.

I have treated in some detail two factors that contributed to Protestantism's compound annual increase at a rate three to six (or more) times the national population's rate of expansion. The most important of the great social disruptions encouraging a shift toward Pentecostalism was the increasing inability of Mayas to live off the land. The rising population began to cross the carrying capacity of their corn and land culture between 1950 and 1964, precisely when Protestantization reached its highest compound annual rate of expansion, namely above 11 percent. Conversion rose because the increasing rate of population expansion (from 1.5 percent per annum prior to this period to 3.5 percent per annum during this period) compromised the corn culture and covenant premises of traditionalist Maya Catholic religion and simultaneously undermined the assumptions of isolation and submission to hierarchy implicit in Ortho-Catholicism, which no longer worked in the hustle-requiring economic domain of a corn-short world.

This long-term process of culture collapse was exacerbated beginning in the mid-1940s by the effective end of municipal isolation (both in premise and in practice) due to two factors. First, Ortho-Catholicism penetrated the indigenous municipalities via its effort to wrest control of worship practices from traditionalist Catholic *cofradía* and *ajq'ijab'* leadership. Second, at much the same time that Ortho-Catholicism sought to end traditionalist Maya Catholic autonomy, national political reforms further savaged the increasingly illusory indigenous municipal isolation. Specifically, democratic constitutional changes begun in 1944–1954 and resumed in 1985 drove electoral reforms. The possibility of elections (even if corrupt), the value of votes, and the linkage of vote counts to national budget subsidies to the *municipios* forced party politics and political bribery into the indigenous communities. Party politics and political money thus further disrupted the cultural ideal of the isolated, self-subsistent village. Ladino party leaders, like the priests before them, hired young Maya bilinguals to broker their entry into the communities. Expanded economic and social opportunities for the Spanish-speaking youths further challenged gerontocratic village control. Moreover, candidates for mayor and other community offices challenged each other, introducing a level of conflict the *pasado* leadership had avoided when they had picked the officeholder or effectively blessed the candidate for which the villagers would vote. What does this have to do with religion and religious change? These were major social upheavals from the indigenous perspective; that changed perspective, forced by subsistence crisis, created an openness to religious resymbolization.

Electoral cycles of party politics visibly and regularly shattered the fiction of indigenous community unity (Dracoulis et al. 2013; Burrell 2013; Hawkins, McDonald, and Adams 2013). Thus, national party politics challenged the indigenous municipal gerontocracy while Ortho-Catholic leadership challenged the indigenous municipality's

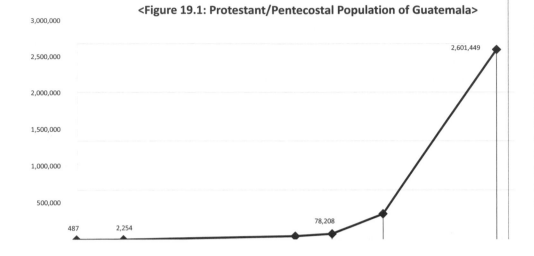

<Figure 19.1: Protestant/Pentecostal Population of Guatemala>

Figure 19.1. Protestant/ Pentecostal population of Guatemala. *Sources*: Secretario de Estado del Despacho de Fomento, Sección de Estadística 1880; Dirección General de Estadística 1897, 1942, 1957, 1971–1972, 1982b; INE 1994, 2002a, 2002b, 2002c, 2003a; Johnson and Grim 2020.

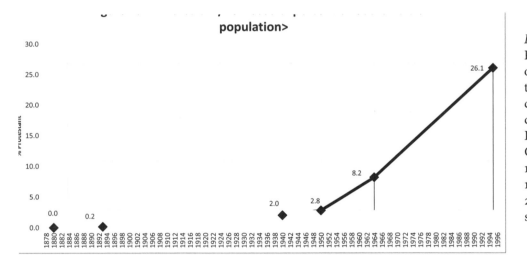

Figure 19.2. Protestant/ Pentecostal percentage of Guatemala's population. *Sources*: Secretario de Estado del Despacho de Fomento, Sección de Estadística 1880; Dirección General de Estadística 1897, 1942, 1957, 1971–1972, 1982b; INE 1994, 2002a, 2002b, 2002c, 2003a; Johnson and Grim 2020.

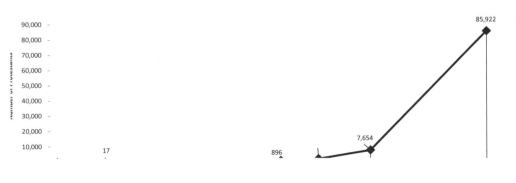

Figure 19.3. Protestant/ Pentecostal population of Sololá. *Sources*: Secretario de Estado del Despacho de Fomento, Sección de Estadística 1880; Dirección General de Estadística 1897, 1942, 1957, 1971–1972, 1982b; INE 1994, 2002a, 2002b, 2002c, 2003a; Johnson and Grim 2020.

Figure 19.4. Protestant/Pentecostal percentage of Sololá's population. *Sources*: Secretario de Estado del Despacho de Fomento, Sección de Estadística 1880; Dirección General de Estadística 1897, 1942, 1957, 1971–1972, 1982b; INE 1994, 2002a, 2002b, 2002c, 2003a; Johnson and Grim 2020.

Figure 19.5. Compound annual growth rate of Protestant/Pentecostal membership in Guatemala and Sololá. *Sources*: Secretario de Estado del Despacho de Fomento, Sección de Estadística 1880; Dirección General de Estadística 1897, 1942, 1957, 1971–1972, 1982b; INE 1994, 2002a, 2002b, 2002c, 2003a; Johnson and Grim 2020.

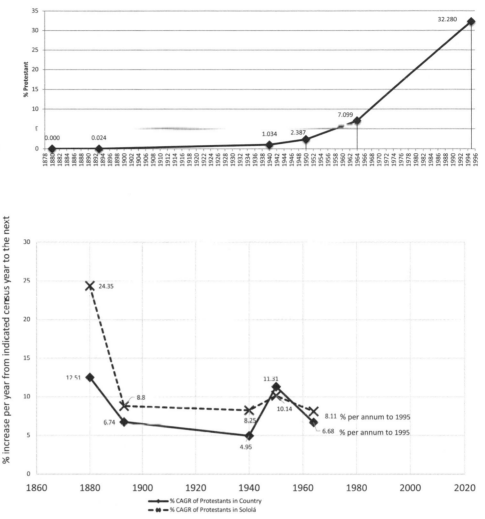

religious gerontocracy for village and hinterland control. Both challenges highlighted the failure of indigenous isolation. Finally, market mechanisms, expanded product consumption, and growth in the importance of nonagricultural wages further penetrated the indigenous communities. With both the religious and the political functions of the *cofradía* compromised, and with new sources of income and external points of reference for securing social status, the internally oriented institutions and the key premises of indigenous status and isolation slowly but surely began to break down (Cancian 1965, 1972, 1992; Brintnall 1979; Smith 1977; Watanabe 1992).

At first, in spite of the political intrusion, in many indigenous communities the elders successfully evaded the disruptive consequences of party politics. In Nahualá and Santa Catarina Ixtahuacán, for example, the *pasados*—those who had passed through ritual offices in the *cofradía*—selected and made known the party candidate they expected the municipality's residents to vote for, which they did. When competition between parties resulted in several candidates in the *municipio*, the *pasados* determined which party's candidate the *pasados* would favor. Their respected opinion was made known and tipped the electoral balance at the municipal level. But slowly, the power of the gerontocracy gave way to the pressure of elections and parties and especially the pressure of money and corruption. Brintnall (1979) tells this story in some detail for the mostly Maya town of Aguacatán. For Santa Catarina Ixtahuacán, Dracoulis and colleagues (2013) show how the old method of selecting mayors increasingly gave way to the new electoral processes. That intervention by electoral process accelerated in about 1986 following the constitutional reforms of 1985. The party system's penetration of the communities amplified the threats to the gerontocracy that the elders had experienced when Ortho-Roman Catholicism sought to regain control from traditionalists. From 1985 to 1995, Ixtahuacán's *cofradía* system rapidly declined, and there were several years of no celebrations. In 1996, the community managed to mount one last celebration, but only because an external NGO supporting indigenous cultural protection funded the costs.

Thus, the international Catholic Church, the national political process, and capitalist markets had penetrated and disrupted the Maya community, the first two explicitly trying to gain dominance over indigenous cultural control of the municipality. In addition, print media, radio, movies, television programs, and advertising penetrated the communities and provoked new wants for products. Consensus gerontocracy lost power. Elders lost respect. Inherited land could no longer support a family. For the community as a whole, land was respected, yet it no longer could be depended on as the key to status, and land could not ensure survival. Corn no longer sufficed. Traditional Maya ways of life lay shattered in what Marx would have called another "great historical upheaval of social conditions." In consequence, the traditionalist religious practices that symbolized and supported the traditional culture of community unity, subordination to family, municipally controlled land, avoidance of caprice and danger from the outside, and the important place of corn slowly lost appeal. Concomitantly, "the outlooks and ideas of men, and consequently their religious ideas" were being "revolutionized" via rapidly increasing adoption of the new Pentecostalisms (Marx and Engels 2008[1850]:94).

In this contested new field of economic market opportunism and political party penetration, the individualist logic of Protestantism made some sense. As taught by American and European missionaries, however, the liturgical form and intellectual content of mainstream Protestantism's theologized rationalism still did not appeal. By contrast, the increasingly desperate liminality that constituted the emerging new Maya social order was made sensible in several ways by the tiny Pentecostal groups that had gotten started in the 1920s. First, Pentecostals preached that the world was corrupt, chaotic, dangerously satanic, beguiling, irredeemable, and close to its end collapse before the coming of Jesus in the millennium. That string of descriptors certainly matched the Mayan and Guatemalan experience of impunity, violence, war, hunger, and precarious existence with insufficient corn. As

landholdings per family diminished, Pentecostal ideas made increasingly good sense. Pentecostal practice felt especially good because it expressed symbolically the lived social chaos that Mayas increasingly experienced. Pentecostal end-of-the-world angst made sense of economic reality in that it matched the Mayas' experience of punishingly small cornfields that could no longer support families in isolated, self-sufficient municipalities. It made sense of political reality as Guatemala's structural violence lurched from Jorge Ubico's 1930s books documenting *mandamiento* labor slavery for Mayas to Fernando Romeo Lucas García's and José Efraín Ríos Montt's 1980s indigenous ethnocide and, later, to the fear and generalized violence of the 1990s post-counterinsurgency milieu. Pentecostalism made sense of painful gender role deterioration as population increases put pressure on households supporting themselves on ever-smaller plots of land. Mayas experienced increased hunger, men's decreased capacity to supply corn, and women's increased need to supplement budgets and feed the many new mouths.

Pentecostalism also made sense because its focus on experiencing the Holy Ghost bodily made the Pentecostal liturgy physically *sensible* in the dual aspects of bodily meaning and bodily perception. The liturgy brings individuals regularly, even daily if they attend each evening's services, to experience in their bodies the reception of the Holy Spirit as a manifestation of Jesus's saving grace. These Pentecostals do not just verbally "accept Jesus" at one named time and date, as required by mainstream Protestant theology. Worldwide, Pentecostals do something more: they receive the Holy Spirit into their bodies and experience this manifestation of divinity inside themselves—and they do it regularly through their animated experiential liturgy. The suffering Mayas certainly needed something more than Protestant thought or Catholic sacraments to save them from the collapse and exclusion that increasingly strangled them. That need became increasingly clear as each generation subdivided the land and passed its shrinking resources to the next. As a result, ecstatic Pentecostalism flourished, sedate mainline Protestant practice withered, and cultural Catholics of both traditionalist and Ortho orientation, whether of Maya or Ladino ethnicity, shrank over time as a percentage of the country's population.

Finally, Pentecostalism made sense because the free provision of healings, the promise (in some congregations) of wealth and success through diligent religious comportment, the sustained social support in rejecting alcohol, and the individualization of responsibility for obedience to law and avoidance of "vices" helped Mayas deal with the harsh but real facts of life as experienced by both them and the urban poor. I elaborate on all these functional and consequentially utilitarian facets of Pentecostal success in chapter 24. At this point I simply state that some institution needed to address the issues faced by Guatemalan Mayas. Unfortunately, no arm of Guatemalan government or civil society was likely to help or save these indigenous people. The Guatemalan government could not help them; it was failing in both security and solvency. Moreover, the Ladino-dominated government did little for indigenous peoples with what money or resources it had because its leaders often were ethnically prejudiced. Nor could indigenes be saved by the newly arriving neoliberal economy. Economic elites wanted more land, not less, and cheap laborers, not citizens. Mayas could not even find salvation in the once self protective *pueblo de indios* ("Indian town") because the autonomous integrity of the indigenous *municipio* had been compromised by Ladinos, by money through state governance penetrations, by the Ortho church's bid for control, and by neoliberal markets. With those intrusions, divisive class differences emerged among Mayas (Brintnall 1979; Watanabe 1992; Hawkins, McDonald, and Adams 2013). In effect, money further corroded the covenant of trust formerly vested in the *municipio*'s indigenous leaders.

Except for the decaying vestiges of protection afforded by their community when they engaged in mass protest, Mayas could depend only on themselves and Jesus. The Pentecostal message of worldly corruption, coming collapse, and reliance on apolitical self-change as the only solution thus spoke truth to the buffeted and anxious souls of many. The Pentecostal message and its anxiously energetic participatory practice resonated with and aptly symbolized the crisis experiences of Mayas and poor urbanites and offered the only safe way to take action to ameliorate the crisis in a violent and untrustworthy state.

The highly expressive liturgy of Pentecostalized Protestantism involved the Mayas and urban poor people in directly experiential (in contrast to Protestant rational and theological) individualism in a small-group setting. It helped develop self-control in familial life according to an external biblical standard (in contrast to Catholic obedience to a priestly hierarchy and to tradition). It honestly manifested a Pentecostal's existential stress through amplified music and persuasive preaching of a soon-to-come end of the world with anticipation of a new millennial order to follow (in contrast to the passive but culturally resistant traditionalism or confrontational Acción Católica). It enshrined insistent, creative, glossolalic prayer (in contrast to traditionalist Maya and Ortho-Catholic standardized chants). The new Pentecostal order generated personal, familial, gendered, and community reformation by individual self-control spread ever wider through evangelization of the surrounding society. The Pentecostal approach made more sense of and better expressed the urgently felt crisis of indigenous subsistence risk, cultural collapse, and exclusion than did verbal Protestantism, land- and corn-based traditionalism, socially conflictive Acción Católica, or hierarchically oriented and quite sedate sacramental Ortho-Catholicism. Pentecostalism made more sense than nonfunctioning democracy or repressive military conservatism—the faith-based secular "isms" available by 1960. In sum, Pentecostalism's strident experiential liturgy and symbolic ideology made strikingly good cultural sense to Mayas. Pentecostalism felt good as an experience, and it provided solutions. In Durkheimian style, Pentecostalism symbolically matched and emotionally vocalized the experienced social crisis and critical deterioration in indigenous and poor urban cultural and physical life conditions. In Marxian terms, Pentecostalism described the worker's and indigenous peasant's real crisis of productive familial life. Indeed, Pentecostal prayer vented the sigh of the oppressed.

Moreover, the Pentecostal practices of gift giving through healing, shared prayers for others, and open sociality bound potential recruits to Pentecostal groups through expectations of reciprocity for gifts and culturally compatible notions of covenant for protection. Pentecostals satisfied their new members' souls by enabling expression of their deepest fears that the cultural and economic world as they knew it, and their survival within it, was at risk and coming to an end. Pentecostalism attracted and connected with both Mayas and urban poor people, converting thousands from among the many relatively unconnected and less participatory cultural Catholics. Pentecostal congregations expanded, split, hived off, and expanded again in multiple locations.

So pre-1970s Pentecostalism triumphed over sedate theological Protestantism and the then-current forms of sedate Maya Catholicism and Ortho-Catholicism, growing faster than any of them although numerically, Pentecostals still constituted only between a quarter and a third of all Guatemalans. Such conversion happened not because individuals chose Pentecostalism rationally for its delivered benefits—as Chesnut (1997); Stark, Iannaccone, and Finke (1996); Iannaccone, Finke, and Stark (1997); Iannaccone, Stark, and Finke (1998); and Stark and Finke (2000), among others, would argue—although the functional benefits built into Pentecostal lifeways helped. Rather, Pentecostalism won out because it resonated with key Maya cultural premises of bodily participation and because it accurately expressed their collapsing, angst-filled cultural experience. Pentecostalism activated the body during worship in ways that could be appreciated by those steeped in the Maya experiential culture. It vocally expressed—loudly and emotionally—the crisis conditions of current collapse and anticipated chaos that Mayas (and urban poor people) experienced or could see descending on them as they sought, but could seldom fulfill, their cultural need to provide for their children's inheritances. Pentecostalism grew too because its practice of avoiding *awas* (vices) helped resolve or elude crisis at the levels of individual, family, and congregation.

Pentecostalism grew also because it requires its members to evangelize others through gift giving, prayer, health, and sociality. That is its key political arm. Pentecostal faith encourages the evangelized spread of a morality that adherents imagine will bring peace, virtue, and humanity to the chaotic and violent Guatemalan state and, indeed, the entire world.

Living by Pentecostal rules and attending Pentecostal religious activities in small communities of coreligionists did, in fact, help solve a number of increasingly pressing problems, and those solutions were cognized as gifts of God acquired through attachment to some particular congregation or denomination. In consequence, Pentecostal faiths drew converts prodigiously. Pentecostalism grew two to three times faster than the 2.8–3.2 percent per annum base rate of population expansion in Guatemala. Figures 19.1–19.4 display data on Protestant/Pentecostal membership in the nation and in the Department of Sololá. Figure 19.5 graphs the compound rates of growth of both through time. From 1880 through 1964, Guatemalan censuses noted whether a person claimed to be Catholic, Protestant, or another religion, or if a person asserted a lack of affiliation or absence of religious belief. Unfortunately, for reasons that I have not been able to determine, the census bureau stopped keeping track of religion in the 1973 population census and subsequently, except for a relatively thorough survey (but not a census) conducted in 1995 by Guatemala's

departments of statistics and health services (INE and MSPAS 1999).[3]

I now examine the numbers used in these censuses to calculate compound annual rates of growth. Because the formula for calculating compound rate of change does not allow division by zero, a starting point of zero for Protestant membership was impossible. By the same token, membership figures close to zero raised the initial rate of growth toward infinity. Thus, I discounted the first Sololá compound rate of return. To make the formula work, I had to assume at least one living Protestant in Sololá in 1880, giving a compound rate of return to the next census (1893) of 24.35 percent. Had I set the initial starting population at five people, the Department of Sololá compound rate of Protestant growth would have been 9.87 percent over the same period. The fact is we do not know what the Protestant membership was in 1880 in Sololá if for no other reason than that the census was manifestly incomplete, with no census figures for several recalcitrant *municipios* in the department. The 1880 census lists 487 Protestants in the country as a whole, but the census takers were not able to enter the Departments of Huehuetenango or San Marcos at all, nor did they attempt to conduct the census in Nahualá or Santa Catarina Ixtahuacán, the most noncompliant towns of Sololá. A few more Protestants in the unsurveyed northwest region would drive down the compound rate of increase substantially. So both the national and the Department of Sololá figures for the period 1880–1893 need to be discounted because any near-zero beginning guarantees a high initial rate of compound annual growth.

From 1893 to 1940, however, Guatemala had a compound annual increase of 6.74 percent among Protestants, a rate that is 5.57 times the compound growth rate of the nation's population during that period. In the Department of Sololá, Protestants expanded at an 8.8 percent rate, compounded annually, over the same forty-seven years. Thus, the Protestant rate of expansion in Sololá was 7.33 times the compound rate of population growth of the nation as a whole and 19.6 times the 0.45 percent annual growth rate of the population of Sololá for that period. Clearly, with these differences in growth rate, Protestantism expanded as a percentage of the nation's and the department's populations. In spite of the high compound annual growth rates, however, the absolute number of Protestants and their percentage of the population in any given territorial unit remained small in these early time periods.

THE CHARISMATIC CATHOLIC
OPENING IN GUATEMALA, 1973–1975

Most Pentecostal expansion came from traditionalist and Ortho-Catholic membership or from those indigenes who had converted to mainline Protestantism, indigenized their worship, and morphed into Pentecostals. With continued and substantial membership losses to the (Protestant) Pentecostals, the Catholic Church's leaders eventually concluded they had to do something. Somehow they had to cauterize the flow of their Catholic membership lifeblood to Pentecostal groups. In Guatemala and elsewhere, some of the response came in the form of highly nationalist complaints by Catholic Church leaders that Protestant *sectas*, led by hordes of prodigiously financed North American ministers, had poached their adherents from Catholic membership and thereby undermined the Catholic cultural basis of Guatemalan national identity. Sarasa (1991) exemplifies such grousing.[4] Official complaints, however, did little to staunch the membership losses. A much more viable response boiled up from the Catholic grassroots in the form of the Catholic Charismatic Renewal movement.

Two of the ethnographic essays in part 1 remark on the origins of Catholic charismaticism in the two studied *municipios*. Here I consolidate and round out their notes in relation to the general system.

First, the formal origin of Catholic charismaticism was in the United States. Cleary (2007:161) notes that "almost all histories" place the beginning of the charismatic movement in Catholicism "at Duquesne University in Pittsburg[h] in February 1967." Cleary, however, challenges this notion, pointing out a second "similar event . . . occurring in Bogotá, Colombia" (172n18, citing Thigpen 2003; Gooren 2012:187). Cleary (2007:161) documents another source of Catholic charismaticism in the preaching and leadership of Father Francis MacNutt in the United States, who "was not drawn to the movement by ties with the Duquesne experience."

The fact of three independent "inventions" of Catholic charismaticism (by adopting and modestly adapting existing Pentecostalism) in two distinct and distant countries, but in close temporal proximity, suggests the existence of a structural cause operating to foment all three instances of charismatic Catholic invention. Some social force selected for or rewarded the openness of communication; the exuberant, tense, angst-laden expression of the liturgy; and the speaking in tongues about the inexpressible.[5] So far as I can tell, however, only the Duquesne movement internationalized, so I confine my remarks to that. Soon after the Duquesne conferences, the participating priests, nuns, and Catholic missionaries instituted a series of retreats and international conferences that distributed the Catholic Charismatic Renewal throughout Latin America and the entire Roman Catholic world (Cleary 2007:161–164; Pastor 1998:1–18). This was rather like the 1906 Azusa Street Pentecostalism led by the Reverend William Seymour and internationalized among Protestants via multiple missions that began worldwide in 1907.

Sometime between 1973 and 1975, Catholics brought the new charismatic practices to western highland Guatemala. The indigenous cook and sacristan who aided the American resident priest in Santa Catarina Ixtahuacán attended a retreat. So also did a parish worker from Nahualá. They likely attended the same retreat. With the blessing of Ixtahuacán's priest and Nahualá's nuns, these two parish workers became the first indigenous converts and leaders of the charismatic *renovación* in their respective municipalities.

The movement has expanded impressively in both Nahualá and Santa Catarina (and throughout Guatemala and the world) ever since. In 2003, Nahualá, for example, sustained some fifty-seven small congregations of charismatic Catholics distributed throughout its semi-urban cantons and rural *aldeas*. Each congregation met every Sunday and several evenings during the week in its own cement-block simple chapel that the faithful of each group had self-financed and built in their rural hamlet, or it met in the home of one of the adherents.

I treat the theological content and liturgical practice of the charismatic movement in more detail in chapter 22. Here I emphasize that substantial similarities exist between a charismatic Catholic meeting and a Pentecostal Protestant meeting. That similarity derives from deliberate copying. In the 1967 Duquesne meetings, Catholics seeking to improve the Ortho church and their personal spirituality learned their techniques from Pentecostal ministers they had invited as teacher-guides. In Guatemala, one could copy by simply attending Pentecostal meetings or by hearing them blasted incessantly from rooftop speakers. The style appealed to and flourished among Maya Catholics. Given the membership losses in Guatemala, the Catholic hierarchy eventually came to accept these Pentecostal practices in regular charismatic meetings held separately from priest-led mass. They viewed these now Catholic-sponsored similarities as a defense against membership losses to Pentecostal congregations.[6] Gooren (2012:193) confirms that such a perspective existed widely: "In Latin America, national bishops' conferences started to promote the Catholic Charismatic Renewal as a way to prevent membership losses to Pentecostalism." Moreover, Catholics recognized several of the social benefits Pentecostalism provided. Those benefits, senior leaders felt, made Protestant Pentecostalism attractive. If Pentecostalism was attractive, they concluded, then Catholicism should allow—indeed, must even foster—something similar. Through charismaticism, a Catholic could have a renewal experience of the Holy Spirit, add the mutually supportive advantages of small-group, teetotaling, Pentecostal practice, and still remain Catholic. A Catholic could be renewed without becoming anti-Catholic; a Catholic could thereby express the same anxieties as Pentecostals and in a similar style.

These advantages may have preempted some of the appeal of Pentecostal practice by incorporating Pentecostalism's attractive features into this renewed Catholicism. In all likelihood, the rapid rise of pentecostal Catholicism in 1975–1995 partly explains the apparent leveling off of Pentecostal Protestant growth during this period, which Gooren (2010) notes in Guatemala. Thus, while Pentecostal expansion from 2000 to 2010 slowed and plateaued, Christian Pentecostalism more widely conceived still expanded rapidly.

The cases of Nahualá and Ixtahuacán confirm Cleary's (2007:171) observation that "the growth of the [Catholic charismatic] movement was less of an innovation by a monopolistic institutional religious supplier than a spontaneous reaction on the part of key individuals and missionaries to events and practices that were simultaneously sparking the growth of Pentecostalism." In the case of Nahualá and Santa Catarina, nuns brought the movement into Sololá because it felt good to them and seemed needed in the church, although they lacked a high-level ecclesiastical push.[7] The Mayas themselves—both Ortho-Catholic and traditional—quickly found the experientiality of charismatic spirit infusion comprehensible and comfortably satisfying. So the charismatic worship style grew rapidly, largely as a popular movement, with many Guatemalan bishops and priests remaining leery and skeptical of it for quite a long time.[8]

I should note that some Catholic leaders now claim the movement as their response to Pentecostal depredations, but that is a post facto rationalization of their late acceptance of it. Catholic charismaticism in Guatemala, and especially in Maya Guatemala, responded to something much deeper than official Catholicism's fear of loss. It responded to the ever-worsening collapse of the capacity to supply by one's own productive efforts the corn that was axial to indigenous identity and essential to adequate nutrition. It responded to the breakdown of protected communal isolationism on which municipal Maya identity had been built. It responded to one's inability to find an adequate place in a non-corn economy. In short, Catholic charismaticism expanded rapidly in Guatemala because it spoke to the same social forces that engendered and fueled Protestant Pentecostalism's acceptance and consequent threat to Ortho-Catholic and traditionalist Maya relevance: collapse of a cultural way of life rooted in dependence on corn and exclusion from any alternative.

ACCUMULATING DESTABILIZERS, 1970–1978

During the 1970s, several factors added cumulatively to the precariousness of life in Guatemala, among them the 1973–1974 economic shock of the oil embargo, governmental incapacity, globalization combined with the impact of expanding state education programs (leading to a divergence of interests), and Guatemala's ever-present but seemingly worsening political ineptitude and electoral corruption.

Oil Embargo

The 1973 oil embargo impacted crop production and added to the Maya crisis by cutting the supply of petrochemicals used to manufacture fertilizer. For a decade prior to the embargo, increasing indigenous use of chemical fertilizers had doubled local crop yields. The embargo changed that dynamic. At first, prices of imported products rose because of supply shortages and failed transportation. But when the oil essential to fertilizer production became available again, the more than fourfold rise in oil prices skyrocketed the peasant's cost for the fertilizer that had mitigated hunger by enhancing the yield of small plots. This made the needed fertilizer inaccessible to many Mayas. Corn production on the small plots fell by about half, which quickly exacerbated the indigenous land shortage crisis that the use of cheap fertilizer had for some years partially masked. This shock, clearly felt in

1974–1975, corresponded with the initial surge in Catholic charismatic membership and with obvious expansion among Protestant-derived Pentecostals.

Governmental Incapacity

Guatemala's high population growth combined with government corruption, ethnic prejudice, and an inability to tax its internal economy continually undermined the government's efforts to provide and improve the public schools and medical services that might have given indigenes and the urban poor better access to the emerging global market economy. For many Mayas, immiserization increased each year as more families fell below the approximately 16 *cuerdas* per household (2.7 *cuerdas* per individual) required to sustain an average family of 5.86 individuals. Some moved to city slums. Some found non-agricultural work. Few found security or satisfaction. The government offered little help (Way 2012).

Globalization, Expanded Education, and the Diverging of Interests

Globalization during the 1970s destabilized the elite sector of the colonial control system in at least three ways. First, the children of elites increasingly acquired international educations and contacts, which provided alternate routes to a means of support. This made absolute social compliance with the networks involved in military and governmental control of the population in the country less attractive and less compulsory. With globalization, elites generated wealth by marketing export crops, importing global consumerism, and developing Guatemala's tourism assets, in addition to the traditional colonial method of controlling the extraction of wealth via government. These divergently funded elites invested their wealth in further industries, which provided attractive alternatives to participating in the existing political and land control structures. But the existence of such alternatives made it increasingly difficult for established elites to control people via political institutions and coercion.

Second, by the 1970s, the Ministry of Education had extended school systems throughout the country so that sixth-grade education became widely available (though not fully used) in the rural hamlets while ninth-grade educations (completion of *básico*) could be acquired in most municipal centers. Secondary education (completion of grades 10–12), however, was neither easily accessible nor

well done by the state, even by the 1990s, especially for the rural Mayas. University degrees and professions came within the reach of many Ladinos but could be accessed by only a few determined and rather lucky Mayas.

The autonomy of the national university system, however, worried state leaders. The military found political critique by students and faculty of the University of San Carlos to be threatening. Military leaders disliked the autonomous status of university funding; to them, the university seemed like a state-funded incubator of communism. So the state pursued a campaign of suppression and intimidation, murdering and disappearing faculty and student leaders who had been alienated by their knowledge of state atrocities perpetrated since the 1960s. More atrocities, however, led to more alienation; and more faculty and student alienation led to more military dissatisfaction and added repression.

Third, globalized communication systems made information about alternatives throughout the nation and the world available to Mayas. Radio, newspapers, television, movies, cell phones, and travel revealed a world of possibilities beyond the *municipio*, indeed, beyond Guatemala, and invited one to consume. In the broadened economy, people could experience the physical comforts and status-enhancing possibilities of consumerism. In short, elites' investment diversity and state education extension created popular dissatisfaction with continued governmental control and corrupt extraction. The colonial element of extraction-funded wealth, invested more diversely, worked against the colonial element of population control. That split the interests of the Guatemalan elites. At the same time, with Mayas' municipal autonomy penetrated by national institutions and expanded education, internal colonialism began to disintegrate. In Marx's framework, bourgeois marketing expansion and state penetration once again sundered the system of internal colonial control and extraction. The system of state-fostered, privately owned coffee capitalism held within itself the seeds of its own destruction. Guatemala teetered on the cusp.

Political Ineptitude and Corruption

Any sampling of Guatemala's newspapers from 1970 to 1978 reveals a nearly continuous string of articles and editorials suggesting that the sources of Guatemala's crisis lay in political ineptitude, corruption, and violence. Indeed, political leadership seemed so inept and corrupt that governance institutions seemed worthy of little more than a good laugh. Writing of the civil war and postwar periods, Diane Nelson (1999:416–417, 2009:130, 137–139, 142, 275, 347n5) elaborates on the importance of popular humor and political jokes in the macabre Guatemalan scene.

I, too, remember the frequent jokes that so many would tell with gusto and laughter between 1971 and 1979. Responding to the brutal violence in the late 1960s and reescalating violence in 1974, Guatemalan students cracked jokes that the workers going house to house to complete the 1974 national population census "were not counting how many of us there are in Guatemala, but how many are left!" Jokes about leaders' stupidity and ineptitude also circulated. Thus, regarding Lucas García, often maligned for lack of intelligence, a joke suggested that when asked by reporters about his favorite composer, Lucas García consulted on the sly his well-educated vice president, Francisco Villagrán Kramer, to learn the name of a composer. "Tell them 'Verdi,'" whispered the vice president and scholar. The president did. When the reporters then asked Lucas García, "Which of Verdi's compositions do you like best?" he thought, "I know the answer to that one without help!" So he replied without consulting his vice president: "My favorite Verdi composition is *Hapi Verdi tu yu, Hapi Verdi tu yu!*" sung to the American and now international "Happy Birthday" song. Almost daily, a piquant new joke would surge through elite and student networks. The jokes suggested that university students and many others had a very low level of confidence in their government's leadership in the mid- to late 1970s.

Obvious electoral corruption also clearly destabilized. Two fraudulent elections (1974 and 1978) indicated to Guatemalans that there was little possibility they might extricate themselves from the control regime peacefully and by democratic means. In 1974, Guatemalans tried to carry out a legitimate election. The best evidence available indicates that the leader of an opposition party, Colonel Efraín Ríos Montt, who later became Guatemala's president but was then a relative unknown, won the 1974 vote (Way 2012:142). I was a doctoral student in the Department of San Marcos and watched the election results with friends on the evening of March 3, 1974. Ríos Montt was ahead on the primitive vote-tally boards shown on local television when, late in the evening, the national broadcasts went blank. The next morning, newspapers announced that the party in power had surged ahead in the overnight count.

Many felt defrauded and excluded—none perhaps more so than Ríos Montt. Later, a political attaché at the US embassy in Guatemala told me that indeed Ríos Montt had won and that the announced result was a falsification. The captors of the election awarded Ríos Montt a consolation prize; they made him ambassador to Spain provided he play along and keep quiet. He did. But something no doubt was rubbed raw in Ríos Montt, for his rise to power, his electoral success, and his place in the army had collapsed. He had been excluded from the leadership club. For Ríos Montt, this experience of personal collapse and exclusion seems as relevant to his subsequent turn to Pentecostal Evangelical religion as the cultural collapse and systemic exclusion that propelled so many Mayas into Pentecostalism or Catholic Charismatic Renewal.

By 1977, on the eve of new elections, the new systems of communication, conflicted economic interests among elites, desperation among urban poor people, and cultural collapse among rural Mayas had brought the Guatemalan social system to a multifaceted crisis. Economically, culturally, socially, and politically, many Guatemalans stood at a tipping point, a critical juncture. They were frustrated with a government of fear. Control interests, however, still reigned. Unelected army officers governed the nation with terror because they feared that they might lose control of the country—their engine of exploitation and self-enrichment.

In this setting of corruption and collapse, one more event added substantially to the sense of loss of control: a major earthquake in 1976.

STATISTICAL ANALYSIS OF 1976 EARTHQUAKE DISRUPTION AS A THEORY OF PROTESTANT GROWTH

A number of scholars argue that the shock and disorganization of the February 1976 earthquake considerably accelerated the Protestantization of Guatemala. Without doubt, the quake hit Guatemalans hard. By rough counts as of early March 1976, the quake killed 22,868 and injured another 77,190 (Espinosa 1976:52). It is likely that additional injured died subsequently of their wounds but missed being included as killed in the early counts. The quake wrecked the physical infrastructure of many towns and villages, completely leveling all buildings in the towns of San Pedro Sacatepéquez in the Department of Guatemala, El Jícaro, Sumpango, Tecpán, and Gualán.

Plate 1. Corn towers over a Maya lass in Xekakixkan, an *aldea* now most closely affiliated with Antigua Santa Catarina Ixtahuacán. Courtesy of Winston K. Scott, 2003.

Plate 2. The agricultural patchwork of Nahualá's tree-denuded western mountainside and small-plot agriculture. Courtesy of Gilbert Bradshaw, 2003.

Plate 3. Women in Nahualá vending on a nonmarket day. Courtesy of John P. Hawkins, 2006.

Plate 4. Old men rest on a park bench in Nahualá. Courtesy of John P. Hawkins, 2006.

Plate 5. A Nahualense man fashions a metate. Courtesy of John P. Hawkins, 2006.

Plate 6. The Nahualá town center and the central Catholic church: the domed church (*left*); the mayoral offices in the double-colonnaded building facing the plaza (*partially behind and to right of church*); market buildings (*across plaza*); housing (*foreground*). Courtesy of John P. Hawkins, 2006.

Plate 7. The Antigua Santa Catarina Ixtahuacán town center, its central Catholic church, and the old, refurbished school used also as the municipal hall and market plaza (*left of the dome*). Courtesy of John P. Hawkins, 2006.

Plate 8. This image of Nueva Santa Catarina Ixtahuacán's housing and streets is typical of the town. Courtesy of John P. Hawkins, 2006.

Plate 9. Alcaldes and *martomuyib'* of Santa Catarina Ixtahuacán in their ceremonial dress. Courtesy of David Radtke, 1985.

Plate 10. Chuchuxelib' of Santa Catarina Ixtahuacán in their ceremonial dress. Courtesy of David Radtke, 1985.

Plate 11. Tambor (drum) and *chirimía* (reed flute) players in Santa Catarina Ixtahuacán. Courtesy of David Radtke, 1985.

Plate 12. Marimba band hired from the *municipio* of Cantel, Department of Quetzaltenango. Cantel used to be on the old footpath leading from Santa Catarina Ixtahuacán to the *municipio* of Quetzaltenango. Courtesy of David Radtke, 1985.

Plate 13. Hanging of San Simón during Holy Week. Courtesy of David Radtke, 1985.

Plate 14. A young man sounds the *k'erk'er* bell substitute during Holy Week. Courtesy of David Radtke, 1985.

Plate 15. Church bells hung with strings of *k'exwäch* flowers during Todos Santos. Courtesy of David Radtke, 1985.

Plate 16. Procession through the arches during Holy Week. Courtesy of David Radtke, 1985.

Plate 17. Ch'i'p Catalina image in a procession during the *feria*. Courtesy of David Radtke, 1985.

Plate 18. Dancers impersonating *mexicanos* in Santa Catarina Ixtahuacán. Courtesy of David Radtke, 1985.

Plate 19. The high altar in Tix's chapel next to his home. The candles in the immediate foreground stand on the edge of the second altar, which represents the surface of the world. Courtesy of Winston K. Scott, 2003.

Plate 20. Traditionalists conduct a ceremony. Courtesy of Frederick H. Hanselmann, 2003.

Plate 21. Colored candles laid out for use in a neotraditionalist ritual. The plastic bags at the center contain copal. Courtesy of Frederick H. Hanselmann, 2003.

Plate 21. Colored candles laid out for use in a neotraditionalist ritual. The plastic bags at the center contain copal. Courtesy of Frederick H. Hanselmann, 2003.

Plate 22. A traditionalist leader pours an alcohol libation. Courtesy of Frederick H. Hanselmann, 2003.

Plate 23. Culto in a Pentecostal church: stacked speakers to left and right of dais, a pastoral mural, the minister preaching near the podium, women and men sitting generally apart. Courtesy of Jennifer Pleasy Philbrick Wayas, 2003.

Plate 24. Band and singers in a Pentecostal church behind a man offering a testimonial from the podium. Courtesy of Jennifer Pleasy Philbrick Wayas, 2003.

Plate 25. The Pentecostal church in Nueva Santa Catarina Ixtahuacán that one author attended. Courtesy of Amelia Sisco Thompson, 2003.

Plate 26. A Pentecostal church exterior. Note the prominent name board and plain modernist design. Courtesy of Adriana Smith, 2003.

Plate 27. A Pentecostal church's interior mural and seating. Courtesy of Adriana Smith, 2003.

Plate 28. Culto in a charismatic Catholic congregation. Note the large speakers to the left and right of the dais. In the deep background is an altar similar to that used in the Ortho mass. Courtesy of Gilbert Bradshaw, 2003.

Plate 29. The altar and crucifix in a charismatic church are positioned similarly to their use in the Ortho mass. *Left*, the local congregational pastor at the altar. Courtesy of Gilbert Bradshaw, 2003.

Plate 30. A panoramic view of Nahualá, where housing occupies much of the arable land. Note the evergreen trees pruned for firewood, leaving only the tops. Courtesy of John P. Hawkins.

Plate 31. Altar structure in the Ortho-Catholic church in Nahualá. The high altar is against the back wall; the middle altar (sacrament table) is used by the living; and candles burn on the lower altar in front of the banister dividing congregational seating from the ritual performance area. Courtesy of John P. Hawkins.

Plate 32. A Pentecostal chapel on Nahualá's periphery (*left background in front of cemetery*). Courtesy of John P. Hawkins.

Plate 33. A Pentecostal chapel on Nueva Ixtahuacán's periphery (*left*). Courtesy of John P. Hawkins.

Also hit hard were Guatemala City, where "88,404 houses were destroyed and 434,934 people [were] left homeless in the Department of Guatemala" and "about one-half that number in the Department of Chimaltenango" (Espinosa 1976:2; see also Espinosa, Husid, and Quesada 1976:52). The quake destroyed 254,750 homes throughout the country and rendered approximately 1.07 million people homeless out of a total population of 3.21 million in the affected departments that Espinosa and colleagues surveyed, causing more than a billion dollars of property damage (Espinosa, Husid, and Quesada 1976:52; data reproduced in table 19.1).

Garrard-Burnett (1998:120–137) argues that the massive dislocations of the quake and the significantly faster and greater aid response by Protestants of all types, compared to the Catholic aid response, triggered an accelerated rate of Pentecostal conversions. I do not believe, however, that the conclusion regarding accelerated Christian Pentecostalization due to disorganization and misery follows from the data regarding deaths, injuries, or destruction of infrastructure, although it is an interesting hypothesis. I suggest that the rise in Christian Pentecostalization as a percentage of the country's population in the period following the quake derived rather from the increased aid, a form of gifting behavior, induced by the occasion of the quake.

Pentecostal mission groups seem to have responded more quickly and in greater quantity than the bureaucratic Catholics, although I could not find figures on donation quantities. Quake aid from religious organizations would have been perceived to be a gift, a godsend. But gifts entail unstated obligations, especially in a covenantal and patrón-oriented social system. Thus, Garrard-Burnett (1998:120–125) is correct in highlighting the impact of differential aid response rates of the religious organizations. She notes that Protestants (actually Pentecostals) responded quickly and nimbly; Catholics did not. If in fact there was a relatively higher amount of Pentecostal or mainline Protestant relief aid and relief interaction following the quake, compared to Catholic efforts, one must grant that the surge in Pentecostal membership derived not from the fear and experience of destruction during the quake and the suffering after, but from the reciprocity power of the gifts distributed by religiously identified groups following the quake.

Although Garrard-Burnett is correct as to the impact of increased aid, she and other scholars are incorrect in placing so much significance on the shock of the destruction.

What is my evidence for this assertion? In the first place, Protestantization—which by 1975 was primarily pentecostalization—had been well under way and considerably accelerated long before the quake. I have already demonstrated that during the more than sixty years prior to the quake, Protestants/Pentecostals experienced greater than 8 percent per annum growth, against a 1–3 percent annual national population growth.

Moreover, there is no statistically significant correlation between quake deaths or injuries and the available proxies for Protestant/Pentecostal membership after the quake. Here I face a bit of a problem. It would have been nice if the Guatemalan government had continued asking about religious affiliation after 1964 in its census every ten years or so. But it did not. On the other hand, one cannot depend on Protestant/Pentecostal/evangélico figures for growth, because each denomination computed its growth according to different measures, because church growth was affected by splits, and because, as Gooren (2010) shows, each denomination's growth came in waves, and the waves did not coincide. So, phenomenal growth in any one denomination does not transfer to all Protestantism or Pentecostalism in Guatemala. For the decade of the 1980s, the only proxy for evangélico membership I have found is the Directorio de Iglesias, Organizaciones y Ministerios del Movimiento Protestante, Guatemala, in which a Guatemalan Evangelical interdenominational agency attempted to list all evangélico congregations by department and municipio, presumably as of 1980 (IINDEF and SEPAL 1981).

Using this listing of congregations by municipio and department, I find no correlation with the recorded percentage of infrastructural damage per department or with the number of Evangelical congregations in 1980, whether absolute number of congregations per department or number of congregations per capita per department. The data from the 1976 quake given in table 19.1, when processed in the Statistical Package for Social Sciences by Pearson correlation, reveal that death, injury, and infrastructural damage, or an index of these three, simply do not correlate with the per capita distribution by department of Evangelical congregations in 1980. In fact, Evangelical membership tended to grow more where the quake hit least.

In 1995, the government health services conducted a survey of health conditions that included a question on religious affiliation (INE and MSPAS 1999; religion data in Johnson and Grim 2020). This survey lumped several

TABLE 19.1. QUAKE DAMAGE IN 1976 AND PROTESTANT CONGREGATIONS IN 1981

DEPARTMENT[a]	POPULATION, 1976[b]	DEATHS FROM QUAKE	QUAKE DEATHS AS % OF DEPARTMENT POPULATION	INJURIES FROM QUAKE	QUAKE INJURIES AS % OF DEPARTMENT POPULATION	% OF STRUCTURES DAMAGED BY QUAKE	# PROTESTANT CONGREGA- TIONS, 1981	PROTESTANT CONGREGATIONS PER CAPITA, 1981
Alta Verapaz	295,424	18	0.006	953	0.323	67.50	213	0.0006615
Baja Verapaz	110,132	152	0.138	718	0.652	82.50	34	0.0002941
Chimaltenango	207,324	13,754	6.634	32,392	15.624	88.00	221	0.0009606
Chiquimula	162,100	50	0.031	378	0.233	50.00	78	0.0004619
El Progreso	76,056	2,028	2.666	7,767	10.212	90.43	69	0.0008499
Guatemala	1,180,171	3,370	0.286	16,549	1.402	68.82	684	0.0005217
Huehuetenango	391,011	10	0.003	50	0.013	n.a.	346	0.0008021
Izabal	178,732	73	0.041	379	0.212	40.00	306	0.0015723
Jalapa	124,529	91	0.073	473	0.380	31.67	111	0.0008156
Jutiapa	239,800	13	0.005	48	0.020	10.00	234	0.0009320
Quetzaltenango	332,127	14	0.004	228	0.069	1.00	373	0.0010165
Quiché	309,385	843	0.272	5,722	1.849	73.00	235	0.0007161
Sacatepéquez	107,456	1,582	1.472	8,855	8.241	71.00	69	0.0005697
Santa Rosa	183,342	40	0.022	291	0.159	1.60	118	0.0006077
Sololá	136,773	110	0.080	300	0.219	10.00	129	0.0008363
Totonicapán	180,003	27	0.015	89	0.049	34.00	85	0.0004158
Zacapa	109,364	693	0.634	1,998	1.827	72.86	179	0.0015469

Notes: [a] These are the only departments for which Espinosa, Husid, and Quesada 1976 provide death, injury, and infrastructure damage data.

[b] Calculated using the compound annual growth rate of each department between 1973 and 1981.

Sources: Dirección General de Estadística 1974, 1982b (populations and congregations per capita); Espinosa, Husid, and Quesada 1976 (deaths, injuries, and infrastructure damage); IINDEF and SEPAL 1981 (congregations and congregations per capita).

departments into regions, for which we have data on religion. By combining my department data on earthquake destruction into the same regions, one can then make rather accurate statistical correlations with 1995 membership and 1976 death and destruction data. There is no statistical correlation by region in Guatemala between deaths, injuries, or percentage of infrastructure damaged by the 1976 quake and the number of *evangélicos* surveyed by region and then used to estimate total Protestant/ Pentecostal membership in those regions (and in the country) in 1995.[9] With no correlation or a negative correlation between either the 1980 proxy for membership by congregation or the 1995 survey of membership, we must therefore discard the theory that Pentecostal/Protestant

growth substantially derived from quake disruption and destruction.

The tallies of death and dislocation attributed to each department caused by Guatemala's 1976 earthquake do not correlate positively or at a statistically significant level with religious affiliation or religious change toward Protestantism in any period for which we have religious affiliation data. The relationship claimed intuitively by some observers that the quake's disruptions pushed conversion to Protestantism (mostly in its Pentecostal forms) simply is not in the data. What is in the data are the corn, land, and other resource correlations with Pentecostalism, as shown in chapter 17.

In sum, the quake inclined North American Protestants

and Pentecostals to send aid. Increased aid—viewed culturally as gifts—attracted members bound by notions of covenant reciprocity, but not in relation to the differing degrees of local destruction. The binding implications of the gifts (Checketts 2005:183–187; Early 2012:19–20), rather than the accumulated despair of the quake, made the difference. Thus, Garrard-Burnett seems correct as to the second half of her hypothesis that Pentecostals' speed of gift giving, close contact, and quantity of aid triggered a surge of conversions, but she and others are not correct that the destruction and misery per se triggered more rapid Protestantization.[10]

So, there is no correlation of the earthquake damage with Protestantization or Pentecostalization. What correlation might there be with Catholic charismaticization? Unfortunately, I have not found any survey or census that distinguishes *carismáticos* from Ortho-Catholics in Guatemala, either in total or by department or *municipio*. Thus I must interpret without the benefit of statistical inference regarding the timing of the charismatic movement's florescence relative to the received theories—mere speculations actually—that earthquake and war lie at the root of the thrust toward Christian Pentecostalization. As I did with the Pentecostal materials, here I deal with the inferences regarding the earthquake and charismaticization of Ortho-Catholicism; in the next chapter I take on the issues of charismaticism and the war.

First, the Christian Pentecostalizing changes burst into being and started to rush through Catholic Guatemala and the *municipios* of Nahualá and Santa Catarina Ixtahuacán in 1973–1975, well before the disruptions of the 1976 earthquake. Subsequently, charismaticism expanded rapidly throughout Guatemala in areas little affected by the quake as well as in areas heavily affected.[11] Thus, the disruptions of the quake seem not a good explanation for the expansion of either branch of spirited religious ecstaticism.

Durkheim (2001[1912]:323) early suggested that religion expresses in symbols the nature of the society and universe in which a people live: "Religion . . . is not only a system of practices, it is also a system of ideas whose purpose is to express the world; we have seen that even the most humble religions"—today we should understand this as *all* religions—"have their cosmology." I have shown that in Guatemala, both Pentecostalism and charismaticism, which I class together as Christian Pentecostalism, have been highly expressive of the chaos, clangor, and fear of subsistence insecurity and the despair of cultural collapse and exclusion. Christian Pentecostalism does indeed express the nature of "the world" as it is experienced by these Mayas, for they live in a chaotic, dangerous, anxiety-producing world made intolerable by the experience of corn culture collapse. In that sense, Christian Pentecostalism, in expressing angst and defining the nature of the world, does indeed embody a cosmology—and a rather sophisticated and accurate one at that.

I turn now to a detailed analysis of the war, its unconscionable brutality, and the supposed effect of that brutality and chaos on Protestant/Pentecostal and Catholic charismatic membership expansion.

NOTES

1. The one civilian-elected exception, Julio César Méndez Montenegro (president from 1966–1970), is widely regarded as having been highly responsive to military control. In short, Montenegro was a puppet of the military. "What lay ahead was a thirty-two-year succession of coups, juntas, civilian-military pacts, and rigged elections as the country became ever more embroiled in counterinsurgency war. From 1954 to 1986, only one president would hail from outside the army high command, and Guatemala would earn its reputation as a 'garrison state'" (Way 2012:69). See also Black 1984 and Schirmer 1998.

2. Garrard-Burnett 2010:60 portrays this spike best in an elegant graph.

3. So far as I am aware, the only place preserving the 1995 religion data gathered by INE and MSPAS is the *World Religion Database* (Johnson and Grim 2020).

4. Sarasa (1991) treats the following topics: Protestants as beneficiaries of North American financing (36–37); the spread of Protestantism as a mechanism of US foreign policy advancement (36–37); Protestants passing useful information to the CIA in exchange for CIA financing (103); Protestantism as a mechanism for spreading "North American individualistic liberalism" (91); and the *invasión religiosa* and *invasión de sectas* (49–50, 54). On the cultural fusion between Catholicism and national identity, I quote: "There exists today an almost Machiavel[l]ian plan to usurp Catholicism from its first place in Guatemala, taking advantage of the great simplicity of its inhabitants which, by the inheritance of two peoples, [who are] extremely [*sumamente*, also translatable as 'above all'] religious, all their life and their activities are linked directly to God." The text then bolds the heading "Guatemalan Identity Threatened," and then continues, "It has taken [*ha costado* is rather stronger than 'It has taken' or, literally, 'It cost.' Perhaps 'It exacted' is closer to the mood] almost 500 years

of catechism to instill the bases of Guatemalan identity, customs [*costumbres*, but note that when used in the singular by a Maya, *costumbre* connotes distinctly Maya traditionalist religious activity], traditions, geographic names, patron saints' festivals, prayers, commemorations, names, celebrations, etc.; to try now to produce a change that destroys all this cultural, religious, and social treasure is a direct and premeditated attack against the integrity of Guatemalan nationality. . . . This is a treacherous, unjust, and irresponsible process. It would constitute the downfall of Guatemala, of its identity" (Sarasa 1991:50, with more of the same on 51).

5.   I have argued that this social force is cultural collapse and systemic exclusion. On why this force should appear among university-educated and apparently middle-class US Catholics in 1967—people in a time and place hardly appearing to be in collapse or exclusion—I invite the reader to suspend judgment until the concluding chapter. There I explore the perception of personal and systemic risk of collapse in increasingly complicated high-speed techno-economies and the experience by many of exclusion therefrom.

6.   The parallels are widely recognized. For the United States, see Mühlen 1975:108; and similar references throughout the essays in McDonnell 1975. Of the charismatics in Nicaragua, Gooren (2012:198) says: "All of these methods [i.e., charismatic ritual practices and social procedures] were directly copied from Pentecostal churches and they were quite successful."

7.   In some ways, the nuns who fostered the infusion of charismaticism into Nahualá and Santa Catarina were just as marginal in a church run by a male hierarchy as were the Mayas receiving the faith. The American priest in Santa Catarina Ixtahuacán was unusual in rather wholeheartedly supporting charismatic innovations, in spite of his fears and reservations regarding the problems that revelatory enthusiasm might bring.

8.   Pastor (1998:15–16, 18, 21–24) describes similar reticence in Argentina's mid-level Catholic hierarchy, which was eventually overcome by episcopal and, later, papal approbation (Thigpen 2003:464–465).

9.   Espinosa 1976 gives no figures for deaths, injuries, or infrastructural damage for five departments that were relatively undamaged, and no infrastructure damage figure for Huehuetenango. These are treated as missing values and not used in the calculation of correlations on these variables.

10.   Here is a challenge for future research. My theory would predict more Protestant/Pentecostal conversions where there was more aid, regardless of the amount of destruction. Nevertheless, I recognize that quake destruction creates immiserization and hastens cultural collapse. I have not been able to find data on amounts of aid by department by religious source of the aid. But I would predict that religiously tied aid, as a proxy of gift giving, better correlates with Protestantization/Pentecostalization than does any quantitative measure or index of deaths, injury, or destruction. Here again, I try to make a clear Popper-style prediction as a test, based on the theory, anticipating that someone more diligent than I can find relevant data in some archive somewhere to challenge or confirm the hypotheses.

11.   I have found no data series that would enable one to separate and analyze statistically charismatic Catholics from other Catholics at different time periods or in different departments.

Chapter Twenty

Cachexy

Religious Movements during Brutal War, 1979–1996

JOHN P. HAWKINS

IN A PRESCIENT ANALYSIS OF society, violence, religion, and change, Durkheim (2001[1912]:158) makes these observations:

In certain historical periods, under the influence of some great collective upheaval, social interactions become more frequent and more active. Individuals seek each other out and assemble more often. The result is a general effervescence characteristic of revolutionary or creative epochs. Now this hyperactivity has the effect of generally stimulating individual energies. People live differently and more intensely than in normal times. The changes are not only those of nuance and degree: man himself becomes other. He is moved by passions so intense that they can be assuaged only by violent, extreme acts of superhuman heroism or bloody barbarism. This explains the Crusades, for example, and so many sublime or savage moments during the French Revolution. Under the influence of general exaltation, the most mediocre and inoffensive burgher is transformed into a hero or an executioner. And all these mental processes are so clearly those at the root of religion that individuals themselves often represent this pressure in an explicitly religious form.

In this chapter I look at issues of violence and religion in Guatemala. From 1979 to 1986, Guatemala tore itself and its citizens apart in a wrenchingly ferocious escalation of its violent counterinsurgency war. Why did Guatemalans shred their society during this period, and what were the religious correlates of the process? In the previous chapter, I explored a number of factors that were destabilizing Guatemala, driving it toward the condition of a failed state. Perhaps a corrupt election triggered the final cascade toward violence.

In the election campaign of 1978, the government staged a repeat of the 1974 stolen election. Two falsified elections in a row drove the moderate center and the often left-leaning students to despair of democracy. University students and others formed clandestine cells and began to resist the patently fraudulent continuance of government control, extraction, and intimidation. The elite beneficiaries of the control regime, conversely, made desperate, grasping efforts to retain hold of their lucrative extractive engine—an internally colonized country (Aguirre Beltrán 1967). Elites tried to keep control by escalating the use of force, intimidation, kidnapping, and torture. They terrorized their compatriots with a special focus on controlling the indigenous peoples by, on occasion, murdering men, raping women, and killing children in front of their parents. Ethnocide and consequent fear ran rampant. In retrospect, state brutality and death squads proved to be the elite's last guttering efforts to keep control of a system undergoing collapse.

But what was the logic of this spasm of violence, this state of cachexy, defined by the *Oxford English Dictionary* as a "depraved condition . . . of a body politic"? In some ways, the 1981–1983 upsurge in state violence mimicked (in its escalated investment in violence aimed at control) the final pre-collapse surge of *cofradía* costs and showy behavior as the *cofradía* system went into decline. In the *cofradía* case, the escalation in ritual investment constituted a final exertion to prove the premises that the gods could be influenced by gifting so as to restore respect for gerontocratic control in the Maya village. Similarly, in the political domain, by increasing the frequency and virulence of state violence against indigenes and upping its brutality, elite actors attempted to prove the premises of colonial control and restore their place in the internal colony. Thus, three forms of social excess responded to the failure of the corn culture. *Cofradía* leaders mobilized excessive offerings to placate the gods; insurgent rebels strove to topple entrenched powers by insurrection; and state leaders fomented excessive violence to maintain control and extraction. Each group responded in parallel according to its perception that social conditions were in fact in collapse. One might even argue that *cofradía* adjustments, insurrection, and governmental repression mimicked excessive Maya local investment and that "milpa-logic" was not a premise of ordinary Maya culture but a last desperate attempt to make indigenous culture work by pouring excessive labor into what little land was left. In this reading, *milpa* logic is an overresponse to current ongoing collapse rather than a bedrock premise of indigeneity, as Annis suggests.

Having outlined the logic of *cofradía* escalation previously, here I examine the parallel logics of increasing violence and terrorizing fear entailed in both government ethnocide and insurgent insurrection.

INVERSION, SUBVERSION, INSURRECTION, AND ETHNOCIDE

To both Marxists and Guatemalan elites, being indigenous meant being poor and miserable. To the Marxists, that meant Mayas were exploited. According to Marxist premises, an increasingly immiserated and exploited population ought to rebel. Marxist insurgent operatives and Marxist military elements tried to mobilize indigenous people in peripheral areas, feeling them susceptible to the call for revolution. Thus, to the Ladinos in control of the government, all of whom presumably understood the Marxist logic, being indigenous equated with being "subversive." Governmental and other conservative elements losing control thus sought to exterminate indigenous people. Using a nonmaterialist approach, I have argued elsewhere (Hawkins 1984) that from the Ladino perspective, being indigenous also equated with being the inverse of the social characteristics and ideologies of Guatemalan Ladino and Euro elites, and vice versa, and this notion of mutually expected inversion added to or culturally confirmed the Ladino logic of indigenes being subversive.

To Guatemalan army leaders, Mayas were the irrationally feared cultural "other," the inverse of human. Therefore, whenever Ladino control was under threat or unstable, the culturally built-in notion of indigenous inverseness suggested the solution: Mayas should be exterminated. Guatemalan elites reacted to internal insurrection (no matter the source, some internal and locally generated, some externally instigated) by crushing indigenes and indigeneity. The result: a spike in violence, which can be seen with remarkable clarity in Virginia Garrard-Burnett's (2010:60) graph of violence frequency in Guatemala. The Guatemalan state fostered brutality, including more than 600 instances of state-perpetrated mass murder, much of it directed against indigenes.

In short, the Guatemalan army and the national police deployed unmitigated, savage methods designed to terrorize the entire population into submission and to exterminate actual, suspected, or simply accused leaders. The reality of any offense did not matter. In the environment of local recrimination and vendetta, a well-placed whisper could get a business competitor or an unwanted suitor conveniently disappeared at no obvious cost. In addition, rape of indigenous women became a condoned state weapon in the government's war to wipe out the indigenous others' supposed purity and therefore their existence (Way 2012:201). Army units and hired thugs attacked all members of protesting, complaining, or activist groups, including students, university professors, urban labor union leaders, Catholic Action leaders, activist priests, and local indigenous development promoters seeking to improve their hamlets. "From the army's point of view, the enemy became not just the guerrillas and their civilian supporters but, eventually, social organization itself"; literally, they "ripped up the social fabric" (Annis 1987:6–7).

But what does this sordid political history have to do with religion? By attacking Maya traditionalists, Ortho-Catholics, and Pentecostals alike, the army made war on the changing "idea which society" was beginning to "have of itself," for those changing ideas implied a loss of Ladino control. These transformations in the idea system were being developed, articulated, and most clearly enacted in the new Christian Pentecostal religions. In Pentecostal and charismatic logic, all society in the Guatemalan setting was corrupt and "worldly," given to abuse of power and the pillage of others. This was indeed revolutionary because it embodied in religion an idea already arrived at by insurrectionists, intellectuals, and university students: society was irredeemably corrupt and in need of change. But now the idea was embraced and incorporated as ritual in the new religions. The idea that a people had of the nature of "society itself"—that Guatemalan society was corrupt—had become sacred.

The difference between Pentecostals and insurrectionists is that Pentecostals and the growing number of charismatic Catholics felt the society could be reformed by peaceful, voluntary, individual ethical change through conversion by the Holy Spirit, one by one. Fed up by past electoral deception, Guatemalans participating in the insurrection chose violence. Somewhere between these two extremes, members of Catholic Action, unionists, and others believed the society could be reformed by protest, confrontation, or disruption of institutions.

There exist some rather horrifying and sobering numeric tallies that measure somewhat the depredations, human suffering, and horrors of the counterinsurgency war. These were consolidated in two attempts to document the atrocities of the war in an effort to bring about reconciliation (Arzobispado de Guatemala 1998; CEH 1999). In these sources one can read the heartrending stories of individuals persecuted. One can also determine something of the volume of violence through the tallies of the massacres by department, deaths by department, and incidents of intimidation by department, per table 20.1.

ETHNOGRAPHIC ANALYSIS OF THE THEORY OF PENTECOSTALISM AS PROTECTIVE COLORATION

In this frenzy of violence, some scholars have argued, the government persecuted Ortho-Catholics more than Protestants because the Catholic Church's turn toward social justice, its preferential option for the poor, and the Catholic effort to confront and break down the institutional structures that maintained poverty and misery made the Catholic leaders, organization, and members a direct threat to elite power. Catholics were indeed persecuted, especially the leadership of Catholic-related organizations intent on securing social justice, including the heads of labor and social unions birthed with Catholic nurturance (such as the Comité de Unidad Campesina), members of Catholic Action, activist priests and bishops, and members of the archbishop of Guatemala's senior staff (Falla 1994:24–30). The argument has been made that such persecution would have made conversion to Protestantism (or the external appearance of conversion) protective and

therefore attractive and thus helps account for Protestant increases (Green 1999:150; Garrard-Burnett 2010:135–136; Stoll 1990:193–203).

Green (1993:161) is particularly clear on this: "Evangelical churches had been growing steadily but unspectacularly for decades when, in the 1980s, the murder of a dozen Catholic priests and hundreds, perhaps thousands, of lay leaders sent a flood of Catholics into evangelical meetings as a haven from repression." She gives details on the village she studied. Before the war, it consisted of 700 "mostly (if only nominally) Catholic. . . . Today there are three hundred people, and all refer to themselves as *evangélicos.*"

The argument that conversion (or the appearance thereof) to Protestantism was protective and that the violence sped conversion rates may well be right, but it is difficult to prove. In part, the notion that conversion to Pentecostalism or Protestantism was protective is problematic because the literature records that the Guatemalan army also attacked, kidnapped, and murdered scores of Pentecostals (Green 1999:186n3; Guzaro and McComb 2010). The army also explicitly attacked Maya Catholic traditionalist shamans.

Falla (1994), who served as a Catholic priest in a war-devastated zone, describes the government's simultaneous persecution of both Catholics and *evangélicos.* Indeed, he affirms that the army attacked all religious systems that held people together or organized them in any way. Traditionalist leaders were executed. So were some Evangelical pastors and leaders (Guzaro and McComb 2010). I suspect that the army attacked all strands of religion because of Durkheim's view that religion embodies and promulgates the idea that a society's members have of themselves. The army suppressed religion in general because organization emerging from religion enabled more effective resistance. As Falla (1994:188, emphases added) puts it, "The army restricted and infiltrated the religious ceremonies, deceived the leaders of the [Catholic] Church, and threatened its members. It killed catechists and *massacred religious groups*, surrounding them during church services and burning them in their temples, *particularly in Evangelical chapels.* The army considered . . . religious activities . . . a screen that fomented subversion." Falla's use of the word "temples" suggests attacks against Protestant or Pentecostal congregations because in Guatemalan Spanish and cultural usage, the word *templo* is used primarily to refer to *evangélico* church buildings. Both the army and the guerrillas applied pressures

DEPARTMENT	POPULATION TOTAL, 1981	MASSACRES TO 1980	MASSACRES TO 1981	MASSACRES TO 1996	# VICTIMS OF RIGHTS VIOLATIONS	# INCIDENTS OF HUMAN RIGHTS VIOLATION	CEH MASSACRE TALLY	% OF RIGHTS VIOLATIONS PER DEPARTMENT	# PROTESTANT CONGREGA-TIONS, 1981	CONGREGATIONS PER CAPITA, 1981
Alta Verapaz	322,008	21	31	63	6,485	2,691	61	9.45	213	0.0006615
Baja Verapaz	115,602	0	4	16	2,799	724	28	4.54	34	0.0002941
Chimaltenango	230,059	2	4	9	332	143	70	6.72	221	0.0009606
Chiquimula	168,863	0	1	1	43	28	8	0.48	78	0.0004619
El Progreso	81,188	0	0	0	38	18	0	0.01	69	0.0008499
Escuintla	334,666	0	0	0	108	78	3	1.03	322	0.0009622
Guatemala	1,311,192	1	1	1	421	234	3	2.74	684	0.0005217
Huehuetenango	431,343	6	22	42	4,776	1,197	88	15.6	346	0.0008021
Izabal	194,618	0	0	1	943	434	3	1.45	306	0.0015723
Jalapa	136,091	0	0	0	0	0	0	0.01	111	0.0008156
Jutiapa	251,068	0	0	0	17	18	0	0.02	234	0.0009320
Petén	131,927	1	4	10	2,099	809	13	3.09	265	0.0020087
Quetzaltenango	366,949	0	1	2	595	439	5	1.92	373	0.0010165
Quiché	328,175	47	109	263	28,806	6,545	344	45.52	235	0.0007161
Retalhuleu	150,923	0	0	0	29	29	1	0.17	117	0.0007752
Sacatepéquez	121,127	0	0	0	3	3	0	0.05	69	0.0005697
San Marcos	472,326	3	7	12	2,718	501	15	2.89	470	0.0009951
Santa Rosa	194,168	0	0	0	6	5	0	0.12	118	0.0006077
Sololá	154,249	0	0	0	46	31	6	2.22	129	0.0008363
Suchitepéquez	237,554	0	0	0	27	14		0.97	223	0.0009387
Totonicapán	204,419	0	0	0	136	103	1	0.55	85	0.0004158
Zacapa	115,712	0	0	0	177	34	1	0.47	179	0.0015469

Sources: Dirección General de Estadística 1982b; Arzobispado de Guatemala 1998; CEH 1999; IINDEF and SEPAL 1981.

designed to induce people to leave all religions, be they traditional, Catholic, Mormon, sedate Protestant, or Protestant Pentecostal (Guzaro and McComb 2010; Samson 2007:37–38).

Locally in Nahualá and Santa Catarina Ixtahuacán, 1973–1975 (beginning with the effective start-up date of Pentecostal expansion through the actual start-up date of Catholic charismatics) was a period of relative peace in these two *municipios*. Protective coloration was hardly needed during peace. Moreover, across the country, the depredations and fears of war had little to do with the surge in numbers of Pentecostals from the 1950s to the 1970s or the start-up of charismatic Catholicism in 1973–1975 and its subsequent rapid florescence. Nevertheless, war, violence, and previous quake disruption in other parts of the country likely were seen by many local Pentecostals as confirming the millennial ideology of collapse embedded in much Pentecostal preaching.

Perhaps the only way to convincingly test the theory that conversion to Protestantism provided protection from state violence would be to determine statistically if Pentecostals or Protestants, as a percentage of the population, suffered more or fewer atrocities than their percentage representation in the population compared to the Catholic percentage of the population. Unfortunately, the two massive archives of data on war atrocities (Arzobispado de Guatemala 1998; CEH 1999) do not record the religious affiliation of the aggrieved, and I find no evidence in the authors' statements of methodology that they systematically or even occasionally asked questions regarding the religion of those interviewed.[1] Perhaps we will never have the data needed to prove or disprove the speculation on the protective coloration offered by Protestantism.

What we do know is that *orejas* (literally, "ears"; government spies, paid informants) lived among the population and reported suspicious people to army commanders. Any Catholic could denounce an *evangélico* to an *oreja* for any reason, and vice versa. Any businessman or jilted lover could likewise denounce the object of their disdain. When citizens or *orejas* reported their intimations, whether well founded or not, to higher authorities, death squads followed in the night. That threat destroyed community trust, which, of course, was the military goal. This rendered any sense of organization, any hope for change, any sense of trust in anything but the military very dangerous indeed. So why

did Christian Pentecostalism—in both its Protestant and Catholic varieties—prosper during insurrection when Ortho-Catholicism did not? My suspicion is that it did so not because it provided protective coloration (although it might have to a degree), but because Christian Pentecostal worship styles better and more openly expressed the cachexy in which people found themselves due to cultural and economic collapse and exclusion now exacerbated by war, and because of legitimate fears they might be targeted anywhere in the country because of their ethnicity, poverty, or resistance based on religious or ethical principles.

STATISTICAL ANALYSIS OF GUATEMALAN POLITICAL VIOLENCE AS A THEORY OF PENTECOSTAL CONVERSION, 1979–1986

I now examine statistically the war theory of Pentecostal expansion, paying attention to violence levels and the academic presumption that war's disorganization and people's fear of violence pushed up Pentecostal conversion rates. The atrocities were many and ghastly, and the task of documenting the war's horrors has already been done well by many (Arzobispado de Guatemala 1998; CEH 1999; Falla 1994; Schirmer 1998; Green 1999; Perera 1993). What matters here is that one of the theories about religious change in Guatemala attributes much of the rise of Protestant Pentecostalism directly to the disruptions and terrors of the war (Stoll 1990:193–203; Green 1999:150; Garrard-Burnett 2010:135–136). Even Gooren's (2015) multifaceted and careful exploration of "internal and external" factors points to war and quake as central contributors to Protestant expansion. In an earlier work, Gooren (2001:184–186, esp. 186n36, 189–192) offers a more complex analysis of general social anomie, but he emphasizes the scholarship on war and earthquake contributing to Protestantization during the 1980s .

Although Green subscribes to the war explanation for the Pentecostal surge, to her credit she identifies data that challenge the war theory. She notes the anthropological documentation of significant Protestantization "prior to the onset of political violence" (Green 1993:161 and, especially, 177n7). She points out that the violence theory also "does not explain ongoing [i.e., postwar] participation" (Green 1993:162). Finally, she observes that the highest rate of Protestant growth (2286 percent, she asserts, but gives no reference or time span for the increase) took place in the Department of Totonicapán, "which sustained relatively little violence." (Totonicapán borders on both Santa Catarina Ixtahuacán and Nahualá, which also experienced relatively little violence.) By contrast, in the Department of El Quiché, "the hardest hit by the war," the "number of [Protestant/Pentecostal] congregations declined by 8.6 percent" (Green 1993:177n8). These statements by Green suggest one should be cautious about the war and violence hypothesis for Protestant expansion.

By comparing data on the war's violence by department (easily gleaned from the memorializations of the war mentioned above), I find that the explanation that attributes the Protestant upturn to the disruptions of war suffers the same two difficulties as the quake-based explanation. In the first place, the turn to Pentecostalism occurred well before the war. Membership numbers indicate that the highest sustained compound annual rates of conversion occurred between 1950 and 1964. This preceded considerably the most savage war violence (November 1981 to November 1982, as seen in Garrard-Burnett's graph [2010:60]), the earthquake (1976), and most of even the longest estimates—thirty-six years—of simmering insurgency and counterinsurgency (1960–1996).

In the second place, the most heavily assaulted regions of the country differed from those where Pentecostals had the most success both in 1981, for which we have data on the number of *evangélico* congregations by department, and in 1995, for which we have a massive government survey. No positive statistical correlations exist between Protestant membership by department as expressed by the 1981 list of congregations, calculating congregations per capita (or what amounts to the same thing, people per congregation), and CEH's reports by department of the war's ravages: massacres, total deaths, or total reported incidents of intimidation. Nor is there a positive correlation with any index composed by summing any combination of these measures and either Evangelical congregations per department or per capita Evangelical congregations per department in 1981. Nor is there any correlation between any of the CEH tallies of war's violence by region with the available 1995 figures on religious affiliation by regions composed of several departments each.[2] Put simply, the theory that war's violence and disorganization accelerated the acceptance of

Protestantism/Pentecostalism or made it firmly situated in the Guatemalan scene simply is not backed by the available numeric data. Finally, if war's dislocation were a primary accelerant of conversion from Catholic to Protestant or Pentecostal membership, then one would expect an early rapid Pentecostal conversion phase in the 1960s in eastern Guatemala, the period when Arana, then a senior military officer, waged a brutal war on what he felt was subversion in the eastern departments. But eastern Guatemala has lagged behind the rest of the country in its degree of Protestantization or Christian Pentecostalization and has been substantially more Catholic (as a percentage) than western Guatemala from the 1960s to the present.

Garrard-Burnett (1997) and Gooren (2010) provide figures that some *evangélico* congregations experienced growth rates of 12, 15, or even 18 percent per annum in the war years. The available data on religion offered by the nonpartisan national census bureau (figure 19.5), however, do not suggest a surge was necessary in this period. For the forty-seven years between the 1893 and 1940 censuses, the Protestant compound rate of growth was 6.74 percent per year. From 1940 to 1950, it was 4.95 percent per year. From 1950 to 1964, long before either heavy war or earthquake violence, it jumped to 11.31 percent per year. After 1964, unfortunately, the government stopped asking about religious affiliation in the national census. As a result, we have no national or department figures on religion until the 1995 Guatemala Demographic and Health Survey as cited in the *World Religion Database* (Johnson and Grim 2020). This study, however, presents data based on cardinally grouped geographic regions (Northwest, Southwest, North [Petén excluded], Northeast, Southeast, and Metropolitan Central) composed of one to five departments each. It gives Catholic and Protestant membership as a percentage of each region. We can estimate the numbers of Protestants/Pentecostals from the percentages per region using the Instituto Nacional de Estadística's (INE n.d.) 1995 population estimate by department to determine the population of each region. That then produces a pretty good estimate of the compound annual rate of Protestant/Pentecostal growth from 1964 to 1995, which turns out to be 6.68 percent for the nation, based on the 1995 Protestant/Pentecostal population of 2.6 million. This 6.68 percent compound annual Protestant growth is more than two times the nation's compound annual population growth rate from 1964 to 1995, and sufficiently accounts for Protestant/

Pentecostalism's fast-increasing percentage of Guatemala's population (figures 19.2 and 19.5).

The 6.68 percent compound annual Protestant growth for the period that includes both earthquake (1976) and war (especially harsh during 1981–1983) is well below the high point in the Protestant/Pentecostal compound annual growth rate of 11.31 percent for the period 1950–1964. Simply put, the high point in Pentecostal expansion preceded the great quake and the most intense period of the war. The decade and a half of 11 percent per annum Protestant/Pentecostal growth included no major quakes and comparatively little war violence. As noted, in the 1960–1964 period, violence was largely confined to departments in eastern Guatemala, where there continues to be the lowest percentages of *evangélico* membership in the nation. There is no need to posit a war surge based on the perhaps inflated figures given by a few Pentecostal groups with possibly self-aggrandizing partisan interests at the same time there are no data on the out-of-favor Pentecostal groups experiencing membership recession.

The appearance of a surge in Protestantism suggested by Garrard-Burnett or Gooren seems a by-product of taking the highest figures given by particular denominations at particular times and using them to project figures for the nation at those times. This procedure, however, is clearly invalid because Gooren's own data show considerable differences in growth rate by denomination for each period addressed. Moreover, Pentecostal denominations show a decided time-related faddishness; first one and then another rolls into first place as the high gainer while former leading denominations decline in rate of gain. To attribute high rates to all Pentecostals based on the religiously partisan "facts" provided by denominations seeking to be high gainers among their peers is most certainly suspect.

I sought more granularity by examining the data for the Department of Sololá. For Sololá, the Pentecostal compound annual growth rate for the period 1964–1995 was 8.8 percent if I impute to Sololá the same percentage of Protestant/Pentecostal membership as the INE and MSPAS 1995 survey (cited in Johnson and Grim 2020) gives to the region in which Sololá is embedded. Using that method, I can estimate the 1995 Protestant/Pentecostal membership of Sololá to be about 85,922. What can be seen, however, is that for both the country as a whole (at 6.68 percent compound annual Protestant/Pentecostal growth) and for the Department of Sololá,

an extraordinary postquake (or postwar) increase in rate of gain among Pentecostals and the few mainline Protestants is not necessary to achieve current membership numbers (figure 19.3) or the Protestant/Pentecostal percentage of the Department of Sololá's population (figure 19.4). Thus, the numbers cited for particular denominations in the literature seem to be selectively picked from among the high-flying denominations of that period and do not account for the fact that at the same time, other denominations of Pentecostalism were withering, cannibalized by the high gainers. Moreover, the membership numbers of those said to be the fastest expanding groups may have been artificially inflated for propaganda purposes by the denomination's record-keeping custodians. In all likelihood, the only impartial record keepers, despite all the difficulties with such data, are the national census takers.

Thus, the only way left open for war to account for Protestantization and Christian Pentecostalization is to depend on a generic explanation. The argument would have to go like this: war violence, whether it touched one's community or department savagely or not, was generally known throughout the country. So an overall fear of war must explain the overall national acceleration in Pentecostal growth, even though that occurred most heavily in the nondisrupted areas. Such an approach, however, constitutes a refusal to grant meaning to the local figures.

First, if war (or earthquake, or both) were the main trigger in Guatemala, how does one explain the fact that the compound annual rate of Protestant expansion for the period preceding the counterinsurgency war was higher than in the period that included the war? Second, if war is such a trigger to Pentecostal expansion, how does one explain the rapid growth in Christian Pentecostalization in Brazil or Ecuador, where no counterinsurgency war ensued? As I show in chapter 26, these countries did indeed experience crises in their political, social, and food production carrying capacity, but they did not experience a war's violence nor did they experience a major earthquake's disruption. In sum, Pentecostal membership by department in Guatemala stands uncorrelated or negatively correlated with both quake damages and war's violence, deaths, intimidation incidents, or massacres (or any composed index of these, for I tried them all), but manifests (as I showed in chapter 17) significant inverse correlations with corn per capita, lands held, and depleting forest resources—all indicators of collapsing indigenous corn culture.

Thus far, I have directed the statistical argument toward Pentecostals of historic Protestant extraction only. What about the Catholic charismatics? To my knowledge, there are no surveys that separate or specify the numbers of charismatics among Catholics in the Guatemalan parishes by municipality, department, or even the nation for any given date. Consequently, I can make no comparable statistical inferences to those I made for Pentecostals. As a result, I must be more intuitive. I can say that Catholic charismaticism initially surged during a period of relative peace in Guatemala (1973–1978) and before the palpable spike in the war's ethnocidal violence expanded to embrace the whole country between 1979 and 1983. I can also say that charismatic expansion continued vigorously during the postwar period. It also seems fair to surmise that some Ortho-Catholics' recourse to noisy charismaticism would not be a likely choice if evasive protective coloration were what was needed at the time.

In sum, the argument that the chaos and depredation of insurgency and the government's 1980s indiscriminate and indescribably violent attacks, rapes, disappearances, and ethnically cleansing war crimes against the indigenous populace accounts for Pentecostal expansion simply does not correlate with religious change by department for any period for which we have data and does not account for the greater rate of Protestant/Pentecostal expansion before the war than during and after. Nor does it help us understand charismatic expansion during the same period. As in the case of quake damage, none of these tallies of the horrors of war correlate positively with Pentecostal expansion anywhere in Guatemala.

ANALYZING CORN, CRISIS, AND RELIGION, 1985–THE PRESENT

In chapter 17, I discussed the emerging crisis in corn and culture as it was experienced and dealt with religiously into the late 1970s. Having now discussed and rejected statistically both the quake damage and the war ravages hypotheses, I return to the issue of corn in the modern period.

In 1995, as already discussed, the Guatemalan National Institute of Statistics did a large survey in which it assessed family health issues. The report (INE and MSPAS 1999, cited in Johnson and Grim 2020) provided the first large regional survey figures on religious affiliation since 1964. The survey asked people to specify whether they were Catholic, *evangélico*, other Protestant, other religion, or no religion. No category broke out Catholic charismatics. By grouping the department data for various years into the same regional sectors as used in the 1995 survey, I analyzed statistically the same questions identified above. Is there a correlation between religion in 1995 and quake effects in 1976, war effects in the region in 1978–1986, or corn and crop land in any period surveyed by the agricultural censuses? The answers to these questions regarding religious affiliation in 1995 are quite straightforward. As I indicated previously, there is no correlation of *evangélico* affiliation in 1995 with the 1976 earthquake regarding either deaths, injuries, or percentage damage of infrastructure (whether in total or per capita by region). There is a strong *negative* correlation between an index I built summing the rank of each region in deaths, injuries, and percentage of infrastructural damage in 1976 and the percentage of *evangélico* presence in 1995. That is, the higher the sum of the ranks of these three kinds of quake damage per capita per department in 1976, the *lower* the percentage of *evangélico* presence in the region in 1995 ($r = -0.726$, $p = 0.032$, one-tailed). Regarding Guatemala's insurrection/civil war, there is no correlation between *evangélico* presence in the geographic regions in 1995 and either massacres or incidents of violence or reports of threats (in either absolute number or per capita) in those regions. There is also no correlation between a region's absolute or per capita human rights violations between 1962 and 1996, as measured by CEH. Conversely, there is a strong *positive* correlation between 1995 *evangélico* percentage per region and the percentage of a region's population having less than the minimum subsistence level of sixteen *cuerdas* of land ($r = 0.948$, $p < 0.000$).[3] Corn shortage, land insufficiency, and culture collapse—not earthquake or counterinsurgency war—explain Guatemala's 1995 religious affiliation figures.

Finally, with regard to war's violence, I note that a large portion of Nahualá's and Santa Catarina's conversion to Christian Pentecostalism has occurred from 1985 to the present. This began considerably after the substantial reduction in counterinsurgency violence in the country but before the formal signing of the Peace Accords in 1996. While 1986–1996 was a period of relative peace, it was also a period of uncertainty, for who knew if the war would flare again? It was also a period of continued population expansion, increasing corn and land shortage per capita, globalization disruption, and relative exclusion from the emerging postwar neoliberal national and worldwide cash economy. In Nahualá and Santa Catarina Ixtahuacán, increasing conversions to the new religions were a 1990s phenomenon, when corn shortage from Mayas' micro landholdings became patently clear. Thus, Christian Pentecostal growth has derived not so much from the threat or disruption of direct violence as from the harder to see but still anxiety-producing erosion of the economic and social conditions that had undergirded a long-held but no longer viable cultural way of life, combined with little apparent access to the visible and tantalizing global and local market alternatives to that collapse. Thus, collapse, exclusion, and indigenous liminality provide the only explanation (so far in the literature) that accounts for the available 1981 and 1995 numeric representations of Pentecostal membership by department or region.

CULTURE COLLAPSE AND EXCLUSION IN THE GUATEMALAN LITERATURE

Here I ask, am I alone in arguing that a cultural collapse of tectonic (if slowly emerging) proportions impacted religious change? Not at all. Green (1993:160) suggests, "Today Mayan communities in the western highlands of Guatemala are in disarray. Town[s] and villages have been ravaged by decades of the slow violence of structural poverty and, since the late 1970s, by a brutal counterinsurgency war. Profound structural transformations have taken place. Two visible signs of structural change are civil militias imposed by the army in 1982 and the prevalence of fundamentalist Protestant churches in rural communities." To Green (1999:165), "fundamentalism"—meaning, I suppose, Evangelical Pentecostalism—in these instances is not so much "a religion of [i.e., responding to] repression, although initially it was for many, nor a religion of advancement, although it has been for a few," but a "religion of survival, and a refuge from suffering" that "offers a space in which people, especially widows, are able to reclaim some personal and social control over their lives." According to Green, the department in which she did fieldwork "probably receives more development aid per capita than anywhere in the *altiplano*." In spite of all this aid, "rather than alleviating the precarious economic situation in which most people live, conditions continue to worsen" (Green 1993:165, citing Smith 1990 regarding

development aid). The fact that "conditions continue[d] to worsen" even with massive aid suggests a programmatic, structural failure in the capitalist and democratic modernization project and clearly manifests what I am calling exclusion. For Green's war widows, this exclusion is life threatening; as widows they lack the familial resources to deal with the social and cultural collapse they experience.

In a similar vein, Early's work *Maya and Catholic Cultures in Crisis* (2012) carefully extends the arguments he made in his 1982 book on Guatemalan demographics. Early argues that the mid-twentieth-century culture crisis was not simply a matter of "Maya poverty" or "a subsistence crisis." Indeed, Early (2012:74) asserts that phrasing the situation in those terms "implies that the crisis was essentially an economic crisis, a lack of resources to acquire physical goods, especially food. While the Maya crisis had its taproot in their loss of land and the self-sufficiency the land provided, the crisis was much more embracing. It was a crisis of physical survival, of the legitimacy of the Maya's social organization, and of the validity of their worldview from which they drew life's meaning, morality, and their self-identity. In brief, it was the crisis of a culture." I found the same.

Christian Pentecostalism is not produced by poverty per se. In my fifty years of returning to do fieldwork and live among the Mayas, principally in San Ildefonso Ixtahuacán and Huehuetenango (1968), in San Marcos and San Pedro Sacatepéquez of San Marcos (1971, 1973–1974), and Nahualá and Santa Catarina Ixtahuacán (summers of 1995–2006, 2009), and on return trips over the years to visit with friends from each, it is my experience that in each of these communities, wealth has increased on average. There are more pickups, more radios, more watches, more two-story houses, fewer straw roofs (now almost none), more tin roofs, fewer adobe houses, more rebar and cinderblock houses, better clothes, fewer bare feet, more shoes, and so on. There is more access to medical clinics and pharmacies and more primary schooling. Thus, it is not poverty and its corrosive effects, glossed by Chesnut (2003a) as "the pathogens of poverty," that have pushed the acceleration of Christian Pentecostalism, as Chesnut and others have argued. The Mayas have always been poor, and over the years, by and large, they have gotten less so. Indeed, Guatemala's indigenous people in the 1920s–1930s were extremely poor, but they had a viable corn-based way of life that enabled sufficient isolation from the surrounding exploiters as to be tolerable, if just barely. Their poverty was culturally consistent; their culture was corn-based, municipally isolated, and broadly shared.

Generally, except for deteriorating land access and ever-lessening self-produced corn resources, the Mayas were poorer monetarily and in terms of western material accoutrements *prior* to the period of 1976–1986 than during that period (deemed to be key to their conversion) or into the present. Poverty is not the issue; culture stress and collapse of corn, land, covenant, and municipal isolation are. But does my observation of increasing wealth not contradict my argument that the Mayas are also excluded? I do not think so. One can have a bit more cash in a market and labor economy and still be actively excluded by ethnic prejudice and a structurally imposed inability to overcome exclusion even though that exclusion is not absolute. Exclusion may be relative and yet surely is made all the more galling both by media visibility and by failure in the bedrock Maya premises of isolation, covenant protection, and corn independence.[4]

Early (2012) concludes that for the Mayas, the traditional covenant no longer held and constituted a breach of cultural integrity. Some Mayas responded by intensifying their celebration of traditional *cofradía* ritual. Others began to seek alternatives in either Catholic or Protestant/Pentecostal religious change. Yet others sought transformation through insurgency. Early details all these approaches to failing subsistence and collapsing culture. In addition, he examines religious intensification through increased adhesion to what he calls "Tridentine Catholicism," which I call Ortho-Catholicism. This core institutional Catholicism eventually issued a call through its bishops for a liberation theology that gave a preferential option for the poor through structural adjustment via Catholic Action. Its alternative consisted in insurgency. Briefly, but importantly, Early (2012:156–159, 396–402, 407) also addresses the attractions of Protestant Pentecostalism and, especially, the rise and attraction of Catholic charismaticism. For Early, these all are Maya attempts to deal with the intertwined subsistence crisis and culture collapse.

Sheldon Annis reached a similar conclusion by 1987. While other scholars focused their attentions on the war's obscene violence, Annis examined religious change and ethnicity. He, like I have, located and explained Protestant/Pentecostal success in relation to Guatemala's economic and cultural collapse. I earlier quoted Annis to the effect that "something more subtle" than earthquake, repression, or war was at work in the religious transformation of Maya Guatemala, and he directs attention to "the growing chaos of a disordered world" entering into indigenous "consciousness." "Growing consciousness of a chaotic and disordered world," however, is a description of cultural breakdown. In the opening paragraphs of *God and Production*, Annis (1987:7) cogently lays out his argument:

> With the countryside embroiled in violence and a Protestant zealot at the helm of the government, one easy interpretation of rising membership in evangelical churches is that being reborn gave villagers a safe-conduct ticket through government-linked repression. A second "easy" interpretation is that during such times of dislocation and extreme psychological stress, villagers responded to the "hot" transcendental qualities of evangelical fundamentalism. If ever there was a time for tears, rolling on the floor, and speaking in tongues, this was it.
>
> As far as they go, these explanations are true. However, they tend to miss the deeper cultural appeal that Protestantism offered many village Indians.

Annis then speaks of "still-inchoate forces" and "deeper cultural appeals" that "had been jelling for years." I believe Annis gets it right—more so than many subsequent scholars dealing with the Pentecostal religious change in Guatemala. He puts the issue squarely on the inability of Mayas to sustain their culture because they could not grow the corn requisite to that culture due to land losses and increasing population. Catholic, colonial, village-oriented, inward-looking "*milpa* logic" is, for Annis, "an elegant expression of what is here called 'Indianness,'" which is also deeply associated with Catholicism. Thus, both indigeneity and Catholicism confront and give way to anti-*milpa* forces of land loss, population growth, market penetration, and an increasingly outward orientation that favors Protestant individualism (Annis 1987:10). "While population . . . has increased dramatically over recent generations, land ownership has become increasingly skewed. The majority find themselves with more and more family members to support on smaller and smaller plots of land" (Annis 1987:36).

By the time of Annis's main fieldwork in 1977–1978, 70 percent of San Antonio Aguas Calientes families (the 40 percent that were absolutely landless plus half of the remaining 60 percent that had some land) owned—and therefore independently controlled—less than 80 percent of the land requisite to sustain the minimum food needs of independent, self-subsistent Maya life. The substantial majority of that 70 percent had nothing at all or very little. Thus, the land and corn "economic equilibrium that was the basis of cultural stability for four hundred years [was] unraveling" (Annis 1987:59) even by the time of Annis's fieldwork, which occurred before the 1980s rise in counterinsurgency violence.

Thus, the qualitative ethnographies of Annis (1987), Green (1999), Early (2012), and Cook and Offit (2013) all confirm the position I have taken on both statistical and ethnographic grounds. The main stimulus to Christian Pentecostalism's growth and acceptability was not quake or war, although these two certainly meshed well with Christian Pentecostal visions of an imminent end of the world. Rather, an inability to provide the corn that is symbolically and physically requisite to being indigenous and fulfilling one's gender role was and remains the underlying basic stressor. Earthquake and war merely accelerated the immiserization and exacerbated the experience of crisis.

Indeed, "even with the best *milpa*-optimizing strategies, subsistence [had] become unattainable for a large and growing proportion of the population, . . . [and] the situation [had] . . . never been worse" for most residents in the *municipio* that Annis studied (1987:63). Thus, "the poorest families [were] so poor that, in a sense, they [were] driven to break the mold and live by a new set of rules" (72), in this case Pentecostal Protestantism. The "chief destabilizer [was] the growing inequity in the distribution of land." The poor and the landless rent from those indigenes (and Ladinos) who have succeeded in accumulating land. Rental "enables the system to accommodate land maldistribution and perpetuate itself" (73), but only as a temporary palliative. The richest people, Annis shows, also drop out of the internal village status display system—Catholicism and *cofradía*—because they can accumulate enough to express their status in terms meaningful to the outside, which requires a different display system (see also Watanabe 1992).

David Stoll (1993b:5) reflects poignantly on these issues: "In societies whose economies are being globalized, whose traditional social structures have heaved apart, where people must fend for themselves in hostile new environments, how can a single, centralized religious hierarchy [he means the Ortho-Catholic Church] satisfy a newly individuated population whose members need to chart their own [and, I would add, new and changed] courses? . . . How can a religious system organized around sacraments satisfy the hunger for personal transformation?" Annis (1987:106) arrives at a related conclusion: "The evangelical chain-letter

is in the mail. . . . The forces that have undercut the replicability of the '*milpa* technologists' world—the same forces that have replaced them with 'dispossessed peasants' and 'petty capitalists'—have prepared the ground for the conversion process. And then, the relatively better economic performance of Protestants, whether at the rich or poor end of the economic scale, has reinforced their spiritual choices with a material rationale."

In his concluding chapter, Annis reflects further on the colonial origins and character of the indigenous condition. In essence Annis independently concludes, as I did in *Inverse Images* (Hawkins 1984), that Severo Martínez Peláez (1970:595–598) and Saussure (1966[1959]) were right. The "Indian" was created by the enslaving institutions of the Spanish colony. Subsequently, à la Saussure, the indigenous person self-maintains indigencity by a meaningful, deliberate, and self-protective opposition to Ladinoness, and vice versa, done by both in the context of institutions of continued oppression. As Annis (1987:140, emphasis in original) puts it:

With conquistador Pedro de Alvarado himself as the founder of the town, San Antonio is in every sense a product of "colonial relations." Its initial "Indianness" was more the Spaniards' creation than the Indians'. Yet over the years, the descendants of those slaves and captives who were settled in San Antonio recreated Indianness in order to meet *their* needs. They built a society that gave to the Hispanic mainstream what it had to but provided the villagers with a stable and dignified culture.

Today, the equilibrium of the town is fractured by a complex bombardment of twentieth-century forces. As a result, Indianness is under siege and changing. This change is probably different from and more profound than any that has previously occurred in the town's 450 years because it affects the community's very idea of itself—who people think they are, what they think their community is and means.

As Durkheim (2001[1912]:314) long ago argued, a community's or a society's "idea of itself" is the "soul of religion." Annis's notion that San Antonio is changing "the community's very idea of itself" is an assertion that the community likely is changing its religion. Religion provides its participants "the very image of . . . real society" through its liturgical practices, its myths and dogmas, and especially through the symbolic vehicle of that religion's images of divinity. Because the Maya people have changed their idea of themselves as radically as they have—which is to say, from secure to precarious, from colonial extraction to market chances, from inward-investing *milpa* logic to outward-seeking wage labor—one would expect them to change their religion, their divinities, and their ritual practices to reflect the changes. And so they have.

The more or less obvious portion of this religious change in Maya Guatemala, from "old" variants of Catholic to "new" variants of Christian Pentecostal, has been an eighty-year process. It will likely take some decades more. Mayas are in the process of changing their religious orientation because they are being forced by a subsistence resource crisis and related cultural failure to change the most basic ideas that they have of themselves and their society. In the Christian symbolic tradition, the "hot" Christian Pentecostal liturgy, end-of-the-world theology, and Spirit-seeking embodiment leads to trance states wherein agitated movement ends with collapse to the floor. This expresses perfectly the crisis of cultural collapse. Of course, not all Mayas changed to the new religions at once, for not all have found themselves equally transformed or equally vexed at the same time or by the same circumstances. People are indeed of different dispositions. But on the whole, and bit by bit, change they have and change they will. Annis (1987:140) writes: "It is this change that has opened the new receptivity to Protestantism, not only in San Antonio but throughout the Guatemalan highlands. Such receptivity, I believe, begins with the stresses and strains that are pulling apart the *milpa*-based economy. As analyzed here, the *milpa* is both the processor of resources and the producer of subsistence, but more broadly it is a metaphor for the 'logic' of traditional Indian culture." It is this logic of indigeneity that has been "pulled apart." Indeed, "as a set of ideas," the social and cultural "logic of the *milpa*" and the cosmic cultural logic of traditionalist Maya "indigenous Catholic religious ideology are inseparable" (Annis 1987:140). Indigenized traditionalist Catholicism and *milpa* logic replicate and sustain each other structurally, even while undergoing change.

In the face of generalized exclusion, the small Christian Pentecostal congregation provides one accepting point of inclusion that is, at the same time, helpful in dealing with a world in chaos and full of dangers. One may not be included in the neoliberal economy, but at least one is accepted by God's little band of fellow congregants and empowered by God through the bodily infusion of

his Spirit. In many regards, the liturgical activities of Christian Pentecostalism thus reflect an agentive pursuit of hope and a deliberate creation of small faith communities of relief. In chapter 24, I elaborate on this agentive reconstruction and the very practical functionalism and the culture change revitalization characteristics associated with the movement.

Being agentive, reconstructive, and usefully functionalist to its adherents, the new Christian Pentecostal religions do not reflect the cynicism of Marx's theory that religion dupes and helps control the masses to the benefit of elites. Rather, the new religions evince a hope that is neither false nor foisted on indigenous people. For most Mayas, the hope generated in Christian Pentecostalism is their only realistic hope. It is based in a valid experience of success derived from their actions and what they see happening to others. This hope is also a faith, for in Christian belief "faith is the substance of things hoped for" (King James Version: Hebrews 11:1). It is an affirmation that their agentive decisions to repremise their worldview, refashion their symbols, reform their behavior, return to a small community of co-practitioners in a new religion, and extend that vision through evangelism will help, heal, and free them as individuals and their compatriots as a nation. It is a hope for change in what is, to them, a shattered cultural world in an otherwise doomed country.

CONCLUSION

Without question, Maya Christian Pentecostal worship displays what can only be called "intense passions." For Durkheim, the intense passions generated by a great collective upheaval display in a double register. One is the register of politics raised to the tumult of dirty internal war. The other is the register of passionate religion.

In the register of politics raised to bloody war, Durkheim (2001[1912]:158) notes that people are "moved by passions so intense that they can be assuaged only by violent, extreme acts of superhuman heroism or bloody barbarism." He references the Crusades and the French Revolution. Today I add Guatemala's savage war violence. No one can read the twelve volumes of historical memory commissioned by the United Nations (CEH 1999), the four volumes of testimony recovered by the Catholic Church (Arzobispado de Guatemala 1998), works by individual scholars (e.g., Green 1999; Manz 2004; Metz 2006;

Montejo 1999; Perera 1993; Smith 1990), or even the Guatemalan newspapers of the time without being revolted by the violence and "bloody barbarism" in the Guatemalan elite's control-motivated and suppression-oriented conduct of the war. As Durkheim says, political behavior in Guatemala, in 1980–1983 in particular, was nothing short of "savage."

Yet, just as surely, in the midst of such savagery, many of the "common burghers" Durkheim spoke of—in this case, ordinary Guatemalan citizens both Maya and non-Maya—responded with private and public "superhuman heroism." In an environment of chaotic war, midnight kidnappings, rape, and pillage, many Guatemalans protected their kin—and sometimes even the Ladino or Maya "other." They found food and work. They hid themselves and others from authorities and from alienated neighbors. Some even challenged authorities and confronted the army and the guerrillas at great personal risk. A few challengers lived. Many others, however, died because they challenged. All such Guatemalans were indeed superhuman heroes.

But altogether too many Guatemalans, including many Mayas forcibly inducted into the army, became "transformed" "under the influence of general exaltation" into "executioners" who raped and tortured and killed, letting themselves become proxies for distant elites (Durkheim 2001[1912]:158).

In Durkheim's (2001[1912]:158) second register, the "mental processes" of political, passionate response to great collective upheaval "are so clearly those at the root of religion that individuals themselves often represent this pressure in an explicitly religious form." In Guatemala's case, the pressure comes from failing subsistence survival and from consequent collapse of the culture and way of life. It comes also from an exclusionary lack of access to the apparent successor mode of production and way of life—the late modern capitalist neoliberalism that now penetrates, disrupts, and extracts from indigenous communities while it excludes. I argue that in 2003, for many, the most effective Guatemalan response to this great collective upheaval of culture collapse did indeed take "an explicitly religious form"—that of Christian Pentecostal ecstatic worship manifesting the characteristics of "more frequent and more active" effervescence during ritual services. These changes happened well before the war. The Guatemalan counterinsurgency war itself was not the great collective upheaval. Indeed,

participating as an insurgent was merely one of many secular responses to the corn shortage preconditions. The Mayas' main response to those preconditions was a growing acceptance of Christian Pentecostalism.

NOTES

1. See, for example, the open database of the CEH study, https://hrdag.org/guatemala/, which does not list the religion of those assaulted.

2. Correlations with massacres by year are insignificant or, if significant, are weak and *negative*, meaning the more massacres per department or per capita per department, the fewer Protestant congregations per capita per department, leaning against (but not disproving) the hypothesis that war fomented Protestantism. There are three exceptions. The correlation of Protestant congregations per capita in 1981 with massacres occurring in 1979 is very weak and statistically insignificant. By contrast, the correlation of Protestant congregations per capita in 1981 with massacres occurring in 1984 is statistically significant ($p = 0.020$) and very strong but *negative* ($r = -0.998$), sharply contradicting the proposition that war foments Protestantism. For 1988 the figures are likewise statistically significant ($p < 0.000$, one-tailed) and strong but *negative*, that is, the areas with more congregations (and presumably more membership per capita) had fewer massacres. Rather than treat massacres by year, one gets a better notion of what was happening by summing the massacres. Taking the total of massacres up to 1980 and also up to 1981, there is no correlation of war's ravages as measured by CEH data with Protestant congregations per department or with Protestant congregations per capita per department. Nor is there any correlation with subsequent Protestant membership percentage by region in 1995. Likewise, if one totals any of the measures of violence for all years (1979–1995), there is no correlation with either Protestant congregations per department in 1980–1981, Protestant congregations per capita in 1980–1981, or Protestant percentage of population by region in 1995. Nor is there any statistically significant correlation of these measures of Protestantism in 1980–1981 or in 1995 with either the number of victims of human rights violations between 1962 and 1996 or the number of incidents of violations reported or aggregated following the conflict. Nor do any of these war violence measures calculated per capita per department correlate with congregations or congregations per capita in 1981 or with Protestant membership in 1995. All such figures have p in the vicinity of 0.45–0.49 for the 1980–1981 congregation figures, and $p = 0.2–0.3$ for the 1995 Protestant percentage of membership.

3.   Note that this 1995 survey of religion omitted sampling in the Petén, so Petén data are not included in the correlations.

4.   John Watanabe, in a personal note referring to a draft of this book, suggests, "In addition to exclusion, [and] despite access to more material goods, lack of control might be another factor here contributing to people's anxieties and felt inadequacies. In a global economy, even when wages or commodity prices are high, no one ever knows when boom will turn to bust or can explain why, so even when times are good, everyone worries about when they are going to turn bad. I would argue that this inability to plan or predict contributes as much to discontent and worry as does any absolute deprivation or felt inequality does." I agree, and in the concluding chapter of this book I develop the idea of uncertainty in Global North economies as an explanation for the expanding acceptance of Christian Pentecostal exuberance among the middle classes and even elites. Such uncertainty no doubt also affects Mayas and others excluded in the Global South.

Chapter Twenty-One

Chaos

The Postwar Generalization of Violence and the Slowing Rates
of Christian Pentecostal Expansion, 1996–2019

JOHN P. HAWKINS

IN THE POSTWAR PERIOD THERE has been a generalizing of nonpolitical violence throughout the urban sector and into the indigenous periphery. Violence used to be largely political and for the most part laser-focused on social organizers and on Mayas in the most marginal areas. Consequently, whom violence might touch used to be somewhat predictable. Today's violence, however, seems a more widespread and largely apolitical, criminal brutality, which is experienced across all sectors of society, mixed in with some continuing political violence. Moreover, corruption, graft, and theft from the resources of the people by agents of the state all continue largely unabated. Only recently are the first hints of an end of political impunity now being felt as a result of twenty-first-century CICIG (Comisión Internacional contra la Impunidad en Guatemala, International Commission against Impunity in Guatemala) investigations. "Ordinary" criminal violence—robbery, assault, kidnapping, extortion, rape—however, seems to have increased, and there is a manifest ineffectiveness of the weakened judicial system. Indeed, less than 2 percent of homicides (and little else) ever go to trial (McDonald and Hawkins 2013b:24), and convictions are rare unless processed through CICIG offices with external investigators, experienced judges, and international pressure. Ordinary criminals therefore run little risk of punishment. Impunity still reigns. The unpredictable violence and concomitant impunity affect and add to the experience of cultural collapse and crisis (Bybee et al. 2013:91; McDonald and Hawkins 2013a, 2013b, 2016). I therefore expect both Catholic and Protestant versions of Christian Pentecostalism to continue to appeal to Mayas, poor urbanites, and a growing section of the increasingly distressed middle class and the peripheral elites.

Nevertheless, I predict that the rate of expansion in Christian Pentecostal membership will slow. Indeed, it must slow down because a large percentage—perhaps close to 70 percent now—of the population is already Christian Pentecostal, either Pentecostal Protestant or charismatic Catholic. For the 1990s, Gooren (2001) documents a trend toward a reduction in the rate of Protestant growth among particular denominational types for which he has membership data. Because mainline, sedate Protestant growth long ago turned flat or declined (Gooren 2015), the relatively recent drop in the rate of *Protestant* increase in fact means a slowing in the rate of *Pentecostal* expansion. At the same time, the Ortho-Catholic fold has been swept by charismaticism, part of the 70 percent of Guatemala's population who are Christian Pentecostal practitioners. Thus, the Christian Pentecostalization of Guatemala is now largely complete, and the rate of increase will necessarily slow.

Finally, if the liminality of the Mayas and urban poor people diminishes because they find a way to gain entry to the encompassing global system of neoliberal markets and digital productivity—that is, if Mayas find dignified and reliable jobs as alternatives to agricultural dependence, and if they find fair and reasonable access to government services, such as education—then I might expect a reversal of rates of Christian Pentecostal growth or even a de-pentecostalization of Guatemala. In this theory, Christian Pentecostal participation will diminish or ritual practice will return to something increasingly sedate when the glossolalic wail—expressing a situation and future too distressing, if not impossible, to put to words—no longer fits. But the anxiety of the marginalized expressed loudly in religion will only "not fit" if systematic exclusion and liminality end. Call me a pessimist, but in Guatemala in 2020, an end of Maya exclusion and liminality appears to be a most unlikely counterfactual.

SEEING CHRISTIAN PENTECOSTALISM AS A REVOLUTIONARY MOVEMENT

Throughout part 2 of this book, I have shown that Guatemala's great historic upheavals in social organization or mode of production have led to successive "revolutions" in the religious ideas Guatemalans have been able to accept. This is because religious ideas help a society's members reflect on their experience. At the same time, and in a way Marx did not comprehend, those ideas become constitutive of people's experience by guiding their perceptions and their decisions. That is, as Weber and Durkheim perceived, novel religious ideas lightly guide decisions such that people's choices begin to rework and reshape society into a confirmation of those ideas. But the revolutions in Guatemalan society and in Guatemalans' ideas about religion have not worked out as Marx thought they would—with physical violence leading to a change of state adequate for the people. For one thing, the enduring social revolution in Guatemala has been the Christian Pentecostal religious movement rather than a political rebellion. Neither has the Christian Pentecostal ideal been implemented, for Guatemala is not yet reformed politically. For the moment, it would appear that only the religious component of the Christian Pentecostal revolution continues to expand. The Marxist revolution, by contrast, has failed or gone into some kind of remission. The contrast that embodies Marx's error can be expressed this way: Christian Pentecostal religion has empowered the masses rather than duped them. Marx was insightful about much, but not about the new religions acting as an opiate or a mechanism simply to deceive and exploit the masses.

In her discussion of the war, Garrard-Burnett (1993:207) suggests that Pentecostalism is a form of revolution. She thus comes close to the idea I present here that these new religions and the various efforts to accomplish political change in Guatemala—whether by direct confrontation via Catholic Action or violence via insurgency—constitute parallel attempts to try to transform the society experiencing a cultural and civil breakdown. Garrard-Burnett (1993:207) expresses the idea this way:

> Latin American Protestantism can be seen as a type of rebellion, the personal protest of the voiceless and powerless. Protestants by definition do not buy into the traditional Catholic-centered status quo, even when they obediently acquiesce to the political or economic "authorities in power." *Evangélicos* may be "model citizens," but their religious identity carries with it a subtext of noncompliance. This suggests that in its own way, evangelical Protestantism could potentially be both more revolutionary and more subversive than conventional forms of political mobilization.

Well said! Garrard-Burnett implies that we should not be overly concerned if some Guatemalan Evangelicals appear to be withdrawn from the political process simply because some might not vote or outwardly demonstrate against injustice (O'Neill 2010:xv–xvi, 2–22). Indeed, I suggest in this book that the Pentecostals take a highly activist political stance because they embody a Foucauldian approach that seeks to inscribe in each individual an orientation toward self-disciplined obedience to law to be applied to all sectors of society. Society therefore does not require state force to maintain social order. The Christian Pentecostal project contrasts sharply with the confrontational and conflictual behavior that some Catholics espouse to deal with Guatemala's corrupt and force-based political institutions. Maya pentecostals thus exemplify the logic of Antonio Gramsci carried forward into Foucault: a society's civil institutions must ideally carry the load of social control by persuasion and not by force, thereby preserving state legitimacy. Protestant and Catholic forms of pentecostalism inscribe in the individual the ideals of a penetrating neoliberalism and of Foucault's notion of governmentality. The individual internalizes a religious first premise that each person is obligated to obey the law. In the end, the internalization approach—early conceived by Gramsci, elaborated by Foucault, and finally put into action by Christian Pentecostalism—may be far more effective political action than what is ordinarily considered by political scientists to be successful, engaged, direct, activist politics.

Garrard-Burnett's and Early's comparisons of Pentecostal religious movements with insurrections, and the parallel of these with my argument, invite reflection on an interesting cultural choice point. Perhaps the key issue is not a choice between various faiths in the supposed marketplace of religions. Rather, the larger issue might be a choice between styles of revolution in the arena of structural transformation. In this view, conversion to Christian Pentecostal religion constitutes one style of revolution. Other possible styles and choices for dealing with the current situation in Guatemala include acceptance and complicity in state repression, insurgency, other forms of resistance to state repression, passive self-protective isolation, participating in global capitalism as a consumer, engaging with international development, and attempting to enhance democracy.

In this reading of Guatemalan life, I see politically justified revolution and Christian Pentecostal religion as alternative adaptive choices or approaches to dealing with a system (the evolved extension of colonialism, corruption, and impunity in Guatemala) that is socially sick (because it still is based on corruption and engages in exploitation and control). That system of corruption and exploitation has been weakened because it has been progressively penetrated and displaced by the emerging alternative system of neoliberal global market capitalism. Finally, even Guatemala's noncolonial and technocratic efforts by people of tremendous good will, who manage the census and the state's local delivery of health, education, roads, utilities, and other services, have been undermined by the state's continued inability to deal with the social pressures that derive from Guatemala's fast population growth and its all too frequent corruption. A combination of insurrectionary groups, elective democracy, liberation theology, Catholic Action, labor unions, and popular protest organizations have reacted to the corrupt and weak but still grasping colonialism by directly confronting power systems and institutional structures. People throughout Guatemala have felt forced to choose among these contenders for structural domination or course change. With the exception of Christian Pentecostalism and perhaps democracy, the adherents of each of the above approaches share one feature: they use force or confrontation to try to goad or impose a needed restructuring on society.

By contrast, politically at least, Christian Pentecostalism constitutes a nonconfrontational approach to the chronic postcolonial illnesses of Guatemalan society. As seen in the ethnography by Thompson and colleagues in this volume, Christian Pentecostalism focuses its confrontations on the interpersonal boundaries of the congregation, thereby seeking to reform its adherents, and across the boundaries of religion in the community,

seeking to attract new followers and undermine Catholicism. Its adherents seek much-needed change, as do the supporters of more direct approaches. Pentecostals, however, do not seek change in the obvious (to Euro-American analysts) political institutions and national structures through confrontation, conflict, or protest. These they prefer to avoid, at least while Pentecostals constitute a minority. Rather, Pentecostals demand that congregants change their own premises at the level of the individual's moral ethos and at the level of the family's and the gender system's normative content, which is inscribed in the minds of individuals. As Garrard-Burnett points out, this Pentecostal (and highly Weberian) approach in effect has flown beneath the controlling elites' paranoid political radar, thus to some degree avoiding confrontation and retribution during and after Guatemala's dirty war.

The Christian Pentecostal project has sought to change the more important loci of the colonial and postcolonial system's structural weaknesses: ethical corruption, Ladino impunity, and indigenous submission. Thus, as Garrard-Burnett suggests, Pentecostalism has been both more revolutionary and more corrosive to Guatemalan and Latin American elite cultural premises than any of Pentecostalism's structure confronting institutional competitors. One can even argue that this nonconfrontationality is enhanced or elaborated by virtue of Saussurean principles that develop meaning clarity by increasing oppositions between elements in a set of objects, which become mutually meaningful via those oppositions.

By being less obvious and less visible, by being nonconfrontational, and by appearing outwardly supportive of governing power structures by advocating for individuals' adherence to law, it appears that Christian Pentecostalism, and perhaps only Christian Pentecostalism (to date, anyway) has survived, succeeded, and even thrived in the environment of state-perpetrated violence in spite of being quite subversive to the premises and logic of state corruption. In this regard, I would argue that Christian Pentecostalism won out as the major Latin American social movement of the second half of the twentieth century and may well be the major social movement of the Christianized Global South in the first half of the twenty-first century.

Nevertheless, the task of bringing about a complete transformation of Guatemalan, Latin American, or Global South societies by virtue of having changed religious premises in a new iteration of Weber's project has not yet succeeded. So far as I know, the application of generalized Christian Pentecostal premises and practices has not yet produced a distinct economy, let alone a moral economy, in any country or region. Nor has the increased percentage of Pentecostal practitioners—with a presumption of having changed premises—led to a correspondingly changed, reformed, honest, counterbalanced, or semi-virtuous polity. Even though Guatemalans have now seated three Evangelical presidents, two have been brought to trial for corruption in office and the third, Jimmy Morales, may well have been a malicious joker (he was a comedian by trade!) since he consolidated power until the 2019 elections. So Christian Pentecostalism has not produced a new society in the sense of providing an integrated cultural, economic, and political apparatus for a new way of life derived from a new religious ideology. At least, not yet. It has, however, clearly expressed the critical need for such.

If Christian Pentecostalism achieves any part of this goal of building a society based on obedience to law and equality of all citizens, rather than on exploitation, it will have succeeded as a revolution and as a revitalization movement. It will have given the power of God to the people by giving the power of society to them through religion. In Durkheim's phrasing, it will have inculcated and renewed in the minds of its participants the social power and interpersonal necessity of a new "social morality."

PART III

Understanding the Christian Pentecostal Wail

Guatemala's Religious Transformation in Synchronic Perspective

---

In *Course in General Linguistics*, Saussure (1966[1959]:14) writes, "Language is a system of interdependent terms in which the value of each term results solely from the simultaneous presence of the others." This fundamental insight about language can be applied to the elements of any communication system, whether a language of words or a language of richer symbols and performances, such as religious behavior. In part 2, I explored the historical and economic sources of Guatemala's current religious diversity and the implications of this history for understanding the directions of religious change from pre-conquest to the twenty-first century. In doing so, I laid out a theory centered on culture collapse and exclusion to account for the relatively recent Maya pentecostal transformation and the intensity and meaning of the Christian Pentecostal wail, which loudly and directly expresses the pain and angst of the Christian Pentecostal's liminal situation.

I now embark on an analysis of Guatemala's religious pluralism using synchronic analysis. I explore present-day manifestations of religious diversity in Nahualá and Santa Catarina Ixtahuacán using the tools of comparison and contrast. Largely by such contrasts, each chapter in this part of the book teases out some aspect of the religious diversity that I have been able to fathom by analysis of contrasting structures, spoken texts, and people's behaviors in the present. The synchronic analyses of part 3 thus complement, triangulate, enrich, and confirm perspectives arrived at by historical analysis.

Another aspect of that comparing and contrasting entails an exploration of Christian Pentecostalism as it manifests around the world. The question here, of course, is whether the data and conclusions drawn from the experience of religious behavior in Nahualá and Santa Catarina Ixtahuacán are unique or whether they exemplify and clarify larger worldwide processes. Put differently, the *data* from these case studies may be wonderful, rich, and insight producing, but the *theories* derived from this study of Nahualá and Santa Catarina Ixtahuacán are interesting only if they apply to religious transformation in other areas of the world—that is, if they are generalizable. So the question is, does this approach work elsewhere?

That inquiry implies the use of the comparative method, which has a long but problematic history in cultural anthropology (Eggan 1954; Radcliffe-Brown 1952, 1957[1948]:76–80, 1961[1952]:chaps. 1–7; Nadel 1952; Salzman 2012). The comparative method is recessive because the primary research method of cultural anthropology—the intensive case study—guarantees the perpetual dilemma of the field: one invests so heavily in analyzing a single case that one has little time or energy left to evaluate comparative materials. Cultural anthropologists are, it would appear, the living embodiment of an otherwise indigenous *milpa* logic: overinvest one's labor locally! Thus, we often fail to get to the question of comparison. But the degree of generalizability is a legitimate issue. Does this new approach generate insight when applied to other people's fieldwork? And in the long term, will it stimulate richer thought and insightful new fieldwork?

Chapter Twenty-Two

The Religions of Nahualá and Santa Catarina Ixtahuacán in Juxtaposition

JOHN P. HAWKINS

IN THIS CHAPTER, I ANALYZE synchronically and comparatively the current religions of Guatemala as exemplified in Nahualá and Santa Catarina Ixtahuacán. I do so in the way I think Ferdinand de Saussure (1857–1913) would have treated religions: as a currently interacting system and as a cognitive set in which each religion derives meaning from its social and ideological contrasts and similarities with the other religions in the local, national, and world milieus.

Saussure, a Swiss linguist foundational to the discipline, sought the basis of meaning in the languages he studied. Meaning, he concludes, derives from the oppositional positioning of words in related word sets operating in a system. "Words," he says, express ideas by "limiting each other reciprocally." Thus, "concepts are . . . defined not by their positive content but negatively by their relations with the other terms of the system. Their most precise characteristic is in being what the others are not" (Saussure 1966[1959]:116–117). His theories apply equally well to the less linguistic, more symbolic systems of meaning—such as religion or identity in society—because there, too, meaning comes in part from opposition between contrastive elements in sets of behavior, sets of symbols, sets of institutions, sets of ideas, or sets of ethnicities.

Given that religious behavior is a system of meaning transmission, Saussure's profound insights on opposition and contrast as a primary source of meaning in language, when applied to religion, suggest one must compare and contrast all the patterns of religious behavior and beliefs expressed in a region if one is to comprehend the meaning embedded in any of them. To that end, our fieldworkers researched and in part 1 of this book laid out the diversity of religions in Nahualá and Santa Catarina. Each religion in Guatemala does indeed take meaning from its contrasts

with other religions in Guatemala—as much as or more than each takes meaning from its own history. In part 2, I examined how the tumultuous processes of Guatemala's history successively birthed and nourished these interrelated faith traditions. Now I compare and juxtapose them all, as simultaneously as possible, as a set of contrasting institutions that mutually limit and define each other.

I have no evidence that Durkheim knew what Saussure had presented in his lectures between 1906 and 1909. At that time, Durkheim would have been working on or finalizing his *Elementary Forms of Religious Life* (1912). In it, Durkheim presents a nearly parallel insight, although not so crisply articulated. He suggests that distinct Australian Aboriginal totemic cults are mutually implicated parts of the same whole, and that totemic variations and rituals must not be studied in isolation but together as a system (Durkheim 2001[1912]:120). Whether or not Durkheim and Saussure knew of each other's work, their analyses certainly vibrate to a similar wavelength. Our research, too, benefits from that wavelength as I compare and contrast the various styles of religion in Nahualá and Santa Catarina Ixtahuacán and, later, around the world.

CATEGORIES OF RELIGIOUS PROFESSION

In Nahualá and Santa Catarina Ixtahuacán, people segment the religious landscape into *católicos* and *evangélicos*. That is the great conceptual divide in the set of religions in this area, and the divide is so important it can be communicated without being spoken. Shortly after our arrival for the 2004 field school, the host family of one student wanted to find out to what religion their guest subscribed. Living in a rural hamlet a forty-minute walk from town, the family spoke no Spanish, and the student spoke only some classroom K'iche'. So the family resorted to pantomime. In K'iche', a sentence beginning with *La* indicates a question will follow. *At* is the second-person singular pronoun. So the conversation proceeded thus: "La at? [accompanied by crossing-on-the-chest motion]." "La at? [with a clapping motion]." Translation: Do you cross (Are you Catholic)? Or do you clap (Are you Pentecostal)? These comprise the two essential categories of religious action and, ultimately, religious thought. When the student said *maj* (no) to each, the host family displayed visible consternation. What on earth could a young woman possibly be if neither *católica* nor *evangélica*?

Religion in Nahualá and Santa Catarina is, of course, a bit more complicated than that. But with this basic binary in mind, I now examine the complexities in the spectrum of faiths in this region, beginning with a tripartite division in Catholicism from the perspective of Mayas.

CATHOLICS: COMPLEXITY AND OVERLAP IN THREE STYLES OF FAITH PROFESSION

Since the conquest of Guatemala almost 500 years ago, the beliefs, practices, and participation of Mayas in Catholicism have been evolving to yield variant practices in the Catholic tradition. In Nahualá and Santa Catarina Ixtahuacán, Catholics recognize and practice three principal approaches to their religion: Maya Catholic traditionalism, Ortho-Catholicism, and *renovación* (renewal or charismatic) Catholicism.

Each variant of Catholicism has a recognizable zone of distinctiveness regarding leadership and belief. A Maya Catholic traditionalist accesses God, Mary, other saints, earth lords, Judas/Maximón, and the ancestors through the services of an *ajq'ij*. (In 2003, the *cofradía* branch of traditionalism was effectively defunct in these *municipios*.) An Ortho-Catholic also addresses God, Mary, and other saints and follows and respects the advice and administration of an ordained priest sent to a parish by the region's Roman Catholic bishop in order to provide the essential sacraments. A charismatic *renovación* Catholic, after attending mass delivered by a priest, worships in additional Sunday and weekday services, usually led by a married couple. In those extra meetings, charismatic Catholics pursue spiritual gifts conferred by embodiment of the Holy Spirit.

The leaders and participants of each of these strands of Catholic faith see themselves—and not the others—as the true or most genuine Catholics, asserting that the Catholics of the other two variants lack something or deviate from authentic, full, properly performed practice, devotion, belief, or enthusiasm. In spite of each style of worship having its distinctive center and each of its members feeling themselves to be the most authentic of Catholics, the ordinary adherents of each practice simultaneously share zones of belief or behavior with one or both of the other styles of Catholicism. They operate somewhat like three overlapping circles in a Venn diagram. At the center of the Venn diagram, all Catholics may attend mass freely; charismatics make a special point of doing so weekly. But many individuals blur the edges by occasionally engaging in one or another of the distinctive practices of the other styles of Catholicism while they affirm their own integrity.

Some also challenge the adequacy of the other strands of Catholic faith. Thus, internally, Catholicism is a contested domain. In part 2, I showed how traditionalist Catholics managing the *cofradía* ritual cycle and Ortho-Catholics implementing the wishes of the priests have contested each other at least since the 1940s and how that conflict opened space for Protestant expansion. From the mid-1970s to the present, neotraditionalists and Catholic charismatics have added their voices to the contest for leadership, legitimacy, and authenticity of practice. The disputes and mutual attributions of inauthenticity hurled between traditionalists and Ortho-Catholics have driven the traditionalist Catholics increasingly to see themselves as independent, to the point that some who were once quite able to be Catholic as traditionalists now reject Catholicism and claim they are practicing a pure Maya religion. Today, Catholic traditionalists, Ortho-Catholics, and Catholic charismatics each claim they offer the purest approach to their religion.

I now consolidate the descriptions and contrasts scattered throughout the ethnographies (part 1) of these three Catholic professions and explore their blurry-edged overlaps.

Traditionalists: Performing *Costumbre* as True Catholicism

Practitioners of Maya Catholic traditionalism consider their liturgy—their *costumbre* (religious custom)—to be old, authentic Catholic (indeed, the only authentic Catholic), and Maya. As late as mid-1980 in Santa Catarina

Ixtahuacán, traditionalism incorporated both the village *cofradía* ceremonies and the shamans who often consulted for individuals or family groups. The corporate *cofradía* activities in Nahualá and Santa Catarina Ixtahuacán, however, have faded and are now just a memory of the elders. What remains vibrant, but only serving a minority of the population, is divinatory and blessing practices and beliefs led by the *ajq'ijab'*.

Today, traditionalist Maya Catholic practice centers on the *ajq'ijab'*, the shamans who provide their private clients (and occasionally a public event) with divinations, blessings, healings, protection, connection with the earth lords and the client's ancestors, and—some fear—curses laid on others in return for cash or payment in kind.[1] An *ajq'ij* is chosen by God, a matter of his *suerte* or *portuna* ("luck" or "fate"). None requires the approval of the Ortho-Catholic priest to perform his (and in fewer cases, her) rituals.

An *ajq'ij* practices in a *sala* (receiving room) in his home or in a dedicated chapel in the home compound or at a client's location. An *ajq'ij* also offers prayers and rituals at suitably symbolic natural sites: springs, caves, unusual rock formations, hilltops, places of transition such as valley passes, crossroads, or places whose names or activities evoke some aspect of the saints or ancestors, such as Catholic church buildings or cemeteries. Occasionally, an *ajq'ij* may be asked to invoke the ancestors' or the Santo Mundo's blessings on a rural community project, such as a new building, a school, a well, or a spring to be tapped for the community's water supply.

Individuals, couples, or family groups may ask for blessing or a divination regarding the auspiciousness of some contemplated new activity, or when faced with severe or persisting reversals of health or with economic misfortune, they may seek a healing or solicit a divination of the misfortune's cause. Through a suitable *ajq'ij*, they may beg for the protective intercession and counsel of their ancestors (Scott el al., this volume). The *ajq'ijab'* aver that they cannot initiate harm. They say they are not *ajits*; that is, they are not *brujos* (witches). Since 1950—and dramatically since 1980—the providers of Maya traditionalist religious services have suffered a substantial public relations defeat. Their prestige in their own communities has declined because of a multipronged cultural attack.

First, most Roman Catholic priests and their trained assistants (formerly in Acción Católica and now the cursillistas) have sought to shut down the *ajq'ijab'* and the *cofradía* leaders since the mid-1940s and more vigorously since the mid-1950s. The *ajq'ijab'* have become alienated as they weather the attacks and disparagement. As time goes on, the *ajq'ijab'* see themselves less and less as the true Catholics or as Catholics at all. Rather, they see themselves more and more as "Maya priests" (*sacerdotes mayas, ajq'ijab'*) doing non-Catholic, "pure" traditional Maya rituals in the "true" religion. The more the international Ortho-Catholics have labeled the *ajq'ijab'* as unorthodox or even pagan, the more the *ajq'ijab'* have actively distanced themselves from the main plaza's church and from interaction with the priest.

Second, Pentecostal discourse expresses vociferous disdain for all traditionalist activities. *Evangélicos* (in Nahualá and Santa Catarina Ixtahuacán, this means Protestant-derived Pentecostals) have openly attacked indigenous traditionalism, labeling the *ajq'ijab'* as *brujos* and pagans in league with the devil. The Pentecostal message gets projected from the religious radio stations, by ministers preaching in church, and in public through the speakers placed on the rooftops of Pentecostal churches and ministers' homes (see Pratt et al., this volume). When not booming out a live meeting, the same speakers incessantly play looped cassettes or CDs of religious messages and Pentecostal music, the words of which challenge and demean both Ortho-Catholic hegemony and traditionalist practice.[2]

Third, the advocates of a national developmentalist culture of science and belief in modernity also see traditionalist Maya culture as backward and restraining progress, useful only for its touristic attraction (Burrell 2013).

In the fourth source of attack, traditionalist leaders were deliberately sought out and executed by the army during the prosecution of the counterinsurgency war. Military persecution combined with public disparagement drove traditionalist practice into hiding.

For all these reasons of former risk and present disdain, traditionalists have become practitioners and custodians of an underground phenomenon, one that few clients readily admit to having used. As John Edvalson (pers. comm.) notes, traditionalist practice has now entered the realm of folklore, and most indigenes now disparage it as "old beliefs." Yet from time to time at public assemblies, bystander-observers can witness the occasional open performance of a traditionalist blessing ritual (Morgan 2005). An *ajq'ij* will perform a ceremony upon the rollover of the 260-day year. It is public and available to those who know and care about such date changes, but attended by relatively few.

In spite of disparagement and professed nonbelief in

the traditionalist practices, many nontraditionalists fear the *ajq'ij*'s power to curse. By the Shakespearean logic of "the lady doth protest too much," the *evangélico*'s vociferous and repeated declamations against the satanic powers of the *ajq'ijab'* become affirmations of traditionalist strength (see Morgan 2005; Scott et al., this volume). Moreover, for those suffering from culture-bound syndromes such as *mal de ojo*, for those with sufficient wealth in land or a trading business that makes them feel secure, and for those who lack experience negotiating modernization, the *ajq'ij*'s divinatory and curing presence can be almost indispensable since Ortho-Catholic official ritual provides nothing to counter or heal the reversals of life. Thus, many apparently Ortho-Catholic Mayas come to and pay the *ajq'ij* for his or her ceremonial knowledge, healing, and practice, thereby blurring the boundaries between traditionalist and Ortho belief.

Clients bring copal, alcohol, sugar, candles, chocolate, bottles of intensely colored Orange Crush soda, and paraphernalia needed to "burn" an offering (Sp. *quemar*; K'i. *käporoj*). Often, they can buy the needed materials from the *ajq'ij*. They receive assurances via culturally appropriate prayers that address the concerns of an agriculturally dependent people, including supplications to the gods of the air, cold, water, and earth that surround them; pleas for protection from the Ladino earth lords or from the betrayals by Maximón/Judas that may capriciously beset them; and conversations with and advice from the ancestors that gave them an inheritance of land.

These divinities, however, work under the supervision or watchful eye of the more distant high gods: Christ, Saint Catherine, Santiago Matamoros, and other saints (per Scott et al., this volume). The high divinities watch over the works of the more world-engaged earth lords, Maximón (a lord of chance, conceived of as a Ladino, who can control one's fate or luck [K'i. *portuna*]), and the ancestors that directly address the clients' needs.[3] Because of this high god supervision, traditionalist practitioners and their clients claim legitimate Catholic affiliation as the true Catholics with the true cosmology.

Some Ortho-Catholics and most *evangélicos* label traditionalists of both Maya Catholic and neotraditionalist orientation as adherents of "Maya religion" or as "of the devil," and therefore their practice is "not a religion." In either case, the two traditionalisms are viewed as non-Christian "paganism." Any traditionalism thus lands outside some nontraditionalist's sense of what is legitimate religion.

Concerning the neotraditionalists, a generally younger set of shamans practice what they call "Maya spirituality." Maya spiritualists have tried to insinuate religious difference into indigenous identity politics by removing the more obvious Catholic and Christian-derived symbols in traditionalist ceremonies. They eschew the mention of Mary or reference to Jesus common in the prayer practice of relatively unpoliticized traditionalists. In some regards, that makes neotraditionalism's criticism of Maya Catholic traditionalism's impurities structurally similar to *renovación* charismaticism's soft critique reformation, rather than full rejection, of Ortho-Catholicism.

Neotraditionalists try to reconstruct what they perceive to be authentically Maya religion from older ethnographies, archaeological accounts, published glyph decipherments, and pop culture studies of the *Popol Wuj*. Thus, the neotraditionalist *ajq'ijab'* of Maya spirituality see themselves not as Catholics, nor even as Christians, but as practitioners of a renewed, restored, and pure Maya religion that they feel existed in Guatemala before the Spanish arrived with Catholicism. It is a religion to which they believe Mayas must return if they are to be true to their inherent natures as Mayas. Although Maya spiritualists tend to compete with the old guard Maya Catholic traditionalists and thereby contest the category of traditionalism and its direction, neotraditionalists nevertheless include Maya Catholic traditionalists and even respect their performances, granting some Maya Catholic traditionalists leadership in formal associations of Maya spiritualists.

As Hanselmann and colleagues (this volume) show, one should keep in mind that traditionalists and neotraditionalists promulgate two distinct worldviews. Maya Catholic traditionalists symbolically value and support the success of the two forms of livelihood most open to Mayas for the last four centuries: hoe cultivation of corn and petty sales in local and itinerant markets. By contrast, neotraditionalists use modified, de-Catholicized, and modernized Maya traditionalist symbolism to create a pan-Maya identity, resist the colonialism they feel is fostered by Ortho-Catholicism, and secure funding, rights, and respect for Mayas generally. However, by advocating for the protection of human rights and preservation of the environment as traditional Maya orientations, neotraditionalists invent customs compatible with, attractive to, and encouraged by NGO-connected globalization and international aid programs aimed at indigenous culture protection. At the end of the counterinsurgency war and just after it, NGOs poured money into the support of "authentic" or autochthonous indigenous culture, especially if this indigenous authenticity affirmed western human rights and ecological standards. As a consequence of these pressures, "pure" Maya neotraditionalist religion in Nahualá and Santa Catarina Ixtahuacán, cleansed of Catholic elements, deliberately has absorbed a substantial modern infusion of green ecotheology and eastern mysticism acquired at international conferences that key Maya Catholic traditionalist and neotraditionalist *ajq'ijab'* have been able to attend because of international funding. Neotraditionalism thus constitutes another pathway in what is actually a bidirectional process of interpenetration and contestation between a mostly Ladino capital city center and a mostly indigenous village periphery. Part of the meaning contrast between Maya Catholic traditionalism and neotraditionalism is the educated ladinoization lurking in the adaptation of traditionalism for political purposes while it is being used simultaneously for identity reconstruction purposes.

Something of the internationally supported resurgent strength of Maya traditionalism is reflected in Nahualá's Association of Maya Priests, a group that brings Nahualá's Maya priests into contact with Maya priests of other communities and with leaders of indigenous nationalism throughout the world. Thus, one reads of the Association of Ecuadoran Shamans, which Andeanizes and standardizes shamanic practice to the extent of issuing certificates of shamanistic legitimacy (Corr 2007:185, 187). So also with the Association of Maya Priests, which likewise offers certificates of legitimacy, which are displayed by several Nahualense shamans. The man who was the head of the Nahualense Association of Maya Priests in 2003, with whom I lived for two summers, is a Maya Catholic traditionalist. He traveled with NGO-sponsored funding to Colombia to an international meeting of indigenous religious leaders. From this experience, he added both ecological and eastern religious tones to his Maya Catholic repertoire. Thus, even the traditionalist Maya Catholic faith makes contact with and becomes changed by association with the political agendas of pan-American and pan-Guatemalan neotraditional indigenous activism. This set of enticing connections, combined with antitraditionalist pressure exerted by Ortho-Catholic priests, bit by bit has led Maya Catholic traditionalists to distance themselves from their once-solid Catholic moorings.

In all these regards, our study of neotraditionalists in Nahualá and Santa Catarina Ixtahuacán confirms Cook

and Offit's (2013:xiii–xiv) observations regarding nearby K'iche'-speaking Momostenango: Maya spirituality "is a religious movement situated culturally and politically within the broader patterns of Guatemalan indigenous cultural activism. . . . It seeks to eliminate Christian influence from Maya religious practice and to return to a pure Maya religion." This makes Maya spirituality an "antisyncretic movement that is in some respects opposed to the syncretized Costumbre tradition from which it emerged" (xiv).

As Larson and colleagues, Scott and colleagues, and Hanselmann and colleagues (all this volume) and Morgan (2005) show, both Maya Catholic traditionalism and neotraditionalism in Nahualá and Santa Catarina Ixtahuacán are on the wane. At the same time, neither Maya Catholic traditionalism nor neotraditionalism can be fully understood without reference to their contrasts with each other and with Ortho-Catholicism. Nor can Guatemalan Ortho-Catholics be understood without reference to their contrasts and struggles with Maya Catholic traditionalists.

Ortho-Catholics: Respecting the Priest as True Catholicism

Roman Catholics recognize the parish priest as their source of authority and their guide to how they ought to maintain or transform their culturally embedded religious behavior. Orientation to a priest connects them to the church hierarchy through the bishop of Sololá. From 1995 through 2010, two priests lived in Nahualá and one priest resided in Antigua Ixtahuacán; from 2000 to 2010, a circuit priest visited Nueva Ixtahuacán to offer mass on Sundays and holy days.

Ortho-Catholic lay leaders—those who assist the priest; clean, maintain, and guard the main church building; ring the bells; lead indoctrination courses; or guide local charismatic congregations—have religious obligations. They should attend mass weekly, meet with the priest for instruction and coordination, and provide various lay-delivered outreach activities. Ortho-Catholics who are active but not in leadership positions feel an obligation to attend mass perhaps as often as once a week. They take care to arrange life-cycle sacraments in their families; they celebrate mass for baptisms, confirmations, marriages, funerals, and other events. They feel they should confess in preparation for these rituals and for mass. They might help prepare for or participate in the processions from the church.

If one is a more marginal, relaxed, or cultural Ortho-Catholic, one attends the life-cycle rituals of self and kin, goes to mass once in a while (perhaps annually or a few times more), tries to be a good person, and is respectful of family, municipal, and religious authority.

When in need or in crisis, Ortho-Catholics (and Catholic traditionalists) may visit the church alone, absent the priest or a call to mass, since the church building is usually open for a visit to importune the saints housed therein. Inside, on weekdays, the church will be largely empty of people except for a few women and occasionally a man on their knees in earnest and often anguished prayer. In their homes, Ortho-Catholics have a house altar, often with a statue of Mary, a bouquet of fresh or plastic flowers, and a lit candle or a tiny electric bulb left on as an offering to honor her. They may address the family altar occasionally with prayers intoned before it or by crossing themselves as they pass in front of it. The people who perform such practices generally self-designate as *católico* and perhaps *muy romano*, but they never would apply the analytical terms of "Ortho" or "mainline" to themselves. The more educated, however, might say they are *ortodoxo* in contrast to traditionalists or *carismáticos*.

Many Catholics participate to some degree in the saints' processions that bless the town as a whole by carrying a statue of a saint mounted on a palanquin (Sp. *andén*), accompanied by a priest, a band, and a crowd of followers. The more devoted parishioners clean, clothe, and otherwise make ready the statues of saints to be carried. On celebratory days, Catholics adorn the procession route with honorific "rugs" of colored sawdust, flower petals, and pine needles laid out in religious pictures or geometric designs. Dozens of lay Catholic adults, classrooms of Catholic school kids, and representatives of Catholic organizations or clubs meet at their designated segment of the route to put down their design prior to the saint's passage. Carried on the shoulders of men and followed by women and men of the faith, the statue of Christ, Mary, or a town's patron saint circumnavigates the town's main perimeter streets, moving counterclockwise as much as streets and paths permit. Announced by a live band or by a battery-operated music system carried in a wheelbarrow, priest, saint, and acolytes process through a series of street-corner shrines. At each one, they stop and bless that section of the town center and, by implication, the hamlets radiating from each quarter.

In all these Catholic lay activities there is no social pressure, small-group awareness, surveillance, or judgment of one another's participation or nonparticipation. Lay Ortho-Catholics come and go to Catholic events as their hearts and devotions dictate, some to many events, many to but a few. No one keeps track. Among Roman Catholics, no one worries if someone has not been to church for quite a while. This contrasts rather starkly with a congregant's and pastor's awareness regarding who is in attendance and who is not in a Pentecostal or Catholic charismatic flock.

Although the Catholic Church is nominally hierarchical, not all its ideas or practices derive from senior ecclesiasts. Individual priests, nuns, or lay leaders may initiate novel activities in their parishes. If successful, such ideas will likely spread, not by hierarchical edict, but by absorption and imitation when Catholic lay leaders meet and exchange ideas at conferences, leadership trainings, and retreats. Information, programs, and workarounds often bypass the inefficiencies of the direct line of hierarchy and homogenize Ortho-Catholicism (and charismaticism) across the nation and even the continent. In general, what works will spread through informal networks and regional assemblies of lay leaders, whether or not it is pushed by a local priest or blessed by a region's bishop. Nevertheless, the personal predilections of the local priest and the bishop do have a distinct impact.

Participating in mass constitutes the main sacrament. The bulk of the ritual consists of the chanting of a written Spanish script, which the priest recites and to which the members respond.[4] The mass is repeated in the same form each offering, varying only slightly according to the season or if it is a high mass, and by the priest's or assistant's brief sermon, homily, or biblical reading. Attending mass brings the adept into submission before God and God's connecting priest. The priest contacts the sacred realm and blesses the sacramental wafer and wine. Lay assistants help the priest distribute the wafer to those consuming the sacrament and circulate among the benches to collect monetary offerings from the attendees. The core liturgy of the Roman Catholic mass remains sedate, manifesting a general tenor of mildness that contrasts sharply with the highly amplified sound, jazzy band improvisations, and human exuberance and anxiety often expressed in Evangelical and charismatic meetings.

Ortho-Catholic symbolism highlights the similarities between the suffering and death of Christ, on the one hand, and one's personal suffering experienced in ordinary life, on the other. Icons visible in church and those used in the Easter pageant visually represent the suffering of Mary; the bleeding and emaciated Christ hangs visibly before the congregation, above a side altar, or in a glass case. Other saints' images in glass cases along walls also display their suffering, bleeding, emaciated, or tortured bodies (although Santa Catarina is always regal, never suffering). Collectively, the images represent the nature of indigenous life with its suffering, pain, and physical difficulty. One could say that the Catholic liturgy and its supporting statuary and paintings represent a worldview in which suffering is expected and endurance is required. The individual suffers in life, as did Christ and the saints as models for life. One can mitigate that suffering by submitting to the authority of the priest, who connects a person to society and to God by receiving confession and by performing mass and life-cycle rituals. Together with privately solicited blessings, asking for the intercession of the saints, public religious practice via the mass helps one confront a life in which privation, suffering, and submission are normative and expected.

I described in part 2 how Maya cultural collapse drove a change to Pentecostalism. One might reasonably ask how a life of expected suffering differs from a way of life that is in existential crisis and collapse. Would not expected suffering have driven Catholics to Pentecostalism much sooner? Is not collapse a form of suffering, and vice versa? The difference is this: suffering can be tolerated and lived with, if cognized as a normal state. Collapse, by contrast, suggests no possibility of continuance in an expected normal state. A clearly present or impending inability to provide for one's family is qualitatively different from an expectation of continuing poverty and hardship shared by all. But in the new system emerging around the collapse, some have indeed gotten ahead. That makes the pain of collapse even more excruciating personally. And the emerging differentiation violates the Maya premise of ethnic equality and mutuality. Collapse of the old system and apparent exclusion from any other system raises anxieties about one's status to a new order of magnitude. The tense, end-of-the-world pentecostalized versions of Christianity liturgically symbolize that deteriorated and collapsed condition of life and the need for something new.

Both traditionalists and Ortho-Catholics claim to be true Catholics and worry about the supposed deviations of the other style of their faith. But as one would suppose, they share many attributes because traditionalists have imitated and borrowed at various periods from the Ortho church. Here I note, for example, the structural similarity

of traditionalist and Ortho altars. There are three altars in Tix's (and any traditionalist *ajq'ij*'s) *sala*: a high altar against the back wall, a middle altar on which the work for the living is performed, and an altar on the floor representing the place of the dead. One finds the same layout in any Ortho-Catholic church (plate 31). Along the back wall is the main high altar where sit the saints and representations of Jesus, God, and/or the *municipio*'s patron saint. Separated from that high altar, there is a table altar on which the priest performs the sacramental work for the living. Toward the worshippers' area, there is a step down to the lower altar where candles are placed on stands or on the floor, lit for the benefit of ancestors gone to the world of the deceased. Structurally, the Ortho-Catholic church's layout and Tix's tripartite altar are identical.

Like the traditionalists, Ortho-Catholics may engage Jesus, Mary, Santa Catarina, or other saints in the central church building, in peripheral chapels dedicated to a saint, or at their home altar. Rather like the traditionalists, Ortho-Catholics can and should help their ancestors by performing the funeral mass, completing the nine evenings of novena prayer, and celebrating mass on the first anniversary of a family member's death. The Ortho-Catholic, however, neither addresses the ancestors as a collectivity nor receives messages from them except by visiting a traditionalist *ajq'ij*. Rather, the Ortho-Catholic commissions a mass or engages in a novena to bless a specific recently deceased ancestor, but not to receive a blessing or communication from an ancestor.

In short, the Roman Catholic Church does not provide Maya Ortho-Catholics with a liturgy with which to converse with their lineage ancestors or receive knowledge, approbation, or advice by divination. Nor does Ortho-Catholicism or its mass provide a means to openly deliver a healing or to defend oneself against or recover from a witchcraft attack. For protection against suspected attack, which is almost always assumed when a sickness is grave or lingers, Ortho-Catholics must consult the traditionalist *ajq'ij* secretively or go to a charismatic meeting (or a Protestant Pentecostal meeting) for healing or expulsion of evil spirits. When they do so, they indeed blur the lines of distinction between these three approaches to Catholicism.

My description and analysis, however, has introduced a distortion. I write as though there *should* be clear boundaries between these approaches to Catholicism, as though participation in them should be mutually exclusive. Catholics themselves see no such necessity. Indeed

Catholicism, as the root meaning of the word suggests, embraces all and has long entertained a broad spectrum of orientations and practices in its various orders and organizations.

Lay leaders and activist members of Ortho-Catholicism, however, actively evangelize among less-involved cultural Catholics in order to sustain Ortho-Catholicism and to staunch its membership losses to Evangelicalism. They encourage all Catholics to be more performative, to be actively Ortho-Catholic, and to stop being passively cultural or actively traditionalist Catholics.

At the priest's behest, male and female lay leaders assist in performing various tasks attendant to mass. They may solicit offerings, sing in the choir, read some portion of the mass or its recommended homilies, or translate into or read in K'iche'. Lay members and employees fill positions—such as *sacristán*—that help the parish priest. Some, called *catequistas*, teach catechism classes to those preparing for confirmation. A few lead or actively participate in spiritual education programs. Some clean the church and its front patio as well as the parish's service and school areas. Others—old men—sit in front of the church building when it is left open to those wishing to pray. They guard its contents, a vestige of the *pasado* gerontocracy sitting in judgment of Maya affairs in front of the Ladino mayor's office (Vogt 1976). But many Catholics engage Catholicism culturally at the family and private level; publicly they attend mass only occasionally and perhaps cross themselves as they pass in front of Catholic churches.

Finally, Roman Catholicism has provided key support services that have aided Catholics with modernization. For example, the Catholic church in Nahualá runs an elementary school and a high school. It operates a clinic staffed by a medical doctor and nurses. In Santa Catarina (both old and new), the Catholic church occasionally has offered a nurse-staffed clinic. It also has fomented a number of economic and social development projects, especially in Santa Catarina Ixtahuacán prior to and following its division, under the inspiration of a development-oriented American priest, resident since 1975, who connects his congregation and its hamlet residents to the charitable economic support of the Seattle diocese where the priest grew up (Checketts 2005; Nuttall 2005; Baronti 2002). But the availability of aid projects depends largely on the networks and interests of a parish's particular priest or nuns. Some are activist in development projects and connected internationally to funding. Some are not.

Church-sponsored aid projects administered from offices housed in a municipal headquarters may serve a widely dispersed population, although our experience is that those in the headquarters town sometimes garner the most benefits. Thus, although Nahualá had a daily Catholic clinic staffed with a doctor and available to members of all religions, none of its hamlets were so served, though, of course, hamlet residents could come to the clinic in the center. And they did, especially on Sundays, thereby combining market, mass, and medical aid. The Catholic school in Nahualá charges tuition, excluding poorer Catholics from attending, although small scholarships and tuition remissions are available to some. Ixtahuacán center had a Catholic-staffed maternity clinic open only occasionally, but none of its highland hamlets had even that. The American priest in Ixtahuacán aggressively fomented local economic development projects, consistent with liberation theology. Such was not obvious in Nahualá, where the priests were Spanish or Guatemalan Ladino throughout most of our field school period. In 2005, however, the seminary in Sololá graduated and ordained a K'iche'-speaking Nahualense priest, apparently the first, and since about 2013, Antigua Santa Catarina Ixtahuacán has had a resident K'iche'-speaking Maya as its priest.

Of the three strands of Catholicism under discussion here, only the Ortho-Catholic hierarchy sponsors nondenominational development projects and aid distribution systems. The funds pay the salaries of local administrators, assist families with children's school supplies, and/or provide food and clothing for the children of impoverished families. But members of all religions think that church-sponsored development projects are always denominational because they believe that a gift received entails reciprocal obligations of affiliation (Checketts 2005; Nuttall 2005; Stratford, Hawkins, and Adams 2020). Neither the client-oriented traditionalists nor the small-congregation charismatics have organized aid, development projects, biomedical delivery systems, or collective secular educational programs. Indeed, Catholic *carismáticos* use an entirely different and nonsecular approach to provide help to local congregants. They seek the Holy Spirit.

Catholic Charismatics: Embodiment by the Holy Spirit as True Catholicism

The third strand of Catholicism, the Charismatic Renewal, responds partly to the threat posed by Pentecostal success in attracting Catholics out of the Ortho faith and partly to the same culture and corn crisis that transformed sedate mission Protestantism into impassioned Pentecostal Evangelicalism. As detailed in chapter 19, since about 1973, Guatemalan Catholics have developed and rapidly expanded their pentecostalized search for solace in the Catholic fold. Adherents call the movement *la renovación* ("the renovation," "the renewal") or, more formally, La Renovación Carismática, and they call themselves *carismáticos* (charismatics). A *carismático* is a Catholic who, in addition to attending mass and recognizing the priest as leader, seeks to experience bodily the manifestation of the Holy Ghost in his or her life, usually with some frequency. *Carismáticos* do so by participating in additional hamlet- or barrio-level congregational meetings on Sundays and weekdays. These meetings are virtually identical to those of *evangélicos*, except that *carismáticos* offer praise to both Jesus and Mary, while Pentecostals laud only Jesus. Involvement in the Catholic charismatic movement offers most of the social advantages of Pentecostal practice and a small congregational community within the fold of the Catholic faith.

In making themselves similar to Protestant Pentecostals, however, *carismáticos* make themselves different from Ortho-Catholics. Among other things, they eschew alcohol consumption,[5] prohibit dancing, abjure the traditional *cofradía* and fiesta system, and reject the world as corrupt. Again like Pentecostals, *carismáticos* emphasize premarital abstention from sexual intercourse, marital fidelity, and attention to family responsibilities. Charismatics also reject any devotions to the Ortho-Catholic panoply of saints, though they express their rejection more gently and respectfully than do Pentecostal *evangélicos*.

Charismatics also differ from Ortho-Catholics by attending Sunday and weekday afternoon meetings in which they seek the Christian Pentecostal experience of having the Holy Spirit enter and infuse their bodies. Such entrance is evidenced by corporal agitation, speaking in tongues, trance collapse to the floor, and/or receiving healings freely proffered. Charismatics differ from Maya Catholic traditionalists and culturally casual Ortho-Catholics by prohibiting alcohol consumption, marimba, secular music, dancing, smoking, and participation in fiestas honoring saints or *municipios*. They reject ritual devotion to the Catholic saints as intermediaries, abjure traditionalist divinities, and prohibit the consultation of an *ajq'ij* (see Pastor 1998:10 for parallels in Argentina). Of course, charismatics also eschew traditionalist divinities of the

second and third tables: Santo Mundo, Maximón/Judas, and the ancestors.

From the perspective of participants and in the movement's guiding principles, the purpose of the Renovación Carismática is not to compete with Pentecostalism and thereby protect Catholicism from the "invasion of the sects" (Coleman et al. 1993:112, 135n5; Stoll 1990:1, 5–6, 40). That, I have noted, is an Ortho-Catholic administrative view. Rather, charismatic Catholics seek a renovation or renewal of the Roman Catholic mother church; they seek to restore an authentic spirit to what they feel has become a listless and despirited core church. *Carismáticos* see themselves as replenishing and rejuvenating the vibrancy of the entire Catholic Church by infusing themselves—and through expansion, eventually the whole church—with the pentecostal gifts of the Holy Spirit. Indeed, charismatics feel that seeking these gifts injects a purifying and completing influence by the respiritualization and reexcitement that they bring to Catholicism; they do not see themselves as in rebellion or stepping away from Catholicism.

Nevertheless, charismaticism is indeed revolutionary and change-oriented both at the personal and at the institutional levels. La Renovación Carismática, however, does not challenge the legitimacy of the Catholic hierarchy directly. Rather, it implicitly challenges the hierarchy by explicitly challenging the sufficiency of the ordinary lived religions of the Ortho-Catholics, marginalized cultural Catholics, and Maya Catholic traditionalists. Charismaticism challenges the traditionalists by providing a spirited alternative in which the individual worshipper, rather than just the *ajq'ij* leader, receives the Holy Spirit into his or her body and enters a trance-like state of collapse or glossolalic expression. Charismaticism challenges the Ortho church by locating revelatory experience and information spontaneously in the congregation, among both men and women, rather than transmitting it by edict only through the male Roman Catholic priesthood.

Like the Pentecostals they mimic, Maya *carismáticos* in Santa Catarina and Nahualá meet frequently. If the congregation is new or small, it likely meets in the *sala* of a leader's house. Larger and more mature groups meet in a cinderblock, one-room chapel that the members of the congregation have funded and labored together to build. Almost every hamlet and urban canton of Nahualá and Santa Catarina Ixtahuacán has one or more such *comunidades*. Often substantially poorer than Pentecostal groups, a few small congregations of *carismáticos* do not have the resources for electronic amplification and music in their church services (see chapter 11). But most do, and their services are noisy and exuberant, with movement, glossolalia, and receipt of spiritual healings.

On Sundays, charismatics from any of the town centers or hamlets we studied begin their religious life with a walk to the town center to attend one of the morning masses. For a charismatic from Nahualá, worship begins on Sunday morning by attending mass in the large church facing the central plaza. In the centers of Antigua and Nueva Ixtahuacán, all Catholics who attended mass did so in provisional sheds during several years when Antigua Ixtahuaquense Catholics repaired the cracks threatening their centuries-old plaza church's walls. At the same time, Nueva Ixtahuaquenses toiled, when they had the money, to build a new retro Spanish baroque building on their plaza. In all three town centers, Catholic renewal charismatics pack the Sunday morning mass in the main plaza church; compared to traditionalists or Ortho-Catholics, many more of them participate. After mass, attendees make their purchases for the week in the Sunday market held in the streets and stalls in each town center. People then walk home or pack themselves and their purchases into the back of a pickup truck or minibus to return to their hamlet for lunch.

At about 3:00 p.m., they enter a local building or home, usually in their hamlet, to attend a two- or three-hour meeting that is Pentecostal in style: exuberant, spirited, electronically amplified, and charismatic in the sense that its preaching, prayers, and music build to a crescendo that emphasizes the corruption of the world, salvation by Jesus only, and embodiment by the Holy Spirit. One may hear speaking in tongues, especially when congregants kneel to have those with the gift of healing lay hands on their heads and offer prayers that cure their ailments. Charismatic meetings, however, exhibit less bodily tension or anxiety than what I have witnessed in an *evangélico* meeting, and I have not seen the crescendo buildup that leads to falling on the floor in trance commonly seen in Pentecostal meetings. A charismatic meeting always occurs with a known set of regular attendees who are expected to be there, and it is led by a well-known and respected local married couple serving as the group's leaders. Of course, visitors are always welcome. They may come forward to be healed, and some convert in response to the social power of reciprocity inherent in receiving the gift of healing.

If the congregation is large enough (and most are), a charismatic group uses an electronic band to produce fast-paced, hyperamplified, "modern" religious music that underscores and enhances the ministrations of the group leader. Whether band-accompanied or not, the liturgy emphasizes repetitious chants of Christological and Marian refrains, songs, sermons by the group's leader insisting on individual moral change, and testimonies by adherents of both genders describing their path from despair to repair. All lay members in good standing have access to the pulpit to sing or testify when urged by the Spirit. Finally, there are manifestations of embodiment by the Holy Spirit: speaking in tongues (but not in all meetings or congregations and not as dominantly as in Evangelical Pentecostal meetings), free healings by prayer (in almost all meetings), bodily motion, and prayerful outcry. As in the Pentecostal Protestant meetings, the presence of strident, pleading, anxious energy is palpable.

Additional worship meetings in the same style occur two or three times on weekday evenings. As do the Evangelicals, many of the charismatic congregants attend most of the sessions held in their particular building. As Charleston and colleagues, Huddleston and colleagues, and Bradshaw and colleagues (all this volume) confirm, charismatic meetings (like Pentecostal practices) consume a substantial number of hours and several evenings of each week. Also like Protestant Pentecostals, *carismáticos* focus theologically on the direct experience of God, bodily received or expressed and confirmed in agitated movement and speaking in tongues as a form of open revelation. The charismatic literature in both English and Spanish emphasizes this point (Mühlen 1975; Healey 1976:29, 41; Breckenridge 1980:19–20, 116, 130; Aldunate 1977:224, 227, 230–237), although the English literature is more explicit: "Catholic pentecostals consider *experiential* religiosity to be more important than assent to faith-propositions" (McGuire 1982:27, emphasis added).

The openness to revelation sets the choice of leadership of the charismatic congregation by revelatory experience against the nomination of leadership by hierarchical submission to the priest. Thus, "in a charismatically renewed Church, the choice of persons for roles of pastoral leadership (e.g., pastors, bishops, popes) would be made solely on the basis of the demonstrated presence in that person of the gifts of the Spirit" (Sullivan 1975:129). This, however, raises tensions with the presumption of management by the Ortho church's hierarchy. Therein lies the challenge that charismaticism presents to Ortho-Catholic leadership.

With so many similarities to the *evangélicos*, how is it that *carismáticos* remain identifiably Catholic? They do so, first, by emphasizing Mary in addition to their focus on Jesus and the Holy Spirit; second, by not emphasizing each congregation's distinctiveness; and third, by clearly subordinating themselves to the municipality's parish priest.

Concerning the first aspect, charismatics continue to preach Mary as the honored mother of God in sermons and songs. My word counts of sermons, however, clearly show a less frequent mention of Mary (compared to mentions of Jesus or the Holy Spirit) than occurs in Ortho-Catholic mass or in other Ortho meetings. Of course, *evangélicos* never mention Mary as an object of veneration. In that regard, *carismáticos* hold a kind of middle ground between Evangelicals and Ortho-Catholics. Both Cleary (2011:89–92) and Gooren (2012:194) note that *marianismo* was eschewed in early charismatic practice but brought back because of the official mainline church's insistence.

On the second issue, while *carismáticos* do divide and subdivide their congregations, they are unlike the ever-fissiparous Pentecostals, for *carismáticos* do not put unique names on their *comunidad* chapels. Charismatic buildings go unlabeled physically. Each is known simply as *la comunidad carismática* until its attendance exceeds the capacity of its building. Then the originating community becomes known as *la primera comunidad*, and the split-off group becomes *la segunda comunidad*, and so on; more advanced numeric designations are added if needed in the town or hamlet. Sometimes, additional communities are labeled by their geographic location in the parish. But the buildings sport no exterior names, and in my experience, none were brightly painted. They were cement gray or whitewashed, although Huddleston and colleagues (this volume) note that the charismatic congregation she attended was painted blue-green, but it too had no name board (see figure 12.1). This absence of a distinct name and (for the most part) the manifestly bland (and Catholic) gray or white exterior contrast sharply with the prominent and unique name or nationwide affiliation emblazoned on each Evangelical chapel and the flamboyant colors that often grace their buildings. Thus, conceptually and visually, charismatic buildings remain part of the Catholic Church; they are not renegade, rebellious, identifiably separate, or pretentious competitors with it.[6]

Third, *carismáticos* must also connect with and convincingly manifest their allegiance to the Ortho-Catholic church's leadership hierarchy. They do so by clearly submitting to the parish priest. A married male *comunidad* leader (equivalent to a Pentecostal congregation's preacher or pastor), assisted by his wife, leads each charismatic congregation. Each male leader, however, has been chosen and vetted by the parish priest, rather than being self-proclaimed, as is common in the fission of a Pentecostal congregation. Charismatic leaders must attend a weekly coordinating meeting presided over by the parish priest. Persistent nonattendance at the coordination meeting or regular absence from mass (without illness or other reasonable excuse) connotes a breakaway movement that Ortho-Catholic leaders view as a step toward independent status and therefore Evangelicalism.

A second mark of subordination to the priest derives from the management of the *comunidad*'s collection of funds. Any funds collected at the Sunday afternoon or weekday meetings should be accounted for and offered to the parish's priest. The priest usually returns these funds (or declines to take them) so that they stay with the local congregation for building maintenance, food after commemorative meetings, electronic repair, or other local costs. Unlike the paid or partially paid Evangelical pastor, the charismatic leader does not draw a stipend from the offerings by the congregants but serves as a nominated volunteer. If the funds go toward maintaining the personal life of the charismatic pastor, then the *comunidad* leader and congregation have begun to become independent and thereby essentially non-Catholic.[7]

Charismatic congregants must also mark themselves as Catholics. They do so by attending mass once a week, usually on Sunday morning, at the central Catholic church facing the municipal square. Indeed, this need to manifest their symbolic connection to Roman Catholicism makes charismatics the numerically preponderant attendees at Sunday mass in all three towns.[8] Furthermore, to ensure the congregation remains oriented to the priest rather than becoming too attached to a local couple, the priest rotates the pastoral *comunidad* leadership, ideally every two years.

Charismatics do not see the similarity they share with Maya Catholic traditionalists, who rotated their *cofradía* leadership annually. Nor do charismatics see the similarity they share with traditionalists when the shaman goes into trance and speaks a foreign language, Spanish, while embodied by an earth lord. (The charismatic goes into a trance and speaks a stream of glossolalia while embodied by the Holy Spirit.) Rather, they note the differences:

Maya charismatics reject alcohol, dancing, and marimba music—all aspects of traditionalist shamanic or *cofradía* ritual. They prohibit any participation in the fire-centered divination rituals that the traditionalist *ajq'ijab'* use to call on saints, ancestors, or earth lords to help the supplicant. Like the Pentecostals and the Ortho-Roman Catholic priests and their adherents, *carismáticos* challenge traditionalists by labeling their practices *brujería* (witchcraft) and satanic. Yet the deep cultural parallels between charismaticism and its first-born cousin, Pentecostalism, on the one hand, and Maya Catholic traditionalism, on the other, remain, even if unacknowledged.

Through these social and symbolic devices, charismatics have remained in the Catholic fold in spite of their difference with Ortho practice and their similarity to Pentecostal worship. They have done so by following a well-trodden path, doing just what the various orders of Dominicans, Franciscans, or Jesuits did centuries ago or what Catholic Action has done more recently: they established a branch of Catholic practice to remedy what they saw as inadequacies and misdirection in the core Catholic Church.

Overlap and Blurring among the Three Professions of Catholicism

No absolute demarcation can be drawn between these three strands of Catholic practice. The distinction between traditionalist Catholic, Ortho-Catholic, and charismatic Catholic becomes blurry because they all claim to be Catholic and because the affiliates of each, under stress, may avail themselves of the unique ritual services provided by the other two.

Many Ortho-Catholics who consider themselves strongly adherent to the parish priest and who think they reject traditionalism engage in practices that any Euro-American Catholic would find quaint, if not strongly traditionalist or even un-Catholic. Even if the priest has spoken against Maya Catholic traditionalist ceremonial behavior, in times of stress, long-term difficulty, misfortune, or sickness, some Ortho-Catholic Mayas will consult a traditionalist *ajq'ij* to find by divination who has used witchcraft to attack them, or they will access a *curandera* to get a cure for traditional illnesses.

Similarly, traditionalist leaders and those who consult them attend mass, avail themselves of the sacraments offered by the priest, and consider themselves good Catholics. Processions that used to be directed by traditionalist *cofradías* now are called for by the priest. Both Ortho-Catholics and traditionalist Catholics will visit the main church to pray before the particular saints symbolically associated with protecting their endeavors and ask for private blessings. They may contract a *promesa*—a promise to abstain from some favored food or other pleasure until what they importune fervently is granted. They may make a pilgrimage. Or they may promise to renew the clothing of the designated saint when an urgently implored blessing is realized through the saint's intercession. In all such matters, the difference between traditionalist Catholic and Ortho-Catholic is minimal.

Likewise, in spite of charismaticism's distinctiveness, several processes operate to overlap or blur the edges between it and Ortho-Catholicism in the congregations of Nahualá and Santa Catarina Ixtahuacán. First, charismatics call themselves Catholics. They do not think of themselves as separate from Roman Catholicism. Second, as already noted, charismatics attend confession and mass. They receive the life-cycle sacraments administered by the priest. Indeed, the priest might not even be aware that most of his congregants attending Sunday morning mass are charismatics, for in the municipality's main church, charismatics, Ortho-Catholics, and Maya Catholic traditionalists seem visually indistinguishable. Adding to the overlap, Ortho-Catholics can attend the Maya Catholic traditionalists' divination or healing, or they can attend the charismatic meeting when in need of healing.

Catholic Complexity and the Ortho Hierarchy's Dilemmas

This blurring of boundaries among the three main types of Catholic orientation and performance in Nahualá and Santa Catarina (and elsewhere) adds to the challenges that Ortho-Catholic leaders face. Some Catholic priests feel they walk a razor-thin middle path as they try to braid together these three strands of Catholicism. Steigenga and Cleary (2007b:9) usefully summarize the essence of Catholic complexity by suggesting we think in terms of a variety of Catholicisms, rather than think of Catholics or of Catholicism as a monolith. Catholicism is indeed a multifaceted system, if not quite a spectrum. Catholicism is not a single entity. Nor is its complexity limited to the three strands or the blurring I elaborate in this book. Here are some of the dilemmas its leaders confront as they deal with this local Catholic diversity and complexity.

Should the Ortho-Catholic hierarchy honor and

sustain the traditionalists? To do so blends Ortho-Catholicism with traditionalism. It honors indigenous culture, which many postwar indigenous activists and many culturally sophisticated Catholic priests have done over the years and see as a good thing. But honoring Maya traditionalist Catholicism as a source of spiritual truth fractures the church's claim that Roman tradition and the voice of the pope combine to provide a definitive source of truth, for it makes Roman tradition and Maya tradition coequal and rivals. Moreover, Maya tradition is certainly not a single thing; each *municipio* and hamlet has evolved its own variants, which its residents see as traditional. Mutual respect of the traditions puts priest and traditionalist shaman in competition for leadership and moral authority. Moreover, sustaining the traditionalists would set the priest in opposition to the far larger block of *carismáticos*, for the latter abjure the traditionalist version of Catholicism as an idolatrous corruption.

On the other hand, honoring and sustaining charismaticism conjures its own problems for Ortho leaders. The priest who nurtured the charismatic movement in Santa Catarina Ixtahuacán and presided in Antigua Santa Catarina until 2017 vocalized the issues. He felt he had to tread lightly with the charismatics and found himself caught in a web of dilemmas. He worried that the revelatory openness of charismatics could be a challenge to a parish priest's leadership and authority. At the same time, he recognized and valued the participatory renewal that charismaticism brings. He feared that if he pressured the charismatics toward the Ortho center, he might lose them to Pentecostalism by wholesale conversion of alienated *comunidades* whose pentecostal charismaticism had pre-adapted them to comfort in Pentecostal churches. Charismatic experience makes Catholics comfortable with pentecostal orientations and practice, which, the priest felt, was likely to facilitate the movement of Catholics into Pentecostal Protestant membership.[9]

Given these issues, which sector should Ortho-Catholic clerical leaders cultivate? Clearly, the local priest and his ecclesiastical superiors are hard pressed to foster both, since charismatics think (and preach) that traditionalists import into Catholicism the workings of the devil. But to foster charismatics will offend the traditionalists and some cultural Ortho-Catholics, for many Ortho-Catholics adhering to the will of the parish priest are rather traditional indigenes in their self-perception and daily life cultural practice. For them, traditionalist Catholicism symbolizes the Mayaness of indigenous life.

In effect, charismatics further divide Catholicism, making it a three-way debate regarding who proffers the purest version of Catholic truth. No matter what he does, an Ortho priest in a Maya *municipio* is likely to push some sector of the Maya populace to the periphery or entirely out of the fold.

Worse yet from the perspective of the parish priest, charismatic pentecostalism challenges the ordained, hierarchical Ortho-Catholic priesthood leadership because a male or female charismatic Catholic being guided by the Spirit can easily receive divine inspiration that runs counter to the will of a priest or bishop. That inherent possibility undermines the Ortho church's claim to being the sole source of authority through a male priesthood. Charismaticism gives lay members of both genders opportunity to preach directly to one another. They do so when prompted by the Spirit. That deprives the Ortho hierarchy of full control of the message and process. Moreover, when a charismatic speaks in tongues incomprehensibly, she or he—not the priest—then speaks for God. And when a message spoken in tongues gets interpreted by what is called the gift of prophecy, it is often a woman who voices the interpretation that conveys God's message to the congregation.[10] Priests, bishops, and the authority of tradition that undergirds the Roman Catholic claim to rightness get shut out in favor of a revelation that jumps directly from God to ordinary lay enthusiasts. This revelatory end run, bypassing the Catholic hierarchy, often flows through women, to the chagrin of Ortho-Catholicism's male-centered hierarchy.

Thus, multiple official sources express nervousness about the contradiction between the hierarchy inherent in the Roman Catholic Church and the revelatory flexibility of the democratized interpretation of tongues. John Healey (1976:99), an American priest who wrote something of a catechism for charismatics, observes, "This kind of equality in Christian action can be difficult for many priests to enter into and accept. In our education and experience we are accustomed, not to equality with laymen and women in doctrinal and devotional areas, but to leadership and the use of authority. To see others take the lead, especially in our presence and without reference to us, can strike some of us as presumptuous and dangerous, even threatening" (see also 100, 107–108). Likewise, the Council of Latin American Bishops recognizes the problematic contrast between "the order, planning, prudence, and discipline" of the church's core "hierarchy" and "the spontaneity, freshness, [and] uncontrollable audacity of the Spirit" inherent in "charismas" (CELAM 1977:56). Indeed, the group devotes six pages (56–62) to the task of suggesting ways to resolve the tension. Charismaticism is indeed a radical challenge to Ortho-Catholic leadership.

Finally, in a process that is largely unperceived by priests to whom I spoke and not addressed in the Catholic literature (to my knowledge), the charismatic movement, by staying in the Ortho church, fundamentally transforms the structure of Roman Catholicism. It does so by creating a de facto married priesthood of both men and women, composed of the married couples who lead, guide, receive revelations, and deliver counsel and healing to the charismatics who worship in the local *comunidad* services, services rarely attended by an ordained Roman Catholic priest. It puts married lay couples in charge of hamlet and canton religious services. Lay members under a married couple's ministration and supervision heal one another in each micro congregation. The Renovación Carismática enables women to perform healings that not even the Ortho-Catholic priest can perform. What the worldwide hierarchy of Catholicism has struggled mightily to avoid—a married priesthood and/or female priests—has in fact occurred in their fold surreptitiously. This de facto married Catholic priesthood is an unintended consequence of the Ortho-Catholic leadership's decision to retain as Catholics those pursuing the gifts of the Spirit in a more energetic, small-community, charismatic liturgy. Through this decision, conservative religious leaders intended to protect Catholics from poaching by Pentecostal Protestants. They lost some control, however, and they acquired a de facto married priesthood as the unexpected and even unseen cost of using charismaticism as a mode of membership preservation.

Another result is that the parish priest has become a supervisor of weekly meetings with charismatic *comunidad* leaders. The parish priest of Nahualá has effectively been made bishop over the fifty-seven or more charismatic communities said to exist throughout the municipality. The official celibate Catholic priesthood has become the senior hierarchical administrative and record-keeping arm of a localized, new, vibrant, adaptive, congregational charismatic Catholic church led by lay married couples who rotate in and out of leadership.

Having noted the contrasts between segments of the Catholic Church and having made brief reference to the similarities between charismatic Catholic Mayas and Pentecostal Mayas, I now discuss in detail the Pentecostals whom the Catholic charismatics have tried to mimic.

EVANGÉLICOS: THE PENTECOSTAL PURSUIT OF EMBODIMENT BY THE SPIRIT AS TRUE RELIGION

In Guatemalan cultural logic, all non-Catholics are considered *evangélicos*, and most who so classify themselves are enthusiastic Pentecostal Protestants. In Nahualá and Santa Catarina, all *evangélicos* are Pentecostal; the sedate Protestant mainline mission practice has no presence.[11] Pentecostal *evangélicos* are Protestants in the sense that they see themselves as opposite of Catholics in belief and practice. We have seen in previous chapters that such institutional opposition is symbolized in the juxtaposition of the ornate and baroque Ortho-Catholic place of worship at the center of town—facing the plaza, mayoral offices, and central market—versus the Pentecostal place of worship, which frequently stands on the town's periphery and, except for bright paint and a name panel, is devoid of architectural intricacy or decoration (plates 25, 26, 32, 33). Pentecostals oppose Catholics verbally at every opportunity and do so publicly by broadcasting live church meetings and recordings of their songs and beliefs from their church rooftops (see Pratt et al., this volume). They actively try to convert Catholics, in their view saving Catholics from their supposed theological and behavioral errors. They are also Protestants in the sense that *evangélicos* derive their historical foundation, administrative organization, and some of their biblical theology from American and European Protestant mission movements that came to Guatemala a century ago (Garrard-Burnett 1998), making them Christ-centered, Bible-guided, individualistic, and vehemently anti-Catholic.

Evangélicos oppose more than just Ortho-Catholics. *Evangélicos* also think all *ajq'ijab'* are in league with the devil, that they are *brujos*, that they have no good in them. Thus, no committed *evangélico* would openly enlist the aid of an *ajq'ij* for blessings, but a weakly committed *evangélico* might well seek the protective countermeasures of an *ajq'ij* if time, Pentecostal faith healings, and the biomedical attentions of doctors did not remove a persistent and debilitating illness. This is so because deeply embedded in the expectations of the culture is the belief that persistent sickness might be caused by a witchcraft attack inspired by envy aroused by the inequality arising from one's success or by the disruption caused by one's failure to abide by the cultural expectations held by other Mayas. While witchcraft is denied in *evangélico* belief, and one's faith should nullify the attacks of the devil directly, for some, doubts emerge when unexplained disease or bad luck persists.

In rather important ways, however, it is quite misleading to think of Pentecostals as Protestants. For example, indigenized Pentecostalism, whether tied to a historic Pentecostal denomination or completely independent, differs considerably from mainline, theological, Bible-centered, rationally interpretive Protestantism. While the Pentecostal movement claims it is centered on the Bible, it has added the freedom to seek and receive the revelations of the Spirit, which they see as fundamental in that Bible. That revelatory freedom makes Pentecostalism (and its Catholic charismatic counterpart) inherently transformative, divergent, fissile, and fundamentally different from its originating Protestantism.

One needs to understand thoroughly the several aspects of the process by which Pentecostals fission into small, relatively independent congregations. Revelatory theology, the open access of congregants to the microphone, leadership charisma, and the limits of the physical meeting space combine to produce a complex but rather predictable developmental cycle of Pentecostal congregations.

Pentecostals' revelatory theology means that anyone can receive the call to minister.[12] Open access to the microphone and the generally participatory and spontaneous style of worship allow anyone to practice their preaching and leadership skills. Pentecostal liturgy thus enables on-the-job training. A charismatic skill in teaching from the Bible constitutes the only prerequisite to ministerial authority beyond a sense of call. That openness to leadership makes conflict in and fission of a congregation both easy and frequent. And fission has its advantages; frequent splits over doctrinal disputes allow rapid adaptation to local needs and guarantee quick indigenization, effectively adapting Pentecostal congregations to the religious needs of every hamlet.

The relatively open *evangélico* access of all members to the pulpit lessens the distance between minister and congregant and thus flattens the religious hierarchy. This contrasts with mainline Catholicism's much more controlled access, wherein one cannot just volunteer to testify or to prophesy if one feels so inclined during the Sunday service. A lay Catholic can volunteer to help the priest, but the priest vets the volunteers who participate in the mass or in other mainline activities and specifies what they must do and say.

In a further flattening of the hierarchy, Pentecostalism

and Ortho-Catholicism differ substantially in the difficulty of pastors' preparation for the ministry. The primary basis for serving as a pastor in the Pentecostal strand of Christianity in Guatemala is some knowledge of the scriptures, a stylized ability to preach that knowledge, a sense of the call, and a shared experience of the needs of the parishioners that can be reflected in one's sermons. Being a pastor presumes an ability to read and speak, but it often requires no formal ministerial training.[13] A Catholic priest, by contrast, requires seven years of university-level study as a seminarian and submission to the ecclesiastical hierarchy. Moreover, the parish priest seldom ministers in the community where he was born, so he is less familiar with local needs and all too often is of a different ethnicity or nationality than his congregants. In similar terms, Stoll (1993b:4–6) contrasts Catholicism's bureaucratic rigidity with Pentecostalism's flexibility via "the decentralized structures of Latin America's Protestants, their multiple leaders competing for followers through charisma, and their emphasis on conversion," all of which, he notes, have "proved to be distinct advantages."

I have already noted that Pentecostal theology focuses on experience of the Holy Spirit. To receive the Spirit bodily, to experience it via prayer in tongues or in the physicality of jumping, dancing, or falling in trance—all these are signs indicating one has received the core religious infusion of a direct experience of God. This theology is not yet explicitly stated in the Nahualense or Ixtahuaquense congregations, but the central place of experientiality over verbal theological and scriptural interpretation (the Pentecostal contrast with mainline Protestants) and the core importance of bodily experience of the Spirit over ingesting a sacrament at least once a week (the contrast with Ortho-Catholics) are made quite explicit in the broader global Pentecostal literature (Macchia 2003, 2006).

Consistent with this notion of the importance of experientiality, the purity of biblical doctrine seems less the issue than fitness to the needs of the micro congregation. The contesting leader offers a vision and a version of needed change. That makes the Pentecostal congregation enormously flexible and quickly adaptive to the needs of its members. At the point of a split, congregants assess their personal needs and the options offered by the nature of the split, the styles of the pastors, and the closeness of their kinship ties to the opposed leaders. They consider also the decisions of other congregants to whom they are related. As Jones and colleagues show in this volume, from this assessment, members confronting a fission choose the flock with which they will align.[14]

If a flock grows without dividing over doctrine and the charisma of leadership, it will likely divide when it exceeds the seating and standing capacity of its physical meeting space unless its leader successfully organizes a monetary collection and labor donation to build a larger cinderblock chapel. In the early stages of its developmental cycle, a small Pentecostal group will meet in the home of the pastor in the *sala*, where house guests or officials are received. Ideally, but not always, this room has no kitchen fire and no or few beds. Rather, it will have some space for benches or plastic chairs to accommodate a crowd, a place to set up stacks of speakers to the left and right of an area that accommodates a pulpit, a few chairs for the pastor and others, and space for the band. The existence of a dedicated *sala* implies that a pastor or prospective pastor has a modestly above average resource base, though such rooms are common enough in homes of those not utterly poor. The pastor's family also will be relatively advanced in its developmental cycle. He will certainly be a father and in all likelihood a grandfather, living in a cluster of homes that house descendants and other kin, some of whose dwellings may face a shared patio. All of this correlates with the underlying Maya values of parenthood, age respect, and wealth respect converted to social service, which undergirded well-being and prestige in indigenous communities for a century or more under the *cofradía* system.

Finally, there is an economic incentive to fission. The leader of the splitting Pentecostal segment gains access to the donations of the followers that join his congregation. Anyone with a bit of personal charisma and a modicum of age-related maturity can learn the skills, receive the call of the Spirit, and split away from an *evangélico* congregation to form a new one. He will attract family and others to attend his meetings, and they will support him financially, if they can. The most successful of such religious leaders might even remedy some of the financial stress deriving from the land and corn crisis.

In spite of change and splitting, the many Pentecostal congregations share a core theology. First, they are resolutely anti-Catholic. In Saussure's terms, they take their meaning as much from their anti-Catholicism—what they are not—as from their internal theology or practice. They assert that Catholicism represents "worldliness" and even the devil. This association of Catholicism with the devil applies especially to Maya Catholic traditionalism's connection with the *ajq'ij*, seen as a sorcerer. *Evangélicos* differentiate themselves from Ortho-Catholics by rejecting alcohol consumption, smoking, dancing, infidelity, fiesta participation, and listening to or playing the instrument iconic to the Catholic fiesta: the marimba (plate 12). Moreover, they adopted these explicitly contrastive prohibitions decades before the charismatics did. Pentecostals claim that one can be saved by connecting oneself directly and only to Jesus, as opposed to Catholics, who, *evangélicos* incessantly point out, seek the intercession of Mary or one of many other saints. Finally, *evangélicos* seek gifts of the Spirit—healing and ecstasy in worship, often accompanied by glossolalia and trance collapse—as their core religious experience, as their equivalent of communion. Any differences in theology or behavioral practice between offshoot Pentecostal groups are relatively minor compared to the shared theology of their anti-Catholic and antitraditionalist stance and their pursuit of a manifestly energetic reception or infusion of the Holy Spirit into one's body, mind, and speech.

Protestant-derived Pentecostalism is indeed distinct, but it is less unique now given the rise of the Renovación Carismática. Since 1973, the liturgical style that characterized the *evangélicos*—seeking the Spirit; offering free healings;[15] engaging in ecstasy, glossolalia, and bodily agitation followed by trance collapse to the floor; avoiding the vices of alcohol and dancing; and promulgating their music and preaching through highly amplified electronic systems—is no longer precisely indexical because all of these aspects have been substantially appropriated by Catholic charismatics. Thus, Catholic charismaticism not only blurs the boundaries between the strands of practice in Catholicism, it also obscures the formerly clear and decisive boundary between Catholicism and the sharply anti-Catholic Protestant Pentecostalism. Indeed, this blurring reinforces the need to consider Protestant-derived Pentecostalism and Catholic Charismatic Renewal as two components of a shared category: Christian Pentecostalism. The implications of what they share as parallel strands of religion can hardly be overstated. They amount to a distinct religious style with a new source of authority.

CHRISTIAN PENTECOSTALISM AS A FOURTH BRANCH OF CHRISTIANITY

I have commented on the parallels between Pentecostalism and Catholic renewal charismaticism in Guatemala and have already used these similarities to suggest a needed analytic category of Christian Pentecostalism. Indeed, compelling reasons demand that Christian Pentecostals, both those derived of Catholic heritage and those derived of Protestant sources, be considered a fourth distinctive Christian tradition, quite different in ideology and outcome from either Roman Catholic, mainline Protestant, or Eastern Orthodox traditions.

For one thing, asserting that "Pentecostalism is a version of Protestantism" strays considerably off the mark. Christian Pentecostalism's emphasis on direct access to experience of the Holy Spirit in one's own body and its insistence on the absolute equality of membership without regard to race or nationality both make it a qualitatively different religious tradition than mainstream sedate Protestantism (with its textual, word-centered, theological orientation), or Ortho-Catholicism (with its hierarchy, sacraments, and adherence to tradition and papal authority), or Eastern Orthodox Catholicism (with its emphasis on ethnic and national distinctiveness and its sense that it endures unchanging). Thus, I argue, Christian Pentecostalism constitutes a fourth genre of Christianity, neither Roman Catholic, nor Protestant, nor Eastern Orthodox in orientation. It is unique because Christian Pentecostalism's truth and charisma derive from one's sense of being embodied by the Spirit and from being experiential, egalitarian, non-national, revelatory, and directly connected to God rather than having one's access to God mediated by a priest, pastor, or saint. It is not verbal or sacramental or national/ethnic regarding this access to God. Here juxtaposition adds to the meaning of each faith strand and urges the separate categorization and equal recognition of Christian Pentecostalism as a major faith.

Second, as I have shown, Protestant-derived Pentecostalism is only part of the pentecostal population. Catholic charismatics constitute the other component. Thus, the view of Pentecostalism as a form of Protestantism obscures the overall process and the parallels between Pentecostalism and Catholic renewal charismaticism.

There has emerged a subdiscipline in anthropology called the anthropology of Christianity. This area seems well anchored in such works as Robbins and Haynes (2014); Robbins's book series on the anthropology of Christianity at the University of California Press, for which he is the general editor; and Cannell (2006). These works, however, focus primarily on Protestant-derived Pentecostalism. Perhaps that discipline has begun to recognize how distinct Christian Pentecostalism is as a

category. Nevertheless, the anthropology of Christianity still underplays Catholic renewal studies and still does not recognize an overarching and combined category of Christian Pentecostalism. But the combined category matters, be it labeled lowercase pentecostalism or uppercase Christian Pentecostalism.

The direct access to the presence of God inherent in Christian Pentecostalism indigenizes quickly, much more quickly than mainline Protestantism, which controls through the textually fixed (but still interpretable) biblical word, or than Roman Catholicism, which controls through hierarchy. Moreover, truth based on the experience of direct embodiment by God is a radically different source of authority than truth by hierarchy and tradition (Roman Catholicism) or truth by complex theology derived from cogitation on a sacred text (mainstream Protestantism).[16] This fourth Christianity thus penetrates and subverts both Ortho-Roman Catholic and historical mainstream Protestant Christianities. More important, the Christian Pentecostal variant creates a new and radically more adaptive Christianity in the Global South by depending not on hierarchy or tradition nor on presumptively pure textual interpretation. It offers the integrative and highly adjustive interaction of text and social context through revelation by the Spirit accorded to and literally penetrating the bodies of all receptive Christian Pentecostal members and pastors and leaders. This democratized revelatory orientation in Christian Pentecostal liturgy privileges—even demands—individual bodily and revelatory experience of the Spirit. That accessible, embodied, revelatory experience is different from and more fissile than even historic Protestantism's fractiousness, which is inherent in textual interpretation. Pentecostalism privileges behavioral divergence and thus, in an evolutionary sense, it privileges immediate adaptivity. Pentecostalism thus democratizes the source of truth and localizes it within the congregation rather than placing it in the biblical word or in the hierarchy that provides sacraments. This localization of authority occurs via revelations that propose solutions to local ecosystem problems. By contrast, mainstream Protestantism privileges logical divergence, and logical divergence takes a much longer time span to build a behavioral response that can address the pressures of an ecosystem.

The differences in source of authority and truth matter. Thus, Pentecostalism's initial derivation from historical Protestant denominations and from the American Protestant holiness movement makes Pentecostalism no more

Protestant than Protestantism's historical derivation from Catholicism makes Protestantism Catholic. The degree of difference regarding root premises is what matters, not the genealogy of the original fission. Having attracted a quarter of all Christians, Christian Pentecostalism and its spirited, ecstatic, bodily experienced, revelatory form available to all congregants demands its place as a new and distinct movement in Christianity. It deserves recognition as a fourth major branch of Christianity alongside Roman Catholicism's internationally integrative hierarchical sacramentalism, Eastern Orthodoxy's nationally and ethnically linked patriarchates, and historic Protestantism's emphasis on theological interpretation of the biblical canon via literacy and education. Each takes its place and meaning by systematic contrast with the major premises and practices of the others.

ESTIMATING THE DEGREE OF CHRISTIAN PENTECOSTALIZATION IN MAYA GUATEMALA

I have outlined the historical evolution of Maya traditionalist, Ortho-Catholic, and Christian Pentecostal forms of religious practice, and I have consolidated and reviewed much detail regarding each strand of religious practice. Some questions remain: How Christian Pentecostal has Maya Guatemala become? What percentage of Mayas connect regularly either with charismatic Catholic communities or with Pentecostal Protestant congregations, the two forms of Christian Pentecostalism in Guatemala?

Today, Christian Pentecostal fervor fires the imagination of peoples throughout Latin America. Steigenga and Cleary (2007b:1, 28n1) suggest that as of 2001, Latin America, "a region that was nearly all Catholic just forty years ago," was 15 percent Protestant. Guatemala, they note, was even more Protestant: "closer to 30 percent, with the vast majority belonging to Pentecostal or Neo-Pentecostal churches." The specific local details are these: in 1940, Guatemala was 99 percent Catholic; Nahualá and Santa Catarina Ixtahuacán were 100 percent Catholic. In 1970, Guatemala was probably 90 percent Catholic; Nahualá and Santa Catarina at that time were still nearly 100 percent Catholic and still chasing the Protestant missionaries out of the *municipios*, though there were a few converts. Today, Guatemala is estimated to be 35–40 percent Pentecostal Protestant, a figure that many Nahualenses and Ixtahuaquenses would agree applies to their *municipios*. In Nahualá and Santa Catarina

Ixtahuacán, much of that change has occurred since 1980 and all of it since about 1973.[17]

This sea change in Pentecostal Protestant presence seems in itself quite remarkable. But the above data on the Pentecostal *Protestant* presence—which involves both the conversion of Catholics and traditionalists as well as the pentecostalization of the historic Protestant denominations—is only half of the story. In the other half, many of Guatemala's Catholics have become pentecostal *carismáticos*. In Nahualá and Santa Catarina, certainly more than half of the Catholics—and by several estimates of residents, as much as 70–80 percent of both *municipios'* Catholics—participate actively in the charismatic movement.

These figures let me calculate the rough math on Christian Pentecostalism in Guatemala. In these *municipios* and in much of the rest of the country, some 35–40 percent of the population is Pentecostal Protestant. That leaves 60–65 percent Catholic. If, however, one takes at face value the estimates that 50 percent to perhaps as much as 70 percent of the country's Catholics have become pentecostal charismatics, then somewhere between 30 percent (the low estimate: 50 percent of the 60 percent who remain Catholic) and 45.5 percent (the high estimate: 70 percent of the 65 percent who remain Catholic) of the total population of Guatemala have become Catholic charismatics, which is to say, pentecostal Catholics. Adding the two, the low estimates suggest at least 65 percent of Guatemalans adhere to ecstatic Christian Pentecostal religions (35 percent Pentecostal, 30 percent charismatic); the high estimates suggest 85.5 percent of Guatemalans practice ecstatic religion (40 percent Pentecostal, 45.5 percent charismatic). No doubt, the high estimate is too high. But that is the direction Guatemala is headed if not there already.[18]

Whether one uses the low estimate or the high one, a truly remarkable transformation of religion in these *municipios* and in Guatemala as a whole has taken place in the space of about eighty years. In two or three generations, these *municipios* have gone from 100 percent (and the country from 99 percent) sedate Ortho-Catholic and traditionalist to somewhere between 65 and 85 percent enthusiastic, ecstatic Christian Pentecostals, whether Pentecostal Protestant or charismatic Catholic.

With these high rates of total pentecostalization in mind, I can address another phenomenon: the apparent plateau in Pentecostal Protestant membership expansion. Steigenga and Cleary (2007b:14) observe that *evangélico* membership numbers have "reached a relatively steady state in some contexts (such as Guatemala, where the percentage of Protestants has not increased sharply since the 1990s)." Gooren (2010) notes the same flattening of growth among Protestants. I suggest that this plateau in Protestantism's growth is due to the substantial pentecostalization of the Catholic Church through the Charismatic Renewal movement. In a word, Catholics have adopted the material and socioeconomic advantages, the gift-giving reciprocities, and the spiritual resonances of crisis-affirming Protestant Pentecostal worship. Catholics likely have inoculated themselves to some degree against the attractions of Pentecostal Protestantism by adopting Pentecostal advantages into an accepted stream of the Catholic renewal tradition. That certainly was the hope of the Ortho-Catholic hierarchy when they finally decided to adopt the movement.

Nevertheless, as Bradshaw and colleagues (this volume) show, charismatics are not as successful as either Pentecostals or Mormons at keeping their youth. Consequently, I doubt that the Charismatic Renewal movement will completely staunch the membership losses to Pentecostalism that Catholics have been experiencing. However, the manifest similarities may slow the Catholic losses to Evangelical Pentecostalism. Taken together, Catholic charismaticism and Protestant Pentecostalism constitute a substantial movement of ecstatic religious change in these villages and in Guatemala as a whole.

CONCLUSION

Throughout this chapter I have reviewed and consolidated the ethnographic information in the chapters of part 1, and I have depended on Saussure's notion that meaning derives from opposition among words in a set. Expanding that idea to the field of religion, I have shown how Mayas find meaning by making direct contrasts between the religions they observe and experience in their region. I have made further contrasts, contrasts that particular Mayas might not have made but would understand and assent to if brought to their attention. Saussure's (1966[1959]:116–117) thought that words "limit each other reciprocally . . . and [are] defined not by their positive content but negatively by their relations with the other terms of the system," when applied to symbolically meaningful religious practices, helps one understand each religion as a part of a total system of lived religions.

When mainline mission Protestantism indigenized its leadership, the religion soon morphed and adapted to the Guatemalan context. As a result, many Catholics and most sedate Protestant evangélico members became ecstatic Pentecostal evangélicos by conversion. Some of the Pentecostalized congregations kept the traditional names of the mainline denominations from which they derived. But regardless of their name, they are Pentecostal because of ecstatic practice. Sedate performance of the Protestant liturgy in the historic style has almost completely disappeared as a ritual practice among Guatemalan Protestants and has totally disappeared from Nahualá and Santa Catarina Ixtahuacán. A similar transformative process has enveloped Latin America (Steigenga and Cleary 2007b:8). Furthermore, ever since a sizable percentage of local Catholics began to imitate Pentecostal practice as congregationally local carismáticos, the Guatemalan Roman Catholic Church has been fundamentally transformed. As charismatics move toward becoming the majority of all Guatemalan Catholics, and since they currently constitute a majority of Catholics attending mass, Ortho-Catholic leaders have become an administrative superstructure of priests and bishops delivering mass to the charismatics, who outnumber the active Ortho-Catholics, the inactive cultural Catholics, and the Maya Catholic traditionalists in attendance at mass or simply living their lives as Catholics. The bulk of the direct spiritual ministration that most Catholics now receive comes through the priest-substitute married couple that guides the local charismatic comunidad. Thus, as Catholic charismaticism expands, ordained Catholic priests increasingly find themselves divorced from contact with the majority of the active members—the charismatics—and also from the remaining relatively inactive cultural Catholics. Generic Christian Pentecostalism has indeed triumphed in Guatemala.

I think neither academics, evangélicos, nor Catholics understand the extent of the change that Pentecostalism and the movement toward pentecostal charismaticism has precipitated in the Roman Catholic Church. For the Pentecostals, this is because they categorize carismáticos as Catholics. They do not see how different carismáticos are from other Catholics. Consequently, the Pentecostals of Guatemala do not perceive carismáticos as spiritual siblings, unified with them as Christian Pentecostals in most of their behavioral and ideological approaches to community life. Rather, Pentecostals think of charismatics as an alien "other" because they claim they are

Catholic. Pentecostals do not realize that their *evangélico* form of bodily experienced Christian Pentecostal religion has emerged as the dominant strand of collective worship even in Catholicism.

Likewise, participants in La Renovación Carismática do not perceive their kinship with Pentecostals. Rather, they see themselves as spirited Catholics. The categorical division between *evangélicos* and *católicos* likewise thwarts academic analysis.

For academics, the division between Protestants and Catholics obscures their similarities, even though those similarities are remarked upon by Mayas themselves. Unfortunately for academics, the intensity of solo fieldwork tends to preclude studying other groups in sufficient depth to see the commonalities. Therein lies the advantage of field school ethnography. The dispersion of field school students throughout the various sectors of religious practice in these two *municipios'* central towns and rural hinterlands—in twice as many religious contexts as discussed in the twelve chapters in part 1—helped me overcome the ethnographer's usual one-site, one religious experience, in-depth approach. As the advocates of multisited ethnography have suggested, the single-site ethnographic method hobbles the anthropologist's ability to address the overarching correspondences and contrasts of performances and meanings as a total and regional system (Marcus 1995, 2009; Falzon 2009).

Beyond this lesson in methodology, what does the high rate and broad acceptance of exuberant pentecostalization suggest about the academic study of religion in Latin America? In 1990, David Stoll wrote a significant and oft-cited book about religious change there. He gave it the title *Is Latin America Turning Protestant?* Stoll recognizes in his book that most of the Protestants he writes about are in fact Pentecostals. Nevertheless, the emphasis in scholarship is still on Catholic-to-Protestant conversion rather than on Catholic to Pentecostal, let alone on what the emphasis should be: conversion from traditionalist Catholic and Ortho-Catholic (and Protestant) to Christian Pentecostal.

The figures discussed above on the overwhelming transformation of both Protestants and Catholics into Christian Pentecostals imply that Stoll and most academics get the emphasis of their question regarding the process of religious conversion in Latin America wrong. I repeat: the issue is not a conversion movement from traditionalist and Catholic to Protestant. Rather, it is from sedate traditionalist and Catholic to ecstatic

Christian Pentecostal. The important issue is conversion from sedate to ecstatic, regardless of denomination. It is from hierarchical and sacramental (in the case of Ortho-Catholic) and textual and mental (in the case of mainline Protestant) to flat (in hierarchy), exuberant (in emotion), and bodily experiential, as Christian Pentecostal. Thus, I suggest that sedate mainline Protestantism, in decline everywhere in the world, was but an initial catalyst that has largely disappeared in Guatemala—used up and spent in initiating the chemistry of converting traditionalists and Ortho-Catholics to Christian Pentecostalism.

I conclude that the most important religious movement in Guatemala, in all of Latin America, and throughout the postcolonial Christian Global South has not been from Catholic to Protestant but from postcolonial sedate and often state-linked denominational Christianities to independent, spirit-infused, ecstatic pentecostal Christianities. Moreover, in Guatemala, the most significant societal movement during the last seven decades has not been from Catholicism to Protestantism, nor from authoritarianism to democracy. Nor has the movement been to insurgent revolution or to liberation theology as applied by Catholic Action. Neither has it been globalization in the sense that Guatemalans have made themselves or their country educationally ready for and socially integrated with the penetrations of global economies. Rather, the most important and profound social movement in Guatemala of the last half of the twentieth century and the first decades of the twenty-first has been the socially transformative process of Christian Pentecostalization.

Pentecostalization responds directly to population expansion, land shortage, and failed agro-dependence associated with a generalized culture collapse among Guatemala's indigenous peoples. Pentecostalism's liturgy and preaching emphasize an end of the world that its adherents are actively and currently experiencing by enduring culture collapse. Compounding the collapse, they find themselves excluded from viable positions in the onrushing and penetrating nation-states that seek to govern and change rural and indigenous areas and urban slums. Thus, the Christian Pentecostal cries for help from God because no other institution exists that assists. The liturgical practices of Christian Pentecostalism, however, do more than just express the angst of collapse and exclusion. As I show in chapter 24, they also respond positively by forming rather tightly articulated micro communities of mutually supportive and mutually caring adherents seeking to establish a new ideology and a new societal outcome.

Before I deal with such functionalities, however, I explore a number of cultural resonances between Christian Pentecostalism and both the formerly vigorous *cofradía*, corporate traditionalism and the shamanic, more private traditionalism. One of the surprising twists that has emerged is this: if traditionalism is contrastive with Ortho-Catholicism, and Ortho-Catholicism is contrastive with the new Christian Pentecostalisms, then, to some degree, the new Christian Pentecostalisms bear some similarity to or share some sympathy with traditionalism! It appears to be a modified version of "the enemy of my enemy is my friend" or structurally similar to the alliance of alternate generations in kinship studies in which the parents of my parents are my protectors and friends. As I show in the next chapter, spirit-enchanted Maya traditionalism indeed shares many sympathies with Holy Spirit–focused Christian Pentecostalisms.

NOTES

1. *Ajq'ij* is from *aj-* ("worker of," "master of," "from the place of," "associated with"), each derived from the root *-aj*, "to (or one's) desire or want." Thus *aj-* has a distinct connotation of lover of, or one who desires or pursues that which is attached after the *aj-* particle. The word *q'ij* means "day," "time," "sun," "light," or "brilliance." The ending *-ab'* (or contextually, *-ob'*) pluralizes animate beings, rendering the term *ajq'ijab'* (also translated as "daykeepers"). The *pasados* (see Larson et al., this volume) who have completed *cofradía* service are in such decline that the more privately oriented *ajq'ijab'* now hold the central stage in Maya traditionalist faith.

2. Molesky-Poz 2004 describes a traditionalist renewal in Santa María Chiquimula, a K'iche'-speaking *municipio* in the Department of Totonicapán. There, Jesuits assigned to administer church affairs in the community promoted a reconciliation between Ortho-Catholic and traditionalist Catholic sensitivities. By being inclusive of traditionalists, these Jesuits succeeded in establishing a number of Maya-affirming workshops and activities that have, according to Molesky-Poz, essentially healed the community and liberated the submerged Maya traditionalism. In some ways this institutional support mirrors the effects of the pan-Maya movement funding and support described in Nueva Ixtahuacán in Hanselmann and colleagues, this volume; and more broadly in Fischer and Brown 1996. Molesky-Poz's orientation toward seeing the ancient Maya roots of current Ortho-tradi-

tionalist rapprochement apparently leads her to not mention the charismatic Catholic movement in the Catholic spectrum and to indicate in only a line or two that 40 percent of the municipality is Protestant (and presumably mostly Pentecostal) (Molesky-Poz 2004:525, 534). After the Jesuit efforts, the community went from zero recognition of traditionalism to all Catholics "practicing both traditions—Catholic and *costumbre*," which perhaps derives from the fact that Maya Catholic traditionalism offers both healing and divination guidance to Maya decision making, which Ortho-Catholicism does not. They are thus complementary theologically and in practice, even if they were competitive politically from 1900 to 1980, with Ortho-Catholicism generally discouraging or even suppressing traditionalist Maya practices.

3. On Maximón in the modern period, Cook and Offit (2013:146–147) say: Maximón is "the wachibal [face, image] for the Guatemalan deity San Simón. San Simón, also called Maximón and sometimes don Pedro . . . [is] identified with Judas Iscariot and with Pedro de Alvarado, [and] San Simón is said to be a god for the merchant because he sold Jesus. . . . San Simón is depicted as a Ladino or gringo, seated in a chair, with a suit and with glasses, and he always wears a broad-brimmed hat and frequently is depicted with a cane in his right hand."

4. The American priest in Antigua Ixtahuacán supervised the translation of the complete missal, so that the mass is available in K'iche', but only he and one or two native K'iche'-speaking priests are able to use the materials (Santa Catarina Ixtahuacán 1995).

5. Charismatics do not come down quite so hard on alcohol as Evangelicals do, perhaps because wine anchors the symbolism of the mass. To reject alcohol totally, rather than reject alcohol's misuse, would undermine Catholicism rather than renew and purify it.

6. As Charleston and colleagues (this volume) show, some *comunidades* may refer to themselves or distinguish themselves from others with individual names, but that is not the usual or primary public referent, and the name is never on the building. In their case study, the congregations were so small they met in members' homes.

7. Priests and parishioners in both Nahualá and Santa Catarina discussed their fear of charismatic units bolting over the thin division separating them from Protestant Pentecostals, but they gave no examples. Chesnut (2003a:72–73, 88) documents several such congregational shifts.

8. Gooren (2012:195) reports the same phenomenon for Nicaragua. Although charismatics constitute a mere 5 percent of Nicaraguan Catholics (among the lowest in Latin America), the charismatic requirement to attend mass makes this 5 percent the majority of attendees at a Nicaraguan mass.

9. The Ortho leadership's primal fear that charismatics will

transform into Pentecostals appears in other areas of the world. Earlier, I noted the fissioning of Pentecostals, the pentecostalization of historical Protestant denominations, and the easy movement of charismatic congregations from the Catholic fold to the Pentecostal Protestant category if the priest was too stringent or dominating. So also in Brazil. Freston (1993:108n2), for example, notes, "Since the 1960s, the historical denominations have produced Pentecostalized breakaways of some size," and among Catholics, "some base communities" have "become independent Pentecostal churches." My colleague John Clark asks, "Why not the reverse?" That is, why doesn't charismaticism prepare the way for *evangélicos* to return comfortably to Catholicism via participation in a charismatic congregation? Gooren (2012:197) reports that in Managua it does. In my own fieldwork, I have indeed encountered individual charismatics who were *evangélicos* previously converted from Ortho-Catholicism. Henri Gooren (2010) also discusses the existence of "backsliders" from Pentecostal Protestantism returning to Catholicism in Guatemala. Nevertheless, I think the dominant movement is from *carismático* to *evangélico* for several reasons. First, an *evangélico* has made a precipitous break with Catholicism and has been socialized against return by Guatemalan evangelism's strident anti-Catholicism. If *evangélico* converts from Catholicism subsequently become dissatisfied, they have a number of options: they can change Pentecostal congregations, found a new congregation, return to either Ortho or charismatic Catholicism, or go inactive regarding all religions.

10.   I have not witnessed this phenomenon of post-speaking-in-tongues interpretation.

11.   Chesnut (2003a:39–40) states, "Pentecostal churches currently account for approximately 75 percent of all Latin American Protestants." Note that in Nahualá, three large congregations of Mormons and a number of Jehovah's Witnesses do not consider themselves (or behave like) Protestants or Pentecostals. They likely would have been included as Protestants in Chesnut's data. Thus, our two data sets are more consistent than the numbers 75 percent (according to Chesnut) and 100 percent (according to me) initially suggest.

12.   In many Pentecostal organizations, no formal ministerial education is required to become a pastor. The resulting openness to the call of Pentecostal ministry culturally parallels the openness of the call to become a traditional healer or *ajq'ij*. See Scott et al., this volume; Wilson 2007. Suffering, more than training, prepares the candidate for the revelatory call.

13.   Some of the larger Pentecostal denominations do have training seminaries that help prepare ministers who are inspired to so serve.

14.   Virtually all studies of Protestantism remark on the fission and factionalism inherent in the Pentecostal tradition. Thus, for Chesnut (2003a:59), "Pentecostalism as a whole benefits from its differentiation. That is, the hundreds, if not thousands of distinct Pentecostal denominations that crowd the popular marketplace allow for a high degree of specialization and niche marketing that targets specific sets of consumers." Bundy (2003:56) draws a detailed descent line for some of the many Chilean denominations he lists. Bergunder's (2008) history of factional division among Pentecostal Protestants in southern India seems endless. Indeed, he defines Pentecostalism not by doctrine or practice but by its genealogical descent by division and subdivision from or communication with a prior Pentecostal group. He takes it as his task as a historian to document through letters and other archival materials the contacts and the splits between groups. Catholic charismatic commentators, such as Mühlen (1975:116–117), also remark on the tendency toward fission inherent in renewal Catholicism's universal access to open revelation and experiential emphasis.

15.   Chesnut sees healing as the primal attractant, the chief product of Pentecostalism in Brazil. He devotes considerable space to an analysis of Pentecostal healing in *Born Again in Brazil* (1997), as he does in *Competitive Spirits* (2003a), where he also treats charismatic Catholic healing. Brown (2011) likewise argues that faith healing is central to worldwide Pentecostal and charismatic growth.

16.   Anderson (2000:30) notes also the verbal, rationalistic theology of mainstream mission Protestantism and its inapplicability to experientially oriented African contexts.

17.   Steigenga and Cleary (2007a) assemble a wealth of comparative data from throughout Latin America. For Guatemala, Steigenga and Cleary (2007b) draw their data from a CID (Consultoría Interdisciplinaria en Desarrollo) Gallup poll and from Gooren (2007). Steigenga and Cleary (2007b:3, 28n1–2) state that between 30 percent (citing https://www.worldchristiandatabase.org/) and 40 percent of Guatemalans are Pentecostal (US Department of State 2005). The Gallup results they cite suggest 22 percent, as self-reported in a national survey (Steigenga and Cleary 2007b:11, 29nn19–21).

Sometimes the differences may be attributed to the indigeneity of a region, sometimes to earlier or later dates of administration of a survey, estimate, or census. One must also be careful of citation circles in which guesstimates get made into truth by repeated citation.

Coleman and colleagues (1993:135n3) cite a paper by Timothy Evans that "provides a careful empirical assessment of the diffusion of Protestantism in Guatemala based on a 1990 survey in three departments. His estimate is a cumulative total of 30 percent Protestant." Two decades later, our 35–40 percent estimate of Pentecostal evangelization of Nahualá and Santa Catarina Ixtahuacán seems reasonably applicable to the nation as a whole.

18. The figures may seem high, but they are not outrageous.

Garriott and O'Neill (2008:394) cite the Pew Research Center (2006) that "as much as 60 percent" of Guatemalans may be, in my terms, Christian Pentecostals (20 percent Pentecostal, 40 percent charismatic).

Chapter Twenty-Three

The Attractions of Cultural Resonance

Christian Pentecostalism as Resymbolized Traditionalism

JOHN P. HAWKINS

THERE EXIST CERTAIN COMPATIBILITIES, RESO-
NANCES, or similarities between what Mayas perceive
as the older Maya cultural beliefs and practices and the
newer Christian Pentecostal beliefs and practices. Such
cultural resonances are to be expected; indeed, they may
have been deliberately chosen for or emphasized in the
newer system. "Almost every revitalization movement,"
writes Anthony Wallace (1956:276), "embodies in its proposed new cultural system large quantities of both traditional and imported cultural material." Catholic and Protestant pentecostalisms find success in part because they
have capitalized on the isomorphisms—some hidden,
some quite obvious—between the new religions' beliefs
and behaviors and one or more deeply held traditionalist premises or practices at the root of indigenous Maya
thought and action. Isomorphisms enhance the acceptability of the new religion because of a sensed compatibility with the traditional Maya Catholic religion and the old
remembered culture.

In this chapter I examine several such correspondences. I suggest that similarities between old institutions and new ease the individual's transition from the
older religious liturgies to the new. Not only do the new
pentecostalisms mesh well with aspects of Maya traditionalism, the new pentecostalisms even restore key and
deeply held Maya beliefs that in some ways had been
under assault or that had simply eroded or corroded
away. Thus, Mayas tap into and return to some traditional cultural premises by adopting pentecostalism,
and that facilitates conversion. Nevertheless, I consider
culture collapse and systemic exclusion to be the primary drivers of Mayas' readiness for conversion. The
symbolic correspondences between old and new simply

help, comfort, and ease the transition of those converting.

The correspondences between Christian Pentecostalism and Maya culture that I treat here include shared
notions of existing in a spirit-suffused world, similarities
in forms of spirit possession, resonances between *cofradía*
and charismatic Catholic group leadership, the underlying importance of experientiality, obedience to law and
conformity to group expectations, withdrawal from the
world, and speaking with a collective voice. While local
cultural factors such as these cannot explain the worldwide acceptance of Christian Pentecostalism, perhaps
they account for why Guatemala displays the highest percentage of Pentecostals in Central America and perhaps
in all of Latin America.

MUTUAL BELIEFS IN AN
ENCHANTED WORLD

Both traditionalist Maya Catholics and Christian Pentecostals share a spirit-suffused, "enchanted" view of the
world they live in. That is not just a Maya attribute, but a
rather widespread indigenous/autochthonous view of the
universe. Several scholars of the Asian pentecostal experience, for example, attribute the acceptability and rapid
expansion of Christian Pentecostalism there to a preexisting and deeply enculturated indigenous spirituality and
comfort with the belief that the universe and its objects
all have a living spiritual component (Yung 2011:43, 45;
Anderson 2011:127; Wiyono 2011:252). The strongly spirit-suffused local religions and indigenous spirituality
are paralleled in Christian Pentecostal beliefs in demon

possession and in divine suffusion throughout the universe, which makes adherents feel like little has changed. Under Pentecostalism, the concepts have been "modernized," however, to a new register (Anderson and Tang 2011). The same occurs among Mayas.

The Mayas in Guatemala live in an enchanted world, a spirit-endowed or spirit-constituted world, as data from Scott and colleagues, Hanselmann and colleagues, and other ethnographic chapters in this volume reveal. Indeed, Samson (2007) makes the enchantment theme central to his analysis of a Protestant congregation among the Maya Mams, and he argues their Protestant Pentecostalism "reenchants" the Maya world. The two worldviews resonate.

In this enchanted world, there are additional resonances. An obvious one is the mutual recognition of Jesus Christ, who exists as an overarching and somewhat detached supervisor in the deep background of the traditionalist's high heaven. He hangs from the cross of the Ortho-Catholic's main church building as God mediated by saints, and he represents the immediate materiality and earthly involvement of the Pentecostal's intimately activist, bodily penetrating, always available, ever-proximate divinity.

RESEMBLANCES IN TRANCE, SPIRIT EMBODIMENT, AND GLOSSOLALIA

Traditionalist Maya and Christian Pentecostal beliefs resemble each other not just on spirit suffusion and on Jesus Christ (with differing degrees of involvement, distant for traditionalist, immediate and frequent for Christian Pentecostal). The two share details regarding the call-up each uses to bring the gods to one's presence. I enumerate some below in order to highlight the similarities.

1.   The traditionalist Maya Catholic believes in spirits suffusing the earth—its mountains, rain, cold, and air.
2.   These spirits can be invoked through chant, song, and prayer and can be brought to presence through the third-order shaman's leadership.
3.   The spirits inhabit the trance-state body of the shaman.
4.   The spirits speak through the shaman to the client in a largely foreign and, for some, partially incomprehensible tongue: Spanish.

5.   The message subsequently gets interpreted and clarified by the *sobrena* (a woman) so that the message is clearly understood by the client-attendees.

The preceding schema is described in detail in Scott and colleagues (this volume). Here are the equivalents in Christian Pentecostal belief and practice:

1.   In both *renovación* Catholic and *evangélico* Protestant forms of Christian Pentecostalism, the physical world is broadly directed by and suffused with the presence of God. Humans can be challenged by demons who can inhabit the world's objects and people.
2.   God in the form of the Holy Spirit is invoked through sermon, song, and prayer and can be brought to presence through the pastor's leadership
3.   The Holy Spirit inhabits the trance-state bodies of all Christian Pentecostal congregants.
4.   Pentecostal glossolalia is foreign and unknown to both K'iche'- and Spanish-speaking people. It follows Spanish phonology yet has none of the grammar of subject, verb, referentiality, and so on essential to any worldly language.
5.   Messages can be interpreted by any member of the congregation, although in most ethnographic reports, it is usually a woman who interprets a glossolalic message (*profesía*) into Spanish or K'iche', thereby giving clarity to the messages brought into the congregation by glossolalic utterance.

No doubt, these clear correspondences between Christian Pentecostal practice and traditionalism contribute to Mayas' acceptance and readiness for spirit-infused Christian Pentecostalism. For example, Mikaela as *sobrena* and the (often) female Christian Pentecostal congregant acting as prophet-interpreter are analogues, the latter a modernized symbolic rendition of the same process as the former.

REPLICATION OF TRADITIONALIST *COFRADÍA* LEADERSHIP ROTATION IN THE CHARISMATIC *COMUNIDADES*

In a Renovación Carismática worship group, the parish priest rotates the leadership couple, ideally every two years. The guide couple serves without pay. In both respects, the charismatic *comunidad*'s leadership mimics the old *cofradía* leadership via regular rotation of service without pay and at considerable personal expense. The charismatic couple and the *cofradía* leader and his *chuchuxel* wife are the *k'amal be*, the "lead rope" or "guide on the road." In this regard, Catholic charismaticism resonates more closely with Maya templates than does Protestant Pentecostal practice, which fosters a permanent pastor who is paid or can access the Sunday contribution funds. Thus, the new Catholic charismaticism as practiced in the Maya community replicates the much older traditionalist Catholic practice embedded in Maya culture for at least a century, but in diminution since the mid-twentieth century.

There are consequences to this particular resonance. Just as the Ortho-Catholic priest seldom visited many of the indigenous municipalities from the eighteenth century to the early twentieth, leaving the *cofradía*-led municipalities quite to their own devices, today the Ortho-Catholic priest seldom visits the many *carismático* Sunday afternoon or weekday services in his parish. No meeting of a *comunidad* that I or our students attended in any year of the field school included an observing or participating priest. Except for the regular leadership meeting of the parish priest with the community's charismatic leaders (conducted at the parish headquarters), the charismatic congregations run quite independently. Thus, I find today's Ortho-Catholic hierarchy's relation to the *carismático comunidades* mimicking the condition of the 1700s to early 1900s, when priests attended a parish as infrequently as once a decade and let operations be decided by the *cofradía* elders. Today, charismatic *comunidades* rarely get an in-person supervisory visit from a priest, and they are run by an unmonitored couple.

The new *carismático* system is as much of an independent challenge to the Catholic priesthood hierarchy as the independent *cofradía* system was prior to and during the 1940s–1950s. The lack of priestly presence in the numerically dominant strand of Catholic practice suggests other parallels with the nineteenth century's lack of Catholic priestly supervision of *cofradía*-centered indigenous municipalities. In the past, the *cofradías* indigenized and ran away with the Ortho church in the form of an uncontrolled, alcohol-infused worship style. Today, the *carismáticos*, locally in *comunidades*, are running away with the bulk of the Ortho church's active membership, engaged in what is, from the Ortho-Catholic leader's perspective, an uncontrolled new revelatory and ecstatic worship style led by married women and men who are not priests. When the ordained ecclesiasts of the Ortho church finally get past

their current benign neglect of the activities of the charismatic *comunidades*, they may be forced to contend politically with the local charismatic leaders to reacquire control, just as they had to wrest control of traditionalist religious practice and church properties from the *cofradistas*. If the Ortho priests try to recapture leadership of the charismatic segments, will they have sufficient priests and nuns to visit the many *comunidades* that have been forming in each parish? Will they have the will to succeed? And if they try, will they be able to reacquire leadership dominance without driving many of the charismatic *comunidades*, a major portion of the Catholic fold, into the hands of the existing and receptive anti-Catholic Pentecostals?

Thus, the past two centuries of *cofradía* independence and subsequent conflict with Ortho-Catholic leadership today repeats in the new symbolic garb of charismaticism. But this symbolic garb is much complicated by the presence of nearly identical but fiercely anti-Catholic *evangélicos*, into which an offended *carismático* congregation can easily morph if challenged by the Ortho hierarchy.

In a similar fashion, Maya women experience nearly equivalent direct involvement in celebratory events as they did during traditionalist *cofradía* fiestas. The *chuchuxelib'*—which is to say, the honored spouses of the *cofradía*'s male leaders—cooked and fed the members of the community that attended the *cofradía* event. Likewise, Christian Pentecostal women—spouses of formal leaders and others who volunteer—cook to feed those who come to a Christian Pentecostal celebratory anniversary or other event. People may get fed at an Ortho-Catholic event, but it looks different from the enthusiastic female volunteerism of the Christian Pentecostal events. At a Christian Pentecostal event, food is cooked on the spot; at an Ortho-Catholic parish-wide event, if there is food, it is often bought and brought to the site.

Finally, I note that Pentecostal congregations, by contrast with Catholic charismatic *comunidades*, do not rotate leadership and do pay their ministers from the congregation donations. Thus, in certain regards, Pentecostal leadership is modeled more on Ladino and Ortho-Catholic governance than on indigenous leadership and cultural styles.

RESONANCES BETWEEN COVENANT, *PROMESA*, AND CONVERSION

Devotion to an Evangelical congregation or charismatic *comunidad* following curing is processually similar to devotion to a saint by *promesa* in the traditionalist and Ortho approaches to the Catholic faith and to the idea of reciprocal covenant in traditionalist and *cofradía* service. All rely on a gift (or solicitation thereof) and a promise of reciprocal devotion after receipt of the gift. In this regard, the Christian Pentecostalization of religion in Guatemala, whether Protestant Pentecostal or Catholic charismatic, is not so radical as might at first appear, but constitutes a modernized transformation of the traditionalist symbol set that practitioners or their progenitors used to carry out the same activities.

Structurally, however, there is a difference. The Protestant Pentecostal and the Catholic charismatic healings bind the receiver to a small community. The Ortho-Catholic *promesa* binds the receiver to an object representing the concept of a divinity or subdivinity (a saint). There is no living community of people that delivered the *promesa*. The traditionalist healing binds the receiver to a cosmology (as do the others) but less to a community because the *ajq'ij* serves individuals and families who do not meet regularly or serve each other, and because he receives payment rather than providing healing as a gift. Thus, only in Christian Pentecostalism is the binding power of gift giving and reciprocity directly mobilized to expand and cement the ties of an existing social group.

SHARED EMPHASIS ON EXPERIENTIALITY

The new Christian Pentecostalism's experiential liturgy and theology resonate with the well-documented Maya practice of learning a task through behavioral observation, without dependence on verbal communication. For example, in his study of Mayas' adaptation to a weaving factory built in the *municipio* of Cantel, Nash (1958a:26–27) remarks that newly hired Mayas assigned to work the mechanical looms did not receive oral or written instructions before performing the complex tasks. Rather, new indigenous employees watched silently for a period of about six weeks until they had seen how the experienced operators resolved the problems that came up. Then the recruits simply took over and ran the machinery. No verbal, theoretical, or school-like exchange occurred. Rather than formal education or verbal instruction, observation and then experience—what I here call experientiality—occasioned unspoken learning and conveyed capacity. In another example, Winston Scott and colleagues (this volume) describe an experiential

orientation during Scott's efforts to learn traditionalist K'iche' cosmology from Tix. Direct conceptual questions did not elicit a verbal response from Tix, Scott's *ajq'ij* mentor. Watching Tix and participating with him, however, did work. When Scott felt he had learned a premise, he could state it, and Tix would reply with yes or no regarding Scott's abstraction. Sometimes Tix even rendered a conceptual elaboration on Scott's submission of the experientially learned (or mislearned) abstraction. But Scott could not get Tix to verbally articulate an abstract concept outside of its experientially descriptive context.

Generic American Protestant Pentecostalism likewise emphasizes experientiality over mainline Protestant ratiocinated discussion. Attempts to theologize Pentecostalism are fairly recent, quite American or European, and as the emerging Pentecostal theologians admit, not successful yet. Pentecostal theologians do recognize bodily experience as a key distinctive aspect of Pentecostalism. Macchia (2003, 2006), a foremost commentator on and theologian in the Pentecostal movement, takes on the task of providing a Pentecostal theology. He begins his book with a discussion of the centrality of experience. The core Pentecostal event in the individual "is essentially an *experience* of self-transcendence motivated by the love of God," which is "culturally mediated" and will consequently "vary . . . from context to context." "But," he says, "I simply cannot imagine this clothing with power unless some kind of powerful *experience* of the divine presence, love, and calling is involved, one that loosens our *tongues* and our *hands* to *function* under the inspiration of the Spirit" (Macchia 2006:14, emphases added). Note the experiential action words: "clothing" as a verb and "experience" that allows body parts "to function." Macchia follows Hollenweger's perspective that Pentecostalism is "a way of doing theology that is not burdened with post-Enlightenment standards of rational discourse" (Macchia 2006:50). Again, Macchia refers to Hollenweger approvingly, agreeing that "doctrinal conceptions among Pentecostals are too diverse" and that the true Pentecostal distinctiveness consists in "forms of *expression* that lie close to the heartthrob of human *experience*" and bring to mind "Harvey Cox's 'primal' *experience*" (2006:50–51, emphases added). "A theology deeply committed to the life of the Spirit cannot neglect aspects of *experience* in Christ that lie outside the limits of rational discourse" (52, emphasis added). Macchia (1120–1121) also argues that "Pentecostals have always favored testimonies, choruses, and prayers over intellectual or critical reflection" and that one should acknowledge a "non-academic" or "devotional theology" that incorporates "prayers, commentaries, devotions, and disputations."

Hollenweger (1972:xviii) wonders about how to use a book, "the means of communication of Protestantism," to reveal adequately the nature of Pentecostalism. The latter is "a movement whose main characteristic is not verbal agreement but correspondence of *sentiments*" and whose "distinguishing feature is the *experience* of the baptism of the Spirit with the 'initial sign of speaking in tongues'" (xviii–xix, emphases added). Hocken (2003:517, emphasis added), in his encyclopedic summation of the charismatic movement (by which Hocken means the worldwide adoption of Christian Pentecostal ecstasy in mainline religions), calls charismaticism "an *experiential* movement" that "has always been strong on faith-affirmation and short on critical reflection." For Macchia (2006:56, emphasis in original), "the Pentecostal . . . 'twist' on the Christian story . . . is pneumatological in emphasis [and] also eschatological, charismatic, and *deeply experiential*. . . . Spirit baptism . . . implies that we do not relate to God as an object of reflection; rather, we are baptized into God as a powerful field of experience."

Dayton (1987:24–26, emphases added) also places "experience" as central to his theology of Pentecostalism. Thus, the key claim of Pentecostalism is that the biblical account of the day of Pentecost "described an *experience* available to believers in all ages" (here, Dayton quotes Menzies 1971:9), and "the modern believer . . . receives the fullness of the Spirit's baptism in separate events or '*experiences*.'" "The availability of the *experience* of Pentecost to every generation" includes "not only the *charismata* such as glossolalia, but [also] . . . divine healing." Thus, "Pentecostalism affirms . . . the integral place of literal miracles of divine healing and insists these are to be *experienced* in our own time."

None of these theologians discuss the *nature* of God in the Protestant style. Rather, they concern themselves with the adherent's bodily *experience* of the Spirit. Likewise, Yong (2005:273) speaks of Pentecostalism's "participatory epistemology," and he locates the "heart beat of pentecostal spirituality [in] the dynamic *experience* of the Holy Spirit" (28, emphasis added). Thus, according to Pentecostalism's theologians, experientiality is American Pentecostalism's distinctive feature, and it is this experientiality that has enabled Christian Pentecostalism, in Durkheim's words, to resist cultural and political enclosure and to internationalize so rapidly.

By embracing experientiality as central, American Pentecostalism as a missionized source is more suited to Maya learning than the antecedent, the*ologica*lly oriented, mainstream Protestantism. The latter never took substantial root because it was too rationally oriented, too textually word-centered, and too verbally taught rather than bodily experienced. A Maya experiences the penetration of the Holy Spirit into her or his body—what an anthropologist would call possession by the spirit—during the pentecostal meeting. She or he sings and moves with the music and utters the prayer plea of the soul in whispers, shouts, groans, tear-filled cries, or glossolalic repetitions of a few unknown syllables. He or she might jump up and down to the music or fall to the floor in trance. In so doing, these Mayas feel they have experienced God in their bodies. A Pentecostal visits the homes of neighbors and blesses the sick, witnesses to others, and ideally, abstains from the behavioral vices of alcohol, infidelity, smoking, or dancing. All these are behaviors to be implemented and experienced. A similar emphasis on experientiality appears throughout Father Jesus María Sarasa's (1991) exegesis on Latin American Catholic Charismatic Renewal.

Generic Christian Pentecostalism emphasizes that *all* congregants can and should experience the reception of the Holy Spirit into their body. This democratization makes all congregants equal and makes religion communal, matching other preexisting core premises of Maya culture: equality, shared experience of poverty, and mutualism of identity and experience in local community. In taking this position, Christian Pentecostalism contrasts with mainline historic Protestantism's verbal and theological focus and with the Ortho-Catholic emphasis on hierarchical contact with God through sacraments administered by a trained priesthood. On both counts of difference, Christian Pentecostalism is more Maya compatible. Just as a Maya learns a complex weaving task by observation and experience, so also with religious tasks. Protestant and Catholic pentecostalisms are markedly performative and collective rather than theological and individual. Thus, Christian Pentecostalism reworks the older indigenous premises or practices regarding the central place of embodied and collective experience in Maya life and thought—which is valued over logic, verbal instruction, explanation, speech, texts, and individuation. K'iche' people, and probably all Mayas, find the experiential, behavioral, egalitarian, and collective emphases of Christian Pentecostalism particularly resonant with their Maya cultural roots.

None of this should be taken to mean that Mayas are not rational. It simply means that Mayas take personal experience and personal testimony to be more certain or reliable than rational or written argument in ascertaining the truth of something. Dabb and colleagues (2013) have shown that K'iche' Mayas prefer a personal testimony of experience to a written document when evidence of truth must be established in court regarding land cases. In this orientation, Mayas differ sharply from Ladinos (Dabb et al. 2013) and mainline Protestants. A K'iche' does not conjure up, store up, or willingly receive an intellectual theology of truth; a K'iche' prefers proof by experience and personal testimony thereof. Given that personal experiences of the Spirit and testimonies thereof by congregants constitute major components of the Christian Pentecostal liturgy, this is a culturally resonant advantage compared to Ortho-Catholicism or historic Protestantism.

To be sure, Mayas' interest in experience does not account for the rise of Christian Pentecostalism among the non-Maya Ladinos of Guatemala, although many Ladinos are but a generation or two distant from Maya extraction. Nor does it account for the relative success of Christian Pentecostalism in other Latin American (non-Maya) regions. Thus, Mayas' cultural compatibility with Christian Pentecostalism cannot be the main explanation for Christian Pentecostal expansion. That is why the primary axis of explanation still rests on culture collapse and exclusion. But Christian Pentecostalism's compatibility with Maya cultural premises does help explain why experiential Christian Pentecostalism has been so exceptionally successful in Maya Guatemala.

SIMILAR EXPECTATIONS OF OBEDIENCE TO LAW

In another line of compatibility, Christian Pentecostalisms advocate the internalization of obedience to a rule of law set by one's micro congregation; this includes obedience to laws of the nation. It hardly needs saying that Spanish colonialism and Ladino internal colonialism imposed obedience to extractive law as a bedrock premise of indigenous obligation. Obedience and conformity to tradition in collective communities long defined indigenous status (Martínez Peláez 1970; Tax 1937), although exploitation was to be self-protectively evaded, of course, using the "weapons of the weak" whenever possible, pace Scott (1985).

Both Protestant-derived and Catholic-derived pentecostalisms reappropriate and internalize obedience to law and, as shown in Thompson and colleagues (this volume), emphasize conformity to a group's iconic behavioral indexes preached in the congregational community. This parallels what was formerly the case at the municipal level regarding an expectation of collective conformity. In these pentecostalisms, however, obedience moves from a collective obligation based on indigenous status relative to Ladino overlords, vetted by a large community (the older municipal Maya solution), to a personal obligation defined by one's individual status before God, judged and vetted by the small congregation (the Christian Pentecostal solution). Divine injunction of the individual obligation, however, leaves no room for evasion. A Christian Pentecostal should obey the law, including the law of the land. This renews the long-established facets of obedience, conformity, and mutuality within self-governing collectivities of indigenous culture. The Maya obligation of collective categorical existence under the law (because one is indigenous by status and judged before one's community and perhaps the Spanish) is transformed and internalized into the Christian Pentecostal obligation of individual obedience to law judged both by one's congregation and by God. God and congregation replace Spaniard and municipality, but the resonance of expected conformity is still there.

PARALLEL DESIRES FOR ISOLATION AND WITHDRAWAL

Mayas sought protection from the Spanish by withdrawal into their *municipios*. That isolation was never perfect; it could not be in a colonial extractive economy. Nevertheless, the Mayas elaborated a variety of institutions to preserve their isolation as much as possible. For the most part, these institutions reduced contact with outsiders and thereby helped protect indigenous municipalities from Ladino depredation and exploitation. I noted throughout part 2, however, that the isolation has substantially broken down.

As Tax (1937) shows, an indigene oriented her or his life toward the natal municipality. This communal orientation within and toward one's municipality as an isolated entity (however fictive the isolation) provided a degree of protection from outside social predators, particularly the Ladino governors. At the same time, key local institutions—especially the religious *cofradías* and age-related respect practices among landholders—delivered social status, but at a local level that was recognized internally only by a *municipio*'s residents, as Cancian (1965) has shown.

All this inward municipal focus was a manifestation in religion and politics of what Annis (1987) calls indigenous "*milpa* logic." Under the premise of *milpa* logic, a family invests its labor, inwardly and prodigiously, into the production of crops on the land it possesses. The same cultural logic applied at the municipal level led one to convert wealth into local and indigenous (rather than national) status through *cofradía* participation. Similarly, *milpa* logic or an orientation toward inward self-reliance would lead Mayas to access local indigenous leadership first rather than consult the Ortho-Catholic priest or the external Ladino leaders of national institutions to solve problems, protect land rights, resolve conflicts, or help them deal with the Ladino world beyond the *municipio*. In times past, one could petition the local indigenous leadership to acquire sufficient additional land from the collectively "owned" municipal holdings so one could raise the corn and beans needed to feed one's family and live one's life as a Maya (Dabb et al. 2013). In times past, respected indigenous leaders from the community adjudicated issues internally to try and avoid sending them up—sometimes literally upstairs—to be adjudicated by an externally appointed Ladino mayor (Vogt 1969). The indigenous cultural focus has long sought municipal autonomy via local leadership and problem solution, even when penetrated by externally imposed Ladino leadership.

Unfortunately, these indigenous municipal structures (economic, religious, and political) that once provided relative isolation, protection, and local guidance have fractured, faded, or failed. They have been overwhelmed by population increase. They have been penetrated and compromised by a variety of Guatemalan political party, nation-state, and global market institutions (Brintnall 1979; Watanabe 1992; Hawkins, McDonald, and Adams 2013) in addition to the arrival of externally imported mainstream Protestant religious institutions. In a word, the Maya position in the colonial way of life, based on corn self-sufficiency and relative isolation with municipal autonomy, has collapsed. Today, that idealized but now substantially breached municipal isolation gets reproduced somewhat via the self-isolating aspects of Christian Pentecostal meetings and via behavioral proscriptions, as

described by Thompson and colleagues (this volume). Protestant and Catholic pentecostals gather with the same congregation of individuals for ten or twenty or more hours a week in meetings whose liturgical style isolates the congregants in a bubble of hyperamplified music, bodily experience, and intense exhortation to avoid "the world" and "worldliness."

That time spent weekly in Christian Pentecostal small-congregation religious meetings seems also a version of *milpa* logic. It is a religious manifestation of inward orientation and of intensive local investment, which parallels (and also democratizes) in modern symbols the *milpa* logic of intensive investment in local social status via *cofradía* service. Investing large quantities of time in a Christian Pentecostal congregation thus reproduces the isolation and the local community orientation of Mayaness. It also connects the Christian Pentecostal to a respected male religious advisor and his female primary religious assistant (his wife)—be they the pastor and *pastora* in Pentecostalism or the married couple that guides the Catholic charismatic *comunidad*. It places one in a mutually helpful congregation usually laced with kin ties to the pastor, just as *cofradía* service connected a web of extended family and neighbors in support of the elder nominated to serve in a senior *cofradía* position. The resonant compatibilities between the traditional perspective of intensive local investment and local isolation in the *municipio* and the Christian Pentecostal perspective of intensive investment in the local congregation and relative isolation within it as a total institution, at least during church meetings, seem to make Christian Pentecostalism a suitable and culturally attractive alternative to the now-defunct system of *cofradía* service.

Thus, in Guatemala, one's *aldea* (hamlet) increasingly replaces the *municipio*, and one's local congregation increasingly replaces hamlet or barrio as the locus of a community of identity in which one deploys the still-present *milpa* logic. Now, however, one invests all one's excess time in spiritual labor instead of investing that excess time in cultivation labor. In either case, the *milpa* logic of spiritual or actual *milpa* investement results in enhanced local status. Active participation as a Christian Pentecostal indexes one's religiosity locally and is done with considerable awareness of the Christian Pentecostal contrast to the less active mode of simply being Catholic as a background form of identity maintained through relatively undemanding family ritual, cultural affirmation, and occasional attendance at mass.

Paradoxically, the Pentecostal connection to the local congregation also links many of the isolated congregations to the nation and even the world if the congregation is connected to an overarching denomination. But this connection is religious, not political. Christian Pentecostals see national government as both external to them and corrupt beyond redemption. National politics are, therefore, neither important nor viable as an immediately approachable moral project. This perspective differs little from the view of traditionalist Mayas over the last 500 years regarding Ladinos and national government, as reported in the older ethnographies, ethnohistorical texts, and dance scripts. In the ethnographies, the Maya who gets even a bit wealthier than his or her peers or who serves in government office must have made a pact with the devil, who in dress, speech, and ethnicity is usually a Ladino. In the indigenous view, unusual wealth must come from outside the indigenous *municipio*, which is the Ladino's world, and brings indigenous subjection. In the old ethnographies, the indigenous Maya sells his or her soul, ethnicity, and future place in heaven for money in the present. The receipt of money, however, binds the unfortunate Maya to an afterlife of enslaved labor forever. In one early ethnography, the Maya who finds wealth will labor forever on coffee plantations in the mountains (Wagley 1949:56–57). That cautionary tale codifies a Faustian bargain that explains the anomaly of indigenous wealth: Mayas who get wealthy and do not share with the community have covenanted with—have sold their souls to—malevonent divinities with Ladino attributes.

So also today, in Pentecostal speech and sermon, the Maya who participates in the utterly corrupt, "worldly" national political field makes a pact with the world, with the *mundo*—the same word that is used for the traditionalist earth lord Santo Mundo. To the Pentecostal Mayas, however, Mundo is the devil and still is Ladino. The 1930s traditionalist's eschewing of money and of contact with the Mundo (the Lord of the World) thus has a surprisingly precise analogue with the twenty-first-century Christian Pentecostal's avoidance of receiving money from an unknown provenance and the related and still-existing assumption that such money generates interaction with an irredeemable "*mundo*—the world" (Checketts 2005). Such connection and such money are seen as corrupt to the core and corrosive to indigenous ethics and indigenous identity.

The Christian Pentecostal ethic of isolation from the world, as expressed in the 1990s–2010s in our ethnographies, attracts Mayas because that isolationism captures the long-term indigenous premises of inwardness and self-support, and the *milpa* logic of intensive, safe, local investment in the local unit—formerly the *municipio*, now the hamlet or canton Christian Pentecostal congregation. Isolation protects one from unsafe external connection. In this case, Christian Pentecostals invest enormous time cultivating the spiritual and mental discipline of their physical body and the social discipline of cultivating their proper place in their residential family and local community of worship. They withdraw from all but municipal political participation and confrontation. They do this instead of investing their excess labor cultivating their cornfields, which, in any event, are now, for most families, insufficient to absorb that labor.

Of course, Mayas still labor as much as they can in whatever small holdings or side commerce their family possesses, and they diversify in a variety of other ways to earn additional money. Nevertheless, as Thompson and colleagues and other contributors in part 1 show, they invest deeply in social status in their small Christian Pentecostal congregation by attending to the bodily practices that bring status through ecstatic receipt of the Spirit, speaking in tongues, and ensuring correct adherence to the group's identifying proscriptions of behavior—the *awas* of Thompson and colleagues' chapter. This supplants and at the same time mimics the *milpa* logic of intensive local investment in the corn plot and in the *cofradía*. The Christian Pentecostal project has thereby transferred the locus of consensus building and community unity from the *municipio*, which due to population growth and national penetration is no longer sustainable as a consensus unit, to one of the several small congregations of 15–200 adherents in each rural hamlet or urban canton. In sum, Christian Pentecostal withdrawal fits rather well with a parallel and centuries-long Maya disinterest in the national political domain (Hawkins 1984).

Maya culture seeks conformity of behavior because that symbolizes a mutuality of status, and it seeks a consensus of opinion among the units identified as part of a local community.[1] Modernity, however, has broken down the *cofradía* structure that formerly allowed the far-flung rural hamlets to collaborate and unite with the governing town center in the ritual renewal of shared municipal consensus. As a result, economically strong or resurgent hamlets, such as Los Guineales in Santa Catarina Ixtahuacán and the Antigua Santa Catarina municipal center that is now effectively a rural hamlet of Nueva Ixtahuacán, now vie for recategorization as subdivided and separated autonomous municipal centers. But achieving local consensus about behavior and opinion is still a valued Maya project. The fact that small Christian Pentecostal congregations can achieve a degree of old-culture consensus and conformity more easily than can the much larger parishes of Ortho-Catholics helps make Christian Pentecostal groupings comparatively attractive.

ANALOGOUS EXPECTATIONS OF MUTUALITY IN A COMMUNITY THAT SPEAKS WITH A COLLECTIVE VOICE

Maya communities have long been known to express their mutuality of status and commitment. That collective and mutual orientation was expressed occasionally in community uprisings during the high violence of the war and when key premises or structures were breached by national or military actions. The notion of speaking with a communal voice spilled out in multiple ways in Santa Catarina Ixtahuacán's path to the relocation of its municipal headquarters town (Hawkins and Adams 2020).

Christian Pentecostal congregations replicate that community and mutuality at the very least in broadcasting their Sunday and weekday congregational voice via rooftop speakers that disperse each congregation's consensus over a wide aural field, even if it further fractures the no longer united *municipio* by attacking traditionalism and Ortho-Catholicism. Glossolalia further symbolizes consensus and mutuality. Who can disagree with an uninterpreted message from God? Assent to the expectations of a congregation's *awas* prohibitions also furthers mutuality. There is consensus in acceptance of the pastor and mutuality in the rotation of former *cofradía* and present Catholic Charismatic Renewal leadership.

Of course, there is consensus with adherents when one agrees to consider oneself Ortho-Catholic. But Ortho-Catholicism injects hierarchy and a degree of anti-mutuality in submission to the priest, who is usually an outsider and appointed not by those served but by the external hierarchy. Likewise, the Catholic custom of making special promises to care for a saint—the *promesa*—in return for a granted favor or needed blessing symbolizes obedience to or subjection to a particular other, be it a worldly *patrón* or an otherworldly *santo*. At the most symbolic religious level that Durkheim holds represents society, one submits to—one renders obeisance and gives gifts to—a saint

that has granted (or that one hopes will grant) favors via the *promesa*. In the worldly enactment of these religious representations of society, one submits to a colonial or postcolonial caudillo in the form of a priest or a distinguished citizen chosen as one's *compadre* (godparent, or ritual kin). In a yet more worldly sense, one submits to the political power of a favor-granting, rich, landed, or political *patrón*. All these are forms of submission, but they show loyalty to a person, not to a law. They contradict the mutuality and communality embedded in Maya culture.

Promised devotion to a saint or its analogue of loyalty to a living *patrón* undermines the notion of focusing on the municipality and speaking with one voice. Both are, rather, manifestations of *personalismo*, of submission to people, of caudillismo. They symbolically enshrine payola for special favors to connected people and contravene the notion of obedience to law. In a word, this folk sector of Ortho-Catholic religious practice replicates precisely Latin American and Guatemalan secular caudillismo politics of subordination and devotion. In a divinely condoned symbolic feedback loop that both Durkheim and Weber would consider exemplary of their theories, the religious practices and beliefs regarding *santo* and *promesa* regenerate the dyadic devotions and subordinations that have corrupted the colonial and military administrations of Guatemala for almost five centuries. Catholicism thus reproduces the top-down, favor-for-submission structure symbolically supportive of Guatemalan Ladino internal colonialism rather than the structures of Maya village autonomy, mutuality, and equality of voice as an ethnically defined community. Thus, in the Maya community, the Christian Pentecostal rejection of submission to saints has far broader implications than simply doing something opposite to what traditionalists or Ortho-Catholics do and believe.

CONCLUSION

Today, colonialism as a social system and municipalism as a protective local Maya enclave of self-sustaining, agriculturally based family independence have disintegrated, leaving Ladinos bereft of expected claims of respect and Mayas bereft of social place, protection, and sustenance. Yet Mayas, even young Mayas, have lingering internalized remembrances of their deep cultural premises and practices. Many express a longing for some kind of return to their cultural heritage. They remember themselves as once having been united. Catholic and Protestant pentecostalisms appeal fundamentally to Mayas because they resonate with these deeply rooted Maya expectations and cultural desires—for unity, consensus, experientiality, small-group orientation and autonomy, obedience to law, local investment, isolation, mutuality, and equality. Evangelical and charismatic congregational fissioning when chapels get full also meshes with Maya familial fissioning: when brothers marry, they fill the family residence with competing spouses and children, and then they hive off to live in relative independence. Today's congregational isolation from the encompassing worldly society matches the former municipal isolation as protection from Ladino contact and exploitation. Finally, the lack of hierarchy in the Catholic charismatic congregation achieved by leadership rotation precisely matches the old *cofradía* rotation.

My emphasis in this chapter has been on the local: on the similarities and resonances between some aspects of K'iche' Maya culture (as expressed via traditionalism in Nahualá and Santa Catarina Ixtahuacán) and the premises and practices of Christian Pentecostalism. I suggest that these resonances ease the process of conversion. It is important to note that one or another of such similarities and resonances also appear to facilitate the processes of conversion to Christian Pentecostalism in many indigenous areas around the world. For example, other literatures point out the importance of an enchanted worldview to Pentecostal acceptance in parts of Asia (Hollenweger 2011:20; Yung 2011:42–44).

Wallace (1956:276) sets the stage for this interpretation when he notes that revitalization movements build into their "proposed new cultural system . . . large quantities of both traditional and imported cultural material." Christian Pentecostalism embraces both traditional and imported components. At the premise level, it keeps or replicates key assumptions of the old worldview. At the symbolic and behavioral levels, it mimics the structure of many iconic practices, but does so in a new manner that is perceived to be modern. As I have shown, Christian Pentecostalism's new symbols imitate and therefore resonate with the spirit-enchanted view of the universe that has always been congenial to the Mayas. In its Christian Pentecostal forms, all people can be embodied by the Holy Spirit, and the devil lurks everywhere to ensnare the unwary. There are analogues to these in traditional Maya thought, although the spirits of the old ways exist in more forms and with more names than the consolidated devil, the singular Jesus, and the Holy Spirit. Other aspects of

Christian Pentecostal worship are imported modernities: bands, electronic amplification, business suits, simple non-baroque meetinghouses, and congregational involvement in sung melodies.

In a process complementary to what Hobsbawm and Ranger (1983) call the "invention of tradition," new religious systems that have in them some parallels to old ways or old premises make their adoption more acceptable and comfortable. By making changes that anticipate a future by using mechanisms felt as resonating with past cultural profundities, revitalization movements like Christian Pentecostalism utilize respected social resources and thereby help make needed mass social change possible. Thus, these "new" but transparent, communal, embodied, experiential, egalitarian, obedience-oriented, *cofradía*-like, isolated Christian Pentecostal versions of religiosity, which call the old "bad," feel more Maya and more traditional than the less transparent, less communal, less embodied, less experiential, less equal, less obedience-oriented, less *cofradía*-like, and less isolated Ortho-Catholic practices. Likewise, Christian Pentecostal practice is more Maya compatible than is historic mainstream Protestantism. It is worth noting, however, that these new Christian Pentecostal liturgies do not just resonate with or mimic Maya culture in a new and modern register. They also simultaneously help solve some key problems arising from collapse and exclusion. They help Mayas deal more effectively with the lives they have been dealt.

NOTE

1. Jardine, Hawkins, and Adams (2020) discuss extensively the importance of consensus in the myths of Santa Catarina Ixtahuacán's municipal foundation. The 1930s–1950s ethnographies document that Maya discourse operated so as to carefully develop collective wisdom in small groups of people who knew each other (Gillin 1952:200). The congregational practice of Christian Pentecostals mimics this aspect of Mayaness.

Chapter Twenty-Four

The Attractions of Practical Consequence

Christian Pentecostalism as a Revitalization Movement in Failing Societies

JOHN P. HAWKINS

ONE WAY TO GAIN FURTHER insight into the pentecostal path to religious change is to see Christian Pentecostalism as providing at least partial solutions to the existential threats people face every day in their sociocultural and environmental interactions. A number of theorists see these benefits or functionalities as though they were "products" created by religions to make those religions more competitive in a vibrant, diverse religious marketplace. However, I argue against this religious marketplace metaphor, suggesting instead that Christian Pentecostalism is a deliberately transformative religious revitalization movement. It is better seen as a magnetic social and idea system than as an element in a happenstance smorgasbord of competing religious providers from which one chooses attractive product solutions. Indeed, "the true justification of religious practices is not in their apparent ends," writes Durkheim (2001[1912]:266), "but in the invisible influence they work on consciousness, in the way they affect our mental state."

ON RELIGIOUS REVITALIZATION MOVEMENTS

Anthony F. C. Wallace (1956, 2003[1956]) systematized the study of nativistic, renewal, revival, adjustment cult, and millenarian religious (and nonreligious) transformations of society under the term "revitalization movements." By his definition, "a revitalization movement is . . . a deliberate, organized, conscious effort by members of a society to construct a more satisfying culture" (Wallace 1956:265, 2003[1956]:10). Revitalization, Wallace (2003[1956]:10)

suggests, "is a special kind of culture change" with four attributes. Wallace then adds a fifth to cover religious versions of revitalization movements:

1. "The persons involved . . . must perceive their culture, or some major areas of it, as a system."
2. "They must feel that this cultural system is unsatisfactory."
3. "They must innovate not merely discrete items, but a new cultural system, specifying new relationships as well as, in some cases, new traits."
4. Finally, "a number of persons" who "collaborate . . . in such an effort" (Wallace 1956:267, 2003[1956]:12) make these innovations with the understanding and "intent" that in some way these changes will heal the ills and dissatisfactions in their society. As Wallace (1956:268, 270, 2003[1956]:13–14, 17) puts it, the revitalization process and indeed all religion "originated . . . in visions of a new way of life by individuals under extreme stress," and these revelatory visions will rectify a "society's troubles" via new rules that, if abided, "promise individual and social revitalization . . . but personal and social catastrophe if they are not."
5. If the solution advocated includes sacred symbols and religious deportment posed as a divinely approved system change, then the movement is a revitalization religion.

Many revitalization movements are in fact revitalization religions because the religious connotations of divine injunction and divine approbation help adherents detach from the old performances and beliefs and motivate them to try the new. By all five attributes above, the varieties of Christian Pentecostalism in Guatemala are religious revitalization movements.

Wallace explicitly contrasts revitalization movements with evolutionary adaptation. Evolutionary adaptation proceeds slowly and without consciously coordinated sudden readjustment. A revitalization movement, by contrast, is a conscious, deliberate, coordinated system transformation resulting from human reconceptualization. Once envisioned, the movement can be expanded by mass collective agreement with the reconceptualizations. Alternatively, it can be expanded by individuals rethinking their view of the world when presented more or less individually with the revitalization practices and premises. This relatively individuated movement toward a revitalization religion is what we mean by conversion.

In this chapter I examine the constructive consequences that have been attributed to involvement in the mental and bodily practices of Christian Pentecostalism viewed as a revitalization religious movement. Some of those consequences are explicitly sought after and understood by Christian Pentecostals themselves as deliberate efforts to transform and improve what they see as a sick society. Protestant-derived Pentecostals, for example, see the culturally dominant Catholic Church and the national societies embracing Catholicism, such as Guatemala, as broken, sick, and corrupt. Catholic charismatic pentecostals likewise see society and the mother church as in need of reformation. They suggest that the Ortho church lacks needed vitality.

Some of the changes and their consequences are perceived more by social analysts than by participants. But the members of a system and those advocating revitalization change cannot be expected to anticipate all of the consequences resulting from their movement. They must merely perceive that parts of their society and culture are an interrelated system, that a significant part of their system is in some kind of crisis or is inadequate or broken, and that the changes proposed are intended to ameliorate the untoward conditions of the crisis. In this regard, all Christian Pentecostals, whether Catholic- or Protestant-derived, believe their society to be corrupt and in crisis, and they believe that their religious activities will bring healing to individuals and through evangelization eventually to the whole of society. These two points are articles of faith in the new religions (Martin 2003).

In certain regards, this chapter may seem like an old-style structural-functional analysis. In that style,

championed by Radcliffe-Brown (1952) and Malinowski (1954) from the 1920s to the 1950s and elaborated by their students from the 1930s to the 1960s, one first identifies a belief or practice that seems incongruous, unwieldy, or incomprehensible to those who share the analyst-author's basic "western" cultural experience. The anthropologist then explores the practice or belief in its context, showing it to be part of an integrated system; revealing its logic and fit in a larger cosmology; and noting the practice's contribution toward bringing about structural reproduction or intellectual coherence in the society. In an ethnography, the structural functionalist seeks to show the interconnectedness, self-consistent rationality, and operational utility of key components of that society.

In the case of religion seen as a revitalization movement, however, one would look at the new institutionalized practices and beliefs to see what changes they bring to the society via agentive decisions of those who choose to adopt and deploy the new practices, beliefs, and symbols because they have judged the underlying system to be inadequate. The question central to this chapter concerns the roles and consequences of the new religious practices and beliefs shared by the new ecstatic religions in Guatemalan society.

Several foundational approaches might be tried. For example, does Christian Pentecostal religion work as a form of class control, as Marx would suggest? Is Pentecostal practice a means by which the Guatemalan elites and the army further and more efficiently delude the masses into being exploited, manipulated, or controlled? These, too, are structural-functional or structural-consequential questions.

Alternatively, does this charismatic change of religion lead to the sacralization of a different idea and symbolic system that guides its adherents to an adaptive transformation generally more congenial to the social interests of the mass of believers than the existing belief and ritual system, as Durkheim would say? Or do the new religions espouse variant systems of principles, symbols, or practices that, when adopted as a mental/cognitive reality through conversion, enable people to deal with a wrecked postcolonial society weakened by corruption and challenged by globalization, as Wallace would extend Durkheim?

Or perhaps Weber, trending toward Geertz, is the right model. Does a new religious conceptualization independently do its work on a society without regard for intended consequence and without necessity of a perception that the society in some sense is deeply troubled and inadequate? I need to be careful here. The religious thinkers of the Reformation knew there were problems in their society that they were attempting to correct, and in that regard, they too are analyzable in terms of Wallace's explicit revitalization model as an extension of Weber's notions of charismatic leadership and change. At the same time, Weber seems to be interested in the longer-term consequences of an ideology after its explicitly recognized impetus for reform gets forgotten.

In this chapter I show that for the most part, the various Christian Pentecostalisms do work to the advantage of their adherents in Guatemala. For example, I show from our Guatemalan Maya ethnographies, as Brusco (1993, 1995) shows in her Colombian data, that Pentecostal change particularly advantages Maya women, given their interest in the family. Thus I side with Durkheim, Weber, and Wallace. In particular, I conclude that the new Christian Pentecostal religions constitute an attempted moral rejuvenation, à la Durkheim, and an attempt at transformational activism, à la Wallace, rather than a deception regarding one's class interests or a mechanism of control by elites, à la Marx. These new religions offer a means of reattachment, remoralization, and resacralization in a society shattered by the cultural collapse of its corn-based institutions. That shattering has made some of Maya society's seemingly older but still continuing religious symbolism and practice—those of traditionalist Maya Catholic and Ortho-Catholic derivation—increasingly marginal. One of the articles of faith in the Christian Pentecostal religions is to contribute to the shared good of society and of individuals in that society. They seem to do so by providing fruitful new cognitive models to guide new behaviors that will, according to the faith, construct a new societal alternative locally. Moreover, they hope that the evangelization and conversion processes will extend the solutions nationally and internationally. The practice of these new liturgies rejuvenates one's sentiments of attachment to and hope for the new local and national frameworks under construction. The new liturgies thus reconstruct one's mental orientation as to how to deal with the messy world.

The new Christian Pentecostal ideologies and their implementation in religious practices are acts of faith. There is no proof that they will work; there is only evidence by experience that their predecessors—the formerly culturally dominant traditionalist Maya Catholic and Ortho-Catholic religions—increasingly have not been working well. Will the adoption of the new premises and practices actually lead to a better society or a better individual life? That is the hope of the converts. The ethnographic evidence of improved, less crisis-ridden lives seems to support that faith. But only time—a century or two of deployment—will tell if this faith in societal change is merited.

In Durkheim's and Wallace's terms, the charismatic aspects of ecstatic religions sacralize important modes of adaptive change and thereby facilitate their adoption. Introduced by revelation to any member of the small community, the contemplated transformations become vested with the ultimate authority of God's imprimatur, made evident in the ecstatic behavioral manifestations of the Holy Spirit when received within the bodies of the worshippers and expressed by humans voicing the testimonio of the Spirit. Given enough stress in the society and its primary religion (in this case, Ortho-Catholicism in 2003 Guatemala) and given experiential participation in an alternative religion, an individual may repremise her or his mind-set to a new configuration.

This act of repremising a sacralized mind-set is conversion. Conversion is the individual-level mental adjustment that consolidates a new orientation or a new approach to perceived existential crisis. As Jones and colleagues (this volume) show, the tellings of such conversions are shaped by interaction in a congregation. Conversion stories are a form of expression, and the way they are experienced is socialized by the congregation. In effect, the new congregation becomes the new focal social unit of the converts, a new source of their identity, and a new model that they imitate and on which they converge. I build on ideas taken from Durkheim (on social structure, moral connection, and social representation), from Weber (on the relentless impact of distinct ideology and charismatic leadership on society), and from Wallace (on purposeful immediate renewal, cultural invention, and synthesis). Taken together, these ground a satisfying analysis of religious change both in Guatemala and throughout the postcolonial Christianized Global South.

In the sections that follow, I discuss several Christian Pentecostal religious practices or injunctions. I relate them to various efforts to improve society—to heal society, if you will. Some of these transformations are consciously sought. Some of the resulting transformations are not sought, or not clearly understood, but are nonetheless consequential to particular levels of society: individual, family, community, nation. Others seem consequential to the emerging processes of globalization.

I group the practices according to the levels of society they most obviously impact. In reality, however, any religious practice operates simultaneously on several levels, from the individual to larger social groupings. Any new practice will have multiple consequences, good and bad, that simultaneously change manifold facets of society, which in their turn will have tertiary effects. To cite but one example, the Pentecostal injunction against drinking alcohol simultaneously reconstructs the addicted individual, changes family interaction, improves family economics, alters underlying gender constructs, and acts on community and culture. It alters economics and patterns of sociality, marriage, kinship, and fictive kinship (*compadrazco*). It probably alters politics. It certainly transforms religion. In short, the consequences of alcohol prohibition reverberate throughout all levels of society simultaneously and are not separable. Thus, the categorizations I offer below of impacts on individual, family, community, and nation, and the order in which I sequence them, are artifacts of the structure of a book and the linear logic needed to communicate via language.

After exploring some benefits that our Maya informants say have resulted from Christian Pentecostal ideology and practice, I note similarities between our findings and the analyses of other scholars exploring similar aspects of the Christian Pentecostal experience in other countries. It is clear that in this field school we discovered nothing new regarding the presumed social benefits of Christian Pentecostal participation. One important takeaway is this: the widespread similarity of consequences across several continents and cultures suggests that seeing Christian Pentecostalism as a revitalization movement attempting to cure social ills applies not just to Guatemala but throughout the postcolonial Christian Global South. On a worldwide basis, Christian Pentecostalism seems to be responsive to the social mechanics and difficulties of mercantile colonial intrusion and population expansion causing local cultural collapse, which is usually followed by colonialism's replacement by exclusionary neoliberal globalism.

RECONSTRUCTING THE INDIVIDUAL

I begin by examining Christian Pentecostal revitalization religion as a deliberate reconstruction of the individual.

Jones and colleagues (this volume) focus on this aspect of reconstructing a disrupted self; all of the Christian Pentecostal chapters (7–13) implicitly touch on the subject. O'Neill (2010) places reconstruction of the self at the heart of the neo-Pentecostal project in urban Guatemala. By "neo-Pentecostal," he refers to Pentecostal congregations not affiliated directly with mainline historic Protestant Pentecostal denominations. O'Neill devotes considerable space to showing how neo-Pentecostal preaching and mutual coaching in small gospel study groups conducted in homes discipline the individual into monitoring and reforming the self. In neo-Pentecostal logic, that reformation of self is considered a form of healing both of the self and of the nation. But that is not the only type of healing going on. A number of studies put physical and mental health and healing at the top of the list of Christian Pentecostal functionalities delivered to congregants (Chesnut 2003a:44–46, 132–134, 153; Brown 2011:3–13).

Mitigating Lack of Health

Mayas, like many others, suffer the "pathogens of poverty" (Chesnut 2003a) in the sense that Mayas frequently are poor. As Early (2012) shows, their poverty leads to nutritional insufficiency, immunological breakdown, inadequate sanitation, limited health care, and other factors that together lead to frequent ill health. A simple illness can ruinously deplete a poor family's resources. Untreated, illness can kill or sideline a wage earner whose income is essential to feed the family. Alternatively, if treatment is sought, the costs of a biomedical cure for an extended serious illness can threaten the household with land loss and even force migration to urban areas when the land one can mortgage to pay for healing runs out (Hawkins and Adams 2007). Either way, ill health and high health care costs can quickly overwhelm a poor family. Mayas thus face a difficult, at times confusing, potentially expensive, and possibly disaster-inducing set of decisions every time a family member gets sick. If land shortage has not already put a Maya family firmly on the cusp of economic and cultural collapse, the ever-present possibility of serious illness certainly does. Thus, finding healing when ill and maintaining physical and mental health as well as cognitive and social order are matters of serious concern to participants in this, as in any, society.

What are the sources of healing help for the Mayas of Guatemala? Two avenues of paid provider-client relationship that work to bring about healing lie within reach of Mayas. In each approach, an individual or family visits a specialist and makes a payment for services rendered. One can follow either route or both at once. In the first, a Maya can seek healing through traditional Maya cultural resources. These include consultations with ethnomedically apprenticed *curanderas* or *curanderos* (curers, female and male), with *comadronas* (midwives), or with bonesetters (Adams and Hawkins 2007; Wilson 2007; Hinojosa 2002, 2004a, 2004b). One visits a particular healer because of her or his known success in treating particular conditions or maladies. In addition to a number of practical and often effective treatment skills, these practitioners use Maya Catholic traditionalist religious symbols to augment the effects of the herbal and body-manipulation treatments they have learned, generally by apprenticeship. In return, they usually receive a gift or payment for their services. Payments end the sense of indebtedness or obligation to the provider for having been healed. The patient entails no follow-on obligation of participation in a group.

Also in the traditionalist Maya cultural panoply of paid provider-client relationships, one can find a cure or receive advice and direction toward acquiring a cure from an *ajq'ij* acting alone or with the assistance of his wife. One pays or gives gifts to the serving *ajq'ij*. One visits the *ajq'ij* for a broader range of concerns than specific healing treatments, and the interaction involves a longer ritual sequence. Scott and colleagues (this volume) show for Nahualá and Santa Catarina Ixtahuacán how traditionalist religious practices involving sortilege, divination, and direct communication with Santo Mundo and the ancestors help reduce the mental consternation engendered by complexity, new decisions, and envy resulting from differential social change. These rituals address both mental and physical illnesses.

In the second avenue of provider-client relationships, a Maya can seek healing by consulting and paying biomedically trained doctors, nurses, and health technicians. Often Mayas consult the biomedical practitioners for "grave" or enduring illnesses when there is no suspicion that they were caused by witchcraft (Adams and Hawkins 2007; Harris 2007). Most of the biomedical doctors come from (or, if indigenous, have effectively passed into) the Ladino cultural system. For indigenous clients seeking healing, that ethnic difference raises issues of access and culturally suitable delivery. But here my focus is on religion and the social implications of healing by religion. Guatemalan-trained biomedical doctors do not use obvious faith symbols in their practice. The idea of healing as a gift of God is not invoked. Rather, notions of training and science dominate. Moreover, biomedical doctors charge the client a fee for service that, compared to Maya incomes, can be quite substantial. There, too, payment cancels the social debt incurred by receiving treatment, whether or not one is healed. The patient acquires no obligation to the biomedical healer; there is no group to join nor are any group-associated obligations incurred.

What routes are there to acquire free healing? Two ways exist for a Catholic, whether Maya or not and whether traditionalist or Ortho-Catholic, to seek religiously sourced healing without consulting a traditionalist healer or an *ajq'ij*. In the first route, a sick Ortho-Catholic or traditionalist who desires specific religious help for his or her malady kneels before one of the saints in the open Catholic church at the center of every *municipio* and makes a *promesa*, a promise or covenant to perform some devotion or sacrifice in return for the blessing of needed healing. A prayer and a promise to be fulfilled upon healing may also be made in a Catholic home at the family altar. The prayer-and-promise modality entails no immediate payment to a practitioner/specialist. But the gift of healing, when received, requires the fulfillment of the promise of reciprocal exchange and presumes a measure of future devotion to that saint.

Alternatively, the Ortho-Catholic can make pilgrimage to a sanctuary known for its healing properties; the Black Christ of Esquipulas is chief among them in Guatemala. Such a trip can be expensive and may also entail the obligations of a conditional *promesa*.

Whether locally sought or by pilgrimage, the ordinary lay Ortho-Catholic member seeking free healing is unsupported by the local Catholic community, and the local Ortho-Catholic priest has no liturgical ability to offer healing.[1] There is no social interaction with a living representative of the Ortho-Catholic community that helps one directly to achieve a ritual healing. Thus, if a religiously sourced healing is desired, the Ortho-Catholic must blur the edges of orthodoxy and seek cures by paying for a blessing in the home of a curer or an *ajq'ij*. In this regard, Ortho-Catholicism contrasts sharply with traditionalist Maya Catholicism because the Ortho-Catholic in Guatemala receives no source of direct healing support during mass nor from priests. Of course, the mass offers an implicit blessing of welfare and can be sponsored as a mass dedicated to one's improvement. But it does not promise direct healing, and sponsoring a mass is not free.

There is, however, another well-known local source of free healing. One can ask for or receive the help of a charismatic Catholic or Pentecostal prayer group that comes to one's home or that can be accessed by attending Christian Pentecostal services. There, healing is offered to all without charge. Indeed, the fact that pentecostalism (both Catholic and Protestant) provides ready access to free healing ranks among its most distinctive and celebrated features.

In Christian Pentecostal church meetings, multiple individuals walk to the front of the hall upon invitation, kneel, and offer themselves for healing prayers. The pastor or a lay healer of either sex may place a Bible directly on the kneeling person's head or touch the supplicant's head with one hand and hold aloft a Bible in the other, praying intensely all the while and moving from supplicant to supplicant. More than one healer may circulate in the meeting. The healing phase in the Christian Pentecostal meeting may be accompanied by manifestations of glossolalia and trance falling to the floor. Whether the proffered prayers do in fact heal the particular ailment or not is beyond the scope of this book. What does matter is that the healings are believed efficacious, that the socially shared *testimonios* bear witness to the actuality of healings, and that belief in the efficacy of the Spirit brings individuals relief and hope.

Individuals of any faith may avail themselves of these free services, but the gifting of a free healing creates a reciprocity pressure to connect with the group offering the gift. This obligation parallels the notion of the cultural obligation an Ortho-Catholic or traditionalist accrues with regard to a saint upon receipt of a gift of healing or problem resolution following a promise made to that saint.

I noted above that the fee paid to the doctor for biomedical services or the fee paid to the *ajq'ij* for ethnomedical services or guidance regarding the cause of an ailment cancels the implicit reciprocity that would have accrued had the client been healed for free. In many Pentecostal services, leaders solicit contributions. Does that solicitation likewise cancel the expectation of accrued reciprocity? In the conduct of a Pentecostal meeting, the contribution-soliciting portion often seems quite disconnected from the healing portion. Perhaps this is the case deliberately. Moreover, the solicitation of contributions during a meeting is sometimes omitted, and one can walk to the front and receive a healing whether or not one has contributed. Thus, the disconnection of fundraising from healing services seems to preclude thinking of the offering as a payment canceling the debt incurred by a healing received.

In an environment of widespread stress- and poverty-induced illness, the fact that the Ortho-Catholic priest has no liturgical way to offer a gift of healing disadvantages Ortho-Catholics vis-à-vis Christian Pentecostals. That same Ortho-Catholic deficit leaves open a structural need for either traditionalist Maya or charismatic Catholic ritual and healing services. Traditionalism thus continues to run parallel to Ortho-Catholicism even if traditionalist divination and healing remain somewhat hidden, an embarrassment to the modernist Mayas. Moreover, traditionalist healers, diviners, and shamans like Tix remain a vibrant, active, continuing option in part because globalization and modernization bring many new and pressing difficulties that disturb the sense of balance that Mayas hold as culturally important. Such disturbances induce culturally linked illnesses that maintain the need for culturally connected curers and diviners.[2] The Ortho-Catholic inability to offer healing except through biomedical clinics also illuminates why the Ortho-Catholic hierarchy eventually came to accept the Charismatic Renewal as a legitimate branch of Catholic practice: Catholicism needed a source of ritually offered free healings and acquired it by imitating the Pentecostals via Charismatic Renewal Catholicism.[3]

To all who seek it in a Christian Pentecostal meeting, the gift of healing is free. In Durkheim's and Mauss's terms, healing is a true generalized gift, subject only to notions of generalized reciprocity. Indeed, people say their healings are a *don de Dios* ("gift of God") or that *xusipaj ri Qajaw chwe* ("Our God [or 'God of us'] gifted it to me") or that *xinucunaj ri Qajaw* ("Our Lord healed me"). In word and thought, healings at Christian Pentecostal meetings (and traditionalist healings) are spoken of as gifts from and mysteries of God, Jesús, or Espíritu Santo (Holy Spirit) or, in the case of traditionalist healings, gifts from these or other usually unseen beings. In providing for free the gift of healing every Sunday and at meetings or house visits during the week, the various Christian Pentecostalisms appropriate to their advantage a Maya cultural expectation of reciprocity through allegiance for gifts given.

These deeply held notions of reciprocity trump any suggestion that conversion and religious affiliation are a matter of rational choice by cost-benefit analysis. Rather than making a rational choice, one takes a gift of healing services freely proffered by evangelistic outreach as a matter of one's chance/fortune/*portuna*. In Maya thought, *portuna* comes as a chance encounter, and it too is a gift of God. Indeed, *portuna* may come as a sign of one's calling via the accidental finding of a clear quartzite crystal among the rocks in the path or as a healing, such as that experienced by Tix (Scott et al., this volume), by Lázaro (Morgan 2005), or with Wilson's (2007) *comadrona*. Ill or distressed lay Catholics may visit the Catholic church building and, kneeling before a favored saint, make a bargain that if they are healed they will dress the saint or serve it faithfully in processions. If cured, that is their *portuna*, and they serve that saint. Or the gift of *portuna* may be brought to one's home by a group of evangelistic healers concerned to give healing to their neighbors. Once received as healing, the chance encounter with *portuna* requires one to take up the path; one must complete the reciprocity implied by one's *portuna*. One reciprocates the gift with devotion and sacrifice to the understood spiritual source of one's *portuna*, just as one serves one's worldly *patrón* as a reciprocal exchange for favors rendered or expected to be rendered. The chance visit by the Christian Pentecostal healers or the receipt of such a precious gift in Sunday Christian Pentecostal services thus occurs within the interpretive framework of a deeply held set of Maya cultural concepts.

The practical question here is, which pathway to one's *portuna* is more likely to open? In a village society where all know one another, including their health status, one's *portuna* when bedridden or ill is more likely to be supplied by an Evangelical committee of healers going house to house than for the ill to rise up, go to the Catholic church, invoke a saint, and make a bargain. Likewise, an ill person is more likely to be visited by the committee than to be out of the house and chance to find a crystal rock on the smooth-packed, clean clay paths, which have been scanned daily by dozens of eyes forced to look downward under the weight of a tumpline-balanced load. Institutionalized outreach by a prayer group giving a freely proffered gift tips *portuna* in favor of the Christian Pentecostals. Thus, healing indeed stands at the center of many people's conversions. But it does so not because free healing is chosen as a lower-cost product offered by a vendor putting religious goods on sale in a marketplace of religions. Rather, it does so because healing is freely given in a culture that believes in generalized reciprocity between humans and divinities wherein gifts must be exchanged and reciprocally balanced by devotion. Again, old Maya culture and new Christian Pentecostal practice resonate.

The broader literature confirms the importance of healing in Christian Pentecostal conversion. "Talk of healing permeates the discourses of personal change" among Bolivian Pentecostals and "extends" to how they "talk about and conceive of their relationship to society" (Wightman 2007:240). Chesnut (1997) argues that healing is the primary attractant among the features that drive the success of spirit-engaged religions in Brazil. Umbanda (Afro-Christian), Pentecostal, and charismatic faiths all prosper, according to Chesnut, because they make faith healing both central to their religious practice and inexpensive. Indeed, faith healing is nominally free to those who attend any Pentecostal or charismatic meeting (Chesnut 1997:51–107; 2003a:7, 44–47, 79–82, 129–134). According to Chesnut (2003a:46), "a serious illness can threaten the very existence of an impoverished household." He is correct, and this danger holds throughout much of the impoverished world. As we have noted elsewhere, the threat of illness portends catastrophe in Nahualá and Santa Catarina Ixtahuacán (Hawkins and Adams 2007:xiii). Because "affordable health care is a scarce commodity, physical illness leads poor Latin Americans to the doors of a Pentecostal house of worship more than any other factor" (Chesnut 2003a:45–46; see also Chesnut 1997:51–72). Chesnut's (2003a:45) research shows that more than half of all converts in his study of religion in Brazil cite an episode of illness and healing as their reason for conversion. In Brazil, "with limited access to the dehumanizing assembly-line medical 'care' of the health posts, Pentecostal faith healing becomes a highly attractive alternative source of health" (Chesnut 1997:72). Tennekes (1985:34) reports the connection of healing and conversion for Chile, and Wilson (1973:123) does so for Argentina. A study of Pentecostalism in Haiti claims that 75 percent of congregants converted as a result of an episode of Pentecostal faith healing (Conway 1980:13). Healing is likewise a "major factor" in the growth of South African Pentecostal and Zionist congregations: "a person joins the church because felt needs are met—and this often means healing from physical sickness and discomfort" (Anderson 2000:120–121).

Around the world, the availability of healing as a free gift of God stands at the heart of pentecostal belief, practice, and mode of expansion. Brown (2011:3, emphasis in original) affirms that "in the Latin American, Asian, and

African countries where pentecostal growth is occurring most rapidly, as many as 80–90 percent of first-generation Christians attribute their conversions *primarily* to having received divine healing for themselves or a family member." Indeed, Brown (2011:14, 19, 21) suggests that "a strong case" can be made that "divine healing is the single most important category—more significant than glossolalia or prosperity—for understanding the global expansion of pentecostal Christianity."

Nahualenses and Ixtahuaquenses see the manifestations of healing in local meetings, at regional meetings where the featured healers come from other countries, and on television broadcasts, CDs, videotapes, and DVDs. These media visually demonstrate the healing process and enable a homogenized pentecostal liturgical healing style to cross international boundaries. It is not just Durkheim's Australian gods who "resist enclosure" in a culture, ethnic group, or tribe. The rituals of pentecostal healing also "internationalize." Indeed, Brown (2011:19) says, "a common pool of divine healing beliefs and practices circulates globally."

One aspect of healing or having been healed is to feel a sense of well-being, to feel joy. Thus far, I have talked primarily about angst regarding collapse and exclusion in the pentecostal context, and I have characterized much of its participatory, collective liturgy and prayer as a "pentecostal wail." How does my depiction of angst square with the manifestations of happiness and joy attributed to Christian Pentecostal religious participation? Does Christian Pentecostalism and its associated liturgies in Pentecostal and charismatic practice only express or give catharsis to pain, stress, risk, or sense of collapse?

Of course not. Pentecostal worship also expresses and embodies a good measure of joy.[4] The experience of joy is, in this case, partly rooted in the fact that pentecostalism as preached asserts that it provides a solution to some of the existential threats experienced in Maya life and that it actually provides a partial amelioration of those threats and societal failings. It works both mentally and physically. Moreover, pentecostals' open access to the congregation's microphone allows them to express their *testimonio* and recount their path out of problems in an at-risk community. This helps them heal. After all, one does not need the presence of a professional therapist to benefit from shared talk about life's difficulties and healings. The practice of an integrated, sacralized, behavioral response to collapse and exclusion and the possession of a cognitive reconceptualization that promises comfort and offers

healing together provide a pathway through and out of chaos. That brings joy. That triggers hope. Indeed, placing oneself and all one's problems in the hands of God is itself a way to remediate chaos and redeem or buffer oneself and one's family from evil. That too brings joy, or at any rate relief, to the individual, and relief perhaps is perceived as joy. The process allows an effervescence of love, appreciation, and communion in the congregation, for the congregation shares that conception through socially articulated testimonies, as shown by Jones and colleagues (this volume). According to Victor Turner (1968, 1969, 1980), sharing travail, which in this case is achieved by sharing testimonies of movement from personal hardship and crisis to healing in a pentecostal fold, itself creates *communitas* in its social and joyful senses of mutual appreciation. Pentecostalism stimulates joy because it offers hope, promise, community, and institutionalized procedures with which an adherent can confront an otherwise hopeless and unpromising situation. The celebration of hope with like-minded congregants is, as Durkheim shows, a source of effervescent pleasure and joy at the same time that such performance can be a distressed and mournful cry, Marx's "protest" arising from and indicating cultural crisis.

Mitigating Alcohol Damage

Both Pentecostal Protestants and charismatic Catholics see alcohol use as a vice that needs both suppression and healing. Alcohol use generates a cascade of problems that many Maya women, including Ortho-Catholic women, freely deplore. As others (e.g., Eber 1995; Brusco 1995) have shown, alcohol consumption pushes a disproportionate percentage of family income to male use and wastes money on empty calories that could feed the children. Alcohol incapacitates some men, making them unavailable to their family. Alcohol consumption removes inhibitions that normally block impulsive or violent behavior arising out of the frustrations of life. Thus, some drunk men hit or otherwise abuse women or children. Incapacitation by alcohol also can lead to a loss of status in the community. Any of these alcohol-induced impediments can add to family crisis and induce increased consumption of alcohol in order to not be distressed by the loss. In too many men, this results in a vicious circle of escalating failure and anxiety being tamped down by increased alcohol use, which leads to further failure and more anxiety.[5]

Alcohol consumption grounds traditionalist ritual. It

lubricates male sociality "in the street." It provides pleasure, especially in the face of difficult circumstances. It anesthetizes the mind against worries, although that leads to poor decisions and further waste. As Wells and colleagues (2020) show, many men stand in precarious economic circumstances in a collapsing culture and must deal with highly contradictory systems. On the one hand, gender roles and ethnic identity urge men to work and provide their family with corn. On the other hand, diminishing inheritances, inflating land prices, and lack of access to paid jobs render these expectations difficult to fulfill. Alcohol's anesthetic properties become useful when one confronts unresolvable contradictions of gender roles or the imminent failure of subsistence.

Women, by contrast, face few social pressures to drink, and most have few opportunities outside the private domestic domain to acquire a taste or need for alcohol. In our ethnographic studies, we encountered very few indigenous women who drank alcohol regularly, but I did see one woman drunk and destitute in the streets of Nahualá versus many such men.

Traditionalist and Maya Catholic religious participation provides little support for avoiding alcohol. Indeed, quite the opposite. Most *ajq'ijab'* consume alcohol as a prominent part of the normal conduct of traditionalist ritual, and drunkenness is common, especially at traditionalist festivals and the week-long celebration of each *municipio*'s patron saint. Until very recently, inebriation was an uncontested and fully expected part of traditionalist ritual, though today a few *ajq'ijab'* eschew alcohol and instead drink Orange Crush, a colorful, sugared, alcohol-free soda. Tix, for example, tried not to drink alcohol, but almost always succumbed as he performed his rituals. And even if avoided by an *ajq'ij*, alcohol is still poured as a libation (plate 22) that is desired and consumed by Santo Mundo and the ancestors called to a divination. Thus, ingestion of alcohol remains a prominent and honored part of traditionalist Maya Catholic ritual.

Roman Catholicism likewise honors alcohol by raising the wine chalice toward heaven at the holiest point during mass. From the earliest historical records to the present-day experience, alcohol has played a prominent part in the celebratory behavior of Catholics at key saints' day celebrations shared with traditionalists. Rounds of drinking punctuate family gatherings after rituals of baptism, communion, marriage, or funeral. Consequently, neither traditionalist nor Roman versions of Catholicism

insulate the individual against alcohol abuse, which can exacerbate one's underlying economic or social problems.

By contrast, Pentecostal Protestant and Mormon congregations support their members by regularly using sermons to strictly prohibit consumption of any alcohol. Though not always successful (as Gooren 2007 has shown), these religions provide a theological justification that helps men sidestep the social pressures and expenses of alcohol consumption and helps their spouses to challenge alcohol use. The charismatic Catholic injunction against alcohol consumption is similarly helpful but complicated by Ortho-Catholicism's openness to alcohol. Catholic charismatics avidly preach against alcohol consumption as part of their renewal of Catholicism. But charismatics cannot completely reject alcohol without rejecting the mass and thereby rejecting Roman Catholicism. So they cannot strictly demonize alcohol use as an unmitigated sin. The youths claim that Ortho-Catholicism is sufficient and that the added restrictions or prescriptions of charismaticism are superfluous. Absent the protective firewall of strict and unequivocal alcohol prohibition, alcohol use can trigger implosion when one's household economy or one's prospect as a youth verges on collapse in a ravaged society. Thus, mainline Catholicism's ritual acceptance of alcohol and fiestas undercuts charismatic preaching against alcohol consumption, a problem alluded to in Bradshaw and colleagues' (this volume) observation that charismatic teenage males have a substantial dropout rate from their parents' charismatic ritual practices and that these youths frequently abuse alcohol.

In spite of the fact that their preachings and social supports do not always work, Pentecostals, Mormons, and charismatics all seek to heal the individual and thereby help heal society in all its multiple levels by supporting abstinence from alcohol.

RECONSTRUCTING FAMILY AND GENDER

The modifications of individual behavior pushed by pentecostalism have consequences in the individual's relationships with others. Most notably, the pentecostal faiths preach a transformation of family and gender relationships, which have been strained, altered, or even shattered by the processes of cultural collapse and economic exclusion.

Mitigating Family and Gender Damage

I have alluded to some of the pressures on the male gender in the previous section. Traditional religion helps individuals communicate with the lineage and family ancestors who provided their inheritance. Access to ancestors and gerontocratic male control in the family made sense under conditions in which people depended on inheritances of usufruct within communally held land and forest resources that were the collective responsibility of senior respected men who had been vetted by passage through the civil-religious hierarchy. The rituals and symbols made sense when those resources were sufficient for the number of families in the *municipio* and when the *municipio* had readily available communal land for expansion as population grew. But that sense of obligation to ancestors because of inheritance grew progressively more tenuous as land became an increasingly scarce resource due to increasing population. That scarcity put family subsistence at risk and jeopardized the balanced covenant with the ancestors who had not given inheritances. Given that men with families have an obligation to provide them corn, land scarcity leading to corn shortage stimulates male anxiety (Wells, Hawkins, and Adams 2020).

As a result of land scarcity and the fact that little non-agricultural work is available, many males have left their natal communities to find work in Guatemalan cities or in the United States. When men leave, however, culturally embedded gender expectations of male priority block the nonmigrating wives from asserting authority in their households. The woman's male children sometimes become insubordinate because they are male: their mother, in their culture, is a female without authority. With family authority systems failing, some youths find quite attractive the group security and authority structure found in nonviolent gangs—more like boys' clubs (Edvalson et al. 2013; Call et al. 2013; Burrell 2013). Alternatively, they might turn to the insentience offered by excessive alcohol consumption (Bradshaw et al., this volume).

In addition, the increasing penetration of the Ladino status system and its attractiveness as a social and economic alternative to the ever more precarious Maya way of life have made Ladino status and Ladino gender norms increasingly a part of indigenous male behavior toward women (Hawkins 1984; Morgan 2005). The dominance, control, and display summarized by the braggadocio of machismo is inherently un-Maya because it contradicts

Maya notions of mutuality, complementarity, and equality. At the same time, machismo can quickly turn into spousal abuse in families where alcohol is used to anesthetize male reactions to their fears or failures to provide adequate corn.

Against this backdrop of problems, the current home- and school-based educations of women leave many women rather unprepared to sustain the household economically if national or international wage remittances from their absent husbands, sons, or sometimes even daughters stop for any reason. Women can weave and sell to tourists or peers (Semus 2005), or they can sell garden produce in the local market, but neither is sufficient to feed a family.

Traditionalist religion offers some support in such circumstances. For one thing, traditionalists perform rituals that can bless a family or protect or cure it from curses rendered by envious enemies. But traditionalist *ajq'ijab'* have little opportunity to preach a message to a large community regarding any of a wide variety of rapidly emerging topics because the *ajq'ij* seldom meets with a collective group larger than a family. The *ajq'ij* does deliver revelatory information and counsel that can strengthen a family when the family consults the ancestors. But an answer from the ancestors who provided one with land or from the earth lord custodians of the land is more likely to be culturally conservative than an answer from the God of the contrastive new pentecostal religions. Traditional gods speaking through traditionalist *ajq'ijab'* give rather traditional solutions to life's perplexities. Moreover, traditionalist concern for the male line of ancestors only works well when living adult males are reliably present and when inheritance is sufficient to sustain successor families, which therefore garners the interest and obedience of successor children (Mendonsa 1982). The threat of disinheritance was more credible and produced greater control over the younger generation in the past, when there was both dependence on land and sufficient wealth in land that an inheritance was possible. But those conditions have changed in many communities (Brintnall 1979). As Annis (1987) has suggested for Pentecostal converts, who are often among the poorest of the poor, landholdings have become so small as to invite starvation. Under these conditions, traditionalist rituals centered on land and ancestors hold less sway, and the *ajq'ij* becomes enmeshed in rituals of protection regarding envy and fears of witchcraft attack.

Roman Catholicism offers little to help the disrupted

family. For a long time, parishes have been too big for a priest to know most of his parishioners or attend to their needs as a therapist or counselor. The priest, even with assistants, is stretched too thin and likely is not of the same ethnicity and culture as his parishioners. Moreover, the set format of the printed call-and-response mass allows little flexibility for the Ortho priest to deal quickly with emergent needs. Even the priest's homily tends to be defined by the external hierarchy: the topic of each suggested biblical passage is tied to an annual calendrical cycle rather than being a sermon prepared in response to immediately felt parishioner needs, as it is in pentecostal services.

Christian Pentecostalism much more directly helps protect and heal the family, which has long been the core domain of a Maya woman. The male pastor's preaching is authoritative and attends to many families' immediate concerns. The various pentecostalisms seek to domesticate men—to reform men and suppress their vices. Sermons orient men toward the household and family as the prime source of status, and they challenge men to leave the street and to stop womanizing. Sermons even advocate that men treat their spouses and children with mildness. The Pentecostal orientation to the familial needs of women in a male-dominated but gender-disrupted society helps account for the disparity between the high number of women and the lower number of men in pentecostal attendance (Brusco 1995:129, 137–138).

Meeting together often in the small Pentecostal or charismatic community reconstitutes to some degree the sense of commitment to a moral community. It allows for the emergence and expression of consensus regarding obedience to laws and moral norms that remain bedrock premises of being Maya (Hawkins 1984:112–113). Women in male-absent or alcohol-impaired households regain the moral compass of a male authority substitute—in the form of the local Pentecostal pastor and his prominent wife (la pastora) or of the charismatic couple appointed as leaders by the priest—to shore up control of the children. Especially in the Pentecostal folds, the local pastor and pastora and other church leaders are often related by kinship or marriage to most of their congregants (Jones et al., this volume). Congregants tend to live close to their pastor, and pastors thus know the members of their flock personally. The pastor, then, can serve as a male role model and support in what Mayas would consider male-deficit families (see Brusco 1986, 1993; Chesnut 2003a). Single mothers can point to this male role model who, as kin and

pastor, preaches a code of behavioral limitations. In Maya culture, a mother needs her children to hear the code of conduct from a male voice. In many cases, the Pentecostal congregation comes close to being a ramage, with the pastor its big-man center of gravity through diverse ties of kinship and affinity. In the Pentecostal congregation, the pastor creates connection with and influence among his parishioners "through pastoral care, church discipline, and preaching, *beyond anything the modern mind can imagine*" (Weber 2002[1905]:105, emphasis in original).

The small-group characteristics of the Evangelical congregation offer other gender-related benefits. Regarding Colombia, Brusco (1993:154) posits an important relation between fissioning and the representation of women's welfare in the Pentecostal setting: "The schismatic nature of the evangelical movement may protect it from becoming exclusively a vehicle for male political interests. The movement works best through small groups that are based on personalistic ties, and its tendency to keep reproducing such groups through schisms when a church gets too large will continue to encourage broad-based, grass-roots involvement by women." The Catholic charismatic movement acquired many of these Pentecostal advantages by imitating Pentecostal openness to offering testimonies. This gives immediate adaptivity and protection to women. They are able to express their issues through access to the microphone when the Spirit impels them. Regular and frequent preaching by a charismatic male role model, a man raised in the local community, helps. The small congregations of mostly kin-connected people live in the nearby environs of the rural hamlet or town canton. Finally, free healings address a key female concern for the welfare of the family.

One difference between Evangelical and charismatic communities concerns the relation of women who are de facto household heads to their respective pastors. The Ortho-Catholic priest rotates a charismatic congregation's leadership every two years, whereas an Evangelical pastor is not rotated. I have noted that charismatic pastoral rotation mimics the older cultural pattern of an annual rotation of cargos in the cofradía system. While such mimicking of the old cofradía leadership rotation can be culturally attractive because it meshes well with the underlying Maya notion of equality in the community, regular rotation somewhat undermines the stability of male leadership resources sought by a woman heading a functionally male-absent household. Catholic charismaticism indeed provides male role models, but its leadership rotation impedes the creation of enduring kin or quasi-kin ties between a stable pastor and the women lacking adequate adult male participation in their households. Perhaps the regular rotation of the *carismático* group leader and the consequent lessened support of the many effectively female-headed families add to the alcohol issues previously discussed and may help explain why Catholic charismatics seem to lose the allegiance of their teenage boys (Bradshaw et al., this volume).

In Nahualá and Santa Catarina Ixtahuacán, Smith and colleagues, Thompson and colleagues, and others in this volume confirm the well-established argument regarding Pentecostal Protestant domestication of the male and the advantage of small congregations often led by a kin-connected male.[6] Brusco (1995:5–6) shows that the Pentecostal liturgy orients males toward family responsibility as the definition of success and goodness. In so doing, Pentecostalism promotes women's practical interests in getting the chores of life done, food on the table, and leadership in the home. It also promotes what Brusco (1993, 1995) has called women's "strategic" gender interests by replacing the man's preconversion mind-set, which rewards "street"-centered public machismo with its conspicuous displays of alcohol consumption, womanizing, and bravado, with a home- and family-centered male mind-set. The Pentecostal redefinition of gender roles does not require that a man be rich or even support the household well. But if one orients toward giving what one has to the family, with full energy and devotion, without waste induced by vice, then that is sufficient sacrifice. No more is required, although material blessings may accrue from the savings engendered by the reorientation. Pastors and members testify in church services to the savings, which are seen as blessings and miracles (Brusco 1995:123–129). This same gender redefinition project holds to a considerable degree for the charismatic Catholic.

In the end, the male symbolic presence at the head of the pentecostal worship service meets a Maya woman's desire for men's participation in and support of a Maya's sense of appropriate household behavior by the young or old of either gender. That constitutes a partial healing of both family and gender. As Brusco (1993:148) succinctly puts it, "In evangelical households the husband may still occupy the position of head, but his relative aspirations have changed to coincide more closely with those of his wife. This last fact is key to the analysis of Colombian Pentecostalism and, I believe, constitutes a change of revolutionary proportions" (see parallels in Brusco 1995:137). In Colombia, as in Guatemala, while the pastor sits on a raised dais facing the congregation in apparent male-dominant leadership, he often preaches to the very practical and woman-centered interests of a better society—defined as families populated by males devoted to family-centered moral behavior. The *evangélico* pastor thereby addresses quite directly the wants and needs of the largest sector of the congregation—the women—inculcating in men the obligations of domestic responsibility, fidelity, honesty, and the avoidance of self- and family-destructive vices. The male pastor thereby continuously heals the social constitution of the family and reformats the social construction of gender, doing so from a perspective congenial to women.[7]

Indeed, the pentecostal pastor cannot stray too far from the real needs of the congregants, for he and his wife come from among them, often without training. He must listen to the concerns as diverse women testify of their pain (*k'ax*). Congregants depend on him to sustain and represent family order. And if the pastor strays from or neglects the real issues of the congregation, and of women especially, the pentecostal's free access to possession by the Spirit allows anyone, and women especially, to inject needed messages and personal angst into the communal awareness via speaking in tongues, which may be followed by a woman's interpretation of that glossolalia into K'iche' as the voice of God to the community. Unlike the relatively set liturgy of the Ortho-Catholic mass, the open access the congregation has to the pulpit and the revelatory character of the Pentecostal and charismatic liturgies enable these religions to stay closely grounded in the experience and needs of the congregation and its female members. Pastors and leaders talk regularly about the travails, experiences, and solutions of daily life that lead to a more integrated family. As Smith and colleagues (this volume) have shown and as Brusco (1993) has shown for Colombia, that means the pentecostal liturgy supports the experience and strategic needs of women for an integrated family, a goal to which virtually all Guatemalan (and Colombian) women aspire culturally. "With conversion, and the breakdown of sex segregation that accompanies it, the condition of the home becomes crucial to the status of men as well as women. Status becomes acquired cooperatively through consumption and investment strategies for the family as a unit" (Brusco 1993:149).

Lindhardt (2012) sees Chilean Pentecostalism as involved in a gender transformation project that clearly parallels discussions by Brusco and the ethnographic data we have presented for Nahualá and Santa Catarina Ixtahuacán. Lindhardt documents the "domestication of men" in 1999–2009 Chile and the transformation of their language away from swearing and wordplay in which double meanings have sexual connotations that demean women. Women in the Chilean Pentecostal churches are empowered in a variety of ways. As in Guatemala, Chilean women have their own groups that they run. They have the backing of church injunctions and doctrines that confer moral authority when they disagree with or even admonish a wayward husband. As Lindhardt observes, Pentecostalism does not just regender the system. Rather, Pentecostalism changes the system's basic premises and thus revolutionizes the system itself. Thus, in Chile, "for Pentecostals, freedom and power are foremost freedom and power to exercise self-control; resist temptations; rework social relationships; [and] transform the domestic sphere, often in accordance with existing feminine standards." Pentecostals in Chile thereby "impose and maintain a little order and clarity in an otherwise messy 'world'" (Lindhardt 2012:191).

O'Neill (2010:115–142) devotes a major chapter to analyzing how the neo-Pentecostal megachurch leaders and members he studied in Guatemala City work to change the male street and bravado scripts or roles. They do so by adopting technologies of small-group discussion and congregational group preaching, which are intended to reorient Guatemalan males toward better family and child-raising orientations. There are, of course, many variations. Green (1993) worked in a Guatemalan community hard hit by insurgency and the government's response of male disappearances—a euphemism for kidnapping, torture, and murder, with sometimes unidentifiable bodies dumped or buried far from where the men were kidnapped. The widows Green studied used many networks to assist them in survival. Most became affiliated with Pentecostal congregations, but some simultaneously availed themselves of Catholic development aid (Green 1993:159–160) or the blessing of a Catholic baptism (172–173). For many widowed women in Green's study, survival strategy trumped religious ideological purity or full conversion.

Before ending this section, I return to the cultural resonance theme of chapter 23. The reconstitution of gender appeals to Mayas and ladinoized poor urbanites, many of whom have Maya roots, because it helps solve problems, which is the point of this chapter. But this is not the only reason, and perhaps not even the most important

reason, that male gender reconstruction, increased family focus, and more balanced male-female equality appeals to Mayas. Pentecostal gender reformation also appeals to Mayas because it meshes with preexisting Maya gender notions of balanced mutual support, which have been severely disrupted by modernization and ladinoization (Wells, Hawkins, and Adams 2020). Mayas experience gender difference as something highly local and place specific. Women, for example, usually wear a municipally identifying variant of traditional women's clothing. Maya women are gender conforming and therefore identity confirming. Men are not, at least not so obviously, since all but the oldest have adopted the clothing of Ladinos and, in many cases, have adopted Ladino vices.

To a Maya, therefore, the pentecostal project to remasculinize the man by reorienting him to family responsibility, greater equality, and mutuality of interest with women is indeed a Maya-compatible project. It makes cultural sense to many Mayas. When successful, conformity in the congregational community feels comfortably indigenous even if it transforms them. The reformation returns them to the most basic Maya cultural assumptions about gender, which include equality, marital balance, parity, and complementarity by collaboration in which men have primary responsibility to raise and bring corn to the house, and women process corn and bring it to the belly while they also bear and raise children. This has been so not only in Nahualá and Santa Catarina Ixtahuacán, but in other Maya communities as well (Gillin 1951:19, 52, 122).

Social investment in congregational community and family become the means of achieving prestige in small, relatively closed, consensus-seeking networks (the congregation) in the municipality that is now too big and too much divided by differing interests. Like the *milpa* logic that Annis (1987) calls the essence of indigenous sensibility and logic, the pentecostal focus on the family is preeminently a local investment of prodigious time in a local social resource existing at the same structural level as one's *milpa* holdings. It entails inward investment in the private domain of household and family, rather than outward investment in the public domain, and is thus consistent with a primary Maya cultural orientation of inwardness. From an indigenous point of view, the Pentecostal project of reconstituting gender is a vastly more important and more accessible political project than reforming the nation. It is a reinstituting of *milpa* logic applied to the family rather than the land. The pentecostal project to rework gender toward equality also harks back to deeply original Maya notions of gender compatibility and complementarity, family focus, and small-group isolation among equals. This they now seek to achieve at the hamlet and subhamlet level of a small congregation instead of at the too-populated, too-complex, and nationally penetrated municipal level.

Mitigating Economic Loss to the Family

Pentecostalism stabilizes or improves many family economies by inculcating an ideology that ideally stops (or tries to restrain) certain expenditures: alcohol purchases, fiesta expenses, and *cofradía* costs. These are all explicitly quite antitraditionalist and anti-Ortho-Catholic prohibitions. Christian Pentecostalisms prohibit as well such activities as gambling, dancing, smoking, and *mujereando* (seeking sexual relations with women other than one's spouse). These practices have come to be viewed by both Catholic *carismáticos* and Pentecostal *evangélicos* (and even some Ortho-Catholics) as wasteful and debilitating (Brusco 1986, 1993, 1995; Flora 1975).

Mitigating Migration Damage

Regular migration has been an important part of indigenous social economics at least since the mid-1800s (McCreery 1994) and, according to Martínez Peláez (1970), since the foundation of haciendas and cochineal production early in the Spanish conquest. But until the 1970s, that labor migration had several characteristics that did not disrupt severely the community and family. First, those performing *repartimiento* migration were able to return to the village and home after a week of labor and perhaps a few days more of walking to and from the assigned work site. Likewise, 1860s–1970s coffee labor migration involved return to the community after a few months. Under *mandamiento* and in response to the labor needs of coffee production into the 1970s, coffee farms sent trucks to each of "their" Maya *municipios* where "their" Maya recruiters had offered loans to meet people's corn and ritual needs. A truckload (*una cuadrilla* ~ a squad) of indigenes from a single *municipio* would travel together to a particular farm (*finca*) and return each year after a few months of labor. Second, migrants would often travel in small groups to work; they would travel and live together as families, as two or more people from a family, or as close kin and co-villagers in a shed (or contiguous zone of a shed) occupied by members of their community

(Carrescia 1982; Bossen 1984:135–136). Third, the labor itself was agricultural and physical, conducted under the watch of a full-time Ladino employee. Migratory farm labor thus matched the parameters of Maya identity formation.

Since the 1970s, labor migration has been less agricultural, less communal, conducted on a longer cycle than a few months' absence each year, and performed at locations farther away than a day's ride in a plantation truck. Today, Mayas of both of our studied communities move permanently to a new city in Guatemala if they are among the fortunate few to get a government or NGO job. The less fortunate migrate permanently or for long periods to the slums of Guatemala City, visiting their home *municipio* when they can.

Beginning in the 1990s and continuing in the twenty-first century, Nahualenses, Ixtahuaquenses, and other Mayas have migrated more and more to the United States, staying for years at a time to work in a variety of yard maintenance, service, food, construction, or clothing manufacturing industries. Unlike the plantation work, when trucks took dozens of workers and even whole families from a single *municipio* to the same farm (often year after year), today's migrants go as individuals or as small groups from a *municipio* to many locations, although they often network so as to end up in a settlement of co-villagers inside the United States (Burns 1993).

How do the various faith traditions under consideration here respond to these new migration patterns?

None of the religious styles prohibit or block migration for work. Traditionalist religious practice, however, does not serve well those who face permanent or long-term absence from the community. Wilson (1995) has shown how the spirits and symbols of traditional faith are tied to specific places. Moreover, a client commissions divinations from a specific, trusted, older *ajq'ij* who likely has not migrated. Thus, traditionalist religious practice does not travel well. As recently as the mid-1980s, the expectation to participate in *cofradía* ritual and take upon oneself the *cargo* or load of service would have impeded migration. Today, the geographic specificity of altars, which are frequently on the prominent mountaintops and ridges that define the limits of municipality and region, still tends to deter the movement of traditionalists.[8] But with land scarce, fewer and fewer find traditionalist practices compelling. Wilson (1995) has shown how the traditionalism that links one to the ancestors who gave inheritance in a specific place becomes less relevant if one moves. In a word, shamanic relevance wanes if one no longer participates much in agriculture because of inadequate inherited land. Finally, the older shaman guides are hard to find in the lands to which the younger migrate for work, and shamans suffer from inadequate replacement as they age and die.

Ortho-Catholicism in the Maya villages also has a place related facet, although it is more portable than traditionalism. In Guatemala, Ortho-Catholicism anchors to the main church building that faces the town's central plaza. This location is shared with government and market buildings that spill into the plaza. Yet, a plaza place focus makes the Catholic Church and its ritual portable, as one can find its core buildings easily in any central city in the Western Hemisphere. Likewise, the Catholic mass is portable, made so by the global reach of Ortho-Catholic hierarchy and the existence of Catholic church buildings throughout the world. The relatively fixed mass, however, does not adapt quickly to the needs of a changing, individuated, and anxious mobile population. Charismatic-style meetings offered at Catholic churches in the United States, however, do address more fully the migrants' needs and liminality.

Pentecostalism offers no impediment to migration. Indeed, *evangélicos* try to plant or pioneer communities in distant locations (Sarasa 1991:64–65; O'Neill 2010:143–169). The ease with which one might find or found a Pentecostal congregation and the fact that the minister need not have specialized religious education also facilitate migration. Anyone can found a Pentecostal congregation anywhere. Moreover, as I have shown at the local level, small pentecostal congregations partially ameliorate the disruptions of male migratory absence by linking de facto female heads of household to a male congregational leader. That provides a respected, resident, and often related man who can serve as a role model and authority figure to the family considering migration. That preexisting structure may facilitate further migration by providing a substitute family system that subtly supports a family's decision for a man to migrate. At the American end of the migration route, the man confronts a life of hardship and risk, lack of language and skills, legal exclusion, consequent liminality, and social isolation, making small-group networking in Christian Pentecostal congregations highly relevant. Here, too, any church can help if it lends a communal hand.

The Pentecostal church thus can be both poignantly expressive of the disruption of migration and also functionally and ideologically helpful to deal with it. Thus, Garrard-Burnett (2007:233) suggests that the IURD (Universal Church of the Kingdom of God), a Brazilian Pentecostal church that has founded congregations and flourished among Brazilian immigrants in the United States, "may not make its [Brazilian] members [in the United States] rich, but it can, indeed, provide them with spiritual capital—that is, a set of beliefs, social networks, a renewed sense of self-worth and purpose—that helps immigrant converts, empowered celestial warriors all, to successfully navigate the rugged terrain of urban America."

In 2003–2010 the indigenous families in Nahualá and Santa Catarina Ixtahuacán faced rending forces. Failure of the corn economy drove many men to migrate to the United States, where they have now lived for years. Marx (Marx and Engels 1948[1848]:11) suggested that capitalism would "tear away" the "sentimental veil" of cultural protections from the family and "reduce the family relation to a mere money relation." What greater "reduc[tion of] the family relation to a mere monetary relation" could one experience than this migratory separation of husbands from wives and children wherein the primary nexus or content of the marriage is the international cash remittance, and the only interaction, sometimes for years on end, consists in phone calls? The damage created by this crass cash nexus is clear. The family sends its responsible male adult and its maturing male teenagers to the United States. It finances their migration by mortgaging a piece of family property, thereby putting personal and ethnic core values concerning land, corn, and family livelihood at increased risk. The migrants must find a job and labor feverishly to repay the 10 percent monthly interest on the mortgage loan to avoid losing their land used as collateral. They are thus cast into debt servitude and separated from their parents, siblings, and future marriage mates for years, some for a decade. They must rend their family to provide for their family.

The protective kin connections in many of the Christian Pentecostal congregations help some families fill gaps caused by that migratory rending. The Pentecostal congregations are small enough for the pastor and *pastora* to know each member of their flock and guide them. The Pentecostal ministers' kinship and shared ethnicity approach to leadership are impossible for the Ortho priests, whose parish sizes make individual acquaintance with all attendees impossible (Foucault 2004:125–129).

RECONSTRUCTING COMMUNITY

With the old order of indigenous municipal community under a measure of assault, the Christian Pentecostal congregation and pentecostal practices in general can impact not just the individual and the family, but also the community and whom (or what level or institution) one considers important to orient to when forming one's community. In the Christian Pentecostal case, this entails focusing on the individual, the family, and the local religious congregation. The latter shifts focus away from the *municipio*.

Finding Community and Relocating Identity in a Smaller Group

In Maya society, the point of attachment for the individual and her or his dominant mental identity focus is now much contested. Without question, the point of attachment and mental focus used to be the *municipio*, as a host of early ethnographies beginning with Tax (1937) have demonstrated. That focus matched the municipality-as-parish organization of Ortho-Catholic administration among the Mayas and the weekly market in the central plaza. But Guatemala's *municipios* have grown too big for traditional institutions such as *cofradía* and plaza-centered Catholicism to integrate the populace, even in small indigenous *municipios* such as Zinacantán, as Cancian (1965, 1972, 1992) has shown.

By contrast, the various pentecostalisms focus on new and much narrower attachment points and identity focus: the individual, the family, and the local congregation. At the same time, Christian Pentecostalism offers a wider connection and emerging identity as a member of a Pentecostal denomination or of the Catholic charismatic movement in the nation and around the globe. With each conversion, the *municipio* recedes as a primary focus. As Anderson (2000:31) points out, the various pentecostalisms, "in contrast to the mainline churches," offer "an 'open invitation' to bring concrete social problems to the church leaders." The flexibilities and bodily interests of the various pentecostalisms, each expressed at the local and micro congregational level, turn out to be more functionalist and adaptive than the older, slower to adjust, and more municipally focused Ortho-Catholicism, which is rooted in a parish coterminous with the *municipio* and led in most cases and until recently by an outsider priest. Indeed, not until almost 500 years after the conquest—in 2015 in Nahualá and 2017 in Antigua Santa Catarina

Ixtahuacán—did these communities receive an indigenous ordained Ortho-Catholic resident parish priest.

The breakdown in municipal focus has evolved through time and seems tied to population increase and to both economic and political penetrations of municipal isolation. As noted in chapter 14, in less than a century (1921–2002), Guatemala's population increased by a multiple of 5.6 (see table 17.1). Municipal populations have generally followed suit. For example, Nahualá's population increased in that period from 16,325 to 51,939 (a 3.2 times increase) and Santa Catarina's from 9,220 to 41,208 (a 4.5 times increase). I would argue (following Cancian 1965, 1992, and others) that this population increase, combined with new external options, has made the *municipios* unmanageable under the old religious-political institutions of *cofradía* and gerontocratic government. Cancian (1965) has shown how the limited number of ranked positions in the *cofradía* section of the civil-religious hierarchy could not accommodate the rapid increase in population. Consequently, all residents in the *municipio* could not acquire positions that affirmed their status in the system. Given a culture of equality and mutualism, that disparity helped corrupt the will of all to maintain the *cofradía* system. The increase in population also overwhelmed the capacity of Ortho-Catholic priests to connect well with the populace. Ortho-Catholic priests could do little more than provide mass to large groups, offer the other sacraments, and run a school or medical station.

Second, the intrusion of alternative national orientations and the rise of new modes of wealth acquisition and expenditure also undermined interest in maintaining *cofradía* participation (Cancian 1965; Brintnall 1979; Watanabe 1992). The marketization of labor from 1860 to the present and the penetration of the communities by diverse class, political, and market opportunities has fractured the egalitarian nature and once-focused intents of the community (Watanabe 1992; Hawkins, McDonald, and Adams 2013). As a result, post-1970, the indigenous municipality seldom was able to act as a unified community, although under the extraordinary pressures of war, some communities, such as Santiago Atitlán, were able to fend off some of the worst depredations of the government and the army via mass manifestations of municipal and ethnic unity. Nevertheless, even though they are now difficult to achieve, consensus and community remain centrally desired goals in Maya culture, repeated in the myth structures that informally educate the residents of

Nahualá and Santa Catarina Ixtahuacán (Jardine, Hawkins, and Adams 2020). In the small Pentecostal and charismatic church groups, Mayas do find and maintain this culturally valued community and consensus. They communicate that consensus to each other through sharing and shaping their *testimonios*.

Today, the Ortho-Catholic mass brings people together, but it does not construct mutually supportive congregational communities in part because one can attend any of several sessions of mass during the week. Consequently, a person attending mass does not meet with a congregation consisting of the same people, week after week, and thus cannot experience a mutually supportive community simply through attendance at church services. Ortho-Catholics do, however, build community at the municipal level by hosting the week of religious celebrations honoring the municipality's patron saint and by celebrating other high rituals and related processions of the Roman Catholic religious calendar at the municipal center. But the parish as a population unit has simply become too big to sustain a more supportive interconnectedness.

By contrast, the Pentecostals and charismatics assemble regularly in much smaller congregations. Because they meet multiple times during the week with the same congregants, they reintegrate and reconstitute their small community frequently. As Durkheim (2008[1912]:418) posits, regular communal religious experience "wakens this sentiment of a refuge, of a shield and of a guardian support which attaches the believer to his cult." "Society is able to revivify the sentiment it has of itself" but "only by assembling" (349). Christian Pentecostals assemble frequently, much more often than do Ortho-Catholics, and consequently, they revivify the sentiments they have of themselves as a society, but at the congregational rather than at the municipal level.

Finding Community around the World

Thompson and colleagues and Wayas and colleagues (both this volume) show that Protestant Pentecostals can build extensive nonlocal connections through itinerant preachers, attendance at regional or national revival camp meetings, listening to the radio or watching other media, and the distribution of purchased or pirated recordings of sermons and songs. Preachers who come to local and regional events from international starting points help build both national and international awareness and connection. In discussing community at this level, however,

I begin to infringe on the issues of building a nation and constructing a global perspective and attachments.

CONSTRUCTING A NATION

In addition to helping restore a sense of local community, Pentecostalism contributes to the development of nationhood. I do not say "reconstructing" a nation or nationhood in this section title because, for Mayas, little sense of nation existed prior to the 1950s. Nothing, therefore, had been broken or disrupted to be reconstructed. The pentecostal contribution toward construction of this new national orientation adds to other social processes developing among Mayas and their evolving imagination of nation. The pentecostal component proceeds along three lines.

Nation Building via Inculcation of Obedience to Law

I argue that Pentecostalism does build nationhood but in ways largely unrecognized by political scientists. O'Neill (2010) throughout his book shows how the members of the urban Pentecostal megachurch he studied are guided by its leader to try to change Guatemala by having Guatemala's citizens transform themselves into moral, self-governing individuals and by extending that self-governance through nation-reaching conversion campaigns. What I find interesting is that O'Neill (2010:32–51) devotes two-thirds of a chapter to showing how state institutions attempt to promote citizens' responsibility for the nation through slogans such as "You Are the City." In one campaign, citizens were invited to wear a rubber band with printed slogans on their wrist; one could pull and snap the band to the wrist to remind oneself to be a better citizen. O'Neill (2010:57–58) notes that he has never seen the government's secular approaches change anyone, but he documents that neo-Pentecostal technologies of self-governance work to considerable effect.

O'Neill also shows that Pentecostalism offers explicitly conscious approaches to healing the nation of its structural violence. The mechanism is through incessant prayer and personal fasting. But O'Neill seems to discount prayer and fasting, seeing them as diversions from the real political work of organizing effective power groups and voting blocs. As O'Neill (2010:xvi) puts it, "Christian citizens of Guatemala . . . are more likely to pray for Guatemala than pay their taxes; they tend to speak in tongues for the soul of the nation rather than vote in general elections; and they more often than not organize prayer campaigns to fight crime rather than organize their communities against the same threat. . . . Christian citizens do a great deal, but they do things that ultimately frustrate Western, ostensibly secular, and deeply liberal expectations of what it means to participate as a citizen of an emerging democracy." I would argue that prayer and fasting are forms of bodily and mental discipline that inculcate in the individual the internalized disposition to obey. Foucault considers some such internalization a necessary basis for neoliberal and democratic society. O'Neill also recognizes this outcome: "Neo-Pentecostals are the self-regulating subjects that postwar Guatemala has long sought" (xiv). Moreover, combining internalized self-discipline with a program of proselyting conversion, pentecostals expand the faith. Adherents recognize that curing the nation of its ills will take time. But given how ineffective (and disruptively violent) the other approaches to change have been, one can hardly criticize pentecostals for imagining and attempting a new and ostensibly nonpolitical approach to national healing. And who can argue that the involvement of civil society in the disciplined inculcation in the minds of an ever-increasing percentage of the society via the religious practice of self-control, self-government, and obedience to law is not a potent way to change, organize, or control society? Certainly Gramsci, Foucault, Bourdieu, Sahlins, Geertz, Weber, Wallace, and Durkheim would agree.

But how is this internalization of obedience to law different than the preexisting culture of obedience to law I have argued already exists as a bedrock premise of Maya indigeneity (in chapters 23 and 24 and in Hawkins 1984:11, 285, 379–381)? The answer lies in the fact that prior forms of obedience were turned toward the *municipio*. People obeyed the social expectations shared by the Maya ethnic sector of a unique *municipio*. They obeyed the advice of their gerontocracy composed of respected *pasados*, not the law of a nation. They obeyed the "law of the saints," as Ruben Reina (1966) deftly puts it, but it was the law of their particular saint linked to their particular *municipio*, not a universal law or the law of an external national or international god. It was the custom of their town, not the law of the nation.

All that shifted, slowly some decades before Ríos Montt and rapidly with him. The process sped up because the new president, placed by a new coup d'etat, advanced the interests of a new Pentecostal religion that used what was for most Mayas in the 1980s a newly accessible medium (TV) to propound what was for Ladinos a startling new message: obey the law and do not steal while in office. More than a few Mayas liked the message, however selectively and unevenly it was administered in practice. Moreover, the Christian Pentecostal emphasis on obedience to law applied not just to Mayas, but also to Ladinos. From a Maya perspective, that, if effected, would be more than just culturally congenial, but factually lifesaving, since much of Maya suffering was a consequence of Ladino notions that as a category and as elites, they were above the law even though, on paper, law formally applied to them.

Nation Building through Church Interconnection

Christian Pentecostals also built nationhood by rituals of outward orientation. Wayas and colleagues (this volume) show the use of song to orient congregations to a larger unit: the country. They do so by reciting all of the departments of the nation as contributors to the work of the kingdom. By referring to the department (or, ambiguously, the department capital), rather than one's own *municipio*, one's focus moves from the local toward the larger whole. The call to parishioners to pray for the nation as well as for themselves builds a national orientation and responsibility.

In addition, substantial groups of a congregation experience and bond with other sections of the country when they travel by bus or pickup to other Pentecostal or charismatic centers to hear sermons or guest revivalists. Traveling guest preachers, some from out of the country, circulate through multiple congregations and further aim the residents away from a strictly local orientation. Indeed, the circulation of international celebrity evangelists builds a worldwide community, a network that transcends the nations involved in Evangelical conversion. It is a network that explicitly seeks to encompass and transform the world. Of course, when Pentecostal preachers treat national topics, this too builds a national orientation, even if they call the nation corrupt. Thus, in a variety of ways, Pentecostals weave themselves into a wide web that references a larger unit than the *municipio*, the traditional focus of indigenous identity and interest. At the same time, they integrate themselves tightly into units of congregational, hamlet- and canton-level community identity much smaller than the *municipio* because of the increasing failure of the *municipio* to serve those ends. I suggest that the political use of prayer to build a national orientation and to inculcate in citizens a national identity deserves more detailed attention than it has received to date.

Nation Building through Withdrawal

A number of scholars have faulted Pentecostalism because they feel Pentecostal beliefs discourage participation in national politics (e.g., O'Neill 2010). Research in Brazil (Freston 1993:73; Ireland 1993), however, challenges this view by showing that local and national political engagement by Pentecostals expands to the degree the Pentecostal community increases as a percentage of national population. Nevertheless, I would argue that apparent withdrawal (or the early phase of withdrawal) has important consequences.

Steigenga's (2001:56, 58) survey data and O'Neill's (2010) ethnography can be instructive in this perspective. Using surveys supplemented with interviews, Steigenga finds that Pentecostal affiliation does not lead to a statistically significant reduction of voting behavior. Steigenga concludes that Pentecostalism does not depoliticize.

O'Neill (2010) uses qualitative methods to address the meanings behind different kinds of political participation in a neo-Pentecostal urban Guatemala City congregation. Out of this, he assembles the logic of Pentecostalized "Christian citizenship." He credits Guatemalan megachurch neo-Pentecostals with fomenting participatory Christian citizenship and active engagement with the nation, but O'Neill still faults them. Explicitly, he sees Pentecostal prayers, fasting, and church attendance on behalf of others and the nation as citizenship of a limited and limiting sort because these Pentecostal activities consume time, energy, and resources that could have been expended in what he considers more effective forms of political participation (O'Neill 2010:xvi). From time to time, O'Neill's end-of-paragraph summative sentences are acerbic one-liners that suggest a degree of disdain for the neo-Pentecostal's approach to Christian citizenship through prayer and fasting. He notes that non-Pentecostal informants generally express "disappointment" in Pentecostal political participation, a feeling he shares as an analyst (199–214). On the whole, he regards the Pentecostal approach to citizenship through private and communal prayer and fasting on behalf of the moral reformation of the Guatemalan nation to be effective at reforming the self, even if standard political science beliefs might consider prayer to be quite ineffective political work (xvi–xvii).

The political science orientation enshrines power manipulation, protest, physical participation, and voting as the preferred political behaviors of real consequence. Prayer, O'Neill deems, is much less effective. Political scientists may feel that any withdrawal from party politics, protesting, and voting short-circuits the Euro-American paradigm for the concrete political work that needs to be done to improve society. Prayer for the nation, as O'Neill makes clear, is real citizenship. But for O'Neill, it also is a fantasy and therefore is wasted effort against real problems that need concrete political action.

Academic critiques of Christian Pentecostal religiosity as an ineffective form of politics hang on highly ethnocentric western assumptions. First, the critique assumes, à la Marx and Freud, that religion is vacuous self-deception. Second, the critique assumes that family activities take place in the private domain rather than in the public domain. It further assumes that public domain activities are political whereas private domain activities are not. Therefore, the Pentecostal focus on the family gets classed as "apolitical" because the family is a private domain and is therefore, in western analytical eyes, a politically inconsequential institution. Likewise, in the current leading edge of Euro-American social philosophy, gendered behavior should be a matter of personal free choice, unregulated, and based on one's inherently natural feelings about oneself. Gender orientation and gendered behavior therefore should not be regulated, judged, or discriminated against in any way.

Pentecostalism takes an entirely different view. In Pentecostalism, the family is the core political institution because in it one learns obedience to law and respect for authority, which are said to be needed for a smooth-functioning nation and a kingdom of God. Pentecostals deem differentiated and prescriptive notions of gender difference essential to family well-being. Maya notions of gender are likewise rather tightly prescriptive and therefore more like Pentecostal notions than the more neoliberal and relaxed notions of gender behavior and identity advanced by western-backed, change-oriented NGO offices serving in Maya communities.

More important, the political science critique of pentecostal prayer behavior fails to recognize prayer as meditative self-discipline wherein one internalizes a critique of the dominant society and its cultural premises. Through prayer, one inculcates that critique into the management of one's own body. Through prayer, one internalizes Foucault's (and before Foucault, Gramsci's) notion that governmentality is ultimately achieved not by state force but by widespread individually internalized assent achieved by participating in nonstate civic institutions and by bodily disciplining the self as a result of civic participation. Each individual influences the others in her or his presence through a variety of nonstate institutions. In this view—to which O'Neill subscribes in his recognition of neo-Pentecostalism as a Foucauldian technology of governance—prayer and fasting are not vacuous. They are rather the most basic inculcation of neoliberal self-governance and responsibility. As O'Neill (2010:57) shows and as I suggest in chapter 20, all other forms of intervention in pursuit of humane governance at the national level have failed. Therefore, Mayas are willing to give pentecostally inscribed self-governance a try. It magnifies the turn toward the inward, inherent in *milpa* logic, which for a long time has been a foundational principle of being Maya. Perhaps it might work, goes their logic, if extended to enough people through evangelization.

The Ortho-Catholic (and somewhat Ladino) project to reform the nation by means of direct participation in political parties, unions, pressure groups, democracy, insurrection, or government retrenchment through violence gets inverted via indigenous pentecostalism. Thus, the pentecostal road to political change entails an evangelizing outreach that inculcates or embeds a moral framework in a spreading web of individuals. One by one, the process converts often apathetic citizens into "Christian citizens" (O'Neill 2010) who theoretically (or as an article of faith, which is the same thing) become self-governing and, hopefully, more moral.

In Foucault's terms, the political project of achieving governmentality is best accomplished—and perhaps can only be accomplished—by building willing, internalized participation by most of the individuals in the state. It must be done through socialization. The institutions doing the socializing cannot be working as obvious handmaidens or prostitutes of the state. In fact, by working on inscribing a political orientation toward the nation and the world, and by helping individuals inscribe in their own body and mind the will to obey law without regard to whether they might "benefit" or not, pentecostalism in fact does the most basic political work held by Foucault to be essential to the operation of modern state power (and capitalism) within the evolving world system. O'Neill and Marx are simply wrong on this point: Using prayer and fasting to inscribe in the body and in the mind a will to obey is indeed political work par excellence. Prayer is not misdirected or

wasted citizenship. Prayer and Christian Pentecostalism attempt to form in the individual mentality an ethical compass and behavioral self-control that may be essential to modern democracy. The pentecostal prayer process harkens to Durkheim's (2001[1912]:266) notion that "the true justification of religious practices is . . . in the way they affect our mental state."

Given the intent of the practice, whether the pentecostal approach to changing society actually works or whether it gets corrupted by greed, power, and/or status may take another century to determine. After all, it took almost a century to figure out that Lenin's political version of Marxist philosophy when applied to a whole country (Russia) and the resulting union of countries (the USSR) would not work. Moreover, with Vladimir Putin's Russian resurgence, we cannot be so sure of Lenin's failure within a century. It took more than three centuries for Weber to see how the ideas and practice of Calvinist Pietism could stimulate, consolidate, and coordinate a capitalist political economy. One should not expect the Christian Pentecostal revolution to be any faster. And whether pentecostalism succeeds or fails at societal reformation, it appears, at least at present, that Christian Pentecostalism will not be as bloody an experiment in reformative ideology and practice as Guatemala's military authoritarianism, Russia's Leninism, or China's Maoism have been as experimental solutions the perplexities of societies in stress.

Considered from a current theoretical perspective, both Catholic and Protestant forms of pentecostalism follow Bourdieu and Foucault in that they discipline the mind by bodily practice and thus attempt to bring people into compatibility with a core political assumption of neoliberal governance: obedience to legitimate law. At the same time, pentecostal practice has kept its adherents out of competition with the most brutal phases of postcolonial Guatemalan governance by elites by discouraging pentecostals from engaging in active forms of institutional confrontation above the local municipality. Weber saw Calvinist Protestantism spurring on capitalism by giving Pietist adherents a religious justification for participating vigorously in the expansion of the local economy: if they proved themselves able to expand the resources with which God had entrusted them by good management and asceticism, that would be a sign they were among the few elect. Their religious anxiety regarding salvation could be allayed, even answered, by successful effort in expanding a worldly endeavor.

Longer term, perhaps pentecostalism will provide the

ideology needed to establish neoliberal governmentality within the moral and structural wreckage of postcolonial nations in Latin America, Africa, and elsewhere in the Christianized Global South. Once citizens are thus inscribed or inculcated, the state need not mobilize overt force to acquire its citizens' compliance. That makes the Christian Pentecostal moral inculcation project doubly attractive to its adherents, but also exceedingly dangerous to democracy. On the good side, first, it creates cohesive congregations that function to ameliorate human suffering. Second, if successful, state force—the bane of Guatemalan life for 500 years because of a morally corrupt, exploitative, ethnically divided colonial state—would not be needed. That, of course, is too utopian, which leads us to the danger side. A disposition toward obedience can be easily abused by a state's leaders, and the consensus orientation of Mayas has already been abused by the Guatemalan nation and its first Evangelical head of state during the civil war.[9] Perhaps one could say, or hope, that if Christian Pentecostalism renders more individuals law-abiding as an end in itself, then Pentecostals could guide state institutions toward greater obedience to law.

In pentecostal logic, the Guatemalan government is so corrupt—their terms are "worldly" and "of the devil" as well as "corrupt"—that it cannot be reformed. Any attempt at direct participation in reform by political confrontation gets blocked or co-opted. The attempt is either undermined, suborned by bribery, or snuffed out by a response of crushing violence. So the pentecostal reform movement has developed by indirect methods through individual conversion. That is the central pentecostal logic. And it is logical. One might say that the Pentecostal assertion that the devil, Satanás, is always present in Guatemala's immoral governmental politics is a Maya equivalent of Acton's trenchant aphorism that "power corrupts and absolute power corrupts absolutely." Because the Guatemalan nation has not had functioning checks and balances, it has operated largely as an absolute power system. In the early twenty-first century, the international order provided CICIG and other oversight systems. It would appear, however, that the checks and balances of these recent international approaches are under threat. Guatemala's president Jimmy Morales Cabrera succeeded in ending the CICIG mandate—it was, after all, investigating him for campaign finance violations—and the institution ceased operations in September 2019 (Escobar et al. 2019; Malkin 2019). In early 2020, the secretary-general of the United Nations pleaded for the Guatemalan government to guarantee the physical safety of CICIG's former staff (Cumes 2020). CICIG not only ceased to exist, but its dispersed former staff feared retribution.

The Evolutionary Success of Apparent Withdrawal

I have suggested there is an academic prejudice against pentecostal religions. This is partly because among many scholars, religion is suspect because it orients behavior toward a seemingly ethereal nonreality. Perhaps the noisy boisterousness of Christian Pentecostalism exacerbates these prejudices (Escobar 1994:114–115). Many academics share with Marx the often unspoken belief that religion is an illusion or a mentally and behaviorally expensive delusion that diverts people from the real work of politics. Thus, one reviewer of an early version of this book suggested that I include an analysis of how Pentecostalism "keeps people" from "examining their lives, [from] thinking independently, [and] from building networks between one another, instead of divisions." Were I to do so, the reviewer implied, I would profitably "show how Pentecostalism is also part of the problem." I would note that yes, pentecostalism keeps people from examining aspects of their lives and from thinking independently, as do all cultures, including the reviewer's. As Henry (1963) shows, culture makes us all stupid by inculcating in us just one set of basic assumptions. Culture thus imposes a narrowed view. That is a clear consequence of culture. Culture necessarily blinds us to the worth of alternative options, just as liberal academic culture has blinded many scholars to the political value of exuberant religious practice.

I would agree that any social change—indeed, any social process—has unintended consequences, especially during the formative period of a socially revolutionary transformation. But pentecostalism is not part of the problem, even if its noisy liturgy and political isolationism irritate some. Pentecostalism's solution vis-à-vis corrupt empowered hierarchy is to avoid enmeshment in politics and therefore avoid corruption of oneself until enough individuals have been ethically reconstructed—they would say morally "reborn"—such that a new society emerges. Given that every other attempt at politico-structural reform has failed rather dismally in Guatemala, who can fault this rather different tactic based on a nonviolent, individualistic approach to inculcating obedience to law? That is the charismatic attempt at a solution to a societal problem. That is religious revitalization.

Like all changes, the Christian Pentecostal transformation will have unforeseen and unintended consequences, some of them negative. But what is more basic to democracy than willing obedience by most of a society's individuals to constitutionally protective good law? Ultimately, this pentecostal project might not succeed, given the possibility that something like Marx's notion of human greed might exist universally. Nietzsche's will to power and power's ability to corrupt may be part of human nature. And if not an intrinsic part of human nature, greed at least seems thoroughly infused in the logic of neoliberal capitalism. If this is so, one can hardly argue with the pentecostal assertion that adherents should avoid the corrupting entanglements in present-day Guatemalan politics.

In Guatemala, the *evangélico* call to Christ gets answered one person at a time, though the call may be extended efficiently to many at once via large meetings and blared from rooftop speakers to the many passing within a sound system's range. In theory, the call to individual morality, when accepted, reforms Guatemala from the grassroots, person by person, through the collective and ostensibly nonpolitical efforts of all believers. That, at any rate, is their faith—their hope for things as yet unseen, their prayer for the future. In their view, the effort will bring about not just a national revolution, but a world revolution. It is a religious approach to Foucault's and Gramsci's goal of individually inculcated governmentality so that the state seldom needs to use overt force.

In that regard, the pentecostal strand of Christianity is a politically revolutionary enterprise. In practice, however, there is no evidence that the supposedly morally inculcated Christian Pentecostal individual can, singly or as a whole, resist political pressures and act any less corruptly on average than others in the society. Pentecostals agree. That is why they avoid the world: because it corrupts. The Pentecostal goal is not to improve the nation by participating in the politics of structural change. That, they say, is an impossible task, a fool's errand. It is a lost cause because structural politics will corrupt those who interact with it. Replete with unending corruption and exploitation, the last five centuries of Guatemalan history seem to confirm the pentecostal contention empirically. So, pentecostals have arrived charismatically at a political alternative that even they do not think of as political. They try to transform people via religion, individually and morally, so that, hopefully, politics as currently known cannot be played in the future. But as already noted, there is no evidence that the pentecostal conversion-and-expansion approach to arriving at clean politics in the future is working.

The pentecostal effort is not just Guatemalan. In the words of one Bolivian pastor, the end result of the pentecostal movement "will be a totally different country because it will be run by men who serve God and justice and therefore become servants of the people, not thieves of the people, not oppressors of the people, but servants of the Bolivian people" (Wightman 2007:249). One must note, however, that such an outcome is hardly a foregone conclusion. Guatemalans have experienced life under three Pentecostal presidents. The first two have been indicted and convicted: one for war crimes (Ríos Montt) and one for massive theft from the national treasury (Jorge Serrano Elías). The third, Jimmy Morales, is literally a professional comedian. By late 2019, Morales had toppled CICIG, the international institution set up to help end judicial impunity in Guatemala. So far, Christian Pentecostalism has changed the politics of Guatemalan corruption not at all.[10]

For Bolivia, Wightman clearly sees that a political implication of the Pentecostal project lies in the reformation of individual ethics made collective by persistent missionary evangelization. "Pentecostals," she says, seek to "heal the nation (*sanar la nación*) . . . as a form of changing the society in which they live." In so doing, "they see their mission as changing Bolivia into a more moral and prosperous society one soul at a time" (Wightman 2007:245–246). The point is this: aggressive evangelization is a necessary adjunct to the individual locus of reform if a revitalization religion is going to be institutionally nonconfrontational but engaged in changing society. Indeed, for individual reform to be a political project, it must entail expansionary evangelization. Marxists, colonialists, and even advocates of democracy have long understood the need for evangelism; they have simply used other means, including force, war, propaganda, and elite prestige. All these have been used to "evangelize" the advance of other "isms." Why would not "withdrawn" Christian Pentecostalism be a potentially successful political project?

Has Christian Pentecostalism had greater reformative impact in Brazil? Perhaps. For example, a non-Pentecostal leader of a Brazilian socialist workers party noted, "Once they are in the party, the evangelicals are really very combative. The people of the Catholic Church have a very vague vision; but not the evangelicals. They have a vision of transformation of society. The evangelicals are able to develop a clear socialist class vision; but the Catholics cannot" (Burdick 1993b:35).

Burdick (1993a:218) portrays the generic Pentecostal as someone "who sees the world as a battleground in which the Devil plays a constant role" and thus can "claim with relative ease that many of the rich are in league with the Devil" and that "the politician or captain of industry [is] a 'tool' of the Devil." I suspect that Mayas of 1930 to the present, whether Pentecostal or traditional, would heartily agree. By contrast, Burdick thinks the Catholic Church in general, and particularly the Ortho-Catholic sector, functions as a mediator and moderator of class conflict—and therefore as a maintainer of class and conflict. Catholics are "taught to think in conciliatory terms." In the class conflict between the poor and the politicians and captains of industry, "the Catholic emphasizes that [Burdick quotes an informant] 'we are both children of God'" (218). In short, Pentecostal belief comes closer to traditional indigenous belief (as expressed in Guatemala) that the rich in a given village get that way by having sold their souls to the Mam equivalent of an earth lord (*witz*) (Wagley 1949:56–57). Compare Wagley's rendition of the Guatemalan concept to the Brazilian Pentecostal belief that "there are employers . . . who sell their souls to the Devil for money. Most of the rich people, the merchants around here, they seek out the Devil to make compacts, there in *macumba* [witchcraft], to make money" (Burdick 1993b:38, brackets and emphasis in original). This mirrors Guatemalan Maya statements almost exactly (Wagley 1957:184–197; Checketts 2005:184).

Ireland (1993:55) has also studied Pentecostalism in Brazil and similarly ties the Pentecostal ideology of only participating in local political change to issues of corruption. Brazilian Pentecostals sustain a vision that the political and economic world is utterly corrupt and therefore difficult, if not impossible, to work within. The only legitimate politics must be local politics for moral, neighborly purposes. One can confront the devil, but only on behalf of those in one's immediate neighborhood.

Around the world, the new Christian Pentecostal religions belong to the people in the local congregations, and they have been indigenized and suffused with change by local revelation, even if the basic framework was originally imported by missionaries and the practices repeatedly coached by traveling evangelists. When Chesnut examines the pentecostal religious project in Brazil, he sees primarily a utilitarian solution set to the "pathogens of poverty." As he puts it, "Above all, popular religiosity is

utilitarian. Concerned with matters of daily survival, the poor seek to manipulate the supernatural, not primarily for rewards in the afterlife, but for divine aid in the here and now," including healing of physical or social ills of poverty, and blessings that lead to a family's more secure material life (Chesnut 1997:67). Chesnut's perspective that religion is a matter of individual utilitarian choice for privatized benefit simply misses the vast social and political scope of the pentecostal revitalization movement. I agree that revitalization pentecostalism in Maya Guatemala has a utilitarian knack for solving or avoiding some problems. By Wallace's definition, however, a revitalization *must* conceive of a society as sick and in need of reform. The movement must aim to reform selected aspects of that sick society. Deliberate reform is necessarily utilitarian. But any revitalization movement is also an idea system about moral, ethical, and therefore ideational reform. It contrasts a vision of a possible future with what it asserts is the apparent untenability of a currently experienced present. That is the unstated political project largely missed by scholars who see Christian Pentecostalism as a self-interested market choice made by adherents for utilitarian gains.

JOINING MODERNITY AND ACCESSING NEWNESS

In chapter 23, I explored how traditionalist Maya culture and pentecostal liturgy and life practice share certain resonances or similarities with key deep premises of Maya thought or with long-standing and once-important Maya practices. Here I highlight the newness of the resonances shared between traditional culture and pentecostal belief and practice. Because cultural aspects of key premises and core practices in the old and sometimes rather nostalgically "lost" traditional life are reproduced in new symbolic garb in the pentecostal present, many Mayas find themselves comforted emotionally when they convert from old traditionalist or Ortho-Catholic to a new pentecostal practice. Through the change they access a slice of modernity otherwise largely denied them. Pentecostalism feels good because, structurally and ideologically, it feels Maya—even if symbolically it has changed. What I emphasize here is that simultaneously, because of the changes, conversion feels modern. While the achievement of modernity and a simultaneous return to indigeneity may seem like an apparent contradiction, in fact revitalization movements have long been recognized as combining new and old (Wallace 1956:276). Indeed, Wallace has asserted that the synthesis of old and new is key to revitalization success. Revitalization movements must tap the deep roots of the old culture as a base, which will be added to or transformed to build acceptance of the new (Wallace 2003[1956]).

For a Maya, joining one or another pentecostal congregation or denomination to access its newness does not need much coaxing. There has been a long-standing interest among Mayas to not be "left behind," a desire to become more "modern" (Checketts 2005). The Mayas' interest in accessing facets of modernity shows up widely in the literature (Way 2012; Everton 1991:231). This makes pentecostalism's symbolic garb of newness an important aspect of pentecostalism's acceptability. For those who suffer subsistence shortage and cultural collapse and who have been effectively excluded from access to an alternative mode of subsistence, pentecostalism offers access to the trappings of modernity in the only institutional sector of the system that Mayas control: their indigenized adjustment cult religious system. Protestant Pentecostal practice and, to a lesser degree, Catholic charismatic pentecostal practice symbolically embrace many forms of newness that connote symbolic inclusion in what Mayas call progress. The Protestant Pentecostals, especially, engage the Mayas' expressed urge to "get ahead" and not be left behind by what they call modernization.

How is this touch of modernity acquired? It is done largely through the pentecostal's contact with the symbols in pentecostalism that connote modernity and newness because of their Saussurean structural contrast with symbols of oldness and the old ways embedded in Ortho and traditionalist Catholicism. Among these forms of newness are lively styles of music lifted from recent media sources, access to the Bible and thus to texts and reading in general, electronic amplification, and adoption of business suits and other European clothing and Spanish language among male leaders. Participating in pentecostalism gives one the sense both of having "found" something old, deeply valued, and lost *and* of having tapped into progress, development, and modernity.

Ortho and traditionalist Catholicism symbolically display connection to and interest in the past; adherence to tradition, after all, is a source of authority in many cultural systems and is explicitly a source of truth and authority in Ortho-Catholicism. This contrasts with Pentecostals' interest in their future, in the New Jeruselem, in "building the kingdom," and in reforming Guatemala, and that contrast is part of what Saussure says gives meaning to both. Recall, for example, that the pentecostal church building likely sports a brightly painted but plain modern façade and a simple interior with nothing more ornate than a background mural idealizing indigenous farm life. One sees no architectural genuflections toward the old or the baroque, which seem Catholic; one sees no spiral columns, no niches for saints, no scalloped shells, no architectural decorations—just bright paints, glossy and durable if affordable, on flat slab construction surmounted by a cross and an outdoor speaker or two. There will be a distinguishing name board outside. A poor congregation might not be able to maintain the paint job or might use poorer building materials, but whatever they do will be as new and modern-looking as they can afford. That is the Pentecostal symbolic signature and orientation (plates 25, 26, 32, 33). A purpose-built charismatic *comunidad* building will be equally non-baroque in construction, but whitewashed (like many a municipality's central Catholic church), gray-toned as untouched building materials, or perhaps given a simple coat of paint. It will not be audaciously painted in multiple colors, but it will nevertheless be distinctly modern even if simple and poor. There will be no external name identification (figure 21.1).

Inside the Pentecostal or charismatic building are rows of bench seating or plastic chairs facing a slightly raised dais. On or in front of the dais are banks of speakers one meter wide by perhaps two meters high to the left and right of a microphone-fitted podium or perhaps bunched all to one side. Chairs on the stand provide seating for the pastor, assistants, and band players. A tangle of cords connects microphones and instruments to a professional-grade sound mixer at the back of the room, whose operator raises and lowers the percentage contributions of pastor's voice and band music sent to the cacophonous output of the speakers. All is modern. The instruments would play well in any western band the world over—trumpets, electric guitars, bass guitar, drums, tambourines, keyboard—all amplified to painful levels. There is no marimba, for that is old, Catholic, and traditional. Pentecostal music (somewhat more so than charismatic music) relies on catchy melodies—sometimes Mexican *ranchera*, sometimes pop or rock covers of American or European contemporary music—played over the radio or available on cassettes and CDs, which are copied with abandon and sold in street markets. The words to the music develop pentecostal Christological refrains; without question, a modern entertainment component lurks in pentecostal liturgy. As several of our ethnographies have remarked, the simple entertainment value of pentecostal *alabanza* singing and band performance, which loudly imitates contemporary music, helps attract youthful adherents.[11]

The wall behind the pentecostal dais may have a mural depicting a pastoral scene of volcanoes and fields, with a few Mayas in traditional garb working with *azadones* (broad bladed hoes). But scattered in the background usually are elements of modernity, often an airplane in the sky or a vehicle on a road, perhaps a Pentecostal church and a school. The glossy colors—pastels and greens, whitewash and burnt orange—highlight fields, work, housing, and corn. These symbols of indigeneity, work ethic, and progress are present, but no symbols connoting traditionalist or old religion. The only things portrayed that might be considered old are the marks of indigenous identity embedded in colorful municipally identified clothing and the depicted agricultural work. All this contrasts sharply with Ortho-Catholic carved wooden icons and somber brown and smoke-darkened paintings of pleading or tortured saints.

During the church service, the Pentecostal pastor invariably dresses in a western-style business suit, shirt, and tie. Band members arrive in western youth dressy casual clothing or may wear suits—all in stark contrast with the Catholic priest's ornate medieval cape. Only the women and old men consistently wear recognizably traditional clothing styles. (In Catholic charismatic meetings, the male group leader may well dress in identifiably local indigenous clothing, but if so, he is likely an elderly individual.) When not on the dais, the Pentecostal pastor sits with his wife and children in the front row of the congregation, facing the stand, or in some cases sunk into a pretentiously overstuffed sofa, the most modern and comfortable seating compared to a simple wooden-block *tem* (seat), a wooden or plastic chair in a Maya house, or the carved and perhaps gilded chair of the Ortho-Catholic priest. The pastor's seat is different from all the other plastic chairs or wooden benches in the Pentecostal meeting place. Connoting the achievement of family unity, economic success, and modern access, the pastor and his family's front-row sofa is an overstuffed symbol of access to modernity, comfort, and even a modicum of wealth.

In the worship service, the pastor reads verses from the Bible or recites memorized verses, always in Spanish. This Spanish orientation holds even though the Bible is generally available in K'iche' in Nahualá's weekly market from both mainline Protestant and Ortho-Catholic publishers.

Leaders and participants sing most songs in Spanish, sometimes singing solo from the podium, sometimes singing in unison as a congregation. Thus, the Pentecostal service (and somewhat less so, the charismatic service) acts as a portal to literacy and education. Through emphasis on literacy and education, pentecostalism increases access to what is perceived to be modern, *lo moderno*. Catholic charismatics explicitly encode the value of newness in their title; it is the Charismatic Renewal, the Renovación Carismática. Both Catholic and Protestant pentecostals aggressively propound their transformative newness. They knowingly and deliberately build a "New Jerusalem," a new kingdom of God on earth. These Pentecostalisms connect Mayas to an international social and political reformation movement perceived to be engaged in transforming a broken and corrupt old Guatemala and reforming their shattered world with something new.

Protestant Pentecostal preaching emphasizes renewal. One hears sermons on shaking off, casting off, or leaving the old and the corrupt. Pentecostals are building a new body and a new nation. They put off the old and put on the new. In this renewal, new premises replace old. New supportive friendships replace street buddies that corrupt or tempt. Spousal and parental relationships are renewed and reconstructed on new lines as the center of one's attention and responsibility. Congregants are regendered and thus are made modern (O'Neill 2010:115–143; Brusco 1993, 1995).

To a degree, an emphasis on individualism is modern (at the same time, it is traditional in isolated familial self-subsistence and short-range kinship genealogies). While pentecostalism coordinates a whole congregation in collective worship, its preaching emphasizes individualism by calling on each person to reform. It seeks to heal the society and the body politic by treating, healing, and changing the individual. The individual is invited to walk forward, kneel before the dais, experience Jesus via reception of the Spirit, and be healed and changed. In all these ways, the pentecostalized individual acquires access to symbols that resonate with modernity.

I described all these details in chapter 22, where Ortho-Catholic and traditionalist Maya religion are contrasted with the various forms of Christian Pentecostalism. I repeat them here to highlight the degree to which this religious juxtaposition, this contrast, is also framed within the concepts of old versus new or modern. These oppositions parallel and give meaning to the contrast between traditionalist and Ortho-Catholic, on the one hand, and both of these with Pentecostal or charismatic

Christian Pentecostal, on the other. Indeed, it is such oppositions and syntheses of old and new that energize revitalization movements.

CHRISTIAN PENTECOSTALISM AS A REVITALIZATION MOVEMENT

I began this chapter by listing the five general characteristics of a religious revitalization movement and asking whether the behavior patterns of Christian Pentecostalism match those attributes. Protestant and Catholic pentecostalisms in Nahualá and Santa Catarina Ixtahuacán do indeed meet Wallace's criteria.

First, Nahualense and Ixtahuaquense Christian Pentecostal leaders and adherents perceive and talk about their society and culture as a system. In Nahualá and Santa Catarina, both Protestant and Catholic pentecostals assert, for example, that only personal ethical transformation will change society, that political corruption impacts multiple aspects of life, and that religion makes a difference in individual, familial, and political life. These are all statements of perceived systemic interconnection. More widely in Guatemala, O'Neill (2010:124–130) documents how members of a congregation of neo-Pentecostals in Guatemala City explicitly talk of changing child care (via the simple act of men touching children) as fundamental to and connected to transforming the family, improving personality, stabilizing gender, and reforming politics. All these statements conceive of society (and its ills) as an interconnected system and, per Wallace's fourth point, portend a deliberately curative alteration of society.

Second, all versions of pentecostalism in Nahualá and Santa Catarina Ixtahuacán vociferously proclaim that the cultural system around them is unsatisfactory. Guatemala, pentecostal adherents say, is sick. It is of the devil. Indeed, they hold that secular Guatemalan society is corrupt to the core. Evangelical Protestant Pentecostals deem traditionalist Maya culture practices and Roman Catholicism as similarly corrupt. Even charismatic Catholics think Ortho-Catholicism has become vapid and unsatisfactory and that the old Maya culture fosters self-destructive excess. Catholicism, considered by Catholic Guatemalans to be a core element of proper culture, needs renewal, the Catholic renovationists say. And they affirm they provide that renewal, though they do not criticize Ortho-Catholicism in public as sharply as do the Pentecostals, who preach that Ortho-Catholicism is fundamentally corrupt and demonic.

All hold both Ortho-Catholicism and secular Guatemalan society to be unsatisfactory, corrupt, broken, and in need of reform.

Third, Nahualá's and Santa Catarina's Christian Pentecostal innovations mix and fuse old and new in a fresh creation. They have innovated by adopting, adapting, and indigenizing both Protestant and Catholic external missionized ideologies and what they perceive to be their own old Maya traditionalism to create a new system.

Fourth, Christian Pentecostals see these innovations as deliberate, curative alterations to what is sick or broken in their overall sociocultural system. Indeed, the pentecostal religions of Nahualá and Santa Catarina Ixtahuacán advocate revolutionary, coordinated, and systematized cultural changes consciously aimed at transforming individual, local, regional, national, and world systems that they see as broken. In Benedict Anderson's (1991) terms, they have "imagined" a new system. They seek "new relationships" and "new traits" that would cure the ills of existing society, if only all would join them. Thus, as Marx (2008[1844]:42) argues, revitalization religions are indeed a direct "protest against real distress" and seek to inject "heart" and "spirit" into the reform of a "heartless world" and a "spiritless situation."

Fifth, by any definition—whether academic or culturally Mayan or Guatemalan—the varieties of Christian Pentecostalism deal with human relations with divinities; they are indeed religions and parts of a religious movement. Thus, point by point, Christian Pentecostal religions in Nahualá, Santa Catarina Ixtahuacán, and other areas of Guatemala meet all of Wallace's definitional criteria of a religious revitalization movement.

Deliberate reform to correct a social or cultural deficit is necessarily an attempt to be utilitarian. The functions include physical and emotional healing, job networking, regendering that reformats the family and household, household economic reform and improvement, nation building, and a religious form of globalization. Clearly, our ethnographies confirm the enormous existing literature identifying the social benefits of (Protestant-derived) Pentecostalism in the constricted postcolonial economies and societies of the Christianized Global South. In addition, our ethnographies of the Renovación Carismática confirm that the same benefits occur in the Catholic Charismatic Renewal. Charismatics have thereby domesticated wildly anti-Catholic Pentecostal Evangelicalism and brought that domesticated pentecostalism into the Catholic household of faith precisely to serve the intensified needs of so many Catholics whose lives, filled with culture crisis, parallel the situation of their Pentecostal co-villagers.

CONCLUSION

Christian Pentecostal liturgy and social theology embody more than just the expression of conditions and emotions. Guatemalan pentecostalisms also entail a resolute and socially effective program of charismatically conceived opportunities to build and deploy the resources at hand: the resources of self, family, congregation, and globally shared faith. These help individuals build or rebuild communities and behaviors that mitigate to some degree the untoward effects of cultural collapse, oppression, exclusion, and liminality. Through various symbolic mechanisms, they help individuals achieve a partial entrance into modernity at the same time that they rebuild a local society. Helping individuals reshape and rebuild a society is, according to Wallace, the goal of revitalization through charismatic reconceptualization. Religious revitalization movements purposefully try to change what their proponents judge to be sick, ill, or corrupted about the society they live in. Becoming pentecostal entails an active choice by the individual first to judge and then to try to change both self and society.

In Wallace's, Weber's, and even Durkheim's perspectives, novel ideas taken on faith as culture and religion can transform and create a new society and culture. Society, they feel, gets restructured in the image of the ideas that its members (or major segments thereof) recite to each other through various symbols communicated in the syntax and context of Christian Pentecostal ritual. To play off von Clausewitz and Marx, religious revitalization is a revolution of society by other means.

The Christian Pentecostal movement and the associated pentecostal utilities are not just parallel responses to a long list of secular efforts to reform society but are in fact far more effective at helping Mayas and urban poor people than any of that list of approaches to poverty or structural violence in Guatemala, including insurgencies, unions, democracy, foreign aid, NGOs, or the continuing parade of repressive, inept, klepto-governments. Moreover, pentecostal congregationalism provides much more effective defenses against what Chesnut calls the "pathogens of poverty" that arise in the context of twentieth- and twenty-first-century globalization than do the

longer-existing forms of traditionalist, Ortho-Catholic, or mainstream Protestant Christian religions in Guatemala.

Following Weber and Wallace, these new ecstatic religions seem to foster a continuous adaptive process. They have structured into their cultural DNA an institutionalized capacity to continuously revitalize and transform. In effect, they have achieved at the grassroots through religion what the Mexican Partido Revolucionario Institucional, for example, could not: Christian Pentecostalism seems to have institutionalized continuous revolutionary change through democratized revelatory experience. The leaders and members of pentecostalism's congregations adapt their religions—their sacred premises, symbols, and practices—in order to equip themselves with an approach to life that, given their resources, works to their benefit in their particular local context. Pentecostalisms—both Protestant and Catholic—give Mayas a cognitive, symbolic, and behavioral approach to life with many micro varieties. Compared to Guatemala's other Christianities—Maya Catholic traditionalism, Ortho-Catholicism, and mainstream denominational Protestantism (and even neotraditionalism as a non-Christian religious performance)—the pentecostal approach solves the most problems, gives its adherents the most resources, and offers them a greater sense of control. It depends little on the untrustworthy state or on unknown outsiders.

To be sure, Maya traditionalism's Ladino-dressed or military-dressed Judas—the duplicitous Maximón who is both an apostle of help and an apostolic and therefore deceiving betrayer—tells Mayas about the world they live in with much accuracy. Catholicism, too, expresses well the Maya experience of pain: Jesus, the model for all humankind to emulate, is raised above the altar of sacramental commitment and displayed as an emaciated, bleeding, and pained body, graphically shown in death throes, slumped on the cross. Catholicism, however, accepts this suffering in a soft voice. One accepts one's fate.

The forms of pentecostalism, by contrast, preach activism. Change the world by changing yourself and converting others. These pentecostalisms tend to be more active and agentive. They better function to provide adherents with supportive social relations and more accessible health sustenance in this chaotic, uncertain time. Christian Pentecostal liturgies accurately portray the painful liminal existence of people caught betwixt and between, of Mayas standing between a breaking-down and rotting-away corn-subsistent colonial way of life and the rise of a largely inaccessible and unsympathetic neoliberal market-oriented way of life. The transformation of society from traditionalist and Ortho-Catholic to pentecostal Protestant *evangélico* and charismatic Catholic confirms the ideas of Weber about religion fitting a people with a new ideology that eventually transforms the society. It precisely follows Wallace's conceptualization of the revitalization movement and adjustment cult as a new religion that takes ideas, symbols, and behaviors of the old religion and culture and blends them with new ideas, symbols, and practices, thereby refitting its adherents and attracting new affiliates to deal better with the world it critiques. The new framework is an experiment in faith—which is to say, an experiment in culture—that attempts to solve problems within a new small-congregational world, fitting adherents with a new cultural order because the rest of their surrounding world excludes them and does little to help them connect to or succeed in that world. Ultimately, this equation of faith and culture helps one understand why religion is indeed what Durkheim calls the "soul of society." When one's cultural place in society is under long-term severe stress, the attraction of a new faith/culture lies in the assessment that individuals make of the possibility that their new way of thinking about and dealing with the world will work better. This they find highly attractive, given their experience that the old way of dealing with and conceiving of that world has generated something quite untenable.

Thus, the new religions indeed express the collective "sigh" of a people, as Marx suggests. However, "religious distress is at the same time the expression of real distress and the protest against real distress" (Marx 2008[1844]:42). In their glossolalia, in their compelling and noisy liturgy, and in their end-of-a-corrupt-world and change-yourself sermons, the new pentecostal religions do express a pained and collective "sigh too deep for words." But they also embody an activist attempt to induce individuals to reform themselves and thereby their society. They advocate the individual agentive choice of a radically distinct moral, political, social, familial, and gendered stance, a stance contrary to the set of premises that built and supported the now collapsing society around them. By faith, they consciously choose a path to collective change. By evangelism, they seek to broaden their movement of individual transformation. They seek to make it communal, societal, national, and even global. It is a movement they feel will reform, refit, and transmute their society as a whole. As O'Neill (2010)

and Wightman (2007) have shown most clearly, Pentecostals see themselves as part of an indigenous, grassroots nation-building and even world-redeeming project. So do the Catholic pentecostals.

By labeling the proposed societal changes a matter of divine mandate, religious sacralization in a religious revitalization movement makes the changes into moral imperatives and thus is profoundly Durkheimian. Religious sacralization allows the new adherent to see "conversion" as a positive moral good rather than as an abandonment or betrayal of tradition or culture. This is one more reason that conversion is not simply a choice of religion from a market shelf of available religions, done for individual advantage.

Quite the contrary. Each religion is deeply implicated and co-constituted by the creative vision and evaluation of people both inside and outside of the convert's congregation. When there is a base religion that represents the majority of its ethnic cultures or citizens, conversion to a new or minority religion evaluates and thus critiques the base culture. In Guatemala's case up to about 1950, that base religion for Mayas was Maya Catholic traditionalism. In living that religion, its adherents continuously evaluated the balance of reciprocities inherent in their notion of mutual covenant with divinity in order to sustain each other. Then, increasingly up to about 1980, the Mayas' base religion included and progressively shifted to Ortho-Catholicism. Ortho-Catholics, too, then had to evaluate, and as a result some shifted to Protestantism. In the background, however, from about 1950 to the present, forms of Pentecostalism and, later, renewal Catholicism have expanded, critiquing society as a whole. Thus, religion always evaluates.

In the words of Marx, the new revitalization religions frame and project a "protest." The new religions always critique society. From about 1980 to the present, the indigenous Christian Pentecostal critique has become increasingly strong, both in the message and in the number of adherents as a percentage of the population. In that regard, Garrard-Burnett (1993:207) and Brusco (1993:146–147, 1995:137) are both correct in seeing Pentecostalism (and, I add, all pentecostalisms, including Catholic pentecostalism) as profoundly revolutionary because it is a critique. In the case of Guatemala, converting people make a wholehearted decision to leave the well-worn, rutted, but now difficult (if not impossible) to follow trail of "old" Maya culture. They leave the customary social road in favor of a tentative and prospective new Maya pathway that—it is hoped and held as a tenet of faith—will eventually lead to a healed self and society.

Durkheim's (2001[1912]:266) assertion that "the true justification of religious practices is not in their apparent ends" does not mean religious practices do not have useful ends. Indeed, by definition, a revitalization movement's leaders and participants consciously seek to accomplish useful, healing, societally corrective ends. I have assembled but a few of those socially corrective procedures and apparent ends for commentary in this chapter. In Durkheim's view, the utilitarian ends are a natural social by-product of the religion having repremised the minds of a society's participants through conversion. This makes Durkheim isomorphic with Weber: Durkheim's "moral" repremising aligns with Weber's transformational new "ethic," which generates a reframed society. The moral premises matter because of the "invisible influence they work on consciousness." I think Durkheim, Weber, and Wallace would all concur that religion's primary impact or justification is to alter the mental state of its adherents. Among the Mayas and widely around the world, the new Christian Pentecostalisms reconstitute ideas of male gender and refocus the interests of men inward toward family welfare rather than outward to the street. They urge all Guatemalans, not just Mayas, to obey both secular and divine law as ultimate sources of societal stability. In a society such as Guatemala that for decades (and, arguably, for five centuries) has been essentially lawless at the state level and caught in violent turmoil and economic chaos, divine support of and human obedience to local law matters. Through prayer, pentecostals practice, inculcate, and discipline that obedience into their bodies. These are bedrock changes instituted by pentecostalism.

The important matter is not so much what the religious practices do usefully, physically, or immediately for the people. In that regard, Chesnut (2003a) and Iannaccone, Finke, and Stark (1997) (as advocates of religious marketplace utility) and Marx (in seeing religion as a materialist manipulation and duping of the masses) are wrong. What matters in the new religions is how liturgical practices discipline people's minds and inculcate in them radical new ideas via the repetitive performance of new ritual tasks. It is a religious instantiation of Bourdieu's (1990) "logic of practice," the logic arising from the practice of ritual. Thus, by prayerful discipline of the body, regular presence at church to revivify the sentiments of moral attachment to the community, and, for men, avoiding alcohol, ending the abuse of women, and turning the intents of their hearts (*kik'ux*) and their minds (*kina'o*, "consciousness" or "sensibility") to the care of children and families and away from sexual or wasteful "wandering in the street," they hope to bring about a more livable society.

We should hope that they succeed. No matter how much any non-pentecostal might be discomforted by the exuberant, agitated noisiness of Christian Pentecostal practice, it may now be taken as fact that the decibel level of their liturgy, their cries, the cacophony, and their glossolalia express with understandable intensity the emotional truth of their almost unspeakable situation. They are desperately liminal people caught between collapse of the old and exclusion from the new, and their hot new religion expresses and seeks to reform that condition.

In the next chapter I show that converts and participants in the Christian Pentecostal experience deem the many benefits and utilities they derive from Christian Pentecostal practice to be "gifts of God" for which they owe God something—reciprocal loyalty. This places gifting and reciprocity at the center of the conversion process analysis, and, I argue, it also makes gifting and reciprocity the *axis mundi* of a better definition of religion.

NOTES

1. The Nahualense Catholic parish supports a biomedical clinic with a doctor and staff. For a number of years prior to the 2000 split, Santa Catarina Ixtahuacán had a prenatal and maternity clinic, operated by regional nuns, that offered services during occasional visits. We did not ascertain the costs, subsidies, or operational procedures in these parish-sponsored Ortho-Catholic clinics.

2. Chesnut (2003a:23, 44–47, 83, 129, 132–134; 1997:28, 35) makes Catholicism's absence of healing services and Christian Pentecostalism's (whether Protestant or Catholic) free delivery of healing the key differentiator that has led to Christian Pentecostalism's swift success. While I disagree with aspects of Chesnut's market-centered approach, without question Christian Pentecostalism's free access to healing is central to its appeal and conversion system (Adams and Hawkins 2007:228–230), but I see conversion as based on the reciprocal consequences of the gift rather than marketplace competition and assessed utility of behavior.

3. I recognize that my analysis here has the religious institutions acting, if not as as competitors, at least as complementary niche service providers, per the religious marketplace theories. My main point is not that religious institutions don't compete for membership. Of course, they do. My point is that rational

market choice by individuals is not the route to conversion. Rather, the social obligation inherent in gift giving and expected reciprocity is.

4. This note embarks on a critique of the extant "theology of joy." One reviewer suggested I should sharpen my use of the word "joy" by bringing to the discussion a theological definition of it. I am not a theologian, and I choose to leave the concept of joy relatively undeveloped for two reasons. First, joy is not central to my analysis. Nevertheless, I recognize that in the Saussurean sense, joy is something of the opposite of the angst and despair of collapse that I do hold central. Thus, joy connects meaningfully to the analysis of angst and collapse. My main reason for leaving joy underdeveloped, however, is that current proponents of a theology of joy seem unable to define joy in a way that is clearly communicable or applicable in a social science inquiry (see, for example, Mathewes 2012:2–3). If theologians cannot define joy, likely I cannot either. I can, however, share the following reflections.

First, theologians do not agree among themselves on the nature or definition of joy. Their disagreement and lack of certitude is evidenced in a website dedicated to the theology of joy (Yale Center for Faith and Culture 2014). What theologians do agree on is that happiness is less intense, more transient, more unstable, and more contextually derived than joy. Such wordplay seems unhelpful to an ethnographer.

Metz (1974:8) remarks that "the Christian message emphasizes joy." One struggles, however, to find a Christian theologian defining the term, as opposed to using, playing with, or simply reflecting on it in culturally expected hagiographic terms. Given that the concept of joy names the emotional reward expected from committed human participation in the Christian tradition, one would think theologians would have elaborated the concept of joy in detail.

Alas, the major multivolume encyclopedias of Christian theology have ample articles on "journalism" and its place in sustaining Christianity, but no entries devoted specifically to "joy." Why do I compare joy to journalism? Because "journalism" is alphabetically proximate to "joy" and thus caught my attention when looking up "joy." The irony is that journalism seems absolutely inconsequential compared to joy in Christian scripture or theology, yet it gets much attention. So, what is out there on joy and on journalism?

Eliade 1987, which has sixteen volumes, has no article on joy and no indexed reference to joy, but almost fifteen columns on journalism's connection to religion. James Hastings edited the *Encyclopedia of Religion and Ethics* (1980). It has no article on joy, but it does contain fleeting index references to the importance of joy in the practice of Jewish life, the Sabbath, marriage, and death, and there is two-thirds of a column on undefined joy in

an article on love. There is nothing on journalism. Jones 2005 has fifteen volumes with no article on joy and no indexed reference to joy except through a "see also" reference to two items of Hindu literature, but it does have thirteen columns on journalism and religion. Komonchak, Collins, and Lane 1987 have no article on either joy or journalism and no index. Fahlbusch et al. 1999 includes two columns on joy by Winkler (1999:3:79) but no definition and no index. Lacoste 2005 has no article on joy and no reference to joy in its index.

What about the status of joy in Christian theology? The theological literature is so vast I could only consult books that included "joy" in their titles. Jürgen Moltmann's (1973) *Theology and Joy* has no definition. I gather from multiple uses in context that joy is the aesthetic appreciation of one's relation to God. That is hardly a definition that social scientists can grasp and use. Moreover, most people have some sense of a relation to God that might constitute appreciation. Who knows what aesthetic versus nonaesthetic appreciation might mean? It seems to imply that if you have some kind of sophisticated perception of a relation with God, then by definition you experience joy. I doubt that can be deployed in any research setting. Metz and Jossua (1974) edited a book called *Theology of Joy*. It includes three essays and an introductory editorial with joy in their titles, but none of these pieces offers a definition. In *The Anchor Bible Dictionary*, Arnold (1992:1022–1023) discusses joy, associates it with "gladness, happiness, and celebration," and gives the occasions when a Christian might expect to feel joy but provides no definition. One gathers, however, that joy is enduring, social, rooted in worship, and based on hope, and it can coexist with hardship and suffering.

The only definition of "joy" that I could find was in Elwell (1984:588): "a delight in life that runs deeper than pain or pleasure" that constitutes "a quality of life and not simply a fleeting emotion" and is "grounded in God himself and flows from him." That too would be a difficult definition for social scientists to work with. Thus, according to Elwell, "the fullness of joy comes when there is a deep sense of the presence of God in one's life" (588). Joy becomes the state of having experienced the presence of God in one's life. Given this definition, pentecostals experience joy when they worship because in worship they seek and experience the presence of God in their bodies; that presence is proven by the ecstatic behavior that they perceive in their bodies as evidenced through glossolalia, being overcome by the Spirit so as to move about or fall to the floor apparently without control, or receipt of healings. Thus, pentecostals experience joy by definition as they express the tensions and risks of their worldly lives through pentecostal experience of the Holy Spirit. God is clearly with them. Indeed, they see and feel that God is in them. Thus the ritual expression of angst produces joy and does so by definition. For Christian Pentecostals, analytically, joy becomes an expectation state achieved by definition when they engage in proper worship. The state of joy is recognizable by having received the signs of the infusion of the Holy Spirit in one's life via enthusiastic participation, receiving and giving of healings, trance possession, and speaking in tongues. Pentecostal worship by definition becomes its own reward: it converts pain to joy through ritual experience.

With regard to my analysis that conversion pressures derive from angst rooted in culture collapse and exclusion, Elwell (1984:588) notes that "there can also be joy in suffering" and yet "one cannot experience joy while being preoccupied with one's own security, pleasure, or self interest." This apparent contradiction raises the possibility that Christian Pentecostal participation sets aside concern over the survival issues that brought a person to conversion. Pentecostal preaching, in various forms, asserts that God will provide, and that expectation (regardless of whether actualized or not) brings relief. Relief then constitutes part of the joy experienced.

The most recent effort to approach a definition of joy comes from the Yale Center for Faith and Culture (2014, 2015) in a project financed by the Templeton Foundation to establish a theology of joy. In their introductory materials, the Yale theologians collectively note, "Joy is fundamental to human existence and well-being, yet it is an elusive phenomenon that resists definition." Moreover, although joy stands "at the center of Jewish and Christian scripture, theology, and practices . . . the very idea of joy has all but disappeared from modern theological reflection, is all but ignored by the social sciences, and is increasingly absent from lived experience. The consequence is a 'flattening out,' a 'graying,' of human life and communities" (Yale Center for Faith and Culture 2015). Guatemalan pentecostal Mayas would agree: both mainline Protestant and Ortho-Catholic ritual seem lifeless and "grayed-out" by comparison with spirited pentecostal worship. Specific theologians collaborating with the Yale Center concur: Mathewes (2012:1, 2–3) affirms that "the ultimate meaning of the word 'joy' remains beyond us." If it is "beyond" the capacity of the full-time theologians to define joy, it is, like I said, beyond my capacity too. Mathewes's attempt at definition—that joy is the emotion felt by a human intimately connected with God and is expressed as "excess" or "rapture"—seems difficult to use in analytical ethnography. It amounts to saying that behavioral exuberance or trance constitutes joy by definition.

Wolterstorff (2014) takes joy as an emotion and uses Robert C. Roberts (2003) to argue that joy as an emotion has an object around which it is organized: evaluative concern or construal. Thus "joy . . . occurs when it's important to one that things be a certain way and one construes them as being that way" (Wolterstorff 2014:3). In short, Wolterstorff dodges the opportunity to define joy and locates it (whatever it is) in the consequences that emerge from consistent religious participation because religion defines what is important and the way important things should be construed. Moreover, participation and belief entail both the way and the construal of a desired reality.

In all these theological attempts at definition, joy and religion become self-referential, mutually confirming, and perhaps coexistent. Joy is what one experiences while engaged in religious performance. Through pentecostal religious participation, joy becomes experienced reality even if the experienced physical conditions—those of the Christian in the Roman Coliseum, in the Guatemalan *milpa* plot, or in the urban slum—are in some external sense abjectly miserable. Nevertheless, I hold that this capacity-by-definition to imbue joy (in the ordinary English sense of profound happiness), no matter the actual condition, is one of the utilitarian "goods" of Christian Pentecostal religion and, likely, all religion.

5. All of these points can be found in a broad swath of literature on the condition of women in indigenous and impoverished urban communities in the Global South. For the Mayas, three of the best are Bossen 1984:175–176, 225; Eber 1995; and Elhers 2000. For Colombia, see Brusco 1986, 1993.

6. For Colombia, see Brusco 1993:143–158, 1995; for Guatemala, O'Neill 2010:115–142; for Chiapas, Mexico, Robledo Hernández 2003:167–169; for Chile, Lindhardt 2012:177–191; for Brazil, Burdick 1993a:87–116; and Chesnut 1997:108–122, 2003a:130–146; for Bolivia, Gill 1990; and for Ghana, Gifford 2004:117–132, 183–185.

7. Steigenga and Smilde (1999), however, find little evidence that evangelical participation in Latin America changes attitudes regarding the legitimacy of women's sociopolitical participation in society beyond the family.

8. One traditionalist shaman I frequented had no cell phone. Another made occasional use of his adult children's cell phones. So far we have not seen the practice of an ill Maya migrant phoning a shaman for the conduct of ritual in his behalf.

9. As a colleague and reviewer notes, "I think Foucault would argue (and I would agree) that given current state technologies of power (and force), when wedded to the righteous conviction of Christian Pentecostal self-embodiment of the Holy Spirit, the result will be, not the inherent sectarianism of Evangelical churches, but the draconian absolutism of religious dictatorship" (John Watanabe, pers. comm.).

10. I do have some interview evidence that elite families think corruption was temporarily restrained during the Ríos Montt presidency.

11.   Durkheim (2001[1912]:282–285) notes the entertainment component of religion. Religion has "its recreational and aesthetic element . . . closely akin to dramatic representations." Rituals

> make men forget the real world in order to transport them into another in which their imagination is more at ease; they entertain. They even have the external trappings of recreation, with the participants laughing and openly enjoying themselves. . . . The state of effervescence in which the assembled worshipers find themselves is necessarily expressed outwardly by exuberant movements that are not easily subordinated to narrowly defined ends. They escape, in part, to no purpose, performed strictly for the pleasure of performing and delighting in something like games. . . . So we may miscalculate when we try to assign each gesture a precise purpose and a well-defined rationale. There are some that serve no purpose at all, they answer simply to the worshipers' feeling that they need to act, to move, to gesticulate. They may leap, turn, dance, shout, and sing, and this agitation may have no discernible meaning. Thus, religion would not be religion if it did not make some place for the free combinations of thought and activity, for play, for art, for all those things that renew the spirit worn down by the constraints of daily labour; the very causes that called religion into existence make it a necessity.

Chapter Twenty-Five

The Attractions of the Gift

Understanding the Conversion Process and Defining Religion

JOHN P. HAWKINS

IN THIS CHAPTER I SEEK to understand the gifts and reciprocities that seem to constitute the fulcrum of conversion and religion in Nahualá, in Santa Catarina Ixtahuacán, and apparently throughout the world. "What rule of legality and self-interest . . . compels the gift that has been received to be obligatorily reciprocated?" asks Mauss (1990[1925]:3–4). "What power resides in the object given that causes its recipient to pay it back? . . . We believe that in [studying and answering] this we have found one of the human foundations on which our societies are built." I have referred to gifting and reciprocity from time to time in prior chapters. Now I consolidate the argument in two components. First, gifting and associated notions of reciprocity better explain individual religious conversion than the idea that people rationally choose in an expanded marketplace of religions among available religious benefits and pay for them with their membership and participation in a given congregation or denomination. Second, from the experience of Mayas in Nahualá and Santa Catarina Ixtahuacán, I elaborate and generalize a definition of religion based on the universally understood linkage between a gift and its expected reciprocities. I suggest that a universally applicable definition and theory of religion can be developed out of gifting behavior.

THE GIFT VERSUS RATIONAL CHOICE AS A THEORY OF CONVERSION

One strand of academic discussion regarding conversion explores the impact of religious diversity seen as a marketplace of religions. The notion is that religious diversity gives rise to competition. That generates variety in the delivery of desired religious products. Religions differ and are made more efficient and helpful when they must compete for the choices of their discerning clients, the members who attach themselves to a congregation or denomination (Iannaccone, Finke, and Stark, 1997).

The marketplace argument suggests that late nineteenth- and early twentieth-century historical conditions in Guatemala gave rise to religious alternatives that ended the monopoly of state-linked Catholicism. During the colonial period, Catholicism was a monopoly, it is said (but only if one ignores nondenominational, autochthonous, popular religion), and was therefore unresponsive to people's needs or wants. The introduction of Protestantism and its fissiparous Pentecostal derivatives, when added to Catholicism, allowed individuals to choose from a diversity of available religions. The supposition is that leaders of religious congregations or denominations that have to compete for market share become more responsive to the needs of individuals in the market, especially if acquiring or retaining adherents provides leaders with some benefit.

In the marketplace approach, denominations or even congregations become something like large and small manufacturers trying to capture market share by introducing ever-better products for those exercising self-benefiting rational choice. The approach holds that the ability of individuals to choose what suits them best forced the formerly unresponsive religious monopoly of Catholicism to become more attuned to the needs of its adherents and produce a better and more competitive line of products. Hence, in the face of competition from Pentecostal Protestantism, Catholic leaders added the Charismatic Renewal to the Catholic line of products. In essence, churches try to produce differentiated niche products that some segment of the potential clientele will "buy." Some of the churches, being like huge companies, split off small start-ups, each advancing an unusual idea. Some make ever more diverse niche products. Some make mass-appeal products. All compete for market share. Individuals select the religious product that best suits their needs and mobilize the available resources with which they can "pay" for those products: a contribution of money or a giving of time, labor, or affirmative commitment to the organization. Presumably they "buy" from the religious outlet offering the required products for the lowest fees.

In the Latin American context, Chesnut (2003a:10–13, 147–160), Carpenter (1999:242–248), and Stewart-Gambino (2001) argue that the benefits for the poor attributed to pentecostal participation via the market diversification of religious products constitutes an explanation for the rapid movement of people out of traditionalism and Ortho-Catholicism and toward conversion to pentecostal religious. This process has occurred most notably throughout Latin America between 1950 and the present. In that marketplace, according to Chesnut, people convert based on rational decisions to acquire the utility values offered by affiliation with a particular style of religious performance. I think Chesnut (among others) correctly emphasizes the substantial and attractive utilities or benefits of pentecostal practice compared with traditionalist or Ortho-Catholic practice given the new conditions. As discussed in the previous chapter, these benefits include healing, hope, small-group community, work ethic, and gender reformation. But I also think that in looking at religious processes as a marketplace, he and others get both the mechanism of conversion and the essence of religion wrong.

Why do analysts tend to get this wrong? The answer lies in the culture system that engulfs most of us. To many of us, the "religious marketplace" is a comfortable metaphor with which to analyze religious change. That tricks us into unthinking acceptance. But the marketplace metaphor fails analytically on several grounds. First, the religious marketplace explanation fails because it is culturally contingent. By this, I mean that the marketplace metaphor encodes as social science theory the experience and culture of a particular society or type of society: Euro-American, post–World War II, market-based global capitalism—a social system in which the market is indeed symbolically and actually central. The logic that underlies the imagination of a religious marketplace centrally

incorporates the valued idea of freedom of choice that we analysts and Euro-American citizens demand to enact in any arena. We demand it because such freedom of choice is considered culturally essential; it is a Euro-American cultural prime. The idea of a marketplace of religions, in which one chooses a religion based on a rational analysis of benefits in relation to costs, replicates the experience of buying any product, be it a car or a tube of toothpaste. A well-stocked US supermarket has fifty to a hundred versions, sizes, and tastes of toothpaste. Yet the essential contents of the various toothpastes are the same: stannous fluoride and diatomaceous grit. So also for automobiles, mobile phones, clothes, and even vegetables. What is important is not that the products are really different, but that we feel validated and individuated if we have made a choice among options that thereby distinguish us from others as individuated and discerning consumers. The notion of a marketplace of religions thus resonates with the core beliefs in a market-centered culture, the free-choice experience of the analyst, and the identity formation occasioned by the ability to purchase and display enough diverse products to make oneself visibly unique and thus an individual. The concept of a marketplace of religions therefore is culturally comfortable. Because the market concept feels so comfortable, it is assumed to be right. Consequently, we readily adopt and use the concept as theory but leave it quite unexamined.

Being culturally contingent on ideas that are core and sacred to a capitalist consumption economy, the idea of a marketplace of religions gets imported into the analysis of Maya religious change even though the marketplace idea does not reflect the underlying thought processes or categories of Maya religious experience or conversion. Mayas talk of "gifts from God" (dones de Dios) received. They note that kujsipaj chqe le qatat-qanan ("our Father/Mother gifts to us"). Mayas do not speak of rationally choosing religions for personal benefit, even though many Mayas do recognize the benefits that accrue from conversion to another religion or from intensification of their behavior and commitment in the religion they already practice. But they do not see those benefits as rationally chosen acquisitions. They see them as gifts from God. Thus, people convert to reciprocate with loyalty on account of having received a gift, the gift of healing, for example. Women who have converted further honor God when they speak of the gift of a husband's or son's change of behavior, or the gift of mutual support in a women's group. In response to such gifts, they reciprocate loyalty, just as they would in response to the gifted largesse of a political patron. The pattern thus follows the gifting and loyal reciprocity owed to a religious *compadre* or a protecting saint that has given a gift to the living and retrieved the *promesa*.

Because of its cultural contingency, the marketplace of religions notion inherits the same intellectual problems that have bedeviled cross-cultural analyses of kinship, problems that Stringer (2008) argues have also undermined the cross-cultural study of religion. Schneider (1984) spent the last decades of his career showing that the western notion of kinship as biological relatedness subverted both the thought and the observations about kinship made by western analysts as they examined other societies. As a result of this bias, we analysts could not see that in some native systems, concepts other than biological relatedness ("blood") held sway in representing and anchoring long-term familial relatedness.

Schneider (1984) shows, for example, that among the Yapese, collaboratively and voluntarily working a piece of land generates enduring, diffuse, mutual obligations and rights—in short, the connectedness, transitivity, and moral obligation of caring that we call kinship. For Yap islanders, shared work on a piece of land, not blood, is the master conceptual symbol of relatedness. This shared work guides the logic of fundamental family formation and connection. Schneider finds that as a result of analysts relying on the comfortable cultural logic of our own society's ideas of blood, sex, and genetic relatedness, in any society that uses symbols other than blood/birth to represent their connectedness, the analyst's western cultural logic has warped the analysis of kinship and gotten kinship wrong. By imposing their own biological ideas onto other people's beliefs and practices, Schneider argues, analysts distort the representation of other cultures.

In Schneider's solution to this distortion, he asserts that some peoples do not have kinship because the way they symbolize their connectedness is not like our western analytical prime of blood, sex, and (later) DNA biology on which the definition of kinship was originally based, having been extracted from the culture of the analyst's experience. However, that solution by Schneider misses the mark because it takes a local western symbol (blood/DNA) of a universal reality (structured reciprocal obligation systems arising out of the universally experienced gifting of birth and childraising) as the reality itself. It therefore denies that some societies have kinship because they do not think or talk about it in our way as defined by our cultural experience. Thus, a local Euro-American

cultural perspective seen as science gets imposed on others. Ethnographies, however, have shown that quite a wide variety of symbols are used for identifying, discussing, and maintaining human small-group domestic connectedness (Schneider 1968, 1984; Delancy 1986).

We must not make the same substitutional mistakes with regard to religion that have been made regarding kinship. We must not confuse a local, comfortable cultural symbol with the underlying structure and universal behavioral process. The cultural comfort inherent in the idea of a marketplace of religions should warn us not to depend on the western marketplace concept—just as the social comfort of blood/DNA as kinship should warn us to not depend on notions of blood connectedness to define kinship nor to impose it on other societies. To not heed this warning may lead us to make the same mistakes regarding religion that we have made for kinship.

Market metaphors also fail because the assumptions on which they are based—dispassionate rationality, complete information accessibility, idealized neoliberal individualism, and free choice—are never wholly present. Thus, the assumptions of rationality, accessibility, and individualism are not only culturally contingent, they are faith-based western myths. In being an unchallenged and unexamined part of western culture, these assumptions constitute secular religion, as it were. The assumptions of full information and rational free choice—or even rational choice with whatever information one has at the moment—are imagined entities, the actual conditions of which are never present in society. They are mystical notions. Applied in the religious domain, these errors commingle and reinforce each other. They result in the distortion of analyses of religion as well as of kinship.

By contrast, I argue, the conversion process does not depend on rational or semi-rational choice to accumulate the most utilitarian benefits at the least cost, a notion that is local and western at best. Rather, the processes of Guatemalan religion and conversion revolve around the sociality and reciprocity of the free gift, a notion that is much more likely to be universal. The religious utilities constitute part of that free gift. The metaphor of the gift, rather than the metaphor of the religious marketplace, better guides one in deciphering and understanding the nature of Guatemalan religious process and conversion as experienced by the K'iche' Mayas.

In the ethnographic chapters of part 1, we describe many occasions when a leader's or a follower's participation in one religion intensifies or shifts to another religion altogether following some chance event considered culturally as a gift from God. These gifts include dreams, accidents, crystalline rocks found on the trail, and sicknesses or accidents followed by healings, often from prayers by visitors to the sick person's home. All these get interpreted as gifts from God. Conversion to a new religion, or intensification of one's religious activity in the old, is the associated reciprocity.

Clearly, the concepts of gifting that undergird kinship interactions trump the concepts that undergird the marketplace as an explanation of the human sociality and morality that Durkheim argues is the basis of religion in all societies. The experiences of kinship and family custodianship as a gift come prior to and are held as more important than the experiences of the marketplace. Schneider (1969) intimates this priority when he tries to link kinship, nationality, and religion as permutations of the same conceptual base. Polanyi (1944:47–52) affirms the priority of gift over market when he places gift, generalized reciprocity, and redistribution before barter and then places barter before market in his presumptive emergence story of modernity.

The concepts of gift giving and reciprocity simply do a better job of explaining the actual emphases of the Mayas regarding their religious conversions than do the ideas of the marketplace and free choice. Throughout the ethnographies of part 1, instances of conversion to a new religion or the intensification of commitment to one's present religion are almost always predicated on an unexpected gift that mitigates, resolves, or is seen to connect with an immediately pressing crisis. Thus, Tix, after much suffering and the deaths of all but one of his children, unexpectedly encountered crystal rocks and saw them as a gifted sign from God that he become a shaman. In such a rock's iridescent crystallinity, Mayas see an affinity with the sun. The root morpheme for "sun" appears in the shaman's title of *ajq'ij*. Traditionalists and Ortho-Catholics receive socially given gifts of healing in pentecostal prayer meetings or church services and interpret these healings as gifts of God. Thereafter, if they make any changes, they are likely to join the Pentecostal or charismatic congregation that gave them those gifts.

The gift that brings a solution obligates the receiver. When the gift is given by a person or group representing a new ideology to a person who is making decisions on the basis of an old ideology but whose life and society are clearly in stress or collapse, then the gift of crisis resolution draws the receiving individual into the debt of the group rendering the gift. Gift giving in the form of free healing, prayers, or supportive social visits thus pulls people in crisis out of the old and into the new group. As they socialize, they drop the old ideology at the same time that they refine and grow into the new one. They do not choose or "buy" Christian Pentecostal healing as an individual act of rationality or benefit acquisition. Rather, they receive pentecostal healing as a social gift, with gratitude, and they respond with culturally expected loyalties and reciprocities. The exchange is social, not individual and rational. Thus, the academic attempt to explain religion and religious change with notions of a "purchase" of the better product, adapted to one's needs, in a rational, informed, neoliberal, free-choice-based globalized religious marketplace fails because it does not capture the cultural logic or the social reciprocities of a Maya's experience of religion. Seeing religious conversion as a response to marketplace diversity does not capture the ethnographic reality.

In sum, the Maya social system is in such crisis that the society's members are pressured toward a cognitive reorientation regarding their covenant premises. People experience the systemic crisis as personal crisis. Perhaps it would be better said that people experience directly the existentially threatening material crisis and the related crucial cultural contradictions that arise in their social system from that material crisis. Thus, they become congenial to the possibility of a cultural critique and a redefinition of the dominant system's cultural ideas and symbols. When someone from the new group (i.e., a church member) gives a gift to someone in the old group, and the gift resolves a problem the individual or family is facing, then the receiving individual, by reciprocity, is primed for switching her or his cognitive orientation and affiliation to the new ways, to the new cultural paradigm, and to the new symbolism, which has resolved the crisis of the old ways through a gift. Gifting throws the culturally flummoxed individual a reciprocally conditioned lifeline that hauls them into the environment of a new ideology with which that individual can process his or her empirically challenged and disrupted worldview. Many accept that gifted offering as a solution and then convert to the new religion. That, I suggest, is the universal mechanism of Mayas' (and others') religious conversion. When the new ideologies and performance pathways become recognized widely as an acceptable and more probably successful solution to the ills or vexations of a society than the old culture's pathways and guidance symbols, then a transformative revitalization social movement, whether religious or not, has emerged in response to felt crisis.

The most successful of the new religions in Guatemala are the ecstatic Christian Pentecostal practices and ideology, far outstripping membership gains made by the mainline Protestants, Mormons, Jehovah's Witnesses, and others. The new becomes successful, which is to say it is adopted increasingly, because the old society and its ways are clearly under stress and inadequate or irrelevant to the conditions and tasks of current life. Living by the old ways thus threatens the biological existence of adherents to the old ways. Thus, practitioners of the old way of society, or a segment of them, are ripe for massive cognitive transformation via religious conversion because the crisis arose in the presence of, and seemingly as a result of, living the old premises. In this pressure cooker, gifts of healing or other social support exchanged across that old-new boundary lead to premise reorientation and potential problem resolution. The relative success of those who switch, compared to those who do not, can be a further stimulus to conversion.

THE GIFT AS BASIS FOR A THEORY AND DEFINITION OF RELIGION

The importance of gifts is not limited to analysis of the conversion process. I suggest that giving gifts to and expecting reciprocities from nonhuman entities constitutes the universal essence of religion and provides the basis for a definition of religion better than Durkheim's analytically vague and manipulable "sacred and set apart" versus "profane" and ordinary or approachable. Scott and colleagues (this volume) show that the Durkheimian sacred-profane division cannot be maintained in the face of traditionalist Maya practice and cosmology. In quite a number of societies, including Maya Guatemala and the United States, sacred-profane turns out not to be a viable subdivision on which to base a definition of religion.

How might the argument for a new definition of religion proceed? First, culture crisis is always existential crisis. That is because a society's cultural concepts define the nature of existence and provide the symbols for evaluating all decisions in life. If the very precepts by which judgments can be made are called into question by the harsh pinch of material reality, judgments cannot be made comfortably nor easily, for the deciders must choose or experiment with old and new pathways. Uncertainty abounds.

Nor can such decisions be reliably made without the consequence of stern judgment by others. Conflict ensues. Social coherence therefore collapses. In addition, as Marx notes, the suggested paths and evaluative symbols guiding an individual's decisions must in fact provide relief at the subsistence, social structural, and personal security levels. If the existing approach is not able to satisfy, the crisis will be physically felt in addition to being mentally discomforting and socially dysfunctional.

Under such circumstances, either an alternative will be created by charismatic leaders inside the particular society or an alternative will be sought and adopted from outside and vested with charismatic hope and sacred character inside. The latter has been Guatemala's path: people have adopted an available outside pentecostal expression and solution. That will persist until the new forms seem by experience to be unworkable. This charismatic cycle unites the emphases of (1) Weber and Wallace on new cultural ideas and symbols propounded by charismatic leaders, (2) Durkheim and Mauss on societal connectedness, religion as a symbol of society, and reciprocal obligation via the gift, (3) Marx on the survival and success of a mode of economic production that provides for social and biological reproduction in a given material substrate, now called an environment, and (4) Giddens on society's evolution by structuration through myriad individual decisions judged by self and others against evaluative symbols provided by religion. These conduce to an emergence of change, and the process may be further accelerated by additional charismatic innovation.

But is the idea of the gift and reciprocity a sound basis for both a general theory of religion and a theory of religious conversion? I would argue that a theory of how individuals experience religion and how religions change through individual conversion ought to be intrinsically related to what religions are by definition and why they persist. Such a linkage would seem a corollary of Occam's razor. In any event, I agree with Durkheim that the great ideas of humankind and human morality derive from the human experience of society. Obviously, humans experience the necessity of society. They also experience gifting and reciprocity. But how are the gift and reciprocity experienced as necessary derivatives of society? I return now to the linkage between gift and birth.

The idea of the gift is initially experienced—and both literally and mentally conceived—during the process of birth. In all societies, women, in giving birth and in nurturing children, take tremendous risk and offer personal sacrifice. That risk taking on behalf of others—the neonate, the family, the society—is always a gift given. Mothers invest a tremendous effort in the task. Any woman might die in childbirth. They all experience the pain of labor and birth. They deplete their bodies and bones to nourish the neonate and suckling child. They sacrifice and work hard to feed and prepare each child for safe entry into society. That risk taking in childbirth, that self-sacrifice in nursing, that investment in raising a child all constitute a great gift both to the newborn and to society. That makes female sexuality and birth the constitutive gifts that initiate both specific kinship reciprocity and generalized reciprocity in society.

The expected reciprocity resulting from those gifts gets codified in a variety of ways in kinship obligation systems. Lévi-Strauss (1967[1949]) argues that women, *as* gifts, get circulated in systems of generalized reciprocity. Lévi-Strauss, however, got it wrong. Rather, women *create* gifts (and social wealth) by risking childbirth. Lévi-Strauss's mistake—and the great error of misogyny and male dominance—comes when the source of the gift, women, gets given as a gift or treated as an object. As in so many societies, Lévi-Strauss's theory mistakenly objectifies women, subjects them to political subordination in social practice, and fails to recognize adequately the value of their gift to society. The reality is that in childbirth and child raising, women give gifts that are foundationally constitutive of society. Gift giving and expected reciprocity make society possible. Women make society possible. The power of society is, therefore, in the gift (and in women) precisely because the gift entails reciprocity—obligation—as a basic condition of humanity. In this view, women are primary, and men are secondary and ancillary. But how men in society have managed to flip and obscure women's primary and formative centrality to society is a subject beyond the scope of this book.

With the notion of gift giving and reciprocity in place as the basis of society, Durkheim is correct in asserting that other foundational ideas flow from the core birth and kinship experiences. Thus, giving gifts to the unseen of the universe—through sacrifices, libations, promises of service, participation in worship, tithing, and so forth—extends the knowledge inherent in the experience of birthing and raising children within society to the surrounding physical environment, indeed to the universe. Gifting obligates the universe, symbolized as deities, to engage in expected reciprocity with the human givers. The fundamentally human attribute of expected

reciprocity for gifts—derived from the universal experience of birth—domesticates and anthropomorphizes the chance pleasures and pains of life by seeing them as gifts and punishments reciprocated by the unseen powers of the universe responding to the adequacy or inadequacy of human gift giving. This fundamentally religious process of gifting and expectation of reciprocity thus incorporates the entire universe into the realm of human thought and sociality. Durkheim (2001[1912]:110) argues just that in his analysis of the correspondence between animal, plant, and environmental totems and their one-to-one reciprocities with the Australian clans and lineages that are their benefactors via sacrifice, avoidance, and responsibility for protection of particular totems. Gifting and reciprocity thus are core to religion and to all societies, even in Durkheim. Gifting and reciprocity operationalize Horton's (1960:212) definition of religion as "an extension of social relationships beyond the confines of purely human society."

Giving gifts to the unseen—to the earth, to sacred beings, or simply to the nonhuman—via offering, sacrifice, or libation, domesticates and humanizes the earth, the unseen, the universe. Gift giving thus incorporates the universe into human society via the expectation of reciprocity. All the impacts, powers, unknowns, and surprises of human existence in the universe become co-opted into and perceived as reward or punishment reciprocities in the universe's gift-based relationship with humans. Gifting and reciprocity derived from the universal social experience of birth underlie the notion of religious covenant expectations with the powers of the universe. This allows humans to make mutually entailed relationships both with each other and with their world, the universe, the environment about them. In Durkheim's terms, the core social experience of birth enables society to domesticate, socialize, and incorporate the imagined universe in a system of reciprocal expectations. Gifting enables the "covenant with earth and rain," as John Monaghan phrased the Nahuatl understanding in the title of his 1995 book.

Gifting to and reciprocity with the unseen forces of the universe thus define religion and make religion what it is: the symbolic and performative mechanism that connects all that is human with all that is not human, thereby humanizing and bringing into reciprocity and covenant the forces and features of nature, of the nonhuman, however culturally conceived. Thus, gifting to the nonhuman, the defining attribute of religion, makes the nonhuman universe humanlike and covenantal. Gifting and reciprocity, derived from the foundational and universal human experience of birth, anthropomorphize the universe and underlie and sustain the human religious experience.

This approach to religion affirms Durkheim's core idea that all human ideas derive from social experience. The idea of society as the gifted integration of all is indeed the "soul of religion." Thus, religion, as the essential idea and spirit of society, as "the idea which society has of itself," is rooted in the universal experience of birth, protective kinship, and reciprocal obligation through gifting.

This definition of religion as gifting to and reciprocity from the unseen powers of the universe creates an intersection between religion as a shared social experience incorporating the universe, and the individual transformative experience witnessed in conversion. In Sahlins's (1981:33–35, 68; 1985:xiv, xvii, 125) terms, there is a structure of conjuncture, an overlapping or intersection of various societal and individual processes. This conjuncture invites a return to the material presented in the first half of this chapter on gifting as the catalyst of personal conversion. As I have shown for Maya Guatemala, the transformative moment of conversion between alternative religions most often flows out of or is triggered by a gift of service or words—often prayers leading to healing—that offers hope to the perplexed, incapacitated, or otherwise desperate. Ultimately, that new hope is the real gift, more important than the proximate gift of the prayer offered, the sociality of the visit shared, or the relief generated by the healing experienced. Gift giving, and especially the gifting of hope, is the real basis of religious transformation in Maya Guatemala, not market availability and the personal choice to "purchase" a religion. Thus, gift giving—via sacrifice, libation, service, and so on in their many forms across all cultures—is the foundation and defining mark both of all religion and of religious conversion.

CONCLUSION

In this book's introduction I suggested that I did not wish to enter a fight regarding the definition of religion. Nevertheless, I have offered here a definition. That throws me into the fray. Therefore a few observations regarding prior efforts to define religion seem apropos.

My initial definition of religion in the introduction centered on beliefs and actions directed toward nonhuman, empowered beings. That definition parallels Tylor's (1871:1:383–385) classic statement that religion embraces the activities associated with "belief in spiritual beings." Such a definition is fully adequate for discussing the ethnography of Maya beliefs and rituals because Mayas, too, so define religion.

But is such a definition applicable worldwide? Perhaps not, because there seem to be systems, like Theravada Buddhism as described by Herbrechtsmeier (1993), that one would not hesitate to call religious but that seem not to have a deity notion. But the modified definition I have given in this chapter, focused as it is on gift giving and reciprocity with the unseen or nonhuman, avoids requiring a belief in deities. It only requires gift giving directed toward the nonhuman or the usually unseen. This definition does work for Guatemala and its various cultures and ethnicities. It might work universally. Are there any societies that make no offerings to nonliving, nonhuman facets of the universe? I do not know of any, but determining the validity of this approach to the definition of religion across the cultures of the world is a debate for others to undertake.

I have defined religion as the system, symbols, practices, and meanings accompanying gift giving and reciprocity with some portion of the nonhuman universe. What this definition does is move analysis from an emphasis on belief to an emphasis on day-to-day doing. Stringer (2008) suggests that the day-to-day things people do to address the family of concepts one might consider religious are a more important aspect of the ethnography of religion than systematized beliefs regarding those things or than systematized ethical beliefs in general. Indeed, Stringer asserts that providing a universal definition of religion is something of a fool's errand, and he is joined in this view by Herbrechtsmeier (1993). I hope they are not correct or I have joined the parade of fools. Nevertheless, Stringer admits we can see family resemblances sufficient to call something religious behavior, even if we cannot define religion. I, however, think that the family resemblances derive from the inherent linkage of gifting and reciprocity derived from birthing, child raising, family concerns, and aging. These generate the inescapable, similar but not identical, universal experience and understanding of gift giving and reciprocity, which is distributed worldwide.

From the universal risks and gifts of birthing, and the life-cycle necessity of reciprocity, we derive the family of resemblances. These understandings of gift giving and reciprocity—when exercised with regard to the unseen powers or presence of the universe, however it is conceived—domesticate and incorporate that universe into human society. Religion makes society coterminous with the universe via gift giving and expected reciprocity with the nonhuman. My expansionist approach in this chapter perhaps now comes closest to the definition offered by Horton (1960:212) more than sixty years ago: religion consists in the "extension of social relationships beyond the confines of purely human society." I think the only thing I add is the mechanism of that universal extension—the gift-reciprocity complex—and the basis of its derivation in all societies: the experience and management of birth and the protection of human maturation. Regardless of any final definition, I think one can safely say that in the gift and its expected reciprocity, Mauss has indeed identified "one of the human foundations on which our societies"—and, I think he would agree, *all* societies—"are built," for on gifting and reciprocity are built both kinship systems and religion.

Chapter Twenty-Six

Culture Collapse and Exclusion across the Christianized World

JOHN P. HAWKINS

IN THE SPACE OF LESS than 120 years, Christian Pentecostalism has swept the globe, accounting for at least a quarter of the world's roughly 2 billion Christians (Barrett and Johnson 2003:287). Some suggest even more astonishing figures: Garriott and O'Neill (2008:381) indicated that "evangelical Christians" by 2020 might grow to as many as a billion adherents, apparently not even counting Catholic charismatics. If the theory of culture collapse that I developed during my experience with Christian Pentecostalism in the communities of Nahualá and Santa Catarina Ixtahuacán is an insightful approach to this new branch of Christianity, then that approach should help one understand the experience of Christian Pentecostals and the expansion of Christian pentecostalization in other parts of the world. The proof—a soft proof, to be sure—must proceed from cross-cultural comparison. To that end, in this chapter I explore Christian Pentecostalism in additional areas of Guatemala, in other countries of Latin America, in two countries in Africa, in southern India, among the Romas in Europe, and in the United States.

I argue that the social conditions of culture collapse and exclusion are sufficiently widespread to account for the internationalization of the gods of Christian Pentecostalism, which seems to have occurred in the Global South (and beyond) and which Durkheim believes is a general religious process. He writes, "The authority of each of these supreme gods is, moreover, not restricted to a single tribe but is equally recognized by a plurality of neighboring tribes" across "a relatively extended geographical area. Their cults, then, have an international character," and their "religious beliefs display a tendency to resist enclosure in a politically delimited society; they have a

natural aptitude for crossing frontiers, becoming diffused and internationalized" (Durkheim 2001[1912]:212). This internationalization may have occurred because the arrival of British colonialism precipitated stress and the perception of impending culture collapse among all of Australia's Aboriginal peoples and merited similar adjustment cult responses. The internationalization of Christian Pentecostalism, however, came later in the colonial cycle. Christian Pentecostalism's international spread is a revitalization movement response to the tricky transition from collapsing colonialism to expanding capitalist globalism. In short, we are dealing with an internationalized notion of culture collapse, an internationalized notion of exclusion or inaccesibility, and an internationalized applicability of the resulting anxieties experienced and expressed in Christian Pentecostal liturgy.

The details vary from place to place—corn culture collapse here, mining culture collapse there, and so forth. The forms of exclusion differ also. But if the Nahualá/Santa Catarina Ixtahuacán theory is correct, the style of religiously expressed anxiety should be present wherever indigenous cultures and Christianized colonialism are in collapse and capitalist globalism is on the rise. To Durkheim, the image of the gods and the form of ritual practices oriented toward them represent the core ideas that a people have about the nature of the society in which they live. This is clearly so for Nahualá and Santa Catarina Ixtahuacán. Do other Christianized peoples in the Global South share the experiences of culture collapse and exclusion seen in Nahualá and Santa Catarina Ixtahuacán, and thus readily adopt the same gods and ritual style? Here, I examine the evidence, starting with reports on Christian Pentecostalism in other areas of Guatemala and extending from there throughout the Global South and into the Digital North.

PENTECOSTAL RECEPTION IN OTHER PARTS OF GUATEMALA

Beyond the work of Annis (1987), to which I have referred extensively in this book, I explore eight other studies of Pentecostalism in Guatemala. One of them also touches on the Catholic Charismatic Renewal. To what degree do these studies fit the theory I propound?

Almolonga and Zunil

Goldin and her collaborators (Goldin and Saenz de Tejada 1993; Goldin and Metz 1991) present excellent data on the differing percentages of Protestant conversion in two contiguous *municipios* of western highland Guatemala: Almolonga and Zunil. Almolonga, she reports, was in the 1980s about 50 percent Protestant;[1] Zunil, by contrast, was about 10 percent Protestant, with one of her key figures indicating just 5 percent (Goldin and Saenz de Tejada 1993:246). How does my corn shortage and exclusion hypothesis of cultural collapse fare in these two communities?

Goldin asserts no significant differences between the two *municipios* as to the amount of land resources held by the majority of the inhabitants in each. She shows that 70 percent of the inhabitants of Zunil and 86 percent of the inhabitants of Almolonga have less than the one *manzana* of land per family necessary for minimum family subsistence. To her, the 16 percent difference between the two communities seems inconsequential: "There is comparatively little theory that permits us to explain unequal development between towns when the towns are roughly equidistant from the core"—that is, Guatemala City—"and have access to roughly the same resources" (Goldin and Saenz de Tejada 1993:248). To account for the religious difference between "two townships with comparable resources . . . [that are] economically distinct," Goldin and Saenz de Tejada note that the two communities have diverged occupationally. Both used to be largely agricultural. Zunil remained so. Almolonga, by contrast, became more mercantile as a result of its smaller land base. Goldin and Saenz de Tejada hold that this occupational difference led to different cognitive outlooks. Almolongueños developed attributes of individualism, entrepreneurialism, and

risk taking needed to manage their new occupational niche. The researchers suggest that these new occupational outlooks predisposed Almolongueños to accept Protestantism more quickly and thoroughly than did the Mayas of Zunil.

Goldin and Saenz de Tejada's analysis is impressive in most regards. But I disagree with their initial assertion that the two communities access "roughly the same" or "comparable" resources. They do not. When more fully analyzed and treated statistically, the 16 percent difference between the two towns in the number of families having less than a minimum subsistence landholding makes the two *municipios* markedly and significantly different.

Goldin uses the 1980 national population census, which shows 7,000 residents in Zunil and 8,000 in Almolonga. From the percentages she gives of the number of families living below minimum subsistence (and cross-checking this with the agricultural censuses) one can calculate the chi-square probability that the distribution of those with one *manzana* or less is due to chance within similar populations. The chance of randomly drawing this difference from the same population is less than one in a hundred.[2] In a word, it is highly improbable that Almolonga's and Zunil's figures are simply randomly differing samples drawn from a similar pool. Statistically, regarding landholdings, the towns are distinctly different.

To see why the 16 percent difference is critical (as I argue) rather than inconsequential (as Goldin and colleagues argue), I examine in greater detail the distribution of arable land in the two communities versus their populations. In Zunil, the 70 percent of Mayas with less than one *manzana* own just 15 percent of the municipality's total arable land. To make ends meet, they rent from the wealthy Mayas and Ladinos of Zunil, who own the rest of the arable land. Compared to Almolonga, Zunil has a rather plentiful supply. The key facts are that Zunil's arable land base of 890 *manzanas* supports 7,000 people. This works out to 0.76 *manzanas* per household (assuming a 6-person average household size) or 24 percent less than what the state considers sufficient for independent subsistence and 20 percent less than what Annis (1987) calculates to be sufficient for survival. By comparison, in Almolonga, just 259 *manzanas* of arable land support 8,000 residents. That works out to 0.194 *manzanas* per family. Because Zunil's larger arable land base supports a smaller population, no one from Zunil rents land outside the *municipio*. The 25 percent deficit argued here could be met with minimal distress to the social fabric by traveling to a *finca* with other members of the community in a *cuadrilla* (squad, truckload of workers). Beyond that, no one had to supplement what was offered by the lands available in the municipality. Zunil as a *municipio* thus remains nominally self-contained (even though ownership of the land is unevenly distributed), relatively autonomous, and agricultural. So Zunil has remained largely corn-growing, with but 4 percent of the land in annuals devoted to truck crops in 1950 and 10 percent of its annuals in truck crops by 1964.

In Almolonga, by contrast, those who have one *manzana* or less (86 percent of the households) own 52 percent of the *municipio*'s arable land base. The remainder (48 percent of Almolonga's 259 arable *manzanas*) is owned by a few larger landowners (14 percent of the population). In Almolonga, the entire population has one-fifth of the arable land necessary for minimum subsistence. This means that 86 percent of the households of Almolonga own, on average, just 0.117 *manzana* each (at six people per family), or slightly more than a tenth of what is needed for minimum subsistence. Moreover, by renting from their richer peers inside the *municipio*, Almolongueños can achieve no better than a fifth of a *manzana* each, on average. This is far below the minimum called for by the state or by Annis (see chapter 17 of this volume). Thus, in Almolonga, the majority of those with less than one *manzana* cannot rent sufficient land in the *municipio* to make up the deficit in land needed for family self-sufficiency. Given Almolonga's population, the culturally essential arable land simply does not exist in the municipality.[3]

There are additional ways to look at Goldin's data that indicate considerable crisis in Almolonga compared to Zunil. One method is to compare the total land base, including available forest. Almolonga has a total land base of twenty square kilometers, giving it a density of 400 people per square kilometer. Zunil's total area of ninety square kilometers gives it a much lower density of 78 people per square kilometer. Thus, Zunil has 5.1 times more resources per capita in total arable land, pasture, and forest with which to buffer and supplement its 24 percent shortfall in arable land than Almolonga has to buffer its 80 percent shortfall in arable land (Morales Urrutia 1961:2:168 for municipal areas).[4] Far from being about equal in resources to Almolonga, Zunil has per capita more than five times the total land resources with which to mitigate its 25 percent arable land deficit.

To make ends meet, Almolonga's Mayas have been forced to diversify occupationally. They have moved toward farming vegetables for cash rather than raising corn for family consumption. They have entered motorized trucking and commercial trade. They have had to buy and rent much land outside their *municipio*. Indeed, 13 percent of Almolonga's arable land base of 259 *manzanas* was devoted to vegetable truck crops in 1964, and much more of it by Goldin's 1980–1988. Almolonga is thus more dependent on market prices and connections to points of sale.

In my judgment, the difference between Zunil's and Almolonga's available land base for the maintenance of a corn-based culture is stark. Even though an ostensibly similar and rather large percentage of both *municipios*' inhabitants—70 versus 86 percent—live below the subsistence survival level of lands owned, the amount of land per capita available for rental in each *municipio* to remedy that ownership shortfall is radically different. Almolonga residents have been forced by land shortage and greater population to break the indigenous paradigm of corn farming and municipal autonomy. They cannot subsist on corn grown in their own *municipio*. They must work and own or rent arable land outside of their *municipio*. In Zunil, by contrast, residents have been able to preserve the indigenous premise of self-containment by renting land from others still living in the *municipio*.

Evidently, Almolonga residents suffer a severe land and corn deficit compared to Zunil residents. The 86 percent of Almolonga's families that live below subsistence maintenance are about ten times worse off than the 70 percent of Zunil's families below subsistence regarding the rentable land in their *municipio*. Almolonga has long been in clear subsistence crisis whereas Zunil is only at the brink of crisis. This land-access disparity fully accounts for the difference in the degree of Protestantization that Goldin reports: Almolonga stands at 50 percent Protestant, including comparatively early first adoption, while Zunil stands at 5–10 percent Protestant, with later first adoption and slower expansion.

I emphasize that the issue driving change to Protestantism in Almolonga is culture collapse and not poverty. Almolongueños are much better off monetarily than the people of Zunil. Indeed, Almolonga has something of a propertied middle class compared to Zunil, but its property is in ten-ton trucks and houses and not in *milpas*. Almolongueños have a thriving trucking and vegetable production industry because they cannot make it on corn, the *axis mundi* of traditionalist Maya Catholic existence and thought. Almolongueños simply do not have the land needed to sustain a corn-based culture or a traditionalist internal and municipal orientation. Nor do Almolongueños have an economic base compatible with the Ortho-Catholic symbols of hierarchy, as Goldin makes clear. Almolongueños must be buyers, sellers, and travelers. They must be in contact with external markets and cannot be isolated corn farmers. They must be on the go, connected, and mercantile. Zunil's corn can be dried and stored for the year; Almolonga's vegetables spoil if not transported and sold immediately. The Almolongueños' mode of production requires independence from hierarchy because they survive now by transporting and selling perishable products in global markets. The Catholic hierarchical orientation does not fit so well. Almolonga is thus in the midst of a severe existential crisis regarding corn and a collapse of its local orientation.

What about exclusion? Almolongueños appear not to be excluded from participation in global markets. They have used their vegetable production to diversify into trading and have carved out a relatively comfortable and less poverty-stricken lifestyle than the people of Zunil have, partly because of the sobriety, work ethic, and commercial networks induced by Protestantism. Almolongueños also seem to be making substantial inroads into education and job diversification.[5] The fact is, however, that Almolongueños fit in the modern world as they did in the colonial one—as the larger system's beasts of burden. Today, Almolongueños load into the trucks they own what they used to load onto their backs or the backs of mules or horses they owned. But Almolongueños still carry and deliver Guatemala's heavy burdens, and in that regard, although richer, they are structurally not much changed from their colonial status. They remain excluded from education, health, and political strength.

In sum, in Almolonga I see a massive resource dissimilarity in land and resources per capita driving collapse of the corn culture. That then drives occupational diversification, economic reorientation, and religious transformation simultaneously and synergistically, such that all the rest of Goldin and Saenz de Tejada's (1993) analysis is absolutely spot-on.

Presbyterian Protestantism and Pentecostal Derivatives in the Department of Quetzaltenango

For the region of Quetzaltenango (which includes Zunil and Almolonga), Bogenschild (1992) shows how mainstream Presbyterian beginnings soon indigenized and morphed into Pentecostal success. In Green's (1993:168–169) summary of Bogenschild, she attributes Protestantization to the disorganization induced "by the disruptive effects of the coffee-boom," which precipitated land expropriations, internal migration, neglect of local fields, low yields, and other issues. "The development of coffee production, the construction of roads, and military conscription displaced economic practices and forms of social organization in the entire western region. The expansion of the Presbyterian mission was rapid and notable in those communities most disrupted by the changes," which forced "impoverished Guatemalans" to "turn to Protestantism not for reasons of social mobility but for basic survival needs." The processes led to "severe loss of corporate community control" and diminished municipal autonomy (168–169).

Samson (2007) and Scotchmer (1986, 1989, 2001) provide the best local ethnographies of mainstream Presbyterianism and its evolution into Pentecostal forms throughout the area. Both Samson and Scotchmer served as missionaries and ministers in the Presbyterian faith before engaging in anthropological research on the administrative and cultural status of Protestantism in this area. Samson's is a decidedly more administrative and institutional account, but he occasionally details the local ethnography of Presbyterian and Pentecostal practice. He confirms my observations, for example, by noting that "small, colorful *templos* . . . dot the contemporary landscape of Guatemala . . . [and] can be spotted from two mountain ridges away because of their bright color amid the earth-colored adobe houses" (Samson 2007:84) and that "evangelicals of all stripes tend to form their religious identity" both behaviorially and symbolically "in contradistinction to Catholicism as well as indigenous religious traditions" (85). Samson notes the Protestant emphasis on "the word," highlighting biblical literacy in programs and the visual and verbal symbols that adorn Protestant *templos* (86–87). His pictures (but not his text) show the huge speakers and electronic amplification of meetings (e.g., his figure 11). Above all, he confirms that even the denominationally named and closely supervised Presbyterian congregations, which he considers mainline and traditionally Protestant, "have a rather informal, if consistent, liturgy and a very Pentecostal 'feel' in terms of style of prayer and the music that is played and sung," with electronic bands and audience participation (90). He continues with a crucial axis of reorientation: "although most services build toward the sermon, as is traditional in Presbyterianism, liturgical practice has clearly been shaped in the local context, where Pentecostal forms are quite prevalent" (91). In short, the denominationally and nominally Presbyterian mainline rural congregations that are counted as Protestant and non-Pentecostal have become quite pentecostalized, as I have argued. Thus, when Scotchmer analyzes his figures on ministerial styles, one can be fairly certain that the "democratic" style of leadership in the large congregations comprising about a third of the area's Protestants, which Scotchmer implies is a more traditional Presbyterian leadership style than the more Pentecostal forms of "hierarchical" and "authoritarian" leadership guiding other split-off congregations, is in fact leading a substantially pentecostal variant of worship in spite of formal names and administrative effort to the contrary (Scotchmer 2001:237–243).

Just how well the culture collapse and exclusion hypothesis fits, I am unable to determine from Samson's and Scotchmer's materials. Both throughout have fleeting references to cultural difficulties, pressures from Ladino society, poverty, and lack of indigenous access. One would have to say that their research reflects the general indigenous condition, and with regard to that, I feel I have proved my case. Local and state social controls have indeed decayed. Today, the state and the economy remain ineffective in indigenous communities (Hawkins, McDonald, and Adams 2013; McDonald and Hawkins 2013a, 2013b, 2013c; Dracoulis et al. 2013; Bybee et al. 2013). The boisterous cry of pentecostalization voices the biting angst of this cultural collapse and exclusion, even in "mainline Protestant" indigenous Presbyterian congregations studied by mainline minister-anthropologists. That cry is not limited to the western highlands. One also finds echoes of this analysis reverberating through early studies of religious change in the Petén.

The Petén

Reina and Schwartz (1974) discuss aspects of Protestantization in four *municipios* in the Petén, based on fieldwork done in 1960. Only three of the *municipios* had sufficient data for me to work with here: Flores, San Andrés, and San José. Among other things, their nuanced study of Protestant reception in the region confirms the Saussurean insight that the religions and towns in an area must be treated as sets and studied by comparison and contrast if one is to extract full meaning from them. Indeed, the four towns and three religions discussed by Reina and Schwartz (1974:162–163) contrast with each other both in practice and in stereotype. These issues of community context bear on the differential rates at which residents in these towns have accepted Protestantism.

San José is the least transformed, least collapsed, and most Maya of the four towns. It has the highest percentage of corn farmers. Moreover, when the corn supply is insufficient, its residents have ready access to and skilled knowledge of the vast Petén forest, which they can use to make ends meet nutritionally or economically. Indeed, Reina and Schwartz (1974) find San José to be the most traditional town, remarking that this judgment is reflected in local stereotype: the religious practices of Joseños are seen as "traditional" in the sense of being not "Ortho-Catholic" rather than being definitively "ancient Maya." Compared to residents of the other towns, Joseños least orient to or interest themselves in modernization and change. As of the fieldwork in the 1960s, the Joseño cultural basis of subsistence had not collapsed, and San José remained virtually 100 percent "folk Catholic" (corresponding to my category of traditionalist Catholic).

Flores is the next least Protestant of the four communities. Economically and politically, it is the apex of local power and the department center. In 1960, it remained 95.5 percent Catholic, with the rest Protestant. Essentially, Flores retained its superior status over the peasant towns of the region: there was no collapse of the elite governing culture. Nevertheless, Reina and Schwartz (1974) identify sectors of the Flores population where Protestantism appeals. Specifically, Protestantism attracts people from the middle class striving for modernization yet excluded by the elite. It provides a vehicle for expressing dissatisfaction regarding the constraints and limitations of the still-enduring colonial system. That reaction to the restraints of the system fits my proposition regarding exclusion, although middle-class Ladino exclusion in 1960s Flores seems not as strongly experienced as was indigenous exclusion in early 2000s Nahualá and Santa Catarina Ixtahuacán.

The third town Reina and Schwartz (1974) discuss, indigenous San Andrés, saw early and rather substantial Protestantization—25 percent by 1960. San Andrés of 1960 was modernizing in the sense of supporting more migrants and greater ethnic complexity, and its residents sought access to Ladino and western products and institutions. Its leaders found ways to install more amenities in their community center than other hinterland towns had acquired. But its residents, I submit, felt both impending collapse and exclusion. San Andrés made almost a complete language shift to Spanish in spite of the fact that a third of its adult residents spoke but did not regularly use a Maya language. Rapid rural transformation took several other forms, and 20 percent of residents were recent Q'eqchi' immigrants. The residents of San Andrés had entered the market as "economic individualists with strong market orientations. They [would] sell large amounts of produce, such as corn, particularly in Flores" (Reina and Schwartz 1974:170), along with their labor. They raised and sold truck crops. They clearly transferred their orientation to the city, finding that work in offices and other urban sites was more prestigious, desirable, and congenial than the dignified, honorable, but difficult labor in the fields.

Were the residents of San Andrés at subsistence risk? Reina and Schwartz (1974) do not give enough information. Could the residents of San Andrés have expanded their land at will and hived off families to clear forest and farm? The authors do not say, but in the 1960s land in the Petén was readily available, which works against my theory. Could the residents of San Andrés have easily used the forest resources, as did the residents of San José? They might not have had the knowledge base. Did they perceive the end of an agricultural life? Apparently so. At least, they greatly diminished their reliance on corn subsistence.

What is clear is that San Andreños "frequently express[ed] dissatisfaction with their level of life, and the economic disparities in the community and between the town and Flores contribute[d] to the discontent. People want[ed] to raise their own standard of living and also want[ed] to match the level of wealthier townsmen and Florenses. Economic disparities, 'selfishness' among the rich, and endemic envy [were] common topics of conversation" (Reina and Schwartz 1974:172). Such comments seem to confirm San Andreños' relative exclusion from the larger society. Indeed, Reina and Schwartz (1974:172) note that "by the late 1920s, the younger Mayeros were not culturally distinguishable from the Ladinos, and by the late 1940s, San Andrés was a thoroughly Ladino town; nevertheless, the Mayeros remained subordinate." In the regional mix of prejudices and economic challenges, the Mayero residents of San Andrés were indeed excluded, and Reina and Schwartz detail how Flores elites repeatedly blocked the transformational initiatives of the surrounding, more Mayero towns. Moreover, the fact that "by the late 1920s, the younger Mayeros were not culturally

distinguishable from the Ladinos," such that "by the late 1940s, San Andrés was a thoroughly Ladino town," suggests a rather rapid cultural collapse and transformation in the space of about twenty years.[6]

Urban Guatemala

Three studies of the place of Protestantism in Guatemala City—Roberts (1968), Gooren (1999), and O'Neill (2010)—complement the rural or small-town indigenous studies. They deserve analysis in part because I have suggested that much of my theoretical framework applies not just to the Mayas, but also to Guatemala's urban poor, in part because many residents of Guatemala City or their forebears are recent migrants from Maya regions. Moreover, the Pentecostal religious interest has moved upward in class. Althoff (2014:285n844) cites a Stoll (1994:108) interviewee who asserts that neo-Pentecostal megachurch members might comprise as much as 5 percent of Guatemala's middle and upper classes, while neo-Pentecostal and Pentecostal members comprise about 30 percent of Guatemala's urban poor.

Way (2012) delivers a social history of Guatemala City that documents the conditions of social collapse faced by the urban poor, the vast majority of Guatemala City's residents, a noticeable percentage of whom were turning Pentecostal by the time of Roberts's fieldwork in the mid-1960s. Way (2012:2, 5) calls poorer parts of the city "a manmade ruin" whose "citizens [have] outpaced the state's ability and willingness to meet their demands" and describes chaos, governmental collapse, and systemic exclusion of poor people from their dream to self-improve (*desarrollarse*). Clearly, for the Maya migrants in the slums, the collapse of corn culture independence is complete.

Way (2012:85) describes the "precariousness of life" among urban families, where "starvation wages . . . confronted people, many of them coming from a fading life of semi-self-sufficiency in the country." "Where labor is worth nothing . . . the social conditions . . . tend to break families and communities apart"; "women had it worse than men, and . . . children had it worst of all" (85, 87). "In twentieth-century Guatemala," writes Way (2012:88), "misery bred chaos, established it as order, and reproduced it in an evolving social landscape." Thus, "from the end of the [1950s] forward, Guatemala City exploded in size and, as part of that dynamic, exploded in misery. From the beginning of the sixties it erupted in violence"

(98). In short, Way provides plenty of material to affirm both social collapse and exclusion in the urban setting.

I use Way's (2012) broader historical context and Roberts's (1973) own ethnography of urban life to help interpret and flesh out what Roberts (1968) writes about Protestantism in two slums of Guatemala City. There, the percentage of adherents of Pentecostal Protestantism is ten times higher than in the country as a whole. In the residential areas studied by Roberts, Pentecostals comprise "approximately 60 percent of Protestants in the sample," with the rest consisting of Jehovah's Witnesses, Seventh-day Adventists, and Southern Baptists. "Only the Presbyterians" provide a historic (and possibly sedate) mainline Protestant presence (Roberts 1968:753n2). Roberts finds doctrinal difference of no practical effect on the parishioners. What is important is that small Protestant congregations and intercongregational visiting provide connections that stabilize recently arrived or otherwise tenuously situated urban residents. Job information, social relationships, healings, and mutual support against vice figure prominently in Roberts's description. His analysis of urban Pentecostalism seems, sociologically, to match what our field school reported fifty years later in rural indigenous areas, in spite of the fact that his urbanites seem little connected to their indigenous roots.

But does this evidence a collapsed cultural or subsistence system? Certainly, the people he studied live an extremely precarious economic life in the city, trying to subsist on petty commerce and occasional jobs. Moreover, "the overwhelming majority of heads of family in this sample are migrants" who came to the city from rural areas of Guatemala. "With one or two exceptions, the entire sample of migrants has made a decision to settle permanently in the city. They have no economic ties (such as land) with their region of origin. These migrants had come to the city because of the difficulty of making a living in the countryside with its low plantation wages; some had come from small farms where land is poor and conditions not suitable for cultivation. In almost all cases, their parents had been small farmers," who were pushed out of their former agricultural way of life by its subsistence untenability (Roberts 1968:756). These urban Guatemalans cannot gain adequate access to the national system; therefore, they avail themselves of the social networking opportunities in Evangelical Protestant or Pentecostal congregations to help keep themselves marginally employed. In my view, Pentecostalism mitigates their exclusion and expresses the pain of that experience.

Henri Gooren (1999) explores the impact of religion on entrepreneurial enterprise and on family organization among Pentecostals in Guatemala City. Through interviews and participant observation, Gooren shows that Pentecostals' avoidance of alcohol and their attention to the welfare of the family as a central male obligation have major consequences on family well-being among those in either the ecstatic Pentecostal or the sedate Mormon fold. A reading of Gooren's life histories suggests, again, that social and economic crisis has led to conversion to Pentecostal congregations and that the Pentecostals he studied are for the most part excluded in some practical sense from connecting with the neoliberal global economic system.

In what is arguably the most sophisticated and interesting study of Pentecostalism in the Guatemalan literature, O'Neill (2010) describes the lives, beliefs, and practices of people engaged with a showy urban neo-Pentecostal megachurch. In outlining "Christian citizenship," O'Neill also paints a thorough picture of neo-Pentecostal belief and practice. The church service is loud, theatrical, and filled with amplified music and images. Prayers often include speaking in tongues. The preaching emphasizes that the individual is responsible for the self and that in disciplining oneself into a condition of correct morality, one improves the nation. Indeed, in O'Neill's description, almost all individual activity is motivated by the idea of saving or improving Guatemala by saving or improving oneself.[7]

O'Neill (2010), Way (2012), and others (O'Neill and Thomas 2011; McAllister and Nelson 2013; Schirmer 1998; Glebbeek 2003; Weld 2014; Levenson 2013; Brenneman 2012) make a well-founded case for the collapse and exclusion theory as an explanation of pentecostal angst in the urban milieu. These conditions also help one to understand neo-Pentecostalism's emerging emphasis on health, wealth, modernization, and development, as well as its appeal among the growing rich, who face the possibility that Guatemala's enormous uncertainty and chaos might undermine their presently favorable situation. This, I submit, accounts for the presence of the estimated 5 percent of the rich who participate in the urban, megachurched neo-Pentecostal faith in Guatemala.

Regional Studies in Guatemala

Althoff's (2014) work diverges from the more typical anthropological approach of studying just one religious group or denomination in just one community. She successfully studies all the main strands of religious practice and philosophy across the nation as a whole, emphasizing the western region that includes the Departments of San Marcos, Huehuetenango, and Quetzaltenango. She interviews adherents and presents a historical ethnography of Maya Catholicism, Ortho-Catholicism, Catholic Action, and charismatic *renovación* Catholicism; the Maya spirituality movement; and Guatemalan Pentecostalism, including mainline Protestantism, denominational Pentecostalism, independent Pentecostalism, and megachurch neo-Pentecostalism.

Althoff's (2014) ethnography and Early's books (2006, 2012) on the historical evolution and more recent practice of Catholicism constitute the best we have on the spectrum of belief and practice in Catholicism. However, Althoff's observations of the many strands of Catholicism and the varieties of Pentecostalism as presently lived are not adequately deep. She provides no interpretation of the meanings embedded in Pentecostalism and simply suggests that it works by suppressing costly and destructive vices and because its leaders responded effectively to the 1976 earthquake and the disruptions of the war in the 1980s. Although her study is richly textured and its subjects provocatively and productively interrelated, Althoff depends too much on the unquestioned assertions in the literature that Pentecostalism flourished because of disruption via quake and war. She does not address the evolving crisis of Maya social and subsistence systems, perhaps because she orients toward issues of ethnic separation and identity maintenance. Thus, I do not see in Althoff the data needed to argue for or against my theories.

In sum, except for indeterminacy on the matter in Althoff's study, it appears that the culture collapse and exclusion approach insightfully organizes the broad swath of data in the aforementioned studies of Pentecostalism in Guatemala.

PENTECOSTALISM ACROSS LATIN AMERICA

I turn now to a consideration of pentecostalism in other parts of Latin America, but with two provisos. First, Guatemala's *renovación* Catholic charismaticism has hardly been studied, as Althoff (2014) makes plain. The same is true regarding the Catholic Charismatic Renewal in the rest of Latin America. Consequently, unless otherwise indicated, the remainder of this section assesses the validity of my theory regarding collapse, exclusion, and uncertainty in relation to Protestant-derived Pentecostalisms, which are relatively well documented with ethnographies. Second, there is more material than I can cover in this book. Therefore, I have selected a sample of the literature from four Latin American countries—El Salvador, Chile, Bolivia, and Brazil—which have ample ethnographic material on religious change and Pentecostalism.

El Salvador

El Salvador mirrors Guatemala regarding the timing and social conditions of its movement toward Evangelicalism. There are, however, important differences. First, El Salvador no longer has a prominent indigenous population since they were largely, though not completely, exterminated in massacres during the 1930s. The remaining, largely non-indigenous peasant sector experienced the collapse of its corn-land balance and exclusion from access to contemporary society because of at least three factors. First, peasant corn agriculture wilted in the face of coffee expansion (Wilson 1983:187–188). Second, Salvadoran peasants experienced a fast-rising population, especially from 1950 to the present. Third, they lived through a terrifying civil war in the 1980s. These factors produced periods of profound chaos and insecurity. Precisely in these periods of culture collapse, Pentecostal Protestant membership surged.

As in Guatemala, an elite rush to wealth via coffee cultivation precipitated a crisis in the peasant way of life. "Beginning in the 1880s, successive regimes abolished communally owned Indian lands and forced subsistence farmers"—corn farmers—"to plant coffee trees. Coffee income grew as a percentage of export revenues from 50 percent in the 1880s to 94 percent in the 1930s and the acreage planted to the crop led to [it increasing] by one half in the years between 1917 and 1934" (Wilson 1983:187). Wilson quotes an early twentieth-century newspaper editor who observed that around 1883, "the land in the country was distributed among the majority of the Salvadorans, but now it is falling into the hands of a few owners" (Wilson 1983:188, citing *Patria*, December 29, 1928, 1). A different observer noted: "The conquest of territory by the coffee industry is alarming. It has already occupied all the high ground and is now descending to the valleys, displacing corn, rice and beans. It goes in the manner of the conquistador, spreading hunger and misery, reducing the former proprietors to the worst conditions" (Wilson 1983:188, citing *Patria*, January 17, 1929, 4). That seems rather like a collapse of the subsistence system among the peasant masses.

What about exclusion? Wilson reports that the Pentecostal movement had its greatest success among poor people in rural areas and in the urban peripheries and slums. He suggests that "educational statistics of the republic were even more dismal than those reported for Guatemala and Honduras, and health services were confined to the folk medicine of the curanderos" (Wilson 1983:188). To keep the masses from rising up, the government engaged in suppression of any form of mass movement; it executed villagers involved in protest or political movements, and it exterminated indigenes in the 1930s. These practices continued into the 1980s. It would appear that in El Salvador, there was indeed corn subsistence collapse and attendant cultural chaos accompanied by exclusion from participation in the new forms of wealth or subsistence production, even though the surviving rural peasant populace was much less indigenous and might not have placed corn at the center of myth and ritual practice as the Mayas did in Guatemala.

Mainline Protestantism entered El Salvador rather like it did in Guatemala: during the 1880s liberal reform movement's effort to undermine Catholic power and acquire coffee lands. But Wilson (1983) shows that Protestantism's growth quickly "plateaued" at one-tenth of a percent and stayed flat until the 1940s. What blossomed, however, were the Pentecostals. Starting in 1915, they planted congregations and grew prodigiously, training and advancing native leaders in the process. From 1935 (membership of 2,000) to 1981 (membership of 75,000), the Asamblea de Dios, the main Pentecostal denomination, doubled every ten years at a compound growth rate of slightly more than 7.2 percent per annum, which was a bit over twice the overall population growth rate. Other congregations probably did as well or better, splitting and expanding to plant new self-sustaining congregations.

Wilson (1983:189) describes 1980s Salvadoran Pentecostal services as "extended prayer sessions, developing occasionally into boisterous displays of emotion, tongues, and ecstasy. Members perceived these episodes of visions, weeping, and healings, accompanied by a sense of prophetic power, as self-authenticating evidence of divine presence." These details parallel Pentecostal practice and perception in Nahualá and Santa Catarina.

For the 1980s, I use Coleman and colleagues' (1993) survey data on religion in El Salvador. In their table 4-1, they show that Protestants have the lowest mean and median income of the religious categories they studied. For survey purposes, they divided respondents' options into four categories: non-affiliators (i.e., asserting no denominational affiliation), Protestants, nonpracticing Catholics, and practicing Catholics (Coleman et al. 1993:114 and table 4-1). Salvadoran Protestants are uniformly poor, with the lowest mean wealth and the lowest standard deviation. Practicing Catholics, by contrast, have the highest recorded wealth, followed by nonpracticing cultural Catholics. Protestants are most like non-affiliators (as distinct from non-attending cultural Catholics) and most different from the wealthiest, who are practicing Catholics (Coleman et al. 1993:114). Coleman and colleagues' data tabulations are statistically significant at robust levels under chi-square analysis, and they position Protestants as the poorest (Coleman et al. 1993:114 and table 4-1), least educated (116 and table 4-2), and second to the least professional (117 and table 4-3), with practicing Catholics the highest in each of these categories by a substantial margin. The frequent similarity between Protestants and non-affiliators in these data sets suggests that Protestants and non-affiliators engaged in a parallel protest or search for new paradigms. This is consistent with my suggestion that Protestantism and indigenized Pentecostalism constitute alternative movements of revolution and labor protest as compared to conflictive aspects of secular revolution and confrontive aspects of secular (but also often Catholic-rooted) labor protest.

Coleman and colleagues' concepts are not exactly analogous with mine, but their finding of lowest income among Protestants (who are, in all likelihood, mostly Pentecostals) corresponds with the collapse of the economy, while the fact that Protestants are both lowest in income and lowest in education correlates with my notion of exclusion from the new order. Coleman and colleagues (1993:131–132) conclude that Protestants in El Salvador "are recruited from the poorest and least educated elements of Salvadoran society," and "contrary to Weberian visions of a Protestant ethic lifting poor converts into higher social strata, our data give little sign that Protestantism has led to upward social mobility in El Salvador."

Coleman and colleagues' pessimism regarding economic improvement under Protestantism in El Salvador contrasts sharply with Brusco's (1993) more positive and intimate ethnographic picture of conversion in Colombia.

Brusco shows that when husbands convert—often years after the wife's conversion—there results an immediate 20–40 percent savings of money not spent on alcohol. Yet more is saved by prohibitions on smoking, gambling, and prostitutes and the prohibition of or disengagement from maintaining secondary concubinage households (Brusco 1993:147). I would add that conversion and transformation probably save the family from loss of work and therefore loss of wages consequent to the incapacities inherent in the aforementioned male behaviors. However, Brusco does not affirm a societal economic change: "Such consumption patterns may not create new economic opportunities in the sense of having a transformative effect on the economy. Yet they often help particular families achieve upward mobility, or at least greater financial security" (150). Sexton (1978) and Annis (1987) affirm substantial familial economic improvement resulting from conversion to Pentecostal Protestantism.

What might account for Coleman and colleagues' divergent view that there is "little sign" of upward mobility or improvement, compared to the more optimistic findings of Weber, Brusco, Sexton, Annis, and others who affirm that Protestantization confers economic advantages? First, the factors advanced by Weber—Calvin's ideas about individualist orientation, occupation as a divine calling, and wealth used productively as manifesting one's election—took some three centuries before they generated a full-blown industrial economy in northern Europe. By contrast, the Pentecostal movement in Latin America has just completed a century of nominal presence and only a half century of exponential growth. It remains a minority presence in the region. Nor has any Latin American country adopted Pentecostalism as its state religion, although Guatemala came close to state fosterage of evangélico religion during the Ríos Montt regime, followed less intensely by Evangelicals Serrano Elías and later Morales.

Second, the survey methodology Coleman and colleagues used in El Salvador missed the fact that Protestant conversion might lead to greater household wealth at a subsequent time. It does so for two reasons. First, there is a time delay between conversion and wealth development that a one-shot questionnaire cannot easily assess. The family savings from reduced alcohol consumption and womanizing that Brusco and others talk about only comes after male household heads convert and change their behavior. The ethnographic record and three of the chapters in this volume (Smith et al., and Thompson et

al., by inference from twice as many women attending as men; and Huddleston et al.) confirm that men's conversion to either Catholic- or Protestant-derived pentecostalisms often follows years after women's conversion (although Jones et al., this volume, find that in Antigua Ixtahuacán in the congregations studied, men generally converted first). Given that women lead many Protestant households while men are absent or nonfunctional, one would not expect to see much improvement economically in households that are—and are likely to remain—led by women. In a word, improvement will be evident only in a percentage of households (most likely those with intact marriages in which the husband also converts), not uniformly in all of them, and even then only some years later.

Next and more important, in a one-time survey any economic improvement subsequent to the conversion of intact couples would be masked by the exponential membership increase drawn from the poor, who most need the congregational support system and who would constitute the bulk of any sample. The improvements that older converts may have experienced would be hidden in the averages generated by the many new converts who are desperately poor. Thus, to prove a Weberian impact on families using survey techniques, one would have to elicit data on length of time since conversion and to acquire estimates of preconversion and current incomes. To my knowledge, neither length of membership data nor self-reported income before and after conversion have been reported anywhere. Given this absence, the case study methods of ethnography, which develop family histories, would seem to provide the more reliable data regarding improvement through time. In all probability, family economies improve through time following some male conversions, *and* researchers are unable to isolate that improvement in surveys during expansionary phases marked by the rapid intake of poor people during crisis, collapse, and exclusion. This quibble aside, Coleman and colleagues' data suggest that the experience of Salvadoran Protestants (who are primarily Pentecostals) does indeed confirm my collapse and exclusion analysis.

Chile

Chile has a long history of Protestant and Pentecostal engagement. Indeed, Chile fostered both the earliest acceptance of Pentecostalism in Latin America and the earliest academic examinations of that movement in Latin America (Willems 1967; D'Epinay 1969), as well as later studies.

By comparing religious change in Brazil and Chile, Willems early recognized the importance of Protestantism as a social movement throughout Latin America. "In both countries the rapid diffusion of evangelizing Protestantism, particularly of its Pentecostal versions, was found to be concomitant with the processes of urbanization and industrialization. In both countries the largest concentrations of Protestants are located in the most urbanized and industrialized areas, while in regions characterized by a continuing predominance of the traditional social order, the number of Protestants has remained comparatively small" (Willems 1967:92). Moreover, "the rapid increase of the Pentecostal sects seems to be related to the presence of numerous rural migrants" (93). Protestantism flourishes in "rural frontier areas" that are being settled by migrants from a variety of sources. In other words, where people have been pushed out of a culture and means of self-support by economic and cultural failure, and where, as migrants, they are trying to form a new way of life, the Pentecostal variant of Protestantism takes root and helps people to negotiate change and build a stable social platform for their disrupted lives. Thus, Willems (1967:122–123) confirms my analysis (or rather, I confirm his) when he says, "The rapid expansion of the Pentecostal sects" occurs among "people exposed to the brunt of cultural changes which they neither control nor understand."

Willems's study, however, does not deal with the conditions that generated migration to the cities. Presumably something dislodged these migrants from their rural way of life and pushed them into urban poverty. I suspect my notion of way-of-life collapse in the rural domain applies. It is hard to imagine that so many would have migrated simply because modernity attracted them out of a perfectly viable and sustainable agriculture system. In Willems's study, however, the reasons for migration away from rural areas remain unstated, and as a result the notion of a way-of-life collapse at the rural origin remains implicit.

For a good ethnography of modern-period Pentecostalism in Chile, I turn to Lindhart's *Power in Powerlessness: A Study of Pentecostal Life Worlds in Urban Chile.* Lindhardt (2012:11) studied the Evangelical Pentecostal Church of Chile over a period of seventeen months between 1999 and 2009. He argues that Pentecostalism is an agentive mechanism for dealing with extremely chaotic and uncertain social conditions. The "most active" of the congregants he studied "belong to the lower socioeconomic sectors of society" (12).

According to Lindhardt (2012:37), "early historical Protestant churches were clearly foreign imports and only managed to attract very few Chilean converts." Historical Protestantism "found sympathy among intellectual liberal elites," whereas "Pentecostalism was from the beginning the religion of the *bajo pueblo* (the low or humble people)" (37). The parallels with historic Protestantism's theological and logocentric incompatibility with Maya culture seem obvious. The introduction of mainline Protestantism had little impact on Chile. Adherents constituted but 1 percent of the population in 1907 (34). Chile's Pentecostalism, by contrast, "was not a missionary import but was born out of a local schism within the Methodist Episcopal Church." In 1910 an American missionary couple, Willis C. and Mary Anne H. Hoover, and their followers founded the first independent Pentecostal church of Latin America.[8]

At first, Pentecostal growth in Chile was slow. "In the 1930s, Chile had become an urban and industrialized nation after three decades of internal migration" (Lindhardt 2012:37). That rapid rural to urban shift amounted to a culture and lifeway collapse. Although a significant middle class arose in the process, "the *bajo pueblo* was mainly left to 'watch the processes of democratization and modernization . . . from the sidelines'" (Lindhardt 2012:38, quoting Sepúlveda 1996:310). To put this in my terminology, the *bajo pueblo* was excluded. "In this context of wide-reaching societal transformations, Pentecostalism started growing, especially after 1940. In 1960, Protestants made up 5.6 percent of the Chilean population" (Lindhardt 2012:38, citing Sepúlveda 1996:317). "Most Pentecostal converts came from the marginal sectors of Chilean society and did not belong to the skilled proletarian working class" (Lindhardt 2012:38). Independent, indigenized Chilean Pentecostalism represented those substantially excluded from Chile's rapid modernization process. They were the *bajo pueblo* who watched "from the sidelines"—an apt expression of both collapse and exclusion.

Protestants constituted 6.7 percent of the Chilean population in 1970. Lindhardt (2012) carefully documents how Chileans feared civil war, on the one hand, and experienced tremendous dislocations, on the other. For the rich, life in Chile under Augusto Pinochet got decidedly better. For the poor, however, life got much worse and became highly unpredictable. Social security was privatized. Modernization brought fuller employment, but policies favored employers. Overall, workers suffered a loss of buying power. Indeed, the buying power of 1990 wages declined below 1970 levels. As a result, according to Lindhardt, even a good working-class job did not guarantee a life outside of poverty. The percentage of people in poverty rose. Life became increasingly difficult for the unemployed, the poor, and the workers who held the low-wage jobs that had proliferated (Lindhardt 2012:41–45). "The economic policies of the [Pinochet] regime resulted in increased poverty, social inequality, and an expansion of the informal economic sector, to which many Pentecostals belong" (50). Lindhardt continues, "For marginal groups that did not experience macro-economic growth as personal success stories and for whom the state and secular organizations did not provide much social security, religious movements that defined themselves in opposition to the 'world'" made sense. In short, Pentecostalism and charismaticism "were likely to have a certain appeal" (50).

From the 1990s to the present, modernization has succeeded in "securing macro-economic growth, [in] reducing poverty, and in enabling educational mobility and a continued boom in construction and consumerism" (Lindhardt 2012:53). But the new regime of economy and polity has brought little security to most workers. With privatization of both health and education systems, the poor are at great risk of health-related impoverishment and have had little access to the credentials and training that would secure for them a middle-class life. The Chilean case confirms my arguments regarding collapse, with radical transformation, risk, and privatization inducing lower-class exclusion and immiserization.[9]

Lindhardt (2012:248) emphasizes the importance of agency and empowerment in Chilean Pentecostalism, declaring that it is not a religion that does things to people but a religion that empowers people to do things:

> By emphasizing their own powerlessness and at the same time establishing an intimate and embodied relationship with transformative divine power, congregants indirectly grant themselves a significant measure of power to shape the social world.
>
> The Pentecostal power of powerlessness is not put to use in political or militant struggles that aim at structural transformation of Chilean society. Rather it is a subjective and intersubjective power that enables congregants to defy the logic of a dominant socio-cultural system, to construct new and meaningful biographies and to symbolically appropriate world history and make it their own. It is a power to create a sense of sacred order in an otherwise messy and ambiguous world.

Lindhardt's summation of Chilean Pentecostalism reminds me of Durkheim's (2001[1912]:266) dictum that the chief importance of religion is what it does to the mind.

Lindhardt's (2012) notion that Pentecostals enhance their agency and control through rejection of a messy, corrupt world replicates and clarifies our ethnographic experience in Guatemala. Pentecostalism brings with it agentive power to organize and transform society by organizing and transforming the constructs that define such things as the individual, gender, family, nation, world, good, and evil. That, to a degree, organizes and even pacifies the chaotic world swirling around the Pentecostal congregants. Emphasizing the agency of its congregants seems to be part of the apparently universal revitalization message of Pentecostalism.

Bolivia

In research conducted in Bolivia, Gill (1993:181) describes a healthy profusion of Pentecostalism in La Paz: "The proliferation of so many new fundamentalist organizations has turned La Paz into a vibrant religious marketplace where practitioners of various sorts compete for the souls of Bolivians." While I disagree with the too-easy use of the term "religious marketplace," Gill's quote does suggest the degree of religious change and diversity, while the "fundamentalist" "vibran[cy]" of religious interest in La Paz intimates its pentecostalization.

Gill lays out the societal context of this Pentecostal fervor. The question is, does it qualify as the collapse of a way of life and exclusion from any viable alternative? According to Gill (1993:181): "The new marketplace of souls has sprung up in a society that, through the 1980s, hovered on the brink of chaos. It spreads among the people who feel helpless because their lives have been disrupted by hyperinflation, unemployment, and tantalizing new symbols of consumption that remain completely out of reach. Familiar institutions—the family, political parties, unions, communities, and the state—are unable to overcome a pervasive sense of despair. The new churches capitalize on this sense of powerlessness."

According to Gill (1993:185–186), the social, political, and economic "situation grew steadily worse through the 1980s," yet "the government's response only aggravated [the people's] plight" until, "faced with an increasingly desperate situation, and having nowhere to turn except a perilous future in the cocaine trade, many were ready to listen to new religious messages." Gill places this surging membership in the 1980s. In short, Bolivian urban migrants had suffered collapse of the paternalistic colonial structures in the countryside, and they were unable to provide for their families because of the shortfall of land. At the same time, in the urban slums they fled to, they suffered exclusion caused by state failure.

Wightman's (2007) study of Pentecostalism in Bolivia confirms Gill's work. Wightman ties the growth of Pentecostalism—from 4 percent of the population in the mid-1980s to 16 percent in 2002—to the rapid urbanization of Bolivia in which migrants came from impoverished rural areas and from mining towns closed by restructuring. They moved into peripheral urban slums in the megacities. "Explosive urban growth has largely corresponded with similarly explosive growth in Pentecostalism," which Wightman (2007:240–241) attributes to "a time of dramatic social, political, and economic change in Bolivia." The national revolution had since the 1950s delivered "sweeping land reform, the nationalization of most major industries (most significantly the mining sector, long the centerpiece of Bolivia's economy), and the establishment of a highly centralized social welfare state" (240–242). Mismanagement and corruption under the centralized government, however, led to a collapse of government services. Economic instability manifested in hyperinflation. As in Guatemala, Bolivian Pentecostalism as both an ideology and a society helped ameliorate the chaos. The implementation of Pentecostal premises created sociality in small groups that abjured incapacitating or expensive vices, and Pentecostalism provided needed healing for free.

Bolivia has had its share of earthquakes, so one cannot abstract quakes from the equation. Bolivia did not, however, have a dirty war on the scale of Guatemala's. What it did have in common with Guatemala was political infighting, indigenous land shortage, a collapsed latifundium system, peasant immiserization, consequent migration to unreceptive cities, hyperinflation, a merry-go-round of unstable governments, and ethnic and economic exclusion of indigenous peoples from access to the modernizing nation. Thus, collapse and exclusion seem a perfectly valid summary of the Bolivian political economy underlying the rapid expansion of Pentecostalism among poor people there.

Unfortunately, I have found no ethnographic studies of charismatic Catholic life in El Salvador, Ecuador, or Bolivia, and thus I cannot offer comparisons with our descriptions and analysis of the Catholic Charismatic Renewal in Nahualá and Santa Catarina Ixtahuacán. Clearly, we need more rich ethnographic studies of Catholic charismatics in other countries.

Brazil

Can the argument for my theory of collapse and exclusion be extended to Brazil? Chesnut (1997:31) sees 1930 as the launching point for Pentecostalism there: "Twenty-nine times more believers claimed Pentecostal affiliation in the mid-1950s than in 1932," he says, citing Endruveit (1975:45), who shows 13,511 Pentecostals in 1932 and 391,975 in 1955. But perhaps it is more helpful to see that increase as a compound growth rate of 15.8 percent per year over the twenty-three-year span, which is an extraordinary rate of gain. Chesnut (1997:39–40) says of Brazilian growth, "The acceleration of the modernization process in the 1950s corresponded with the takeoff of Pentecostal growth in the first years of the decade. . . . Astronomic growth rates continued in the 1960s. Brazilian Pentecostals multiplied by a factor of thirty-three from 1955 to 1970" (citing Endruveit 1975:45). Here, Chesnut errs. Endruveit (1975:44) says the 1970 Pentecostal population of Brazil was 1.296 million. Dividing by the 1955 population yields a multiple of 3.3, not "thirty-three,"[10] and a compound annual growth rate of 8.3 percent for those fifteen years. By comparison, Brazil's population was almost 35 million in 1932 and almost 62.5 million in 1955 for a compound rate of gain of 2.57 percent per annum for that period, and 95.1 million in 1970, yielding a compound annual rate of gain of 2.82 percent for 1955–1970.[11]

Why the takeoff in Brazilian Pentecostalism in the 1930s and the decelerated but still very high rate from 1955 to 1970? Among the reasons for Pentecostal expansion in Brazil, Chesnut (1997:27–28) cites disease and the Pentecostal provision of free ritual healing, given poor people's utterly inadequate access to curing services from national health care or the Catholic health ministries. Beyond healing, Chesnut (1997:32) sees Brazilian Pentecostalism as "a church of the poor that expanded among those who had been pushed to the margins of economic, social, political, and religious life." He notes that Pentecostals' "rigid code of conduct . . . kept the evil world at bay while creating a sense of group solidarity and distinctiveness."

Brazil, even more so and earlier than Guatemala, underwent a process of rapid urbanization. Says Chesnut (1997:35), "The demand for healing," and thus for

Protestant Pentecostalism, "surged partly in response to the stress of rapid social change. Brazil in the early 1950s was suffering the process of modernization. . . . Economic policy favoring industrialization led to divestment in the agricultural sector, which sent waves of economic refugees to the cities."

In my terms, Brazilians suffered the social and cultural breakdown of an agricultural production system geared for export. That breakdown led to urban migration. But the migrants found themselves excluded in an inadequately serviced urban slum environment. To be sure, these data imply structural collapse rather than cultural collapse, but one cannot expect the fine details of collapse in each society to be the same. Nevertheless, cultural stress, if not collapse, would surely have been concomitant. "Excluded from the modernization process," Brazil's favela dwellers "responded enthusiastically to modern Pentecostalism's timeless message of healing" (Chesnut 1997:36). In other words, Brazilian urban migrants experienced the chaos and angst of the collapse of the old system and exclusion from entrance into the new global economy and services.

Not all of Brazil's displaced residents went to the city. Rural Pentecostal membership also expanded in areas of new agro-based migration and colonization. Chesnut records that although "the mushrooming favelas of the urban periphery continued to serve as the main suppliers of Pentecostal converts, . . . some of the fastest growth has occurred in the areas of agricultural colonization." For different areas of the country, he records Pentecostal growth rates of 291, 400, and 605 percent in the decade of the 1960s.

In sum, in the 1980s Chesnut saw severe exclusion of the poor in Brazilian society and an ever-faster expansion of Pentecostalism. He describes "the increasing immiseration of the lost decade of the 1980s," which included "a debt crisis, runaway inflation, and chronic unemployment and hunger [that] raised the misery index for the poor and for large sectors of the shrinking middle class." Indeed, "between 1982 and 1987 domestic consumption declined 25 percent . . . [and] the percentage of national income accruing to the poorest 50 percent of the population dropped from an already paltry 17.4 percent in 1960 to an astonishing 11 percent in 1990" (Chesnut 1997:47, citing Burns 1993:471, 476, for percentages). Chesnut's analysis rings of collapse and exclusion.

Chesnut's work, however, relies on the concept of the pathogens of poverty. Against these pathogens, Protestant Pentecostalism and Catholic charismaticism constitute a healing balm (Chesnut 1997:48, 83, 168, 172). I suggest, however, that it is not poverty per se that has fostered the acceptance and growth of Pentecostalism. Poverty existed before Pentecostal expansion, as did the other pathogens Chesnut identifies: lack of health, lack of education, lack of power. But neither mainline Protestantism nor ecstatic Pentecostalism took substantial hold under those preexisting conditions. So it was not just poverty (a subjective but also relative term) but a breakdown in the rural Brazilian subsistence, power, control, and cultural systems that disengaged rural people from both the exploitations and the protections of their local patrónes. This breakdown individualized them and put them at greater risk. People migrated when they lost faith in the possibility of survival in their former rural territories—which is to say, when they experienced a collapse of culture. The analogy with regard to the rise of Pentecostalism in Guatemala seems remarkably close.

If Chesnut paints with too broad a historical brush, one can look at more detailed ethnographies of Pentecostalism in Brazil, such as Ireland's (1993:45) study of Campo Alegre, a pseudonym for "a town of twelve thousand on the perimeter of Recife." For decades, Campo Alegre functioned as a port serving the local sugar industry. That industry, however, collapsed, leaving Campo Alegre residents without means of support. Yet migrants kept coming to Campo Alegre because residents in the rural areas had been deprived of the patronage—the coronelismo—that they had learned to depend on (Ireland 1993:47). With the "destruction of small scale production" (52), something quite akin to the Maya's milpa deficit, Campo Alegre residents and migrants entered a period of even greater existential crisis. One of Ireland's (1993:52) informants describes the source of their angst:

It [the local world of craft and subsistence production] is disappearing. But people need manioc flour, yams, sweet potatoes, and no one knows who is going to plant these things. Because the rich man wants what? Sugarcane. Or he wants to get the poor off the land to carve it up into expensive lots. . . . And what's the little man, who wants to plant and look after himself while living in town, going to do? Nobody knows. The little man has nothing to eat and nothing to sell now. When he loses his plot, how can he consume? . . . As it is, we don't have enough to maintain ourselves.

Collapse and exclusion suffuse this informant's comments.

I could go on, country by country or with more cases per country, throughout Latin America. Ample material exists for extended comparisons in Mexico (e.g., Dow and Sandstrom 2001) and Colombia (Brusco 1993, 1995), the latter of which I have cited extensively. I now shift, however, to explore two cases of Christian Pentecostal expansion in Africa.

PENTECOSTALISM IN AFRICA

Christianized Africa south of the Sahara has been beset by the institution of western colonialism and then its end, the collapse of national economies, civil wars and ethnocide, the rise of HIV infection, governmental instability, and a widespread notion that elites extract wealth illegally, control people by force, and stand above the law. All these contribute to a pattern of social and cultural collapse, instability, and exclusion. These conditions of social breakdown parallel or exceed those experienced in Guatemala. In such chaotic conditions, a substantial segment of Africa's mission-generated mainline Protestants have indigenized and Pentecostalized. Many of the area's traditionalists, Ortho-Catholics, and mainline colonially derived Protestants have converted to Pentecostalism or have pentecostalized their Catholic religious practice through equivalents of *la renovación* (charismatic Catholicism).

I limit myself to examining two analyses of African countries: Marshall's (2009) study of the "Pentecostal revolution" in Nigeria and Gifford's (2004) examination of Pentecostal life in Ghana.

Nigeria

Marshall notes the early arrival of Protestant missionaries and the beginnings of pentecostalization in the 1930s, but neither religion experienced significant growth at that time. For Marshall (2009:51), the transformative "born-again revival in Nigeria begins in the 1970s, gathering momentum through the 1990s and continuing to grow to the present." Did anything approximating cultural collapse and social exclusion from alternatives occur during or just prior to this 1970s–1990s period to account for the timing of this Pentecostal expansion?

The British occupied Nigeria from 1900 to 1960, throughout which time an independence movement

slowly emerged. With independence granted in 1960, local tribal interests reemerged. The country burst into the Biafran civil war in 1967, which lasted until 1970. During this war, perhaps a million people (out of some 60 million) died of starvation and violence. In the early 1970s, the discovery of oil fueled extractive carnage.

Marshall's (2009:96) perspective on the nature of government and society during this period resonates with my argument. She locates "a turning point in Nigeria's postcolonial history" in 1970. To Marshall, the main conditions contributing to the situation of deprivation and cultural cachexy in Nigeria include "the effects of the civil war and the oil boom," "the dramatic economic crisis of the early 1980s," and the "disastrous political heritage of the Second Republic." These led to "deep popular disaffection with government and fundamentally destabilized many of the mechanisms that had enabled the great majority of Nigerians to confront the ordeal of everyday life" (96).

Marshall (2009:96) speaks of "intensified . . . themes of insecurity, violence, and corruption" resulting from the oil boom and quotes Ihonvbere and Shaw (1998:49), who document a total disenchantment with the "insecurity, uncertainty, violence, bitter politics, and the deepening socio-economic crisis . . . accompanied by corruption, and waste that had characterized civilian rule since 1960." This "predatory and extractive exercise of power" had been "well established during the colonial period" (Marshall 2009:97). According to Ihonvbere and Shaw (1998:112, as quoted in Marshall 2009:102), the extraction and chaos amounted to "the transparent rape of the country." Marshall (102) summarizes a fifteen-year period of "successive military rule, austerity, unfinanced structural adjustment, increasing division, growing authoritarianism and state violence, the almost total collapse of state services, the dramatic impoverishment of the middle class, the descent into absolute poverty of the great majority, and the resounding failure of traditional strategies of social mobility and success." As in Guatemala, the Nigerian government and its elites evinced corruption to the core. In short, Marshall's study suggests that Nigeria from the 1970s to the present fits well within a model of collapse, exclusion, and uncertainty fueling the rise of Pentecostalism.

But did Nigerian Pentecostalism serve as a revitalization movement? Marshall (2009), like Lindhardt (2012), argues that Pentecostalism's discourse against corruption and the chaos of the world constituted a highly political—indeed, "revolutionary"—activism that both helped individuals and families who converted and constituted an authentic effort to transform untenable conditions. Meanwhile, sedate mainline Christianity in Nigeria withered because it "appeared to offer little in the way of solutions for the reestablishment of moral mastery and the control of untrammeled powers" (Marshall 2009:110–111). As in Guatemala, the historic Protestant denominations that had introduced Christianity to Nigeria experienced significant declines in membership. Only Pentecostalism thrived. "The revival" via Pentecostalism, Marshall (113) notes, "was primarily fueled by the enthusiasm of the youth and of women, the two social categories most affected by both the boom and the economic downturn. . . . Converts re-created the bonds of social solidarity and reconstructed networks of social support. . . . Churches and fellowships presented themselves as the 'new family.'"

The transformative impact of Pentecostalism on gender and family was palpable: "Marriage strategies changed, as conversion came to be seen as a way of finding a reliable and serious spouse," and "marriage came to be mediated by the approbation and critical eye, not of the extended family, but of the pastor and fellow believers" (Marshall 2009:113). As in Guatemala, but better documented here, Marshall (116) shows that "powerful forms of discursive rescripting" meshed "a global Pentecostal doctrine with a local ontology of power, something that mission or orthodox Christianity had failed to do. This gave plausibility to new practices of deliverance that are part of Pentecostal orthodoxy everywhere."

Marshall's book adds a rich trove of data and analysis to the understanding of how Pentecostal belief and practice constitute an agentive approach to dealing with a collapsed social environment. The relation I posit between the breakdown of culturally controllable lifeways, exclusion from any subsequent sustainable way of life, and Pentecostalism as a restorative revitalization fits Nigeria's conditions and accounts for the timing of Nigeria's Pentecostal surge starting in the 1970s and continuing to the present.

Ghana

Gifford (2004) delivers a detailed ethnography of Pentecostal Christianity in Ghana that confirms that Marshall's (2009) Nigerian study is not an anomaly. Gifford links the expansion of Pentecostal congregationalism to existential survival issues. To be sure, he affirms the many utilitarian benefits of Pentecostalism described in the literature.

Underlying all, however, Gifford (2004:ix) argues that "the new churches" "flourish mainly because they claim to have the answers to Ghanaians' existential problem[s] and especially to their most pressing existential problem, economic survival."

According to Gifford (2004:1), from independence in 1957 to 1978, Ghana's leaders could be characterized by their "'big man' rule, personality cult, corruption and . . . disregard of the rule of law." By 1978, Gifford (3) contends, "Ghana bordered on collapse." Yet conditions got worse: "Bad rains, with the resulting poor harvests, and then the forced repatriation from Nigeria of up to 1 million Ghanaians without proper papers, mean that around 1982–3, Ghana reached its nadir; the country simply could not cope." In 1983 the government of Jerry John Rawlings led the country into "structural adjustment," which was touted "in the West as an economic success story but by the middle of the 1990s it was clear that this programme . . . was not working, . . .[and] Ghanaians . . . did not need convincing; life was incredibly hard. By the late 1990s there was widespread poverty with 70 percent of the population earning under US$1.00 a day" (Gifford 2004:3–4). Gifford shows that the minimum daily wage would buy but 2.8 loaves of bread. The medical system was in shambles, with 80 percent of doctors fleeing the country within five years of graduation. "Education collapsed. . . . The country was almost totally dependent on foreign aid" (4). The agricultural sector also collapsed, yet Ghana was an agriculturally dependent country (5). "After seventeen years of IMF [International Monetary Fund] supervision," Rawlings presided "over an economy in a state of collapse" (6). From independence to the present—and especially from 1972 to the present—the ordinary Ghanaian has indeed lived a life in a state of collapse, exclusion, and uncertainty.

Was there also a subsistence crisis that led to a cultural crisis? I do not have data on the Ghanaian adoption of any particular crop as sacred, equivalent to the Mayas' reverence for corn. But the data I do have show that population has risen prodigiously, that land is short for most, and that this disparity between land and population drives massive urbanization.

Like Guatemalans, Ghanaians have experienced a population explosion. From a bit fewer than 2.3 million people in 1921, Ghana's population ballooned to 18.9 million in 2000, the effective date of Gifford's analysis. The annual rate of population increase reached 3.2 percent in the 1920s, dipped to 1.6 percent in the 1930s, and shot back up to 4.1 percent in the 1940s. The rate of increase hovered between 2.4 and 2.8 percent per annum for the five decades between 1950 and 2000 (Gaisie et al. 2005:xvii).

During this period of population expansion, Ghana's land base has stayed the same. Agricultural dependence is still considerable, but diminishing. In 2000, 50–53 percent of Ghana's working population age fifteen or older was engaged in agriculture, down from 57 60 percent in agriculture from 1960 to 1984 (Gaisie et al. 2005:98, 99). Unemployment in 2000 jumped to more than 10 percent, rising from 6 percent in 1960 and 1970 and 2.8 percent in 1984 (Gaisie et al. 2005:100).

In the only national agricultural census available, taken in 1984, there is considerable evidence of subsistence distress. For the country as a whole, the national census reported that 66 percent of landholders had fewer than 1.99 acres (the census's minimum category) to support them. Converted to Guatemala's measure, 1.99 acres is 18.5 *cuerdas* or 1.16 *manzanas*. One may take this figure as equivalent to the minimum subsistence level necessary for a family in Ghana, and it is close to the minimum requirement for a peasant family's agricultural subsistence in Guatemala.

Ghanaian census procedures focused on household units with land and did not count the landless. Therefore, in addition to the 66 percent of landholders who were below the minimum for subsistence, one must separately estimate the number of landless. Using Gaisie and colleagues' (2005:18) figures, there were 1.85 million agricultural landholders in Ghana. If one multiplies this by 5 or 6 family members per agricultural landholder, there were between 9.25 million and 11.1 million people dependent on agricultural landholdings for sustenance. This implies two facts. First, between 75 and 90 percent of Ghana's 1984 population of 12.3 million were agriculturally dependent. And second, between 9.7 and 24.8 percent of Ghana's population was landless. Adding the landless to the 66 percent of landholders with substandard farms yields the possibility that at least 75.7 percent and perhaps as much as 91 percent of Ghana's population lived below the minimum needed for subsistence agriculture in 1984. These figures give some notion of the pervasive subsistence crisis in Ghana, an essentially agricultural country.

More recent ethnographies of Pentecostalism in Ghana confirm Gifford's analysis. Meyer (2015:8–9), for example, suggests that Pentecostalism, "popular since the 1980s, . . . had a strong appeal for those disappointed by the perceived incapacity of the state to bring about 'development.'" Such a perspective suggests exclusion. In this setting Pentecostalism would, "with its emphasis on the capacity of the Holy Spirit to induce personal change, enable ruptures and ever new beginnings, effect miracles, follow and protect born-again Christians wherever they went, and bring about health and wealth," articulating a "strand of Christianity that fit exceptionally well into the new climate of millennial capitalism" (8 9). Both Gifford (2004:27–30) and Meyer (2015) detail many striking similarities between Ghanaian and Guatemalan Pentecostal liturgical and daily religious practices.

I have not been able to find firm figures on the timing and expansion of Pentecostal practice in Ghana. Gifford (2004:27) casually suggests 1979 as a "convenient" start date for "the beginning of Accra's charismatic Christianity" and says that during the period from 1979 to 2002, the Ortho-Catholic and mainline historical Protestant churches were "in many ways . . . eclipsed by something quite new, the charismatic sector . . . although some in Ghana use the term 'neo-Pentecostal'" (27, 23). Olupona (2003:15), however, places the beginnings of the charismatic pentecostal movement in West Africa more generically "in the 1970s, a decade after the period when most African countries obtained independence from the colonial government." Clearly, the twenty- to thirty-year period immediately preceding Gifford's fieldwork was the core period of expansion. In his rendition, Ghana in the period 1972–1978 "bordered on collapse," in 1982–1983 went through a "nadir" of institutional "collapse," and in 2000 had "enormous problems, and [was] economically on its knees" (Gifford 2004:1, 4–5, 19).

In the year 2000, according to Burgess and van der Maas (2003:111), Ghana's historic denominational Pentecostals had a combined membership of 858,349 (19 percent of all pentecostals). Charismatics practicing renewal in the historic Protestant and Catholic denominations numbered 889,035 (20 percent of pentecostals). Neo-charismatics operating independently of denominational affiliation but derived mostly from the Protestant tradition surpassed both at 2.7 million (61 percent of pentecostals). Thus, the total adherents of renewal faiths, what I call pentecostals or Christian Pentecostals, amounted to 4.5 million (23.7 percent of Ghana's total population).

In 2000 Ghana's total population was between 18.9 million (Gaisie et al. 2005:217) and 20.2 million (Platte 2010 for the rest of the figures in this paragraph). The Christian population in Ghana totaled 11.2 million (55.4 percent of 20 million). Of these, the mainline historic

Catholic faith included 1.9 million people (9.5 percent of the total population), while historic Protestant denominations in four main branches embraced a total of 3.8 million. Combined, the historic Protestant and Catholic denominations totaled some 5.7 million people. The total of exuberant pentecostals likely included at least the 4.5 million whom Barrett, Kurian, and Johnson (2001:111) list as pentecostal/charismatics (40 percent of all Christians) and might also have included the 1.5 million listed as Evangelicals. If one includes the latter 1.5 million, pentecostal religion had been embraced by 53 percent of Ghanaian Christians, most joining in the twenty years preceding Gifford's 2000–2002 fieldwork.

In Ghana, pentecostalism surged but it has had no war. It does have moderate seismic activity, but during this time of surge there were no significantly destructive earthquakes. Yet, war and quake are the two commonly cited explanations of the Pentecostal surge in Guatemala. What Ghana does share with Guatemala is a problematic ratio of population to available land indicating crisis, ample evidence of national collapse, and some evidence of local collapse in the traditional cultural systems. The Ghanaian culture and country indeed are in turmoil. The urban environment and the governmental system are chaotic at best. Collapse and exclusion seem an apt explanation for the 1970s–2000s pentecostal florescence in Ghana, most likely with the same symbolic resonances that I have argued are communicated by pentecostal practice in Guatemala.

Pentecostalism in Africa: A Summation

To conclude, neither Ghanaians nor Nigerians experienced earthquake disruption on the order of Guatemala, although Ghana is moderately seismic. Of the two African countries, only Nigeria shares with Guatemala the experience of civil war. The only factor all three share that is relevant to my theory of Christian Pentecostal expansion is this: Nigeria, Ghana, and Guatemala all experienced a subsistence catastrophe at the population-land interface. These subsistence catastrophes exposed their indigenous cultures to the breakdown of axial local practice and symbol in traditionalist religions. The same subsistence failure disrupted colonially imposed mainline Christian religions in the rural areas. All three nations experienced massive and rapid urbanization with no public services. All three suffered governmental and societal malfeasance and corruption. Clearly, individuals in all three countries

confronted a society that had collapsed locally and that excluded nationally.

Given these facts, and given what Durkheim, Weber, Marx, and Wallace theorized, all three societies should have experienced similar changes in their traditional and colonial religious practices and ideologies. And they have. They have all substantially Pentecostalized their Christianity, moving toward ecstatic, Spirit-embodying practice.

In postcolonial Africa, as in Guatemala and in Latin America more broadly, Christian Pentecostalism accurately expresses the angst of culture collapse, exclusion, and liminality. It operates as a revitalization and as a critique of local and national society. It reconstructs supportive relations to replace those lost through migration, death, alcohol, anomie, and the collapse of traditional and colonial institutions. Christian Pentecostalism teaches agentive, adaptive behavior locally appropriate to and modified by revelation received in the religious community. It fosters gender and family reorganization. It strives to suppress racial and ethnic distinctions. Pentecostalism constitutes the only response so far devised that enables a growing sector of the poor to conceptualize and construct a meaningful and workable response to state failure, societal chaos, economic exploitation, and exclusion. I now turn to southern India, where Christianity may have gotten its start as early as the sixth decade CE.

PENTECOSTALISM IN INDIA

According to local myth, in the year 52 CE, Saint Thomas the Apostle brought Christianity to a small portion of the population inhabiting the southern tip of India. Historical evidence, however, exists only for fourth-century origins via traders from the eastern patriarchates (Bergunder 2008:15; Abraham 2004:133–134). No matter the date, ministers and traders from the eastern patriarchates certainly influenced India's early Christianity for many centuries. Then, in the late 1400s and early 1500s, Portuguese contact with India brought the already existing eastern rites under Roman Catholic control and succeeded to a degree in romanizing the by-then indigenized Indian practice of Thomasine Syrian patriarchate Christianity (Palackal 2004:151–153).[12]

Mainline Protestant missionaries went to India in the 1800s with British colonization but had little success in converting the Thomasine Roman Catholics or the people of any of India's other religions. Pentecostal missionaries who had participated in the Azusa Street revivals arrived in India in 1907 (Bergunder 2008:24). It is difficult to assess Pentecostal success, because India's census figures do not differentiate Catholics, Protestants, or Pentecostals among those listed as Christians. Nevertheless, the Pentecostal version of spirited and Spirit-infused bodily experience seems to have flourished much better than the sedate, logocentric, theological mainline Protestantism. Indeed, mainline Protestants and Catholics supplied the bulk of Pentecostal converts. That much of the story parallels Guatemala fairly precisely.

So does Indian Pentecostal practice. Michael Bergunder (2008), a historian, documents the dizzying fissiparousness of Pentecostal congregations in India, as does Thomas (2008). There is open access to the pulpit, the ability to consult the Bible, charismatic ministerial leadership, and the expectation and practice of gifts of the spirit, including healings and speaking in tongues. An assistant pastor can split a congregation if he has a variant view on how to better live life in a given locality. The ecstaticism of the Azusa experience—speaking in tongues, spirit possession, exorcism, exuberance, bodily activity during worship, and emphatic amplification of feelings by music—all find expression in Indian Pentecostalism (Thomas 2008; Palackal 2004; Rapaka 2013).

As in Guatemala and other locations, the historical mainstream denominations have morphed toward a pentecostal style regardless of denominational name (Thomas 2008). Peter Schmitthenner (pers. comm., 2016) confirmed that morphing. Schmitthenner is a historian focused on British colonial India. He also is the child of Lutheran missionary parents who served in India from 1952 until their retirement in 1981. In our discussions about Pentecostalism, Schmitthenner recounted how he took his father back to India in 2006 to visit the congregations his father had founded and guided in his ministerial youth. After some twenty-five years away from the mission field, his father said that he simply did not recognize the congregations he had founded because they had thoroughly Pentecostalized (Schmitthenner, pers. comm., 2019). Not just in Guatemala, but also in India and Ghana, the mainline historic Protestant denominations pentecostalize in practice at the congregational level, even though they may retain a Protestant denominational name.

What about the collapse of one's way of life and culture or exclusion from alternatives? Southern India is organized by caste, with Dalits (also called untouchables), like the Mayas and Guatemala's urban poor (Tumin 1952;

Gillin 1951), at the bottom of the country's hierarchy of prestige and opportunity. Dalits are also the major sector of society to pentecostalize.

Also like Guatemala, much of India's population has been agriculturally dependent. Has the country followed a similar path regarding population expansion relative to the carrying capacity of the cultivable land? It would appear so. Kumar (1992:104, 123–124) reports regular famine in the Madras Presidency, a colonial political-administrative unit in southern India where Christianity took root. Indeed, famines occurred cyclically in every decade of the 1800s but one, with devastating results. Kumar reports losses of between a third and a half of the population from even a single famine. Wilson (2016:318–321) confirms famine and dislocation in India during the same time span and for the southern half of the subcontinent. The regularity of famine in the main Christianized region of southern India suggests an early land, production, and lifeway crisis equivalent to or even greater than that experienced by Guatemalan peasant Mayas in the 1950s–1970s. Beyond the frequent famines, Kumar details the tremendous impact of the British as they disorganized and reorganized landholdings in the Madras region. Such landholding changes in a primarily agricultural society would constitute a kind of collapse. Tharoor (2016) confirms the excruciating cultural and social disruptions imposed by British colonialism aimed at commercial extraction, as does Wilson (2016:326–331).

Of what religious consequence was this disruption? Kumar (1992) indicates that in the mid-1850s—in the midst of both frequent famine and overwhelming British colonial disruption—southern India's Madras region experienced tremendous religious upheaval that manifested in the form of ecstaticism, end-of-the-world belief, and speaking in tongues. In short, the pressure of a collapsing land-to-population ratio and colonialism generated the classic signs of pentecostal/charismatic renewal half a world away from and half a century before the official emergence of Pentecostalism at the hands of the Reverend William Seymour in 1906 on Azusa Street in Los Angeles. But did it occur only among India's Christians? Or was it a general phenomenon of traditionalist possession cults under stress, as documented by Lewis (1971) among autochthonous societies elsewhere in the world? I do not know. But there is substantial evidence that among Christians at least, Christian Pentecostal behavior appeared in multiple locations decades before 1906 (or even 1900) when it could have been exported out of the

United States by letters or missionary diffusion (Rapaka 2013:24–34).

The apparently independent invention of Christian Pentecostalism in India, Chile, and the United States strongly augurs for the structuralist explanations advanced in this book rather than diffusionist explanations of transmission by missionary work. Where diffusion succeeded, one may assume it was because colonially induced cultural collapse and exclusion had made the recipients ready for change. Finally, a thorough study of the documents from this region and time might establish whether colonially delivered Christianity was particularly or uniquely inclined toward a fundamentalist ecstatic revitalization response to cultural stress or whether it paralleled the patterns of ecstaticism or fundamentalism elsewhere in the world, as documented by Lewis (1971) and by Marty and Appleby (1991, 1993, 1994, 1995) and other volumes published by the University of Chicago's Fundamentalism Project.

Skipping forward, Bergunder (2008) argues and Thomas (2008) confirms that the Pentecostal movement in Indian Christianity surged in the 1970s and, as evidenced in Bergunder's charts, clearly accelerated in the 1980s–1990s. Why then, and among whom? The latter I can assess more easily. Bergunder shows that the two largest social sources of Pentecostal converts were the untouchable Dalits and the agricultural caste of Nadars. Roberts (2016) confirms a concentration of Pentecostalism among the Dalits, as does Rapaka (2013). Thomas (2008) focuses on Pentecostal Dalits but notes that the higher-caste Syrian Christians, though also largely very poor, converted and tried to exclude Dalits from the Pentecostal congregations. Certainly, the disparaged ethnicity of the Dalits—the primary social source of Pentecostal conversions—parallels the Maya experience. Did the Dalits suffer some kind of social, cultural, or subsistence collapse and some kind of exclusion in the period preceding and during the Pentecostal expansion?

Roberts (2016) gives a detailed ethnography of urban slum Christianity in Chennai, southern India, that hints at a process that might have constituted cultural collapse. In his study, Christians are exclusively Dalits, but not all Dalits are Christian. Indeed, most are Hindus. Exclusion is not difficult to find in his ethnography; it is the essence of being an untouchable Dalit. But what about culture collapse? Roberts goes to great length to show that prior to Gandhi's rebellion against British colonial rule, Dalits were not considered Hindus. They were simply "other," polluting and perhaps not even human. In the 1940s, however, British colonial census policy and Hindu nationalism vis-à-vis Muslims made it essential that Hindus start to count Dalits as Hindus if they wanted a majority of votes to control the government. The relative nonhumanity of Dalits as a category ended as Hindus claimed, counted, and politicized Dalits, but Hindus kept the Dalits excluded. I suspect that being reclassed as Hindus, rather than being simply "other," constituted a major culture change.[13] Did the Dalits come under severe subsistence or caste structural deterioration, as my theory would predict if their Thomasine, Roman Catholic, or mainline Protestant Christianity was pentecostalizing? I do not have information for the twentieth century. Here again, my theoretical approach could be tested by a young ethnographer or historian.

The second part of the theoretical equation asks, was there some kind of exclusion? The very notion of Dalits as untouchable reeks with exclusion. But as John Watanabe (pers. comm., 2019) reminded me, Dalits had "been excluded for a very long time, so why convert now?" First, I would bet that the 1970s, a time associated with vibrant Pentecostal expansion, was also associated with the beginnings of Indian access to or impact by neoliberal globalization. Second, I am also willing to bet that the anthropological discovery and recognition of a vibrant Pentecostal presence came much later than the actual period of its highest compound annual growth rate, its period of real flourishing, as in Guatemala. I suspect that following the collapse of the British Raj, Gandhi's efforts on behalf of Dalit equality, independence, Muslim-Hindu separation strife, and the 1950s–1960s beginnings of India's modernization and movement into the new world system, Dalit Christian conversions expanded at a much higher compound annual rate than from the 1970s to the present. Certainly, more deep ethnographies of Pentecostal and, especially, charismatic Catholic religious transformation in southern India are needed.

PENTECOSTALISM IN EUROPE AND THE UNITED STATES

I now shift from an exploration of the rise of Pentecostalism in the postcolonial Global South to an exploration of Pentecostalism's presence in the postindustrial North.

European Romas

Perhaps the most obvious example of a people undergoing cultural collapse and clear exclusion can be found in Europe's Roma population, who are also known as "Gypsies," Romanis, or Gitanos. Their long-standing way of life as a mobile yet quasi-corporate and isolated people seems increasingly untenable in present day Europe. Discrimination against the Romas, especially in eastern Europe, has long been and still remains rampant. Some governments seem to use national social services to commit genocide by adoption (Chai 2005). In this process, government agents report poverty, racially imposed joblessness, and cultural deviation from the national norm as evidence of the unsuitability of Roma home life. On the basis of such reports, state officers place Roma children in orphanages or foster homes where they are reeducated or adopted out of the country, thereby interrupting the cultural and biological reproduction of the Roma community. This constitutes a slow but systematic form of ethnic cleansing. The Romas are kept as liminal and marginal beings in the European context both by self-choice and by imposed prejudices.

In my theory, such a people would be ripe for pentecostalization, and web sources on Roma life confirm that some two-thirds of Romas now engage in Pentecostal worship.[14] Whether these online data are accurate or whether they are simply partisan jeremiads created to support a Pentecostal evangelist agenda, I cannot say. Atanasov (2010) provides a detailed but religiously motivated description of Roma Pentecostals in Bulgaria from which one can extract some comparative data. Although some Romas were always sedentary, many have been labeled "formerly travelers" (Atanasov 2010:33). The adjective "formerly" regarding the lifeway of traveling suggests some degree of culture collapse while Atanasov's assertion that "they have been oppressed, marginalized, despised, and are still considered outsiders" (39) implies exclusion. Clearly, Roma life has come under transformative assault in a broad array of European nations by state institutional forces that try to settle Romas in particular places to live sedentary lives. In addition, powerful forces of prejudice among non-Romas and an internal focus among Romas on their own local community lead to separation, discrimination, and exclusion (Thomas 2003). Drawn in via conversion, perhaps half or more of all Romas participate vigorously in Pentecostal worship.

Gay y Blasco's (2000) more nuanced account of Romas in Spain confirms much of what Atanasov describes. Gay y Blasco (2000:12) asserts that Pentecostal participation among Spain's Gitanos became considerable in the 1990s, with about a third to as much as half the population in her study area claiming such affiliation (Gay y Blasco 2002:176). Pentecostalism has become a way of overcoming the fissiparousness of Gitano life and forging the overarching framework of a "new diasporic modality" that synthesizes both a "transformation and [a] continuity," thereby reworking Gitano culture (Gay y Blasco 2000:10). According to Gay y Blasco (2000:12), "Evangelism . . . define[s] personal and communal identities within a framework of rapid social change and of great pressures for acculturation or assimilation." Pentecostalism enables the Gitanos of various bands to interact and reduces their tendency toward feuding. It minimizes the disruptions of alcohol. The Pentecostal movement has also developed among "the converts . . . a novel interest in other Gitanos and even other Gypsies" (15), paralleling the way pentecostalism overcomes the isolating municipal orientation of indigenes in Guatemala. Thus, "at the core of these Evangelical innovations, lies a changed perception of the self and the group in time" (16). In addition, she finds a significant perception of gender role modification believed favorable to Gitana women (Gay y Blasco 2012:4–9). Gay y Blasco (2000:19) suggests in the Gitano Pentecostal enthusiasm the operation of a revitalization movement, the Pentecostal Gitanos seeing the non-Pentecostal Gitanos as backward, corrupt, and in need of change and "modernization" to heal themselves.

I suggest that the increasing crisis in Romas' subsistence strategies and the breakdown of their traveling way of life constitute a kind of cultural assault, if not collapse. Gay y Blasco (2000:4–5, 2002:175–176) notes for the Spanish Gitanos the end of rural and mobile life beginning in the 1950s and details other facets of the cultural pressure and exclusion to which they have been subjected. I note further that the Romas remain excluded from new modes of subsistence in Spain and elsewhere and that state resettlement, reeducation, removing children to orphanages, and foster-care programs constitute part of the assault on their culture. Finally, I suggest that Roma Pentecostalism responds as a revitalization movement and adjustment cult by blending the core premises of Roma culture with new constructions and by offering a legitimate ritual for expression of the pain and liminality brought on by living a severely threatened cultural existence.

The Origins of US Pentecostalism:
Azusa Street and Its Precursors

My sociocultural interpretation of the growth of pen-tecostalism worldwide should also account for the ori-gins of Pentecostalism in the United States. The gen-erally acknowledged beginning of Pentecostalism as a regular practice with a coherent belief system, and the conscious attempt to spread the practice to the world, can be traced to Bonnie Brae and Azusa Streets in Los Angeles, California. It commenced with a speaking-in-tongues event under the tutelage of William J. Seymour, generally acknowledged as the founder of Pentecostal-ism, on April 9, 1906 (Borlase 2006:116–118; Liardon 2006:96–97; Hyatt 2006:1; Espinosa 2014:55). I think it is appropriate to treat in some detail the US origins of Pentecostalism. Both the life of Seymour and the social context of the first Pentecostal movement ought to con-form substantially to the theories I have developed from our exploration of Christian Pentecostalism in Nahualá and Santa Catarina Ixtahuacán.

William Seymour was born in 1870 in Centerville, Louisiana, the son of an emancipated African Ameri-can couple. Seymour grew up amid the post–Civil War social collapse in the black community of Louisiana. To be sure, the slave system had been crushed by war. For African Americans, however, the brief hope of equality and the promise of entry into a viable life in Reconstruc-tion society was dashed by the imposition of Jim Crow laws (Martin 1999:31–40). Blacks were liminal, caught between collapse and exclusion. Indeed, they have been isolated, restricted, terrorized, and excluded from the end of Reconstruction in 1877 until the civil rights transfor-mations of the 1960s and to the present (McMillen 1989). Thus, the hypothesis of this book—that Pentecostalism flourishes under conditions of culture collapse and exclu-sion—fits well the origins and development of Pente-costalism in African American communities (Espinosa 2014:48, 58; McMillen 1989).

As a young man looking for work and probably for escape from the travails of Jim Crow life, Seymour migrated north, busing tables and helping in hotels in Memphis, Tennessee, likely in 1891; in St. Louis, Missouri, in 1893; and in 1895 in Indianapolis, Indiana, where he found religious community and conversion in the "all-black Simpson Chapel Methodist Episcopal Church" (Martin 1999:66, 68, 70). There, "Seymour's life had new purpose. He was no longer traveling from place to place

just to escape the poverty and oppression of the South. Now he was a spiritual pilgrim" (71). Martin notes that Seymour soon "found a new church home among the stricter Holiness sects" (72), eventually choosing to affil-iate with the Apostolic faith. In 1900, Seymour moved to Chicago, where "it is unlikely" that Seymour would have missed connecting with John Alexander Dowie, a "faith healer and founder of the Christian Apostolic Church" (74). Seymour likely appreciated and absorbed both the healing and Dowie's emphasis on racial equality through "integrated seating in his facilities" (75). Both the integra-tionist perspective and the emphasis on healing became arrows in Seymour's future spiritual quiver.

Seymour relocated in 1901 to Cincinnati, Ohio, where he attended the Reverend Daniel S. Warner's Eve-ning Light Saints Holiness Church. In Cincinnati, Sey-mour experienced "sanctification," the spiritual assur-ance of God manifested in the believer's soul. Among the Evening Light Saints, Seymour learned to expect "an unprecedented outpouring of the Holy Spirit before Jesus returned" (Martin 1999:77), an expectation that would later unfold in Pentecostal practice. The Evening Light Saints also radically (for the time) pushed integra-tion: "There were 30 black leaders" who "worked hand in hand" with whites (77). The Evening Light Saints and the closely associated Church of God adhered to strict standards of behavior. To integration, Seymour seems to have added sanctification, the expectation of "unprece-dented outpouring," and the idea of living by strict stan-dards. Principle by principle, Seymour seemed to collect the main tenets of a future Pentecostalism as he traveled across the land.

In Cincinnati, Seymour survived a bout with small-pox that scarred his face and left him substantially blind in one eye. The fire of pox brought with it a transforma-tion. In return for the gift of health, Seymour commit-ted to change: instead of serving people by bringing them food in restaurants, as he had done to support himself in almost every city, he would serve people by bringing them God in churches. Under Warner's tutelage, Seymour sought and received God and was ordained a minister (Borlase 2006:50–55; Espinosa 2014:49).

Seymour left Cincinnati in 1902. He appears to have received "spiritual advice and training from Charles P. Jones," another holiness preacher, in "the winter of 1904–1905" in Jackson, Mississippi (Martin 1999:87). Jones preached that the second sanctification definitely had to be "experienced." During this time, Seymour likely added the arrow of experientiality to his expanding quiver of concepts.

Seymour then moved to Houston, Texas, at least by 1905, hoping to find relatives lost during the chaos of slavery and postwar Reconstruction. I distill the crucial Houston connections from three sources (Borlase 2006:57–82; Espinosa 2014:46-51; Martin 1999:87–96). In Houston, Seymour intersected by chance with three persons—Lucy Farrow, Charles Parham, and Neely Terry—in ways that would alter the path of Seymour's life and fundamentally change the course of Christian history and practice. While in Houston, Seymour "attended a Black Holiness congregation pastored by Lucy Farrow," who had been "born a slave in Virginia," had been sold "further south," and after the war had migrated to Houston (Martin 1999:89). Her congregation was small; widowed with two living children, she supplemented her pastoral income with cooking and cleaning for others.

Parham arrived in Houston in 1905 by another path. As a Holiness preacher, he had established a residential Bible college in Topeka, Kansas, that, by 1900, taught the expectation of gifts of the spirit as described in the Acts of the Apostles. His students identified glossolalia as most important among those gifts. Together, they embarked on prayer and fasting that resulted in an outburst of glossolalia early in the morning of January 1, 1901, the start of the new century and an apt time for renewal in the holiness tradition.[15] Parham extended his ministry, holding successful revivals, with manifestations of the Spirit via glossolalia, in Galena and Baxter Springs, Kansas; Joplin, Missouri; and finally, in 1905, in Houston, Texas. There, Parham employed Farrow to assist his ministry as a cook. When it came time to return to Topeka, he asked Farrow to join his family as a governess. She accepted. Farrow appointed Seymour, a certified minister, interim pastor of her flock and left with Parham for Kansas.

In Kansas, Farrow witnessed and then experienced the glossolalia which Parham preached. During his absence, however, Parham's ministry in Topeka had fallen into disrepair and Parham, perhaps with Farrow's encouragement, decided after a few months to return to Houston and open his Bible college there.

In Houston, Farrow encouraged Parham to accept Seymour as a Bible college student. Being black in Jim Crow Texas and given Parham's racial prejudices, Seymour listened from the outer hallway, or through a window, unable to sit in the same room with the white students. Seymour rejected Parham's racism but absorbed his ideas

regarding the necessity of receiving the Spirit as manifest by glossolalia. Not allowed to approach the dais, however, Seymour did not personally experience glossolalia in Texas.

Enter Neely Terry. Sometime between Farrow's departure for Topeka and Seymour's attendance at the Houston Bible college, Terry, a resident of Los Angeles and friend of Farrow's, came to Houston to visit relatives. While in Houston, she attended Farrow's congregation and there saw and heard Seymour preach. She was impressed. When she returned, she persuaded her church group to invite him to Los Angeles as a ministerial candidate. He accepted. With some financial help from Parham and the Texas congregation, Seymour made the journey to Los Angeles. As he stepped off the train in early February 1906 and made his way to Bonnie Brae Street to lead meetings there, this disheveled, pox-scarred, half-blind preacher changed forever the path of Christian religious history.[16]

Seymour's ideas were too radical for Terry's co congregants, however, and they rejected him. Penniless, Seymour boarded for free with a skeptical but tolerant Edward Lee, who served in a local black mission to the poor. Over time, Seymour's sincerity, intensity, and conversations with Lee overcame Lee's skepticism. On April 9, 1906, Lee asked Seymour to lay hands on him. Seymour did—and Lee spoke in tongues, as did others that day under Seymour's guidance. Seymour preached the reception of the spirit but did not himself experience glossolalia until three days later. Word of these manifestations spread through Lee's ministerial connections. At first, Seymour and his congregants held enthusiastic meetings in Lee's house and others on Bonnie Brae Street, with Seymour preaching. These meetings overflowed the houses, spilled into the street, and eventually were moved to renovated quarters in an abandoned warehouse on Azusa Street.

Enthusiastic, glossolalic, trance-inducing meetings flowered. Word of mouth and newspaper reports expanded their fame. Pentecostalism had been born successfully in 1906 Los Angeles.

But why did this transformative reception of the spirit spread in Los Angeles, whereas the same spiritual manifestations in Kansas and Texas did not? Why was Seymour successful but Parham was not? And why did this spirituality flower in 1900–1906 versus some other time?

I start with the location. Los Angeles, even in 1905–1906, billed itself as the "city of dreams" (Flamming 2005), the "Land of Promise" (Carr 1935:129). The city and region had begun to advertise itself as a new mecca of freedom, opportunity, and wish fulfillment. In addition, Los Angeles was undoubtedly less constrained by Jim Crow laws and had a less racist culture than most places in the United States. But for black people, it was no city of dream fulfillment. Society in Los Angeles bore down on African Americans with prejudice, segregation (Flamming 2005:4–5, 50–51, 55–58; Carr 1935:95, 246, 248), and systematic exclusion (Flamming 2005:60–91; Martin 1999:101–118).

Los Angeles was also the last possible stop on the nation's hope-generating westward trek in pursuit of the self-improvement, success, and attainment proffered in the American dream, a core idea of US culture.[17] One could not go farther west in the American search for betterment, for the next step was the Pacific Ocean. "Los Angeles," writes Carr (1935:6) in his chatty history of the city and environs, "marks the end of the chapter. It is the end of the trail. We stand on the shores of the Pacific looking out across the face of the waters to the old home [from] whence we came." "Go west, young man," the idea that for generations had fired the minds of Americans with dreams of land and opportunity for the taking, could go no further. Hence, arrival at the Pacific in part triggered Seymour's existential crisis.

Stopped by the Pacific Ocean and realizing—consciously or unconsciously—that he could not move farther west to pursue the American dream and that he had no means of escape from the failure of that dream, Seymour deployed the arrows of his spiritual experience, which he had picked up city by city and contact by contact as he zigzagged north, east, west, south, and then west again in his life journey. Seymour preached that all people, black or white, could experience equality (Espinosa 2014:56–61, 96–108). That was his key critique of US society. If equality were not possible in ordinary society, all people could at least experience equality before God through receipt of the Pentecostal gifts: bodily experience of the Holy Spirit, physical and mental healing, and speaking in tongues. Such gifts were available to anyone. They were gifts from God.

Thus, in Los Angeles, Seymour's message of Pentecostal readiness struck home and took root. Men and women—of African, European, Latin American, and Asian descent—met together, prayed together, and laid hands on each other for healing, all in peace and equality, all breaking the fetters of Jim Crow. They spoke in tongues. People of both genders and diverse ethnicities sang, danced, laughed, prayed, and fell on the floor together, immobilized in trance, "slain" by the Holy Spirit's entry into their bodies (Espinosa 2014:53–68). As Espinosa (14, 32) puts it, they "transgressed" the lines of color division and threatened the order of society. And in so doing, they were also preaching and practicing the end of the illness of US society; they were indeed engaged in a religious revitalization movement.

Word spread of the spiritual zeal among Seymour's parishioners. Indeed, Seymour commissioned parishioners and visiting Protestant ministers who had received the Spirit to depart and spread the message and style of Spirit reception around the world. Many did. In the United States, an Azusa Street diaspora of ministers and missionaries led to the foundation of Pentecostal groups in Oregon. Seymour converted pastors and ministers who already held senior leadership positions in several denominations. He thereby Pentecostalized the Assemblies of God and the Burning Bush holiness movement in Indiana, Oklahoma, Arkansas, Missouri, Texas, North Carolina, and "throughout the South, sweeping in Holiness leaders and movements like . . . [the] Fire Baptized Holiness Church, the Pentecostal Free-Will Baptist Church, and the Church of God (Cleveland, TN)" (Espinosa 2014:319–320, 325, 329). By the end of 1907, Seymour's apprentices in the theology and practice of Pentecostal worship had established missions and made converts in Liberia, South Africa, Egypt, Lebanon, Palestine, Sweden, Norway, England, Scotland, Ireland, India, Japan, China, Korea, Australia, New Zealand, Chile, Mexico, Venezuela (in 1910), Canada, Brazil, Argentina, and Puerto Rico (in 1916; Espinosa 2014:324). The pentecostal style that today flourishes in Guatemala and throughout the Protestant and Catholic pentecostal world was thus born in and nurtured from Los Angeles.

In the United States and other countries, the movement fostered charismatic but relatively unlettered preachers who shared the trials of life with their parishioners. All congregants had access to the pulpit and, later, the microphone. Many spoke in tongues. "Prophetesses" interpreted what had been said, ensuring that women's grievances were heard in the community. People of all races and stations, but mainly the poor, experienced equally the manifestations of the presence of the Holy Spirit in their bodies through boisterous song, intense prayer, bodily agitation, and much-needed healings. As they framed their practice, anyone who wanted it could have unmediated, untheologized, egalitarian access to an experience of God in their minds and bodies. All could manifest that experience by speaking in tongues the messages too profoundly painful—or joyful—to be expressed in words. Their messages were then interpreted by others and expressed the consensus of the congregation in an open, responsive, change-enabling revelatory style. Pentecostals promulgated the notion that their only salvation lay in these gifts of God.

But Pentecostals also urged strict adherence to the laws of God (as they interpreted the Bible), abjuring vices and urging care for one another. No one other than God and their little community of congregants would or could cure them, for the world was utterly corrupt. All could be healed of bodily and spiritual afflictions by praying and by claiming Christ as their only protector and source of salvation. In a world of disease and hardship, all needed both bodily and spiritual healing. Pentecostalism offered precisely the egalitarian and supportive mini-society that people need when they are caught in that limbo between a collapsed old society and an exclusionary new one. Moreover, these characteristics spread around the world with considerable uniformity. The pentecostal God and rituals internationalized, as Durkheim (2001[1912]) said they would, in part because they spoke to shared problems of collapse and exclusion experienced in the Christianized postcolonial Global South.

Given the blockage represented by the Pacific Ocean, fulfillment of the American dream had to lie in another dimension, not in the physical. Seymour found it in a set of religious principles and practices. That is why Seymour's quest materialized in Los Angeles and soon flourished around the world.

Why did Seymour succeed where others, like Parham, did not? I submit that Seymour's revitalization succeeded because his religion initially crossed racial barriers, thus charismatically breaching one of US society's most profound social ills. In that regard and at that point in time, Seymour's Pentecostalism became a revitalization movement, proclaiming the illness of society and establishing a clear path to change and improve it. Parham, by contrast, did not integrate his congregations. He neither critiqued nor corrected the main structural ill of US society. Indeed, he promoted racial segregation. Seymour's Pentecostalism succeeded because Americans of all races, but black people especially, faced the collapse and exclusion embedded in racism, and he preached and practiced a solution. His revitalization movement gathered energy against the corruption of the racism in the society in which it was embedded. It succeeded because new religions bring

innovation, and Seymour's innovation brought social healing. The post–Civil War political process certainly had not achieved the end of color-based discrimination. Jim Crow saw to that. Yet in this new religion, blacks and whites attended church and worshipped together. They laid hands on each other, healed each other, and fell down in the spirit together. Many, even some whites, found the message that "race was irrelevant" to be compelling. Unfortunately, factionalism combined with Jim Crow pressures and prejudices to quickly resegregate the Pentecostal movement and give rise to race-based Pentecostal denominations (Espinosa 2014:126–142).

Beyond a striving for unconditional equality, Seymour's experience highlights one additional parallel between the Pentecostal florescences in Los Angeles and in Guatemala: earthquakes. Annis (1987:1–3) describes how the Pentecostal preachers in Guatemala drew metaphors of sinfulness and the need for change from the massive 1976 earthquake that leveled great swaths of the country. They called the quake a sign of God's wrath toward Guatemalans for their sins, God's call for Guatemalans to repent and convert. These same beliefs had appeared seventy years earlier in the United States following the San Francisco quake. At the time of the quake in Guatemala, Protestantism was about a hundred years old there and Pentecostalism perhaps fifty. Seymour, however, had brought his congregation to Pentecostal glossolalia, their sign of God's grace, only nine days before the earthquake that shook both San Francisco and Los Angeles. Yet the style of American Pentecostalism and much of the message had already been established pre-quake. The quake was not the cause of Pentecostal success in either Guatemala or Los Angeles; revitalization was.

The subsequent spread of American Pentecostalism followed the US fault lines of race and class. Pentecostalism reached into all areas of the country, but it succeeded and spread most brilliantly among black people and poor whites in the South, in rural areas, and in urban slums, all areas undergoing the constraints of collapse and exclusion vis-à-vis the cultural dream.

Having argued for the influence of collapse and exclusion on Pentecostalism in terms of economics and racism—the failure of some sectors to access the American dream—I now reargue the case for the widespread adoption of Pentecostalism specifically in 1906. I do so in relation to the great transformation of the United States from a hand- and animal-powered society to an industrial power no longer centered on farming. Both the industrialization of the United States and the concomitant movement of farms, farming, and farmers from primary to secondary place in the prestige system of the country derived from increased use of internal combustion engines and fossil fuels. These were momentous cultural events. Old forms of labor and culture collapsed. Mule- and horsepower no long fed America. Machines did. In the process, farm people migrated to urban centers.

I show this cultural and structural change in graphs of three sets of figures, one on animal power, one on population distribution in relation to farms, and one on farm size. Since colonial times, the American farm system had been powered by humans and animals as a primary source of work energy. From the Civil War to the end of the Great Depression, however, farm systems once dependent on animal power and hand labor slowly underwent eclipse, if not outright collapse. Farms and farmers increasingly used portable industrial machinery driven by motors using fossil fuels to do their agricultural work. Figure 26.1 graphs the inexorable move from a farm system based on human and animal power to a farm system worked by industrial machines. The use of live animal power peaked in 1920 and then steadily dropped until 1960. The drop, however, was even more precipitous than these figures indicate because this chart includes not just working horses and mules (which diminished in number), but also "pet" horses used strictly for pleasure and sport (which increased in number). Were figures available on mules alone or on work and transportation horses alone, the reduction in farm dependence on animal power might show up even more starkly, for the use of horses as pets and for sport by the comfortable classes likely masks the precipitous drop in animal power used on the nation's farms and roads. Figure 26.2 portrays the animal-to-mechanical restructuring of the farmer's way of life at two points: 1920 and 1962. The chart underscores the immense transition to motorized farm operations.

In figure 26.2, live horsepower drops from 22 million to 3 million head; mechanical horsepower, by contrast, rises from 18 million to 382 million animal-equivalent units, what we now call the "horsepower rating" of engines. The steady rise in the use of tractors, both in number of units and in horsepower, can be seen in figure 26.3, where they are displayed as a percentage of 1960 figures. Clearly, the culture of farming with animal power was vanishing, a culture in transition if not in collapse, between 1890 and 1940, and clearly was under stress between 1900 and 1910,

the period during which Parham tinkered with Pentecostalism and Seymour delivered full-blown, enduring Pentecostal success.

A second way to look at the transformation of farm culture explores changing farm size, number of farms, and farming population in absolute numbers and as a percentage of US society. Figure 26.4 shows the rapid reduction of farm size from 1850 to a low point in 1880, just twenty-six years before the Azusa Street birth of Pentecostalism. The reduction in farm size was precipitated by inheritance subdivisions brought on by population increase. From 1890 to 1920, farm size remained essentially flat, though the US population (figure 26.5) continued to rise. The number of people resident on US farms reached a high point about 1910 and then began a slow decline until about 1940, when the farm population started to drop rapidly (figure 26.5).

With people moving away from farm dependence, farms no longer had to be chopped into pieces for inheritance. And with increased use of tractors as a source of power, mini-farms could be—indeed, had to be—consolidated to run more efficiently. This process simultaneously depopulated and industrialized the farms. The turning point in the curve of both processes—the fulcrum indicating collapse of the old way of life—occurred soon after the 1901 speaking-in-tongues event in Parham's Kansas and the 1906 start of Azusa Street Pentecostalism. Thus, for example, the farm population reached its maximum in 1910 (figure 26.5). In the same year, average farm size reached its nadir. By 1920, farm size had begun to increase under the new processes of consolidation brought on by mechanization and industrialization. The number of farms reached a maximum in approximately 1920 and then began to drop. According to Marx, such rapid change in the modality of farm culture and its risks should have impacted religion. It did. There followed the rapid pentecostalization of American religion from a handful of first adherents at Bonnie Brae Street and a few hundred attendees at Azusa Street to some 75 million American Pentecostal and Charismatic Renewal adherents in 2000 (Burgess and van der Maas 2003:277).

From the first data available (1840), one sees in table 26.1 (column 4) a continuous decrease in farmers as a percentage of the US population. The country was urbanizing and industrializing. All of this indicates a transition to what US representative Champ Clark in 1909 called the industrial or "intensive" mode of farming. More precisely, family farming powered by animal labor and done

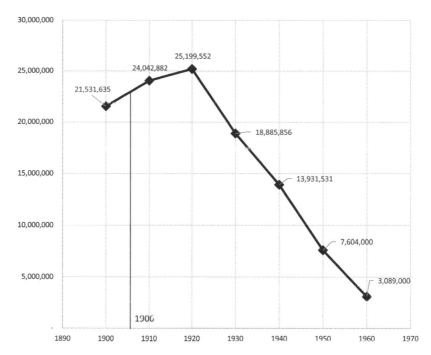

Figure 26.1. US horse and mule census, 1900–1960. Note the 1906 mark for the beginning of Pentecostalism in the United States. *Source*: Kilby 2007:176.

Figure 26.2. Available farm power, US farms. *Source*: Economic Research Service, US Department of Agriculture, 1966:2.

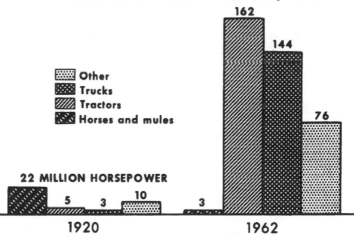

AVAILABLE FARM POWER, U.S.

Figure 26.3. Rise of tractors and tractor "horsepower" on US farms. *Source*: Economic Research Service, US Department of Agriculture, 1966:4.

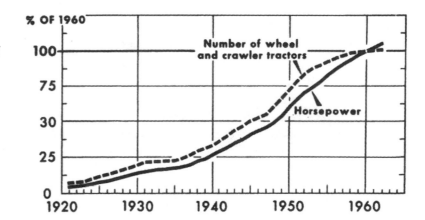

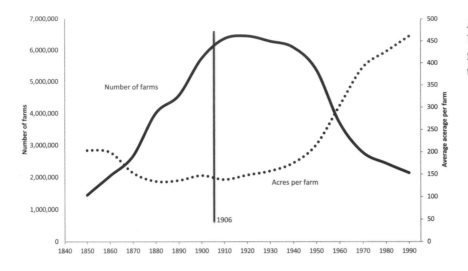

Figure 26.4. Number and acreage of US farms by year. Note the 1906 mark for the beginning of Pentecostalism in the United States. *Source*: Bellis 2019.

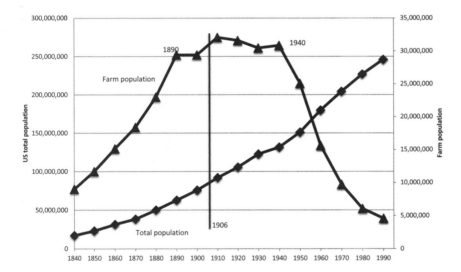

Figure 26.5. US population and farm population. Note the 1906 mark for the beginning of Pentecostalism in the United States. *Source*: Bellis 2019.

in relative isolation was in collapse. America's industrial orientation was on the rise, along with industrial farming. With the number of farmers rapidly declining and farm size fast rising, the rural and urban poor were subjected to even more of a squeeze.[18]

The process of societal change and the associated angst are well summarized in an Associated Press dispatch of Clark's concern, as printed in the Ottawa *Evening Citizen*:

> Washington, D.C., Dec. 29 [1909]—"The present high price[s] for farm products have come to stay; the rural population is playing out; the present census, if it classes the unincorporated villages as towns, will show between 60 and 65 per cent of population in towns," declared Representative Clark of Missouri, the minority leader in

the house yesterday. "At the present rate, in 20 years the United States will cease to be an exporting nation for agricultural products, except as to cotton.

> "One of the principal causes of the high prices of farm products is in the world movement of people towards the towns and cities. While a few people in towns and cities have gardens, and raise chickens and occasionally pigs, practically the entire town and city population are non-producers of anything to eat, but are consumers only. For the first time last year, Argentine [*sic*] beat us in exporting corn; and Argentine and Brazil are now fixing to take the frozen meat trade from us. Until we adopt the intensive system of agriculture we have nearly reached our limit of agricultural output." (Disappearing Farms 1909:2)

TABLE 26.1. US FARM POPULATION AND MECHANIZATION

YEAR	US POPULATION	ESTIMATED FARM POPULATION	FARMERS AS % OF LABOR FORCE	# OF FARMS	AVERAGE ACREAGE PER FARM	TOTAL ACREAGE IN FARMS	ACREAGE PER CAPITA, US POPULATION	ACREAGE PER CAPITA, US FARM POPULATION	FARM POPULATION PER FARM	# OF HORSES AND MULES
1840	17,069,453	9,012,000	69							
1850	23,191,786	11,680,000	64	1,449,000	203	294,147,000	12.68	25.18	8.06	
1860	31,443,321	15,141,000	58	2,044,000	199	406,756,000	12.94	26.86	7.40	
1870	38,558,371	18,373,000	53	2,660,000	153	406,980,000	10.55	22.15	6.91	
1880	50,155,783	22,981,000	49	4,009,000	134	537,206,000	10.71	23.38	5.73	
1890	62,941,714	29,414,000	43	4,565,000	136	620,840,000	9.86	21.11	6.44	
1900	75,994,266	29,414,000	38	5,740,000	147	843,780,000	11.10	28.69	5.12	21,531,635
1910	91,972,266	32,077,000	31	6,366,000	138	878,508,000	9.55	27.39	5.04	24,042,882
1920	105,710,620	31,614,269	27	6,454,000	148	955,192,000	9.04	30.21	4.90	25,199,552
1930	122,775,046	30,455,350	21	6,295,000	157	988,315,000	8.05	32.45	4.84	18,885,856
1940	131,820,000	30,840,000	18	6,102,000	175	1,067,850,000	8.10	34.63	5.05	13,931,531
1950	151,132,000	25,058,000	12.2	5,388,000	216	1,163,808,000	7.70	46.44	4.65	7,604,000
1960	180,007,000	15,635,000	8.3	3,711,000	303	1,124,433,000	6.25	71.92	4.21	3,089,000
1970	204,335,000	9,712,000	4.6	2,780,000	390	1,084,200,000	5.31	111.64	3.49	
1980	227,020,000	6,051,000	3.4	2,439,510	426	1,039,231,260	4.58	171.75	2.48	
1990	246,081,000	4,591,000	2.6	2,143,150	461	987,992,150	4.01	215.20	2.14	

Sources: Bellis 2019; Kilby 2007.

Representative Clark saw an end to the older method of production: "we have nearly reached our limit of agricultural output" with family farms "ceas[ing] to export" and the "rural population . . . playing out." Here was the competitive angst: a new mode of production—"the intensive system of agriculture" or what would come to be known as industrial agriculture—was needed, or the United States would be eclipsed by such entities as Argentina and Brazil. Between 1900 and 1910, the mode of production in the United States was clearly at its fulcrum point, transitioning from hand labor and animal power to motorized industrialization. The farm culture associated with manual labor was at risk and in collapse. But that was not all that was in transition.

At approximately the same time, around 1905, there was another major change: the emergent idea of relativity and uncertainty in all things physical. Johnson (1983:1)

argues that "the modern world began on 29 May 1919, when photographs of a solar eclipse . . . confirmed the truth of a new theory of the universe." I would quibble with that date. The old Newtonian cosmology had been under assault for several years, and 1919 only "confirmed" the emerging truth that was first published by Einstein in 1905. Science was making its presence felt in new ways, transforming the world. There was a host of transformative scientific and science-related technical inventions taking hold in society during the late 1800s and early 1900s: the first gas-powered auto in 1885, the first films in 1895, the first mechanically powered air flight in 1903, and so forth. Indeed, I argue that the modern world began when it was possible to conceive of relativity applying to physical things, as Einstein proposed in 1905, thereby challenging the Newtonian paradigm of the solid nature of the universe. Thus, virtually simultaneously with the rise of Pentecostalism in 1906, the old cognitive paradigm of Newtonian absolutes that defied the common senses threatened to collapse, to be replaced with Einstein's less accessible relativistic paradigm.

The theory of relativity affected not only physics, but "at the beginning of the 1920s the belief began to circulate, for the first time at a popular level, that there were no longer any absolutes: of time and space, of good and evil, of knowledge, and above all of value. Mistakenly but perhaps inevitably, relativity became confused with relativism" (Johnson 1983:4). Amid the movement of American life from agriculture to industry and science, such transformative thought provided fertile ground for the counterpoint of Pentecostalism's moral certitudes.

Are the nearly simultaneous inventions of Pentecostalism, relativity, scientific invention, industrialization, and urbanization unrelated coincidences? I doubt it. They are interrelated responses to a new cultural and societal condition in which educational access and novel thought would be the keys to success rather than the acquisition of land or business by inheritance or by state-sponsored homestead giveaways and westward movement. Whatever the cause, in the early twentieth-century United States, science, earth, society, and religion all quaked in unison.

CONCLUSION

Throughout this chapter I have explored the international distribution of a new God—the Christian Pentecostal God—and the beliefs and practices of his simultaneously mournful and joyful devotees. As Durkheim (2001[1912]:212) says of Australia's tribal gods, the Christian Pentecostal God has "resisted enclosure within a politically delimited society." Indeed, the pentecostal God has jumped from the United States to Guatemala, Mexico, and all of Latin America. He has sailed also to the many nations in Africa with a Christian colonial past. The same pentecostal God has traveled to southern India and quite possibly got an independent start there (Rapaka 2013:24–34). Indeed, the Christian Pentecostal God and practices have become the expansive and even dominating form of Christianity throughout the Global South among both Catholics and Protestants. The Christian Pentecostal God and practices have even taken center stage in the Christianity emergent in several nations without a significant Christian colonial

past, among them China and Korea, whose Pentecostal experiences I have not the space to explore.

The pentecostal God "resisted enclosure" in the American milieu. Indeed, he has become a pentecostal God on a global scale, suffused through the postcolonial Christianized Global South, apparently for essentially the same reason: because the social processes of colonialism, inadequate decolonization, and population explosion have led to widespread cultural collapse and stress among indigenous and impoverished peoples, while newer modes of capitalism have remained inaccessible and exclusionary to indigenous peoples. Thus, the Christian Pentecostal God thoroughly internationalized, first, because he and his symbolic accoutrements organize a generic, broadly useful, culturally adaptable, and rather portable vision of how to solve individual and societal problems in a postcolonial social context of local cultural collapse and relative exclusion from imported, largely western, socioeconomic alternatives, and second, because he encourages an accurate expression of the pain of that cultural collapse and exclusion. Today, the context of societal similarity stretches far wider than the ecology of colonial contact and Aboriginal distress that Durkheim analyzed using the then-available Australian ethnographies. Today, the sources of pentecostal internationalization include (1) state-based and international public health programs that increase populations, causing otherwise stable indigenous agriculture subsistence systems and their sustaining cultures to become inadequate and collapse, and (2) the absence of access to alternatives in a world left underdeveloped by extractive and often corrupt derivatives of colonialism. These two conditions extend across the postcolonial, Christian, missionized Global South and provide fertile ground for the internationalization of Christian Pentecostalism.

In this context, the new religions, the new gods, the new beliefs, the new angsts, the new prohibitions, and the new prophecies all inculcate new sets of assumptions that define an emerging and expanding view of society and the universe. In Durkheim's perspective, society is changing the idea it has of itself, and that means change in religion. Members of society are changing the ideas they have of society and of their relations to each other. These changes include new assumptions about how to live life and how to decide what needs to be decided. This is so because decisions made at any of the small and large points of life with the old ideologies and religions as guides are manifestly inadequate. The new Christian Pentecostal God and his associated ritual pathways teach people how to express the angst of newly arising social dilemmas and how to at least partially solve those problems. In this regard, Christian Pentecostalism is a religious revitalization movement throughout the world.

For most of the common era, Catholicism's variants ordered European and Mediterranean people's lives through submission to sacraments provided by a priesthood hierarchy. Beginning in about 1450, mainstream Protestantism's various construals have added individualism, a work ethic, and a (western) rational, logical, word-centered, textual theology. But with the failure of local subsistence systems, the Catholic hierarchy became an inflexible impediment, a straitjacket. Likewise, the logic of mainstream, sedate Protestant interpretation no longer sufficed. Words and theology promising postworldly salvation were not enough to help indigenous postcolonial peoples deal with culture collapse and exclusion. Hoped-for salvation could not prevent impending starvation or rectify its presence. Something more active, embodied, and expressive was needed. In the half century before 1900, several charismatic religious events flickered but waned—in India, Wales, the United States, Chile, and elsewhere. The Christian ecstatic response to modernity's pressures consolidated in Azusa Street Pentecostalism and has spread like wildfire internationally: Christian Pentecostalism.

Although I offer worldwide comparisons in this chapter, I am acutely aware of Durkheim's dictum that "we can usefully compare only facts that we know well." The facts I know well are the Guatemalan materials. But Durkheim (2001[1912]:80) goes on: "Now, when we try to encompass all sorts of societies and civilizations, we cannot know any with the necessary competence." I have certainly exceeded the limits of my anthropological competence by dealing with the rise and context of Christian Pentecostalism in so many societies in this chapter. What I have done must be taken only as a hint that the approach I advocate may prove fertile if applied by anthropologists and others to the areas they deeply understand. Only in-depth comparisons can make thorough assessments of the validity of this approach. While likely to be in error on many points, my approach, if it stimulates further research, will have fulfilled my purpose and made a contribution to an understanding of our shared humanity and of the nature of religion and religious change in cultures around the world.

NOTES

1. In a 10 percent survey in 1988, Almolonga was 52 percent Catholic, 48 percent Protestant, with a population of about 12,000 (up from the 1980 census figure of 8,000).

2. Here are the data:

COMMUNITY	TOTAL POPULATION	POPULATION IN HOUSEHOLDS OWNING	
		≤ 1 MANZANA	> 1 MANZANA
Almolonga	8000	6880	1120
Zunil	7000	4900	2100

The χ^2 for the above is 5667.9152, and thus the probability of drawing this distribution by chance from a nonskewed population is less than 0.01 percent. Conclusion: the populations and land situations of the people of Almolonga and those of Zunil are substantially and significantly different.

If one divides the above population figures by 6 to get an approximation of the number of households that are at or below one *manzana* versus above one *manzana*, the χ^2 figure is 94.9126, with, again, $p < 0.01$. Statistically, the two communities differ substantially and significantly.

3. In Zunil, 85 percent of the 890 arable *manzanas* is owned by 30 percent of the population (12 percent Ladino and 18 percent Maya).

4. Dirección General de Cartografía (1961–1962, vol. 2) lists Zunil as "approximately 92 sq. km." and Almolonga as "approximately 20 sq. km." This difference in the areas of the two *municipios* enhances my argument. At 90 and 20 square kilometers, the chi-square probability of randomly drawing this difference of land and population distribution from a single system is less than 0.01. Statistically, Goldin's equality hypothesis must be rejected.

5. The comfortable, almost middle-class lifestyle of Almolongueños needs one further comment relative to pentecostalization. First, if poverty (whether absolute or relative) were the driver of pentecostalization, then, according to Goldin's data, Zunil would be the pentecostalizing municipality, not Almolonga. Goldin and colleagues' (Goldin 2011; Goldin and Saenz de Tejada 1993) reports, however, clearly indicate that the richer and more comfortable town is the one that has Protestantized. Their data also show that Almolonga's citizens, though comfortably well off, are the ones who have suffered the most culture change. The Almolonga-Zunil case clearly suggests that the driver of Protestantization is not poverty per se, but transformational culture collapse. Almolongueños have dealt with the inadequate arable land

in their *municipio*, vis-à-vis the population, by entering the trucking and transportation business and taking advantage of their favorable location for planting vegetable crops for cash sale.

6. Before Schwartz's health utterly failed, he read an early draft of this book. In our discussions, he confirmed the value of my analysis for his early work in the Petén, and he indicated that he intended to collaborate in a restudy of religious change in the region. Perhaps someone can honor his intent by engaging in such a restudy of the relevant towns in the Petén-Flores region and the multiplicity of religions now present there, possibly using the multisited field school model reflected in this book and detailed in Hawkins 2014 and Hawkins and Adams 2014.

7. Although O'Neill (2010) mentions evangelistic outreach at several points, he does not adequately tie the goal of outreach conversion into the analysis of how the project of self-monitoring behavior actually self-disciplines and thus corrects the nation's central problem of a culture undermined by elite corruption and inability or refusal to obey law. In spite of my critique, I find O'Neill's book to be a remarkably penetrating and useful analysis.

8. Nevertheless, the behavior following the schism may have had some input from Pentecostal events in Azusa Street. "In 1907," the Hoovers "received a letter from a missionary friend . . . who wrote about a Christian revival, where people had been baptized by the Holy Spirit, spoken in other tongues, fallen to the floor, and had various visions. After this the Hoovers started corresponding with leaders of other churches in India, Venezuela, Norway, and the United States, which had had similar experiences" (Lindhardt 2012:35). In describing their Chilean congregation, the Hoovers noted the "laughing, weeping, shouting, singing, foreign tongues, visions and ecstasies during which the individual fell to the ground and felt himself caught up into another place, to heaven, to paradise, in splendid fields, with various kinds of experience: conversations with God, the angels or the Devil" (Lindhardt 2012:35, quoting Hoover 1977:41). Lindhardt does not specify whether the Chilean congregations had already and independently manifested exuberant, Spirit-filled pentecostal practices before their Azusa Street contact or whether they were influenced in that direction through correspondence with Azusa Street Pentecostals.

9. The picture is not entirely dark, however. Lindhardt (2012) shows that the youths are beginning to succeed in acquiring educational access. If so, my theory would expect this more successful generation to be less pentecostal than the parental generation unless the continued risk of collapse or exclusion remains a dominant cognitive orientation. In this regard, I note Gooren's (2015) observation that the ten largest Pentecostal denominations in Chile experienced flat to declining growth from 1995 to 2000. Unfortunately, one cannot take these large denominations as a proxy for the whole movement because fission among Protestants and Pentecostals generates new congregations and new growth, which are no longer counted in the original large denomination. Moreover, focus on the largest Pentecostal denominations misses the impact of the Catholic Charismatic Renewal in the ecstatic movement.

10. Endruveit states the erroneous "thirty-three" in his 1975 text, and Chesnut carries that forward in 1997.

11. Data for population of Brazil in 1955 and 1970: https://www.populationpyramid.net/brazil/1955; data for population of Brazil in 1932: https://web.archive.org/web/20110408193914/http://www.populstat.info/Americas/brazilc.htm.

12. Thomas 2008 suggests throughout that Thomasine Christianity survived the Latin onslaught rather well, leaving much of Thomasine Christianity operational among the Syrian and Dalit castes. The complexities Thomas notes of Syrian versus Dalit modes and rates of adoption into Pentecostal practice lie well beyond the scope of this chapter.

13. Thomas (2008) confirms Roberts's (2016) assertions regarding Dalits' orientation toward social and political equality and that Pentecostalism provided an access bridge to modernity (as they saw it).

14. See, for example, http://crossculturalencounters.blogspot.com/search/label/History%20of%20the%20Gypsy%20Pentecostal%20Movement%20in%20Spain; http://crossculturalencounters.blogspot.com/search/label/The%20Gypsy%20Image; http://www.economist.com/node/21557784.

15. The reception of the Spirit, manifest as glossolalia, on the morning of the first day of the new century, whether mythically reconstructed or not, provides an apt symbol of new religious beginnings. Under Parham's leadership and personal behavior, however, pentecostal experiences did not "take" widely or spread. Why not? I must be speculative here, but I think this is because Parham's version expressed the anxiety of the time but did not offer a solution to the chief problem and contradiction of US society: racism. In Parham's renewal, nonwhites were excluded. It thus did not provide a revitalization solution to nor critique a key problem. Thus, Parham's work should be considered a precursor spark to the flourishing fire stoked at the Bonnie Brae and Azusa Street meetings in 1906, in which Seymour identified and preached a colorblind solution to the racial ills that beset US society.

16. I have found Borlase (2006) the most satisfying biography, and I have used him as the final arbiter of the details of Seymour's life. Espinosa's (2014) documents helped more than his harder-to-follow history, which is marred by a thinner emotional portrayal of Seymour's character. Martin (1999) was also central to my understanding of Seymour.

17. The dream of escape and of gaining riches by moving rather

exactly matches the dreams of many Guatemalans, both Maya and non-Maya. Many Mayas dream of and hear about phenomenal hourly wages to the north. They then mortgage land to migrate to the United States, where they hope to earn enough to redeem their land and fund a business or a home. They still encounter discrimination, however, this time because of the weaknesses inherent in their undocumented status. Many do find a better economic opportunity structure than is available to indigenes in Guatemala. Promoted by *coyotes*, local rumor, and the prominent construction of three-story concrete houses by a few successful returnees, legal or illegal migration to the United States offers the hope of escape, riches, and a return with an infusion of cash to generate a new life.

18. These figures are problematic because they apply at the national level. As the nation expanded westward, the ecology of farming changed toward dry-land and ranching practices. Farm size necessarily rose. These ecological factors impacted the Homestead Act, which was revised from 160-acre grants to 320 acres for dry-land areas and, later, 640 acres for cattle ranch expansion in the yet drier western United States. To avoid the impact of this ecological change on my figures, I would need to prove farm size expansion within particular ecosystems. This might be done by state, or within ecological areas. Perhaps someone will find such figures and challenge or better confirm my analysis.

Conclusion

Accounting for Current Pentecostal/Charismatic Appeal in the Digital North

JOHN P. HAWKINS

"TODAY, CHRISTIANITY IS LIVING THROUGH a reformation that will prove to be even more basic and more sweeping than the one that shook Europe during the sixteenth century," writes Harvey Cox (2011:xvi–xvii). "The epicenter of Christianity is no longer in Europe (or in its North American extension) but in . . . the Global South." The phenomenal growth and general attributes of Christian Pentecostalism in Guatemala that we have depicted in this book exemplify that second reformation and epicenter shift in Christianity.

The summary of my thesis is this: Christian Pentecostalism converted people and grew—in Guatemala and in the Global South—for two reasons. The first is the disruption of the collapse and exclusion complex I have identified. During the nineteenth century and especially the twentieth, indigenous peoples throughout the Global South experienced high stress from indigenous and urban culture collapse and exclusion resulting from the decay of colonial administrations and the disruptions and exclusions of global capitalist penetration and restructuring. Part of that collapse and disruption derived from national and missionary health services and related sanitation improvements that triggered population expansion to the point local cultures could no longer sustain family subsistence within their traditional cultural pathways, given their lands and resources.

The second reason for Christian Pentecostalism's spread is its response to that disruption. Christian Pentecostals' answers to the cascade of difficulties glossed as modernization have been enormously successful because its liturgy and the life practices enjoined upon *evangélicos* and *carismáticos* have enabled adherents to accurately express the chaos and cacophony in their lives of collapse and exclusion. At the same time, those expressive and other liturgical mechanisms and the preached prohibitions and lifestyles have enabled adherents to solve at least partially a significant number of problems inherent in living in chaos and scarcity. Many of these generally beneficial small-group social responses are couched in the idiom of gifting. The gifts—including healing, small-group support, and gender restructuring—not only work to solve perceived problems, but also draw in additional adherents via the cultural implications of reciprocity.

People find the gifts inherent in the Christian Pentecostal lifestyle and liturgy to be effective aids as they confront the collapse of their culture and their exclusion from neoliberal society. Christian Pentecostalism's experiential, crisis-centered, end-of-a-corrupt-world, angst-expressive style appeals culturally, and its small-group structure and free gift giving are welcomed socially. It promotes access to literacy, abstinence from alcohol, sexual discipline, male gender reformation, work reliability, family orientation, and connection to evangelist world networks. All these constitute a system of gifts that both help people live with the stresses they experience and bind people to the gift-giving groups. Because the behavioral injunctions solve problems to a degree, Christian Pentecostalism increasingly makes sense to many Mayas and to a broad range of others both in and beyond Guatemala who, in a shattering world, have lost all hope. Moreover, some parts of Christian Pentecostalism make sense because they resonate with deeply held indigenous cultural premises. Other parts make sense because they help pentecostalized Mayas adapt to the emerging global market system. Finally, Christian Pentecostal liturgy feels good because it offers Mayas a legitimate place to express the anxieties generated by land shortage, culture collapse, food insecurity, and the generalized sense of risk and violence in Guatemalan society.

The practical result of these compatibilities is a religious style that appeals to excluded and at-risk peoples. Protestant and Catholic pentecostalisms thus have expanded rapidly in Guatemala, and they continue to grow around the world. They have attracted so many adherents because in the postcolonial Global South, people are pressed out of their heritage cultures and effectively excluded from the penetrating new systems. What remains accessible to them is religion, old and new. Around the world, the new Christian Pentecostal religions confront collapse and exclusion with revitalization movements that critique and change society via individuals' adoption of moral injunctions promulgated by the congregation and its leaders.

My approach to religion (see chapter 25) reflects Guatemalan Maya beliefs that these solutions to their problems are gifts from God. Maya concepts of gifts and covenant thus parallel the work of Mauss and Malinowski regarding gifts and reciprocity. Brown (2000:164) argues that the linkage of gift giving and reciprocity is likely a human cultural universal. I accept that proposition. I suggest that the universal linkage between gift giving and reciprocity arises out of the shared social experience of the risks taken by women giving birth and the gifts given in society and within the family that derive from the tasks of protecting and raising children. If so, the nature of religion links it intimately with nationality, for states have an interest in reproduction, and religion is often used as a state symbol or a symbol of tribe and society. Religion also links directly to kinship, as Schneider (1969) suggests and Durkheim (2001[1912]) observes, because kinship relates to birthing, and birthing generates gifting and reciprocity. Moreover, via gift giving and reciprocity, religions share in the attributes of kinship defined as relationships of "a code for conduct enjoining diffuse, enduring solidarity" (Schneider 1984:53; see also Schneider 1969:120). All this confirms Durkheim's fundamental observation that all of the ideas fundamental to human existence derive from the experience of society, and that experience gets encoded in religion such that religion becomes the soul of society by promulgating, sacralizing, and representing those core ideas.

Throughout this book, I have combined Mauss's ideas on the power of the gift with Weber's ideas on how certain key elements of a religion change behavior and, eventually, the structure of society. Weber and Wallace further show how charismatic leaders create new ideas to reform society when old ideas no longer generate sustainable behavior. I set all these thoughts in the context of Marx's remarkably insightful concept that social change will be generated—forced, actually—by the pressures of continuously transforming modes of production when those modes no longer sustain the underlying premises of a culture and society.

Guatemalans have indeed experienced a series of "great social upheavals," as Durkheim puts it, or "great historical upheavals," per Marx. For Mayas, the greatest of these upheavals has been the loss of their ability to produce the corn that stands at the center of their culture and traditional religion. Guatemala's Mayas have expressed the pain, anxiety, and sense of broken covenant attendant to that disruption—that upheaval—in their movement toward the pentecostal liturgy of distress, which voices the anguish and uncertainty of their lives. The new Christian Pentecostalisms are a "protest," as Marx suggests, of religion. They are a lamentation arising from the anxiety this loss of culture occasions and an institutional framework that supports profound decisions to reform at the individual level so as to ameliorate what these Mayas (and other people elsewhere) protest and deeply lament. Thus, I have combined and used the ideas of Marx, Weber, Durkheim, Mauss, and Wallace to explore the ongoing religious transformation of Nahualá and Santa Catarina Ixtahuacán. Moreover, I have shown that these ideas apply in many other locations in the Christianized postcolonial Global South.

ON SECULARIZATION, ALIENATION, AND RELIGIOUS ANGST IN THE DIGITAL NORTH

In the remainder of this chapter I shift my gaze from Guatemala and the Global South to what one might call the Digital North. In particular, I explore in a rather speculative way the implications of this study for my own society, the United States, as an example of religious change in the Digital North. I have partially done so in the previous chapter, when I examined the origins of Azusa Street Pentecostalism. Here, however, I examine more recent events. Note that I have not done fieldwork nor studied the literature extensively for this chapter; I have simply lived in the United States as an anthropologically informed observer.

I know that the pentecostal movement is not limited to marginal peoples caught between cultural collapse and exclusion nor to Americans of more than a century ago during the birth of the Pentecostal experience.

There is, after all, a widespread movement toward charismatic expression in many of the mainline, sedate religious denominations in US society today. In these mainline Catholic and Protestant denominations, pentecostal behavior infuses the Spirit into people's bodies and brings spirited behavior into their worship patterns. Furthermore, the rise of the neo-Pentecostal megachurches and the widespread acceptance of them suggests that pentecostalization is increasingly relevant in mainstream American and European society.

But that global spread seems to embrace a contradiction with regard to the thesis of this book. Does not mainstream acceptance of pentecostal practice in the Digital North contradict the notion that pentecostalism appeals to people experiencing cultural collapse and systemic exclusion?

I approach this question through examination of the now-contested hypothesis that western society is becoming increasingly secular and of the notion that people in society have become alienated. The argument works like this. As science increasingly takes over sectors of the belief system, as education covers many types of learning (even teaching civic morals), and as politics handles what once were religious issues regarding obedience to authority and law, religion diminishes in importance, power, and institutional domain.[1] Indeed, religion becomes primarily a guide relevant to life only in the private, personal, and domestic domain (Durkheim 2001[1912]:324–327). Moreover, as individualism, choice, and freedom from restraint become increasingly important in defining courtship, marriage, and gender and in structuring the individual's moral path, religion's place even in organizing the individual and domestic domains becomes diminished and is called into question.

For Weber, part of that increasing insignificance has occurred as the work ethic has become detached from religious justification. Work has been made a secular aspect of individual self-expression and self-worth. Work gives a person "identity." Weber (2002[1905]:115, emphases in original) trenchantly characterizes this process: "The idea of the *obligation* of man to the possessions entrusted to him, to which he subordinates himself as servant and steward or even as 'moneymaking machine,' lies on life with its chill weight. *If* he will only persevere on the ascetic path, then the more possessions he acquires, the heavier becomes the feeling of responsibility to preserve them undiminished to God's glory and to increase them through tireless labor." Weber's male pronouns are dated,

but his core idea is not. In a secular and individualist society, one feels a responsibility to work. But many no longer feel that work is a tool with which to build "God's glory," as the Protestant ethic would enjoin. One feels it, rather, as a method with which to build one's own social status and glory. Ego—not God, not Durkheim's society as God—becomes the center. In either the former religious situation or the current secular case, one tries to "increase" one's possessions "through tireless labor." But, Weber says, some now excel at such tireless labor entirely without religious justification. Weber (2002[1905]:115) then asks rhetorically, "Which of us with eyes to see has not met people of this persuasion," that is, people tirelessly laboring without religious justification "right up to our own time?" And who among us has not heard, to quote Weber (119) again, "the comforting assurance that the unequal distribution of this world's goods was the special work of the providence of God?" One current answer to Weber's latter question is that the rich have rightfully earned their portion of the current distribution of wealth by their good decisions and astute risk taking. Today, we are told, the "unequal distribution" results not from "the hidden hand of God's grace" and the "working out" of God's "secret purposes, of which we know nothing," as Weber (2002[1905]:119) phrases the Protestant ethic. Rather, today, the unequal distribution is said to result from the working out of the complexities of the economy, of which we still know very little and of which too much is still held secret. Thus, God and the economy become equally mystified and mutually substitutable. Fate happens: some people get rich because the free-market economy—having become God—wills it.

In the Pietist world that Weber (2002[1905]:121, for all quotes in this paragraph) studied, "concern for outward possessions . . . should sit lightly on the shoulders." Material concerns should be worn "like a thin cloak." In capitalism's evolution, however, material concerns have become central, and religious justification for material gain has diminished. As Weber observes, materialism now sits like "a shell as hard as steel." The "outward goods of this world" have "gained increasing and finally inescapable power over men, as never before in history." Thus, by Weber's day, the religious spirit had "fled" from the materialist cloak so that it had become a "steel shell" or, in other translations, an "iron cage" that captured the capitalist participants. But had the religious spirit fled from this shell for all time? "Who knows? Certainly, victorious capitalism has no further need for this [religious spirit as a] support now that it rests on the foundation of the machine." As a result, a fully secular "'duty in a call-ing' haunts our lives like the ghost of once-held religious beliefs." One's job begets one's identity, without which one cannot live. Pursuit of jobs and pursuit of wealth now constitute the core of one's being, replacing pursuit of God. One's own grace, shown via wealth, becomes central.

Here is Weber's source of meaninglessness and alien-ation in modern society. It is not Marx's alienation—caused when the fruits of the worker's labor are structur-ally stolen from him or her or when the labor is rendered unfulfilling by being broken into boring, repetitive com-ponents, mere segments of the total production. Rather, for Weber, alienation comes from corruption within the self resulting from the removal of a moral or religious rationale for work at the same time that work has become central and consuming. Here also are resonances with Durkheim's notion that the core issue of religion, and indeed of all social life, concerns the building of moral justifications that make life meaningful. Life is rendered meaningless when, in Weber's terms, "doing one's job" becomes both centrally important and yet "cannot be directly linked to the highest spiritual and cultural val-ues." To be sure, according to Weber, work may be felt to be more than mere economic coercion. That is, some may work for more than just to pay the bills. Neverthe-less, today as in Weber's time, the individual "usually makes no attempt to find any meaning" in work (Weber 2002[1905]:121).

Thus, according to Weber, the evolution of modernity has gone from Pietist asceticism, in which work glorifies God and signals one's selection among the redeemed, to individualist devotion to work, in which work glorifies, honors, and forms the defining attribute of "self." Self replaces God. The transition, says Weber, leads to civi-lizational meaninglessness. The circular referentiality of "work," "self," and "identity" isolates women and men. Humankind has been alienated by that isolation, but not just from the objects men and women produce. In mov-ing from sacred to secular, humankind is alienated from society itself because, as Durkheim theorizes, religion is what connects and maintains humans' attachment to society and moralizes us into sentient rather than alien-ated and desensitized human beings. If this is indeed so, should we be at all surprised that people, via religious institutions—Durkheim's soul of society—embark on a strident and spirited critique of society's meaninglessness or its corruptions? That, in fact, has been the Christian Pentecostal message—a critique of current society.

CRITIQUING MARX

Marx, too, critiques industrializing society. In part of that critique, he considers religion to be an illusion that keeps the working class compliant to the exploitations of the elites. Weber and Wallace, by contrast, see religion as a source of charismatic transformation. Charismatic ideas and charismatic leaders transform society. Through the power of sacralized ideas and the consequences of the internalized bodily disciplines linked to those ideas, people slowly work change on the society and economy through millions of little decisions guided by ideology and symbol. It is a process that Giddens (1984, 1993) has called structuration. In religious revitalization, however, the transformation in cosmology and behavior can occur quite rapidly; the old premises or behaviors are replaced by newly invented or externally borrowed ones con-sciously intended to correct the nature of society.

Wallace investigated the source of social charisma. One source is prophetic reconceptualization deriving from one's experience of culture crisis from overpopula-tion, colonialism, or the penetrations of global markets and media. Handsome Lake, for example, was an Iroquois prophet seeking to restructure Iroquoian society when it was confronted by the overwhelming impacts of migra-tion and new technology arriving from Europe (Wallace 2003[1971]). An extensive cargo cult literature derives from Wallace and Weber. There have been other revi-talization movements, the one led by William Seymour prominent among them.

Ultimately, Durkheim helps one understand why revi-talization-directed charisma must exist from time to time. "Religious forces . . . consist . . . of transfigured collec-tive forces, that is moral forces. They are made of ideas and feelings that awaken in us the spectacle of society," he writes (Durkheim 2001[1912]:240). Society and its indi-viduals are symbiotic. On the one hand, the individual cannot survive without an organized, supportive society that provides viable subsistence along with a modicum of personal and social security, predictability, and a coher-ent ideology and conception of the cosmos. On the other hand, society cannot survive without individuals being securely attached—socially, culturally, morally—to oth-ers around them and able to make coordinated decisions in their culture's "game of life," all by internalizing and deploying roughly the same rules, strategies, and evalua-tion-guiding symbols. The idea of society that is the soul of religion, a core idea of Durkheim, is in each individual both a moral compass and a leap of faith that generates behavior in a structured society of individuals dealing with a changing environment. If the rules and strategies taught via a culture and confirmed in a religion do not work to produce a viable life, and if the symbols do not help one make sound evaluations of situations and establish adequate goals, one can expect social and religious revitalization change.

Marx thus did not get right the exploitation component of religion. At least during the charismatic transformative period, Christian Pentecostal revitalization and adjustment cult religions have been the source of legitimate, if experimental, courses of action that are in fact revolutionary. Christian Pentecostal revitalizations generate genuine and highly socializing human expression rather than facilitate Mayas' exploitation. They are a source of profound processes of reconceptualization and reimagination that empower individuals to act in socially responsible ways. Humankind therefore has the prospect and the power, through cumulative action based on social critique and premise reconceptualization, to heal society via individualized behavioral change and prayerful focus on a moral whole.

Marx failed to see the agentive and transformative potential of revitalization religions. He did not foresee that, as in Guatemala and throughout much of the Global South, a peaceful religious movement largely ignored by governments would come to dominate the social scene more effectively than any overt protest or violent revolution. Except for seeing religion as protest, Marx substantially missed the transformative power of revitalization religion. I nearly missed theorizing the movement—in spite of having been dressed down by the economist described in the preface.

Finally, in spite of transforming the premises and practices of a quarter of all Christianity, the Christian Pentecostal movement remains largely underappreciated, sometimes disparaged, and until recently, little studied by scholars. Many academics seem uncomfortable with the stridency of Christian Pentecostal worship. According to Marx, the structures of property distribution that define capitalism, combined with greed (or, to put it in more academic terms, an internalized striving for profit, power, social status, and comfort) lead to conflict and instability. If the critique of modern society advanced by Marx and still agreed to by many can be so trenchant, why should academics be surprised or offended by the equally scathing Christian Pentecostal analysis? The Christian Pentecostal critique simply uses different symbols—and not even so different. To say that the world is corrupt—that it is, symbolically, "of the devil"—and that people must throw off the chains of their vices is little different than Marx's message to the proletariat to rise up against capitalism and throw off the chains of their oppressors. The difference is that Christian Pentecostalism alters the location and means of change; it focuses on changing the individual by personal but nonviolent and institutionally nonchallenging decisions. Marx, by contrast, advocates directly confronting derelict social institutions, with violence if necessary.

Yet the Christian Pentecostal message is also a real protest against the binding conditions of society. Should not, therefore, the pentecostal critique of western society be expressed with passionate, Spirit-filled rancor—as loud as an arousing political speech or as spirited as a crowd singing "The Internationale"? Indeed, given the perspectives of Marx, Durkheim, Weber, and Wallace, is it not rather easy to understand the Christian Pentecostal wail and the absolute need for behavioral reformation in the United States as much as in Guatemala? And is not change needed in other countries caught in the continuing chaos of collapsed European colonialism? We academics should appreciate and even empathize with the people in the postcolonial Christianized Global South who have so rapidly accepted the Christian Pentecostal message that revitalization is urgently needed.

Thus I argue that Christian Pentecostalism is cognitively rational. This is, after all, a world where perhaps 40 percent of the US population has experienced collapse and exclusion as automation and the global migration of industries remove jobs while local education systems fail to prepare too many underserved students for success in science and technology. Meanwhile, the upper 20 percent wonder whether and how the late modern global capitalist production system they benefit from can be maintained, given the threats of climate change, maldistribution of wealth, class instabilities, political gridlock, and, most recently, the COVID-19 (novel coronavirus) shutdown. The social critiques of Marx, Gramsci, and Foucault; the commentaries of Pope Francis, Gandhi, and the Buddha; and the basic teachings of pentecostalism about the corrupt nature of human life in the world differ only in detail and symbol, not in content. They differ in style and in the locus of their approach to a solution. Nevertheless, all note some form of alienation, and all have sought to aid the world's marginalized peoples.

PERCEIVED RISK OF COLLAPSE IN THE DIGITAL NORTH

Christian Pentecostal practice is not just a rising phenomenon among marginal peoples. Pentecostal practice has also entered the mainline sedate religions in the Digital North. Parishioners of the mainline denominations who practice pentecostal liturgies and seek its spiritual gifts are formally known in theological literature as charismatics, whether Catholic or Protestant. Pentecostalism has gained widespread middle-class acceptance in the Digital North via the megachurches of neo-Pentecostalism. Why such interest among those who seem not to be in collapse and not at all excluded, but who come from the center of American and, increasingly, European life? Are my approach and my theory wrongheaded? Or is something beyond subsistence collapse and social exclusion going on?

That something, I suggest, is a growing cultural understanding of the difficulties of living with increasing techno-social complexity. What are these difficulties?

First, as technological complexity and the rate of change increase, many individuals throughout the Digital North, particularly rural people and ethnic minorities, get excluded from the educations and other tools they need to integrate with high-speed technological change. That exclusion constitutes not just alienation from the latest forms of modernity but also a collapse of the American dream and therefore a collapse of at least one foundational premise of American culture. So they too experience cultural collapse.

Second, it appears that the combination of capitalism, science, technology, and democracy produces increasingly fragile, complex, and difficult to manage cultural and political economies based on ever-accelerating change. The continual pursuit of technological development seems assured. Moreover, risk and angst increase as the rate of change increases. Why? Among other reasons, with increased complexity comes an increased threat of breakdown and increased individual vulnerability, even for elites. Thus, as Marx asserts, ever-escalating risk and angst are inherent to modern society. As vulnerability and risk become more obvious, one can predict that the Christian Pentecostal expression of angst will increasingly pervade mainstream European and American Christian consciousness, religious theology, and practice. Christian Pentecostal anguish will move from the founding peripheral denominations into segments of the historic denominations and from them to generalized cultural acceptance.

Such is already the case. The more incomprehensibly complex our societies become, the more pertinent the Christian Pentecostal expression of angst will seem intellectually and emotionally. My logic here is not new. As Berger (1999:7) puts it, "Modernity, for fully understandable reasons, undermines all of the old certainties; uncertainty is a condition that many people find very hard to bear; therefore, any movement (not only a religious one) that promises to provide or to renew certainty has a ready market." Donald Trump's nationalism is one manifestation of this "ready market" for supposed solutions to uncertainty; Christian Pentecostalism is another. Indeed, in the United States, these two seem to share a considerable overlap.

The apocalyptic instability that Marx and Engels (1948[1848]:12, for all quotes in this paragraph) suggest is inherent in modern capitalist society derives from that society's drive to be "constantly revolutionizing" itself with improved technology and other transformations. As a result, the "known" and "solid" conventions are "swept away, . . . antiquated before they can ossify." Indeed, social conventions "melt into air" and are "profaned." This has been the Guatemalan experience: various forms of *cofradía* have evaporated; traditionalism has declined as a popular religion; rotational, unpaid local government functions have ceased; men and families migrate; and so on. It is the American experience, too, with the difference that change is celebrated in the United States until the pace becomes disorienting, people get left out of the new way of life, and major segments of the population engage in a politics of resentment and revenge because they find themselves without access to whatever is defined as modern and desirable and, like Guatemalan Mayas, seem to have no place in the new system. They see themselves, like the Mayas, as falling behind.

If this is so, then my theory would predict that the near-collapse of the US and world financial systems in 2007–2008 and the threats to the contracting economies of southern Europe—specifically Greece, Spain, Italy, and Portugal—should have precipitated a significant expansion among Pentecostals and Catholic charismatics in these areas. Here is another place where the logic of my approach can be tested, à la Karl Popper (1965, 1968).

To be sure, small congregations and differentiated practices will solve some of the problems that coreligionists, both men and women, experience. But church organization and practice cannot remove the underlying risk that complexity brings to industrial and postindustrial modes of sustenance and production. If the complexity of modernity is indeed both inherent and unstable, the new pentecostal wail will continue to expand into the more privileged sectors of Christian society worldwide. Moreover, as techno-modernism continues to spread around the world, some version of this anxiety will likely penetrate all traditional and world religions—Islam, Buddhism, Hinduism, and so forth—without distinction. Marty and his coeditors (Marty and Appleby 1991, 1993, 1994, 1995) have already documented the beginnings of this process in their multivolume study of fundamentalism and its instabilities around the world. The rise of fundamentalism in Islam, concurrent with Islam's forced proximity to, comparison with, and exclusion from western modalities, seems obvious. Likely, the Hindu world will follow as urbanization, climate change, water shortage, and monsoon excess impinge further on India's people.

Thus, the new Christian Pentecostal wail will not abate, even in places of improving economic security, because it does not derive primarily from poverty, relative deprivation, or simple lack of market access. It responds rather to the perception that one's culturally affirmed way of life has collapsed or that it could collapse with utter unpredictability. Marx and anthropologists have critiqued western society; Christian Pentecostal preachers extend the critique. The Christian Pentecostal wail is thus the sigh of peoples who have come to agree with Marx on the nature of the problem, but who have chosen an individualist, nonviolent path toward a religious solution. So far, at least in the Global South, this path seems to be more revolutionary and more peaceful than anything proposed by Marx or his followers.[2] We will see how it plays out in the Digital North.

ON THE LONG-TERM CONSEQUENCES OF RELIGIOUS ANGST

Weber argues that a religious premise (that God has predetermined a limited number of people, the elect, who will be saved in heaven) generated a religious angst implicit in wanting an answer to the question, how can I determine if I am one of the saved? The answer was that effective and expansive works in the world were a sign of having been chosen. If you accumulated an ever-expanding portion of

God's creation in the world, effectively collaborating in the expansion of God's creative work, then you showed that you were one of God's elect. You thereby proved your election to heaven and allayed your anxiety. Thus, a purely religious premise led to a psychologically driving question, the answer to which supported the expansion of capitalism and manifested one's divine approbation in the eyes of God. This led to a world-affirming and world-engaging brace of Protestant ascetic religions that set individuals free to try to manage a portion of that world without enjoying (in their view, wasting) too much of it via conspicuous consumption. Fueled by this world-accepting style of religion, capitalism, without being depleted by consumption, became the dominant world order. A religious premise generated a religious angst that contributed to an unexpected real-world outcome of stunning proportions. In Weber's (2002[1905]:35, emphasis in original) words, the "consequences of purely religious motives" led to "cultural effects" that were "unforeseen and *unwished for* consequences . . . far removed from, or even in virtual opposition to, everything that they themselves"—the religious reformers and their adherents at the time—"had in mind."

By thinking of the conversion process from sedate to enthusiastic religions in Guatemala as a revitalization movement, I have taken a somewhat reversed approach to Weber's analysis regarding unanticipated outcomes. Instead of starting with a religious premise that led to angst and, eventually, a question the answer to which results in a specific form of worldly behavior, I started with a worldly condition: subsistence failure and culture collapse. The experience of subsistence failure has led to a worldly angst ("How will my family and I survive?") and to a questioning of religious covenant ("Are my root culture's traditionalist and Ortho-Catholic assumptions about reciprocity between Mayas and God correct, given that my Maya world appears to be falling apart?"). According to Wallace, an answer of no in this significantly stressful environment would lead to the decision to adopt a new set of assumptions. That happened, via Christian Pentecostal assumptions, as portrayed throughout this book.

That conclusion sends my analysis directly back to Weber. Will any of the new assumptions in Christian Pentecostalism generate enough angst among its believers to drive pentecostals to behave sufficiently differently in the world so as to restructure it? So far, the answer seems to be a definite yes with regard to restructuring men's relations to spouse, family, and gender, and a provisional yes with regard to obedience to law and the work ethic. Both obedience to law and the work ethic are often remarked on at the local municipal level, but any societal transformation resulting from obedience to law seems utterly unproven—having no discernible impact at the national level in Guatemala in the political and economic domains. Curiously, the outwardly world-rejecting Christian Pentecostalisms become world-affirming by pursuing local solutions—arrived at by revelation—to the real-world problems of the culturally destroyed. Will some other Christian Pentecostal premise generate a motivating angst that leads to a question, the answer to which produces an unanticipated world-level outcome? Perhaps in 200 more years, we will know.

Finally, do we even need the threat of collapse to account for the continued presence of vibrant religion in modernity? Throughout the last 50,000 years of human evolution, every society that has left any evidence beyond stone tools and rock-ringed fire pits has produced at least some materials that we only seem able to interpret as symbols suggesting that people have long possessed cosmological ideas that entailed gift giving to unseen beings and forces. Given this *longue durée* of religion, perhaps I can safely surmise that the Protestant trajectory that leads to Weber's stone-cold analysis of modern capitalism as a dispirited worship of "work ethic as ultimate being" would unnerve humans at some by now DNA-encoded visceral level and generate a revitalization religion. Given the coevolution of brain, religion, and society, do we even need a perception of cultural collapse or societal instability to account for vibrant religiosity? Would not a culture without religion be a "culture against man," to use Henry's (1963) pithy phrase? Would not a culture without religion be an inhuman culture? And would not some charismatic leader, responding to that inhumanity, surely reinvent vibrant religion?

CONCLUSION

The Christian Pentecostal wail, blaring in Nahualá and Santa Catarina Ixtahuacán from 4 a.m. to 11 p.m. and sometimes throughout the night from the loudspeakers of *evangélico* and *carismático* congregational buildings and even some homes, is the harbinger of those Guatemalans desperately seeking familial stability, economic viability, and political security in an alienating world of global transformation. They find their world crosscut by incomprehensible and, for K'iche' Maya villagers, almost insuperable ethnic and class exclusions. The cry of Christian Pentecostalism in highland Maya Guatemala, throughout most of Latin America, and across the Global South is legitimate, widespread, and growing. The cry needs to be heard for what it is: an expressive and self-protective response to pervasive insecurity and exclusion that attempts to establish the social conditions necessary for family integrity, mental and bodily health, and adequate sustenance in a dignified and secure way of life.

In the Guatemalan case, as Marx and Engels (1968[1848]) predicted, the "sober senses," through which many Mayas "are compelled" to contemplate their land shortage as their "real conditions of life," indicate that the society can no longer function based on corn and colonial modes of governance. It can therefore no longer be cognized using the hierarchical Catholic or the earthy, agricultural, and caprice-laden traditionalist symbols that for 450 years guided a colonial society premised on earth-based subsistence and colonial structures of control and extraction.

These allusions to Marx are deliberate and help one understand the Christian Pentecostal movement in Guatemala and around the world. The religious transformation of Maya Guatemala has occurred simultaneously with other major social movements and cannot be understood apart from them. For Guatemala, the co-occurring social movements include failed revolutionary politics, a revanchist civil war, the unsuccessful efforts of Catholic liberation theology, the demonstrated impotence of a half century of international development aid, and a series of democratically elected but corrupt governments.

All these institutions have attempted change but have failed the Mayas. Only Christian Pentecostal religious revolution has survived, thrived, and helped solve their problems. It has done so, as Brusco (1995) has clearly shown and as this book confirms, by reconstructing gender—especially masculinity—and by providing new forms of psychosocial and physical healing. To perhaps 70 percent of Guatemalans, only these Christian Pentecostalisms are believed to have any chance of improving the individual's, the family's, Guatemala's, or the world's future, a view O'Neill (2010) so carefully documents. In Guatemala, only the religious revolution has triumphed.

But revitalization religion has not triumphed thoroughly. Christian Pentecostalism has not solved the underlying sustenance crisis nor guaranteed Mayas' inclusion in an alternative system of provision. It has only bent the gender structure to provide a temporary palliative. It is a useful workaround that helps in the moment. But it only delays a reckoning because Christian Pentecostalism, although it seems (and promises) to help individuals improve economically, does not yet provide a viable mode of family production in a secure societal and cultural context.

Therefore, one may legitimately ask, how long can the message embodied in the Christian Pentecostal wail remain unattended? I do not know. Today, the Christian Pentecostal wail is the loudest and also the most peaceful voice of social truth and social action in Guatemala and perhaps in the world. It is a distressed and mournful keen that speaks of systemic state and local subsistence failure, social exclusion, intellectual confusion, and individual angst. So far, it is also the most effective human response to these problems and anxieties, with results far less wrenching and far more enduring than revolutionary war.

As Harvey Cox (2011:xvii, for all quotes in this paragraph) affirms, Christian Pentecostals are living through a momentous period that "will prove to be even more basic and more sweeping" than the Reformation "that shook Europe." "The questions in dispute at the time" of the Reformation, he writes, "now appear increasingly provincial." These questions, posed in the 1400s–1500s, largely concerned ways of relating humans to their church. Does one need to pay a church for absolution from sin? Can a lay individual consult the sacred text? How can I determine if I am among the saved? These were narrow questions indeed, although in the long view of history, Weber shows that Luther's and especially Calvin's answers to such questions had telling implications for the concepts of individualism, freedom, submission, will, access to information, and work ethic in Euro-American societies.

I agree with Cox that the questions now posed by leaders of the Christian Pentecostal movement are by no means as narrow as those proffered in the Reformation. Today they ask, what is the nature of the world? How does one live within it? Is it enough for people to relate to God and to each other by inviting God into their church and by ingesting God's physical substance via sacraments (the Ortho-Catholic solution), or should they prepare themselves to receive God directly into their bodies in ways that manifestly activate them? Is it enough to bring God into the minds of parishioners via biblical access, study, and interpretation and to accept

Jesus verbally at a named time and place (the mainline Protestant solution)? Or should one bring the spirit of God into one's body, speech, and action regularly via enthusiastic worship, trance, glossolalia, healings, and the gifting of these behaviors to others, all of which show that one is saved (the Christian Pentecostal solution)? These Christian Pentecostal questions are not provincial at all. So one might expect in the longer run of history that Christian Pentecostal answers to these questions may well have consequences commensurately "more far-reaching and radical" than those of the capitalism that Weber says had emerged unexpectedly from the Reformation's questions by his time.

Throughout this book, I have shown that Christian Pentecostalism is, as Cox (2011:xvi–xvii) suggests, "shaking the foundations" of local life at the level of individual behavior and family constitution. It is shaking the foundations of Ortho-Catholicism, although the Roman Catholic hierarchy may not be aware of that fact yet, for the exuberant Catholic Charismatic Renewal confers on Catholicism a de facto married priesthood at a micro congregational level precisely when the official church's priesthood is in desperate trouble, largely unable to recruit and apparently unable to control priests' sexuality. It is shaking the foundations of mainstream Protestantism, which, like Ortho-Catholicism, is losing its membership lifeblood: except for its charismatic components and Pentecostal offshoots, sedate Protestantism is in numerical decline (Johnson and Ross 2009:172, 192). Christian Pentecostalism has overtaken historic Christian denominations in places as diverse as Guatemala, El Salvador, Bolivia, Chile, Ghana, Nigeria, and India. The decline in mainstream Protestant religiosity also has suffused the United States and Europe. By virtue of its basic Evangelical expansionist premise, Christian Pentecostalism appears poised to shake the political foundations of several societies and already may have shaken the political foundations of Guatemala, having provided three *evangélico* presidents (Ríos Montt, Serrano Elías, and Morales). Christian Pentecostalism also has provided Brazil with its first Pentecostal president, Jair Messias Bolsonaro. Of course, Evangelical religions have already impacted elections in the United States on the Republican side from Ronald Reagan through Trump. This it has done in fewer than 120 years.

But as of yet, Christian Pentecostalism has not unleashed a transformative new system of economics, statecraft, or policy, whether guided by religion or not, and certainly has created nothing as transformative as the global capitalism that Weber says the Reformation ushered in. If given the same 400 years as between the first reformers and Weber's trenchant analysis, will Christian Pentecostalism have the capacity to shake the foundations of the world and produce something as different from global capitalism as global capitalism is from fifteenth-century European mercantile city-statism? Time will tell.

Time will tell if the three Christian Pentecostal mustard seeds raise up some great new plant. The first seed is the notion of individual responsibility for obedience to law and constructing an ethical self. The second seed is the obligation to resist enclosure by evangelizing others. The third seed is the manifestation of experiential commitment to the first two seeds via embodiment of the Spirit. The moral repremising inculcated by bodily practice in its adepts may indeed shake the foundations of Christian history as Christian Pentecostal practitioners explicitly seek a new and changed society under the cultural codes of their new God.

Regardless of the outcome, change in society is the Christian Pentecostal hope. It is a matter of faith. Does one resign oneself to living with chaos and collapse—to suffer and put up with it, to *soportarlo*, as the Guatemalans say and so many do? Or does one reform at least oneself to stabilize a tiny sector of that chaos? Can one expand one's island of peace by touching others with a freely given gift of the Spirit? That is the faith. Given the alternatives they have tried and found wanting, many Guatemalans find the new faiths and practices enormously attractive. Perhaps their faith will indeed reshape the world. In any event, academics should try diligently to understand the process of religious change, the meanings within it, the conditions that drive it, and the results that may yet come of it.

Even the most cynical academics would surely agree that the world needs considerable reshaping. Perhaps Christian Pentecostals have got it right; perhaps the moral and ethical reform of the individual focused on obedience to law and attention to family, combined with vigorous person-to-person outreach through gifting, may well do more than political restructuring, institutional change, structural adjustment, neoliberalism, revolutionary violence, authoritarianism, economic aid, globalized consumerism, or even democratic elections. All these have been tried and found ineffective, at least in Guatemala and throughout much of the Global South. By contrast, the Christian Pentecostal movement has expanded prodigiously and peacefully, so that today some 250 million Protestant Pentecostals and nearly as many Catholic charismatics—about a quarter of all Christians—have thought the effort of self-discipline and shared outreach worth a try.

The new Christian Pentecostalisms invite the refugees from Ortho-Catholicism and mainline Protestantism to abandon hierarchy, displace sacraments, and sideline theological discussion. In place of these, they substitute congregational equality through enthusiastic participation, bodily experience of God via reception of the Spirit, and disciplined self-reformation. Nothing more is required beyond sharing the gift through Evangelical proselyting, largely through service-oriented gift giving, including predominantly the healing of the body and (hopefully) society.

Christian Pentecostalism has become an international religion and a worldwide revitalization movement. It has become the fourth great branch of Christianity. Its God crosses many borders because the problems of colonialism and the difficulties of garnering subsistence and safety acutely challenge peasant and indigenous peoples around the world. Catholic and Protestant pentecostal practices symbolize the severity of the crisis through the Christian Pentecostal wail, glossolalia, and trance collapse. They also provide a modestly successful set of behavioral therapies for reconstructing oneself and the nation. Generic Christian Pentecostalism is a highly portable way to try to domesticate the chaos of life in failing societies or in failing sectors of society, specifically those experiencing cultural collapse and exclusion. Christian Pentecostal healings fill an urgent need. Glossolalia enables adherents to to cry out the unbearable sociocultural conditions in which they live. These varieties of Christian Pentecostalism are legitimate and effective attempts by people, as active agents, to heal themselves and their society in a shattering world.

NOTES

1. The logic of secularization has long been with us. Religion once was central to the concept of how society operated. Marx, however, took religion out of the driver's seat and made it and spiritual ideology epiphenomena of political economy. Or take Durkheim on science: "Once the authority of science is established, . . . one can affirm nothing that science denies, [and] deny nothing that it affirms. . . . Faith no longer exerts the same hege-

mony as before over the systems of ideas that we can continue to call religious. It is countered by a rival power that, born from it, submits it henceforth to its criticism and control. And all indicators predict that this control will become ever more extensive and effective, with no possibility of assigning a limit to its future influence" (Durkheim 2001[1912]:326).

2. I would not include China in the Global South, but certainly it has radically improved the lives of many of its citizens. But the cost in blood and suffering during China's cultural revolutions has been enormous.

References

Abraham, Natalia. 2004. Hindu Customs and Practices in Christian Ceremonies: The Case of the Malabar Church. In *Christianity and Native Cultures: Perspectives from Different Regions of the World.* Cyriac K. Pullapilly, Bernard J. Donahoe, David Stefancic, and William Svelmoe, eds., 133–149. Notre Dame, IN: Cross Cultural.

Adams, Betty Hannstein. n.d. The Life Cycle of Modern Coffee: Production and Processing Systems Used on Finca Oriflama. Unpublished manuscript available from walteradams2002@gmail.com or john_hawkins@byu.edu.

Adams, Richard, and Santiago Bastos. 2003. *Las Relaciones Étnicas en Guatemala, 1944–2000.* Antigua, Guatemala: Centro de Investigaciones Regionales de Mesoamérica.

Adams, Walter Randolph. 1999. Alcohol Production and Consumption in a Highland Guatemalan Maya Community. *Bulletin of the Alcohol and Drug Study Group* 34(2):1–9.

Adams, Walter Randolph, and John P. Hawkins, eds. 2007. *Health Care in Maya Guatemala: Confronting Medical Pluralism in a Developing Country.* Norman: University of Oklahoma Press.

Aguirre Beltrán, Gonzalo. 1967. *Regiones de Refugio: El Desarrollo de la Comunidad y el Proceso Dominical en Mestizo América.* Mexico City: Instituto Indigenista Interamericano.

Ajpacajá Túm, Florentino Pedro. 2001. *Tz'onob'al Tziij: Discurso Ceremonial K'ichee'.* Guatemala City, Guatemala: Cholsamaj.

Aldunate, P. Carlos. 1977. Fenomenología Pastoral. In *Renovación en el Espíritu: Movimientos Carismáticos en America Latina.* Consejo Episcopal Latinoamericano, ed., 223–243. CELAM document no. 33. Bogotá, Colombia: Impresa LTDA for the Secretriado General del CELAM.

Althoff, Andrea. 2014. *Divided by Faith and Ethnicity: Religious Pluralism and the Problem of Race in Guatemala.* Boston: De Gruyter.

Anderson, Allan H. 2000. *Zion and Pentecost: The Spirituality and Experience of Pentecostal and Zionist/Apostolic Churches in South Africa.* Pretoria: University of South Africa Press.

———. 2011. Revising Pentecostal History in Global Perspective. In *Asian and Pentecostal: The Charismatic Face of Christianity in Asia.* Allan Anderson and Edmond Tang, eds., 118–140. Eugene, OR: Wipf and Stock.

———. 2013. *To the Ends of the Earth: Pentecostalism and the Transformation of World Christianity.* New York: Oxford University Press.

Anderson, Allan, and Edmond Tang, eds. 2011. *Asian and Pentecostal: The Charismatic Face of Christianity in Asia.* Eugene, OR: Wipf and Stock.

Anderson, Benedict. R. 1991. *Imagined Communities: Reflections on the Origin and Spread of Nationalism.* 2nd ed. New York: Verso.

Annis, Sheldon. 1987. *God and Production in a Guatemalan Town.* Austin: University of Texas Press.

Araneda, Kelly C. 2005. "The Commitment": Transformations of Courtship and Marriage in Santa Catarina Ixtahuacán. In *Roads to Change in Maya Guatemala: A Field School Approach to Understanding the K'iche'.* John P. Hawkins and Walter Randolph Adams, eds., 99–123. Norman: University of Oklahoma Press.

Arnold, Clinton E. 1992. Joy. In *The Anchor Bible Dictionary.* Vol. 3. David Noel Freedman, ed., 1022–1023. New York: Doubleday.

Arzobispado de Guatemala. 1998. *Guatemala: Nunca Mas.* 4 vols. Guatemala City, Guatemala: Oficina de Derechos Humanos del Arzobispado de Guatemala.

Asociación CODEIN [Asociación Comunitaria de Desarrollo Integral Nahualá]. 2008. *Reconstrucción de la Memoria Histórica del Municipio de Nahualá y Sistematización de Principios y Valores.* Guatemala City, Guatemala: Asociación CODEIN.

Atanasov, Miroslav A. 2010. *Gypsy Pentecostals: The Growth of the Pentecostal Movement among the Roma in Bulgaria and Its Revitalization of Their Communities.* Lexington, KY: Emeth.

Baer, Hans A., Merrill Singer, and Ida Susser. 1997. *Medical Anthropology and the World System: A Critical Perspective.* Westport, CT: Bergin and Garvey.

Balch, R. 1980. Looking behind the Scenes in a Religious Cult: Implications for the Study of Conversion. *Sociological Analysis* 41(2):137–143.

Baronti, David Scott. 2002. Sound Symbolism Use in Affect Verbs in Santa Catarina Ixtahuacán. PhD diss., Department of Anthropology, University of California, Davis.

Barrett, David B., and Todd M. Johnson. 2003. Global Statistics. In *The New International Dictionary of Pentecostal and Charismatic Movements.* Rev. ed. Stanley M. Burgess and Eduard M. van der Maas, eds., 284–302. Grand Rapids, MI: Zondervan.

Barrett, David B., George Thomas Kurian, and Todd M. Johnson. 2001. *World Christian Encyclopedia: A Comparative Survey of Churches and Religions in the Modern World.* 2nd ed. 2 vols. New York: Oxford University Press.

Barth, Fredrik. 1969. *Ethnic Groups and Boundaries: The Social Organization of Culture Difference.* Boston: Little, Brown.

Basso, Ellen B. 1985. *A Musical View of the Universe.* Philadelphia: University of Pennsylvania Press.

Bateson, Gregory. 1936. *Naven: A Survey of the Problems Suggested by a Composite Picture of the Culture of a New Guinea Tribe Drawn from Three Points of View.* Cambridge: Cambridge University Press.

Bauer Paiz, Alfonso. 1965. *Catalogación de Leyes y Disposiciones de Trabajo de Guatemala del Período 1872 a 1930.* Guatemala City, Guatemala: Universidad de San Carlos de Guatemala, Facultad de Ciencias Económicas, Instituto de Investigaciones Econónomicas y Sociales.

Beckford, J. A. 1978. Accounting for Conversion. *British Journal of Sociology* 29:235–245.

Bellis, Mary. 2019. History of American Agriculture. *ThoughtCo.* https://www.thoughtco.com/history-of-american-agriculture-farm-machinery-4074385.

Berger, Peter. 1990[1967]. *The Sacred Canopy: Elements of a Sociological Theory of Religion.* Garden City, NY: Doubleday.

———. 1999. The Desecularization of the World: A Global Overview. In *The Desecularization of the World: Resurgent Religion and World Politics.* Peter L. Berger, ed., 1–18. Washington, DC: Ethics and Public Policy Center.

Bergunder, Michael. 2008. *The South Indian Pentecostal Movement in the Twentieth Century.* Grand Rapids, MI: Eerdmans.

Bidegain, Ana María. 1985. *From Catholic Action to Liberation Theology: The Historical Process of the Laity in Latin America in the Twentieth Century.* Working Paper no. 48. Notre Dame, IN: Helen Kellogg Institute for International Studies, University of Notre Dame.

Black, George. 1984. *Garrison Guatemala.* New York: Monthly Review Press.

Bogenschild, Thomas E. 1992. The Roots of Fundamentalism in Liberal Guatemala: Missionary Ideologies and Local Responses, 1882–1944. PhD diss., University of California, Berkeley.

Booth, Wayne C. 1995. The Rhetoric of Fundamentalist Conversion Narratives. In *Fundamentalisms Comprehended.* Martin E. Marty and R. Scott Appleby, eds., 367–395. Fundamentalism Project, vol. 5. Chicago: University of Chicago Press.

Bord, Richard J., and Joseph E. Faulkner. 1983. *The Catholic Charismatics: The Anatomy of a Modern Religious Movement.* University Park: Pennsylvania State University Press.

Borlase, Craig. 2006. *William Seymour: A Biography.* Lake Mary, FL: Charisma House.

Bossen, Laurel. 1984. *The Redivision of Labor: Women and Economic Choice in Four Guatemalan Communities.* Albany: State University of New York Press.

Boudewijnse, Barbara. 1991. The Development of the Charismatic Movement within the Catholic Church of Curaçao. In *Popular Power in Latin American Religions.* A. F. Droogers et al., eds., 175–195. Saarbrucken, Germany: Breitenbach.

Bourdieu, Pierre. 1990. *The Logic of Practice.* Stanford, CA: Stanford University Press.

Bouyer, Louis. 1990. Spirituality for the Coming Years. In *Catholicism and Secularization in America: Essays on Nature, Grace, and Culture.* David L. Schindler and Louis Bouyer, eds., 80–92. Huntington, IN: Our Sunday Visitor Press.

Breckenridge, James F. 1980. *The Theological Self-Understanding of the Catholic Charismatic Movement.* Washington, DC: University Press of America.

Brenneman, Robert. 2012. *Homies and Hermanos: God and Gangs in Central America*. New York: Oxford University Press.

Brintnall, Douglas E. 1979. *Revolt against the Dead: The Modernization of a Mayan Community in the Highlands of Guatemala*. New York: Gordon and Breach.

Brown, Candy Gunther. 2011. Introduction: Pentecostalism and the Globalization of Illness and Healing. In *Global Pentecostal and Charismatic Healing*. Candy Gunther Brown, ed., 3–26. Oxford: Oxford University Press.

Brown, Donald E. 2000. Human Universals and Their Implications. In *Being Humans: Anthropological Universality and Particularity in Transdisciplinary Perspectives*. Neil Roughley, ed., 156–174. New York: De Gruyter.

Brusco, Elizabeth E. 1986. The Household Basis of Evangelical Religion and the Reformation of Machismo in Colombia. PhD diss., City University of New York.

———. 1993. The Reformation of Machismo: Asceticism and Masculinity among Colombian Evangelicals. In *Rethinking Protestantism in Latin America*. Virginia Garrard-Burnett and David Stoll, eds., 143–158. Philadelphia, PA: Temple University Press.

———. 1995. *The Reformation of Machismo: Evangelical Conversion and Gender in Colombia*. Austin: University of Texas Press.

Bundy, David D. 2003. Chile. In *The New International Dictionary of Pentecostal and Charismatic Movements*. Rev. ed. Stanley M. Burgess and Eduard M. van der Maas, eds., 55–58. Grand Rapids, MI: Zondervan.

Bunzel, Ruth. 1959. *Chichicastenango*. Seattle: University of Washington Press.

Burdick, John. 1993a. *Looking for God in Brazil: The Progressive Catholic Church in Urban Brazil's Religious Arena*. Berkeley: University of California Press.

———. 1993b. Struggling against the Devil: Pentecostalism and Social Movements in Urban Brazil. In *Rethinking Protestantism in Latin America*. Virginia Garrard-Burnett and David Stoll, eds., 20–44. Philadelphia, PA: Temple University Press.

Burgess, Stanley M., and Eduard M. van der Maas, eds. 2003. *The New International Dictionary of Pentecostal and Charismatic Movements*. Rev. ed. Grand Rapids, MI: Zondervan.

Burns, Allan F. 1993. *Maya in Exile*. Philadelphia, PA: Temple University Press.

Burrell, Jennifer L. 2013. *Maya after War: Conflict, Power, and Politics in Guatemala*. Austin: University of Texas Press.

Bybee, Eric Ruiz, John P. Hawkins, James H. McDonald, and Walter Randolph Adams. 2013. "Saved from Being Lynched": Reinvention of Customary Law in Nahualá. In *Crisis of Governance in Maya Guatemala: Indigenous Responses to a Failing State*. John P. Hawkins, James H. McDonald, and Walter Randolph Adams, eds., 86–114. Norman: University of Oklahoma Press.

Calder, Bruce J. 1970. *Crecimiento y Cambio de la Iglesia Católica Guatemalteca, 1944–1966*. Estudios Centroamericanos no. 6, Seminario de Integración Social Guatemalteca. Guatemala City, Guatemala: Editorial José Pineda Ibarra/Ministerio de Educación.

———. 2001. The Role of the Catholic Church and Other Religious Institutions in the Guatemalan Peace Process, 1980–1996. *Journal of Church and State* 43(4):773–797.

Call, Tristan P., John P. Hawkins, James H. McDonald, and Walter Randolph Adams. 2013. "There Is No Respect Now": Youth Power in Nahualá. In *Crisis of Governance in Maya Guatemala: Indigenous Responses to a Failing State*. John P. Hawkins, James H. McDonald, and Walter Randolph Adams, eds., 218–242. Norman: University of Oklahoma Press.

Cancian, Frank. 1965. *Economics and Prestige in a Maya Community: The Religious Cargo System in Zinacantán*. Stanford, CA: Stanford University Press.

———. 1972. *Change and Uncertainty in a Peasant Economy: The Maya Corn Farmers of Zinacantán*. Stanford, CA: Stanford University Press.

———. 1992. *The Decline of Community in Zinacantán: Economy, Public Life, and Social Stratification, 1960–1987*. Stanford, CA: Stanford University Press.

Cannell, Fenella, ed. 2006. *The Anthropology of Christianity*. Durham, NC: Duke University Press.

Carlsen, Robert S., and Martin Prechtel. 1994. Walking on Two Legs: Shamanism in Santiago Atitlan, Guatemala. In *Ancient Traditions: Shamanism in Central Asia and the Americas*. Gary Seaman and Jane S. Day, eds., 77–111. Niwot: University Press of Colorado.

Carmack, Robert M., ed. 1988. *Harvest of Violence: The Maya Indians and the Guatemalan Crisis*. Norman: University of Oklahoma Press.

Carpenter, Robert. 1999. Esoteric Literature as a Microcosmic Mirror of Brazil's Religious Marketplace. In *Latin American Religion in Motion*. Christian Smith and Joshua Prokopy, eds., 235–260. New York: Routledge.

Carr, Harry. 1935. *Los Angeles: City of Dreams*. New York: Appleton-Century.

Carrescia, Olivia, dir. 1982. *Todos Santos Cuchumatán*. New York: Icarus Films.

CEH [Comisión para el Esclarecimiento Histórico]. 1999. *Guatemala: Memoria del Silencio*. 12 vols. Guatemala City, Guatemala: Oficina de Servicios para Proyectos de las Naciones Unidas.

CELAM [Consejo Episcopal Latinoamericano]. 1977. *Renovación en el Espíritu: Movimientos Carismáticos en America Latina*. Bogotá, Colombia: Impresa LTDA for the Secretriado General del CELAM.

Centro Carismático el Minuto de Dios. 1976. *Obispos y Carismas*. Bogotá, Colombia: Editorial Carrera.

Chai, Jolie. 2005. Forced Removal of Romani Children from the Care of Their Families. European Roma Rights Centre. http://www.errc.org/roma-rights-journal/forced-removal-of-romani-children-from-the-care-of-their-families.

Checketts, Nathan. 2005. "By the Sweat of Thy Brow": Development, Religion, and Culture in Santa Catarina Ixtahuacán. In *Roads to Change in Maya Guatemala: A Field School Approach to Understanding the K'iche'*. John P. Hawkins and Walter Randolph Adams, eds., 175–188. Norman: University of Oklahoma Press.

Chesnut, R. Andrew. 1997. *Born Again in Brazil: The Pentecostal Boom and the Pathogens of Poverty*. New Brunswick, NJ: Rutgers University Press.

———. 2003a. *Competitive Spirits: Latin America's New Religious Economy*. Oxford: Oxford University Press.

———. 2003b. A Preferential Option for the Spirit: The Catholic Charismatic Renewal in Latin America's New Religious Economy. *Latin American Politics and Society* 45(1):55–85.

Christenson, Allen J. n.d. *K'iche'-English Dictionary and Guide to Pronunciation of the K'iche'-Maya Alphabet*. http://www.famsi.org/mayawriting/dictionary/christenson/quidic_complete.pdf.

———. 2001. *Art and Society in a Highland Maya Community: The Altarpiece of Santiago Atitlán*. Austin: University of Texas Press.

———, trans. and ed. 2003. *Popol Vuj: The Mythic Sections— Tales of First Beginnings from the Ancient K'iche'-Maya*. Provo, UT: Foundation for Ancient Research and Mormon Studies.

Chuchiak, John F., IV. 2005. In *Servitio Dei*: Fray Diego de Landa, the Franciscan Order, and the Return of the Extirpattion [*sic*] of Idolatry in the Colonial Diocese of Yucatan, 1573–1579. *Americas* 61(4):611–646.

Cleary, Edward L. 2007. The Catholic Charismatic Renewal: Revitalization Movements and Conversion. In *Conversion of a Continent: Contemporary Religious Change in Latin America*. Timothy J. Steigenga and Edward L. Cleary, eds., 153–173. New Brunswick, NJ: Rutgers University Press.

———. 2011. *The Rise of Charismatic Catholicism in Latin America*. Gainesville: University Press of Florida.

Coleman, Kenneth M., Edwin Eloy Aguilar, José Miguel Sandoval, and Timothy J. Steigenga. 1993. Protestantism in El Salvador: Conventional Wisdom versus the Survey Evidence. In *Rethinking Protestantism in Latin America*. Virginia Garrard-Burnett and David Stoll, eds., 111–142. Philadelphia, PA: Temple University Press.

Conway, Frederick J. 1980. Pentecostalism in Haiti: Healing and Hierarchy. In *Perspectives on Pentecostalism: Case Studies from the Caribbean and Latin America*. Stephen D. Glazier, ed., 7–26. Washington, DC: University Press of America.

Cook, Garrett W. 2000. *Renewing the Maya World: Expressive Culture in a Highland Town*. Austin: University of Texas Press.

Cook, Garrett W., and Thomas A. Offit. 2013. *Indigenous Religion and Cultural Performance in the New Maya World*. Albuquerque: University of New Mexico Press

Corr, Rachel. 2007. Conversion to Native Spirituality in the Andes. In *Conversion of a Continent: Contemporary Religious Change in Latin America*. Timothy J. Steigenga and Edward L. Cleary, eds., 174–195. New Brunswick, NJ: Rutgers University Press.

Cox, Harvey. 2011. Foreword. In *Global Pentecostal and Charismatic Healing*. Candy Gunther Brown, ed., xvii–xxi. New York: Oxford University Press.

Crapo, Richley H. 2003. *Anthropology of Religion: The Unity and Diversity of Religions*. New York: McGraw-Hill.

Cumes, Willian. 2020. ONU pide a Guatemala que Garantice Seguridad de Antiguo Personal de la Cicig. *Prensa Libre*, January 10. https://www.prensalibre.com/ahora/guatemala/politica/onu-pide-a-guatemala-que-garantice-seguridad-de-antiguo-personal-de-la-cicig.

Dabb, Curtis W., James H. McDonald, John P. Hawkins, and Walter Randolph Adams. 2013. A Land Divided without Clear Titles: The Clash of Communal and Individual Land Claims in Nahualá and Santa Catarina Ixtahuacán. In *Crisis of Governance in Maya Guatemala: Indigenous Responses to a Failing State*. John P. Hawkins, James H. McDonald, and Walter Randolph Adams, eds., 115–148. Norman: University of Oklahoma Press.

Dayton, Donald W. 1987. *Theological Roots of Pentecostalism*. Metuchen, NJ: Hendrickson.

de Certeau, Michel, and Steven Rendall. 1984. *The Practice of Everyday Life*. Berkeley: University of California Press.

De Hoyos, Deborah Pratt, John P. Hawkins, and Walter Randolph Adams. 2020. Bringing in the New Dawn: The Struggle for Education and Community Reconstruction in Antigua Santa Catarina Ixtahuacán. In *Making a Place for the Future in Maya Guatemala: Disaster, Resettlement, and Indigenous Development in Santa Catarina Ixtahuacán*. John P. Hawkins and Walter Randolph Adams, eds. Unpublished book manuscript in possession of editors.

Delaney, Carol. 1986. The Meaning of Paternity and the Virgin Birth Debate. *Man*, n.s., 21(3):494–513.

D'Epinay, Christian Lalive. 1969. *Haven of the Masses: A Study of the Pentecostal Movement in Chile*. London: Lutterworth.

Diez de Arriba, Pbro., and R. P. Luis. 1989. *História de la Iglésia Católica en Guatemala: Crisis*. Vol. 2. Guatemala City, Guatemala: N.p.

Dirección General de Cartografía. 1961–1962. *Diccionario Geográfico de Guatemala*. 2 vols. Guatemala City, Guatemala: Tipografía Nacional de Guatemala.

Dirección General de Estadística. 1897. *Censo, 1893*. Guatemala City, Guatemala: Dirección General de Estadística.

———. 1921. *Censo de la República de Guatemala*. Guatemala City, Guatemala: Dirección General de Estadística.

———. 1924. *Censo de la Población de la República Levantado el 28 de Agosto de 1923, 4° Censo: Parte II*. Guatemala City, Guatemala: Tipografía Nacional.

———. 1942. *Quinto Censo de la Población de la República Levantado el 7 de Abril de 1940*. Guatemala City, Guatemala: Tipografía Nacional.

———. 1954. *I Censo Agropecuario, 1950*. Vol. 1: *Agricultura*. Guatemala City, Guatemala: Dirección General de Estadística.

———. 1957. *Sexto Censo Nacional de Población, 1950*. Guatemala City, Guatemala: Dirección General de Estadística.

———. 1968. *II Censo Agropecuario, 1964*. Vol. 1: *Características Generales, Concentración y Tenencia de la Tierra*. Guatemala City, Guatemala: Dirección General de Estadística.

———. 1971a. *II Censo Agropecuario, 1964*. Vol. 2: *Uso de la Tierra, Cultivos*. Guatemala City, Guatemala: Dirección General de Estadística.

———. 1971b. *II Censo Agropecuario, 1964*. Vol. 5: *Panorama de la Estructura Agropecuaria de Guatemala*. Guatemala City, Guatemala: Dirección General de Estadística.

———. 1971–1972. *VII Censo de Población, 1964*. 3 vols. Guatemala City, Guatemala: Dirección General de Estadística.

———. 1974. *VIII Censo de Población y III de Habitación, 26 de Marzo de 1973: Resultados de Tabulación por Muestreo, Población*. Ser. 2, vol. 1. Guatemala City, Guatemala: Dirección General de Estadística.

———. 1982a. *III Censo Nacional Agropecuario, 1979*. Vol. 1: *Número y Superficie de Fincas y Características Principales*. Guatemala City, Guatemala: Dirección General de Estadística.

———. 1982b. *Censos Nacionales, IX de Población, IV de Habitación: Cifras Preliminares*. Guatemala City, Guatemala: Dirección General de Estadística.

Disappearing Farms: United States Ceasing to Be an Exporting Nation. 1909. *Evening Citizen* (Ottawa, Canada), December 29, 2. http://news.google.com/newspapers?id=4pouAAAAIBAJ&sjid=5tgFAAAAIBAJ&pg=4970,3524511&dq=history+farm+population+us&hl=en.

Douglas, Mary. 1966. *Purity and Danger: An Analysis of Concepts of Pollution and Taboo*. London: Routledge and Kegan Paul.

Douglas, William. 1968. Santiago Atitlán. In *Los Pueblos del Lago de Atitlán*. Seminario de Integración Social Guatemalteco, ed., 229–276. Guatemala City, Guatemala: Seminario de Integración Social Guatemalteco.

Dow, James A., and Alan R. Sandstrom, eds. 2001. *Holy Saints and Fiery Preachers: The Anthropology of Protestantism in Mexico and Central America*. Westport CT: Praeger.

Dracoulis, Donald Y., John P. Hawkins, James H. McDonald, and Walter Randolph Adams. 2013. "The System Changed to Voting": Respect, Electoral Democracy, and the Public's Anger toward Mayors in Santa Catarina Ixtahuacán. In *Crisis of Governance in Maya Guatemala: Indigenous Responses to a Failing State*. John P. Hawkins, James H. McDonald, and Walter Randolph Adams, eds., 50–85. Norman: University of Oklahoma Press.

Durkheim, Émile. 1949[1893]. *The Division of Labor in Society*. 3rd ed. Translated by George Simpson. Glencoe, IL: Free Press.

———. 1961[1912]. *The Elementary Forms of the Religious Life*. Translated by Joseph Ward Swain. New York: Collier.

———. 1965[1895]. *The Rules of Sociological Method.* New York: Free Press.

———. 2001[1912]. *The Elementary Forms of Religious Life.* Translated by Carol Cosman. Edited by Mark S. Cladis. Oxford: Oxford University Press.

———. 2008[1912]. *The Elementary Forms of Religious Life.* Translated by Joseph Ward Swain. Mineola, NY: Dover.

Early, John D. 1982. *The Demographic Structure and Evolution of a Peasant System: The Guatemalan Population.* Boca Raton: University Presses of Florida.

———. 2006. *The Maya and Catholicism: An Encounter of Worldviews.* Gainesville: University Press of Florida.

———. 2012. *Maya and Catholic Cultures in Crisis.* Gainesville: University Press of Florida.

Eber, Christine. 1995. *Women and Alcohol in a Highland Maya Town: Water of Hope, Water of Sorrow.* Austin: University of Texas Press.

Economic Research Service, US Department of Agriculture. 1966. *Demand for Farm Tractors in the United States: A Regression Analysis.* Agricultural Economic Report no. 103. Washington, DC: US Government Printing Office. http://naldc.nal.usda.gov/naldc/download.xhtml?id=CAT87201824&content=PDF.

Edvalson, John, James H. McDonald, John P. Hawkins, and Walter Randolph Adams. 2013. Gangs, Community Politics, and the Social Production of Space in Nahualá. In *Crisis of Governance in Maya Guatemala: Indigenous Responses to a Failing State.* John P. Hawkins, James H. McDonald, and Walter Randolph Adams, eds., 195–217. Norman: University of Oklahoma Press.

Eggan, Fred. 1954. Social Anthropology and the Method of Controlled Comparison. *American Anthropologist* 56(5):743–763.

Elbow, Gary Stewart. 1972. Cultural Factors in the Spatial Organization of Three Highland Guatemalan Towns. PhD diss., University of Pittsburgh.

Elhers, Tracy Barach. 2000. *Silent Looms: Women and Production in a Guatemalan Town.* Austin: University of Texas Press.

Eliade, Mircea. 1959. *The Sacred and the Profane: The Nature of Religion.* Translated by Willard R. Trask. New York: Harcourt, Brace.

———, ed. 1987. *The Encyclopedia of Religion.* 16 vols. New York: Macmillan.

Elwell, Walter A. 1984. *Evangelical Dictionary of Theology.* Grand Rapids, MI: Baker Book House.

Endruveit, Wilson. 1975. Pentecostalism in Brazil: A Historical and Theological Study of Its Characteristics. PhD diss., Northwestern University.

Engels, Friedrich. 2008[1873 1886]. Dialectics of Nature [Extracts]. In *On Religion* by Karl Marx and Friedrich Engels, 152–193. Mineola, NY: Dover.

———. 2008[1882]. Bruno Bauer and Early Christianity. In *On Religion* by Karl Marx and Friedrich Engels, 194–204. Mineola, NY: Dover.

———. 2008[1886]. Ludwig Feuerbach and the End of Classical German Philosophy. In *On Religion* by Karl Marx and Friedrich Engels, 213–268. Mineola, NY: Dover.

———. 2008[1887]. Juristic Socialism. In *On Religion* by Karl Marx and Friedrich Engels, 269–272. Mineola, NY: Dover.

———. 2008[1890a]. Engels to Bloch. In *On Religion* by Karl Marx and Friedrich Engels, 273–277. Mineola, NY: Dover.

———. 2008[1890b]. Engels to C. Schmidt. In *On Religion* by Karl Marx and Friedrich Engels, 278–286. Mineola, NY: Dover.

England, Nora C. 2003. Mayan Language Revival and Revitalization Politics: Linguists and Linguistic Ideologies. *American Anthropologist* 105(4):733–743.

Erickson, Stephen Dane, John P. Hawkins, and Walter Randolph Adams. 2020. "We Must Move On": The Relocation of a K'iche' Maya Town in Ten-Year Perspective. In *Making a Place for the Future in Maya Guatemala: Disaster, Resettlement, and Indigenous Development in Santa Catarina Ixtahuacán.* John P. Hawkins and Walter Randolph Adams, eds. Unpublished book manuscript in possession of editors.

Escobar, Irving, Kenneth Monzón, Andrea Orozco, and Carlos Álvarez. 2019. Morales, Arzú y Vásquez Habrían Hablado sobre Decreto para Respaldar Cese de Cicig, Según Diputado. *Prensa Libre*, February 11. https://www.prensalibre.com/guatemala/politica/morales-arzu-y-vasquez-han-hablado-sobre-poner-fin-al-mandato-de-cicig-segun-diputado/.

Escobar, J. Samuel. 1994. Conflict of Interpretations of Popular Protestantism. In *New Face of the Church in Latin America.* Guillermo Cook, ed., 112–134. Maryknoll, NY: Orbis.

Espinosa, Alvaro F., ed. 1976. *The Guatemalan Earthquake of February 4, 1976: A Preliminary Report.* Geological Survey Professional Paper no. 102. Washington, DC: US Government Printing Office.

Espinosa, Alvaro F., Raul Husid, and Antonio Quesada. 1976. Intensity Distribution and Source Parameters from

Field Observations. In *The Guatemalan Earthquake of February 4, 1976: A Preliminary Report*. Geological Survey Professional Paper no. 102. Alvaro F. Espinosa, ed., 52–66. Washington, DC: US Government Printing Office.

Espinosa, Gastón. 2014. *William J. Seymour and the Origins of Global Pentecostalism: A Biography and Documentary History*. Durham, NC: Duke University Press.

Everton, Macduff. 1991. *The Modern Maya: A Culture in Transition*. Albuquerque: University of New Mexico Press.

Fahlbusch, Erwin, Jan Milič Lochman, John Mbiti, Jaroslav Pelikan, and Lukas Vischer, eds. 1999. *The Encyclopedia of Christianity*. Grand Rapids, MI: Eerdmans.

Falla, Ricardo. 1978. *Quiché Rebelde: Estudio de un Movimiento de Conversión Religiosa, Rebelde a las Creencias Tradicionales, en San Antonio Ilotenango, Quiché (1948–1970)*. Guatemala City, Guatemala: Editorial Universitaria.

———. 1994. *Massacres in the Jungle: Ixcán, Guatemala, 1975–1982*. Boulder, CO: Westview.

———. 2001. *Quiché Rebelde: Religious Conversion, Politics, and Ethnic Identity in Guatemala*. Austin: University of Texas Press.

Falzon, Mark-Anthony. 2009. Introduction. In *Multi-Sited Ethnography: Theory, Praxis and Locality in Contemporary Research*. Mark-Anthony Falzon, ed., 1–23. Surrey, England: Ashgate.

Feld, Steven, and Aaron A. Fox. 1994. Music and Language. *Annual Review of Anthropology* 23:25–53.

Fischer, Edward F. 1996. Induced Culture Change as a Strategy for Socioeconomic Development: The Pan-Maya Movement in Guatemala. In *Maya Cultural Activism in Guatemala*. Edward F. Fischer and R. Mckenna Brown, eds., 51–73. Austin: University of Texas Press.

———. 1999. Cultural Logic and Maya Identity: Rethinking Constructivism and Essentialism. *Current Anthropology* 40(4):473–499.

———. 2001. *Cultural Logics and Global Economics: Maya Identity in Thought and Practice*. Austin: University of Texas Press.

———. 2003. Strategic Identities and Subversive Narratives: On Being Maya in a Globalized World. *Vanderbilt Journal of Luso-Hispanic Studies* 1(1):149–166.

———. 2006. *Broccoli and Desire: Global Connections and Maya Struggles in Postwar Guatemala*. Stanford, CA: Stanford University Press.

Fischer, Edward F., and Carol Hendrickson. 2003. *Tecpán,*

Guatemala: A Modern Maya Town in Global and Local Context. Boulder, CO: Westview.

Fischer, Edward F., and R. Mckenna Brown, eds. 1996. *Maya Cultural Activism in Guatemala*. Austin: University of Texas Press.

Flamming, Douglas. 2005. *Bound for Freedom: Black Los Angeles in Jim Crow America*. Berkeley: University of California Press.

Flinn, Frank K. 1999. Conversion: Up from Evangelicalism; or, The Pentecostal and Charismatic Experience. In *Religious Conversion: Contemporary Practices and Controversies*. Christopher Lamb and M. Darrol Bryant, eds., 51–72. London: Cassell.

Flora, Cornelia Butler. 1975. Pentecostal Women in Colombia: Religious Change and the Status of Working-Class Women. *Journal of Interamerican Studies and World Affairs* 17(4):411–425.

———. 1976. *Pentecostalism in Colombia: Baptism by Fire and Spirit*. Cranbury, NJ: Associated University Presses.

Foster, George M. 1960. *Culture and Conquest: America's Spanish Heritage*. New York: Wenner-Gren Foundation for Anthropological Research.

———. 1965. Peasant Society and the Image of Limited Good. *American Anthropologist* 67(2):293–315.

Foucault, Michel. 1982. The Subject and Power. *Critical Inquiry* 8(4):777–795.

———. 2004. *Security, Territory, Population: Lectures at the Collège de France, 1977–1978*. Translated by Graham Burchell. New York: Palgrave.

Frase, Ronald. 1975. A Sociological Analysis of the Development of Brazilian Protestantism. PhD diss., Princeton Theological Seminary.

Freixedo, Salvador. 1983. *Curanderismo y Curaciones por la Fé*. Barcelona, Spain: Martínez Roca.

Freston, Paul. 1993. Brother Votes for Brother: The New Politics of Protestantism in Brazil. In *Rethinking Protestantism in Latin America*. Virginia Garrard-Burnett and David Stoll, eds., 66–110. Philadelphia, PA: Temple University Press.

Friedel, David, Linda Schele, and Joy Parker. 1993. *Maya Cosmos: Three Thousand Years on the Shaman's Path*. New York: Morrow.

FUNCEDE [Fundación Centroamericana de Desarrollo]. 1994. *Diagnóstico del Municipio de Santa Catarina Ixtahuacán, Departamento de Sololá*. Guatemala City, Guatemala: FUNCEDE, Impresos Unidos del Norte.

———. 1995. *Diagnóstico del Municipio de Nahualá, Departamento de Sololá, Guatemala, Centro America*. Guatemala City, Guatemala: FUNCEDE, Impresos Unidos del Norte.

———. 1997a. *Diagnóstico del Municipio de Nahualá, Departamento de Sololá, Guatemala, Centro America*. Guatemala City, Guatemala: FUNCEDE.

———. 1997b. *Diagnóstico del Municipio de Santa Catarina Ixtahuacán, Departamento de Sololá, Guatemala, Centro America*. Guatemala City, Guatemala: FUNCEDE.

Gaisie, S. K., Edith K. Mote, Chuks Mba, Philomena E. Nyarko, K. A. Twum-Baah, T. K. B. Kumekpor, Omar B. Ahmad, and Tesfay Teklu. 2005. *Population Data Analysis Reports*. Vol. 1: *Socioeconomic and Demographic Trends Analysis*. N.p.: Ghana Statistical Service. www2.statsghana.gov.gh/nada/index.php/catalog/3/download/39 (accessed September 29, 2015).

Gall, Francis. 1981. *Diccionario Geográfico de Guatemala*. Vol. 1. Guatemala City, Guatemala: Instituto Geográfico Nacional.

———. 1983. *Diccionario Geográfico de Guatemala*. Vol. 3. Guatemala City, Guatemala: Instituto Geográfico Nacional.

Gálvez Borrell, Víctor, and Alberto Esquit Choy. 1997. *The Mayan Movement Today: Issues of Indigenous Culture and Development in Guatemala*. Guatemala City, Guatemala: FLASCO/Editorial Serviprensa.

García Añoveros, Jesús María. 1995. La Iglesia en la Diócesis de Guatemala. In *Siglo XVIII Hasta la Independencia*. Vol. 3 of *Historia General de Guatemala*. Cristina Zilbermann de Luján, ed., 57–82. Guatemala City, Guatemala: Associación de Amigos del País and Fundación para la Cultura e el Desarrollo.

Garrard-Burnett, Virginia. 1993. Conclusion: Is This Latin America's Reformation? In *Rethinking Protestantism in Latin America*. Virginia Garrard-Burnett and David Stoll, eds., 199–210. Philadelphia, PA: Temple University Press.

———. 1997. El Protestantismo, 1954–1990. In *Epoca Contemporánea de 1945 a la Actualidad*. Vol. 6 of *Historia General de Guatemala*. J. Daniel Contreras R., ed., 265–277. Guatemala City, Guatemala: Asociación de Amigos del País and the Fundacion para la Cultura y el Desarrollo.

———. 1998. *Protestantism in Guatemala: Living in the New Jerusalem*. Austin: University of Texas Press.

———. 2004. Inculturated Protestant Theology in Guatemala. In *Christianity and Native Cultures: Perspectives from Different Regions of the World*. Cyriac K. Pullapilly, Bernard J. Donahoe, David Stefancic, and William

Svelmoe, eds., 536–548. Notre Dame, IN: Cross Cultural.

———. 2007. Stop Suffering? The Iglesia Universal del Reino de Dios in the United States. In *Conversion of a Continent: Contemporary Religious Change in Latin America*. Timothy J. Steigenga and Edward L. Cleary, eds., 218–238. New Brunswick, NJ: Rutgers University Press.

———. 2008. Priests, Preachers, and Politics: The Region's New Religious Landscape. *Current History* 107(706):84–89.

———. 2010. *Terror in the Land of the Holy Spirit: Guatemala under General Efraín Ríos Montt, 1982–1983*. Oxford: Oxford University Press

Garriott, William, and Kevin Lewis O'Neill. 2008. Who Is a Christian? Toward a Dialogic Approach in the Anthropology of Christianity. *Anthropological Theory* 8(4):381–398.

Gay y Blasco, Paloma. 2000. Gitano Evangelism: The Emergence of a Politico-Religious Diaspora. Paper presented at the Sixth EASA Conference, Krakow, Poland, July 26–29. http://www.transcomm.ox.ac.uk/working%20papers/WPTC-01-04%20Gayyblasco.pdf.

———. 2002. Gypsy/Roma Diasporas: A Comparative Perspective. *Social Anthropology* 10(2):173–188.

———. 2012. Gender and Pentecostalism among the Gitanos of Madrid: Combining Approaches. *Romani Studies* 22(1):1–18.

Geertz, Clifford. 1973. Religion as a Cultural System. In Geertz, *The Interpretation of Cultures*, 87–125. New York: Basic.

Giddens, Anthony. 1984. *The Constitution of Society: Outline of the Theory of Structuration*. Berkeley: University of California Press.

———. 1993. *New Rules of Sociological Method: A Positive Critique of Interpretative Sociologies*. 2nd ed. Stanford, CA: Stanford University Press.

Gifford, Paul. 2004. *Ghana's New Christianity: Pentecostalism in a Globalizing African Economy*. Bloomington: Indiana University Press.

Gill, Lesley. 1990. Like a Veil to Cover Them: Women and the Pentecostal Movement in La Paz. *American Ethnologist* 17(4):708–721.

———. 1993. Religious Mobility and the Many Words of God in La Paz, Bolivia. In *Rethinking Protestantism in Latin America*. Virginia Garrard-Burnett and David Stoll, eds., 180–198. Philadelphia, PA: Temple University Press.

Gillin, John P. 1951. *The Culture of Security in San Carlos:*

A Study of a Guatemalan Community of Indians and Latinos. New Orleans, LA: Tulane University, Middle American Research Institute.

———. 1952. Ethos and Cultural Aspects of Personality. In *Heritage of Conquest: The Ethnology of Middle America.* Sol Tax, ed., 193–222. New York: Macmillan.

Glebbeek, Marie-Louise. 2003. *In the Crossfire of Democracy: Police Reform and Police Practice in Post-Civil War Guatemala.* Utrecht, Netherlands: Rozenberg.

Goldin, Liliana R. 2011. *Global Maya: Work and Ideology in Rural Guatemala.* Tucson: University of Arizona Press.

Goldin, Liliana R., and Brent Metz. 1991. An Expression of Cultural Change: Invisible Converts to Protestantism among Highland Guatemala Mayas. *Ethnology* 30(4):325–338.

Goldin, Liliana R., and María Eugenia Saenz de Tejada. 1993. Uneven Development in Western Guatemala. *Ethnology* 32(3):237–251.

Gooren, Henri. 1999. *Rich among the Poor: Church, Firm, and Household among Small-Scale Entrepreneurs in Guatemala City.* Amsterdam, Netherlands: Thela Latin America.

———. 2001. Reconsidering Protestant Growth in Guatemala, 1900–1995. In *Holy Saints and Fiery Preachers: The Anthropology of Protestantism in Mexico and Central America.* James W. Dow and Alan R. Sandstrom, eds., 169–203. Westport, CT: Praeger.

———. 2002. Catholic and Non-Catholic Theologies of Liberation: Poverty, Self-Improvement and Ethics among Small Scale Entrepreneurs in Guatemala City. *Journal for the Scientific Study of Religion* 41(1):29–45.

———. 2007. Conversion Careers in Latin America: Entering and Leaving Church among Pentecostals, Catholics, and Mormons. In *Conversion of a Continent: Contemporary Religious Change in Latin America.* Timothy J. Steigenga and Edward L. Cleary, eds., 52–71. New Brunswick, NJ: Rutgers University Press.

———. 2010. The Pentecostalization of Religion and Society in Latin America. *Exchange* 39:355–376.

———. 2012. The Catholic Charismatic Renewal in Latin America. *Pneuma* 34(2):185–207.

———. 2015. The Growth and Development of Non-Catholic Churches in Chile. *Review of Religious Research* 57(2):191–218.

Green, Linda. 1993. Shifting Affiliations: Maya Widows and Evangélicos in Guatemala. In *Rethinking Protestantism in Latin America.* Virginia Garrard-Burnett and David Stoll, eds., 159–179. Philadelphia, PA: Temple University Press.

———. 1999. *Fear as a Way of Life: Mayan Widows in Rural Guatemala.* New York: Columbia University Press.

Griffith, Marie. 2002. Female Suffering and Religious Devotion in American Pentecostalism. In *Women and 20th Century Protestantism.* Margaret Lamberts Beddroth and Virginia Lieson Brereton, eds., 184–208. Urbana: University of Illinois Press.

Gutiérrez González, Juan. 1977. Orar en Lenguas: Hacia una Oración Mas Profunda? In *Renovación en el Espíritu: Movimientos Carismáticos en América Latina.* Consejo Episcopal Latinoamericano, ed., 93–125. CELAM document no. 33. Bogotá, Colombia: Impresa LTDA for Secretariado General del CELAM.

Guzaro, Tomás, and Terri Jacob McComb. 2010. *Escaping the Fire: How an Ixil Mayan Pastor Led His People Out of a Holocaust during the Guatemalan Civil War.* Austin: University of Texas Press.

Hall, David. 1997. *Lived Religion in America: Toward a History of Practice.* Princeton, NJ: Princeton University Press.

Hanamaikai, Heather, and Ryan Thompson. 2005. "Girls Don't Talk": Education and Gender in Nahualá. In *Roads to Change in Maya Guatemala: A Field School Approach to Understanding the K'iche'.* John P. Hawkins and Walter Randolph Adams, eds., 167–173. Norman: University of Oklahoma Press.

Harris, Jason. 2007. "Someone Is Making You Sick": Conceptions of Disease in Santa Catarina Ixtahuacán. In *Health Care in Maya Guatemala: Confronting Medical Pluralism in a Developing Country.* Walter Randolph Adams and John P. Hawkins, eds., 27–43. Norman: University of Oklahoma Press.

Hart, Thomas. 2008. *The Ancient Spirituality of the Modern Maya.* Albuquerque: University of New Mexico Press.

Hastings, James, ed. 1980. *Encyclopedia of Religion and Ethics.* 13 vols. New York: Scribner's.

Hatch, Tara Seely. 2005. "Sit Properly": Elementary Education in Nahualá. In *Roads to Change in Maya Guatemala: A Field School Approach to Understanding the K'iche'.* John P. Hawkins and Walter Randolph Adams, eds., 151–166. Norman: University of Oklahoma Press.

Hawkins, John P. 1984. *Inverse Images: The Meaning of Culture, Ethnicity, and Family in Postcolonial Guatemala.* Albuquerque: University of New Mexico Press.

———. 2014. The Undergraduate Ethnographic Field School as a Research Method. *Current Anthropology* 55:551–590.

Hawkins, John P., and Walter Randolph Adams, eds. 2005a. *Roads to Change in Maya Guatemala: A Field School Approach to Understanding the K'iche'*. Norman: University of Oklahoma Press.

———. 2005b. Fostering Field School Ethnography. In *Roads to Change in Maya Guatemala: A Field School Approach to Understanding the K'iche'*. John P. Hawkins and Walter Randolph Adams, eds., 3–36. Norman: University of Oklahoma Press.

———. 2007. Preface. In *Health Care in Maya Guatemala: Confronting Medical Pluralism in a Developing Country*. Walter Randolph Adams and John P. Hawkins, eds., xiii–xvii. Norman: University of Oklahoma Press.

———. 2014. A Guide for Leaders: Some Considerations when Operating a Publication-Oriented Ethnographic Field School. Supplement A to Hawkins, The Undergraduate Ethnographic Field School as a Research Method. *Current Anthropology* 55(5):551–590, https://www.journals.uchicago.edu/doi/suppl/10.1086/678137. Available from the author, john_hawkins@byu.edu.

———. 2020. *Making a Place for the Future in Maya Guatemala: Disaster, Resettlement, and Indigenous Development in Santa Catarina Ixtahuacán*. Unpublished book manuscript in possession of editors.

Hawkins, John P., James H. McDonald, and Walter Randolph Adams, eds. 2013. *Crisis of Governance in Maya Guatemala: Indigenous Responses to a Failing State*. Norman: University of Oklahoma Press.

Hayden, Brian, and Margaret Nelson. 1981. The Use of Chipped Lithic Material in the Contemporary Maya Highlands. *American Antiquity* 46(4):885–898.

Healey, John B. 1976. *Charismatic Renewal: Reflections of a Pastor*. New York: Paulist Press.

Heath, Dwight B. 1987. Anthropology and Alcohol Studies: Current Issues. *Annual Review of Anthropology* 16:99–120.

———. 1988. Emerging Anthropological Theory and Models of Alcohol Use and Alcoholism. In *Theories on Alcoholism*. C. Douglas Chaudron and D. Adrian Wilkinson, eds., 353–410. Toronto, ON: Addiction Research Foundation.

———. 1990. Coca in the Andes: Traditions, Functions and Problems. *Rhode Island Medical Journal* 73:237–241.

———. 1991. Uses and Misuses of the Concept of Ethnicity in Alcohol Studies: An Essay in Deconstruction. *International Journal of the Addictions* 25:607–628.

Henry, Jules. 1963. *Culture against Man*. New York: Random House.

Herbrechtsmeier, William. 1993. Buddhism and the Definition of Religion: One More Time. *Journal for the Scientific Study of Religion* 32(1):1–18.

Hinojosa, Servando Z. 2002. "The Hands Know": Bodily Engagement and Medical Impasse in Highland Maya Bonesetting. *Medical Anthropology Quarterly* 16(1):22–40.

———. 2004a. Bonesetting and Radiography in the Southern Maya Highlands. *Medical Anthropology* 23(4):263–293.

———. 2004b. The Hands, the Sacred, and the Context of Change in Maya Bonesetting. In *Healing by Hand: Manual Medicine and Bone Setting in Global Perspective*. Kathryn S. Oths and Servando Z. Hinojosa, eds., 107–129. Walnut Creek, CA: AltaMira.

Hinshaw, Robert E. 1975. *Panajachel: A Guatemalan Town in Thirty-Year Perspective*. Pittsburgh, PA: University of Pittsburgh Press.

Hobsbawm, Eric, and Terence Ranger. 1983. *The Invention of Tradition*. Cambridge: Cambridge University Press.

Hocken, Peter D. 2003. Charismatic Movement. In *The New International Dictionary of Pentecostal and Charismatic Movements*. Rev. ed. Stanley M. Burgess and Eduard M. van der Maas, eds., 477–519. Grand Rapids, MI: Zondervan.

Hoenes del Pinal, Eric. 2008. Ideologies of Language and Gesture among Q'eqchi'-Maya Mainstream and Charismatic Catholics. PhD diss., Department of Anthropology, University of California, San Diego.

Hollenweger, Walter J. 1972. *The Pentecostals: The Charismatic Movement in the Churches*. Minneapolis, MN: Augsburg.

———. 2011. The Contribution of Asian Pentecostalism to Ecumenical Christianity: Hopes and Questions of a Barthian Theologian. In *Asian and Pentecostal: The Charismatic Face of Christianity in Asia*. Allan Anderson and Edmond Tang, eds., 13–21. Eugene, OR: Wipf and Stock.

Hoover, Willis C. 1977. *Historia del Avivamiento Pentecostal en Chile*. Santiago, Chile: Eben-Ezer.

Horst, Oscar H. 1956. An Analysis of Land Use in the Rio Samala Region of Guatemala. PhD diss., Ohio State University.

Horton, Robin. 1960. A Definition of Religion and Its Uses. *Journal of the Royal Anthropological Institute of Great Britain and Ireland* 90(2):201–226.

———. 1967. African Traditional Thought and Western Science. Part I: From Tradition to Science. *Africa: Journal of the International African Institute* 37(1):50–71.

Horwatt, Karin. 1988. The Shamanic Complex in the Pentecostal Church. *Ethos* 16(2):128–145.

Houston, Stephen H. 2008. Te-Mu and Te-Ma as "Throne." *Maya Decipherment: Ideas on Ancient Maya Writing and Iconography*, April 24. https://decipherment. wordpress.com/2008/04/24/te-mu-and-te-ma-as-throne.

Houston, Stephen, David Stuart, and Karl Taube. 2006. *The Memory of Bones: Body, Being, and Experience among the Classic Maya.* Austin: University of Texas Press.

Hyatt, Eddie, ed. 2006. *Fire on the Earth: Eyewitness Reports from the Azusa Street Revival.* Lake Mary, FL: Creation House.

Iannaccone, Laurence R., Rodney Stark, and Roger Finke. 1998. Rationality and the "Religious Mind." *Economic Inquiry* 36(3):373–389.

Iannaccone, Laurence R., Roger Finke, and Rodney Stark. 1997. Deregulating Religion: The Economics of Church and State. *Economic Inquiry* 35(2):350–364.

Ihonvbere, Julius Omozuanvbo, and Timothy M. Shaw. 1998. *Illusions of Power: Nigeria in Transition.* Trenton NJ: Africa World Press.

IINDEF [Instituto Internacional de Evangelización a Fondo] and SEPAL [Servicio Evangelizador para América Latina]. 1981. *Directorio de Iglesias, Organizaciones y Ministerios del Movimiento Protestante, Guatemala.* Guatemala City, Guatemala: IINDEF y SEPAL.

INE [Instituto Nacional de Estadística]. n.d. *Proyecciones de Población, 1995–2000.* Vol. 1. CD. Guatemala City, Guatemala: INE.

———. 1994. *X Censo de Población y V de Habitación: Población y Vivienda a Nivel de Lugar Poblado.* CD. Guatemala City, Guatemala: INE.

———. 2002a. *Base de Datos del XI Censo de Población y VI de Habitación.* CD. Guatemala City, Guatemala: INE.

———. 2002b. *Censos Nacionales XI de Población y VI de Habitación: Características de la Población y de los Locales de Habitación Censados.* CD. Guatemala City, Guatemala: República de Guatemala.

———. 2002c. *Lugares Poblados con Base en el XI Censo de Población y VI de Habitación.* CD. Guatemala City, Guatemala: INE.

———. 2003a. *Características de la Población y de los Locales de Habitación Censados, Censos Nacionales XI de Población y VI de Habitación, 2002.* Guatemala City Guatemala: INE.

———. 2003b. *IV Censo Nacional Agropecuario.* Vol. 1: *Características Generales de las Fincas Censales y de Produc-*
toras *y Productores Agropequarios.* CD. Guatemala City, Guatemala: INE.

———. 2004a. *IV Censo Nacional Agropecuario.* Vol. 2: *Número de Fincas Censales, Superficie Cosechada, Producción Obtenida de Cultivos Anuales y Temporales y Viveros.* CD. Guatemala City, Guatemala: INE.

———. 2004b. *IV Censo Nacional Agropecuario.* Vol. 3: *Número de Fincas Censales, Superficie Cultivada y Producción Obtenida de Cultivos Permanentes y Semipermanentes.* CD. Guatemala City, Guatemala: INE.

INE and MSPAS [Instituto Nacional de Estadística and Ministerio de Salud Pública y Asistencia Social]. 1999. *Salud Materno Infantil en los Departamentos del Altiplano.* Guatemala City, Guatemala: INE, MSPAS, and other institutions.

Instituto Brasileiro de Geografia e Estatística. 1946. *Recenseamento Geral do Brasil, 1° de Setembro de 1940: Sinopse do Censo Demográfico, Dados Gerais.* Rio de Janeiro, Brazil: Serviço Gráfico do Instituto Brasileiro de Geografia e Estatística.

Ireland, Rowan. 1993. The *Crentes* of Campo Alegre and the Religious Construction of Brazilian Politics. In *Rethinking Protestantism in Latin America.* Virginia Garrard-Burnett and David Stoll, eds., 45–65. Philadelphia, PA: Temple University Press.

Jardine, Spencer J., John P. Hawkins, and Walter Randolph Adams. 2020. Origin Narrative, Relocation, and Identity via Invention of Tradition in Nueva Santa Catarina Ixtahuacán. In *Making a Place for the Future in Maya Guatemala: Disaster, Resettlement, and Indigenous Development in Santa Catarina Ixtahuacán.* John P. Hawkins and Walter Randolph Adams, eds. Unpublished book manuscript in possession of editors.

Jiménez de Báez, Yvette, ed., with Raquel Mosqueda and Marco Antonio Molina. 2002. *Lenguajes de la Tradición Popular Fiesta, Canto, Música y Representación.* Mexico City: El Colegio de México, Centro de Estudios Lingüísticos y Literarios.

Johnson, Paul. 1983. *Modern Times: The World from the Twenties to the Eighties.* New York: Harper and Row.

Johnson, Todd M., and Brian J. Grim, eds. 2020. *World Religion Database.* https://www.worldreligiondatabase.org. Leiden: Brill.

Johnson, Todd M., and Kenneth R. Ross, eds. 2009. *Atlas of Global Christianity, 1910–2010.* Edinburgh: Edinburgh University Press.

Johnson, Todd M., and Sun Young Chung. 2009. Christianity's Centre of Gravity, AD 33–2100. In *Atlas of Global Christianity, 1910–2010*. Todd M. Johnson and Kenneth R. Ross, eds., 50–53. Edinburgh: Edinburgh University Press.

Jones, Chester Lloyd. 1940. *Guatemala, Past and Present*. Minneapolis: University of Minnesota Press.

Jones, Lindsay, ed. 2005. *Encyclopedia of Religion*. 15 vols. 2nd ed. New York: Thomson Gale.

Kalberg, Stephen. 1980. Max Weber's Types of Rationality: Cornerstones for the Analysis of Rationalization Processes in History. *American Journal of Sociology* 85(5):1145–1179.

Kamsteeg, F. 1991. *Pentecostal Healing and Power: A Peruvian Case*. Fort Lauderdale, FL: Breitenbach.

Keane, Webb. 1997. Religious Language. *Annual Review of Anthropology* 26:47–71.

Keil, Charles. 1987. Participatory Discrepancies and the Power of Music. *Cultural Anthropology* 2(3):275–283.

Kilbourne, Brock, and James T. Richardson. 1989. Paradigm Conflict, Types of Conversion, and Conversion Theories. *Sociological Analysis* 50(1):1–21.

Kilby, Emily R. 2007. The Demographics of the U.S. Equine Population. In *The State of the Animals*. D. J. Salem and A. N. Rowan, eds., 175–205. Washington, DC: Humane Society Press. http://www.humanesociety.org/assets/pdfs/hsp/soaiv_07_ch10.pdf.

Komonchak, Joseph A., Mary Collins, and Dermon A. Lane. 1987. *The New Dictionary of Theology*. Wilmington, DE: Michael Glazier.

Kovic, Christine. 2007. Indigenous Conversion to Catholicism: Change of Heart in Chiapas, Mexico. In *Conversion of a Continent: Contemporary Religious Change in Latin America*. Timothy J. Steigenga and Edward L. Cleary, eds., 199–217. New Brunswick, NJ: Rutgers University Press.

Kumar, Dharma. 1992. *Land and Caste in South India: Agricultural Labour in the Madras Presidency during the Nineteenth Century*. Delhi, India: Manohar.

Lacoste, Jean-Yves. 2005. *Encyclopedia of Christian Theology*. 3 vols. New York: Routledge.

LaFarge, Oliver. 1947. *Santa Eulalia: The Religion of a Cuchumatán Town*. Chicago: University of Chicago Press.

Lambeck, Michael. 1998. Taboo as Cultural Practice among Malagasy Speakers. In *Religion in Culture and Society*. John R. Bowen, ed., 117–138. Boston: Allyn and Bacon.

Lange, Barbara Rose. 1996. Gender Politics and Musical Performers in the Isten Gyülekezet: A Fieldwork Account. *Journal of American Folklore* 109(431):60–76.

Larson, Clayton G. 2006. Four Forms of Fetishism: Tradition and Economic Change in a Guatemalan Village. *Human Mosaic* 36(2):26–41.

Lawless, Elaine J. 1983. "Shouting for the Lord": The Power of Women's Speech in the Pentecostal Religious Service. *Journal of American Folklore* 96(382):434–459.

———. 1988. "The Night I Got the Holy Ghost": Holy Ghost Narratives and the Pentecostal Conversion Process. *Western Folklore* 47(1):1–19.

Leach, Edmund Ronald. 1965[1954]. *Political Systems of Highland Burma: A Study of Kachin Social Structure*. Boston: Beacon.

Levenson, Deborah T. 2013. *Adiós Niño: The Gangs of Guatemala City and the Politics of Death*. Durham, NC: Duke University Press.

Lévi-Strauss, Claude. 1955. The Structural Study of Myth. *Journal of American Folklore* 68(270):428–444.

———. 1967[1949]. *The Elementary Structures of Kinship*. Rev. ed. Translated by James H. Bell and John R. Sturmer. Edited by Rodney Needham. London: Eyre and Spottiswoode.

———. 1974. *Tristes Tropiques*. New York: Atheneum.

Lewis, I. M. 1971. *Ecstatic Religion: An Anthropological Study of Spirit Possession and Shamanism*. Harmondsworth, England: Penguin.

Liardon, Roberts. 2006. *The Azusa Street Revival: When the Fire Fell*. Shippensburg, PA: Destiny Image.

Lindhardt, Martin. 2012. *Power in Powerlessness: A Study of Pentecostal Life Worlds in Urban Chile*. Leiden, Netherlands: Brill.

Long, T., and J. Hadden. 1983. Religious Conversion and Socialization. *Journal for the Scientific Study of Religion* 24:1–14.

López Cortés, Eliseo. 1990. *Pentecostalismo y Milenarismo: La Iglesia Apostólica de la Fe en Cristo Jesús*. Mexico City: Universidad Autónoma Metropolitana/Iztapalapa.

Macchia, Frank D. 2003. Theology, Pentecostal. In *The New International Dictionary of Pentecostal and Charismatic Movements*. Rev. ed. Stanley M. Burgess and Eduard M. van der Maas, eds., 1120–1141. Grand Rapids, MI: Zondervan.

———. 2006. *Baptized in the Spirit: A Global Pentecostal Theology*. Grand Rapids, MI: Zondervan.

MacLeod, Murdo J. 1973. *Spanish Central America: A Socioeconomic History, 1520–1720*. Berkeley: University of California Press.

Malinowski, B. 1954. *Magic, Science and Religion*. Garden City, NY: Doubleday.

Malkin, Elisabeth. 2019. Guatemala Expels U.N.-Backed Anti-Corruption Panel, Claiming Overreach. *New York Times*, January 7. https://www.nytimes.com/2019/01/07/world/americas/guatemala-corruption-commission-united-nations.html.

Manz, Beatriz. 2004. *Paradise in Ashes: A Guatemalan Journey of Courage, Terror, and Hope.* Berkeley: University of California Press.

Marcus, George E. 1995. Ethnography in/of the World System: The Emergence of Multi-Sited Ethnography. *Annual Review of Anthropology* 24:95–117.

———. 2009. Multi-Sited Ethnography: Notes and Queries. In *Multi-Sited Ethnography: Theory, Praxis and Locality in Contemporary Research.* Mark-Anthony Falzon, ed., 181–196. Surrey, England: Ashgate.

Marcus, George E., and Michael M. J. Fischer. 1986. *Anthropology as Cultural Critique: An Experimental Moment in the Human Sciences.* Chicago: University of Chicago Press.

Marcus, Joyce. 2003. Advances in Maya Archaeology. *Journal of Archaeological Research* 11(2):71–148.

Marshall, Ruth. 2009. *Political Spiritualities: The Pentecostal Revolution in Nigeria.* Chicago: University of Chicago Press.

Martin, David. 1990. *Tongues of Fire: The Explosion of Protestantism in Latin America.* Cambridge, MA: Blackwell.

Martin, Francis. 2003. Healing, Gift of. In *The New International Dictionary of Pentecostal and Charismatic Movements.* Rev. ed. Stanley M. Burgess and Eduard M. van der Maas, eds., 694–698. Grand Rapids, MI: Zondervan.

Martin, Larry. 1999. *The Life and Ministry of William J. Seymour and a History of the Azusa Street Revival.* Joplin, MO: Christian Life Books.

Martínez Peláez, Severo. 1970. *La Patria del Criollo: Ensayo de Interpretación de la Realidad Colonial Guatemalteca.* Guatemala: Universitaria.

Marty, Martin E., and R. Scott Appleby. 1991. *Fundamentalisms Observed.* Fundamentalism Project, vol. 1. Chicago: University of Chicago Press.

———. 1993. *Fundamentalisms and the State: Remaking Polities, Economies, and Militance.* Fundamentalism Project, vol. 3. Chicago: University of Chicago Press.

———. 1994. *Accounting for Fundamentalisms: The Dynamic Character of Movements.* Fundamentalism Project, vol. 4. Chicago: University of Chicago Press.

———. 1995. *Fundamentalisms Comprehended.* Fundamentalism Project, vol. 5. Chicago: University of Chicago Press.

Marx, Karl. 2008[1844]. Contribution to the Critique of Hegel's Philosophy of Right. In *On Religion* by Karl Marx and Friedrich Engels, 41–58. Mineola, NY: Dover.

———. 2008[1855]. Anti-Church Movement—Demonstration in Hyde Park. In *On Religion* by Karl Marx and Friedrich Engels, 127–134. Mineola, NY: Dover.

Marx, Karl, and Friedrich Engels. 1948[1848]. *The Manifesto of the Communist Party: Authorized English Translation.* Edited and annotated by Friedrich Engels. New York: International Publishers.

———. 1968[1848]. *The Communist Manifesto.* Translated by Paul M. Sweezy. New York: Modern Reader Paperbacks.

———. 2008[1846]. German Ideology. In *On Religion* by Karl Marx and Friedrich Engels, 73–81. Mineola, NY: Dover.

———. 2008[1850]. Review of G. Fr. Daumer's *The Revolution of the New Age.* In *On Religion* by Karl Marx and Friedrich Engels, 90–96. Mineola, NY: Dover.

Mathewes, Charles. 2012. Toward a Theology of Joy. http://faith.yale.edu/sites/default/files/mathewes_toward_a_theology_of_joy.pdf.

Mauss, Marcel. 1990[1925]. *The Gift: The Form and Reason for Exchange in Archaic Societies.* Translated by W. D. Halls. New York: Norton.

Maynard, Kent. 1993. Protestant Theories and Anthropological Knowledge: Convergent Models in the Ecuadorian Sierra. *Cultural Anthropology* 8(2):246–267.

McAllister, Carlota, and Diane M. Nelson. 2013. *War by Other Means: Aftermath in Post-Genocide Guatemala.* Durham, NC: Duke University Press.

McBryde, Felix Webster. 1933. *Sololá: A Guatemalan Town and Cakchiquel Market-Center.* New Orleans, LA: Tulane University.

———. 1945. *Cultural and Historical Geography of South West Guatemala.* Washington, DC: US Government Printing Office.

McCreery, David. 1994. *Rural Guatemala, 1760–1940.* Stanford, CA: Stanford University Press.

McDonald, James H., and John P. Hawkins. 2013a. Conclusion: Fear, Control, and Power in an Unpredictable World. In *Crisis of Governance in Maya Guatemala: Indigenous Responses to a Failing State.* John P. Hawkins, James H. McDonald, and Walter Randolph Adams, eds., 218–258. Norman: University of Oklahoma Press.

———. 2013b. Introduction: Crisis of Governance and Consequences of Indeterminacy in Postwar Maya Guatemala. In *Crisis of Governance in Maya Guatemala: Indigenous*

Responses to a Failing State. John P. Hawkins, James H. McDonald, and Walter Randolph Adams, eds., 13–49. Norman: University of Oklahoma Press.

———. 2013c. Prologue. In *Crisis of Governance in Maya Guatemala: Indigenous Responses to a Failing State*. John P. Hawkins, James H. McDonald, and Walter Randolph Adams, eds., 3–12. Norman: University of Oklahoma Press.

———. 2016. Valor Humano, Anarquía Endémica y Gubernamentalidad Precaria en Guatemala. *Mesoamérica* 37(58):40–66.

McDonnell, Kilian, ed. 1975. *The Holy Spirit and Power: The Catholic Charismatic Renewal*. Garden City, NY: Doubleday.

McGuire, Meredith B. 1982. *Pentecostal Catholics: Power, Charisma, and Order in a Religious Movement*. Philadelphia, PA: Temple University Press.

McMillen, Neil R. 1989. *Dark Journey: Black Mississippians in the Age of Jim Crow*. Chicago: University of Illinois Press.

Melendez, Guillermo. 1992. The Catholic Church in Central America: Into the 1990s. *Social Compass* 39(4):553–570.

Mendonsa, Eugene L. 1982. *The Politics of Divination: A Processual View of Reactions to Illness and Deviance among the Sisala of Northern Ghana*. Berkeley: University of California Press.

Menzies, William. 1971. *Anointed to Serve*. Springfield, MO: Gospel Publishing House.

Merriam, Alan P. 1955. Music in American Culture. *American Anthropologist*, n.s., 57(6):1173–1181.

———. 1964. *The Anthropology of Music*. Chicago: Northwestern University Press.

Metz, Brent. 2006. *Ch'orti'-Maya Survival in Eastern Guatemala*. Albuquerque: University of New Mexico Press.

Metz, Johann Baptist. 1974. Editorial: Joy and Grief, Cheerfulness, Melancholy and Humour; or, The Difficulty of Saying Yes. In *Theology of Joy*. Johann Baptist Metz and Jean-Pierre Jossua, eds., 7–12. New York: Herder and Herder.

Meyer, Birgit. 2015. *Sensational Movies: Video, Vision, and Christianity in Ghana*. Berkeley: University of California Press.

Miller, Mary Ellen, and Meghan E. O'Neil. 1999. *Maya Art and Architecture*. 2nd ed. London: Thames and Hudson.

Molesky-Poz, Jean. 2004. The Dawning of Something Ancient, yet New: Reconciliation and Inculturation in the Guatemalan Highlands. In *Christianity and Native Cultures: Perspectives from Different Regions of the*

World. Cyriac K. Pullapilly, Bernard J. Donahoe, David Stefancic, and William Svelmoe, eds., 519–535. Notre Dame, IN: Cross Cultural.

———. 2006. *Contemporary Maya Spirituality: The Ancient Ways Are Not Lost*. Austin: University of Texas Press.

Moltmann, Jürgen. 1973. *Theology and Joy*. London: SCM Press.

Monaghan, John. 1995. *The Covenants with Earth and Rain: Exchange, Sacrifice, and Revelation in Mixtec Sociality*. Norman: University of Oklahoma Press.

Montejo, Victor. 1999. *Voices from Exile: Violence and Survival in Modern Maya History*. Norman: University of Oklahoma Press.

Montoya, Matilde. 1970. *Estudio sobre el Baile de la Conquista*. Guatemala: Editorial Universitaria.

Morales Urrutia, Mateo. 1961. *La División Política y Administrativa de la República de Guatemala, con Sus Datos Historicos y de Legislación*. 2 vols. and 2 supps. Guatemala City, Guatemala: Iberia.

Morgan, Jesse. 2005. Standing at the Crossroads: Culture Change in Nahualá as Seen through the Eyes of Javier, a Maya Elder. In *Roads to Change in Maya Guatemala: A Field School Approach to Understanding the K'iche'*. John P. Hawkins and Walter Randolph Adams, eds., 61–96. Norman: University of Oklahoma Press.

Mühlen, Heribert. 1975. The Charismatic Renewal as Experience. In *The Holy Spirit and Power: The Catholic Charismatic Renewal*. Kilian McDonnell, ed., 107–117. Garden City, NY: Doubleday.

Municipio de Cantel. 1991. *El Baile de la Conquista*. Guatemala City, Guatemala: Editorial Piedra Santa.

Nadel, S. F. [Siegfried Frederick]. 1946. A Study of Shamanism in the Nuba Mountains. *Journal of the Royal Anthropological Institute of Great Britain and Ireland* 76(1):25–37.

———. 1952. Witchcraft in Four African Societies. *American Anthropologist* 54(1):18–29.

Nash, Manning. 1958a. *Machine Age Maya: The Industrialization of a Guatemalan Community*. Memoirs of the American Anthropological Association. Vol. 60, no. 2, pt. 2. Menasha, WI: American Anthropological Association.

———. 1958b. Political Relations in Guatemala. *Social and Economic Studies* 7:65–75.

———. 1967[1958]. *Machine Age Maya: The Industrialization of a Guatemalan Community*. Chicago: University of Chicago Press.

Nelson, Diane M. 1999. *A Finger in the Wound: Body Politics in Quincentennial Guatemala*. Berkeley: University of California Press.

———. 2009. *Reckoning: The Ends of War in Guatemala*. Durham, NC: Duke University Press.

Nuttall, Kristyn Roser. 2005. "We Are Very Capable": Women and Development in Santa Catarina Ixtahuacán. In *Roads to Change in Maya Guatemala. A Field School Approach to Understanding the K'iche'*. John P. Hawkins and Walter Randolph Adams, eds., 191–209. Norman: University of Oklahoma Press.

Oakes, Maud. 1951a. *Beyond the Windy Place: Life in the Guatemalan Highlands*. New York: Farrar, Straus, and Young.

———. 1951b. *The Two Crosses of Todos Santos: Survivals of Maya Religious Ritual*. New York: Pantheon.

Olupona, Jacob K. 2003. Africa, West (Survey). In *The New International Dictionary of Pentecostal and Charismatic Movements*. Rev. ed. Stanley Burgess and Eduard M. van der Maas, eds., 11–21. Grand Rapids, MI: Zondervan.

O'Neill, Kevin Lewis. 2010. *City of God: Christian Citizenship in Postwar Guatemala*. Berkeley: University of California Press.

O'Neill, Kevin Lewis, and Kedron Thomas, eds. 2011. *Securing the City: Neoliberalism, Space, and Insecurity in Postwar Guatemala*. Durham, NC: Duke University Press.

Orsi, Robert A. 2005. *Between Heaven and Earth: The Religious Worlds People Make and the Scholars Who Study Them*. Princeton, NJ: Princeton University Press.

Owen, Roger C., Nancy E. Walstrom, and Ralph C. Michelsen. 1969. Musical Culture and Ethnic Solidarity: A Baja California Case Study. *Journal of American Folklore* 82(324):99–111.

Palackal, Joseph J. 2004. Interface between History and Music in the Christian Context of South India. In *Christianity and Native Cultures: Perspectives from Different Regions of the World*. Cyriac K. Pullapilly, Bernard J. Donahoe, David Stefancic, and William Svelmoe, eds., 150–161. Notre Dame, IN: Cross Cultural.

Paloutzian, Raymond F., James T. Richardson, and Lewis R. Rambo. 1999. Religious Conversion and Personality Change. *Journal of Personality* 67(6):1047–1049.

Pastor, Angela. 1998. *Los Curas Carismáticos*. Buenos Aires, Argentina: Libro Latino.

Pattridge, Blake D. 1994. Catholic Church in Revolutionary Guatemala, 1944–54: A House Divided. *Journal of Church and State* 36(3):527–540.

Perera, Victor. 1993. *Unfinished Conquest: The Guatemalan Tragedy*. Berkeley: University of California Press.

Pew Research Center. 2006. *Spirit and Power: A 10-Country Survey of Pentecostals*. Washington, DC: Pew Research Center on Religion and Public Life. https://www.pew-forum.org/2006/10/05/spirit-and-power/.

Pitts, Walter. 1991. Like a Tree Planted by the Water: The Musical Cycle in the African-American Baptist Ritual. *Journal of American Folklore* 104(413):318–340.

Platte, Daniel, ed. 2010. *Cambridge Dictionary of Christianity*. Cambridge: Cambridge University Press. https://www.vanderbilt.edu/AnS/religious_studies/CDC/ (accessed September 6, 2019).

Polanyi, Karl. 1944. *The Great Transformation: The Political and Economic Origins of Our Time*. Boston: Beacon.

Poling, T., and J. Kenny. 1986. *The Hare Krishna Character Type: A Study in Sensate Personality*. Lewiston, NY: Edwin Mellen.

Popper, Karl R. 1965. *Conjectures and Refutations: The Growth of Scientific Knowledge*. New York: Basic.

———. 1968. *The Logic of Scientific Discovery*. New York: Harper and Row.

Prado Ponce, Eduardo. 1984. *Comunidades de Guatemala (Recopilación)*. Guatemala City, Guatemala: Impresos Herme.

Radcliffe-Brown, A. R. 1952. The Comparative Method in Social Anthropology. *Journal of the Royal Anthropological Institute* 81:15–22.

———. 1957[1948]. *A Natural Science of Society*. Glencoe, IL: Free Press.

———. 1961[1952]. *Structure and Function in Primitive Society: Essays and Addresses*. Glencoe, IL: Free Press.

Rapaka, Yabbeju (Jabez). 2013. *Dalit Pentecostalism: A Study of the Indian Pentecostal Church of God, 1932–2010*. Lexington KY: Emeth.

Rappaport, Roy A. 1968. *Pigs for the Ancestors*. New Haven, CT: Yale University Press.

———. 1999. *Ritual and Religion in the Making of Humanity*. New York: Cambridge University Press.

Redfield, Robert. 1946. Notes on San Antonio Palopo. Microfilm collection of manuscripts on Middle American cultural anthropology, University of Chicago. https://www.crl.edu/microfilm-collection-manuscripts-middle-american-cultural-anthropology (accessed May 22, 2020).

Reina, Ruben E. 1966. *The Law of the Saints: A Pokomam Pueblo and Its Community Culture*. New York: Bobbs-Merrill.

Reina, Ruben E., and Norman B. Schwartz. 1974. The

Structural Context of Religious Conversion in Petén, Guatemala: Status, Community, and Multicommunity. *American Ethnologist* 1(1):157–191.

Robbins, Joel, and Naomi Haynes, eds. 2014. The Anthropology of Christianity: Unity, Diversity, New Directions. Special issue, *Current Anthropology* 55, supp. 10.

Roberts, Brian. 1968. Protestant Groups and Coping with Urban Life in Guatemala City. *American Journal of Sociology* 73(6):753–767.

———. 1973. *Organizing Strangers: Poor Families in Guatemala City*. Austin: University of Texas Press.

Roberts, Nathaniel. 2016. *To Be Cared For: The Power of Conversion and Foreignness of Belonging in an Indian Slum*. Berkeley: University of California Press.

Roberts, Robert Campbell. 2003. *Emotions: An Essay in Aid of Moral Psychology*. New York: Cambridge University Press.

Robledo Hernández, Gabriela Patricia. 2003. Protestantism and Family Dynamics in an Indigenous Community of Highland Chiapas. In *Women of Chiapas: Making History in Times of Struggle and Hope*. Christine Eber, ed., 161–170. New York: Routledge.

Rode, Stephen Shem. 2007. "If We Do Not Eat Milpa, We Die": The Cultural Basis of Health in Nahualá. In *Health Care in Maya Guatemala: Confronting Medical Pluralism in a Developing Country*. Walter Randolph Adams and John P. Hawkins, eds., 69–85. Norman: University of Oklahoma Press.

Rodseth, Lars, and Jennifer Olsen. 2000. Mystics against the Market: American Religions and the Autocritique of Capitalism. *Critique of Anthropology* 20(3):265–288.

Rojas Lima, Flavio. 1968. Los Otros Pueblos del Lago. In *Los Pueblos del Lago de Atitlán*. Seminario de Integración Social Guatemalteco, ed., 277–340. Guatemala City, Guatemala: Seminario de Integración Social Guatemalteco.

———. 1988. *La Cultura del Maíz en Guatemala*. Guatemala City, Guatemala: Ministerio de Cultura y Deportes.

Ruether, Rosemary Radford. 1989. *Women-Church: Theology and Practice of Feminist Liturgical Communities*. San Francisco, CA: Harper and Row.

Sahlins, Marshall. 1981. *Historical Metaphors and Mythical Realities: Structure in the Early History of the Sandwich Islands Kingdom*. Ann Arbor: University of Michigan Press.

———. 1985. *Islands of History*. Chicago: University of Chicago Press.

Salazar, Oswaldo. 1996. *Historia Moderna de la Etnicidad en Guatemala: La Visión Hegemónica de 1944 al Presente*. Guatemala City, Guatemala: Universidad Rafael Landívar.

Salzman, Philip Carl. 2012. *Classic Comparative Anthropology: Studied from the Tradition*. Long Grove, IL: Waveland.

Samson, C. Mathews. 2007. *Re-Enchanting the World: Maya Protestantism in the Guatemalan Highlands*. Tuscaloosa: University of Alabama Press.

Sanford, Victoria. 2003. *Buried Secrets: Truth and Human Rights in Guatemala*. New York: Palgrave.

Santa Catarina Ixtahuacán. 1995. *Misal K'iche': Parroquia Reech Santa Catarina Ixtahuacán, Diócesis Reech Sololá*. Guatemala City, Guatemala: Cholsamaj.

Sarasa, Jesus María. 1991. *Los Protestantes en Guatemala*. No publication data except hand-placed ink stamp "Gobierno Ecco [Eclesástico] Metr. [Metropolitiano] de Santiago de Guatemala," and handwritten "Con Licencia Eclesiastica Libro corriente, fol 397, #4008; Guatemala, 13 de Deciembre de 1991." Brigham Young University Archives, Provo, UT.

Saunders, George R. 1995. The Crisis of Presence in Italian Pentecostal Conversion. *American Ethnologist* 22(2):324–340.

Saussure, Ferdinand de. 1966[1959]. *Course in General Linguistics*. Edited by Charles Bally and Albert Schehaye. Translated by Wade Baskin. New York: Philosophical Library.

Schirmer, Jennifer. 1998. *The Guatemalan Military Project: A Violence Called Democracy*. Philadelphia: University of Pennsylvania Press.

Schlesinger, Stephen C. and Stephen Kinzer. 2005. *Bitter Fruit: The Story of the American Coup in Guatemala*. Rev. ed. Cambridge, MA: Harvard University Press.

Schneider, David M. 1968. Virgin Birth. *Man* 3:126–129.

———. 1969. Kinship, Nationality and Religion in American Culture: Toward a Definition of Kinship. In *Forms of Symbolic Action: Proceedings of the 1969 Annual Spring Meeting of the American Ethnological Society*. Robert F. Spencer, ed., 116–125. Seattle, WA: American Ethnological Society.

———. 1984. *A Critique of the Study of Kinship*. Ann Arbor: University of Michigan Press.

Scotchmer, David. 1986. Convergence of the Gods: Comparing Traditional Maya and Christian Maya Cosmologies. In *Symbol and Meaning beyond the Closed Community: Essays in Mesoamerican Ideas*. Gary H. Grossen, ed., 197–226. Albany, NY: Institute for Mesoamerican Studies.

———. 1989. Symbols of Salvation: A Local Mayan Protestant Theology. *Missiology* 17:293–310.

———. 2001. Pastors, Preachers, or Prophets? Cultural Conflict and Continuity in Maya Protestant Leadership. In *Holy Saints and Fiery Preachers: The Anthropology of Protestantism in Mexico and Central America*. James A. Dow and Alan R. Sandstrom, eds., 235–262. Westport CT: Praeger.

Scott, James C. 1985. *Weapons of the Weak: Everyday Forms of Peasant Resistance*. New Haven, CT: Yale University Press

Scott, Shauna L. 1994. "They Don't Have to Live by the Old Traditions": Saintly Men, Sinner Women, and an Appalachian Pentecostal Revival. *American Ethnologist* 21(2):227–244.

Searcy, Michael T. 2011. *The Life-Giving Stone: Ethnoarchaeology of Maya Metates*. Tucson: University of Arizona Press.

Secretario de Estado del Despacho de Fomento, Sección de Estadística. 1880. *Censo General de la República de Guatemala Levantado en el Año de 1880*. Guatemala City, Guatemala: Establecmiento Tipografico de El Progreso.

Semus, Rebekah. 2005. "Because We Weave Together": Women, Work, and Dominance in a Nahualá Extended Family. In *Roads to Change in Maya Guatemala: A Field School Approach to Understanding the K'iche'*. John P. Hawkins and Walter Randolph Adams, eds., 139–148. Norman: University of Oklahoma Press.

Sepúlveda, Juan. 1996. Reinterpreting Chilean Pentecostalism. *Social Compass* 43(3):299–318.

Sexton, James D. 1978. Protestantism and Modernization in Two Guatemala Towns. *American Ethnologist* 5(2):280–302.

Siebers, H. 1991. *Indian Religion and the Catholic Church in Guatemala*. Fort Lauderdale, FL: Breitenbach.

Sinclair, Bronwyn M. 2007. Wild Greens Every Day, That Is All We Ate. In *Health Care in Maya Guatemala: Confronting Medical Pluralism in a Developing Country*. Walter Randolph Adams and John P. Hawkins, eds., 166–178. Norman: University of Oklahoma Press.

Skinner-Klee, Jorge. 1954. *Legislación Indigenista de Guatemala*. Mexico City: Instituto Indigenista Interamericano.

Slootweg, H. 1998. *Pentecostal Women in Chile: A Case Study in Iquique*. London: Scarecrow.

Smith, Carol. 1990. The Militarization of Civil Society in Guatemala: Economic Reorganization as a Continuation of War. *Latin American Perspectives* 17(4):8–41.

Smith, G. D. 2019. Faith and Revealed Truth: Part I. *Catholic Culture*. https://www.catholicculture.org/culture/library/view.cfm?recnum=5804#vi.

Smith, Waldemar R. 1977. *The Fiesta System and Economic Change*. New York: Columbia University Press.

Stanzione, Vincent James. 2003. *Rituals of Sacrifice: Walking the Face of the Earth on the Sacred Path of the Sun, a Journey through the Tz'utujil Maya World of Santiago Atitlán*. Albuquerque: University of New Mexico Press.

Stark, Rodney. 1998. Catholic Contexts: Competition, Commitment and Innovation. *Review of Religious Research* 39(3):197–209.

Stark, Rodney, and Roger Finke. 2000. *Acts of Faith: Explaining the Human Side of Religion*. Berkeley: University of California Press.

Stark, Rodney, Lawrence R. Iannaccone, and Roger Finke. 1996. Religion, Science, and Rationality. *American Economic Review* 86(2):433–437.

Starkloff, Carl F. 1997. Church as Structure and Communitas: Victor Turner and Ecclesiology. *Theological Studies* 58(4):643–668.

Stavenhagen, Rodolfo. 1970. Classes, Colonialism, and Acculturation: A System of Interethnic Relations in Mesoamerica. In *Masses in Latin America*, Irving L. Horowitz, ed., 235–288. New York: Oxford University Press.

———. 1975. *Social Classes in Agrarian Societies*. New York: Doubleday, Anchor.

Steigenga, Timothy J. 2001. *The Politics of the Spirit: The Political Implications of Pentecostalized Religion in Costa Rica and Guatemala*. Lanham, MD: Lexington.

———. 2007. The Politics of Pentecostalized Religion: Conversion as Pentecostalization in Guatemala. In *Conversion of a Continent: Contemporary Religious Change in Latin America*. Timothy J. Steigenga and Edward L. Cleary, eds., 256–279. New Brunswick, NJ: Rutgers University Press.

Steigenga, Timothy J., and Edward L. Cleary, eds. 2007a. *Conversion of a Continent: Contemporary Religious Change in Latin America*. New Brunswick, NJ: Rutgers University Press.

———. 2007b. Understanding Conversion in the Americas. In *Conversion of a Continent: Contemporary Religious Change in Latin America*. Timothy J. Steigenga and Edward L. Cleary, eds., 1–32. New Brunswick, NJ: Rutgers University Press.

Steigenga, Timothy, and David Smilde. 1999. Wrapped in the

Holy Shawl: The Strange Case of Conservative Christians and Gender Equality in Latin America. In *Latin American Religion in Motion*. Christian Smith and Joshua Prokopy, eds., 173–186. New York: Routledge.

Stewart-Gambino, Hannah W. 2001. Review: "Religious Consumers" in a "Religious Marketplace." *Latin American Research Review* 36(1):193–206.

Stoll, David. 1990. *Is Latin America Turning Protestant? The Politics of Evangelical Growth*. Berkeley: University of California Press.

———. 1993a. *Between Two Armies in the Ixil Towns of Guatemala*. New York: Columbia University Press.

———. 1993b. Introduction. In *Rethinking Protestantism in Latin America*. Virginia Garrard-Burnett and David Stoll, eds., 1–19. Philadelphia, PA: Temple University Press.

———. 1994. "Jesus Is Lord of Guatemala": Evangelical Reform in a Death-Squad State. In *Accounting for Fundamentalisms: The Dynamic Character of Movements*. Martin E. Marty and R. Scott Appleby, eds., 99–123. Chicago: University of Chicago Press.

———. 2013. *El Norte or Bust! How Migration Fever and Microcredit Produced a Financial Crash in a Latin American Town*. Lanham, MD: Rowman and Littlefield.

Stratford, Starr Peterson, John P. Hawkins, and Walter Randolph Adams. 2020. Developing a Dream: Community, State, and NGO Relations during the Construction of Nueva Santa Catarina Ixtahuacán. In *Making a Place for the Future in Maya Guatemala: Disaster, Resettlement, and Indigenous Development in Santa Catarina Ixtahuacán*. John P. Hawkins and Walter Randolph Adams, eds. Unpublished book manuscript in possession of editors.

Stringer, Martin D. 2008. *Contemporary Western Ethnography and the Definition of Religion*. London: Continuum.

Stromberg, Peter G. 1993. *Language and Self-Transformation: A Study of the Christian Conversion Narrative*. Cambridge: Cambridge University Press.

Stross, Brian. 2007. Eight Reinterpretations of Submerged Symbolism in the Mayan Popol Wuj. *Anthropological Linguistics* 49(3–4):388–423.

Sullivan, Emily R. 2007. Sadness in the Highlands: A Study of Depression in Nueva Santa Catarina Ixtahuacán. In *Health Care in Maya Guatemala: Confronting Medical Pluralism in a Developing Country*. Walter Randolph Adams and John P. Hawkins, eds., 194–214. Norman: University of Oklahoma Press.

Sullivan, Francis A. 1975. The Ecclesiological Context of the Charismatic Renewal. In *The Holy Spirit and Power: The Catholic Charismatic Renewal*. Kilian McDonnell, ed., 119–138. Garden City, NY: Doubleday.

Sullivan-González, Douglass. 1998. *Piety, Power, and Politics: Religion and Nation Formation in Guatemala, 1821–1871*. Pittsburgh, PA: University of Pittsburgh Press.

Susumu, Shimazono. 1986. Conversion Stories and Their Popularization in Japan's New Religions. *Japanese Journal of Religious Studies* 13(2–3):157–175.

Tarn, Nathaniel. 1997. *Scandals in the House of Birds: Shamans and Priests on Lake Atitlán*. New York: Marsilio.

Taube, Karl A. 1992. *The Major Gods of Ancient Yucatan*. Washington, DC: Dumbarton Oaks Research Library and Collection.

———. 1996. The Olmec Maize God: The Face of Corn in Formative Mesoamerica. *Pre-Columbian* 29–30(Spring–Autumn):39–81.

———. 2000. Lightning Celts and Corn Fetishes: The Formative Olmec and the Development of Maize Symbolism in Mesoamerica and the American Southwest. In *Olmec Art and Archaeology in Mesoamerica*. Mary E. Pye and John E. Clark, eds., 297–337. Washington, DC: National Art Gallery.

Taussig, Michael T. 1980. *The Devil and Commodity Fetishism in South America*. Chapel Hill: University of North Carolina Press.

Tax, Sol. 1937. The Municipios of the Midwestern Highlands of Guatemala. *American Anthropologist* 39:423–444.

———. 1946. The Towns of Lake Atitlán. Microfilm collection of manuscripts on Middle American cultural anthropology, University of Chicago. https://www.crl.edu/microfilm-collection-manuscripts-middle-american-cultural-anthropology (accessed May 22, 2020).

Taylor, Bryan. 1976. Conversion and Cognition: An Area for Empirical Study in the Microsociology of Religious Knowledge. *Social Compass* 23(1):5–22.

Tedlock, Barbara. 1981. Quiché Dream Interpretation. *Ethos* 9(4):313–330.

———. 1982. *Time and the Highland Maya*. Albuquerque: University of New Mexico Press.

———. 1987. Zuni and Quiché Dream Sharing and Interpreting. In *Dreaming: Anthropological and Psychological Interpretations*. Barbara Tedlock, ed., 105–131. New York: Cambridge University Press.

———. 1991. Role of Dreams and Visionary Narratives in Mayan Cultural Survival. *Ethos* 20(4):453–476.

———. 2005. *The Woman in the Shaman's Body: Reclaim-*

ing the Feminine in Religion and Medicine. New York: Bantam.

Tedlock, Dennis, trans. 1996. *The Popol Vuh: The Mayan Book of the Dawn of Life*. New York: Touchstone/Simon and Schuster.

Tennekes, Hans. 1985. *El Movimiento Pentecostal en la Sociedad Chilena*. Iquique, Chile: Centro de Investigación de la Realidad del Norte.

Tharoor, Shashi. 2016. *Inglorious Empire: What the British Did to India*. Brunswick, Australia: Scribe.

Thigpen, T. Paul. 2003. Catholic Charismatic Renewal. In *The New International Dictionary of Pentecostal and Charismatic Movements*. Rev. ed. Stanley M. Burgess and Eduard M. van der Maas, eds., 460–467. Grand Rapids, MI: Zondervan.

Thomas, S. L. 2003. Gypsies. In *The New International Dictionary of Pentecostal and Charismatic Movements*. Rev. ed. Stanley M. Burgess and Eduard M. van der Maas, eds., 683–686. Grand Rapids, MI: Zondervan.

Thomas, V. V. 2008. *Dalit Pentecostalism: Spirituality of the Empowered Poor*. Bangalore, India: Asian Trading Corporation.

Thompson, Ryan, and Heather Hanamaikai. 2005. "All Men Are like That": Gender Roles and the Sociocultural Context of a Rape in Nahualá. In *Roads to Change in Maya Guatemala: A Field School Approach to Understanding the K'iche'*. John P. Hawkins and Walter Randolph Adams, eds., 125–137. Norman: University of Oklahoma Press.

Tumin, Melvin M. 1952. *Caste in a Peasant Society*. Princeton, NJ: Princeton University Press.

Turner, Victor W. 1957. *Schism and Continuity in an African Society: A Study of Ndembu Village Life*. Manchester, England: Manchester University Press.

———. 1967. *The Forest of Symbols: Aspects of Ndembu Ritual*. Ithaca, NY: Cornell University Press.

———. 1968. *The Drums of Affliction: A Study of Religious Processes among the Ndembu of Zambia*. London: International African Institute.

———. 1969. *The Ritual Process: Structure and Anti-Structure*. Chicago: Aldine.

———. 1980. *The Forest of Symbols: Aspects of Ndembu Ritual*. Ithaca, NY: Cornell University Press.

Tylor, Edward B. 1871. *Primitive Culture: Researches into the Development of Mythology, Philosophy, Religion, Art, and Custom*. London: John Murray.

United Nations Food and Agriculture Organization. 1958. *Coffee in Latin America: Productivity Problems and Future Prospects*. Vol. 1: *Colombia and El Salvador*. N.p.: United Nations Food and Agriculture Organization.

US Department of State. 2005. *International Religious Freedom Report, 2005*. https://2009-2017.state.gov/j/drl/rls/irf/2005/51641.htm.

Valladares, León A. 1993. *Culto al Maíz en Guatemala*. Guatemala City, Guatemala: Impreofset Oscar de León Palacios.

———. 2002[1957]. *El Hombre y el Maíz: Etnografía y Etnopsicología de Colotenango*. Guatemala City, Guatemala: Litografía MacDonald.

van den Hoogen, L. 1991. *The Romanization of the Brazilian Church: Women's Participation in a Religious Association in Prados, Minas Gerais*. Fort Lauderdale, FL: Breitenbach.

van Gennep, Arnold. 1960[1909]. *The Rites of Passage*. Translated by Monika B. Vizedom and Gabrielle L. Caffee. Chicago: University of Chicago Press.

Vogt, Evon Z. 1969. *Zinacantán: A Maya Community in the Highlands of Chiapas*. Cambridge, MA: Harvard University Press.

———. 1976. *Tortillas for the Gods: A Symbolic Analysis of Zinacanteco Rituals*. Cambridge, MA: Harvard University Press.

Von Tempsky, Gustav Ferdinand. 1858. *Mitla: A Narrative of Incidents and Personal Adventures on a Journey in Mexico, Guatemala, and Salvador in the Years of 1853 to 1855: With Observations on the Modes of Life in Those Countries*. J. S. Bell, ed. London: Longman, Brown, Green, Longmans, and Roberts.

Wagley, Charles. 1949. *Social and Religious Life of a Guatemalan Village*. Memoirs of the American Anthropological Association. Vol. 71. Menasha, WI: American Anthropological Association.

———. 1957. *Santiago Chimaltenango: Estudio Antropologico-Social de una Comunidad Indígena de Huehuetenango*. Translated by Juaquin Noval. Guatemala City, Guatemala: Tipografía Nacional.

Wagner, Regina. 2001. *The History of Coffee in Guatemala*. Bogotá, Colombia: Villegas Editores for Anacafe.

Wallace, Anthony F. C. 1956. Revitalization Movements. *American Anthropologist* 58(2):264–281.

———. 2003[1956]. Revitalization Movements. In *Revitalizations and Mazeways: Essays on Culture Change*. Vol. 1. Edited by Robert S. Grumet, 9–29. Lincoln: University of Nebraska Press.

———. 2003[1971]. Handsome Lake and the Decline of the

Iroquois Matriarchate. In *Revitalizations and Maze-ways: Essays on Culture Change.* Vol. 1. Edited by Robert S. Grumet, 57–67. Lincoln: University of Nebraska Press.

Warren, Kay B. 1978. *The Symbolism of Subordination: Indian Identity in a Guatemalan Town.* Austin: University of Texas Press.

———. 1998. *Indigenous Movements and Their Critics: Pan-Maya Activism in Guatemala.* Princeton, NJ: Princeton University Press.

Watanabe, John. 1992. *Maya Saints and Souls in a Changing World.* Austin: University of Texas Press.

Way, J. T. [John Thomas]. 2012. *The Mayan in the Mall: Globalization, Development, and the Making of Modern Guatemala.* Durham, NC: Duke University Press.

Weber, Max. 1946a. The Protestant Sects and the Spirit of Capitalism. In *From Max Weber: Essays in Sociology.* Hans H. Gerth and C. Wright Mills, eds., 301–322. New York: Oxford University Press.

———. 1946b. Science as a Vocation. In *From Max Weber: Essays in Sociology.* Hans H. Gerth and C. Wright Mills, eds., 129–156. New York: Oxford University Press.

———. 1978[1968]. *Economy and Society: An Outline of Interpretive Sociology.* Edited by Guenther Roth and Clauss Wittich. Berkeley: University of California Press.

———. 1996. *The Protestant Ethic and the Spirit of Capitalism.* Translated by Talcott Parsons. Los Angeles, CA: Roxbury.

———. 2002[1905]. *The Protestant Ethic and the Spirit of Capitalism.* Edited and translated by Peter Baehr and Gordon C. Wells. New York: Penguin.

Weiner, Tim. 2007. *Legacy of Ashes: The History of the CIA.* New York: Doubleday.

Weiss, Arnold S. 1987. Psychological Distress and Well-Being in Hare Krishnas. *Psychological Reports* 61:23-35.

Weiss, Arnold S., and Andrew L. Comrey. 1987. Personality and Mental Health of Hare Krishnas Compared with Psychiatric Outpatients and "Normals." *Personality and Individual Differences* 8(5):721-730.

Weld, Kristen. 2014. *Paper Cadavers: The Archives of Dictatorship in Guatemala.* Durham, NC: Duke University Press.

Wells, Mark, John P. Hawkins, and Walter Randolph Adams. 2020. "To Maintain the Family": Economic Constraints, Traditional Culture, and the Crisis of Manhood in Nueva Santa Catarina Ixtahuacán. In *Making a Place for the Future in Maya Guatemala: Disaster, Resettlement, and Indigenous Development in Santa Catarina Ixtahuacán.* John P. Hawkins and Walter Randolph Adams, eds. Unpublished book manuscript in possession of editors.

Whipple, Kristine. 2006. Cultural Construction of Communication: Language, Space, and Kinship among the Maya-K'iche'. *Journal of Inquiry: Student Cross-Cultural Field Research* 2:139–159.

White, Leslie A. 1959. *The Evolution of Culture: The Development of Civilization to the Fall of Rome.* New York: McGraw-Hill.

Wightman, Jill M. 2007. Healing the Nation: Pentecostal Identity and Social Change in Bolivia. In *Conversion of a Continent: Contemporary Religious Change in Latin America.* Timothy J. Steigenga and Edward L. Cleary, eds., 239–255. New Brunswick, NJ: Rutgers University Press.

Willems, Emilio. 1967. *Followers of the New Faith: Culture Change and the Rise of Protestantism in Brazil and Chile.* Nashville, TN: Vanderbilt University Press.

Wilson, Bryan. 1973. *Magic and the Millennium.* London: Heinemann Educational.

Wilson, Everett A. 1983. Sanguine Saints: Pentecostalism in El Salvador. *Church History* 52(2):186–198.

———. 2003. Latin America. In *The New International Dictionary of Pentecostal and Charismatic Movements.* Rev. ed. Stanley M. Burgess and Eduard M. van der Maas, eds., 157–167. Grand Rapids, MI: Zondervan.

Wilson, Jon. 2016. *The Chaos of Empire: The British Raj and the Conquest of India.* New York: Public Affairs.

Wilson, Kevara Ellsworth. 2007. "Your Destiny Is to Care for Pregnant Women": Midwives and Childbirth in Nahualá. In *Health Care in Maya Guatemala: Confronting Medical Pluralism in a Developing Country.* Walter Randolph Adams and John P. Hawkins, eds., 125–147. Norman: University of Oklahoma Press.

Wilson, Richard. 1995. *Maya Resurgence in Guatemala: Q'eqchi' Experiences.* Norman: University of Oklahoma Press.

Winkler, Klaus. 1999. Joy. In *The Encyclopedia of Christianity.* Erwin Fahlbusch, Jan Milič Lochman, John Mbiti, Jaroslav Pelikan, and Lukas Vischer, eds., 3:79. Grand Rapids, MI: Eerdmans.

Wiyono, Gani. 2011. Pentecostalism in Indonesia. In *Asian and Pentecostal: The Charismatic Face of Christianity in Asia.* Allan Anderson and Edmond Tang, eds., 248–278. Eugene, OR: Wipf and Stock.

Wolterstorff, Nicholas. 2014. Joy and Human Well-Being.

http://faith.yale.edu/sites/default/files/wolterstorff_
joy_and_human_wellbeing.pdf.

Woods, Clyde. 1968. San Lucas Tolimán. In *Los Pueblos del Lago de Atitlán*, Seminario de Integración Social Guatemalteco, ed., 201–228. Guatemala City, Guatemala: Seminario de Integración Social Guatemalteco.

Yale Center for Faith and Culture. 2014. Consultations. http://faith.yale.edu/joy/2014-consultations.

———. 2015. Theology of Joy and the Good Life. http://faith.yale.edu/joy/about.

Yong, Amos. 2005. *The Spirit Poured Out on All Flesh*. Grand Rapids, MI: Baker Academic.

Yukes, Jolene. 2007. "No One Wants to Become a Healer": Herbal Medicine and Ethnobotanical Knowledge in Nahualá. In *Health Care in Maya Guatemala: Confronting Medical Pluralism in a Developing Country*. Walter Randolph Adams and John P. Hawkins, eds., 44–68. Norman: University of Oklahoma Press.

Yung, Hwa. 2011. Pentecostalism and the Asian Church. In *Asian and Pentecostal: The Charismatic Face of Christianity in Asia*. Allan Anderson and Edmond Tang, eds., 30–45. Eugene, OR: Wipf and Stock.

Zier, Christian J. 1980. A Classic-Period Maya Agricultural Field in Western El Salvador. *Journal of Field Archaeology* 7(1):65–74.

Contributors

Walter Randolph Adams received a master's of science in nutritional anthropology from the University of Pennsylvania, a PhD in anthropology from Michigan State University, and a postdoctorate from Brown University's Center for Alcohol and Addiction Studies. A primary focus of his studies has been on the biological, cultural, and psychological components that contribute to binge drinking and its sequelae. Adams served as the field school codirector during its 1995–2006 operations. He considers that experience a highlight of his career. Indeed, he "marvels and continues in awe at how each of the students has grown, bloomed, blossomed, and flourished, each in their own ways."

Gilbert "Gil" Bradshaw worked in 2004 at a Latin American political think tank in Washington, DC. Graduating with honors in 2005 from Brigham Young University with a bachelor of arts in history and a minor in anthropology, Bradshaw followed his wife to law school at Brigham Young University, and he worked in Mexico City as a student law clerk. Upon graduation, Bradshaw worked at a Wall Street law firm in its Latin American transactions department. Afterward, he worked for a company based in Medellín, Colombia, at which point he earned a master of laws in taxation from the UCLA School of Law. Currently, Bradshaw is a tax policy analyst, consulting with Latin American governments, particularly Mexico, on tax policy. Bradshaw is an adjunct professor at the University of Southern California Law School.

Aileen S. Charleston's first ethnographic experience in Guatemala opened both her eyes and her heart, and she has dedicated the rest of her career to social justice, human rights, and conflict resolution. She considers her experience in Antigua Santa Catarina Ixtahuacán to be one of the most meaningful times of her life and regrets that she was never able to enrich the lives of the people

there the way they have enriched hers. Charleston completed her master's degree on international sustainable development and conflict resolution at Brandeis University and obtained her BA in Latin American studies and French from the University of Texas at Austin. She is currently the gender justice coordinator at Oxfam International and is passionate about women's rights, discovering new places, beaches, and her children.

John J. Edvalson graduated from Brigham Young University in 2004 and went on to study anthropology at the University at Albany, State University of New York. He returned to Nahualá first for language studies in K'iche' and then to conduct doctoral-level fieldwork. Edvalson currently resides in Albany, NY, where he works as a library assistant for Albany Public Library. His family has accompanied him to Guatemala several times, and he has many good memories of the people and culture.

Frederick H. "Fritz" Hanselmann completed a BA in anthropology at Brigham Young University and then went to Indiana University to earn an MPA, with a focus on underwater resource management, as well as an MA and a PhD in anthropology. He is an underwater archaeologist and faculty in the Department of Marine Ecosystems and Society and part of the Exploration Sciences Program at the Rosenstiel School of Marine and Atmospheric Sciences at the University of Miami, where he directs the Underwater Archaeology Program. His exploration and research ranges from submerged prehistoric deposits in springs and caves to historic shipwrecks in Latin America and the Caribbean. Fritz also focuses on capacity building and training for archaeologists and heritage managers in less developed countries and fosters the development of marine protected areas and underwater preserves. Hanselmann led archaeological survey off the mouth of the Chagres River in Panama and directs the Río Chagres

Maritime Landscape Study and the Lost Ships of Henry Morgan Project.

John P. Hawkins earned his PhD from the University of Chicago in 1978 and is professor emeritus of anthropology at Brigham Young University. He retired in 2014 after forty years of service there. His research has focused on Guatemala since 1968. Together with Walter Adams, he directed the Brigham Young University Anthropology Department Field School in Nahualá and Santa Catarina Ixtahuacán from 1995 through 2006 and again in 2009. That experience provided both the most important research and the most satisfying and enduring student-faculty relationships of his career. See Hawkins 2014 and Hawkins and Adams 2014 for his philosophy on and procedures for the conduct of ethnographic field schools.

Nicole Matheny Huddleston graduated from Brigham Young University in 2005 with a BA in sociocultural anthropology and then received an MA in applied anthropology from the University of North Texas in 2007. Her master's research explored traditional and biomedical healing beliefs and practices among Latinos in northern Texas. Since 2007, Huddleston has continued her social science research as a research consultant, conducting qualitative and quantitative studies on a wide variety of topics and working with clients from varying industries.

Michael H. Jones graduated in 2004 from Brigham Young University with a BA in cultural anthropology and then attended the University of Kentucky's School of Dentistry, where he met his wife, Brooke. After earning his DMD in 2010, Jones completed advanced education during his general dentistry residency at Scott Air Force Base and then moved to Tokyo, Japan, for three years. Jones then worked for three years providing dental services to the migrant labor force in northern Maine. He is currently in private practice in Jefferson City, Missouri. Mike and Brooke Jones have five daughters.

Clayton G. Larson participated in the field school in Nueva Santa Catarina Ixtahuacán between August and December 2002. He returned to Nueva Santa Catarina Ixtahuacán with his new wife and infant child in 2005 and again in 2007 to complete graduate research. Larson is a doctoral candidate in anthropology at Tulane University. He is currently studying how trends in K'iche' Maya names reflect shifting identities.

Benjamin Pratt's participation in the field school during the summer of 2003 was a pivotal experience in preparation for his future studies, research, and work. After graduating from Brigham Young University in 2006 with a bachelor of arts degree in anthropology and a minor in psychology, Pratt earned a master's of social work from the University of Houston and was a social work fellow with the Leadership Education in Adolescent Health program at Baylor College of Medicine in 2007–2008. Pratt spent the next five years as a practicing social worker, first as a therapist at an inpatient residential treatment facility for at-risk youth, and then as a social worker and social work administrator at the George E. Wahlen Department of Veteran's Affairs Hospital in Salt Lake City, Utah. In 2013, Pratt resumed his graduate studies at Purdue University, earning a master's of science in sociology in 2015. He is currently pursuing doctoral studies in the Organizational Behavior and Human Resource Management program at Purdue University. In 2004, Pratt married Mauri Stotts. They are the proud parents of two daughters and two sons.

Winston K. Scott graduated from the University of Utah in 2003 with a BA in anthropology. He continued fieldwork in Guatemala with Kaqchikel, K'iche', and Q'eqchi' Maya language communities. Scott conducted his doctoral dissertation research in Senahú, Guatemala, in the Alta Verapaz province. He received a doctorate in cultural anthropology from the University at Albany, State University of New York, in 2012.

Adriana Smith first visited Guatemala as an undergraduate anthropology student at Brigham Young University in 2002 in the Guatemala field study program and for the following three years worked as the program's field facilitator: recruiting, teaching the field preparation course, and supporting students' work in the field. She graduated from BYU in 2005 with a BA in anthropology and minors in women's studies and international development. She then earned a master's of public health with an international public health focus from Boston University in 2008 and was involved in public health projects in Massachusetts, Bolivia, and Vietnam while at Boston University. She returned to Guatemala in 2008 to work for grassroots NGOs fostering sexual and reproductive health and HIV prevention. Smith currently works with several health and development organizations in Guatemala as an independent consultant. She lives in Guatemala City and has established a home and family in that beautiful country.

Amelia "Amy" Sisco Thompson's firsthand ethnographic experience in the field gave her a taste for telling people's stories. Soon after returning to the United States, she began contracting with a consulting firm in Chicago, studying Latin American populations in southern California. This led to a full-time job at a product design firm in Portland, Oregon, where she was able to utilize the research methodology used in Guatemala on the entirely different American consumer culture. Eventually she felt her powers were being used for evil as she served to tighten the hold of corporate America on the masses. She then earned a master's in the art of teaching, with an emphasis on middle-school social studies. As luck and fate would have it, she finished her degree just in time to get married and start a family. She and her husband, Clayton, have four children who are, by far, their greatest achievements. Thompson continues to enjoy the art of telling stories and is a frequent contributor to several magazines and a freelance copywriter.

Jennifer Pleasy Philbrick Wayas graduated from Brigham Young University in 2004 with a BA in anthropology and received a JD from the University of Idaho College of Law in 2011. She met her husband, Jon, during the first year of law school. They currently live in Utah with their three boys. Wayas works as an attorney in Salt Lake City, where she continues to use the interviewing, observation, critical thinking, and Spanish skills she acquired during her field study experience in Guatemala.

Index

Abbreviations and conventions used in this index: SCI=Santa Catarina Ixtahuacán. Page numbers followed by an f (as in 203f) indicate a figure; page numbers followed by a t (as in 207t) indicate a table.